MW01055973

Houghton Mifflin Harcourt

GEORGIA

JOURNEYS

COMMON CORE

Program Authors

James F. Baumann · David J. Chard · Jamal Cooks
J. David Cooper · Russell Gersten · Marjorie Lipson
Lesley Mandel Morrow · John J. Pikulski · Héctor H. Rivera
Mabel Rivera · Shane Templeton · Sheila W. Valencia
Catherine Valentino · MaryEllen Vogt

Consulting Author

Irene Fountas

Cover illustration by Brandon Dorman.

Printed in the U.S.A.

ISBN 978-0-544-16492-5

4 5 6 7 8 9 10 0918 22 21 20 19 18 17 16 15 14
4500481181 C D E F G

Houghton
Mifflin
Harcourt

GEORGIA JOURNEYS

COMMON CORE

Unit 1

Lesson 1

Lesson 2

Lesson 3

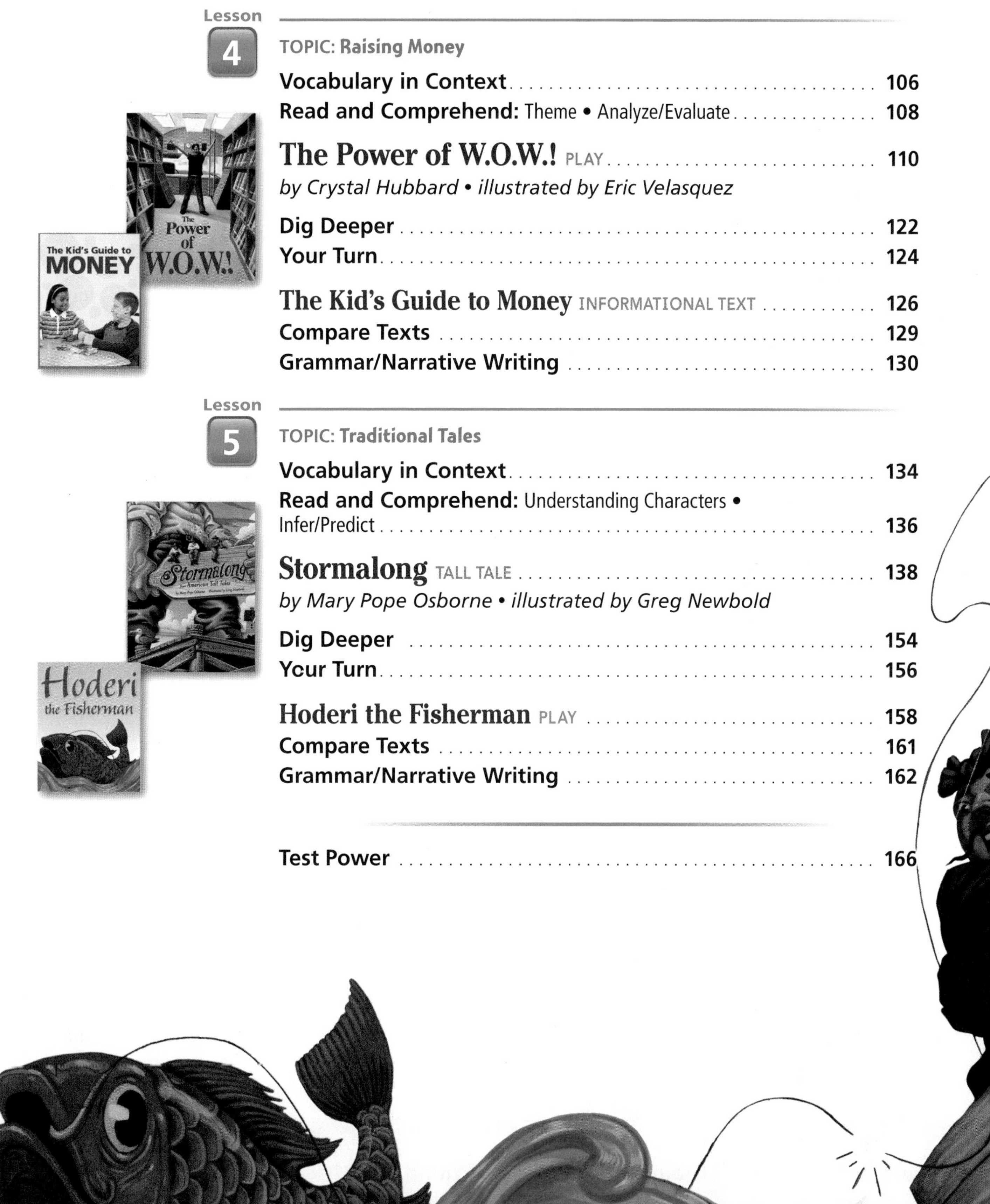

The Power of W.O.W.!
The Kid's Guide to MONEY
Stormalong
Hoderi the Fisherman

Unit 2

Lesson 6

Lesson 7

Lesson 8

Lesson 9

Lesson 10

Discovering Mars: The Amazing Story of the Red Planet
INFORMATIONAL TEXT
by Melvin Berger

Unit 3

Lesson

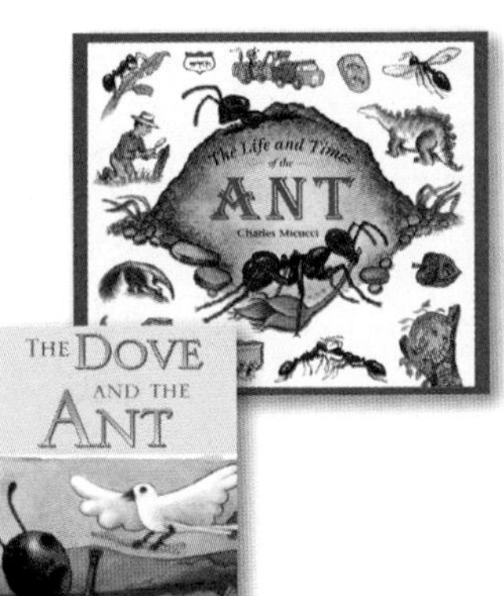

Lesson

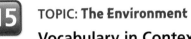

Unit 4

Lesson 16

TOPIC: Individual Contributions

Lesson 17

TOPIC: Service Animals

Lesson 18

TOPIC: Traditional Tales

Lesson 19

Lesson 20

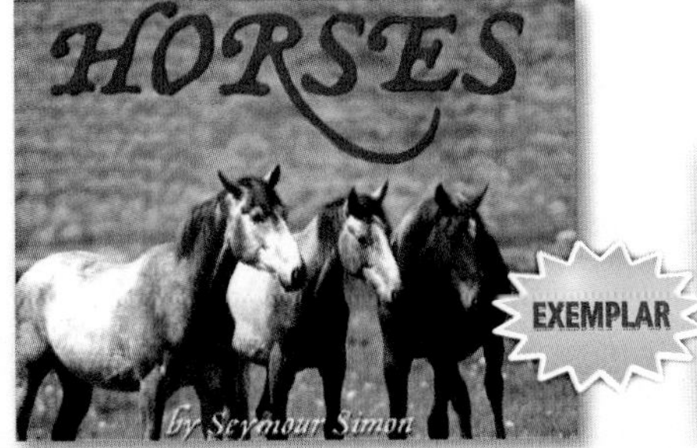

Horses
INFORMATIONAL TEXT
by Seymour Simon

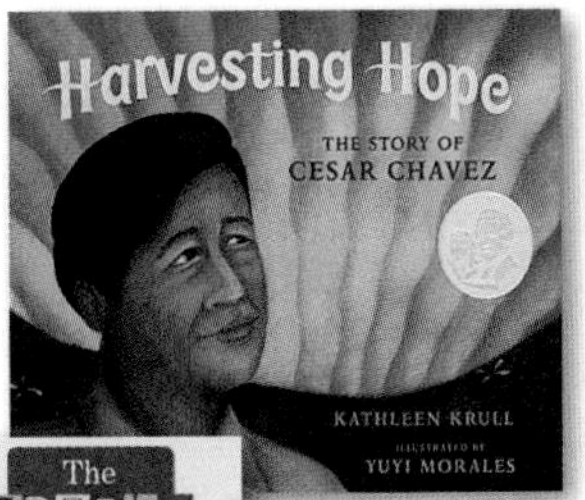

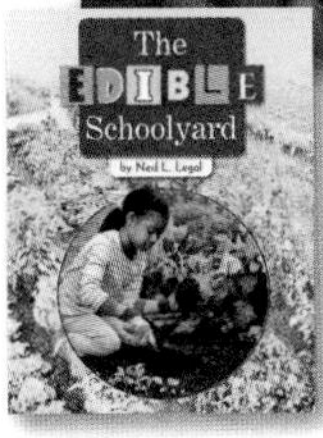

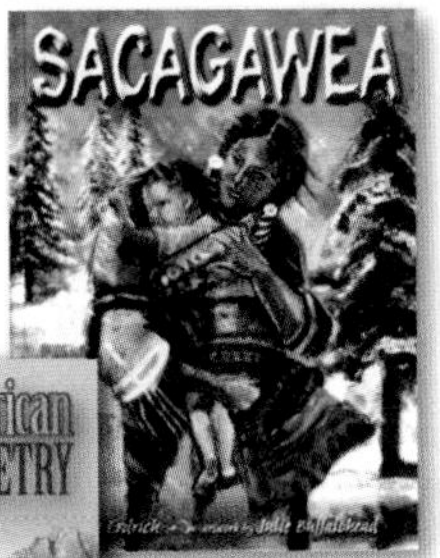

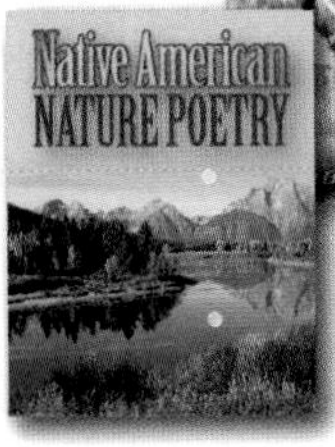

Unit 5

Welcome, Reader!

You're about to set out on a reading journey that will take you from the underwater world of a Japanese folktale to the American wilderness of Sacagawea in 1804. On the way, you'll learn amazing things as you become a better reader.

Your reading journey begins with a story about a remarkable dog named Winn-Dixie.

Many other reading adventures lie ahead. Just turn the page!

Sincerely,

The Authors

Unit 1

Lesson 1

Because of Winn-Dixie

Because of BookEnds

TARGET VOCABULARY

comfort
mention
mood
properly
intends
consisted
positive
advanced
peculiar
talent

Vocabulary Reader

Context Cards

ELACC4L6 acquire/use vocabulary, including academic and domain-specific

Vocabulary in Context

1 comfort

Friends often comfort each other. They help each other get through hard times.

2 mention

Do not mention one friend's faults to another. Keep them to yourself instead.

3 mood

Friends remain friends even when one is in a bad mood, or emotional state.

4 properly

Friends often greet each other properly. A handshake is the correct way.

- Study each Context Card.
- Use two Vocabulary words to tell about an experience you had.

5 intends

This girl intends to keep in touch with a friend. She plans to send e-mail every day.

6 consisted

This lively day consisted of, or was made up of, bike riding and fresh air.

7 positive

These friends are positive that they're having a good time. They are sure of it.

8 advanced

With his advanced chess skills, this man can teach his young friend to play.

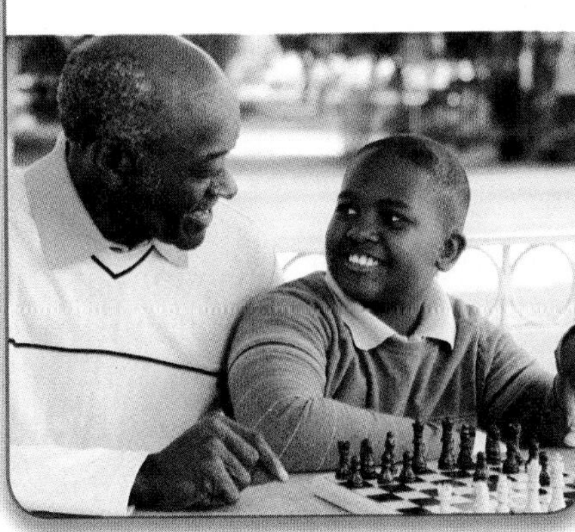

9 peculiar

Friends may act in peculiar, or unusual, ways when taking photos.

10 talent

These friends share a talent for music. This ability gives them hours of fun.

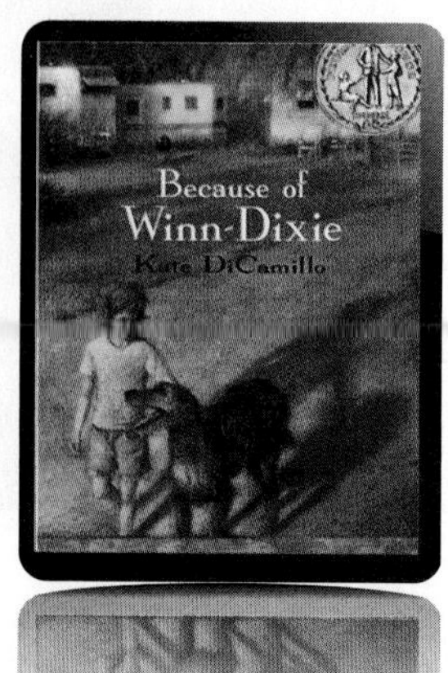

Read and Comprehend

TARGET SKILL

Story Structure As you read "Because of Winn-Dixie," ask yourself what the most important parts of the story are. The story's events make up the **plot**. Look for details that help you picture the **setting,** or where and when the story takes place. Keep track of new **characters** as they are introduced. Use a graphic organizer like this one to help you.

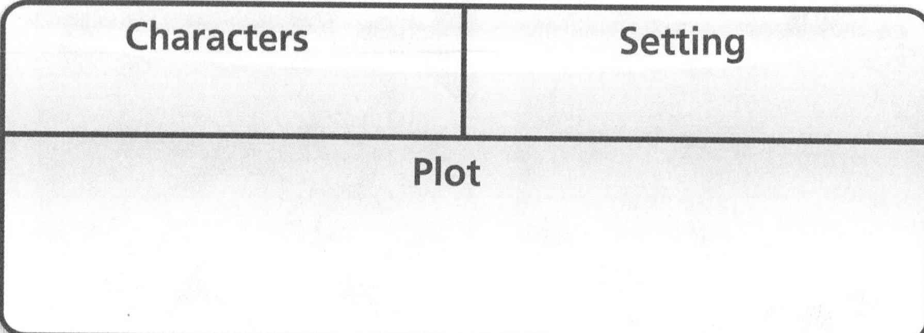

Characters	Setting
Plot	

TARGET STRATEGY

Summarize When you **summarize** a story, you tell who the characters are and briefly retell the main events. Summarizing can help you understand and remember a story. As you read "Because of Winn-Dixie," pause at the end of each page to briefly summarize what you have just read to make sure you understand it.

ELACC4RL1 refer to details and examples when explaining what the text says explicitly and when drawing inferences; **ELACC4RL3** describe a character, setting, or event, drawing on details; **ELACC4RL2** determine theme from details/summarize

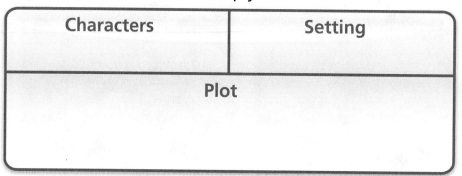

PREVIEW THE TOPIC

Helping Others

Doing favors, helping with chores, and volunteering for community projects are all ways of helping others. Sometimes we can help others just by talking or listening to them.

"Because of Winn-Dixie" is a story about how one person can make a newcomer feel at home in a new place. How the characters interact can show readers what it means to be a friend.

Lesson 1

ANCHOR TEXT

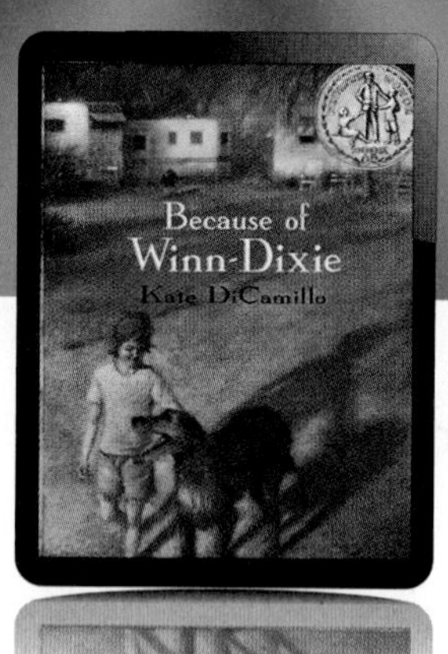

TARGET SKILL

Story Structure Examine details about characters, setting, and plot.

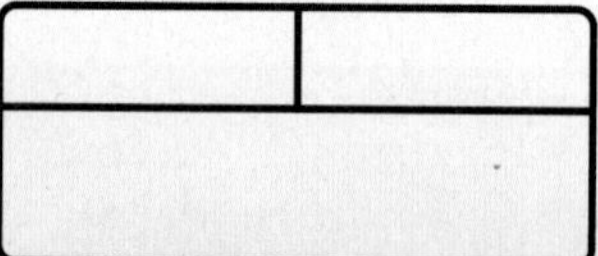

GENRE

Realistic fiction has characters and events that are like people and events in real life. As you read, look for:

- a setting that could be a real place
- a plot with a beginning, a middle, and an ending
- characters who have feelings that real people have

ELACC4RL2 determine theme from details/summarize; **ELACC4RL3** describe a character, setting, or event, drawing on details; **ELACC4RL6** compare and contrast the point of view from which stories are narrated; **ELACC4RL10** read and comprehend literature

Go Digital

MEET THE AUTHOR

Kate DiCamillo

Kate DiCamillo grew up in Florida, where this story takes place. She wrote *Because of Winn-Dixie* during the first time in her life that she did not own a dog. DiCamillo believes that looking closely at the world and paying attention are the most important ways to become a good writer.

Because of WINN-DIXIE

BY KATE DICAMILLO

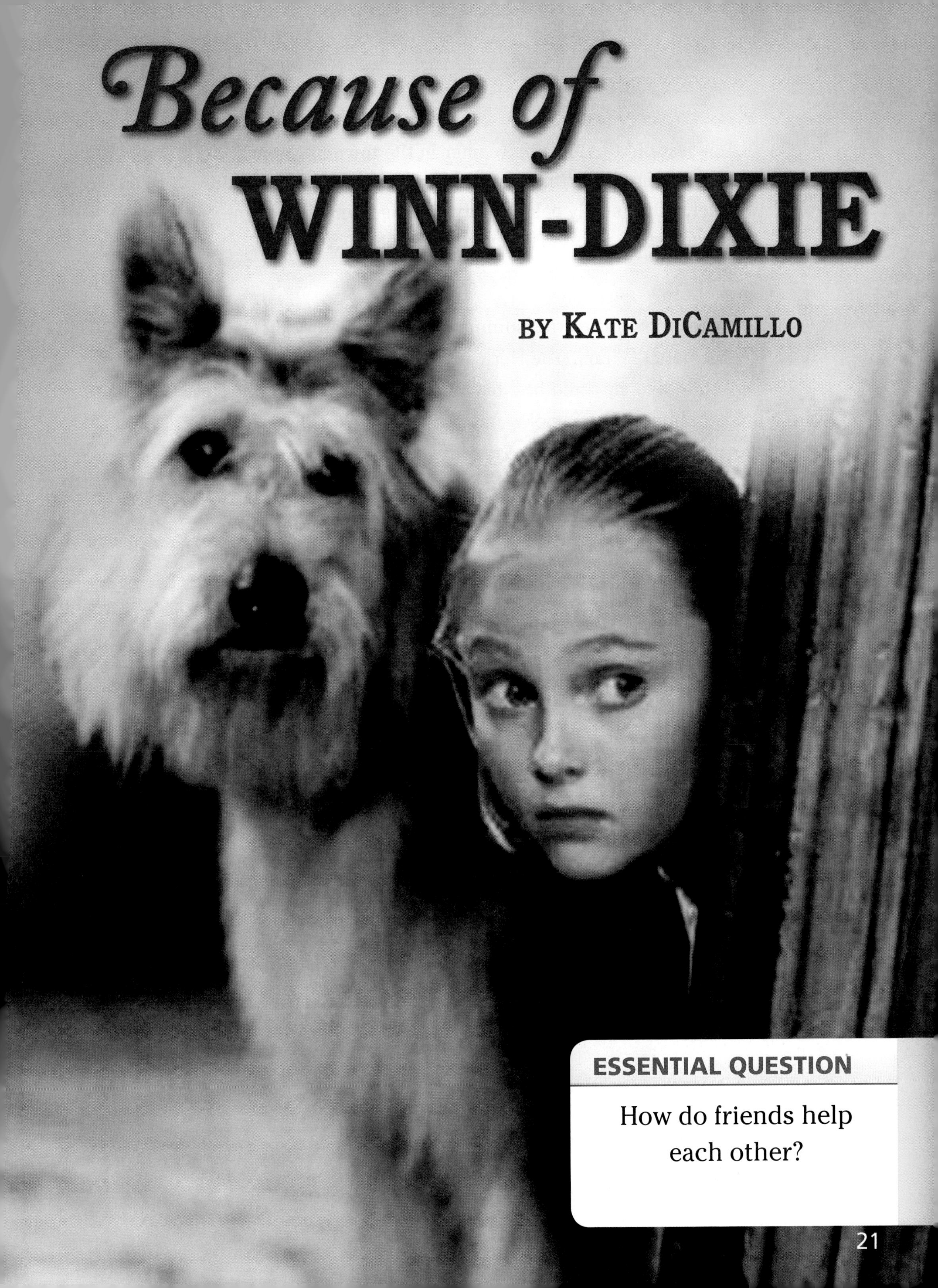

ESSENTIAL QUESTION

How do friends help each other?

Ten-year-old Opal is a newcomer in the town of Naomi, Florida. She hasn't made any friends yet and feels a little lonely. Opal's only pal is a very big dog, named after the grocery store where she found him: Winn-Dixie.

I spent a lot of time that summer at the Herman W. Block Memorial Library. The Herman W. Block Memorial Library sounds like it would be a big fancy place, but it's not. It's just a little old house full of books, and Miss Franny Block is in charge of them all. She is a very small, very old woman with short gray hair, and she was the first friend I made in Naomi.

It all started with Winn-Dixie not liking it when I went into the library, because he couldn't go inside, too. But I showed him how he could stand up on his hind legs and look in the window and see me in there, selecting my books; and he was okay, as long as he could see me. But the thing was, the first time Miss Franny Block saw Winn-Dixie standing up on his hind legs like that, looking in the window, she didn't think he was a dog. She thought he was a bear.

This is what happened: I was picking out my books and kind of humming to myself, and all of a sudden, there was this loud and scary scream. I went running up to the front of the library, and there was Miss Franny Block, sitting on the floor behind her desk.

"Miss Franny?" I said. "Are you all right?"

"A bear," she said.

"A bear?" I asked.

"He has come back," she said.

"He has?" I asked. "Where is he?"

"Out there," she said and raised a finger and pointed at Winn-Dixie standing up on his hind legs, looking in the window for me.

"Miss Franny Block," I said, "that's not a bear. That's a dog. That's my dog. Winn-Dixie."

"Are you positive?" she asked.

"Yes ma'am," I told her. "I'm positive. He's my dog. I would know him anywhere."

ANALYZE THE TEXT

Point of View From what point of view is the story told? What words signal the point of view?

Miss Franny sat there trembling and shaking.

"Come on," I said. "Let me help you up. It's okay." I stuck out my hand and Miss Franny took hold of it, and I pulled her up off the floor. She didn't weigh hardly anything at all. Once she was standing on her feet, she started acting all embarrassed, saying how I must think she was a silly old lady, mistaking a dog for a bear, but that she had a bad experience with a bear coming into the Herman W. Block Memorial Library a long time ago and she never had quite gotten over it.

"When did that happen?" I asked her.

"Well," said Miss Franny, "it is a very long story."

"That's okay," I told her. "I am like my mama in that I like to be told stories. But before you start telling it, can Winn-Dixie come in and listen, too? He gets lonely without me."

"Well, I don't know," said Miss Franny. "Dogs are not allowed in the Herman W. Block Memorial Library."

"He'll be good," I told her. "He's a dog who goes to church." And before she could say yes or no, I went outside and got Winn-Dixie, and he came in and lay down with a "*huummmppff*" and a sigh, right at Miss Franny's feet.

She looked down at him and said, "He most certainly is a large dog."

"Yes ma'am," I told her. "He has a large heart, too."

"Well," Miss Franny said. She bent over and gave Winn-Dixie a pat on the head, and Winn-Dixie wagged his tail back and forth and snuffled his nose on her little old-lady feet. "Let me get a chair and sit down so I can tell this story properly."

"Back when Florida was wild, when it consisted of nothing but palmetto trees and mosquitoes so big they could fly away with you," Miss Franny Block started in, "and I was just a little girl no bigger than you, my father, Herman W. Block, told me that I could have anything I wanted for my birthday. Anything at all."

ANALYZE THE TEXT

Flashback Which details in the text tell you that a flashback is part of this selection? Why has the author included this flashback?

Miss Franny looked around the library. She leaned in close to me. "I don't want to appear prideful," she said, "but my daddy was a very rich man. A very rich man." She nodded and then leaned back and said, "And I was a little girl who loved to read. So I told him, I said, 'Daddy, I would most certainly love to have a library for my birthday, a small little library would be wonderful.'"

"You asked for a whole library?"

"A small one," Miss Franny nodded. "I wanted a little house full of nothing but books and I wanted to share them, too. And I got my wish. My father built me this house, the very one we are sitting in now. And at a very young age, I became a librarian. Yes, ma'am."

"What about the bear?" I said.

"Did I mention that Florida was wild in those days?" Miss Franny Block said.

"Uh-huh, you did."

"It was wild. There were wild men and wild women and wild animals."

"Like bears!"

"Yes ma'am. That's right. Now, I have to tell you, I was a little-miss-know-it-all. I was a miss-smarty-pants with my library full of books. Oh, yes ma'am, I thought I knew the answers to everything. Well, one hot Thursday, I was sitting in my library with all the doors and windows open and my nose stuck in a book, when a shadow crossed the desk. And without looking up, yes ma'am, without even looking up, I said, 'Is there a book I can help you find?'

"Well, there was no answer. And I thought it might have been a wild man or a wild woman, scared of all these books and afraid to speak up. But then I became aware of a very peculiar smell, a very strong smell. I raised my eyes slowly. And standing right in front of me was a bear. Yes ma'am. A very large bear."

"How big?" I asked.

"Oh, well," said Miss Franny, "perhaps three times the size of your dog."

"Then what happened?" I asked her.

"Well," said Miss Franny, "I looked at him and he looked at me. He put his big nose up in the air and sniffed and sniffed as if he was trying to decide if a little-miss-know-it-all librarian was what he was in the mood to eat. And I sat there. And then I thought, 'Well, if this bear intends to eat me, I am not going to let it happen without a fight. No ma'am.' So very slowly and very carefully, I raised up the book I was reading."

"What book was that?" I asked.

"Why, it was *War and Peace*, a very large book. I raised it up slowly and then I aimed it carefully and I threw it right at that bear and screamed, 'Be gone!' And do you know what?"

"No ma'am," I said.

"He went. But this is what I will never forget. He took the book with him."

"Nuh-uh," I said.

"Yes ma'am," said Miss Franny. "He snatched it up and ran."

"Did he come back?" I asked.

"No. I never saw him again. Well, the men in town used to tease me about it. They used to say, 'Miss Franny, we saw that bear of yours out in the woods today. He was reading that book and he said it sure was good and would it be all right if he kept it for just another week.' Yes ma'am. They did tease me about it." She sighed. "I imagine I'm the only one left from those days. I imagine I'm the only one that even recalls that bear. All my friends, everyone I knew when I was young, they are all dead and gone."

She sighed again. She looked sad and old and wrinkled. It was the same way I felt sometimes, being friendless in a new town and not having a mama to comfort me. I sighed, too.

Winn-Dixie raised his head off his paws and looked back and forth between me and Miss Franny. He sat up then and showed Miss Franny his teeth.

"Well now, look at that," she said. "That dog is smiling at me."

"It's a talent of his," I told her.

"It is a fine talent," Miss Franny said. "A very fine talent." And she smiled back at Winn-Dixie.

"We could be friends," I said to Miss Franny. "I mean you and me and Winn-Dixie, we could all be friends."

Miss Franny smiled even bigger. "Why, that would be grand," she said, "just grand."

And right at that minute, right when the three of us had decided to be friends, who should come marching into the Herman W. Block Memorial Library but old pinch-faced Amanda Wilkinson. She walked right up to Miss Franny's desk and said, "I finished *Johnny Tremain* and I enjoyed it very much. I would like something even more difficult to read now, because I am an advanced reader."

"Yes dear, I know," said Miss Franny. She got up out of her chair.

Amanda pretended like I wasn't there. She stared right past me. "Are dogs allowed in the library?" she asked Miss Franny as they walked away.

"Certain ones," said Miss Franny, "a select few." And then she turned around and winked at me. I smiled back. I had just made my first friend in Naomi, and nobody was going to mess that up for me, not even old pinch-faced Amanda Wilkinson.

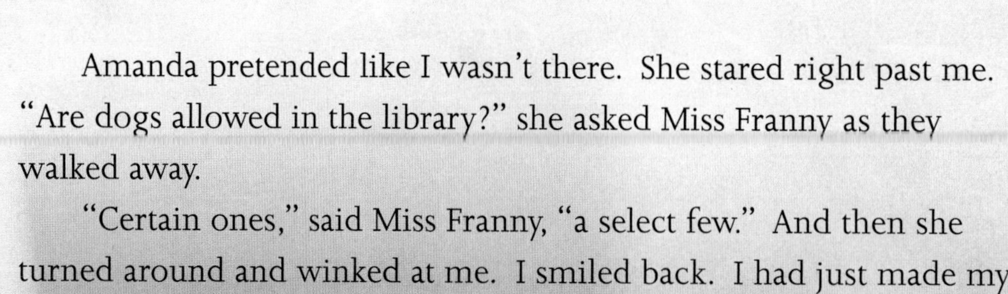

ANALYZE THE TEXT

Story Structure What story events have led to Opal making her first new friend in Naomi? How has the setting affected these events?

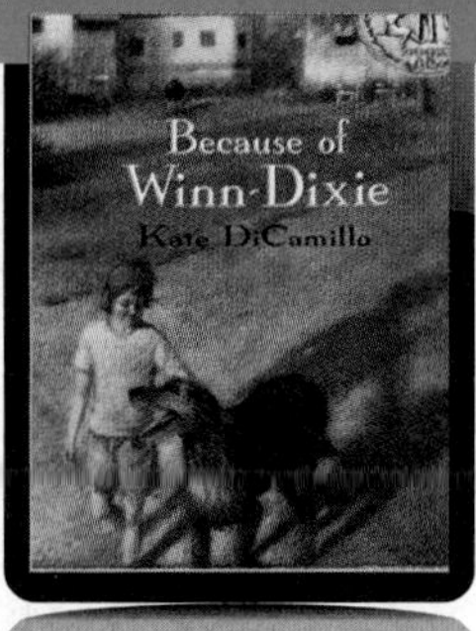

Dig Deeper

How to Analyze the Text

Use these pages to learn about Story Structure, Point of View, and Flashback. Then read "Because of Winn-Dixie" again to apply what you learned.

Story Structure

"Because of Winn-Dixie" is a realistic fiction story about a girl who moves to a new town. Fiction stories have a beginning, a middle, and an ending. The **plot** is the story's events. These events are usually told in the order they happen. **Characters** are the people in a story. The **setting** is the time and place where the story events happen.

You can use text evidence, or details, from "Because of Winn-Dixie" to describe the characters, the events, and the setting. Who are the most important characters in "Because of Winn-Dixie"? Look back at the beginning of the story. What is the first event?

Characters	Setting
Plot	

ELACC4RL1 refer to details and examples when explaining what the text says explicitly and when drawing inferences; **ELACC4RL3** describe a character, setting, or event, drawing on details; **ELACC4RL6** compare and contrast the point of view from which stories are narrated

Point of View

Point of view is the standpoint from which a text is written.

- When a story character is the narrator, the story is told in **first-person point of view.** The narrator uses the words *I, me*, and *my*.
- When an outside observer is the narrator, the story is told in **third-person point of view**. The narrator uses the words *he, she,* and *they* to tell about the characters.

Flashback

Authors sometimes tell about an event that happened before the time in which the main story is set. This is called a **flashback**. Think about the story Miss Franny tells Opal. What event does she tell about and when did it take place?

Your Turn

RETURN TO THE ESSENTIAL QUESTION

Review the selection with a partner to prepare to discuss this question: *How do friends help each other?* Use text evidence from the story and your experiences to explain your ideas to your partner.

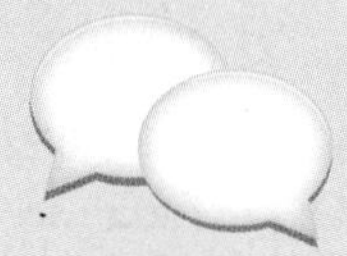

Classroom Conversation

Continue your discussion of "Because of Winn-Dixie" by explaining your answers to these questions:

1. Why do you think the author chose to tell the story from a first-person point of view?
2. Why do Miss Franny and Opal become friends?
3. How can you tell that Miss Franny and Opal will remain friends?

HOW DO YOU SAY IT?

Discuss Formal and Informal Language
Author Kate DiCamillo uses some formal language to show readers what Miss Franny is like. Phrases such as "Yes, ma'am" and "Why, that would be grand" help you get the sense that Miss Franny is old-fashioned. List other reasons you might use formal language instead of informal language. Compare your list with a partner's list, and talk about your examples.

WRITE ABOUT READING

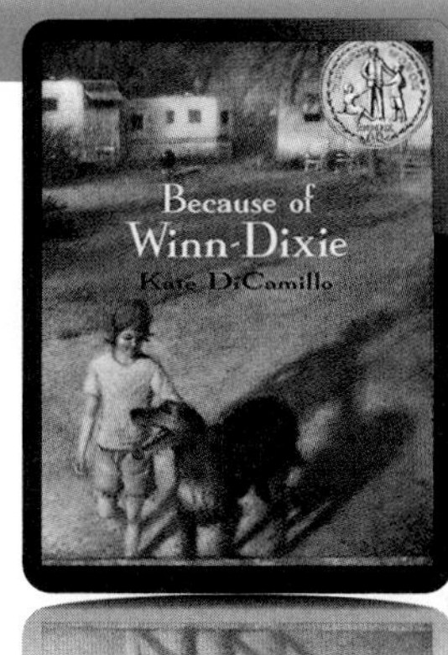

Response Sometimes an author writes a story within a story. What is the flashback in "Because of Winn-Dixie"? Do you think the story would be as interesting without this flashback? Write a paragraph or two that identifies the flashback and gives your opinion of it. Use words and phrases such as *for instance* to link your opinions with reasons and details from the text.

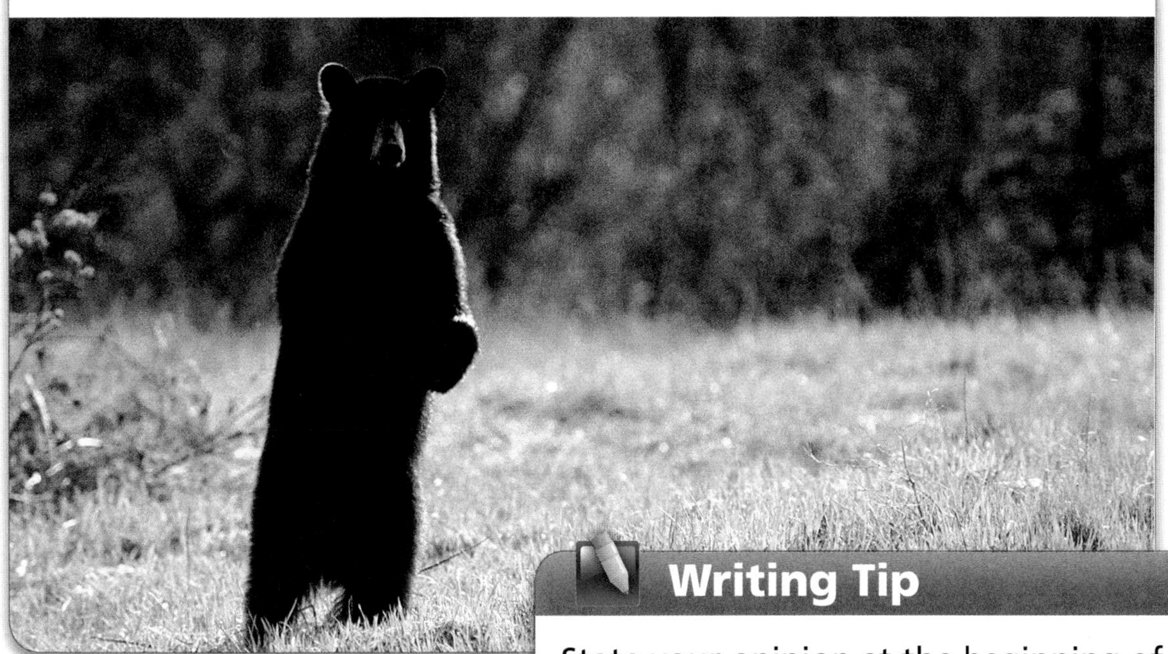

Writing Tip

State your opinion at the beginning of your response. At the end, provide a concluding sentence that sums up your opinion.

COMMON CORE **ELACC4RL3** describe a character, setting, or event, drawing on details; **ELACC4W1b** provide reasons supported by facts and details; **ELACC4W1c** link opinion and reasons using words and phrases; **ELACC4W9a** apply grade 4 Reading standards to literature; **ELACC4SL1a** come to discussions prepared/explicitly draw on preparation and other information about the topic; **ELACC4SL1d** review key ideas expressed and explain own ideas and understanding; **ELACC4L3c** differentiate contexts that call for formal English and informal discourse

Lesson 1

INFORMATIONAL TEXT

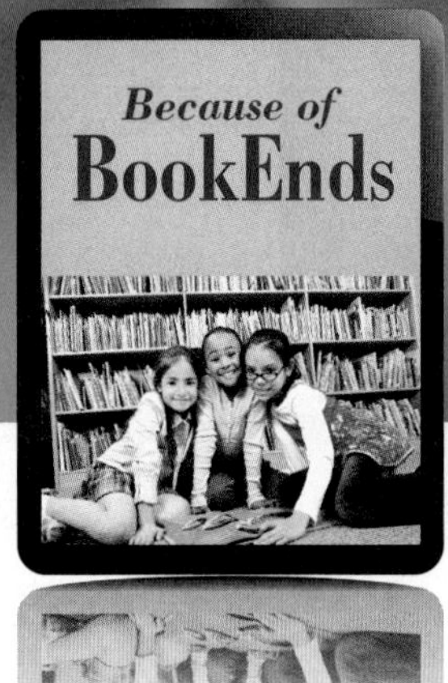

GENRE

Informational text, such as this magazine article, gives facts and examples about a topic.

TEXT FOCUS

Graphs Informational text may include a bar graph, a diagram that uses bars to compare measurements or amounts. Study the graph on page 38. Note the title and the details. Explain the information in the graph.

ELACC4RI7 interpret information presented visually, orally, or quantitatively

Because of BookEnds

by John Korba

Think about what you're doing right now. You're learning something new. How are you doing it? You're reading a book.

You learn all kinds of things from books—things that are fun, or important, or even peculiar. Books can make you smile and can comfort you when you're sad.

What if you didn't have this book, or any books? An eight-year-old boy named Brandon once thought about that, and then he had a great idea.

A Little Boy's Big Idea

One day in 1998, Brandon Keefe was home from school with a cold. His mother, Robin, had to go to a meeting, so she took Brandon with her. The meeting was at a place called Hollygrove in Los Angeles, California. Hollygrove is a community organization for children and families.

Not all children's libraries are as well stocked as this one. That's where BookEnds comes in.

At the meeting, Brandon played in a corner. The adults were in a serious mood. They wanted to buy books for the children's center, but they didn't have much money. Brandon thought about this. He was positive he could use his problem-solving talent to help.

The next day Brandon was back at school. His teacher talked to the class about helping the community and asked for ideas. Brandon told the class about the children's center and its need for books. Then he announced his idea to hold a giant book drive.

Brandon's class organized the book drive. Soon, donations of new and used books poured in. Teams of volunteers, which consisted of students, teachers, and administrators from the school, collected and sorted the books. Meanwhile, Brandon did not mention this project to his mother.

Then one day Robin drove to school to pick up Brandon. He was waiting in the driveway with a great surprise: 847 books for the new library!

"That was one of the best days of my life," said Robin.

BookEnds Is Born

Robin knew there were many places that needed children's books. She saw that Brandon's idea could help them, too, so she started an organization called BookEnds.

BookEnds helps school kids set up book drives and get the books to children who need them. Since 1998, BookEnds volunteers have donated more than a million books to more than three hundred thousand children.

Brandon is an adult now. He is still involved with BookEnds and intends to stay involved.

You Can Do It, Too!

Do you and your schoolmates have many books that you'll never read again? Then your school might want to hold a book drive.

Step 1: Find a place that needs books.

Step 2: Collect books that are still in good shape.

Step 3: Sort the books properly by reading level. (You don't want children to get books that are too easy or too advanced.)

Step 4: Deliver your books and watch the smiles appear!

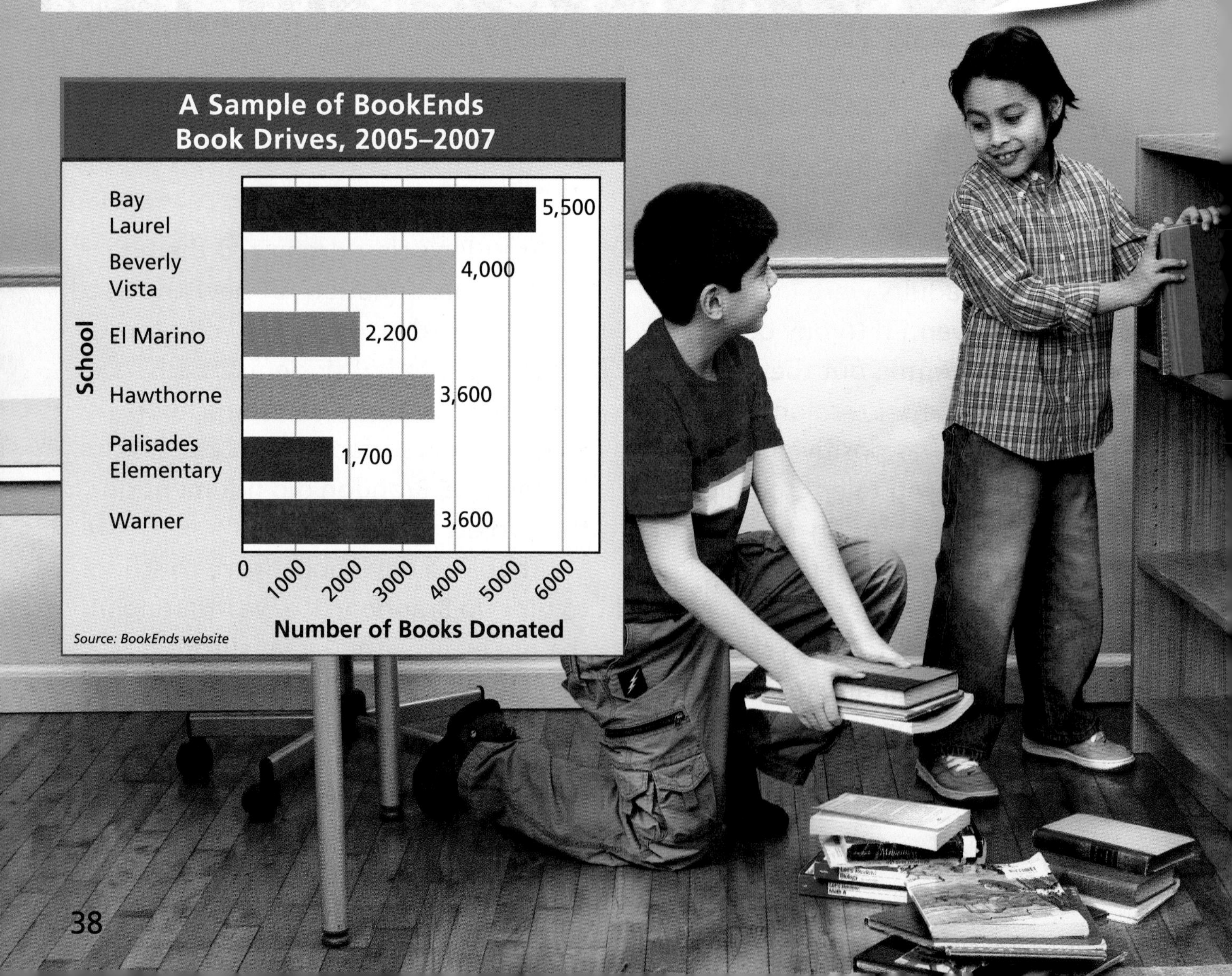

Compare Texts

TEXT TO TEXT

Compare Actions How do the characters in "Because of Winn-Dixie" and the student in "Because of BookEnds" help others? Find text evidence in each selection of someone helping someone else. Work with a group to compile a list. Then add to the list other ideas for helping.

TEXT TO SELF

Write a Narrative Think about a time you made a new friend. Write about that experience and why it was important to you. Be sure to include descriptive details about the place and time to help readers visualize the story. Share your story with a group.

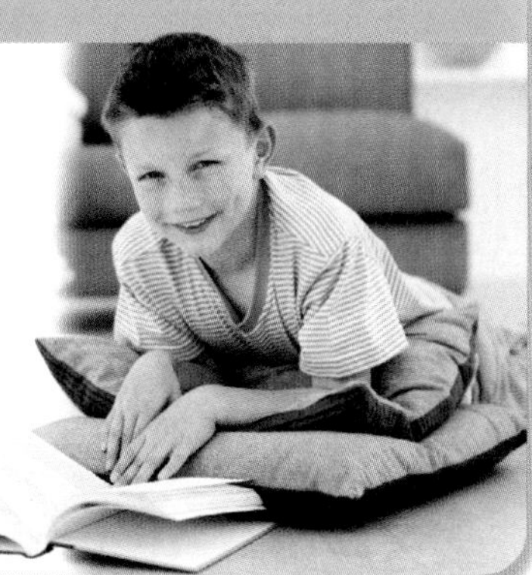

TEXT TO WORLD

Write a Proposal Think of a place in your community that might like to receive a donation of books. Write a step-by-step plan for how you and your classmates might organize a book drive. Then pitch the idea to your class.

ELACC4RL3 describe a character, setting, or event, drawing on details; **ELACC4W3b** use dialogue and description to develop experiences and events or show characters' responses; **ELACC4W10** write routinely over extended time frames and shorter time frames

ELACC4L1f produce complete sentences, recognizing and correcting fragments and run-ons; **ELACC4W3d** use concrete words and phrases and sensory details; **ELACC4L3a** choose words and phrases to convey ideas precisely

Grammar

What Is a Sentence? A **sentence** is a group of words that tells a complete thought. Every sentence has a subject and a predicate. The **simple subject** is the main word that names the person or thing being spoken about. The **simple predicate** is the main word or words that tell what the subject is or does. A simple sentence has one subject and one predicate.

Complete Sentences

A small woman (simple subject) sits (simple predicate) at the desk.

Many children (simple subject) visit (simple predicate) the library.

A **complete subject** contains all the words that tell who or what is doing the action in a sentence. A **complete predicate** includes all the words that tell what the subject of the sentence is or does.

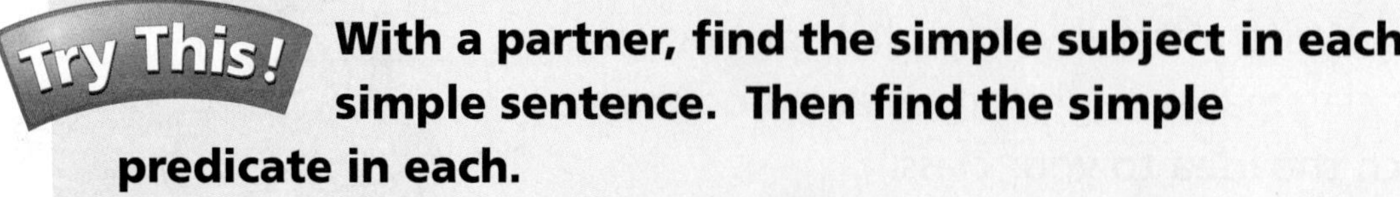

With a partner, find the simple subject in each simple sentence. Then find the simple predicate in each.

1. Several students borrow books from the library.
2. The new book about dogs is popular.
3. The kind librarian stands by the door.

You can create interesting sentences by adding descriptive words to a simple subject. The simple subject and the words that describe it make up the complete subject.

Sentence	Descriptive Words
 The dog peeked into the window.	 big brown

New Complete Sentence

The big brown dog peeked into the window.

Connect Grammar to Writing

As you revise your descriptive paragraph, make sure each sentence has a subject and a predicate. Add descriptive words to simple subjects to make them complete subjects.

ELACC4W3d use concrete words and phrases and sensory details; ELACC4W10 write routinely over extended time frames and shorter time frames; ELACC4L3a choose words and phrases to convey ideas precisely

Narrative Writing

Word Choice A good **descriptive paragraph** has clear, colorful details to describe real or imaginary places. For example, the author of "Because of Winn-Dixie" describes the library as "just a little old house full of books." Find places in your paragraph to add vivid details to keep readers interested. Use the Writing Traits Checklist below as you revise your writing.

For a story, Vanessa drafted a description of an apartment. Later, she added more details to help her readers picture it.

Writing Traits Checklist

- **Ideas** Did I include vivid details?
- **Organization** Did I put my details in a logical order?
- **Word Choice** Did I use sense words and phrases?
- **Voice** Did I give my description a special mood or feeling?
- **Sentence Fluency** Did I write smooth, complete sentences?
- **Conventions** Did I use correct spelling, grammar, and mechanics?

Revised Draft

Mrs. Henry's apartment was very small and cheery. When you walked in, it always smelled ~~good~~ like pancakes. There were two sunny windows and funny photographs on the walls, such as a Chihuahua on a doll chair. Mrs. Henry's sofa had a fuzzy blue cover that she crocheted herself, and by her sofa was a table covered with ~~interesting things~~ seashells, china birds, and family pictures.

Final Copy

Mrs. Henry's Place

by Vanessa Brune

Mrs. Henry's apartment was very small and cheery. When you walked in, it always smelled like pancakes. There were two sunny windows and funny photographs on the walls, such as a Chihuahua on a doll chair. Mrs. Henry's sofa had a fuzzy blue cover that she crocheted herself, and by her sofa was a table covered with seashells, china birds, and family pictures. The best thing was the fish tank with goldfish and blue-and-red striped guppies. In the sand at the bottom of the tank, a scuba diver explored for treasure. The diver's air tube bubbled quietly as the fish swam in smooth circles or darted around. Mrs. Henry's apartment was a fascinating place to visit.

Reading as a Writer

What makes Vanessa's details vivid? Where can you add clear and colorful details in your description?

In my final paper, I added some vivid details. I also made sure I had written complete sentences.

Lesson

2

Vocabulary in Context

TARGET VOCABULARY

injustice
numerous
segregation
nourishing
captured
dream
encounters
preferred
recall
example

Vocabulary Reader

Context Cards

ELACC4L6 acquire/use vocabulary, including academic and domain-specific

1 injustice

Some people spend their entire lives fighting injustice, or unfairness.

2 numerous

If numerous people sign a petition, their many voices can change the laws.

3 segregation

Laws on segregation once kept African Americans and white Americans separate.

4 nourishing

Many groups hope to end hunger by giving people healthy, nourishing food.

- Study each Context Card.
- Make up a new context sentence that uses two Vocabulary words.

5 captured

Some leaders have captured, or caught, people's attention with moving speeches.

6 dream

Many people have a dream of fair treatment for all. It is their goal.

7 encounters

Brief encounters, or meetings, with heroes can inspire kids to work for change.

8 preferred

Some Americans have preferred, or chosen, to work for change as a group.

9 recall

Most people can look back and recall a situation when they were treated unfairly.

10 example

It is easy to admire a leader who sets an example of fairness and equality.

Read and Comprehend

TARGET SKILL

Author's Purpose As you read "My Brother Martin," think about the **author's purpose,** or reason for writing. Does she want to inform, entertain, or persuade readers? For clues, look at text evidence. Pay attention to the details the author chooses to support her points. Note what kind of words she chooses to describe people and events. Use a graphic organizer like this one to help you figure out and explain the author's purpose.

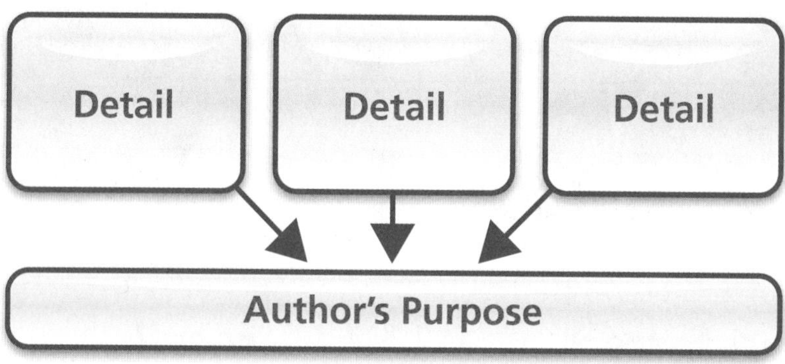

TARGET STRATEGY

Monitor/Clarify As you read "My Brother Martin," **monitor**, or pay attention to, your understanding of individual words as well as ideas. If something does not make sense, stop to **clarify** it, or make it clear. You can clarify by rereading the sentence or paragraph and using context clues.

ELACC4RI8 explain how an author uses reasons and evidence to support points; **ELACC4RF4c** use context to confirm or self-correct word recognition and understanding

PREVIEW THE TOPIC

Civil Rights

Civil rights are the rights that every person has as a citizen of the United States. Until the 1960s, many African Americans did not have the same civil rights as other Americans.

One of the most powerful leaders in the fight for civil rights was Dr. Martin Luther King Jr. He led peaceful protests that eventually led to changes in the laws about the rights of all Americans. In "My Brother Martin," his sister tells about childhood experiences that inspired her brother to spend his life fighting for civil rights.

Lesson 2

ANCHOR TEXT

TARGET SKILL

Author's Purpose Use text details to figure out the author's reasons for writing.

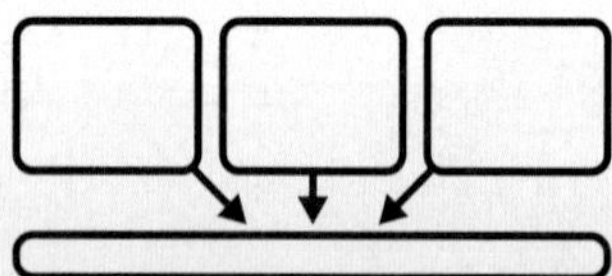

GENRE

A **biography** tells about a person's life and is written by another person. As you read, look for:

- information about why the person is important
- opinions and personal judgments based on facts

COMMON CORE **ELACC4RI3** explain events/procedures/ideas/concepts in a text; **ELACC4RI8** explain how an author uses reasons and evidence to support points; **ELACC4RI10** read and comprehend informational texts; **ELACC4L5.b** recognize and explain the meaning of idioms, adages, and proverbs

MEET THE AUTHOR

CHRISTINE KING FARRIS

Christine King Farris is the sister of Dr. Martin Luther King Jr. *My Brother Martin* is her second book about the famous civil rights leader. The first is *Martin Luther King: His Life and Dream.* In addition to being a writer, she is also a college instructor and a speaker.

MEET THE ILLUSTRATOR

CHRIS SOENTPIET

Originally from South Korea, Chris Soentpiet was adopted by a Hawaiian family when he was eight years old. He met members of his birth family while researching his book *Peacebound Trains.* Research and accuracy are very important to Soentpiet. He uses live models, makes costumes for them, and photographs the models before he begins painting.

my brother MARTIN

A SISTER REMEMBERS
GROWING UP WITH THE REV. DR. MARTIN LUTHER KING JR.

by CHRISTINE KING FARRIS
illustrated by CHRIS SOENTPIET

ESSENTIAL QUESTION

What might lead a person to try to change the world?

We were born in the same room, my brother Martin and I. I was an early baby, born sooner than expected. Mother Dear and Daddy placed me in the chifforobe drawer that stood in the corner of their upstairs bedroom. I got a crib a few days afterward. A year and a half later, Martin spent his first night in that hand-me-down crib in the very same room.

The house where we were born belonged to Mother Dear's parents, our grandparents, the Reverend and Mrs. A. D. Williams. We lived there with them and our Aunt Ida, our grandmother's sister.

And not long after my brother Martin—who we called M. L., because he and Daddy had the same name—our baby brother was born. His name was Alfred Daniel, but we called him A. D., after our grandfather.

They called me Christine, and like three peas in one pod, we grew together. Our days and rooms were filled with adventure stories and Tinkertoys, with dolls and Monopoly and Chinese checkers.

And although Daddy, who was an important minister, and Mother Dear, who was known far and wide as a musician, often had work that took them away from home, our grandmother was always there to take care of us. I remember days sitting at her feet, as she and Aunt Ida filled us with grand memories of their childhood and read to us about all the wonderful places in the world.

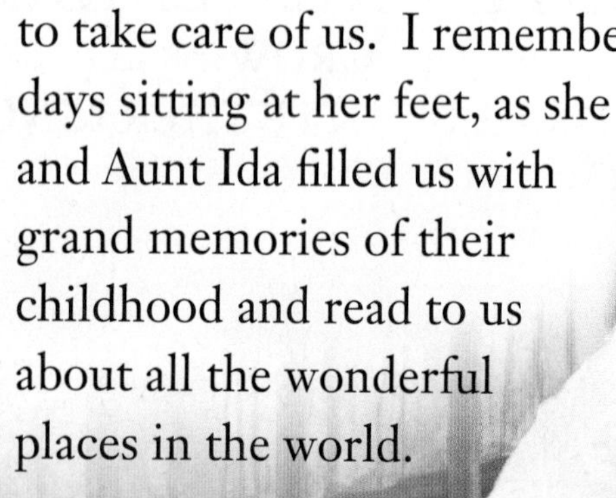

And of course, my brothers and I had each other. We three stuck together like the pages in a brand-new book. And being normal young children, we were almost *always* up to something.

Our best prank involved a fur piece that belonged to our grandmother. It looked almost alive, with its tiny feet and little head and gleaming glass eyes. So, every once in a while, in the waning light of evening, we'd tie that fur piece to a stick, and, hiding behind the hedge in front of our house, we would dangle it in front of unsuspecting passersby. Boy! You could hear the screams of fright all across the neighborhood!

Then there was the time Mother Dear decided that her children should all learn to play piano. I didn't mind too much, but M. L. and A. D. preferred being outside to being stuck inside with our piano teacher, Mr. Mann, who would rap your knuckles with a ruler just for playing the wrong notes. Well, one morning, M. L. and A. D. decided to loosen the legs on the piano bench so we wouldn't have to practice. We didn't tell Mr. Mann, and when he sat . . . *CRASH!*
Down he went.

But mostly we were good, obedient children, and M. L. did learn to play a few songs on the piano. He even went off to sing with our mother a time or two. Given his love for singing and music, I'm sure he could have become as good a musician as our mother had his life not called him down a different path.

But that's just what his life did.

My brothers and I grew up a long time ago. Back in a time when certain places in our country had unfair laws that said it was right to keep black people separate because our skin was darker and our ancestors had been captured in far-off Africa and brought to America as slaves.

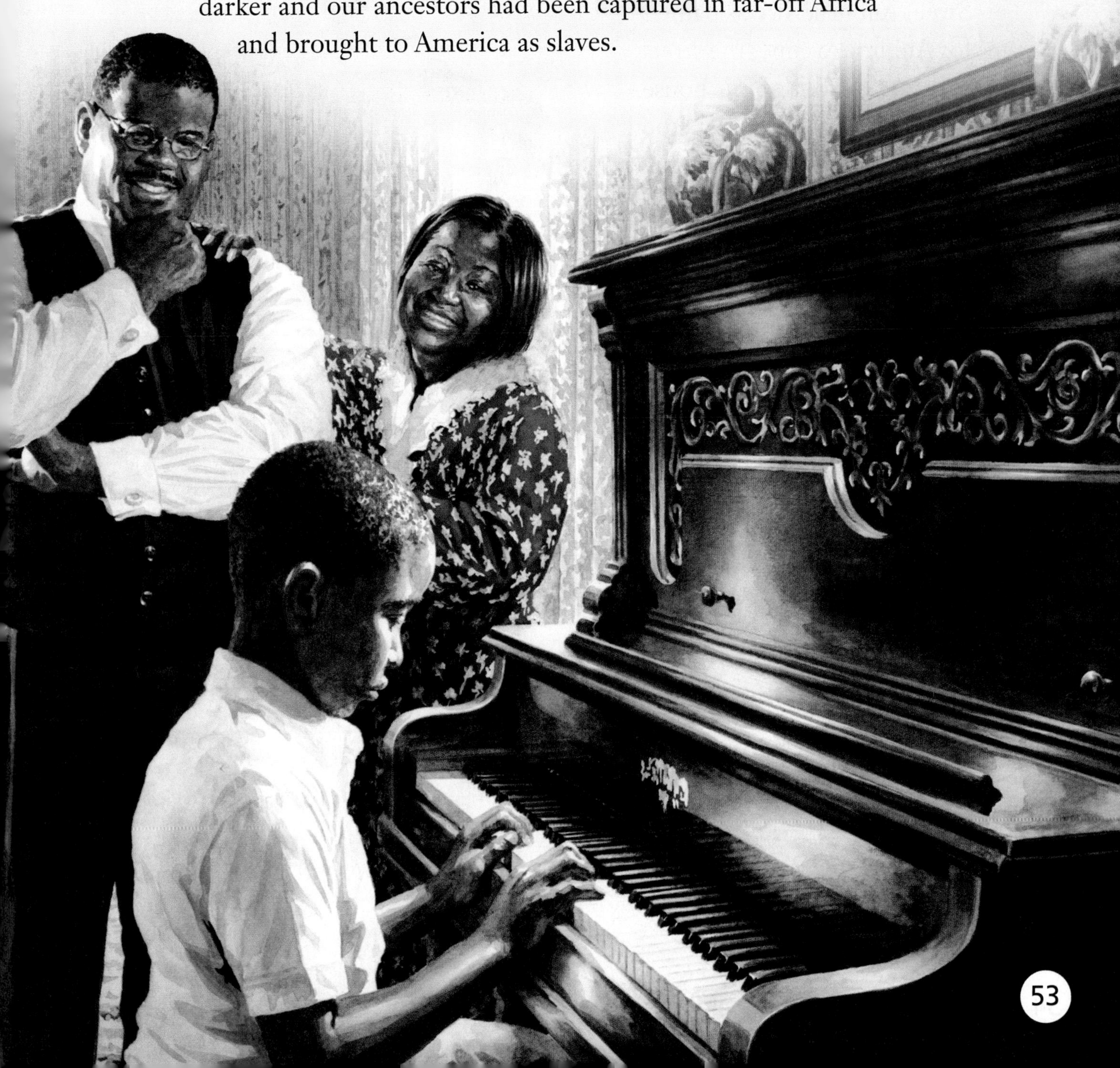

Atlanta, Georgia, the city in which we were growing up, had those laws. Because of those laws, my family rarely went to the picture shows or visited Grant Park with its famous Cyclorama. In fact, to this very day I don't recall ever seeing my father on a streetcar. Because of those laws, and the indignity that went with them, Daddy preferred keeping M. L., A. D., and me close to home, where we'd be protected.

We lived in a neighborhood in Atlanta that's now called Sweet Auburn. It was named for Auburn Avenue, the street that ran in front of our house. On our side of the street stood two-story frame houses similar to the one we lived in. Across it crouched a line of one-story row houses and a store owned by a white family.

When we were young all the children along Auburn Avenue played together, even the two boys whose parents owned the store.

And since our house was the favorite gathering place, those boys played with us in our backyard and ran with M. L. and A. D. to the firehouse on the corner where they watched the engines and the firemen.

The thought of *not* playing with those kids because they were different, because they were white and we were black, never entered our minds.

Well, one day, M. L. and A. D. went to get their playmates from across the street just as they had done a hundred times before. But they came home alone. The boys had told my brothers that they couldn't play together anymore because A. D. and M. L. were Negroes.

And that was it. Shortly afterward the family sold the store and moved away. We never saw or heard from them again.

ANALYZE THE TEXT

Explain Historical Events What happened here? Why were the white children no longer allowed to play with M. L. and A. D.?

Looking back, I realize that it was only a matter of time before the generations of cruelty and injustice that Daddy and Mother Dear and Mama and Aunt Ida had been shielding us from finally broke through. But back then it was a crushing blow that seemed to come out of nowhere.

"Why do white people treat colored people so mean?" M. L. asked Mother Dear afterward. And with me and M. L. and A. D. standing in front of her trying our best to understand, Mother Dear gave the reason behind it all.

Her words explained the streetcars our family avoided and the WHITES ONLY sign that kept us off the elevator at City Hall. Her words told why there were parks and museums that black people could not visit and why some restaurants refused to serve us and why hotels wouldn't give us rooms and why theaters would only allow us to watch their picture shows from the balcony.

But her words also gave us hope.

She answered simply, "Because they just don't understand that everyone is the same, but someday, it will be better."

And my brother M. L. looked up into our mother's face and said the words I remember to this day.

He said, "Mother Dear, one day I'm going to turn this world upside down."

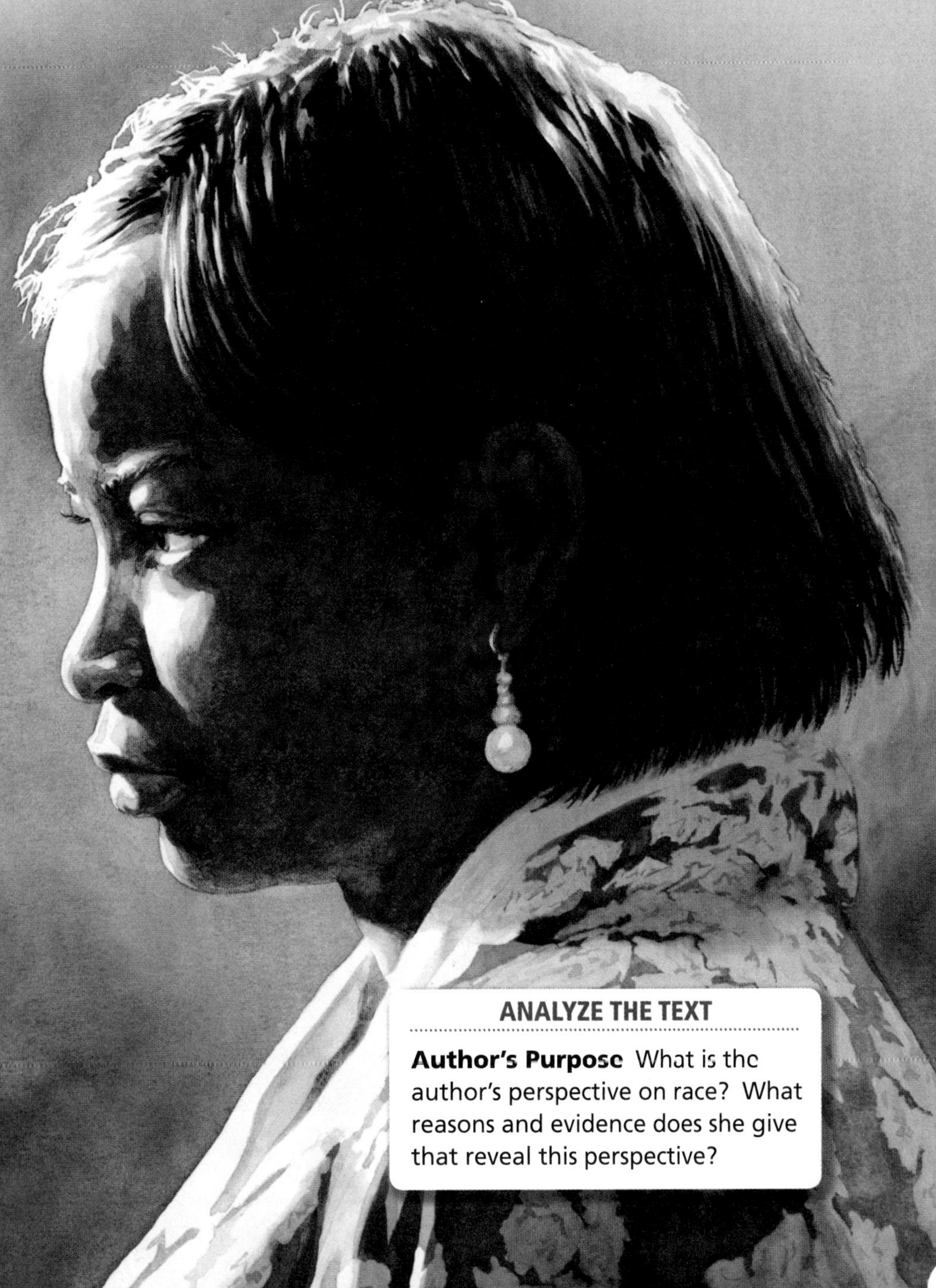

ANALYZE THE TEXT

Author's Purpose What is the author's perspective on race? What reasons and evidence does she give that reveal this perspective?

In the coming years there would be other reminders of the cruel system called segregation that sought to keep black people down. But it was Daddy who showed M. L. and A. D. and me how to speak out against hatred and bigotry and stand up for what's right.

Daddy was the minister at Ebenezer Baptist Church. And after losing our playmates, when M. L., A. D., and I heard our father speak from his pulpit, his words held new meaning.

And Daddy practiced what he preached. He always stood up for himself when confronted with hatred and bigotry, and each day he shared his encounters at the dinner table.

When a shoe salesman told Daddy and M. L. that he'd only serve them in the back of the store because they were black, Daddy took M. L. somewhere else to buy new shoes.

Another time, a police officer pulled Daddy over and called him "boy." Daddy pointed to M. L. sitting next to him in the car and said, "This is a boy. I am a man, and until you call me one, I will not listen to you."

These stories were as nourishing as the food that was set before us.

Years would pass, and many new lessons would be learned. There would be numerous speeches and marches and prizes. But my brother never forgot the example of our father, or the promise he had made to our mother on the day his friends turned him away.

And when he was much older, my brother M. L. dreamed a dream . . .

. . . that turned the world upside down.

ANALYZE THE TEXT

Idioms What does the idiom "turned the world upside down" mean? How could you confirm its meaning?

COMPREHENSION

Dig Deeper

How to Analyze the Text

Use these pages to learn about Author's Purpose, Explaining Historical Events, and Idioms. Then read "My Brother Martin" again to apply what you learned.

Author's Purpose

"My Brother Martin" describes Dr. Martin Luther King Jr.'s childhood in Atlanta. Why do you think his sister, Christine, wrote this biography? What was the **author's purpose**, or reason for writing it? To answer, notice the particular points the author includes and the **reasons** and **evidence** used to support them. Putting together these details can help you determine the author's purpose.

Look back at page 56 for details that help to reveal the author's purpose. What does the author say about the laws in her city when she and her brothers were growing up?

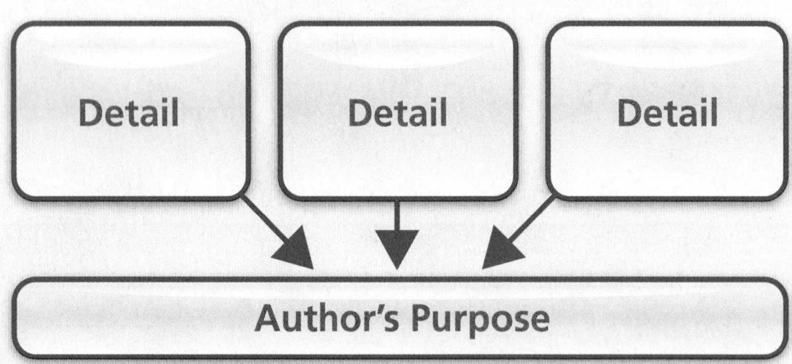

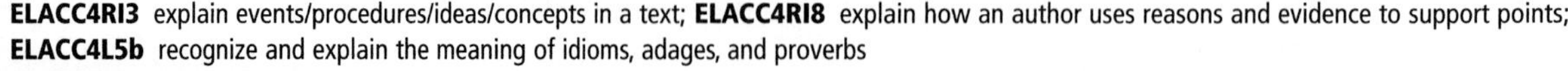
ELACC4RI3 explain events/procedures/ideas/concepts in a text; **ELACC4RI8** explain how an author uses reasons and evidence to support points; **ELACC4L5b** recognize and explain the meaning of idioms, adages, and proverbs

Explain Historical Events

Authors of biographies tell not only about a person's life but also about the **historical events** that took place during that person's life. To understand historical events, think about the information in the text that tells about what happened and why. For example, in "My Brother Martin," the author says that her family rarely went to picture shows. This was because of laws that kept black people separate.

Idioms

An **idiom** is a phrase that means something different from what the individual words suggest. For instance, Mr. King could have bitten his tongue when pulled over by the police officer, but instead he spoke out. The idiom *biting his tongue* means "keeping quiet." Idioms help make ideas more powerful.

Your Turn

RETURN TO THE ESSENTIAL QUESTION

Review the selection to prepare to discuss this question: *What might lead a person to try to change the world?* As you discuss, take turns identifying key events and text evidence, telling why they are important. Answer each other's questions.

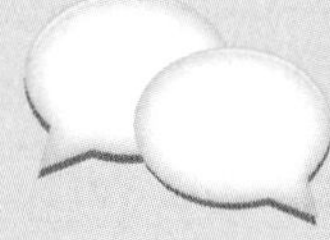

Classroom Conversation

Continue your discussion of "My Brother Martin" by explaining your answers to these questions:

1. How do you think having strong role models affected M. L.'s desire to create change?
2. In what way is Dr. Martin Luther King Jr. a role model for others?
3. Do you think M. L.'s parents were right to shield the children from segregation? Why?

FREE AT LAST!

Make a Timeline In a small group, look back through the selection and list the most important events in M. L.'s childhood. Then use the list to create a timeline of these events. Add illustrations to your timeline to help show what was happening at important times.

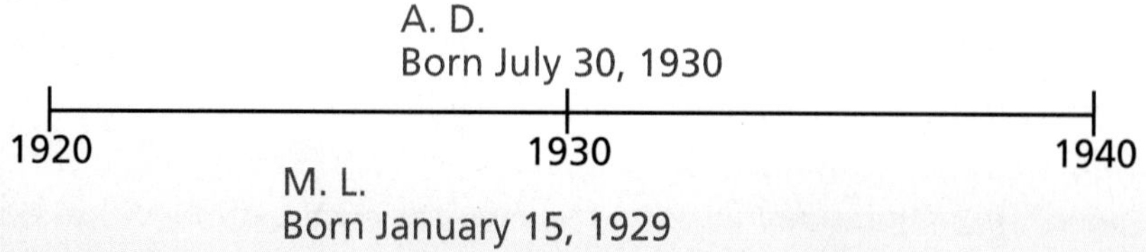

WRITE ABOUT READING

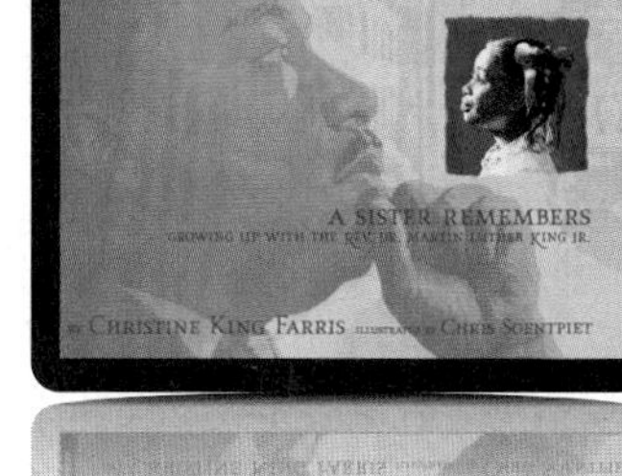

Response What did "My Brother Martin" teach you about Dr. Martin Luther King Jr.'s childhood? Write a paragraph explaining what you learned and which details you found most interesting. Use facts and examples from the selection to explain your ideas. End your paragraph with a strong conclusion.

Writing Tip

Begin your paragraph with an introduction. Make sure that each sentence in your paragraph has a subject and a predicate.

COMMON CORE **ELACC4RI3** explain events/procedures/ideas/concepts in a text; **ELACC4W1d** provide a concluding statement or section; **ELACC4W9b** apply grade 4 Reading standards to informational texts; **ELACC4SL1c** pose and respond to questions and make comments that contribute to the discussion and link to others' remarks; **ELACC4SL1d** review key ideas expressed and explain own ideas and understanding

Lesson 2

POETRY

GENRE

Poetry, such as this lyrical poetry, uses the sound and rhythm of words to suggest images and express feelings.

TEXT FOCUS

Poet's Message Poets often use descriptions and images to express feelings and convey a message to the reader. Discuss the images Langston Hughes uses in each poem. What is his message to the reader in each poem?

ELACC4RL2 determine theme from details/ summarize; **ELACC4RL10** read and comprehend literature

Go Digital

Langston HUGHES: A Poet and a Dreamer

Langston Hughes was a famous African American poet whose words inspired and affected people all over the world. Like Dr. Martin Luther King Jr., Hughes believed that a person's dream, or goal, could change the future. In the following poems, Hughes writes about dreams and why they are so important.

Langston Hughes, 1902–1967

As a child, Langston Hughes moved from city to city in the Midwest. Without a permanent home, he found comfort in reading. Books were as nourishing to him as food. He grew into a strong reader and writer. He published his first poems and stories when he was in high school.

As a young man, Hughes traveled the world. He wrote about his encounters with all kinds of people. At home, he had to deal with the unfair laws of segregation that kept people apart because of race. He thought deeply about injustice.

Hughes moved to Harlem, an African American neighborhood in New York City. Harlem became the place he preferred to all others. Here, writers, artists, and musicians were creating great works of art. Hughes's career as a writer blossomed. He went on to write numerous poems, stories, plays, and articles. Many of his works captured the culture and experiences of African Americans, to be shared with readers around the world.

Langston Hughes is known as one of the most important poets of the twentieth century. His work has set an example for writers to come.

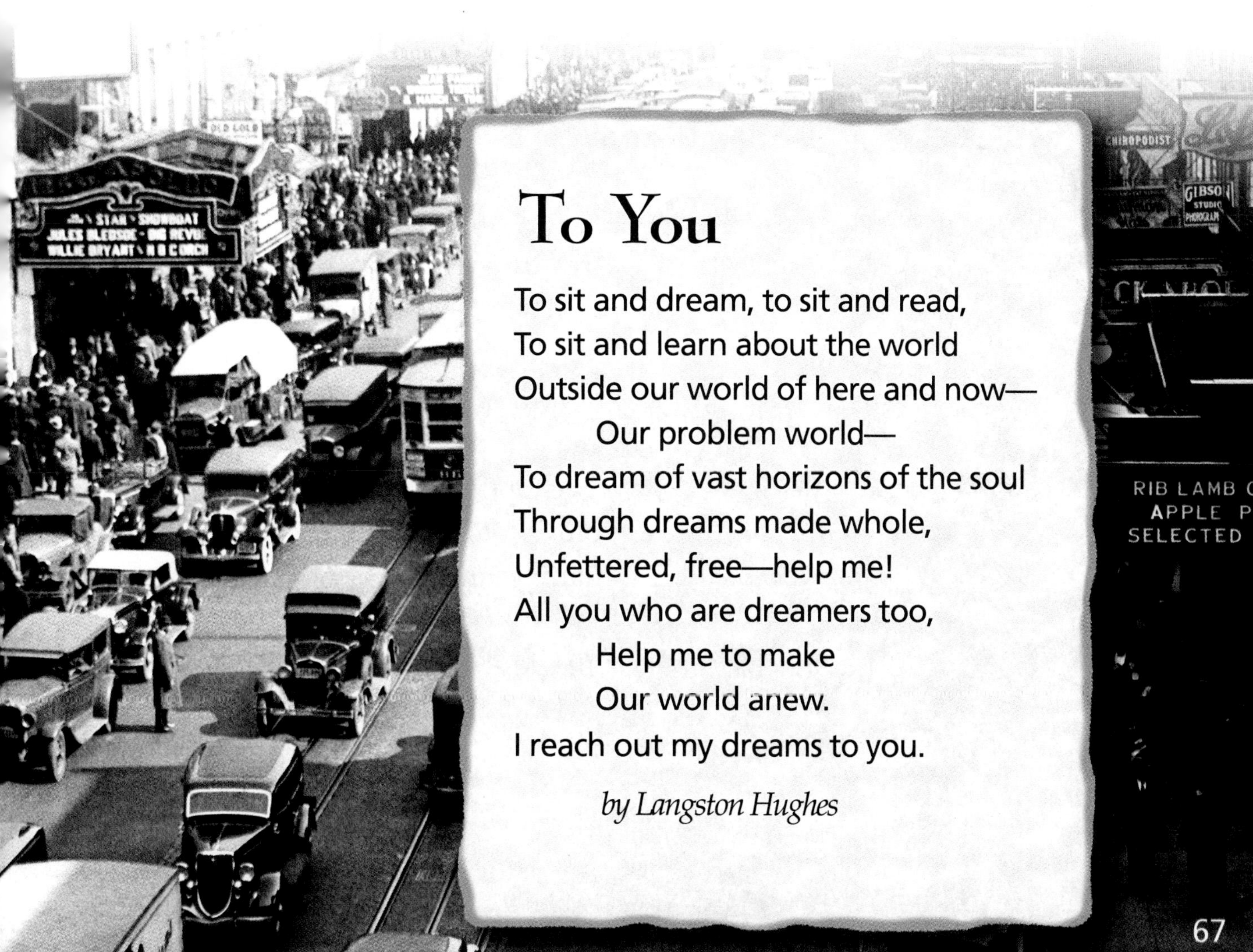

To You

To sit and dream, to sit and read,
To sit and learn about the world
Outside our world of here and now—
    Our problem world—
To dream of vast horizons of the soul
Through dreams made whole,
Unfettered, free—help me!
All you who are dreamers too,
    Help me to make
    Our world anew.
I reach out my dreams to you.

by Langston Hughes

Dreams

Hold fast to dreams
For if dreams die
Life is a broken-winged bird
That cannot fly.

Hold fast to dreams
For when dreams go
Life is a barren field
Frozen with snow.

by Langston Hughes

The Dream Keeper

Bring me all of your dreams,
You dreamers,
Bring me all of your
Heart melodies
That I may wrap them
In a blue cloud-cloth
Away from the too-rough fingers
Of the world.

by Langston Hughes

Write a Dream Poem

Do you have a special dream? Write a poem about it. Try to recall the important details and show how you feel. Your dream might be big or small. It might be something you hope to accomplish tomorrow, next month, or in many years.

See where your dreams take you!

Compare Texts

TEXT TO TEXT

Compare and Contrast Dr. Martin Luther King Jr. and Langston Hughes both talked about dreams. How were their dreams the same? How were their dreams different? Discuss your ideas with a partner.

TEXT TO SELF

Write Paragraphs Dr. Martin Luther King Jr. and Langston Hughes both dreamed about making the world a better place. Write about a dream you have for making your neighborhood, your city, or even the world better.

TEXT TO WORLD

Compare Forms Prose is writing that is made up of sentences and organized into paragraphs. Poetry is writing that is made up of lines. Many poems are organized into groups of lines called stanzas, or verses. Compare the poem "Dreams" to the biography "My Brother Martin." How is each kind of text organized? How does each text teach you something about the world around you? Make notes on your findings and compare them with a partner's.

ELACC4RL1 refer to details and examples when explaining what the text says explicitly and when drawing inferences; **ELACC4RL2** determine theme from details/summarize; **ELACC4RL5** explain major differences between poems, drama, and prose/refer to their structural elements; **ELACC4W10** write routinely over extended time frames and shorter time frames

ELACC4L1f produce complete sentences, recognizing and correcting fragments and run-ons

Grammar

What Are the Four Kinds of Sentences? A sentence that tells something is a **statement.** A statement ends with a period. A sentence that asks something is a **question.** A question ends with a question mark. A sentence that tells someone to do something is a **command**. A command ends with a period or an exclamation mark. A sentence that shows strong feeling is an **exclamation**. An exclamation ends with an exclamation point.

Sentence	Kind of Sentence
M. L. had an older sister.	statement
Do you have brothers or sisters?	question
Listen to his famous speech.	command
That speech is so inspiring!	exclamation

Take turns reading each sentence below with a partner. Tell what kind of sentence it is.

1. How can I help spread Dr. Martin Luther King Jr.'s message?
2. Help me find my copy of his sister's book.
3. I'll give it to a friend.
4. That's a good idea!

Avoid using too many statements when you write. Turn some statements into questions, commands, or exclamations. This will make your writing livelier and help to keep your readers' attention.

Statements	Varied Sentence Types

We are writing poetry this week. I wrote an awesome poem. It's about my dreams for the future. Maybe you would like to hear it.	Can you believe we're writing poetry this week? I wrote an awesome poem! It's about my dreams for the future. Listen to it!

 Connect Grammar to Writing

As you revise your story, look for opportunities to use questions, commands, and exclamations as well as statements.

ELACC4W3b use dialogue and description to develop experiences and events or show characters' responses; **ELACC4W4** produce writing in which development and organization are appropriate to task, purpose, and audience; **ELACC4W10** write routinely over extended time frames and shorter time frames; **ELACC4L3a** choose words and phrases for effect; **ELACC4L3b** choose punctuation for effect

Narrative Writing

✔ Word Choice When the author of "My Brother Martin" says that segregation was "a crushing blow" and that her family's pride was "nourishing," her words help us understand her feelings. In your **story**, use words that capture thoughts and actions. Also choose punctuation for effect. Use the Writing Traits Checklist below as you revise your writing.

Victor drafted a story about a boy who stood up for his rights. Later, he added some words that describe more clearly what his characters think and do.

Writing Traits Checklist

- ✔ **Ideas**
  Did I show the events vividly?
- ✔ **Organization**
  Did I tell the events in order?
- ✔ **Word Choice**
  Did I use words that describe?
- ✔ **Voice**
  Does my dialogue sound natural?
- ✔ **Sentence Fluency**
  Did I use a variety of sentence types?
- ✔ **Conventions**
  Did I use correct spelling, grammar, and punctuation?

Revised Draft

James could hardly believe his luck. His ~~James's~~ new house was right next to a basketball court. He grabbed ~~got~~ his ball and raced ~~went~~ over.

A boy was already shooting baskets.

"Can I shoot some?" James asked.

"Not now," said the boy. "I was here first." His face and voice were ~~was~~ unfriendly. ~~His voice was unfriendly too~~.

James sat on the bench. He waited patiently for a whole hour and then asked again.

Final Copy

Fair Play: A Story

by Victor Alvez

James could hardly believe his luck. His new house was right next to a basketball court. He grabbed his ball and raced over.

A boy was already shooting baskets. "Can I shoot some?" James asked.

"Not now," said the boy. "I was here first." His face and voice were unfriendly.

James sat on the bench. He waited patiently for a whole hour and then asked again. The boy just kept on shooting baskets. James's face grew hot. At last he stood up. "Hey!" he said in a loud, firm voice. "This court's for everyone, not just you."

The boy stopped. His look of surprise turned to an embarrassed grin.

"Yeah, you're right," he said. "It's your turn." Then he said, "My name's Cole. What's yours?"

Reading as a Writer

How does Victor make the story more exciting? How does Victor describe his characters and their actions?

In my final paper, I added words to better show what my characters think and do. I made sure I used a variety of sentences, including an exclamation for effect.

Lesson 3

My Librarian Is a Camel

From Idea to Book

Vocabulary in Context

TARGET VOCABULARY

isolated
virtual
access
devour
impassable
remote
obtain
preserve
extremes
avid

Vocabulary Reader

Context Cards

ELACC4L6 acquire/use vocabulary, including academic and domain-specific

1 isolated

An island that is isolated lies far from any other land.

2 virtual

A virtual library is online or on a computer, not in a physical location.

3 access

If you need to go online, go to a place with Internet access.

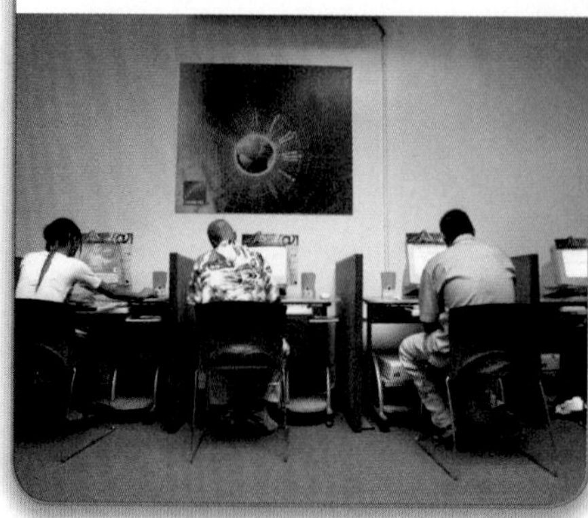

4 devour

Some people love to read so much that they devour books.

- ▶ Study each Context Card.
- ▶ Discuss one picture. Use a different Vocabulary word from the one on the card.

5 impassable

Sand covered the road, making it impassable, or blocked.

6 remote

Sometimes, the easiest way to get to a remote village is by boat.

7 obtain

Hospitals obtain, or get, blood from people who donate it.

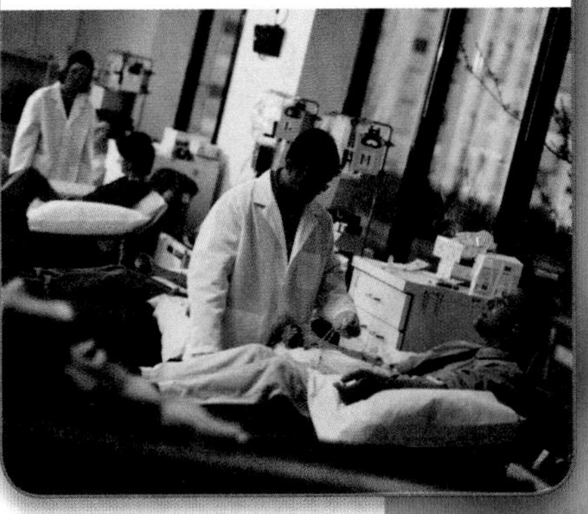

8 preserve

Sometimes people dress up to preserve, or remember, their culture's history.

9 extremes

A zebra's colors show extremes. Its black and white stripes are opposites.

10 avid

Nathan likes baseball, but he is also an avid reader. He loves books.

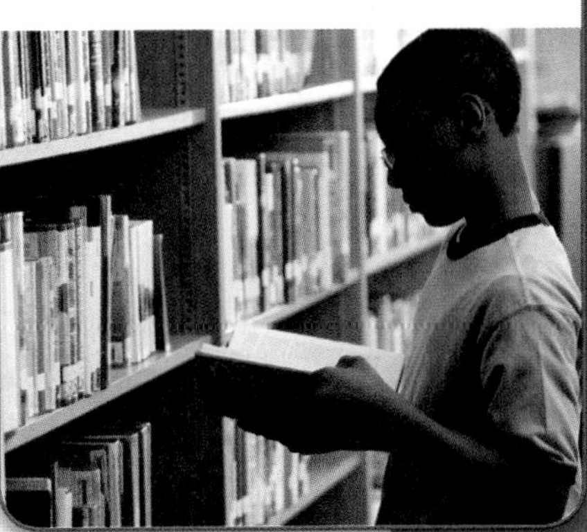

Read and Comprehend

 TARGET SKILL

Cause and Effect The structure of a text is the way in which the ideas are organized. Nonfiction selections may be organized by sequence of events, by similarities and differences, and by causes and effects. A **cause** is an event that makes another event happen. An **effect** is what happens as a result of the cause.

As you read "My Librarian Is a Camel," look for a pattern of causes and effects. In each new section of text, ask yourself, *What is happening? Why is it happening? What effect does it have?* Use a graphic organizer like this one to show the causes and effects.

Cause	Effect
•	•
•	•
•	•

TARGET STRATEGY

Visualize As you read, use details from the text to help you form mental pictures of the people, places, and things the author is describing. **Visualizing** people and places can help you better keep track of what you read.

COMMON CORE **ELACC4RI5** describe the overall structure of a text or part of a text

PREVIEW THE TOPIC

Media

The term *media* refers to all kinds of information and entertainment sources, such as books, newspapers, magazines, TV, radio, and the Internet. In most places around the world, finding books to read and movies to watch is quick and easy. But what happens when people live in isolated corners of the earth, without libraries, Internet access, and even roads to travel on?

"My Librarian Is a Camel" tells how children in remote locations get their hands on books.

Lesson 3

ANCHOR TEXT

TARGET SKILL

Cause and Effect Think about how the text is organized. Look for and explain cause-and-effect relationships, or how one event leads to another.

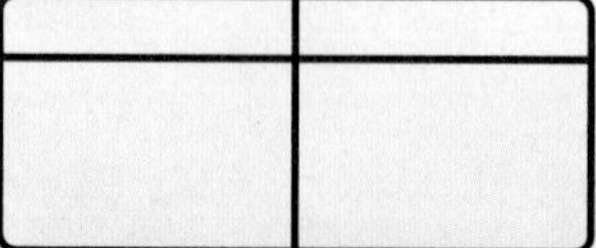

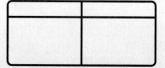

GENRE

Informational text gives facts and examples about a topic. As you read, look for:

- headings that begin sections of related information
- photographs and captions
- graphics to help explain the topic, such as maps, photographs, and captions

ELACC4RI4 determine the meaning of general academic and domain-specific words and phrases; **ELACC4RI5** describe the overall structure of a text or part of a text; **ELACC4RI7** interpret information presented visually, orally, or quantitatively

Go Digital

MEET THE AUTHOR

Margriet Ruurs

Margriet Ruurs travels the world, sharing her love of books with children. She has taught reading and writing in countries as far away as Pakistan, Indonesia, and Malaysia. She has written more than twenty books and has even opened a book-themed bed-and-breakfast!

My Librarian Is a Camel

How Books Are Brought to Children Around the World

by Margriet Ruurs

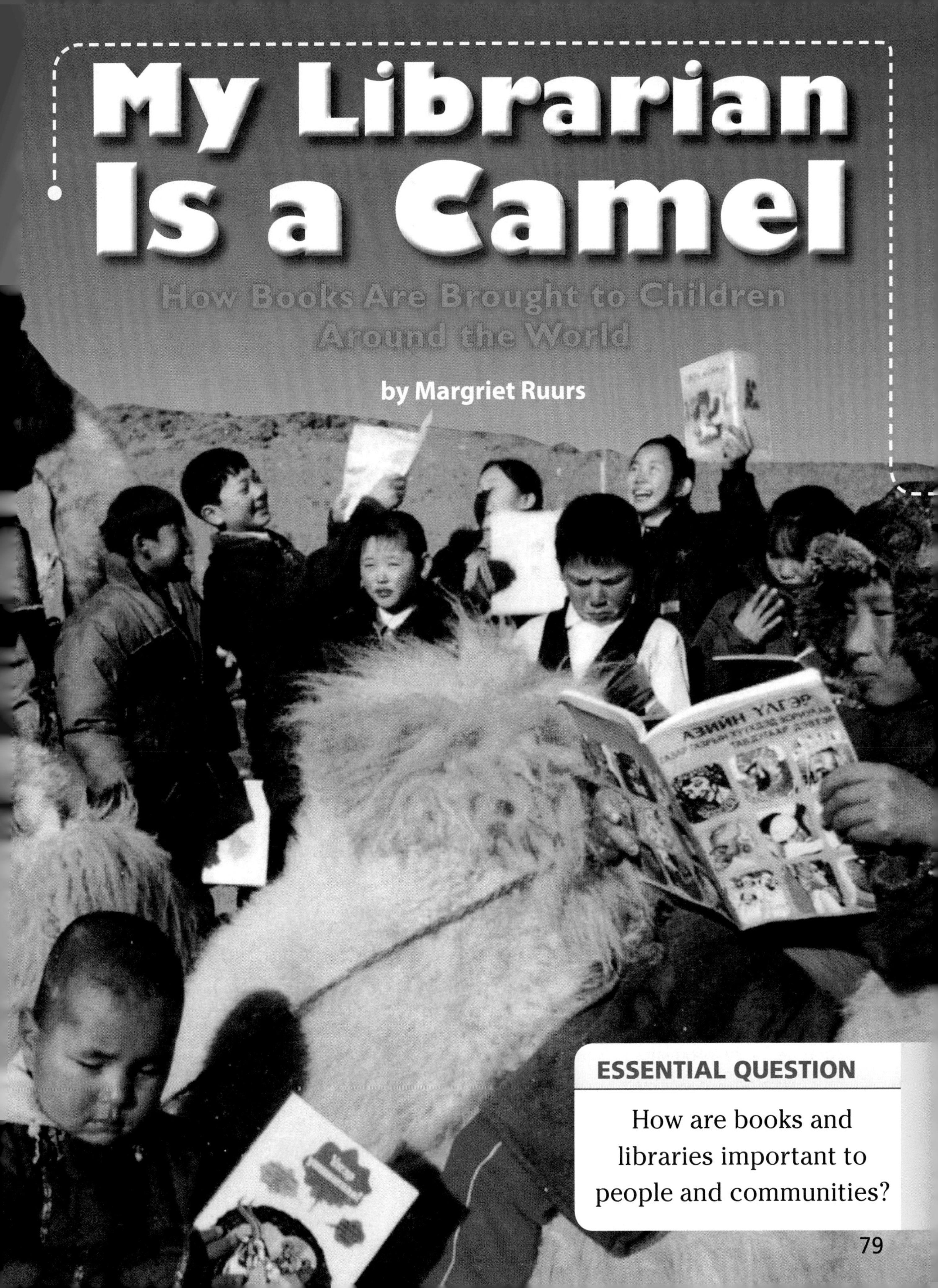

ESSENTIAL QUESTION

How are books and libraries important to people and communities?

Not every community has a library. Read on to learn more about some of the unique ways librarians deliver books to communities in distant areas!

CANADA

Nunavut, which means "Our Land" in the language of the Inuit people, is a huge territory in Canada's north. The arctic region stretches from the North Pole to Arviat in the south, and from Kugluktuk in the west to Panjnirtung in the east. The distances are huge, and many villages are very isolated. The Northwest Territories reach from Nunavut in the east to the Yukon in the west.

Larger towns like Iqaluit, Tuktoyaktuk, and Yellowknife have their own public-library buildings, but many communities are just too small. Some communities, like Fort Liard, have a virtual library, which offers Internet access. But even if the community does not have any kind of library building, the Northwest Territories public library system offers books to everyone in the far north through their Borrower-by-Mail program.

Tyson Anakvik, Colin Igutaaq, James Naikak, and Cameron Ovilok are friends in Cambridge Bay, Nunavut. They request library books by e-mail or by phone. A mobile library doesn't bring the books to their village; the books are sent through the mail. The Borrower-by-Mail program will send children any books they'd like to read. If the library doesn't have a book in its system, librarians will borrow the book from another library in Canada and mail it. They even include a stamped, addressed envelope, so the children won't have to pay to return the book.

The boys take their young friend Liza for a ride on their sled as they walk to the post office to pick up their books. The boys look forward to reading that night. On winter days, the sun does not come above the horizon, and when the thermometer reads minus 50 degrees, the children like to curl up with a good book by the woodstove. While the northern wind howls across the tundra, they read fantasy and action novels. Liza is excited about finding good picture books in the package.

They can keep their books for up to six weeks. After that, they'll pack them up and walk to the local post office to mail the books back to the library. Then they'll check the mail every day . . . until another big brown package arrives with new books to devour in their remote corner of Canada's Arctic.

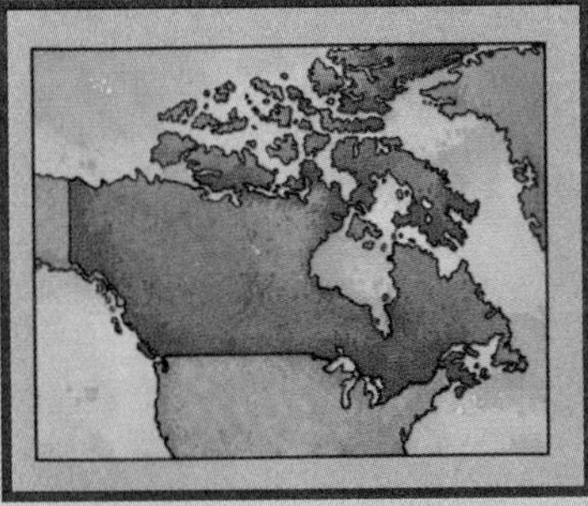

Canada

Capital: Ottawa

Estimated population: 30,532,900

Canada, located in North America, is the second-largest country in the world. The most easterly point of Newfoundland is closer to England than it is to Calgary, Alberta. From east to west, Canada is so wide that there are six time zones within its borders. Canada has two official languages, English and French, and native Canadians also speak their own languages. The original people of the North are called Inuit, and they speak Inuktitut.

FINLAND

In the middle of Aboland Archipelago is a big water called Gullkrona, meaning "Golden Crown." It was given its name by Queen Blanka of Namur (1316–1363). According to an old legend, while on a voyage to Finland, Queen Blanka promised her golden crown to the most beautiful thing she would see along the way. This turned out to be the bay in the south of Finland, and so she let her crown sink into the waves! The bay is now called Gullkrona Bay.

The south coast of Finland skirts the Gulf of Finland. The archipelago, in the southwest, consists of thousands of rocky islands. Some islands have only summer visitors, but others are populated year-round. People in this area of Finland speak both Finnish and Swedish. Since 1976, the Pargas Library has been bringing books to the people of these islands by book boat: *Bokbåt* in Swedish or *Kirjastovene* in Finnish.

The boat, called *Kalkholm*, meaning "Limestone Island" in Swedish, measures 4 meters wide and 12 meters long. It carries about six hundred books. The boat, with a crew consisting of a librarian and an assistant, sails among the islands, making about ten stops. Kids come scrambling down the rocky shores to collect their books. Since winters are severe in Finland, the boat goes out only from May to October.

Maj-Len, the chief librarian in Pargas Stad, oversees the operation of the book boat. "Reading has become very important to our book-boat children," she says. "If the book boat didn't come, they might not be reading at all. They are always happy to see us and their supply of new books."

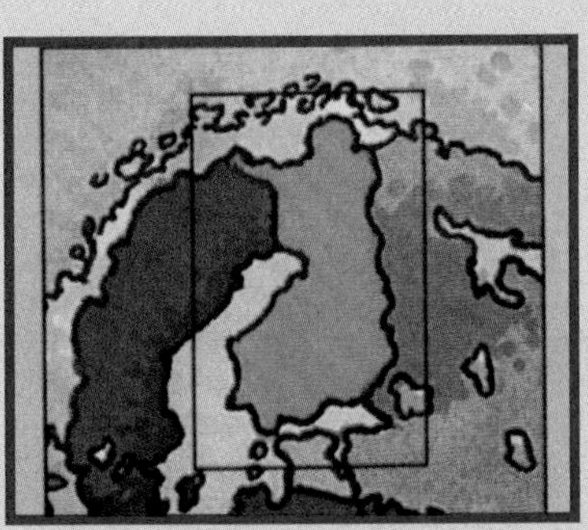

Republic of Finland

Capital: Helsinki

Estimated population: 5,156,000

Finland lies in North Europe. At least a third of the country is north of the Arctic Circle. The country has two official languages, Finnish and Swedish. Other languages include Lappish and Romany.

Lapland is a region that stretches across Norway, Sweden, Finland, and part of Russia. Most of Lapland is within the Arctic Circle, and parts of it are under snow and ice year-round.

In Northern Lapland, four towns share a mobile library bus, which also carries children's books. What makes this bus special is that the service is shared by communities in three countries: Finland, Sweden, and Norway.

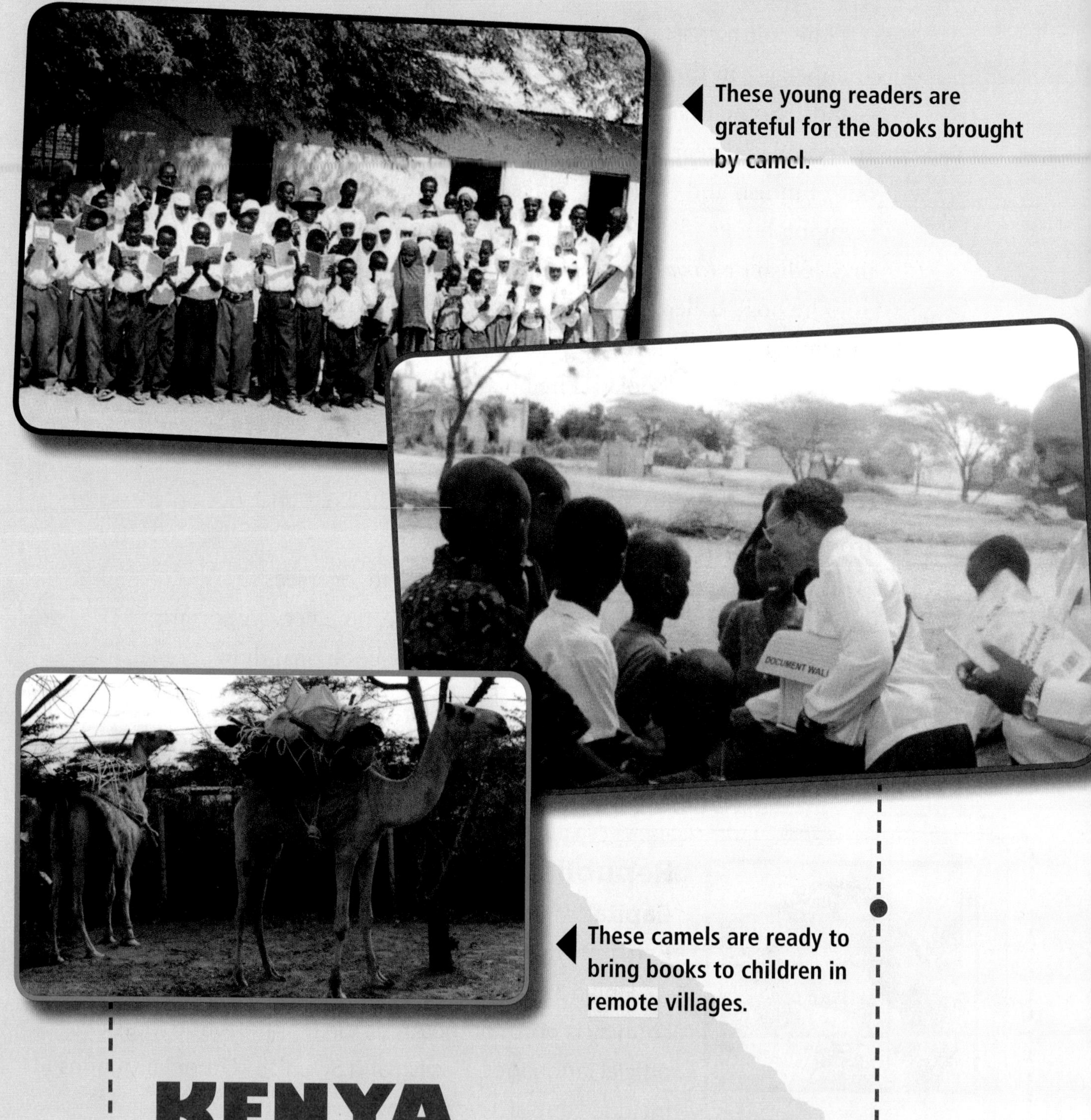

These young readers are grateful for the books brought by camel.

These camels are ready to bring books to children in remote villages.

KENYA

The roads to Bulla Iftin, two hundred miles northeast of Nairobi, are impassable because of the desert sand, even for cars with four-wheel drive. But young people who live in nomadic villages in the area are hungry for books. So librarians use the most economical means of transportation—camels!

Library camels are on the road five days a week. They can carry heavy loads and need little water in the heat of the desert. One camel may carry as many as five hundred books, weighing about four hundred pounds. A driver and a librarian divide the books into two boxes. They saddle them on the camel's back, which is covered with a grass mat for protection. A second camel carries a tent that serves as the library roof.

The students of Bulla Iftin eagerly await the arrival of the camels. When the library caravan finally reaches the village, the children watch as the librarian pitches the tent and displays the books on wooden shelves. The librarian places the grass mats on the ground in the shade of an acacia tree, making a place where the children can sit. The students can treasure their new books for two weeks. When the library camels return, the children can trade their books for new ones.

ANALYZE THE TEXT

Interpret Visuals How do the map and flag in each section connect to the text? Why do you think the author included them?

Republic of Kenya

Capital: Nairobi

Estimated population: 32,000,000

Kenya is a country in East Africa. Kenya's climate varies. The coast, which lies on the Indian Ocean, is hot and humid. Inland, the climate is temperate, but the northern part of the country is dry. The official language is English. The national language is Kiswahili.

MONGOLIA

For centuries, people in Mongolia have led a nomadic lifestyle, moving across the steppe, a vast grass-covered plain, with their herds. Many people are still herders of livestock, moving with their herds as they graze. The life of the nomads has not changed very much since the old days except that nowadays the herders like to use "iron horses," meaning motorbikes, instead of real horses. Very few people have telephones, television, or access to computers, but most people can read! There is almost no illiteracy in this country.

Jambyn Dashdondog is a well-known writer of children's books in Mongolia. He was looking for a way to bring books to the many children of herders' families, who live scattered across the Gobi Desert. A horse-drawn wagon (as well as a camel) is used to carry books into the desert.

Together with Mongolian Children's Cultural Foundation, Mr. Dashdondog was able to obtain a minibus and ten thousand books, mostly donated by Japan. The Japanese books are being translated into Mongolian, and Mr. Dashdondog makes trips with the minibus to bring the books to children in the countryside.

The book tour is called *Amttai Nom* which means "candy books." Why? Because before they share the books, the children are given food, including some sweets. After the children listen to stories and choose books, Mr. Dashdondog asks: "Which was sweeter: books or candies?" And the children always answer: "BOOKS!"

"I just returned from a trip to visit herders' children in the Great Gobi Desert," said Mr. Dashdondog, who has visited nearly ten thousand children in the past two years. "We covered some fifteen hundred kilometers in two weeks. And this was in winter, so it was cold and snowy. We had no winter fuel for our bus, so we had to use summer fuel, and the fuel froze at night, making the bus stall. But we weren't cold: the stories and their heroes kept us warm!"

ANALYZE THE TEXT

Domain-Specific Vocabulary How are words such as *nomadic, steppe, livestock,* and *countryside* related? How does this connect with the topic of the text?

Mongolia

Capital: Ulaanbaatar

Estimated population: 2,300,000

Mongolia is a vast country in northeast Asia, more than one and a half million square kilometers in size. With fewer than two and a half million people living in it, there is lots of empty space throughout the land. The official language is Khalkha Mongol.

To preserve traditional culture and traditions, children are being taught the old Cyrillic Mongolian script, which is written vertically from top to bottom.

The country has high mountain ranges as well as vast desert plains, with the Gobi Desert in the southeast. Snow leopards, wild horses, and ibex still roam the Gobi Desert. Most of the roads that run through Mongolia are unpaved and rough. The climate is one of extremes: cold in winter, hot and very dry in summer.

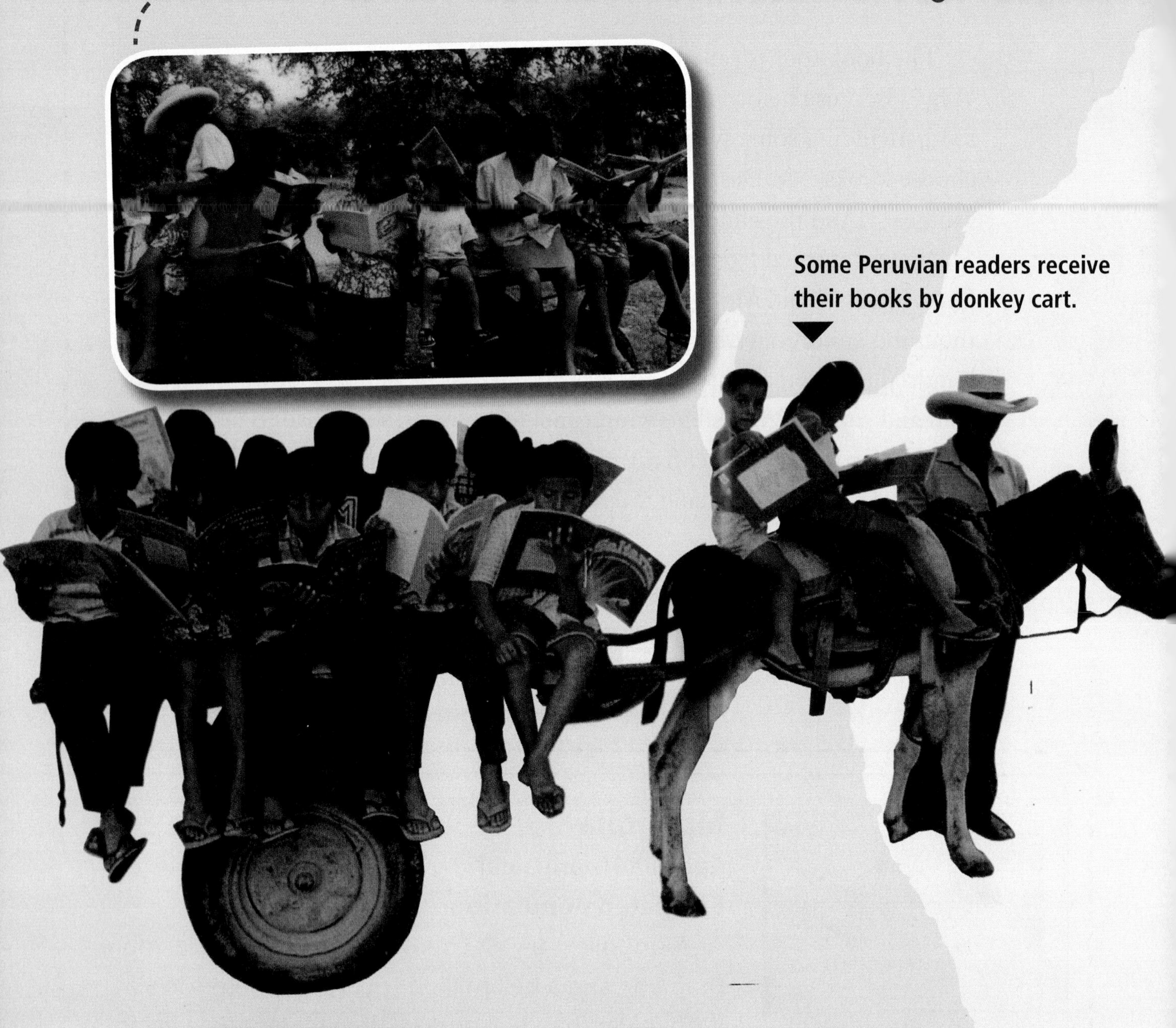

Some Peruvian readers receive their books by donkey cart.

PERU

Children in Peru can receive their books in several different, innovative ways.

CEDILI – IBBY Peru is an institution that delivers books in bags to families in Lima. Each bag contains twenty books, which families can keep for a month. The books come in four different reading levels so that children really learn how to read. The project in Spanish is called *El Libro Compartido en Familia* and enables parents to share the joy of books with their children.

In small, rural communities, books are delivered in wooden suitcases and plastic bags. These suitcases and bags contain books that the community can keep and share for the next three months. The number of books in each suitcase depends on the size of the community. There are no library buildings in these small towns, and people gather outside, in the plaza, to see the books they can check out. In the coastal regions, books are sometimes delivered by donkey cart. The books are stored in the reading promoter's home.

In the ancient city of Cajamarca, reading promoters from various rural areas select and receive a large collection of books for their area. The program is called *Aspaderuc*. The reading promoter lends these books to his or her neighbors, and after three months, a new selection of books goes out to each area. Books in this system are for children and adults.

And last but not least, *Fe Y Alegria* brings a collection of children's books to rural schools. The books are brought from school to school by wagon. The children, who are excited about browsing through the books when they arrive, are turning into avid readers.

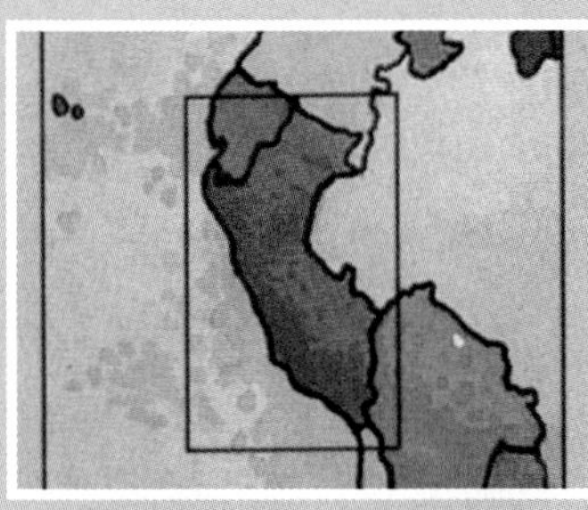

Republic of Peru

Capital: Lima

Estimated population: 28,000,000

Peru, in South America, borders the South Pacific Ocean, between Ecuador and Chile. The tropical coast, the Andes Mountains, and the Amazon River make Peru a diverse and interesting country. The Peruvian people speak Spanish. Quechua is the country's other official language. Peru's history includes the Inca civilization, which occupied much of the South American continent five hundred years ago.

▲ The elephant library is headed for remote villages in northern Thailand.

THAILAND

In Omkoi, a region of northern Thailand, there are no schools or libraries. Tribal people cannot read or write. The government of Thailand hopes to change that with a literacy program that includes bringing books to remote villages in the jungle.

A number of these villages can be reached only on foot. This makes transportation difficult, especially during the rainy season. How do you get books to people who need them most, when they live in hard-to-reach mountainous regions of northern Thailand? Elephants!

The Chiangmai Non-Formal Education Center had the idea to use elephants as libraries. Elephants are already being used here to plow the paddy fields and to carry logs and crops. Now more than twenty elephants in the Omkoi region are used to carry books. The elephant teams spend two to three days in each village. Each trip covers seven or eight villages, so it takes each elephant team eighteen to twenty days to complete a round-trip.

The Books-by-Elephant delivery program serves thirty-seven villages, providing education for almost two thousand people in the Omkoi region. They have even designed special metal slates that won't break when carried on the elephants' backs across the rough terrain.

These slates are used to teach Thai children to write and read. (There are also two-person teams carrying books to about sixteen villages, bringing learning materials to another six hundred people.)

In Bangkok, the capital of Thailand, old train carriages have been transformed into a library. The train is called *Hong Rotfai Yoawachon*, which means "Library Train for Young People." The train serves the homeless children of Bangkok. The Railway Police Division in Bangkok realized there was a need for a safe place for street children, so they refurbished the old train carriages at the railway station, where many of the kids were hanging out. The police restored the trains to their old glory, complete with wood paneling and shining copper light fixtures. They turned the railway cars into a library and a classroom. Here the children learn to read and write. The police have even transformed the area around the train into a garden, where they grow herbs and vegetables.

ANALYZE THE TEXT

Cause and Effect Why did the Chiangmai Non-Formal Education Center put together the Books-by-Elephant program? What is the effect of the center's efforts?

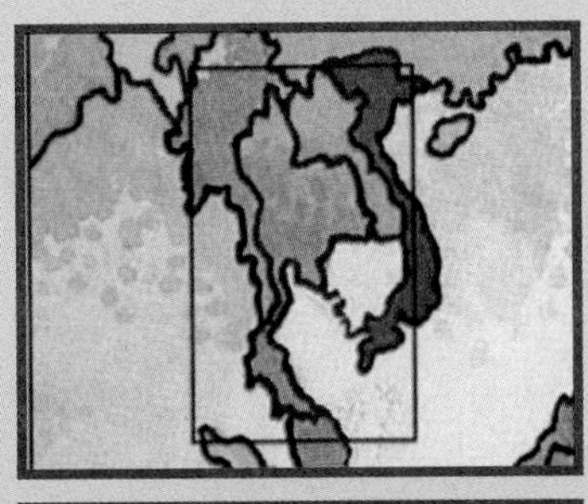

Kingdom of Thailand

Capital: Bangkok

Estimated population: 62,860,000

Thailand (TIE-land), which means "the land of the free," lies in Southeast Asia. The climate varies from season to season: dry in January and February, hot in March and May, wet from June to October, and cool in November and December. The official language of the country is Thai.

COMPREHENSION

Dig Deeper

How to Analyze the Text

Use these pages to learn about Cause and Effect, Interpreting Visuals, and Domain-Specific Vocabulary. Then read "My Librarian Is a Camel" again to apply what you learned.

Cause and Effect

"My Librarian Is a Camel" tells about six remote places in the world and how the children who live there get books to read. The selection is organized into six sections with the same text structure. Each section describes a different **cause-and-effect relationship**. For example, the section about Canada explains that many villages in the Nunavut region are too small and too remote to have their own libraries. As a result, the Borrower-by-Mail program was started.

Turn to pages 84–85. What is the cause of the roads being impassable in this part of Kenya? What is the effect of the roads being impassable?

Cause	Effect
•	•
•	•
•	•

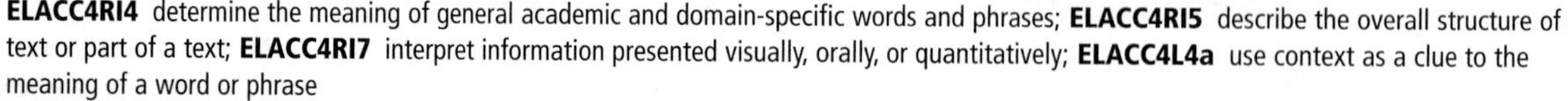
ELACC4RI4 determine the meaning of general academic and domain-specific words and phrases; **ELACC4RI5** describe the overall structure of a text or part of a text; **ELACC4RI7** interpret information presented visually, orally, or quantitatively; **ELACC4L4a** use context as a clue to the meaning of a word or phrase

Interpret Visuals

Each part of "My Librarian Is a Camel" includes a special feature called a **sidebar.** A sidebar is a separate section that is set off from the main text. It gives information that's not included in the main text. The sidebar on page 85 shows a map of Kenya and the Kenyan flag. These **visuals,** along with the photographs and captions on page 84, help you learn more about Kenya and its people.

Domain-Specific Vocabulary

Special areas of knowledge are called **domains.** Every domain has its own set of important words. These words are called **domain-specific vocabulary.** "My Librarian Is a Camel" is a social studies selection. It includes vocabulary such as *tundra* and *archipelago*, which describe types of land. Look for context clues for these words in the text. For example, *thousands of rocky islands* is a clue to the meaning of *archipelago*.

Your Turn

RETURN TO THE ESSENTIAL QUESTION

Turn and Talk Review the selection with a partner to prepare to discuss this question: *How are books and libraries important to people and communities?* Take turns reviewing and explaining the key ideas. Ask questions to clarify each other's ideas. Use text evidence to support your answers.

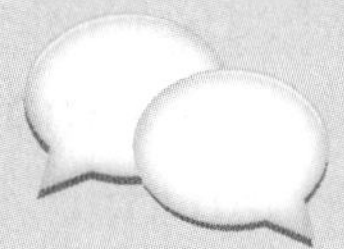

Classroom Conversation

Continue your discussion of "My Librarian Is a Camel" by explaining your answers to these questions:

1. Why might people work hard to provide library services?
2. Why do you think the children from Mongolia say that books are sweeter than candy?
3. Do you think everyone should have access to books? Why or why not?

RESEARCH A COUNTRY

Make a Poster In "My Librarian Is a Camel," the author includes information for each country. Choose one country to research. Then make a poster that gives details about the country, such as its location, its culture, and some famous cities or sights. Include visuals that illustrate key details about the country.

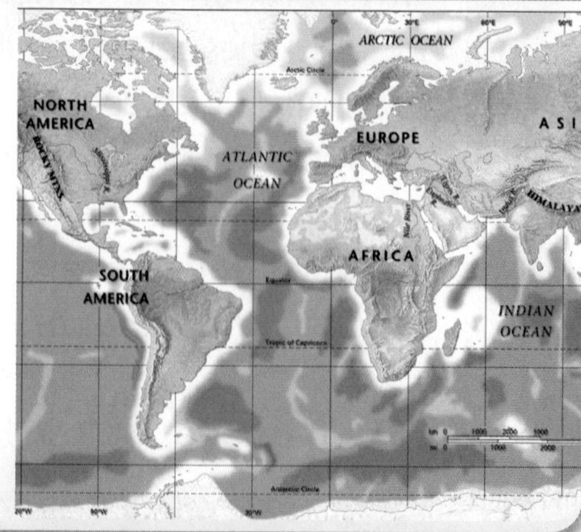

WRITE ABOUT READING

Response Think of the different libraries described in "My Librarian Is a Camel." Write one paragraph explaining which library you would most like to use and why. Be sure to support your opinion with details and examples from the text. Make sure to mention the country where that library is located and how the books get to the library.

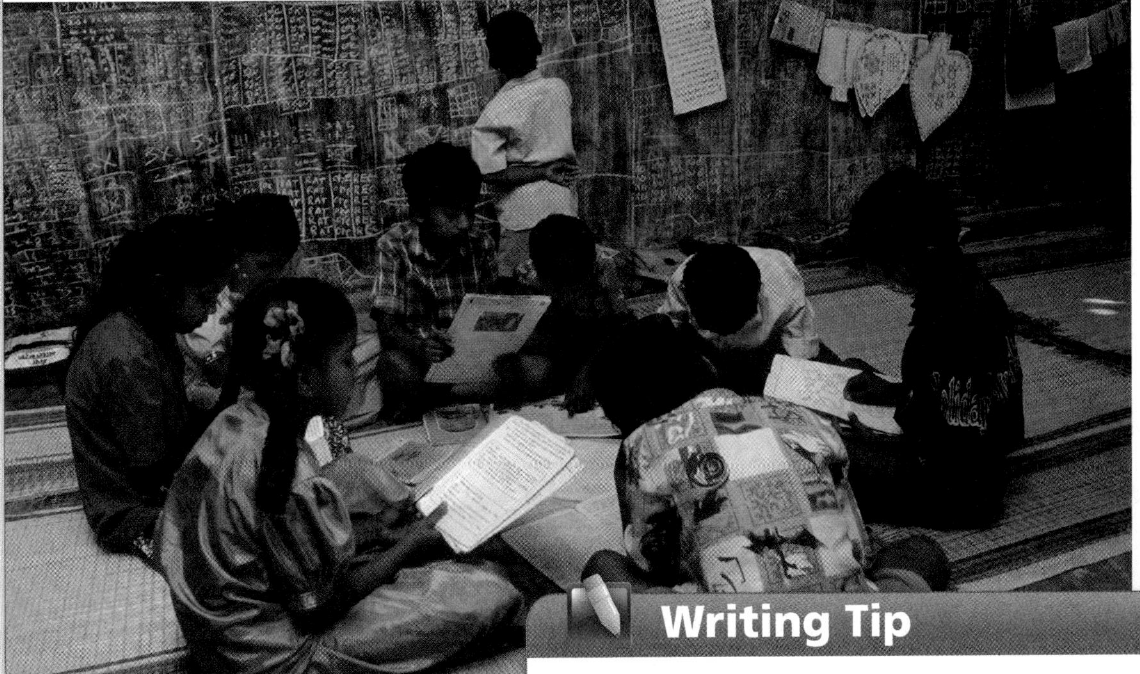

Writing Tip

As you write your response, try to use more than one kind of sentence. For example, use punctuation for effect by including an exclamation to show a feeling of excitement or surprise.

COMMON CORE **ELACC4RI1** refer to details and examples when explaining what the text says explicitly and when drawing inferences; **ELACC4W1b** provide reasons supported by facts and details; **ELACC4W7** conduct short research projects that build knowledge through investigation; **ELACC4W9b** apply grade 4 Reading standards to informational texts; **ELACC4SL1a** come to discussions prepared/explicitly draw on preparation and other information about the topic; **ELACC4SL1d** review key ideas expressed and explain own ideas and understanding; **ELACC4L3b** choose punctuation for effect

Lesson 3

INFORMATIONAL TEXT

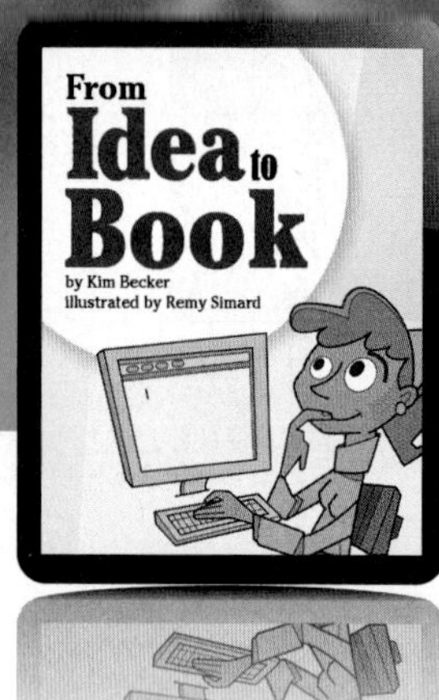

GENRE

Informational text, such as this article, gives information about a topic. Informational text often includes visuals, such as photographs and diagrams.

TEXT FOCUS

Procedures Informational text often explains how something is created or built. The procedures are explained step by step and are often shown in a chart or diagram. Look for the diagram in this article.

ELACC4RI3 explain events/procedures/ideas/concepts in a text; **ELACC4RI7** interpret information presented visually, orally, or quantitatively; **ELACC4RI10** read and comprehend informational texts

From Idea to Book

by Kim Becker
illustrated by Remy Simard

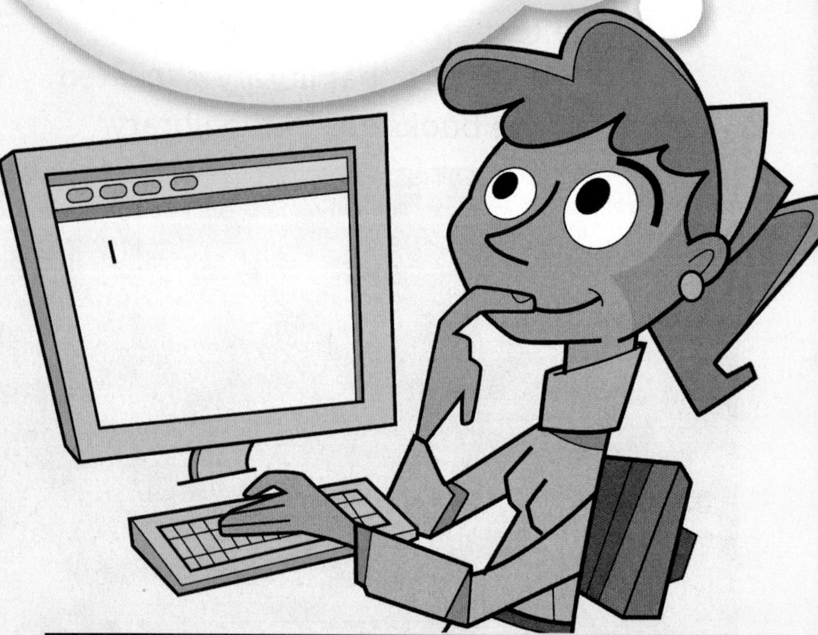

Have you ever wondered how a book is made? It takes a lot of people to make a book. It can take months, or even years, for a book to go from an idea to a finished product.

A book begins when an author comes up with an idea for a book. Authors get ideas in different ways. They may get ideas from their own lives, from watching the world around them, or from reading.

Next, an author may plan the book by making an outline. Sometimes authors do research to gather information. They may read books or articles. They may interview people or visit places.

Then, the author begins to write. Authors may write for months or years to finish a manuscript. A manuscript is the text an author produces for publication. Sometimes authors make many changes or even start over during the writing process.

Finally, the author sends the completed manuscript to a publisher. If the publisher decides to publish the book, the author works with an editor. An editor reads the manuscript. Then, he or she recommends changes to improve the book. A copyeditor reads the manuscript to correct any grammatical errors.

After an author makes the suggested changes, a designer may decide how the book will look. The designer may choose the size, shape, and type styles for the book. Some picture book authors create their own illustrations. If not, an illustrator is chosen to create pictures for the book.

First, the designer or illustrator decides what scenes to illustrate. He or she plans what pictures should go on which pages. Next, the illustrator makes sketches of pictures that will go on each page. As they sketch, illustrators decide how the characters and setting will look. They use techniques such as perspective and point of view to clearly show story events.

The sketches are sent to the publishing company. The editor makes sure the pictures clearly tell the story. The designer checks how the words and pictures will fit together on the pages. He or she may make suggestions for improving the art.

After the design changes are made, the illustrator begins creating the final pictures. The illustrator chooses what tools to use, such as paint, pastels, crayons, or a computer. As the illustrator works, he or she may make many changes to the illustrations. The illustrator may change the colors, the perspective, or the composition of pictures. It may take months to create all the pictures.

How a Book Is Made

An author writes a manuscript.

An editor helps the author revise the manuscript and prepare it for publication.

The printer prints the pages. The pages are bound and trimmed. The book cover is added.

The books are stored in a warehouse until they are purchased by stores and libraries.

The finished art is then sent to the publisher. The designer adjusts how the pictures and words fit together on the pages. The completed pages are sent to the printer. Many books are still made into books with paper pages. However, many titles are available as eBooks, or electronic books.

The printer uses huge printing presses to make the pages. Many pages of a picture book can be printed on one big sheet of paper. Printing presses can print thousands of pages in just a few hours. The big sheets of printed pages are then sent to the bindery. Here they are folded into booklets called signatures. The signatures are gathered, along with the endpapers, and stitched together. The bound signatures are trimmed along the edges. Then, they are glued into the book cover. The finished books are then sent to the publisher's warehouse. They are stored there until they are purchased by libraries and bookstores.

A designer often chooses a style for the book and the illustrator. The illustrator then makes the sketches.

The editor and designer check that the words and pictures work together.

The illustrator creates the final artwork.

The designer finishes the pages. The pages are sent to the printer or to be made into an eBook.

E-readers have changed how some books are made. Publishers sell some books as eBooks. However, some authors do not use a publisher at all. Instead of sending a manuscript to a publisher, some authors turn their manuscripts into eBooks themselves. Many websites offer services that help authors convert their manuscripts into an e-reader format. Some websites offer the help of eBook designers who make sure photos or illustrations match the words. Finally, an author's eBook is uploaded to virtual bookstores on the Internet. Customers can purchase and download eBooks from these websites.

Compare Texts

TEXT TO TEXT

Compare Texts With a partner, compare "My Librarian Is a Camel" and "From Idea to Book." Discuss these questions: *How is "My Librarian Is a Camel" organized? How is "From Idea to Book" organized? Is each selection fiction or nonfiction?* After you have discussed your ideas, work with your partner to write a response to each question.

TEXT TO SELF

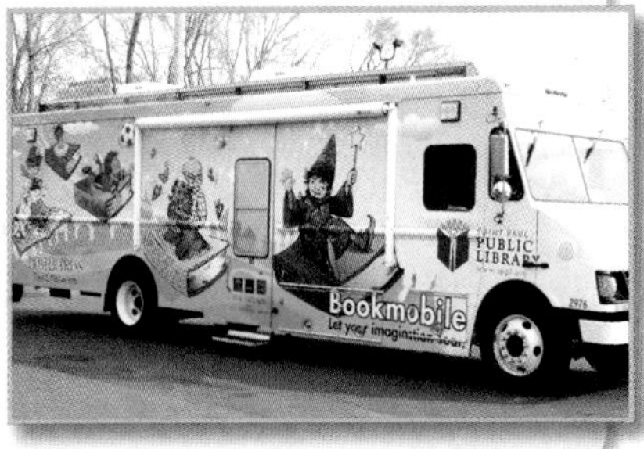

Make a Plan Imagine you live in a community that does not have access to a library. Write a letter to the closest library proposing a way for books to be delivered to your community. Use ideas from "My Librarian Is a Camel" and from your own imagination.

TEXT TO WORLD

Librarian Wanted Imagine that Miss Franny Block from "Because of Winn-Dixie" was tired of living in Naomi, Florida, and wanted a change of scenery. Which library described in "My Librarian Is a Camel" do you think she might like to work in? Think about what Miss Franny Block likes and doesn't like to help you answer this question. Then write a paragraph explaining your opinion. Provide reasons and details to support your opinion.

ELACC4RI1 refer to details and examples when explaining what the text says explicitly and when drawing inferences; **ELACC4RI5** describe the overall structure of a text or part of a text; **ELACC4W1a** introduce a topic, state an opinion, and create an organizational structure; **ELACC4W1b** provide reasons supported by facts and details

ELACC4L2b use commas and quotation marks to mark direct speech and quotations from a text

Grammar

What Are Quotations? A direct **quotation** is the exact words that someone says. Use quotation marks (" ") before and after a direct quotation to set it apart from the other words in the sentence. Also use quotation marks to set off the dialogue in a story. Begin a new paragraph with each change of speaker. Use quotation marks whenever you quote an author's exact words. A comma should separate a quote from a **dialogue tag** that states who is being quoted.

Quotation Marks in a Dialogue

"It's been foggy all summer," moaned Lesley. "I'm so tired of gray skies and drippy plants!"

Simon joked, "Well, if you were a redwood tree, you wouldn't mind. You would cheer every gray day, and you would love the feeling of water dripping from your branches."

Copy each sentence. Add quotation marks and a comma to set off the direct quotation.

1. The library is my favorite place Sarah said.
2. Danielle replied I like it, too!
3. I prefer fiction stories Sarah stated.
4. The author says the Books-by-Elephant program serves thirty-seven villages.

Using quotation marks can be tricky. If you use them incorrectly, you can confuse readers. When you proofread your writing, be sure that you include only the speaker's exact words inside the quotations. Also make sure that you have placed the comma in the correct place to make it clear who is speaking.

Incorrect Quotation	Correct Quotation

"May I borrow this book about Mongolia Jared asked?" Of course replied the librarian.	"May I borrow this book about Mongolia?" Jared asked. "Of course," replied the librarian.

Connect Grammar to Writing

As you edit your narrative writing this week, look closely at the dialogue between characters. Make sure you have used quotation marks and commas correctly. Correct any errors you notice. Punctuating dialogue correctly is an important part of good narrative writing.

ELACC4W3b use dialogue and description to develop experiences and events or show characters' responses; **ELACC4W10** write routinely over extended time frames and shorter time frames; **ELACC4L3b** choose punctuation for effect

Narrative Writing

Voice In "My Librarian Is a Camel," the dialogue—what the people say to each other—shows how real people speak and how they feel. Good writers often use **dialogue** in **narrative writing** to show what characters say, how they feel, what they are like, and how they respond to experiences.

Iris wrote the first draft of a dialogue between a brother and sister. Then she revised her draft. She made the dialogue more natural and chose punctuation for effect.

Writing Traits Checklist

- **Ideas** Did I include some gestures and actions?
- **Organization** Does the sequence make sense?
- **Word Choice** Did I use words that fit my characters?
- **Voice** Does my dialogue show how the characters feel?
- **Sentence Fluency** Did I use different kinds of sentences?
- **Conventions** Did I use quotation marks correctly? Did I choose punctuation for effect?

Revised Draft

Ashley and Daniel's dad had the flu.

"Let's make him get-well cards," Ashley said.

Daniel made a face. "Boring!" ~~"I don't like making cards."~~

"Well, what else would Dad like?"

"I know," said Daniel. "Let's bake brownies!"

"~~Would they be~~ For him or for you? Dad's got the stomach flu!"

Final Copy

The Get-Well Gift

by Iris Panza

Ashley and Daniel's dad had the flu. "Let's make him get-well cards," Ashley said.

Daniel made a face. "Boring!"

"Well, what else would Dad like?"

"I know," said Daniel. "Let's bake brownies!"

"For him or for you? Dad's got the stomach flu!"

"Oops. Duh. I forgot. Hmmm."

Suddenly, Ashley slapped the table. "You gave me a great idea! We can make him a surprise gift certificate. When he's better, he can turn it in, and the surprise will be—"

"Homemade brownies!" Daniel said. "Let's go for it!"

Reading as a Writer

What did Iris add to make her dialogue show what the characters are feeling? How can you make the dialogue in your narrative show how the characters feel and respond to the situation?

In my final dialogue, I included more natural language and expression. I used punctuation to show feeling and excitement.

Lesson 4

Vocabulary in Context

The Power of W.O.W.!

The Kid's Guide to MONEY

☑ TARGET VOCABULARY

assist
burglaries
innocent
scheme
regretfully
misjudged
suspect
favor
speculated
prior

Vocabulary Reader

Context Cards

ELACC4L6 acquire/use vocabulary, including academic and domain-specific

1 assist

Everyone appreciates people who assist, or help, others to solve a problem.

2 burglaries

Finding robbers who commit burglaries is a job for the police.

3 innocent

If you are accused of mischief and are not innocent, be honest! Admit your mistake.

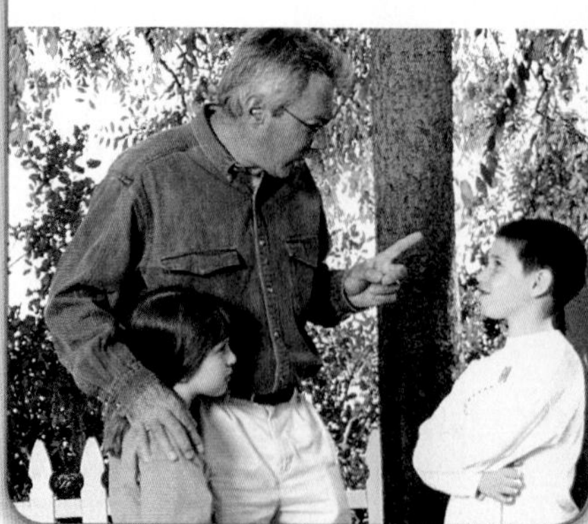

4 scheme

When a solution involves many steps, a scheme, or plan, is helpful.

▶ Study each Context Card.

▶ Ask a question that uses one of the Vocabulary words.

5 regretfully

At times people must regretfully, or sadly, admit that a problem can't be solved.

6 misjudged

People who have bought too little pet food have misjudged how much pets eat.

7 suspect

This teacher has a good idea who hid the desk keys. She has a suspect in mind.

8 favor

If an adult helps you solve a problem, you might mow his or her lawn as a favor.

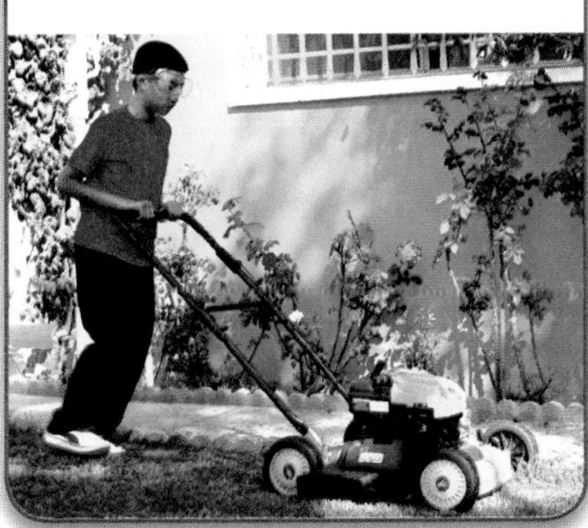

9 speculated

This weather reporter has speculated, or supposed, that winter frosts are over.

10 prior

Checking a map prior to a road trip can help you know where to go beforehand.

Read and Comprehend

TARGET SKILL

Theme As you read "The Power of W.O.W.!," notice how the characters and their actions come together to teach a lesson to the audience. This lesson is the **theme** of the play. To figure out the theme, look at how the play's setting, the cast of characters, and the characters' actions in each scene work together to teach the audience a lesson. Use a graphic organizer like this one to help you see how these elements come together to create the theme.

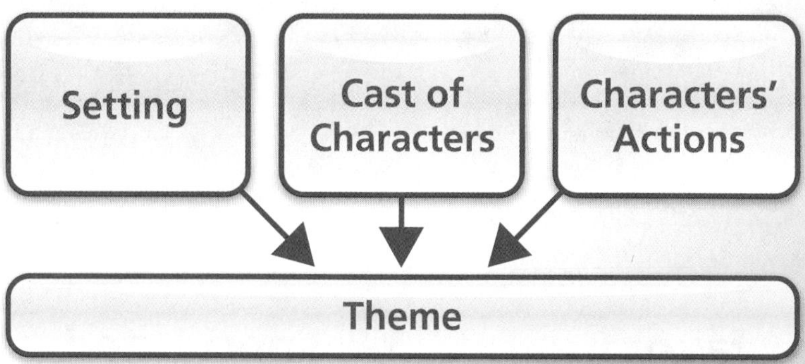

TARGET STRATEGY

Analyze/Evaluate As you read "The Power of W.O.W.!," **analyze** by asking yourself why the characters in the play say and do certain things. **Evaluate** by asking what is the effect of their actions. The answers to these questions can help you understand the author's message.

COMMON CORE **ELACC4RL2** determine theme from details/summarize

PREVIEW THE TOPIC

Raising Money

A community is a group of people who live in the same area or share a common interest. Being part of a community means that people work together and help each other. People can help out in their communities by picking up litter, planting trees, and raising money to help support schools, libraries, or other local resources.

You may not realize it, but every little bit of help makes a big difference when working together to help your community. In "The Power of W.O.W.!" you'll learn how a group of young people helps their community by raising money.

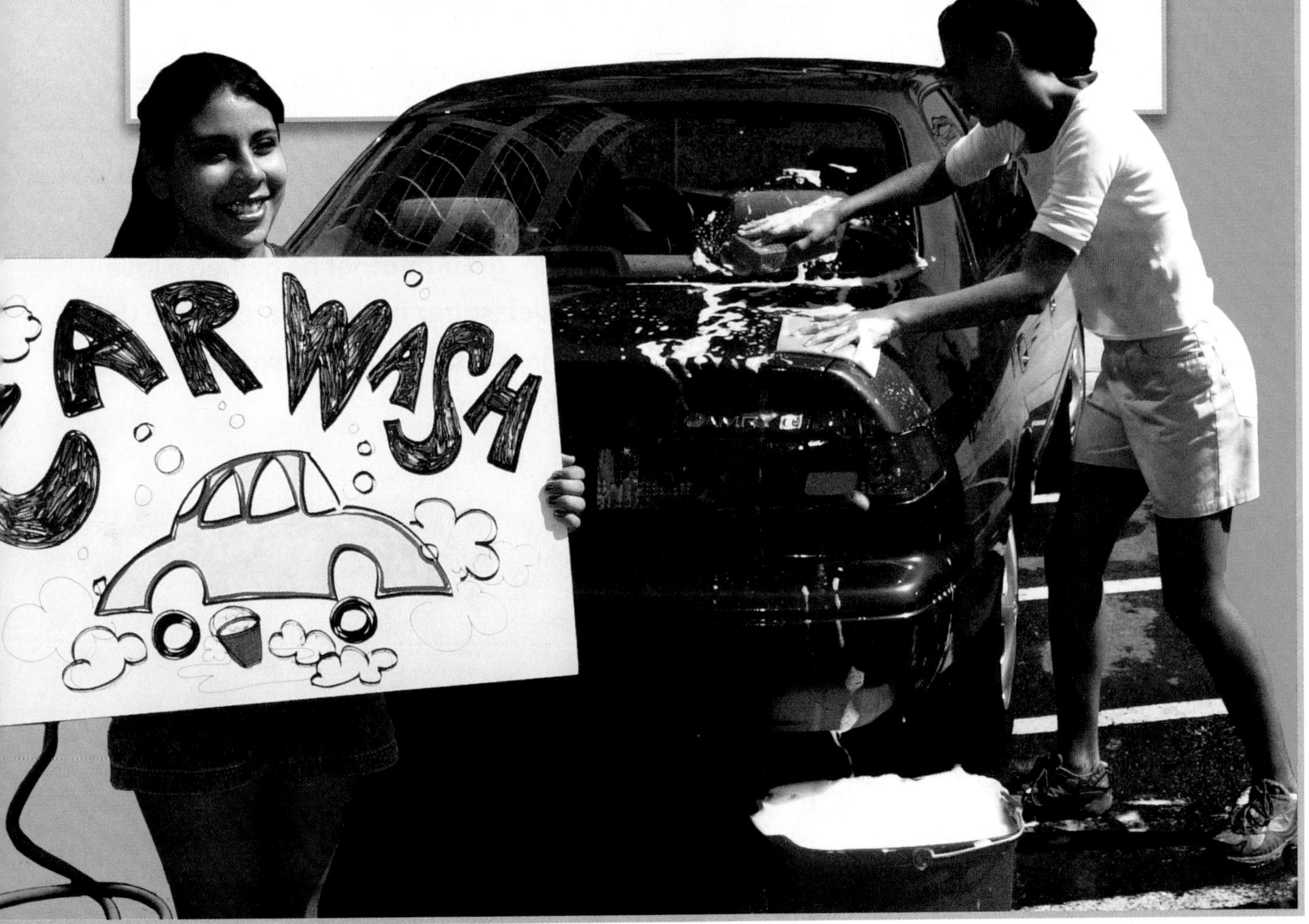

Lesson 4

ANCHOR TEXT

TARGET SKILL

Theme Examine characters' thoughts and actions to recognize the play's theme.

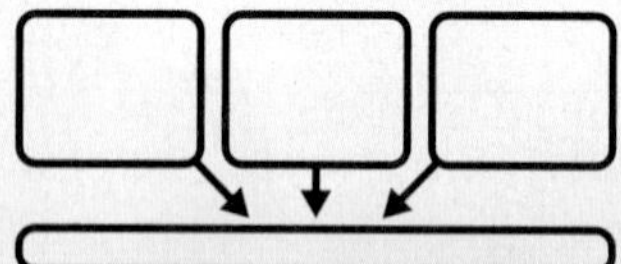

GENRE

A **play** is a story that can be performed for an audience. As you read, look for:

- characters' actions and feelings shown through dialogue
- acts that are divided into scenes
- a plot with a problem and a resolution

ELACC4RL2 determine theme from details/summarize; **ELACC4RL3** describe a character, setting, or event, drawing on details; **ELACC4RL5** explain major differences between poems, drama, and prose/refer to their structural elements

Go Digital

MEET THE AUTHOR

Crystal Hubbard

As a child growing up in St. Louis, Missouri, Crystal Hubbard dreamed of being a writer. She lives near Boston, Massachusetts, with her family and two goldfish named Eyeballs and Rocks. Hubbard has written for Boston-area newspapers and especially likes writing sports biographies.

MEET THE ILLUSTRATOR

Eric Velasquez

Eric Velasquez owes his love of the arts to his family. From his parents he learned to appreciate drawing and film; from his grandmother he gained a love of music. Velasquez has illustrated more than 300 book jackets. He has also written several books of his own.

The Power of W.O.W.!

by Crystal Hubbard
illustrated by Eric Velasquez

ESSENTIAL QUESTION

Why might people raise money for a cause?

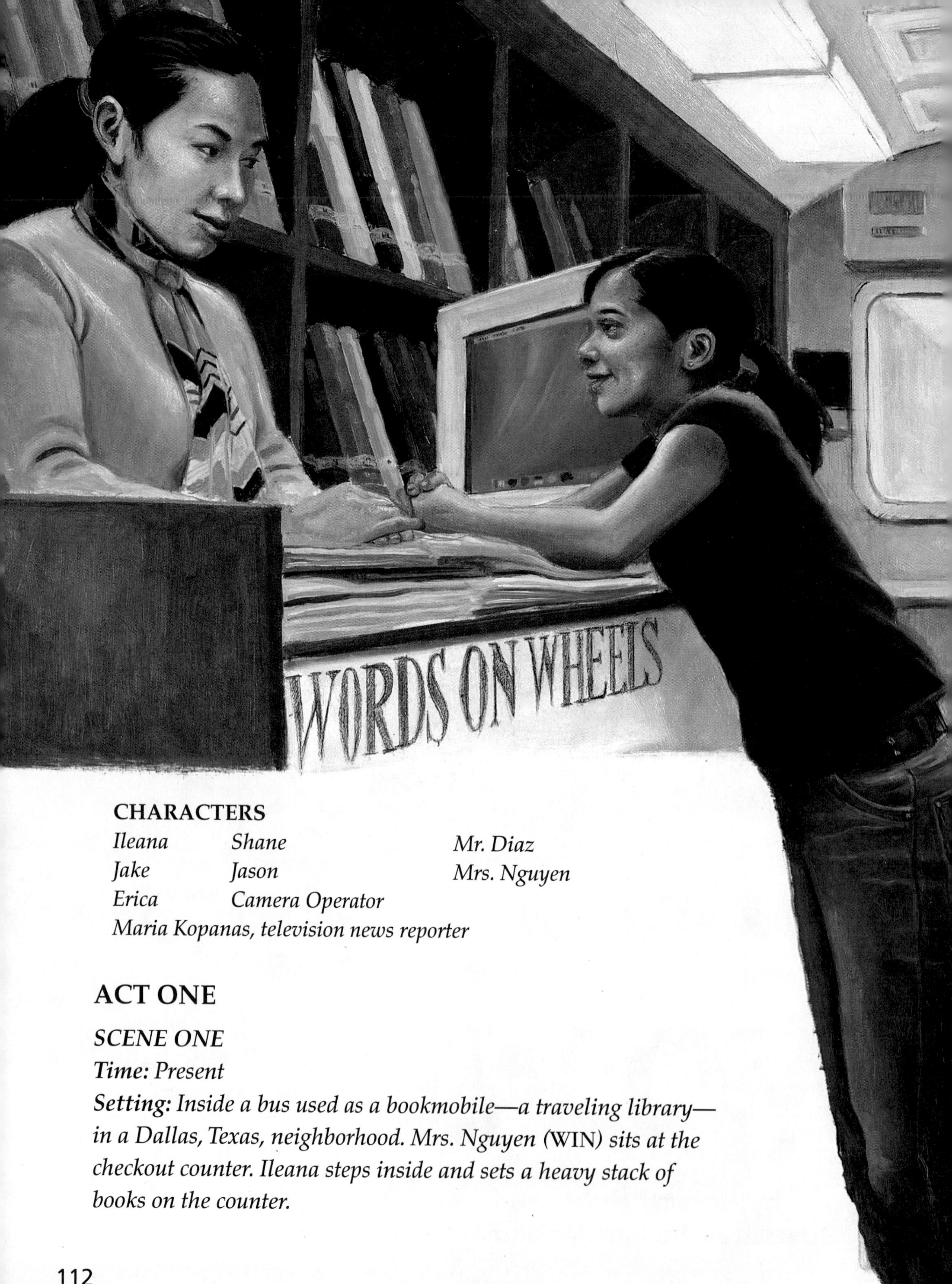

CHARACTERS

Ileana	*Shane*	*Mr. Diaz*
Jake	*Jason*	*Mrs. Nguyen*
Erica	*Camera Operator*	

Maria Kopanas, television news reporter

ACT ONE

SCENE ONE

Time: *Present*

Setting: *Inside a bus used as a bookmobile—a traveling library—in a Dallas, Texas, neighborhood. Mrs. Nguyen (WIN) sits at the checkout counter. Ileana steps inside and sets a heavy stack of books on the counter.*

Mrs. Nguyen: Hi, Ileana! How did you enjoy the books?

Ileana: I liked everything but the Greek mythology. *(Pause)* I *loved* that!

Mrs. Nguyen: *(Smiling)*: I almost misjudged you. Which myth was your favorite?

Ileana: The one where King Midas turns everything to gold. That wish didn't work out too well.

Mrs. Nguyen: *(Sighing)*: I wouldn't mind having the Midas Touch today.

Ileana: Why? Is something wrong?

Mrs. Nguyen: *(Forcing a smile)*: Nothing *you* need to worry about. By the way, we just got the latest Sam Thorne mystery. It's called *The Case of the Pet Store Burglaries.* I won't give away who the prime suspect is . . .

Ileana: I think you're changing the subject, Mrs. Nguyen.

Mrs. Nguyen: *(Looking down regretfully)* I'm afraid Words on Wheels won't be back after next week.

Ileana: What?? Why not?

Mrs. Nguyen: Words on Wheels is a pilot program. The prior plan—for this past year—was for the library to fund W.O.W. But the year's almost up. Now there's no more money to pay for gas or to buy new books. I'll have to go back to the downtown branch.

Ileana: But that's too far away! The only time my grandmother can use a computer is when the W.O.W. bus comes. And I'll never get to see you, Mrs. Nguyen. Can't the library give you some more money?

Mrs. Nguyen: The library does its best to assist us, but the money doesn't go as far as we'd like. We rely on community support, and people just don't seem to be interested in contributing to W.O.W.

Ileana: I have some money saved. You can have it—all of it.

Mrs. Nguyen: *(Smiling sadly)* That's very generous, Ileana, but I'm afraid it would take King Midas to save W.O.W., and I doubt if he's going to show up.

ANALYZE THE TEXT

Allusion What does the allusion to the Midas Touch add to the play?

SCENE TWO

Setting: *Shane's backyard. Ileana, Shane, and Jason are sitting at a picnic table, sipping juice and munching snacks.*

Shane: *(Shaking his head)* Wow. That's bad news about W.O.W.

Ileana: Could we do without the puns, Shane? This is serious.

Shane: *(Looking innocent)* What did I say?

Jason: So, what did Mrs. Nguyen mean by "community support"?

Ileana: She meant that donations from people in the community help pay for the library's special programs.

Jason: Well, we're the community, and if we want to save W.O.W., we have to find a way to make money to pay for it.

Ileana: Does anyone have something we can sell? A rare baseball card?

Shane: I'd sell my bike, but I need it to get to school.

Ileana: Right. Maybe there's something we could do to raise money.

Shane: I could ask my brother. He and his friends raised money for their school picnic last year.

Jake: *(Calling from the back door)* Hey, Squirt. Mom says your friends can stay for dinner. We're having mutant chicken.

Ileana: *(Looking confused)* Mutant chicken?

Shane: Jake and I used to fight over the drumsticks, so my mom uses skewers to attach extra legs to a regular chicken. *(To Jake)* Hey, we have a question.

Jake: *(Sits at picnic table)* Make it fast. I'm a busy man.

Ileana: We need a way to make some cash. The W.O.W. program ran out of money. So tell us how your class paid for last year's picnic.

Jake: We did a lot of things. *(Picks up a handful of snacks)* You could have a bake sale.

Jason: Is that what you did?

Jake: Nope. We held a car wash one Saturday morning, and we earned enough money to pay for the picnic.

Ileana: (*Perking up*) A car wash!

Jason: Let's do it!

Shane: Works for me.

Jake: Whoa. Hold on. You can't just stand on the street and yell "Car Wash!" You have to organize it. You need a place and supplies. You especially need a water source, and you have to advertise.

Shane: (*Resigned*) Wow. I guess it's going to take a lot of work to save W.O.W.

Ileana: You did it again, Shane.

Shane: Oops. Sorry.

Jake: (*To Ileana and Jason*) Tell you what. If you guys are staying for mutant chicken, we can discuss ways to save W.O.W.

Ileana: Great!

ACT TWO

SCENE ONE:

Setting: *Diaz Bakery. Mr. Diaz stands beside a counter next to a glass case filled with pastries. Ileana, Shane, and Jason enter the shop wearing hand-lettered buttons that read "P.O.W.W.O.W." Each of them carries a stack of papers of assorted colors.*

Mr. Diaz: *Hola, niños*[1]. (*He reads buttons.*) What's "pow-wow"?

Shane: It stands for "Please Open Wallets for Words on Wheels." Ileana thought of it.

Mr. Diaz: What scheme are you kids cooking up now?

Ileana: (*Taking a deep breath*) We'd like to ask you for a favor, Uncle Carlos. Words on Wheels needs money so it can keep coming to the neighborhood.

Mr. Diaz: (*Reaching for his wallet*) So, you'd like a donation?

[1] *Hola, niños*.: Hi, kids.

ANALYZE THE TEXT

Elements of Drama How does the description of the setting help you follow the story?

Ileana: Not that kind of donation. See, we'd like to have a car wash this Saturday to raise the money. Our parents donated all the cleaning supplies and we used the W.O.W. computer and printer to make advertisements. (*She hands Mr. Diaz a bright-blue flyer, which he reads.*)

Jason: All we need now is a place to hold the car wash.

Mr. Diaz: (*Chuckling softly*) And that's where I come in, right?

Ileana: Well, you are a part of the community, Uncle Carlos.

Mr. Diaz: True. (*He rubs his chin.*) The hummingbird cake recipe Mrs. Nguyen found online last month has been one of my best sellers. Sure. You can use my parking lot. You can hook up your hose right to the building.

Ileana: (*Slaps high-fives with Shane, Jason, and Mr. Diaz*) *Gracias,*[2] Uncle Carlos! Thank you!

Shane: You won't be sorry. Just think of all the people who'll want to buy pies and cakes while we're washing their cars.

Jason: (*Turns to Ileana and Shane*) The next step is to get the word out. We have to add the location to these flyers and hand them out. Let's stick to the places that we know. I'll go to the Spotless Cleaners and to Teddy's Barbershop and see if we can put flyers there. Mr. Diaz, may I leave a stack of flyers for your customers?

Mr. Diaz: Of course, and I'll give a discount on baked goods to anyone who lets you wash their car.

Jason: *Muchas gracias,*[3] Mr. Diaz.

Mr. Diaz: *De nada,*[4] Jason.

Shane: I'll go to Big Hit Card store and Dr. Bonzo's Used CDs.

Ileana: And I'll take my flyers to Mrs. Romero's Market, the Bead Shop, and the Flower Basket.

Mr. Diaz: (*Impressed*) You're very organized.

Ileana: The bookmobile has a lot of information on fundraising.

Shane: That's the power of W.O.W.

Mr. Diaz: After you finish handing out your flyers, meet back here and I'll show you the power of a hummingbird cake!

2 *Gracias*: Thank you.
3 *Muchas gracias*: Thank you very much.
4 *De nada*: You're welcome.

SCENE TWO

***Setting:** Parking lot of Diaz Bakery. Jake uses a hose to rinse his father's car. Shane and Jason towel-dry a second car. Erica accepts a few bills from the driver and hurries over to Ileana, who holds the cash jar.*

Erica: (*Excitedly*) How much do we have so far?

Ileana: (*Sarcastically*) A whopping sixty-five dollars.

Erica: We've been out here for three hours and that's it?

Ileana: I thought for sure we'd have tons of cars. I guess . . . (*Her voice trails off as she stares over Erica's shoulder.*)

Erica: (*Turns to see*) Hey, check out the van. We should charge extra to wash that big silver pole on top.

Jake: (*Jogging over with Shane and Jason*) That's the Dallas News 7 van! We're going to be famous.

Maria Kopanas: (*She exits the van while the driver shoulders a video camera. They walk over.*) Hi, my name is Maria Kopanas. I'm a reporter for Channel 7.

Shane: I've seen you on the news.

Maria: Well, today you're the news. My Aunt Della owns Spotless Cleaners, and she told me about the car wash today. May I speak to the organizer?

(*Ileana reluctantly allows the others to push her forward.*)

Maria: Do you mind if I ask you a few questions?

Ileana: (*Shyly*) I guess not.

Camera Operator: We're on the air in five . . . four . . . three . . . (*Raises two fingers, then one, and points to Maria*)

Maria: (*Speaking into microphone*) I'm Maria Kopanas with five remarkable young people. They decided to do something after learning that their beloved bookmobile, Words on Wheels, lacked the funds to operate. I'll let them introduce themselves. (*Holds microphone to each*)

Ileana: Hi. I'm Ileana, and this is my sister Erica.

Erica: I can say my own name! (*Sweetly, to camera*) I'm Erica. And Diaz Bakery makes the best bread in town!

Jason: I'm Jason.

Jake: I'm Jake.

Shane: He's my brother. I'm Shane. (*Waving*) Hi, Mom!

Maria: (*To Ileana*) Why is the bookmobile so important to you?

Ileana: It's the only way a lot of kids in my neighborhood can get library books and use a computer. The downtown branch is too far away, so it's nice to have a library come to us. (*Showing her button*) P.O.W. stands for "Please Open Wallets"—or "Power of Words."

Erica: Yeah, a book can give you an adventure.

Jason: Or teach you something.

Shane: Or make you laugh.

Maria: (*Speaking to camera*) Some have speculated that when a community is in trouble, no one's around. But here's a group of kids who have come together to help one of their own. What about you? It's a beautiful day for a car wash, folks!

Camera Operator: And we're out. Nice job, Maria.

Maria: Thanks. But before we head back to the station, I think the news van could use a good wash.

SCENE THREE

***Setting**: Parking lot of Diaz Bakery. Kids, parents, and the camera operator are washing a long line of cars. The W.O.W. bus lumbers into the parking lot. Mrs. Nguyen exits the bookmobile.*

Ileana: Look, Mrs. Nguyen! (*Holding up the money jar*) This is all for W.O.W.

Mrs. Nguyen: Ileana, this is unbelievable!

Ileana: After Maria Kopanas put us on the news, tons of cars showed up. I don't know if there's enough money here to save W.O.W., but it looks like a good start, doesn't it?

Mrs. Nguyen: That's what I came to tell you, Ileana. Thanks to your flyers and the news story, people have promised to help. (*She pulls envelopes from her pocket.*) All of these contain checks! They're from Spotless Cleaners, Teddy's Barbershop, the Bead Shop, Mrs. Romero's Market, Channel 7, your parents, and so many others in the neighborhood. W.O.W. can keep running for a long time to come!

Ileana: (*Jumping in the air*) Wow! Guys! We saved W.O.W.!

Shane: I couldn't have said it better myself.

ANALYZE THE TEXT

Theme What do the characters learn by the end of the play? How does this relate to the theme?

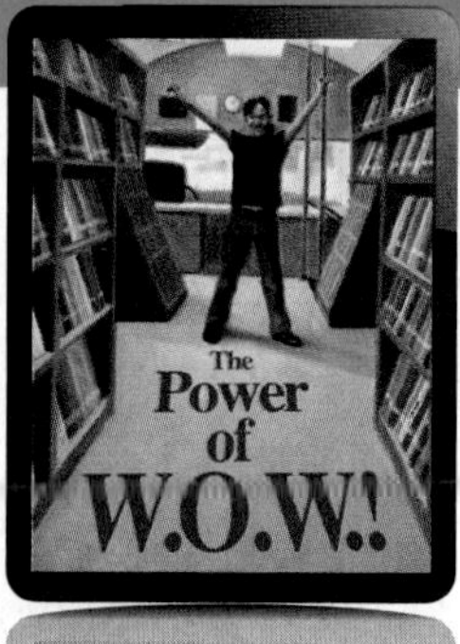

COMPREHENSION

Dig Deeper

How to Analyze the Text

Use these pages to learn about Theme, Elements of a Drama, and Allusion. Then read "The Power of W.O.W.!" again to apply what you learned.

Theme

"The Power of W.O.W.!" is a play that makes a point. All of the elements in the play come together to teach a lesson to the audience. This lesson is the **theme** of the play.

Use details about the play's setting, the cast of characters, and the characters' actions in each scene to figure out the theme of the play. A graphic organizer like the one below can help you see how the story elements come together to create the theme. You can often determine a story's theme by thinking about what the characters learn. Turn to pages 114–115. What lesson do the characters learn about helping others on these pages?

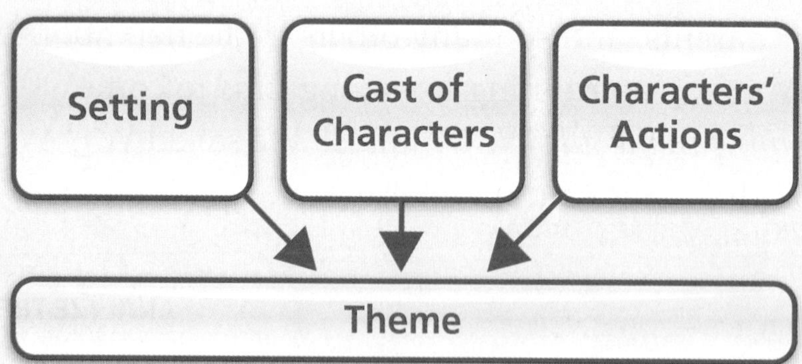

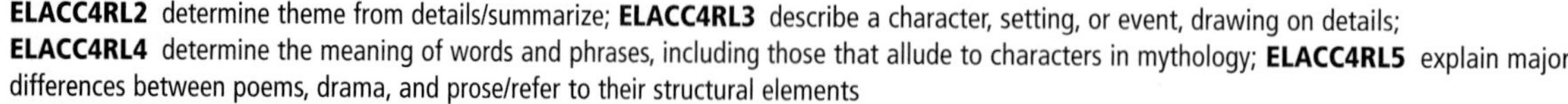
ELACC4RL2 determine theme from details/summarize; **ELACC4RL3** describe a character, setting, or event, drawing on details; **ELACC4RL4** determine the meaning of words and phrases, including those that allude to characters in mythology; **ELACC4RL5** explain major differences between poems, drama, and prose/refer to their structural elements

Elements of a Drama

Drama, such as "The Power of W.O.W.!," have these structural elements:

- **cast of characters**—a list of people or animals in the story
- **dialogue**—plot is told through what characters say or think to themselves
- **stage directions**—instructions about how actors should move and speak on stage

Like prose or other stories, dramas also have a **setting**—where and when the stories take place.

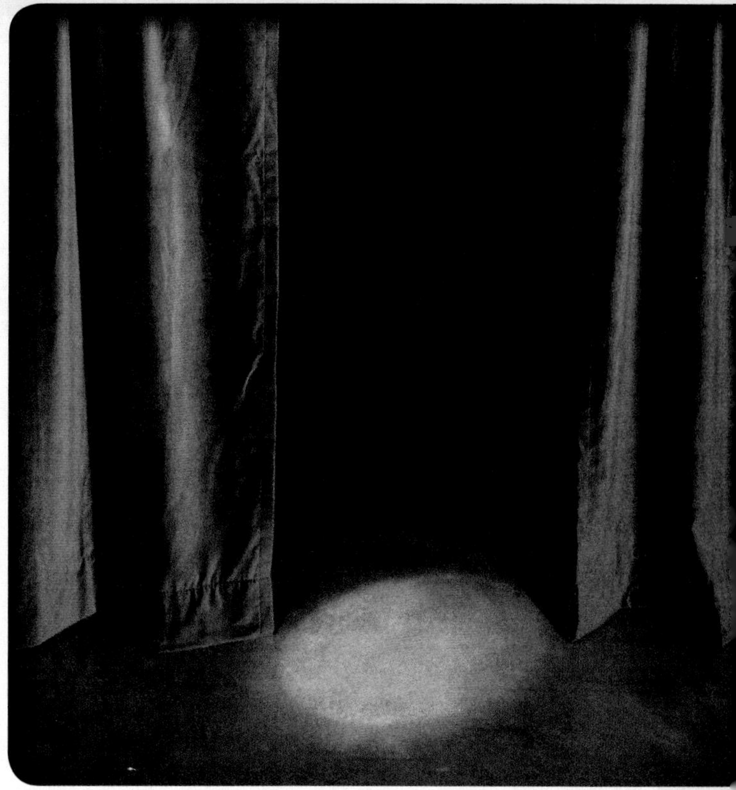

Allusion

When an author includes a reference to a famous person, place, event, or other story, the author is using an **allusion.** Authors use allusions to give details about characters or events in an interesting, descriptive way. For example, a story character caught in a storm might say, "I guess Neptune is really angry now!" In Roman mythology, Neptune is the god of the sea and is responsible for storms at sea.

Your Turn

RETURN TO THE ESSENTIAL QUESTION

Turn and Talk Review the selection with a partner to prepare to discuss this question: *Why might people raise money for a cause?* Use text evidence from the play to support your answers. Make sure your comments link to what your partner says so the discussion stays on track.

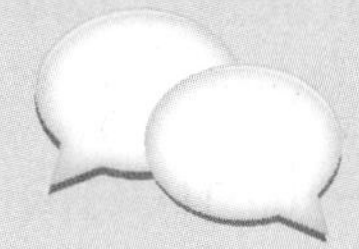

Classroom Conversation

Continue your discussion of "The Power of W.O.W.!" by explaining your answers to these questions:

1. Why do you think so many drivers went to the car wash after the TV news report?
2. What kind of power do the students show in the play?
3. What are some other ways Ileana and her friends could have helped save W.O.W.?

PLACES, EVERYONE

Perform a Scene With a group, choose one scene from the play to act out. Work together to assign roles. Take time to rehearse. Your performance should match the directions in the play. Then perform your scene for the class. Discuss how your presentation connects to the text of the play.

WRITE ABOUT READING

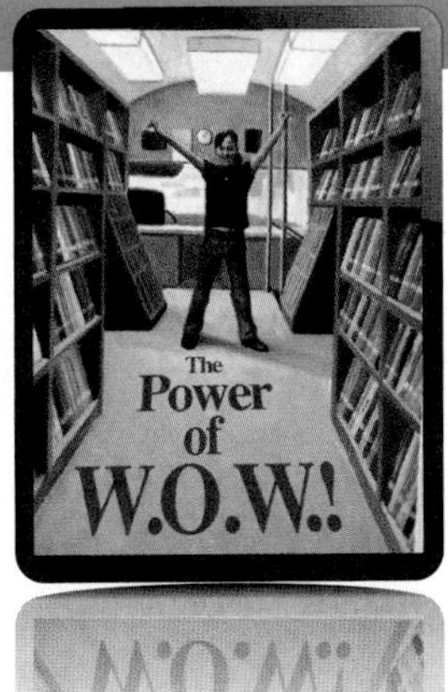

Response "The Power of W.O.W.!" shows that taking action can have a positive effect on a community. What would you do if you found out your favorite after-school activity or community program was going to end? Write a paragraph explaining what you might do to help that activity or program continue. Include what effect you think your actions might have.

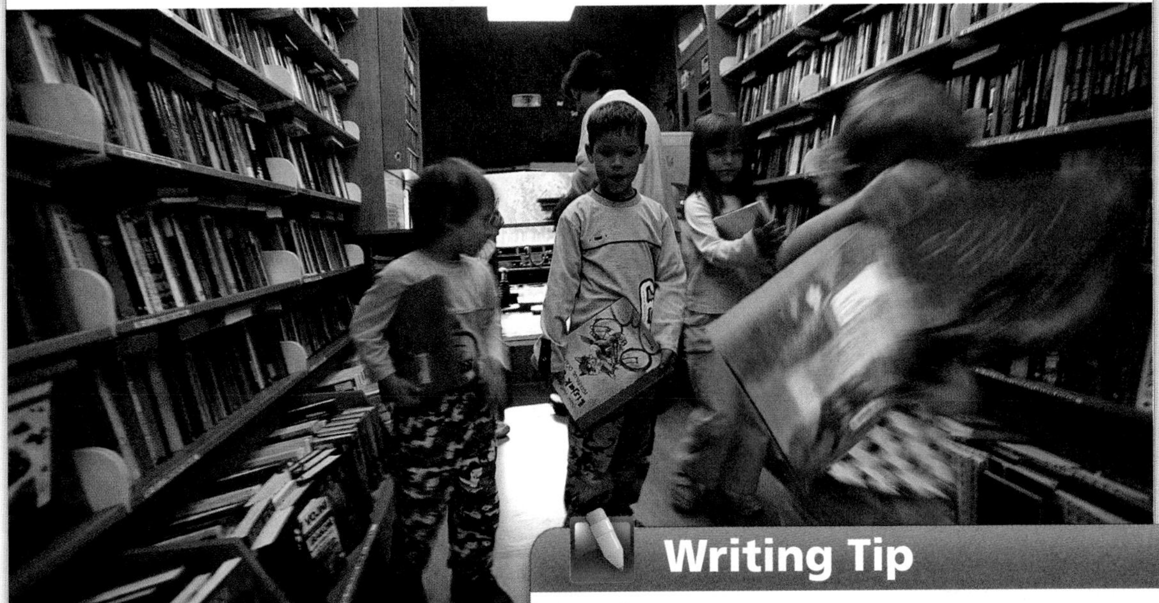

Writing Tip

Make sure that all your sentences are complete. Check by identifying the subject and predicate in each sentence.

ELACC4RL2 determine theme from details/summarize; **ELACC4RL7** make connections between the text and a visual or oral presentation of it; **ELACC4W10** write routinely over extended time frames and shorter time frames; **ELACC4SL1c** pose and respond to questions and make comments that contribute to the discussion and link to others' remarks

Lesson 4

INFORMATIONAL TEXT

GENRE

Informational text gives factual information about a topic. The information is often organized under headings. Informational text often includes visuals, such as charts, graphs, and photographs.

TEXT FOCUS

Charts provide information in a visual way. They often provide examples for the information in the article.

ELACC4RI7 interpret information presented visually, orally, or quantitatively; **ELACC4RI10** read and comprehend informational texts

 Go Digital

The Kid's Guide to MONEY

by Steve Otfinoski

Spending Your Money

What do you do with money? You can spend it, save it, invest it, or give it away.

Budgeting Your Spending

Spending your money on the things you want may be a lot of fun. But spending has its own set of responsibilities. You have to make sure you don't buy so many things you want that you don't have money for things you need. One way to be sure you have enough money to pay for everything you need is to make a budget. A **budget** is a plan for managing your money on a regular basis. When you follow a budget, you have enough money to meet all your expenses.

Five Steps to Making a Budget

Step 1: Figure out your weekly income, the money you receive from all sources. Count only the money you get regularly, for example, a weekly allowance or money earned from a steady job such as delivering newspapers.

Step 2: Every week, make a list of the things you need to spend money on, such as bus fare, school supplies, and lunches.

Step 3: Make a list of the things you want but could get along without if you had to. These could include going to a movie or buying snacks or a tape.

Step 4: Now list any things that you need to save for.

Step 5: Subtract your needs (the total amount from Step 2) from your income. You can spend or save whatever's left. This is your weekly budget.

Even if you don't have much of a weekly income, it's still a good idea to create a budget. Managing your money is a habit that's best to develop early in life—starting right now!

Once you plan your budget, it's important to stick to it. Keep track of your spending and budget goals in a notebook. You might want to call it your Money Management Book. Add up each week's total spending. If you managed to keep within your budget that week, you should give yourself a great big pat on the back and 27 hip-hip-hoorays.

Here is a sample weekly budget:

Total weekly income: $10.00

NEEDS	
lunch/milk tickets	$2.00
bus fare (to piano lesson)	$1.50
Total needs:	$3.50
Total weekly income:	$10.00
Total weekly needs:	$3.50
Money remaining:	$6.50

WANTS	
snacks at school	$3.00
movie	$3.50
Total wants:	$6.50
Saving for new bike	$2.00
Giving donation	$1.00

Budget notes:
I need to rethink my "want" spending.
I really want to go to the movies this week,
so if I bring my own snacks to school I can cut
that expense and still have money to save for
the bike and make a donation to charity.

Money Jars

Here's one way to make sure you stick to your budget. Take four empty glass or plastic jars and write the following labels on them: NEEDS, OTHER SPENDING, SAVINGS, and GIVING. Put the jars on your dresser or a desk in your room. Every week take your money and split it into the four jars, according to your budget. Take the money out of each jar as you need it.

Compare Texts

TEXT TO TEXT

Compare Concepts Explain the main idea of "The Kid's Guide to Money" in your own words. Then explain the details that support it. Now think about Ileana and her friends. What could they learn from "The Kid's Guide to Money"? What could they add to "The Kid's Guide to Money"? Present your ideas in a small group. Remember to speak clearly so that your classmates can understand you.

TEXT TO SELF

Write About Teamwork In "The Power of W.O.W.!," a group of kids saves their community's bookmobile. Think about a time when you worked with a group to help others. Write a paragraph that describes your group's goal, the steps you took to reach the goal, and the result.

TEXT TO WORLD

Community Services "The Power of W.O.W.!" shows how important a library can be to a community. Work with a partner to brainstorm some of the different services that are important to your community. Discuss why each of these services is important to your community and who it helps.

ELACC4RL9 compare and contrast the treatment of similar themes and topics; **ELACC4RI2** determine the main idea and explain how it is supported by details/summarize; **ELACC4RI9** integrate information from two texts on the same topic; **ELACC4SL4** report on a topic or text, tell a story, or recount an experience/speak clearly at an understandable pace

ELACC4L1f produce complete sentences, recognizing and correcting fragments and run-ons; **ELACC4L2a** use correct capitalization

Grammar

What Are a Sentence Fragment and a Run-On Sentence?
A sentence tells a complete thought. It has a subject and a predicate. A group of words that does not tell a complete thought is called a **sentence fragment.**

Sentence Fragments	Corrected Sentences
Had a car wash.	The students had a car wash.
Is making fifty dollars!	The group is making fifty dollars.

A **run-on sentence** has two complete thoughts, or sentences, that run into each other. The end punctuation of the first sentence is missing. Often a run-on sentence is also missing the capital letter that begins the second sentence.

Run-On Sentences	Corrected Sentences
The library gives money it is not enough.	The library gives money. It is not enough.
The kids had a car wash they made money.	The kids had a car wash. They made money.

With a partner, identify each group of words as a sentence fragment or a run-on sentence. Then tell how each should be corrected.

1. needs books to read.
2. Not all families in our community.
3. A library van comes to our town we borrow books.

When you write, make sure each sentence contains a subject and a predicate. You can fix a sentence fragment by adding the missing subject or predicate. To correct a run-on sentence, separate the two complete thoughts with a period. Make sure each sentence begins with a capital letter.

Sentence Fragment	Run-On Sentence
 Is almost out of money.	 Mr. Diaz is helping he is letting us use his lot.
New, Complete Sentence	**New, Complete Sentences**
 The van program is almost out of money.	 Mr. Diaz is helping! He is letting us use his lot.

Connect Grammar to Writing

As you edit your fictional narrative next week, make sure each sentence has a subject and a predicate. If a sentence has two complete thoughts, correct the run-on by splitting it into two sentences. Begin each sentence with a capital letter.

ELACC4W3a orient the reader by establishing a situation and introducing a narrator or characters/organize an event sequence; **ELACC4W4** produce writing in which development and organization are appropriate to task, purpose, and audience; **ELACC4W5** develop and strengthen writing by planning, revising, and editing

Narrative Writing

Reading-Writing Workshop: Prewrite

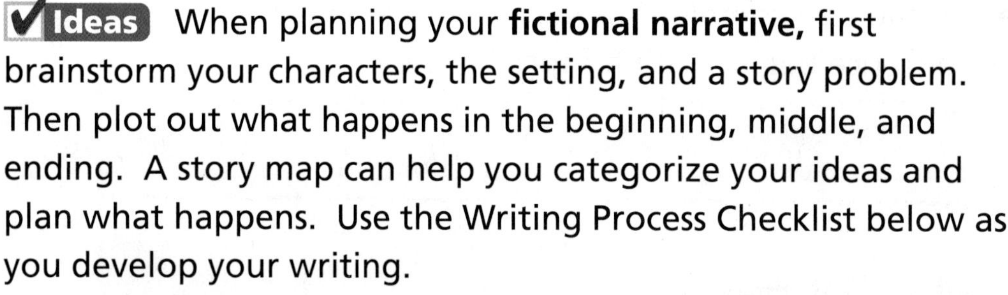

✔ Ideas When planning your **fictional narrative,** first brainstorm your characters, the setting, and a story problem. Then plot out what happens in the beginning, middle, and ending. A story map can help you categorize your ideas and plan what happens. Use the Writing Process Checklist below as you develop your writing.

Mei Ann thought of ideas for her story. She circled the ones to write about. Then she developed her ideas in more detail using a story map.

Exploring a Topic

Who? a dog walker

[two friends]

a young guitarist

Where? [attic]

city park

talent show

What? [find a mysterious box]

loses a dog

wants to win a contest

Writing Process Checklist

▶ Prewrite

- ✔ Did I think of ideas that my audience and I will both enjoy?
- ✔ Are my characters and setting worked out?
- ✔ Did I plan a problem for my characters?
- ✔ Did I think of exciting events for the middle of the story?
- ✔ Did I decide how the story problem will turn out?

Draft

Revise

Edit

Publish and Share

Story Map

Setting	Characters
Attic: dusty, full of toys, furniture, camping equipment	Matt: afraid of spiders, smart Sarah: bossy, brave Sarah's mom

Plot

Beginning: Sarah discovers a locked suitcase.

Middle: Sarah and Matt can't figure out how to open the suitcase. Sarah's mom brings some old keys. Inside the suitcase is an old newspaper and a jacket with a ring in the pocket.

Ending: Matt reads the newspaper and learns that a jewelry thief used to live in Sarah's house. They return the ring to the jewelry-store owner.

Reading as a Writer

Which parts of Mei Ann's story map sound interesting to you? What interesting events and details can you add to your own story map?

As I filled out my story map, I added details about the setting, characters, and events. I organized my ideas into a specific sequence.

Lesson 5

Vocabulary in Context

TARGET VOCABULARY

seafaring
tidal
foaming
outcast
yearning
memorable
betrayed
condition
shortage
horrified

Vocabulary Reader

Context Cards

ELACC4L6 acquire/use vocabulary, including academic and domain-specific

1 seafaring

Both of Jen's parents are sailors. Her seafaring childhood was exciting.

2 tidal

An earthquake in the ocean caused a great tidal wave.

3 foaming

Foaming waves crashed against the sea wall, spraying mist into the air.

4 outcast

The lonely girl felt like an outcast in her new town. She did not know anyone.

- Study each Context Card.
- Tell a story about two or more pictures, using the Vocabulary words.

5 yearning

After traveling for months, Daniel felt a yearning to be home.

6 memorable

The vacation was very memorable. She will never forget it.

7 betrayed

If someone betrayed you, he or she let you down.

8 condition

Abe has a fever. In his condition, he should be resting.

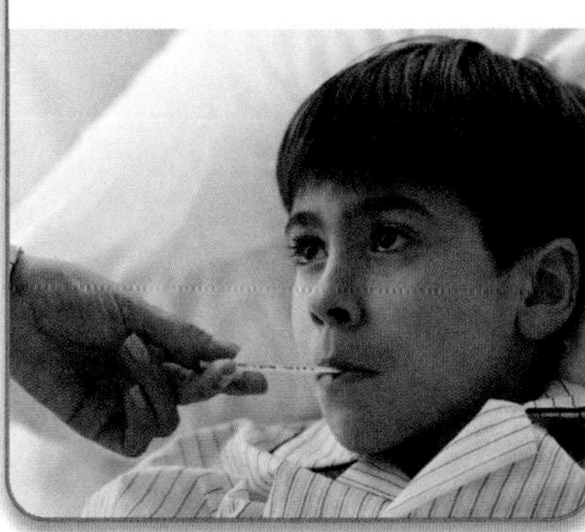

9 shortage

There are long lines for gas because of the gas shortage.

10 horrified

He was horrified when he accidentally dropped his plate of food.

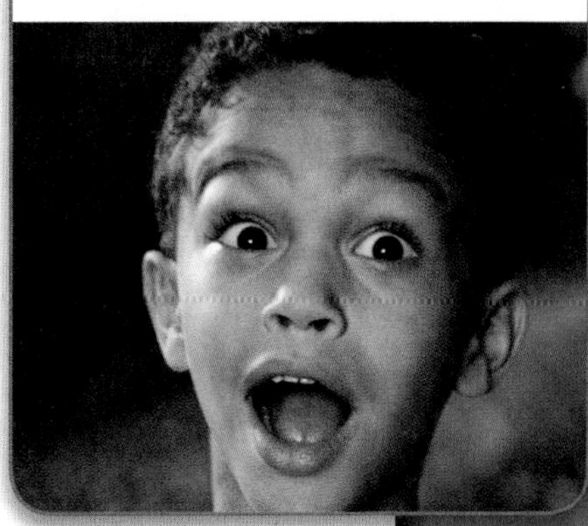

Read and Comprehend

TARGET SKILL

Understanding Characters As you read "Stormalong," look for details in the text that help you understand the personality of the **main character.** Pay attention to how Stormalong feels, what he does, and what his relationships are like with other characters. Use a graphic organizer like the one below to help you understand Stormalong and the changes he experiences.

Thoughts	Words	Actions

TARGET STRATEGY

Infer/Predict When you **infer**, you use details in the story to figure out something that the author has left unsaid or has not stated directly. As you read, infer what kind of person Stormalong is. Then **predict** what he might do next, based on clues the author has given and what you have inferred.

COMMON CORE **ELACC4RL1** refer to details and examples when explaining what the text says explicitly and when drawing inferences; **ELACC4RL3** describe a character, setting, or event, drawing on details

PREVIEW THE TOPIC

Traditional Tales

A traditional tale is a story that is told and retold through the years. Traditional tales were passed on from one generation to the next by word of mouth.

"Stormalong" is a traditional tale about a thirty-foot-tall sailor named Alfred Bulltop Stormalong. American sailors began singing about Stormalong in the 1830s, when fast-moving boats called clipper ships sailed between cities. Over time, tales about Stormalong spread. His strength, courage, and kindness became legendary. Singing together about Stormalong's fantastic deeds helped sailors tackle hard work on the rolling ocean waves.

Lesson 5

ANCHOR TEXT

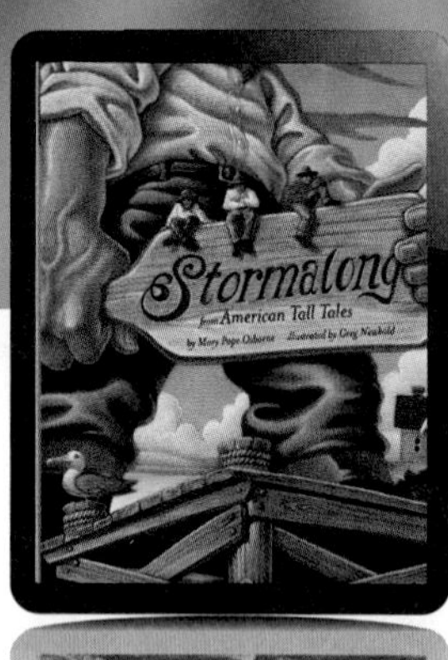

Stormalong
from American Tall Tales
by Mary Pope Osborne illustrated by Greg Newbold

 TARGET SKILL

Understanding Characters
Examine the characters' relationships and how they change throughout the story.

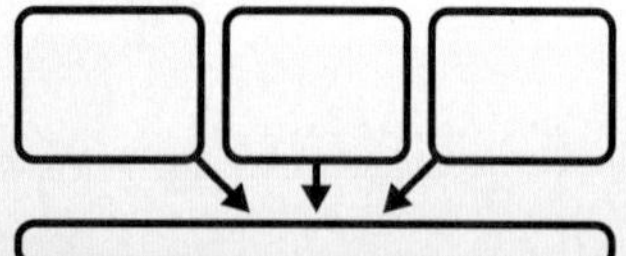

 GENRE

A **tall tale** is a humorous story about impossible or exaggerated happenings. As you read, look for:

- events that could not happen in real life
- exaggerations about the strength and abilities of a story character
- stories about American folk heroes and legends

ELACC4RL3 describe a character, setting, or event, drawing on details; **ELACC4RL4** determine the meaning of words and phrases, including those that allude to characters in mythology; **ELACC4RL10** read and comprehend literature

 Go Digital

MEET THE AUTHOR

Mary Pope Osborne

Mary Pope Osborne, author of the Magic Tree House series, has written more than fifty books. As a child, she traveled widely with her family, and as a young adult, she continued to seek adventure. Once she slept in a cave on the Greek island of Crete! Osborne's love of research has led to many other journeys through her writing.

MEET THE ILLUSTRATOR

Greg Newbold

Greg Newbold always loved art and began drawing and painting at a very early age. He has illustrated many children's books and has even made designs for advertisements. Newbold also teaches college art classes.

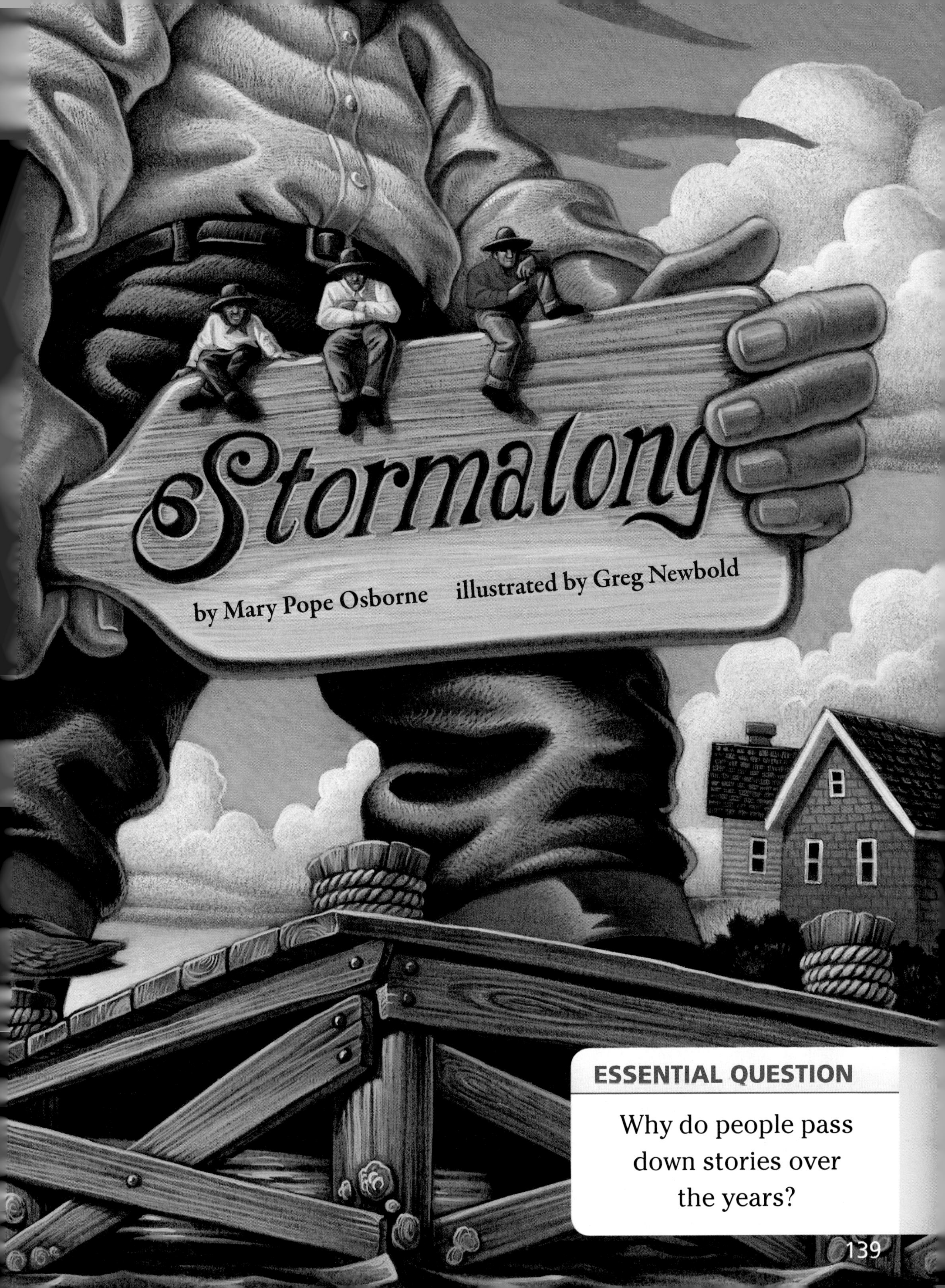

ESSENTIAL QUESTION

Why do people pass down stories over the years?

One day in the early 1800s a tidal wave crashed down on the shores of Cape Cod in New England. After the wave had washed back out to sea, the villagers heard deep, bellowing sounds coming from the beach. When they rushed to find out what was going on, they couldn't believe their eyes. A giant baby three fathoms tall—or eighteen feet!—was crawling across the sand, crying in a voice as loud as a foghorn.

The villagers put the baby in a big wheelbarrow and carried him to town. They took him to the meetinghouse and fed him barrels and barrels of milk. As ten people patted the baby on the back, the minister said, "What will we name him?"

"How about *Alfred Bulltop Stormalong*?" a little boy piped up. "And call him Stormy for short."

The baby smiled at the boy.

"Stormy it is!" everyone cried.

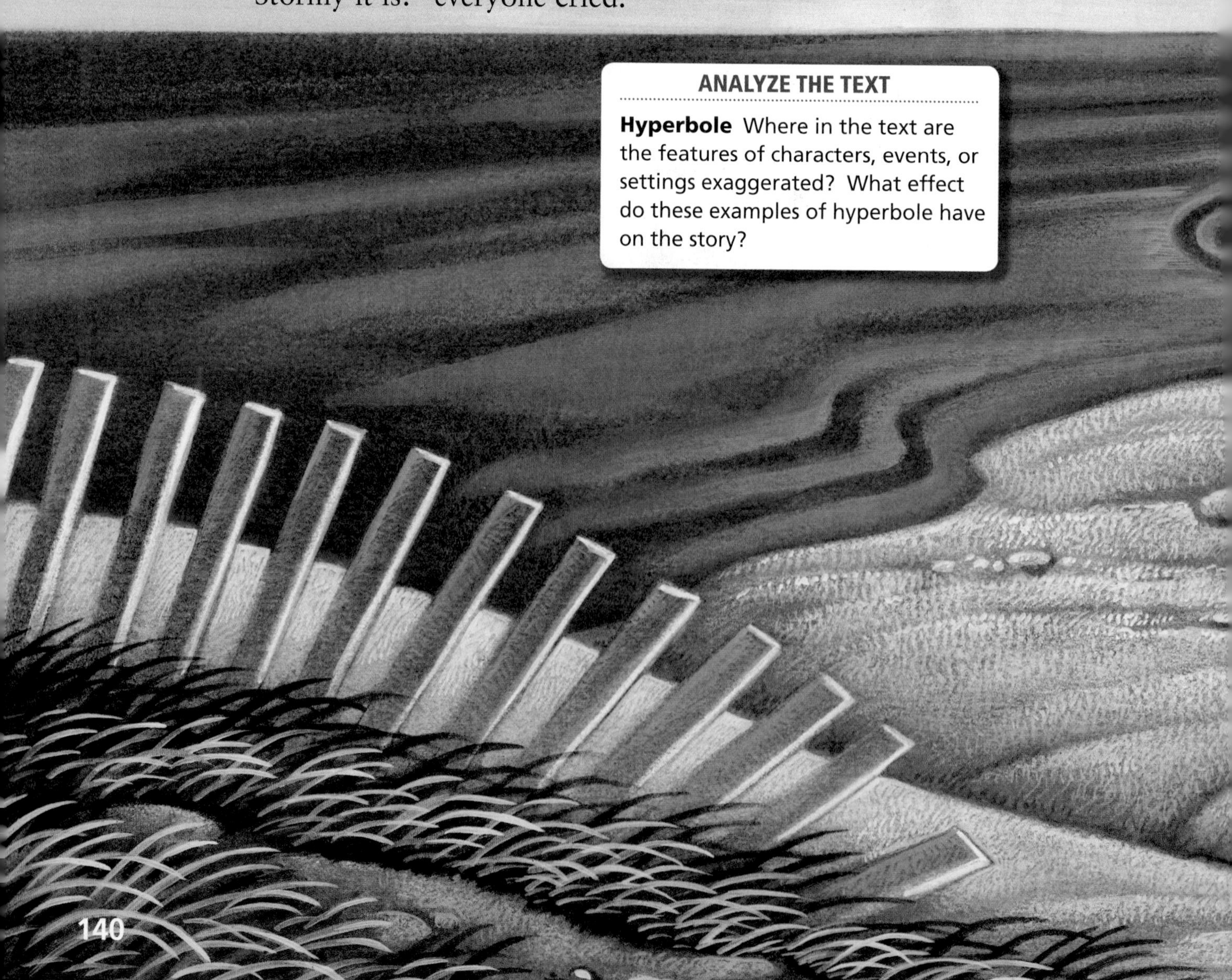

ANALYZE THE TEXT

Hyperbole Where in the text are the features of characters, events, or settings exaggerated? What effect do these examples of hyperbole have on the story?

As he grew older Stormy was the main attraction of Cape Cod. He didn't care for all the attention, however. It reminded him that he was different from everyone else. After school he always tried to slip away to the sea. He liked to swim out into the deep water and ride the whales and porpoises. Stormy's love for the ocean was so strong that folks used to say he had salt water in his veins.

By the time Stormy was twelve, he was already six fathoms tall—or thirty-six feet! "I guess you're going to have to go out into the world now," his friends said sadly. "The truth is, you've grown too big for this town. You can't fit in the schoolhouse, and you're too tall to work in a store. Maybe you should go to Boston. It's a lot bigger than Cape Cod."

Stormy felt like an outcast as he packed his trunk, hoisted it over his shoulder, and started away. And when he arrived in Boston, he discovered something that made him even sadder. Although the city had more buildings than Cape Cod, they were just as small. Worse than that, his huge size and foghorn voice scared the daylights out of everyone he met.

"A sailor's life is the only one for me," he said, staring longingly at Boston Harbor. "The sea's my best friend. It's with her that I belong." And with his back to Boston, Stormy strode toward the biggest Yankee clipper docked in the harbor, *The Lady of the Sea*.

"Blow me down!" said the captain when Stormy stood before him. "I've never seen a man as big as you before."

"I'm not a man," said Stormy. "I'm twelve years old."

"Blow me down again!" said the captain. "I guess you'll have to be the biggest cabin boy in the world then. Welcome aboard, son."

ANALYZE THE TEXT

Point of View Who is telling this story? What evidence in the text tells the story's point of view?

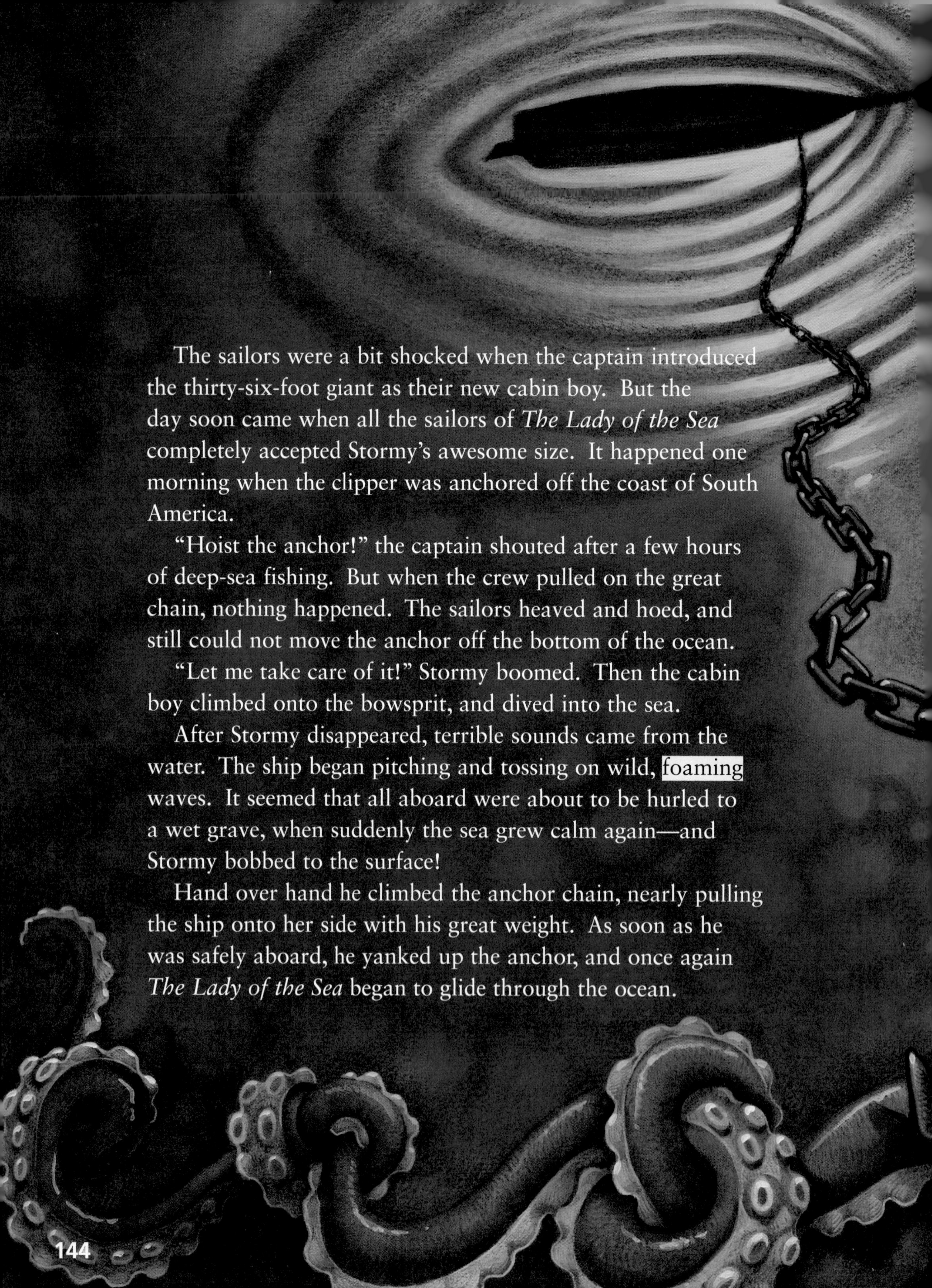

The sailors were a bit shocked when the captain introduced the thirty-six-foot giant as their new cabin boy. But the day soon came when all the sailors of *The Lady of the Sea* completely accepted Stormy's awesome size. It happened one morning when the clipper was anchored off the coast of South America.

"Hoist the anchor!" the captain shouted after a few hours of deep-sea fishing. But when the crew pulled on the great chain, nothing happened. The sailors heaved and hoed, and still could not move the anchor off the bottom of the ocean.

"Let me take care of it!" Stormy boomed. Then the cabin boy climbed onto the bowsprit, and dived into the sea.

After Stormy disappeared, terrible sounds came from the water. The ship began pitching and tossing on wild, foaming waves. It seemed that all aboard were about to be hurled to a wet grave, when suddenly the sea grew calm again—and Stormy bobbed to the surface!

Hand over hand he climbed the anchor chain, nearly pulling the ship onto her side with his great weight. As soon as he was safely aboard, he yanked up the anchor, and once again *The Lady of the Sea* began to glide through the ocean.

"What happened?" cried the crew.

"Just a little fight with a two-ton octopus," said Stormy.

"Octopus!"

"Aye. He didn't want to let go of our anchor."

"What'd you do to him?" the others cried.

"Wrestled eight slimy tentacles into double knots. It'll take a month o' Sundays for him to untie himself."

From then on Stormy was the most popular sailor on board. Over the next few years his reputation spread too, until all the Yankee clipper crews wanted him to sail with them.

But Stormy still wasn't happy. Partly it was because no ship, not even *The Lady of the Sea*, was big enough for him. She would nearly tip over when he stood close to her rail. All her wood peeled off when he scrubbed her decks. And giant waves rolled over her sides when he sang a sea chantey.

Worst of all, Stormy was still lonely. The clipper's hammocks were so small that at night he had to sleep by himself in a rowboat. As he listened to the other sailors singing and having a good time, he felt as if his best friend, the sea, had betrayed him. Maybe it was time for the giant sailor to move on.

One day, when *The Lady of the Sea* dropped anchor in Boston, Stormy announced to his friends that he'd decided to give up his seafaring life. "I'm going to put an oar over my shoulder and head west," he said. "I hear there's room enough for any kind of folks out there, even ones as big as me."

"Where will you settle down, Stormy?" a sailor asked.

"I'm going to walk till the first person asks me, 'Hey, mister, what's that funny thing you got on your shoulder there?' Then I'll know I'm far enough away from the sea, and I won't ever think about her again."

Stormy walked through the cities of Providence and New York. He walked through the pine barrens of New Jersey and the woods of Pennsylvania. He crossed the Allegheny Mountains and floated on flatboats down the Ohio River.

Pioneers often invited Stormy to share their dinner, but these occasions only made him homesick, for folks always guessed he was a sailor and asked him questions about the sea.

It wasn't until Stormy came to the plains of Kansas that a farmer said, "Hey, mister, what's that funny thing you got on your shoulder?"

"You asked the right question, mate," said Stormy. "I'm going to settle down on this spot and dig me some potatoes!"

And that's just what Stormy did. Soon he became the best farmer around. He planted over five million potatoes and watered his whole crop with the sweat of his brow.

But all the time Stormy was watering, hoeing, picking, and planting, he knew he still had not found a home. He was too big to go square dancing in the dance hall. He was too big to visit other farmhouses, too big for the meetinghouse, too big for the general store.

And he felt a great yearning for the sea. He missed the fishy-smelling breezes and salt spray. Never in the prairies did a giant wave knock him to his knees. Never did a hurricane whirl him across the earth. How could he ever test his true strength and courage?

One day, several years after Stormy's disappearance, the sailors of Boston Harbor saw a giant coming down the wharf, waving his oar above his head. As he approached, they began to whoop with joy. Stormy was back!

But as happy as they were to see him, they were horrified when they discovered how bad he looked. He was all stooped over. His face was like a withered cornstalk, and there were pale bags under his eyes.

After word spread about Stormy's condition, thousands of sailors met to talk about the problem.

"We've got to keep him with us this time," one said.

"There's only one way to do it," said another. "Build a ship that's big enough."

"Aye!" the others agreed. "We can't be having him trail behind us at night in his own rowboat!"

So the New England sailors set about building the biggest clipper ship in the world. Her sails had to be cut and sewn in the Mojave Desert, and after she was built, there was a lumber shortage all over America. It took over forty seamen to manage her pilot's wheel—unless, of course, the captain happened to be Alfred Bulltop Stormalong, who could whirl the ship's wheel with his baby finger!

Stormalong named the clipper *The Courser*. On her maiden voyage, he clutched *The Courser*'s wheel and steered her out of Boston Harbor. As he soared over the billowing waves, his cheeks glowed with sunburn, his hair sparkled with ocean spray, and the salt water began coursing through his veins again.

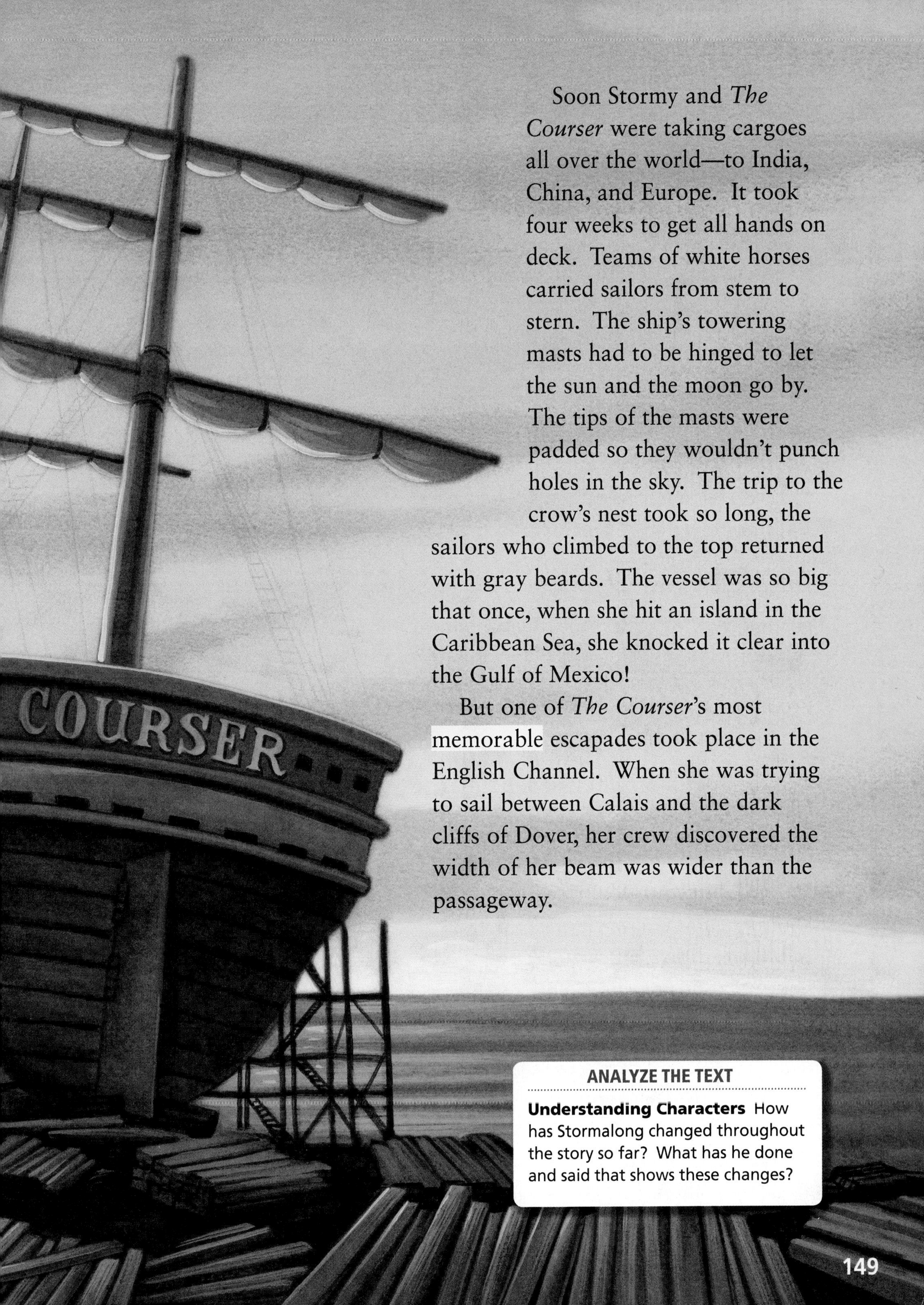

Soon Stormy and *The Courser* were taking cargoes all over the world—to India, China, and Europe. It took four weeks to get all hands on deck. Teams of white horses carried sailors from stem to stern. The ship's towering masts had to be hinged to let the sun and the moon go by. The tips of the masts were padded so they wouldn't punch holes in the sky. The trip to the crow's nest took so long, the sailors who climbed to the top returned with gray beards. The vessel was so big that once, when she hit an island in the Caribbean Sea, she knocked it clear into the Gulf of Mexico!

But one of *The Courser*'s most memorable escapades took place in the English Channel. When she was trying to sail between Calais and the dark cliffs of Dover, her crew discovered the width of her beam was wider than the passageway.

ANALYZE THE TEXT

Understanding Characters How has Stormalong changed throughout the story so far? What has he done and said that shows these changes?

"It's impossible to wedge her through!" the first mate cried. "We have to turn back!"

"Hurry, before she crashes on the rocks!" said another.

"No, don't turn her back!" bellowed Stormy from the captain's wheel. "Bring all the soap on deck!"

The crew thought Stormy had lost his mind, but they went below and hauled up the three-ton shipment of soap just picked up in Holland.

"Now swab her sides until she's as slippery as an eel," Stormy ordered.

"Aye!" the sailors shouted, and they sang a chantey as they plastered *The Courser*'s sides with white soap.

"Now we'll take her through!" said Stormy. And as the ship's sails caught the wind, Stormalong eased her between the Dover cliffs and Calais. Ever since then the white cliffs of Dover have been as milky white as a whale's belly, and the sea below still foams with soapsuds.

For years Stormalong was the most famous sea captain in the world. Sailors in every port told how he ate ostrich eggs for breakfast, a hundred gallons of whale soup for lunch, and a warehouseful of shark meat for dinner. They told how after every meal he'd pick his teeth with an eighteen-foot oar—some said it was the same oar he once carried to Kansas.

But it was also said that sometimes when the crew sang chanteys late at night, their giant captain would stand alone on the deck, gazing out at the sea with a look of unfathomable sorrow in his eyes.

After the Civil War, steamships began to transport cargo over the seas. The days of the great sailing ships came to an end, and the courageous men who steered the beautiful Yankee clippers across the oceans also began to disappear.

IN
MEMORY
OF
B. STORMALONG

No one remembers quite how old Stormalong died. All they recollect is his funeral. It seems that one foggy twilight thousands of sailors attended his burial. They covered him with a hundred yards of the finest Chinese silk, and then fifty sailors carried his huge coffin to a grave near the sea. As they dug into the sand with silver spades and lowered his coffin with a silver cord, they wept tears like rain.

And for years afterward they sang about him:

Old Stormy's dead and gone to rest—
To my way, hey, Stormalong!
Of all the sailors he was the best—
Aye, aye, aye, Mister Stormalong!

Ever since then seamen first class put "A.B.S." after their names. Most people think it means "Able-Bodied Seaman." But the old New England seafaring men know different. They know it stands for the most amazing deep-water sailor who ever lived, Alfred Bulltop Stormalong.

COMPREHENSION

Dig Deeper

How to Analyze the Text

Use these pages to learn about Understanding Characters, Point of View, and Hyperbole. Then read "Stormalong" again to apply what you learned.

Understanding Characters

"Stormalong" is a tall tale about a larger-than-life sailor nicknamed Stormy. Like people in real life, every story **character** is unique. To figure out what a character is like, look for text evidence about what he or she thinks, says, and does.

Paying attention to what Stormy thinks, says, and does will help you understand what he is like and what his relationships with other characters are like. Reread pages 146–147. What do Stormy's thoughts, words, and actions tell you about him?

Thoughts	Words	Actions

ELACC4RL3 describe a character, setting, or event, drawing on details; **ELACC4RL4** determine the meaning of words and phrases, including those that allude to characters in mythology; **ELACC4RL6** compare and contrast the point of view from which stories are narrated

Point of View

Point of view is the standpoint from which a text is written. Remember that most stories are written in first-person or third-person point of view.

- In **first-person point of view,** a story character is the narrator. The narrator uses the words *I, me,* and *my*.
- In **third-person point of view,** an outside observer is the narrator. The narrator uses the words *he, she*, and *they* to tell about characters. A third-person narrator knows what all the characters are thinking.

Hyperbole

Hyperbole is a device authors use to "stretch the truth," or exaggerate characters' actions and abilities. Writers of tall tales use hyperbole to make characters seem larger than life. For example, the author compares Stormy's voice to a foghorn, a device that makes a loud moaning noise to warn sailors of approaching land.

Your Turn

RETURN TO THE ESSENTIAL QUESTION

Review the story to prepare to discuss this question: *Why do people pass down stories over the years?* As you discuss, take turns naming stories that have been passed down for generations.

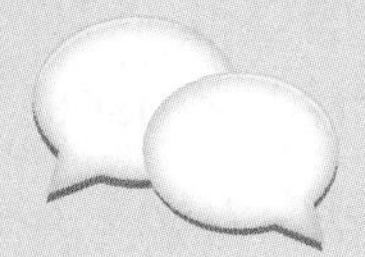

Classroom Conversation

Continue your discussion of "Stormalong" by explaining your answers to these questions:

1. What do you think was the author's purpose for writing this story?
2. What made Stormalong such a legend among sailors?
3. Do you think Stormalong ever felt as if he belonged? Tell why or why not.

LOCAL LEGEND

Write a Song With a partner, write your own humorous song about a huge baby or other tall-tale character that comes to your town. Include a description of the main character and a problem his or her arrival creates. How does your town solve this problem? Decide on a tune for your song and perform it for the class.

WRITE ABOUT READING

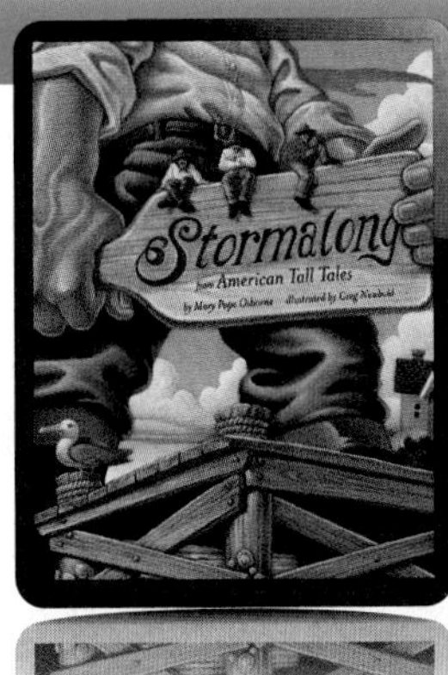

Response Stormy struggled his whole life to fit in. Write a paragraph about why he struggled so much. Use examples and details from the story to support your answer. Also include your thoughts about why people feel the need to fit in. Remember to end the paragraph with a concluding statement.

Writing Tip

To capture your readers' attention, open your paragraph with an interesting introduction. Then state two or three reasons why Stormy struggled.

ELACC4RL3 describe a character, setting, or event, drawing on details; **ELACC4W1b** provide reasons supported by facts and details; **ELACC4W1d** provide a concluding statement or section; **ELACC4W9a** apply grade 4 Reading standards to literature; **ELACC4SL1a** come to discussions prepared/explicitly draw on preparation and other information about the topic

Lesson 5

FOLKTALE

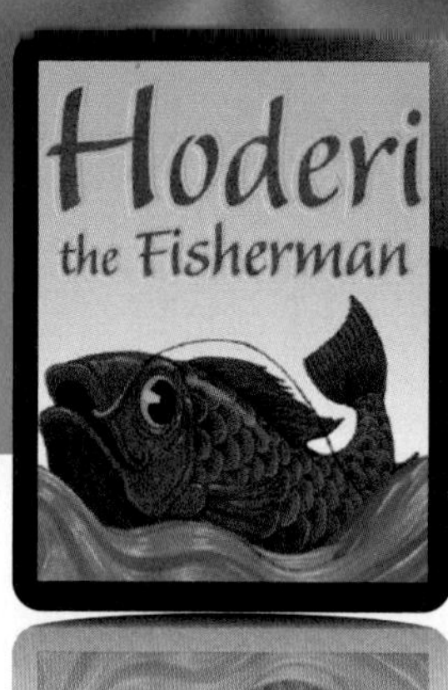

GENRE

A **folktale** is a story that the people of a country tell to explain or entertain. This folktale is in the form of a play.

TEXT FOCUS

Scenes help show when the setting, or time and place, changes in a play. Scenes also separate the action of the play into different sections. How does each scene differ from the others?

ELACC4RL5 explain major differences between poems, drama, and prose/refer to their structural elements

Hoderi the Fisherman

retold by Kate McGovern

Cast of Characters

Narrator
Hoderi (hoh DEH ree)
Hikohodemi (HIH koh hoh DEH mee)
Katsumi (kat SOO mee)
Sea King

Scene 1

[Setting: A small Japanese fishing village in the 1500s.]

Narrator: One day, two brothers—Hoderi, a hunter, and Hikohodemi, a fisherman—decide to trade jobs for a day.

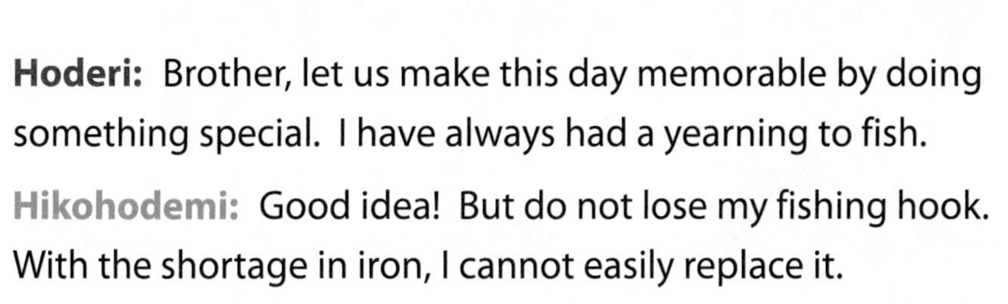

Hoderi: Brother, let us make this day memorable by doing something special. I have always had a yearning to fish.

Hikohodemi: Good idea! But do not lose my fishing hook. With the shortage in iron, I cannot easily replace it.

Narrator: Alas, Hoderi is not a seafaring man. The first fish he catches swims away with the fishing hook.

Hoderi: *[To Hikohodemi]* I am afraid I lost your hook.

Hikohodemi: *[Looking horrified]* Hoderi! You betrayed my trust! By now the sea's tidal shifts have taken it far away.

Hoderi: *[Sorrowfully]* Then I shall search the entire sea until I find it. *[Hoderi dives into the water.]*

Scene 2

[Setting: Underwater, near the Sea King's palace.]

Narrator: Soon, Hoderi meets Katsumi, a Sea Princess.

Katsumi: Welcome! What brings you to our palace?

Hoderi: Forgive me. I am looking for a lost fishing hook. It belongs to my brother.

Katsumi: Perhaps my father, the Sea King, can help.

Narrator: Hoderi tells the Sea King his story.

Sea King: The condition of the sea can make it dangerous, friend. We will help you search.

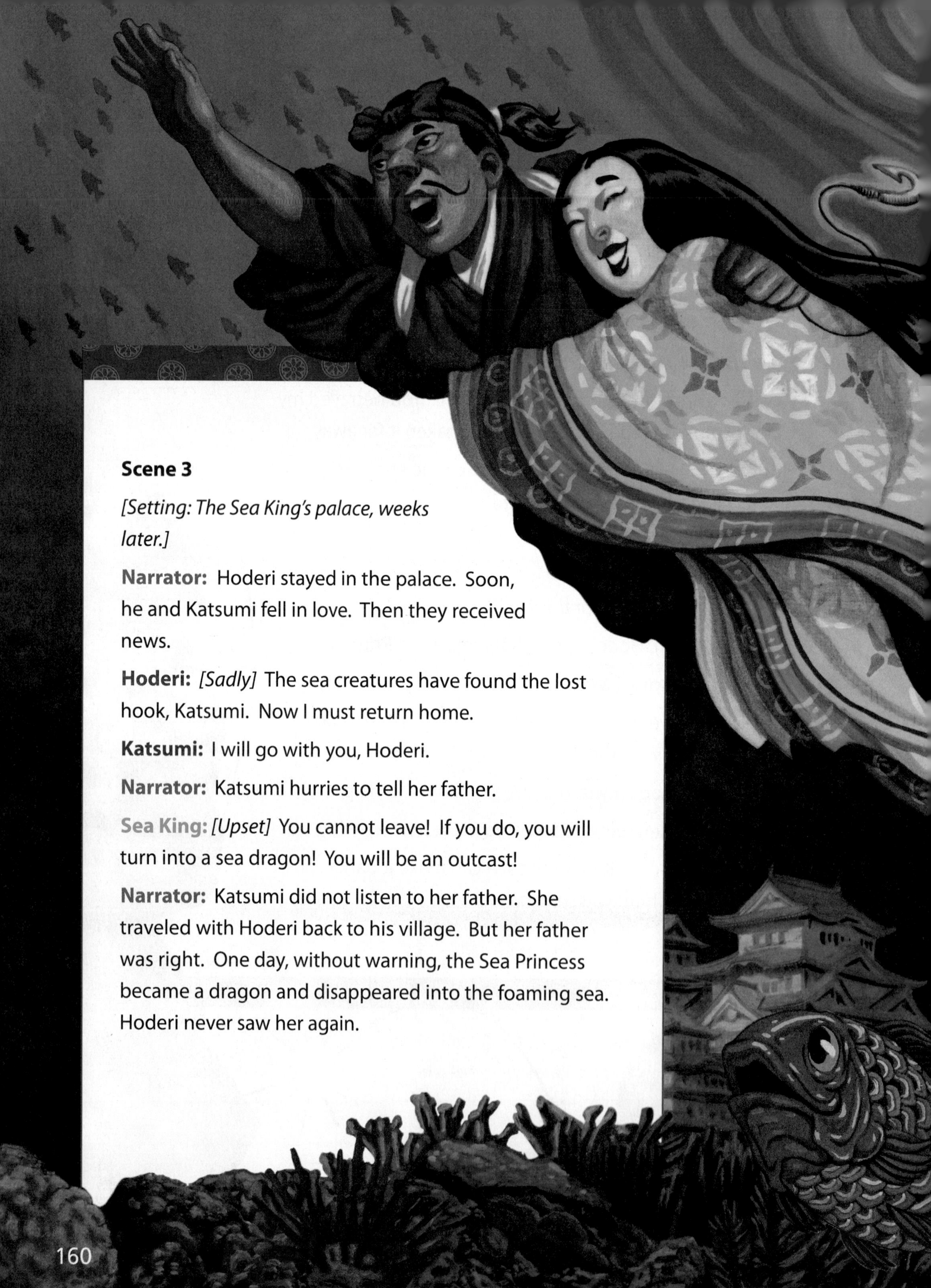

Scene 3

[Setting: The Sea King's palace, weeks later.]

Narrator: Hoderi stayed in the palace. Soon, he and Katsumi fell in love. Then they received news.

Hoderi: *[Sadly]* The sea creatures have found the lost hook, Katsumi. Now I must return home.

Katsumi: I will go with you, Hoderi.

Narrator: Katsumi hurries to tell her father.

Sea King: *[Upset]* You cannot leave! If you do, you will turn into a sea dragon! You will be an outcast!

Narrator: Katsumi did not listen to her father. She traveled with Hoderi back to his village. But her father was right. One day, without warning, the Sea Princess became a dragon and disappeared into the foaming sea. Hoderi never saw her again.

Compare Texts

TEXT TO TEXT

Discuss Theme The theme of a story is the author's message, or the lesson the author wants readers to learn. With a partner, talk about the lesson that readers can learn from "Stormalong" and from "Hoderi the Fisherman." Then work together to write a sentence that sums up the theme both stories communicate.

TEXT TO SELF

Describe an Interest In "Stormalong," the main character is happy only when he realizes his true calling as a sailor. Think of an activity, such as a sport, game, or hobby, that makes you especially happy. Write a short paragraph describing this activity. Explain why you like it so much.

TEXT TO WORLD

Research Steamships The era of the clipper ships described in "Stormalong" ended when ships powered by steam were invented. Use one online and one print source to learn about steamships. Then create a list of facts about steamships, including how they changed the way goods were transported. Share what you learned with the class.

ELACC4RL2 determine theme from details/summarize; **ELACC4RL9** compare and contrast the treatment of similar themes and topics; **ELACC4W7** conduct short research projects that build knowledge through investigation; **ELACC4W8** recall information from experiences or gather information from print and digital sources/take notes, categorize information, and provide a list of sources

COMMON CORE **ELACC4L2a** use correct capitalization

Grammar

What Is a Proper Noun? A noun names a person, place, or thing. A **proper noun** names a particular person, place, or thing. A proper noun always begins with a capital letter. Some examples are names, states, languages, and book titles. Some words, such as *Uncle*, *Mom,* and *Jr.*, can be used as names or parts of names. These words are also proper nouns.

Proper Nouns
During the Civil War (historical event), Abraham Lincoln (name) issued the Emancipation Proclamation (historical document).
Mona read *Harriet Tubman: Conductor of the Underground Railroad* (book) and "The Underground Railroad" (article) for summer reading.
Mona heard Uncle John (words used as a name) say that many Americans (nationality) helped African American slaves escape to New York (state) or Canada (country).

Rewrite the sentences below, correctly capitalizing the words in bold type.

1. **paul bunyan and babe the blue ox** is another tall tale about a giant.
2. **pablo** and **aunt lola** saw a statue of **paul bunyan** in **bemidji, minnesota**.
3. They learned that **americans** started reading stories about **paul bunyan** during **world war I**.

When you use proper nouns in your writing, be sure to capitalize the appropriate words. This will help your readers know that you are using the names or titles of particular people, places, and things.

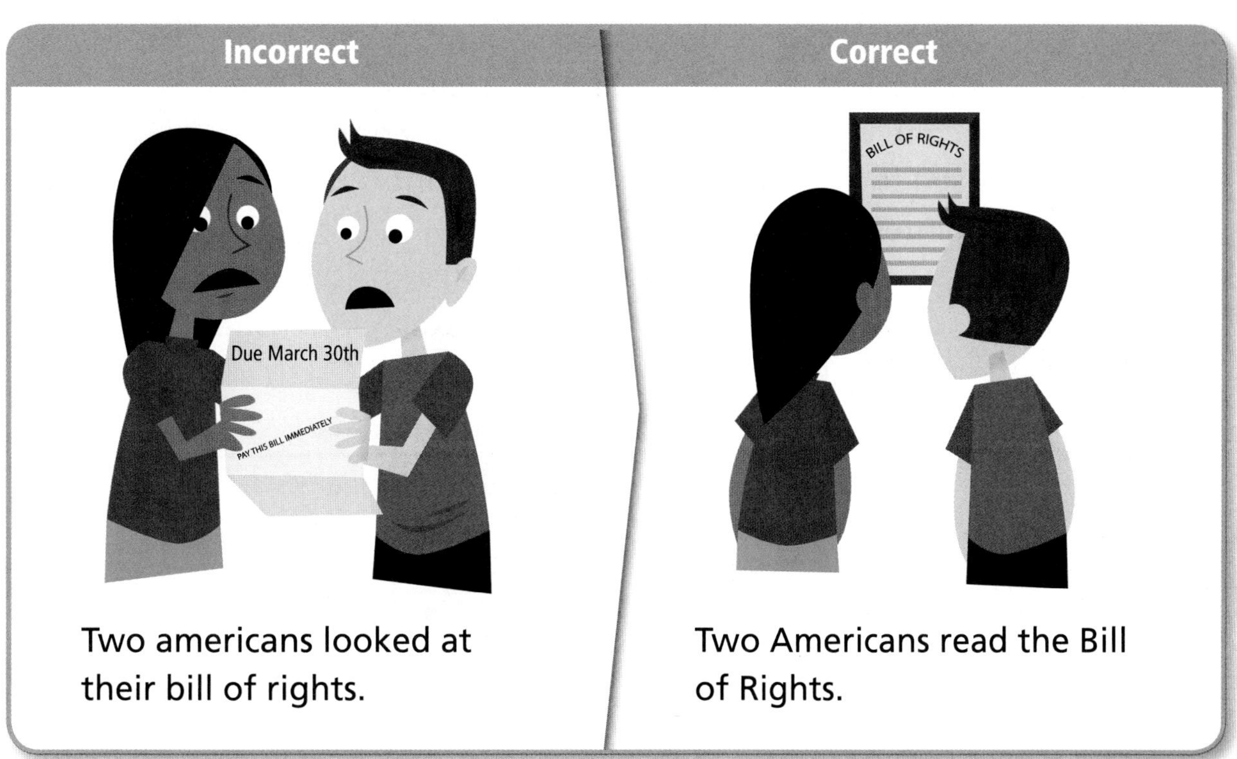

Incorrect	Correct
Two americans looked at their bill of rights.	Two Americans read the Bill of Rights.

 Connect Grammar to Writing

As you edit your narrative, check to make sure that you have capitalized all the proper nouns in your writing. If necessary, rewrite proper nouns so that they are capitalized correctly.

COMMON CORE **ELACC4W3a** orient the reader by establishing a situation and introducing a narrator or characters/organize an event sequence; **ELACC4W3b** use dialogue and description to develop experiences and events or show characters' responses; **ELACC4W3c** use transitional words and phrases to manage the sequence of events

Narrative Writing

Reading-Writing Workshop: Revise

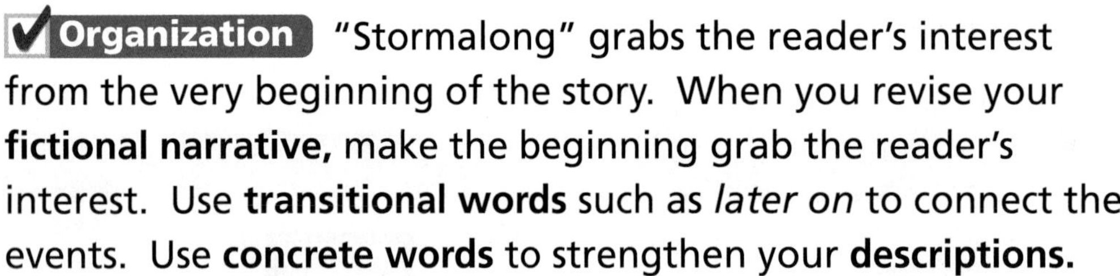

Organization "Stormalong" grabs the reader's interest from the very beginning of the story. When you revise your **fictional narrative,** make the beginning grab the reader's interest. Use **transitional words** such as *later on* to connect the events. Use **concrete words** to strengthen your **descriptions.**

Mei Ann revised the beginning of her story by introducing the setting in an interesting way. Later, she revised her opening paragraph by adding a transitional phrase to make the sequence of events clearer. She replaced dull words with exact ones. She also made sure all proper nouns were capitalized.

Revised Draft

"Achoo!" Sarah sneezed in the dusty air. ^It was the first time sarah had entered the attic of her new house. The room was dark and dusty. ^After a few minutes, Sarah's eyes got used to the dark. She saw camping gear, old ~~things~~ ^toys, and furniture stacked against the walls. "This place is so cool!" she said.

Matt didn't agree. "There are probably ~~bugs~~ ^spiders up here!"

"We can't turn back now!" Sarah said.

Writing Process Checklist

Prewrite

Draft

▶ **Revise**

- ✔ Did I introduce the characters and setting in an interesting way?
- ✔ Have I used transitional words?
- ✔ Did I use exact words and dialogue?
- ✔ Did I capitalize proper nouns?

Edit

Publish and Share

Final Copy

In the Attic

by Mei Ann Lee

"Achoo!" Sarah sneezed in the dusty air. It was the first time Sarah had entered the attic of her new house. The room was dark and dusty. After a few minutes, Sarah's eyes got used to the dark. She saw camping gear, old toys, and furniture stacked against the walls. "This place is so cool!" she said.

Matt didn't agree. "There are probably spiders up here!"

"We can't turn back now!" Sarah said. Then she pointed to an old brown suitcase. "I wonder what's in that." Sarah tried to open the suitcase, but it was protected by a heavy lock. "We'll never get this open!" she said. Just then the attic door creaked open, and Mom appeared. She held several keys on an old string.

"Let the exploration begin," she said.

Reading as a Writer

Which parts of Mei Ann's opening help set the stage for the story? Is the sequence of events clear? How can you add transitional words to make sure readers follow the events in your story?

In my final draft, I used exact words. I also made sure to use transitional words to connect events. I checked that I used quotation marks for the dialogue.

Read the passages "The Name of the Game" and "A New Friend." As you read, stop and answer each question using text evidence.

The Name of the Game

Javier and his family had relocated to Bay City only a few weeks ago. It had been hard to leave his friends and relatives in Mexico and come to a place where everything was different.

 What is the meaning of the word *relocated* in this passage? Explain how you determined the meaning.

At Javier's new school, many kids smiled at him. Some boys in his class even made room for him at the lunch table. Still, Javier worried that he would never make friends. He was learning more English every day, but he still had difficulty carrying on a conversation with the other kids. Javier had to concentrate so much on the strange-sounding words that he sometimes got a headache trying to understand people.

Other things were different, too. In Mexico, everyone in the family came home and ate lunch together. Everyone talked and laughed, and no one was in a hurry. Now Javier ate lunch at school. He was not used to the cafeteria food, and everyone had to eat so quickly.

Most of all, Javier missed playing *futbol*. In Mexico, Javier and his friends played *futbol* whenever they could. Sometimes their familes played in the evenings, and the games went on until it got too dark to see. Here in Bay City, no one seemed to play Javier's favorite game.

Then one day at recess, one of the boys called, "Hey, Javier! Do you want to play football with us?"

At last, here was something familiar, something Javier loved! When the game began, though, it turned out to be not at all what Javier had expected. This was American football. It was fun but not the same. When Javier walked back to class, his shoulders dropped a little bit.

"I don't think the kids here know how to play *futbol*," Javier told his family that night at dinner.

ELACC4RL2 determine theme from details/summarize; **ELACC4RL3** describe a character, setting, or event, drawing on details; **ELACC4RL4** determine the meaning of words and phrases, including those that allude to characters in mythology; **ELACC4RL6** compare and contrast the point of view from which stories are narrated

"Maybe you'll need to learn how to play American football," his mother suggested.

Javier took his mother's advice and tried playing American football. He enjoyed playing this new game well enough, but he still really missed the game he used to play. On Saturday afternoon, he grabbed his old round black-and-white ball and took it to the park. He was dribbling it across the grass when he heard someone call his name and saw some kids from his class waving to him.

"Can we play soccer with you?" one of them yelled to Javier. Javier was confused. What was this soccer they were talking about?

"Come on, Javier, pass the ball to me!" another called.

Javier grinned and kicked the ball. Before he knew it, he was in the middle of the game he loved best. When they finally stopped playing, the kids gathered around Javier.

"You're a great soccer player, Javier!" one of his new friends exclaimed. "Did you play soccer a lot in Mexico?"

Javier figured it out. He smiled as he told them, "In Mexico, the game you call soccer is called *futbol*."

The other kids looked surprised. "Well, let's play some more *futbol*!" one of them said. Javier grinned. Whatever it was called, he was delighted to be playing his favorite game again.

What is the theme of this passage? Use details from the passage to support your response.

A New Friend

A few weeks ago, our teacher introduced a new student to our class. Her name was Rosita, and she had just moved here from Mexico. When we passed each other, I smiled at her and said, "Welcome to our class. My name is Maddie." She smiled back, but she seemed shy.

My friends and I invited Rosita to sit with us at lunch in the cafeteria. A couple of times, though, I noticed that Rosita was frowning. I wondered if maybe she didn't feel well. She didn't talk much, either. I hoped it wasn't because she didn't like us.

How would you describe Maddie, the girl who wrote this passage? Give examples to support your response.

One afternoon, my friends and I invited Rosita to play soccer with us in the park. She said she didn't know how to play soccer, but we said we would teach her. "Please come, Rosita," I urged her. "Soccer is a lot of fun, and I bet you'll learn in a jiffy."

"What is a jiffy?" Rosita asked, looking confused. I realized she probably didn't understand some of the words we used. If I moved to Mexico, I suppose I would have difficulty understanding people, too.

When we got to the park and Rosita saw the soccer ball, her eyes began to sparkle. The first time the ball was passed to her, she dribbled it a short way and passed it neatly off to Taylor on her left.

Taylor lofted the ball into the air with her foot, attempting to put it into the goal. Taylor's kick was going too high, but suddenly Rosita was there. She faked around a defender, leaped high into the air, and headed the ball right into the goal.

Everyone cheered and gave Rosita high-fives. "I thought you said you didn't know how to play soccer," I laughed.

"I did not know this word *soccer*," Rosita replied, "but I do know this game. In Mexico, we call it *futbol*."

Rosita had learned a new English word, and the rest of us had learned a new Spanish word. I was pretty sure we had made a great new friend, too.

How are the points of view of "A New Friend" and "The Name of the Game" different?

Unit 2

Lesson 6

Vocabulary in Context

TARGET VOCABULARY

alarmed
reacted
convey
daring
luminous
awe
indescribable
extraordinary
fade
conferring

Vocabulary Reader

Context Cards

ELACC4L6 acquire/use vocabulary, including academic and domain-specific

1 alarmed

The young girl was alarmed, or scared, by what she heard on the radio.

2 reacted

The couple's favorite song came on the radio. They reacted with smiles.

3 convey

The crowd cheered to convey its support for the team.

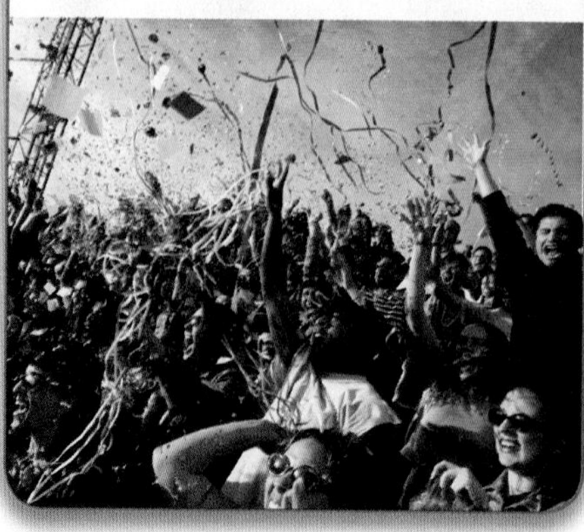

4 daring

Only a daring person can be a mountain climber. She must be very brave.

- Study each Context Card.
- Use a dictionary to help you learn the meanings of these words.

5 luminous

On a clear night, a full moon is luminous. It is very bright in the sky.

6 awe

The couple was in awe at what they were seeing. They were shocked!

7 indescribable

What the man saw was indescribable. He could not put it into words.

8 extraordinary

The boy watched as the basketball player made an extraordinary, or amazing, shot.

9 fade

The music on the radio began to fade as it became quieter and quieter.

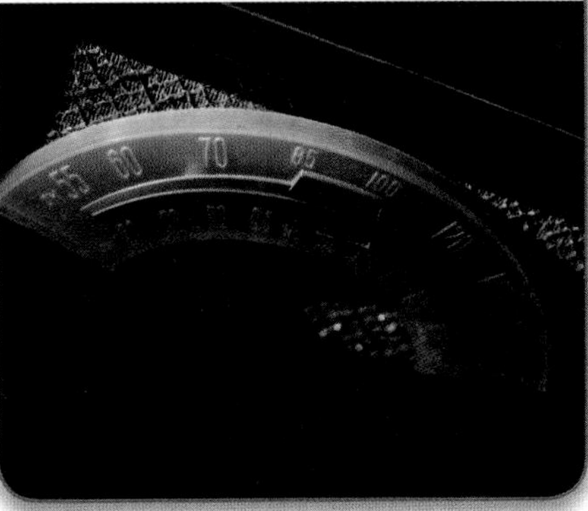

10 conferring

The TV reporter is conferring with the police to discuss the details of the accident.

Read and Comprehend

TARGET SKILL

Story Structure As you read "Invasion from Mars," ask yourself what the most important parts of the story are. Look for text evidence that helps you picture the **setting**, or where and when the story takes place. Keep track of new **characters** as they are introduced, and pay careful attention to what the characters do, think, and say. Pay attention to the **plot,** or what happens. Use a graphic organizer like the one below to help you.

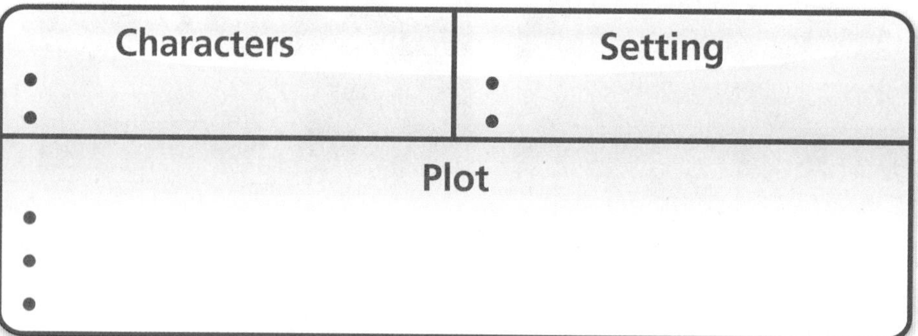

TARGET STRATEGY

Infer/Predict When you **infer**, you try to figure out something that is not directly stated in the text. Use text evidence from the radio commentary to help you infer what is happening and to **predict** what might happen next.

COMMON CORE

ELACC4RL1 refer to details and examples when explaining what the text says explicitly and when drawing inferences; **ELACC4RL3** describe a character, setting, or event, drawing on details

PREVIEW THE TOPIC

Performance Arts

The performance arts include dancing, singing, acting, playing musical instruments, and reading stories in front of an audience. Often people go to a theater or concert hall to see performances, but radio and television carry live and recorded performances, too.

One of the most famous radio performances in history was a live broadcast of a science-fiction drama based on a book called *The War of the Worlds*. You are about to read an excerpt, or a part, of that famous performance. You'll find out why it shocked America.

Lesson 6

ANCHOR TEXT

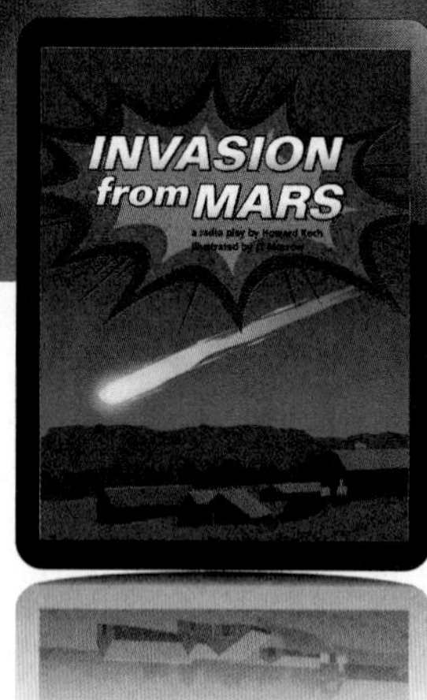

 TARGET VOCABULARY

Story Structure Explain the elements that make up the story. Identify the characters, setting, and plot events.

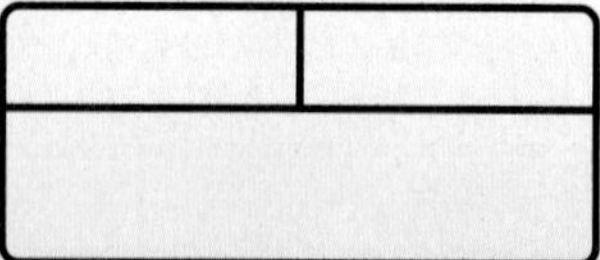

 GENRE

A **play** is a story that can be performed for an audience. As you read, look for:

- text that consists mainly of dialogue
- characters' actions and feelings shown through dialogue
- stage directions

ELACC4RL3 describe a character, setting, or event, drawing on details; **ELACC4RL5** explain major differences between poems, drama, and prose/refer to their structural elements; **ELACC4RL10** read and comprehend literature; **ELACC4L3c** differentiate contexts that call for formal English and informal discourse

 Go Digital

MEET THE AUTHOR

Howard Koch

Howard Koch began his career as a lawyer, but he quickly discovered that the profession didn't provide him the kind of creative outlet he wanted. He first started writing plays for theater, and soon Orson Welles hired Howard to rewrite classic and modern literature for radio plays. Later, Howard would move to Hollywood, where he would write the screenplay for one of the most famous movies of all time, *Casablanca*.

MEET THE ILLUSTRATOR

JT Morrow

JT Morrow grew up in a small town in Tennessee. As a kid, he drew constantly and fell in love with all styles of art. "I like my work to be an explosion of color," JT says, and he brings that love of color to all his pieces. Today, JT draws and paints in many different styles, often parodying well-known classics.

INVASION from MARS

a radio play by Howard Koch
illustrated by JT Morrow

ESSENTIAL QUESTION

How are performances similar to and different from written stories?

On the night of October 30, 1938, Orson Welles and the Mercury Theater Company broadcast the radio play *Invasion from Mars*, adapted from the novel *The War of the Worlds* by H. G. Wells. Listeners who tuned in after the broadcast began were alarmed by what they heard. In this scene from the play, newsman Carl Phillips is broadcasting live from the New Jersey farm where a strange metal cylinder has crash-landed. How would you have reacted to hearing these words on your radio?

Phillips: Well, I've never seen anything like it. The color is sort of yellowish-white. Curious spectators now are pressing close to the object in spite of the efforts of the police to keep them back. They're getting in front of my line of vision. Would you mind standing on one side, please?

Policeman: One side, there, one side.

Phillips: While the policemen are pushing the crowd back, here's Mr. Wilmuth, owner of the farm here. He may have some interesting facts to add. . . . Mr. Wilmuth, would you please tell the radio audience as much as you remember of this rather unusual visitor that dropped in your backyard? Step closer, please. Ladies and gentlemen, this is Mr. Wilmuth.

Wilmuth: I was listenin' to the radio.

Phillips: Closer and louder, please.

Wilmuth: Pardon me!

Phillips: Louder, please, and closer.

Wilmuth: Yes, sir—while I was listening to the radio and kinda drowsin', that Professor fellow was talkin' about Mars, so I was half dozin' and half . . .

Phillips: Yes, Mr. Wilmuth. Then what happened?

Wilmuth: As I was sayin', I was listenin' to the radio kinda halfways . . .

Phillips: Yes, Mr. Wilmuth, and then you saw something?

Wilmuth: Not first off. I heard something.

Phillips: And what did you hear?

Wilmuth: A hissing sound. Like this: sssssss . . . kinda like a fourt' of July rocket.

Phillips: Then what?

Wilmuth: Turned my head out the window and would have swore I was to sleep and dreamin'.

Phillips: Yes?

Wilmuth: I seen a kinda greenish streak and then zingo! Somethin' smacked the ground. Knocked me clear out of my chair!

Phillips: Well, were you frightened, Mr. Wilmuth?

Wilmuth: Well, I — I ain't quite sure. I reckon I — I was kinda riled.

Phillips: Thank you, Mr. Wilmuth. Thank you.

Wilmuth: Want me to tell you some more?

Phillips: No . . . That's quite all right, that's plenty.

ANALYZE THE TEXT

Formal and Informal Language
Would you describe Carl Phillips's language use as formal or informal? Why? How does his language compare with how Mr. Wilmuth talks?

Phillips: Ladies and gentlemen, you've just heard Mr. Wilmuth, owner of the farm where this thing has fallen. I wish I could convey the atmosphere . . . the background of this . . . fantastic scene. Hundreds of cars are parked in a field in back of us. Police are trying to rope off the roadway leading into the farm. But it's no use. They're breaking right through. Their headlights throw an enormous spot on the pit where the object's half buried. Some of the more daring souls are venturing near the edge. Their silhouettes stand out against the metal sheen.

(*Faint humming sound*)

One man wants to touch the thing . . . he's having an argument with a policeman. The policeman wins. . . . Now, ladies and gentlemen, there's something I haven't mentioned in all this excitement, but it's becoming more distinct. Perhaps you've caught it already on your radio. Listen: (*Long pause*) . . .

Do you hear it? It's a curious humming sound that seems to come from inside the object. I'll move the microphone nearer. Here. (*Pause*) Now we're not more than twenty-five feet away. Can you hear it now? Oh, Professor Pierson!

Pierson: Yes, Mr. Phillips?

Phillips: Can you tell us the meaning of that scraping noise inside the thing?

Pierson: Possibly the unequal cooling of its surface.

Phillips: Do you still think it's a meteor, Professor?

Pierson: I don't know what to think. The metal casing is definitely extraterrestrial . . . not found on this earth. Friction with the earth's atmosphere usually tears holes in a meteorite. This thing is smooth and, as you can see, of cylindrical shape.

ANALYZE THE TEXT

Story Structure How does the interview with Professor Pierson add to the plot? What new information do you learn?

Phillips: Just a minute! Something's happening! Ladies and gentlemen, this is terrific! This end of the thing is beginning to flake off! The top is beginning to rotate like a screw! The thing must be hollow!

Voices: She's a movin'!

Look, the darn thing's unscrewing!

Keep back, there! Keep back, I tell you!

Maybe there's men in it trying to escape!

It's red hot, they'll burn to a cinder!

Keep back there. Keep those idiots back!

(*Suddenly the clanking sound of a huge piece of falling metal*)

Voices: She's off! The top's loose!

Look out there! Stand back!

Phillips: Ladies and gentlemen, this is the most terrifying thing I have ever witnessed . . . Wait a minute! *Someone's crawling out of the hollow top.* Someone or . . . something. I can see peering out of that black hole two luminous disks . . . are they eyes? It might be a face. It might be . . .

(*Shout of awe from the crowd*)

Phillips: Good heavens, something's wriggling out of the shadow like a gray snake. Now it's another one, and another. They look like tentacles to me. There, I can see the thing's body. It's large as a bear and it glistens like wet leather. But that face. It . . . it's indescribable. I can hardly force myself to keep looking at it. The eyes are black and gleam like a serpent. The mouth is V-shaped with saliva dripping from its rimless lips that seem to quiver and pulsate. The monster or whatever it is can hardly move. It seems weighed down by . . . possibly gravity or something. The thing's raising up. The crowd falls back. They've seen enough. This is the most extraordinary experience. I can't find words . . . I'm pulling this microphone with me as I talk. I'll have to stop the description until I've taken a new position. Hold on, will you please, I'll be back in a minute.

(*Fade into piano*)

ANALYZE THE TEXT

Elements of Drama What is the purpose of the stage directions in the text? How might they affect how the actors read the play?

Announcer Two: We are bringing you an eyewitness account of what's happening on the Wilmuth farm, Grovers Mill, New Jersey. (*More piano*) We now return you to Carl Phillips at Grovers Mill.

Phillips: Ladies and gentlemen (Am I on?). Ladies and gentlemen, here I am, back of a stone wall that adjoins Mr. Wilmuth's garden. From here I get a sweep of the whole scene. I'll give you every detail as long as I can talk. As long as I can see. More state police have arrived. They're drawing up a cordon in front of the pit, about thirty of them. No need to push the crowd back now. They're willing to keep their distance. The captain is conferring with someone. We can't quite see who. Oh yes, I believe it's Professor Pierson. Yes, it is. Now they've parted. The professor moves around one side, studying the object, while the captain and two policemen advance with something in their hands. I can see it now. It's a white handkerchief tied to a pole . . . a flag of truce. If those creatures know what that means . . . what anything means! . . . *Wait!* Something's happening!

(*Hissing sound followed by a humming that increases in intensity*)

A humped shape is rising out of the pit. I can make out a small beam of light against a mirror. What's that? There's a jet of flame springing from that mirror, and it leaps right at the advancing men. It strikes them head on! Good Lord, they're turning into flame!

(*Screams and unearthly shrieks*)

Now the whole field's caught fire. (*Explosion*) The woods . . . the barns . . . the gas tanks of automobiles . . . it's spreading everywhere. It's coming this way. About twenty yards to my right . . .

(*Crash of microphone . . . then dead silence*)

COMPREHENSION

Dig Deeper

How to Analyze the Text

Use these pages to learn about Story Structure, Elements of Drama, and Formal and Informal Language. Then read "Invasion from Mars" again to apply what you learned.

Story Structure

A **story's structure** is made up of its characters, setting, and plot. The **characters** are the people and other creatures involved in the story. The **setting** is where and when the story takes place. The **plot** is what happens in the story. It is made up of a series of events.

Look for text evidence to help you understand and describe characters, setting, and plot events. For example, in the beginning of "Invasion from Mars," the radio host introduces Mr. Wilmuth as "the owner of the farm here." This clue tells you that the story takes place on a farm. Details and evidence such as the picture of the old-fashioned radio and the date in the introduction tell you that the story takes place in 1938.

What details and text evidence can you find to help you describe the characters and plot events?

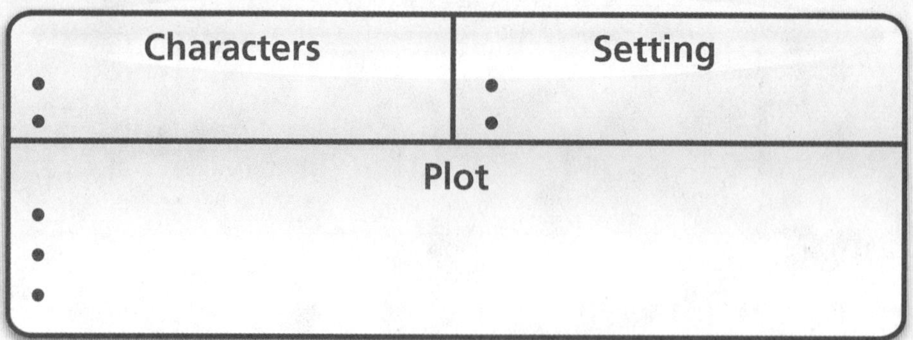

ELACC4RL3 describe a character, setting, or event, drawing on details; **ELACC4RL5** explain major differences between poems, drama, and prose/ refer to their structural elements; **ELACC4RL7** make connections between the text and a visual or oral presentation of it; **ELACC4L3c** differentiate contexts that call for formal English and informal discourse

Elements of Drama

Reading a drama is a different experience than watching or hearing one. When you listen to a drama, you rely on the narrator's **descriptions** and the characters' **dialogue** to understand the story. Dialogue is what characters say. When you read a drama such as "Invasion from Mars," you see the **stage directions** that describe sound effects and tell actors how to speak and act.

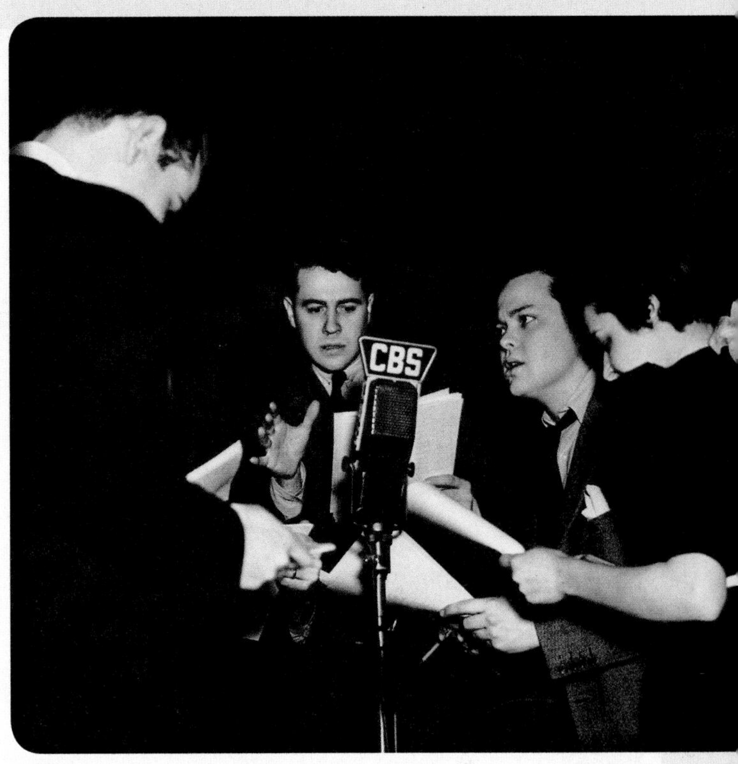

Formal and Informal Language

Just like people in real life, characters in a story use formal or informal language depending on the situation and their background. Professor Pierson uses **formal language.** He speaks in complete sentences and uses some specialized science words. He does not use slang expressions, such as *kinda* or *zingo.* Professor Pierson's use of formal language makes him sound like an expert on science.

Your Turn

RETURN TO THE ESSENTIAL QUESTION

Review the selection with a partner to prepare to discuss this question: *How are performances similar to and different from written stories?* As you discuss, take turns reviewing and explaining your ideas using text evidence from "Invasion from Mars."

Classroom Conversation

Continue your discussion of "Invasion from Mars" by explaining your answers with text evidence:

1. Do you think Carl Phillips is scared by the object?
2. How do the descriptions of sounds contribute to the play?
3. Do you think it was wrong to deliberately scare listeners, or was the radio broadcast just entertainment? Explain.

ACT IT OUT

Readers' Theater In a small group, choose one scene. Select a director and choose roles. Take time to rehearse, and make sure your performance matches the dialogue and stage directions. Then perform the scene for the class. Discuss how your performance differed from the print version of the story.

WRITE ABOUT READING

Response In the play "Invasion from Mars," a reporter describes events to the radio audience as they happen. Imagine you heard the broadcast. Summarize the story in one or two paragraphs. Be sure to set the scene and to tell the events in order. Remember to provide a conclusion for your summary.

Writing Tip

Be sure to use transitional words and phrases to show the sequence of events. Use a variety of sentence types to keep your writing interesting.

ELACC4RL2 determine theme from details/summarize; **ELACC4RL5** explain major differences between poems, drama, and prose/refer to their structural elements; **ELACC4RL7** make connections between the text and a visual or oral presentation of it; **ELACC4W9a** apply grade 4 Reading standards to literature; **ELACC4SL3** identify reasons and evidence a speaker provides to support points

Lesson 6

INFORMATIONAL TEXT

 GENRE

Informational text, such as this article, gives information about a topic. The information can be organized under headings. Informational text often includes photographs.

 TEXT FOCUS

Historical text is a kind of informational text that tells about a topic in history. It is usually told in sequential order with dates as well as transitional words to help readers keep track of events. Historical text often includes a timeline that shows a series of events. What does the timeline in this article show?

ELACC4RI3 explain events/procedures/ideas/concepts in a text; **ELACC4RI7** interpret information presented visually, orally, or quantitatively; **ELACC4RI10** read and comprehend informational texts

Go Digital

The History of RADIO

by Vivian Fernandez

The Beginning of Radio

We can't see them, but radio waves are all around us. In the late 1800s, Guglielmo Marconi used radio waves to send and receive a signal through the air. At first, the signal only went short distances. Marconi kept working, and soon he was sending signals over several miles.

By the early 1900s, people were using radio technology to send and receive messages across oceans. However, these messages were not voices. They had to be sent in Morse code. Then, on December 24, 1906, Reginald Fessenden made the first transmission of speech and music. He had found a way to change the sounds of voices and music into a signal that could be carried by radio waves.

Orson Welles directed and performed in many radio plays.

Radios in the Home

By the 1920s, more and more people had radios at home. Families listened to the radio like we watch television. Many listened to music, but soon radio stations came up with different kinds of programs, which were often broadcast live. Families could listen to the radio to hear music, comedies, and stories. One show was maybe too exciting. On October 30, 1938, Orson Welles presented "The War of the Worlds." Millions of people listened to the radio show about an alien attack, and some believed that what they heard was real.

Another kind of radio drama told stories about families. They were called "soaps." This is because soap makers paid for most of these shows. Saturday mornings and after school were times for children's shows. *Buck Rogers in the Twenty-fifth Century, Superman,* and *Popeye* were some children's shows.

The radio was also a way for families to hear about news. On March 12, 1933, President Franklin D. Roosevelt gave the first of his "fireside chats." Later, during World War II, radio stations reported what was happening.

After World War II, people turned away from radio to television. Many radio programs stopped airing. Some shows that had been on the radio, such as *The Lone Ranger,* were now on television.

The Future of Radio

Today, radio has a lot of competition. Besides television and movies, many people turn to the Internet for entertainment and news. Internet radio does not use radio waves, but like radio, you can listen to music and shows anywhere. Regular radio is limited by how far radio signals can reach. In time, we will see if radio survives this new kind of competition.

TITANIC SINKS FOUR HOURS AFTER HITTING ICEBERG;
866 RESCUED BY CARPATHIA, PROBABLY 1250 PERISI
ISMAY SAFE, MRS. ASTOR MAYBE, NOTED NAMES MISSI

Many people first heard about the sinking of the *Titanic* over the radio.

Millions of Americans listened to President Roosevelt's "fireside chats" on the radio.

Early Days of Radio

1895 Guglielmo Marconi sends and receives first radio signal through the air

1901 Marconi receives first radio signal across the Atlantic Ocean

1906 Reginald Fessenden sends first transmission of human voice

1912 A message about the RMS *Titanic* sinking is sent through radio transmission, saving many lives

1920 First radio commercial broadcast in the United States reports results of presidential election

1921 First broadcast of baseball and football games

1922 First radio commercial in the United States (for real estate in New York)

1926 First national network is formed: National Broadcasting Company (NBC)

1895 1900 1905 1910 1915 1920 1925 1930

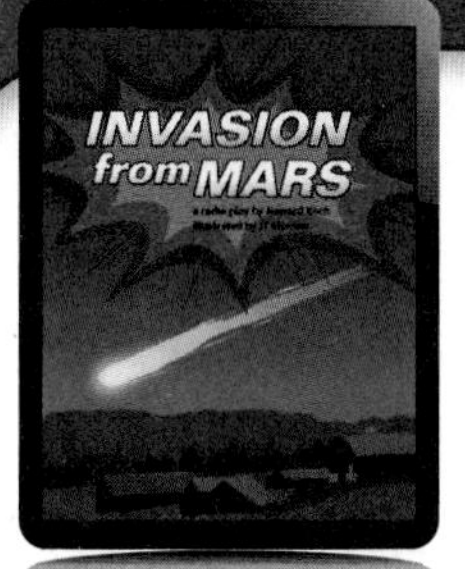

Compare Texts

TEXT TO TEXT

Analyze Radio Based on what you read in "The History of Radio," does it seem like radio plays such as "Invasion from Mars" were a common form of entertainment in the 1930s? Discuss your ideas with a partner. Use text evidence to support your ideas.

TEXT TO SELF

Analyze Reactions How do you think you might have reacted if you had heard "Invasion from Mars" in its first broadcast? Would you have thought that it was real? Write a paragraph explaining your thoughts.

TEXT TO WORLD

Compare Genres Look back at the play "Invasion from Mars." How would it have been told as a story? How is a play similar to and different from a written story? How is it similar to and different from a poem? Share your answers with a partner.

ELACC4RL5 explain major differences between poems, drama, and prose/refer to their structural elements; **ELACC4RI1** refer to details and examples when explaining what the text says explicitly and when drawing inferences; **ELACC4W10** write routinely over extended time frames and shorter time frames

ELACC4L3a choose words and phrases to convey ideas precisely

Grammar

What Is a Verb? A verb is a word that can show action. When a verb tells what people or things do, it is called an **action verb.** When a verb tells what someone or something is like, it is called a **linking verb.** Most linking verbs are forms of the verb *be,* such as *am, is, are, was,* and *were*.

Action Verb	Linking Verb
Phillips reported from the site.	The people were scared.

A verb may be more than one word. The main verb tells what the action is. The **helping verb** comes before the main verb and tells more about the action. Some helping verbs are *has, have, had, should, would, could, can,* and *may.*

helping verb — main verb
Aliens have landed in a field.

helping verb — main verb
People had gathered in the field.

Try This! **Work with a partner. Find the sentences with action verbs. Find the sentence with a linking verb. Point out the sentences with a main verb and a helping verb.**

1. Mr. Wilmuth watched the spaceship.
2. The spaceship hatch should open.
3. The aliens were scary.
4. The aliens have asked for a snack.

You can make your writing clearer and more interesting by choosing stronger verbs.

Sentence with Weak Verb	Sentence with Stronger Verb
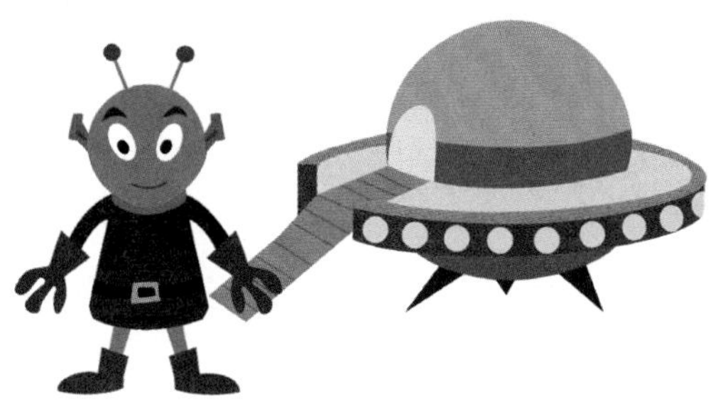 The alien came out of the spaceship.	 The alien climbed out of the spaceship.
 A crowd is in the field.	 A crowd has gathered in the field.

Connect Grammar to Writing

As you revise your news report, replace weak verbs with stronger, precise verbs to help keep the reader interested and engaged.

ELACC4W2a introduce a topic and group related information/include formatting, illustrations, and multimedia; **ELACC4W2b** develop the topic with facts, definitions, details, quotations, or other information and examples; **ELACC4W2d** use precise language and domain-specific vocabulary; **ELACC4L3a** choose words and phrases to convey ideas precisely

Informative Writing

Ideas "Invasion from Mars" is a radio play told in the form of a news report. When you write a news report, use precise language to draw the reader in and explain exactly what happened. Develop your topic by providing facts, concrete details, and examples.

Juan drafted a news report about a memorable night in his town. He added quotations and precise language to help the reader get a sense of the night's excitement.

Revised Draft

Pierson, FL—

at the Pierson Police Department ^The ~~police~~ phones ^began ringing on August 12th ^when bright ~~l~~Lights ~~had been seen in~~ ^streaked across the night sky.

"I couldn't believe what I was seeing," said Silvio Garcia^, a farmer. "My little boy asked if it was an alien invasion."

Writing Traits Checklist

- **Ideas** Did I answer *who, what, where,* and *when*?
- **Organization** Does the order of my ideas make sense?
- **Word Choice** Did I use precise language?
- **Voice** Is my tone appropriate for a news report?
- **Sentence Fluency** Did I combine sentences to vary their length?
- **Conventions** Did I use correct spelling and grammar?

Final Copy

Lights in the Sky

by Juan Ramos

Pierson, FL—The phones at the Pierson Police Department began ringing on August 12th when bright lights streaked across the night sky.

"I couldn't believe what I was seeing," said Silvio Garcia, a farmer. "My little boy asked if it was an alien invasion."

The Pierson Police received nearly a dozen calls from alarmed residents reporting Unidentified Flying Objects (UFOs).

Dr. Jorge Santos, an astronomer, says the lights in the sky were not alien spaceships. "It's the Perseid meteor shower," he explained. "It happens every August."

Dr. Santos says there is no reason to be scared. The streaks of light are caused by meteoroids, which are space rocks that burn up in the atmosphere and rarely reach Earth. "Lay back on a blanket, eat some snacks, and enjoy the show," Santos recommends.

Reading as a Writer

Which words did Juan replace to make his writing clearer? How can you make your news report more effective? What definitions should you add?

In my final paper, I replaced weak and vague words with stronger, more precise words to show my ideas. I included a definition for *meteoroid.* I also combined two sentences to vary my sentence length.

Lesson 7

COMING DISTRACTIONS
Questioning Movies
How Do They Do That?

Vocabulary in Context

TARGET VOCABULARY

entertaining
promote
focus
advertise
jolts
critics
target
thrilling
angles
generated

Vocabulary Reader

Context Cards

ELACC4L6 acquire/use vocabulary, including academic and domain-specific

1 entertaining

Going to a movie has been a fun and entertaining pastime for generations.

2 promote

Moviemakers show clips of exciting scenes to promote their movies.

3 focus

Moviemakers use cameras to focus, or concentrate, on each film shot.

4 advertise

Posters advertise movies. People know a film is coming when they see the poster.

- Study each Context Card.
- Use a dictionary to help you pronounce these words.

5 jolts

Movies often include chase scenes so that viewers feel jolts, or bursts, of excitement.

6 critics

Critics give reviews of movies. Many people pay attention to these reviewers' opinions.

7 target

Some movies are made for kids. Kids are the target audience.

8 thrilling

Seeing a movie on a giant screen can be thrilling. Many people find it exciting.

9 angles

A movie scene is usually filmed from several angles, or positions.

10 generated

Sometimes a movie's success is generated, or created, mainly by word of mouth.

Read and Comprehend

TARGET SKILL

Fact and Opinion As you read "Coming Distractions: Questioning Movies," notice the facts and opinions that the author provides. A **fact** is a statement that can be proved true by checking a reference book or another resource. An **opinion** is a statement that expresses a thought or a belief. Also notice how the author uses reasons and evidence to support the facts and opinions he states. Use a graphic organizer like the one below to help you separate facts from opinions.

Fact	Opinion

TARGET STRATEGY

Summarize When you **summarize** a text, you briefly restate the most important ideas in your own words. Summarizing can help you understand and remember what you read. As you read "Coming Distractions," stop after each section to summarize the important parts of the text and to confirm your understanding.

COMMON CORE

ELACC4RI2 determine the main idea and explain how it is supported by details/summarize; **ELACC4RI8** explain how an author uses reasons and evidence to support points

PREVIEW THE TOPIC

Media

Communication is the exchange of information. A great deal of the information we receive comes from media. There are different types of media, and each type has a purpose. Newspapers and magazines inform readers about recent events and other news. Radios fill the air with music. TV shows and movies entertain us.

"Coming Distractions" explores how movie directors, in their particular form of media, use special tricks to influence the way audiences feel.

Lesson 7

ANCHOR TEXT

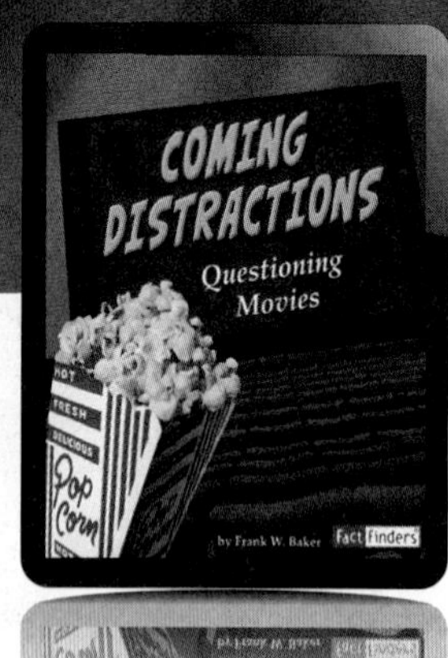

COMING DISTRACTIONS
Questioning Movies
HOT
FRESH
DELICIOUS
Pop Corn
by Frank W. Baker
Fact Finders

TARGET SKILL

Fact and Opinion Look for statements that are facts and statements that are opinions. Notice how the author uses reasons and evidence to support his points.

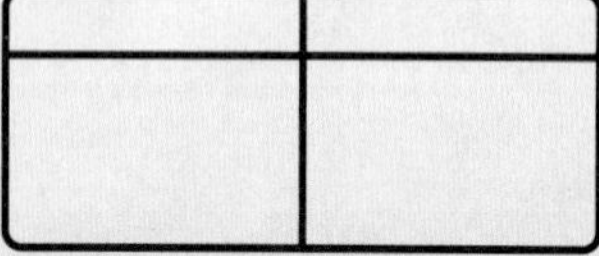

GENRE

An **informational text** gives facts and examples about a topic. As you read, look for:

- text structure, or the ways the ideas and information are organized
- facts and details about a subject
- photographs and captions

ELACC4RI8 explain how an author uses reasons and evidence to support points

 Go Digital

MEET THE AUTHOR

Frank W. Baker

Frank W. Baker was once a television news reporter. Today he travels around the United States, encouraging students to question messages in the media. Movies are only one of his concerns. He also cautions young people about toy commercials that may be dishonest, about the health risks of not exercising enough, and about the problems caused by eating too much junk food.

Coming Distractions

Questioning Movies

by
Frank W. Baker

ESSENTIAL QUESTION

How are movies a form of communication?

Movies are fun. There's no doubt about that. But sometimes movies don't give us the whole story. And that can be a problem. But never fear! There is an easy way to make sure we aren't influenced without knowing it. Think about what you see and ask questions.

What Is Left Out of the Message?

Every time cinematographers look through their camera they frame their shot. They focus on one thing. But just as important as what's in their frame is what isn't. Sometimes moviemakers leave things out of the frame or out of the script on purpose. But why would they do that? Well, there are a few reasons.

The "Numbing" Effect

One reason filmmakers leave things out is simply a length issue. If our legs fall asleep because the movie is too long, we're not going to like it. Moviemakers have to decide what to keep and what to cut.

LINGO
frame: to focus the camera on an object or scene

Painting a "Bad" Picture

Sometimes movies leave things out that would make them lose momentum. Fast-paced, action-packed car chase movies are exciting to watch. Violent fight scenes are thrilling to see. But movies don't always show the effects of these actions.

Watching people clean up the damage or go to the hospital just isn't as fun. So even though the movie is entertaining, we have to remember that it's not really how things would go down in real life.

ANALYZE THE TEXT

Fact and Opinion What reasons does the author give to support the opinion he shares in the first sentence?

Cameron Diaz in *Charlie's Angels* makes fighting in heels look easy.

Painting a "Pretty" Picture

Think about a movie dealing with ordinary people with real problems. Maybe a dad loses his job. Even without a job, the family still has a brand new car, a beautiful home, and fashionable clothes. How can they afford it? Moviemaking magic, that's how. A leading man doesn't look as good driving a rusty old car. A leading lady, even when she's fighting the bad guys, wears high heels. These tricks make for entertaining viewing, but they don't paint an accurate picture of real life.

Try It Out!

Imagine that you're writing a screenplay about your life. It's getting long, so you have to decide what to leave out. Make a list of things you would not put in a movie about you. Here are some things to consider:

- **Do you show your bad habits? Why or why not? If you don't, does that change the story of the real you?**
- **Do you include situations where you got in trouble? Why or why not?**

How Does the Message Get My Attention?

So now we know studios think a lot about who the movie is for, what they'd put in the movie, and what to leave out. But how do they get the word out? Movie studios advertise their movies like crazy. They market their films in places where their target audience will see it. Trailers for *Revenge of the Mighty Hamburger* won't be running during the evening news. Kids aren't watching TV then. But they'll be all over the TV right around the time school lets out!

Movie studios use more than trailers to grab our attention. They use every marketing trick in the book.

Movie posters tell about important features of a movie. They list the title, the stars, and what happens.

Stars of the movie give lots of interviews on TV, on the radio, in magazines, and even on Web sites. Moviemakers hope the more you hear about the movie, the more interested you'll be.

Blogs, or Web logs, are becoming a popular way to promote movies. Bloggers write about movies to create more buzz.

Movie critics get to see movies before the public. Their reviews carry a lot of weight. Many people will go to see a movie that gets "two thumbs up."

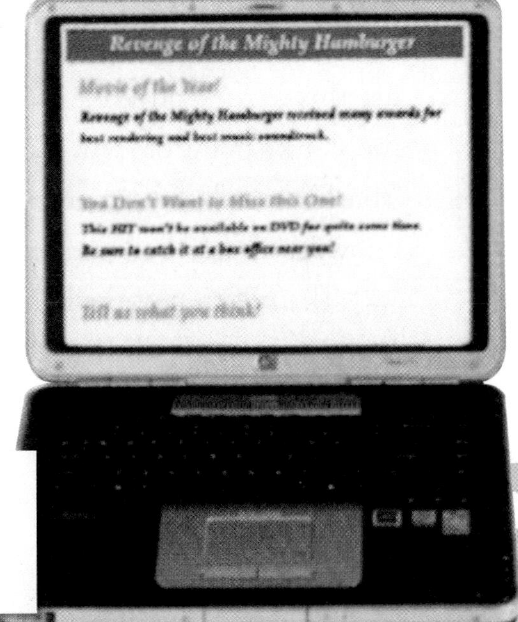

Blogs are sometimes used to market movies.

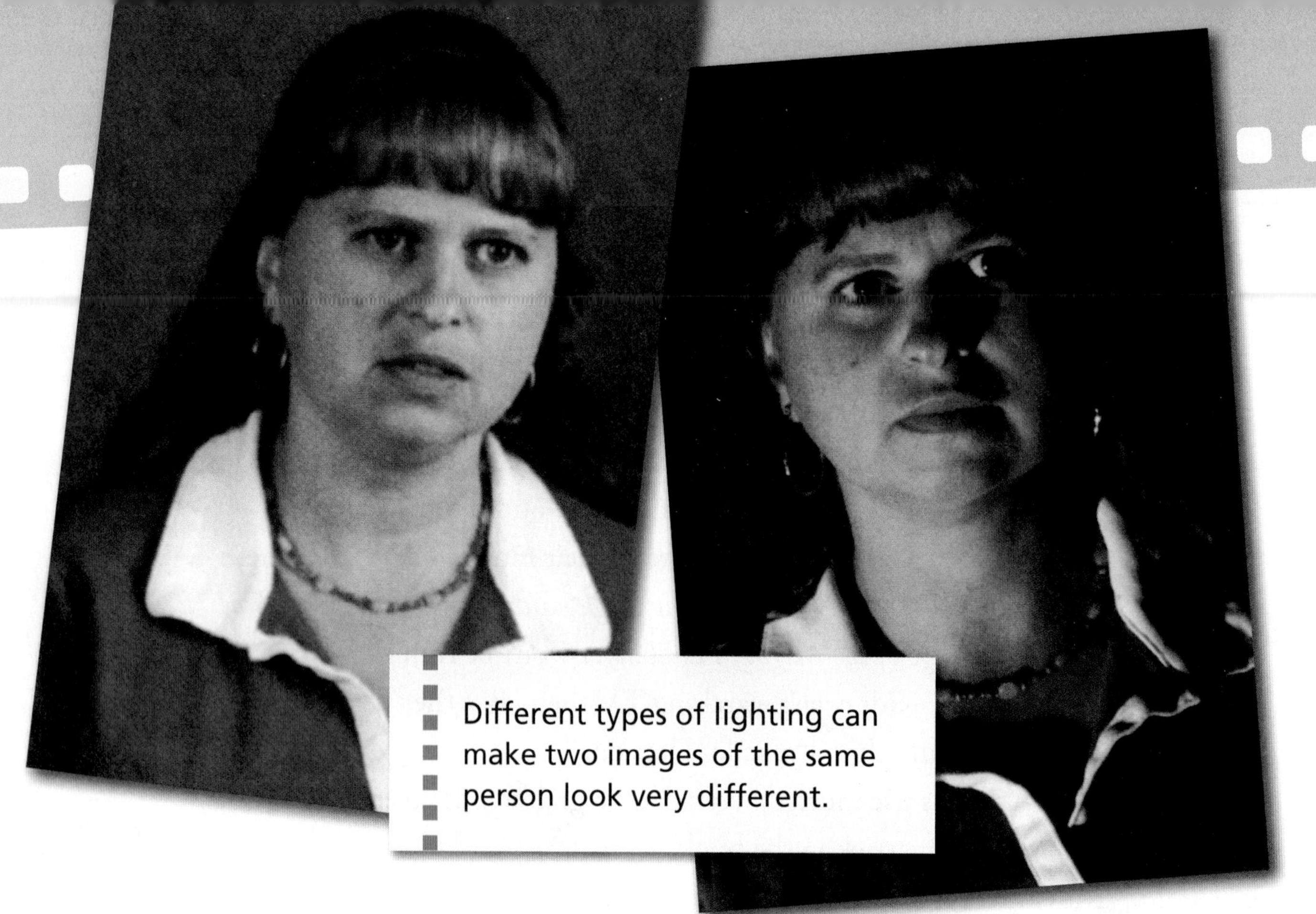

Different types of lighting can make two images of the same person look very different.

Mixing Up a Movie

It takes a lot of ingredients to mix up a film. These ingredients all have to work together to keep us in our seats. Why does that matter? Well, if we aren't interested, we won't buy the products featured in the film or tell our friends to buy tickets.

In a movie, we see only what the camera sees. And moviemakers use this to their advantage. In a scene in *Jaws*, the director wanted the shark's point of view. So the camera became the shark. When the "shark" moved, the camera was panned. We don't see the shark, but we know it's after the swimmer.

The position of the lights can tell us a lot about what's happening. A character in a well-lit area is safe and happy. When a person's face is half in shadow, half in light we know she is doing something evil.

Moviemakers use CGI (Computer Generated Imagery) to keep the action going. Dangerous or imaginary scenes can be digitally created to look like anything they want. The character Gollum from the *Lord of the Rings* trilogy was made using CGI.

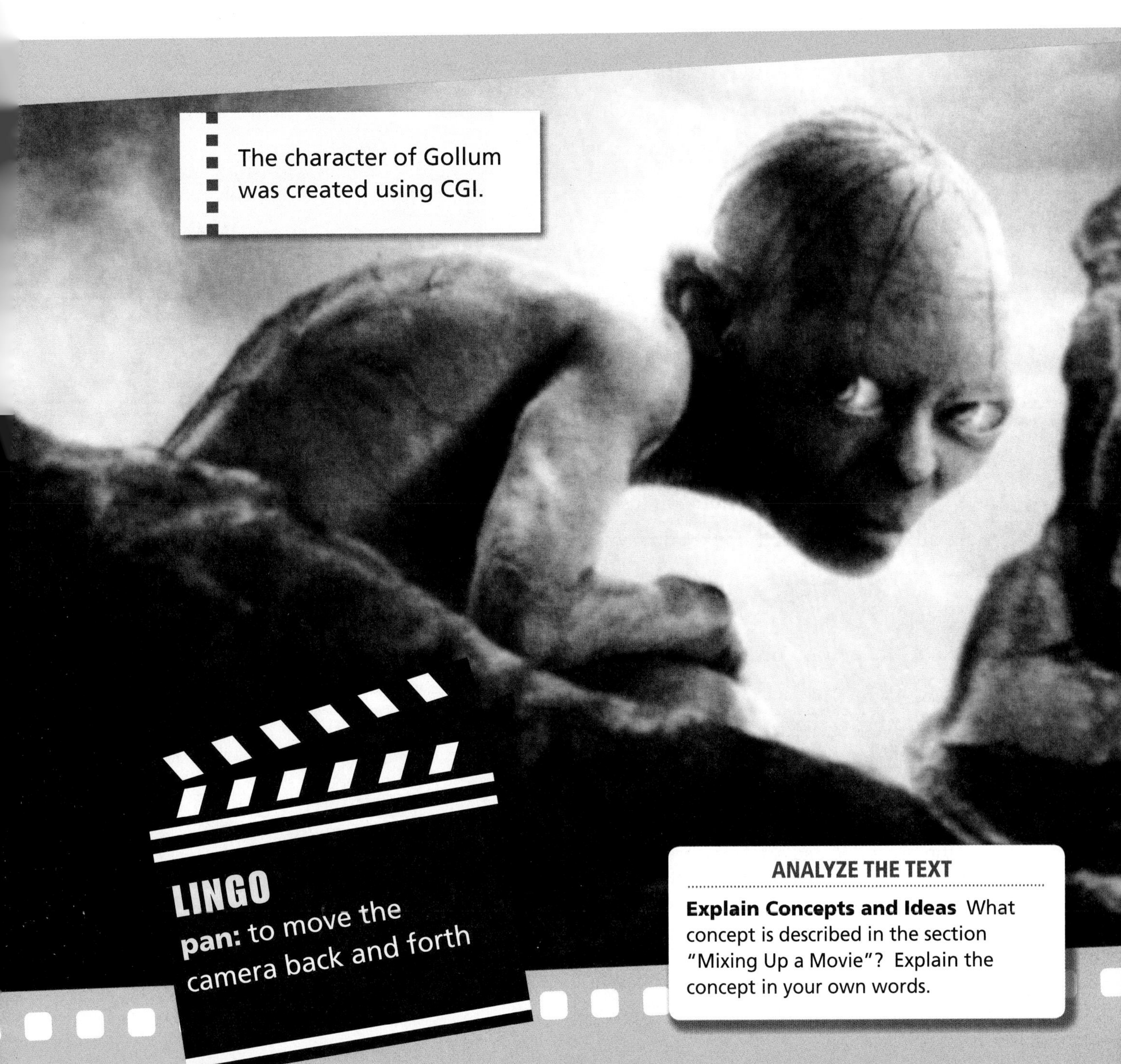

The character of Gollum was created using CGI.

LINGO

pan: to move the camera back and forth

ANALYZE THE TEXT

Explain Concepts and Ideas What concept is described in the section "Mixing Up a Movie"? Explain the concept in your own words.

Could you imagine *Star Wars* without the music? Music is a great trick to keep our attention. Generally, we don't even think about the music. But without it, movies just wouldn't be as exciting. Did you know editors dub in the sound track after the movie is filmed? The actors may not even hear the finished sound track until they see the final cut of the movie.

LINGO

dub: adding a sound track to a movie after filming is complete

Jolts Per Minute

Lighting, music, camera angles, and special effects are all ingredients that make movies exciting and fun. But moviemakers have other tricks they use to keep us watching. One of these tricks is called jolts per minute (JPM). JPMs are fast, exciting quick cuts or action sequences that get you excited.

ANALYZE THE TEXT

Domain-Specific Vocabulary What do the terms *dub* and *action sequence* mean? What do they have to do with the topic of making movies?

LINGO

quick cut: fast scene changes that are meant to jolt and excite you

Try It Out!

Music can play a big role in a movie's JPMs. Suppose *Revenge of the Mighty Hamburger* needs a sound track. Get out your CD collection. Pick out some songs that would fit these scenes.

- The Mighty Hamburger is rolling down the hill on his skateboard going 60 miles per hour. The cops are chasing him and getting closer and closer.
- The Mighty Hamburger and a beautiful cheeseburger take a stroll along the beach at sunset.

Did you use different kinds of music for each scene? Why or why not? Could you use something other than music to beef up a movie's JPMs?

The End

Movies are great entertainment. And sometimes they even teach us a thing or two. That's why we watch them. What's cool, though, is that we don't have to believe everything a movie shows. It's totally our choice. So let's go pop some popcorn, watch a movie, and enjoy asking questions.

COMPREHENSION

Dig Deeper

How to Analyze the Text

Use these pages to learn about Fact and Opinion, Explaining Concepts and Ideas, and Domain-Specific Vocabulary. Then read "Coming Distractions: Questioning Movies" again to apply what you learned.

Fact and Opinion

Informational texts, such as "Coming Distractions," often contain a mix of **facts** and **opinions.** A fact is a statement that can be proved true by checking a reference book or an online resource. An opinion is a statement that expresses a feeling or belief. An opinion cannot be proved.

Authors of informational text must give reasons and evidence to support their opinions. Often, writers support their points by giving facts. Turn to page 204. What opinions does the author state on this page? How do you know they are opinions? What facts does the author present to support his opinions?

Fact	Opinion

ELACC4RI1 refer to details and examples when explaining what the text says explicitly and when drawing inferences; **ELACC4RI3** explain events/procedures/ideas/concepts in a text; **ELACC4RI4** determine the meaning of general academic and domain-specific words and phrases; **ELACC4RI8** explain how an author uses reasons and evidence to support points; **ELACC4L6** acquire/use vocabulary, including academic and domain-specific

Explain Concepts and Ideas

Imagine that you want to explain an idea or a concept you learned about in "Coming Distractions." How would you begin? First, choose the concept you would like to explain, such as how moviemakers use camera angles and light. Reread the part of the text that discusses this concept. Make sure you fully understand what the author has said. Then explain the concept in your own words.

Domain-Specific Vocabulary

Authors often use specific words to express their ideas clearly. Words that are used mainly in one type of business or field of study are called **jargon** or **domain-specific vocabulary.** The word *pan* is an example of movie jargon. *Pan* is used in the movie business to describe the way a camera follows a moving object or gives a wider view of a scene.

Your Turn

RETURN TO THE ESSENTIAL QUESTION

Turn and Talk Review the selection with a partner to prepare to discuss this question: *How are movies a form of communication?* As you talk with your partner, refer to text evidence. Also take turns explaining the key ideas in your discussion.

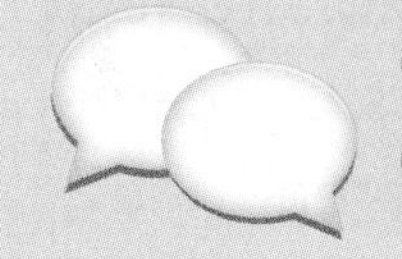

Classroom Conversation

Continue your discussion of "Coming Distractions" by explaining your answers to these questions:

1. What factors might a director consider when deciding what to leave out of a scene in a movie?
2. What questions might you ask the next time you see a movie?
3. Why do you think it is important to ask questions when you watch movies?

LIGHTS, CAMERA, ACTION!

Summarize Write a summary of a fiction selection you have already read or of your favorite story. Be sure to include important details about the characters, setting, and events. Then explain which techniques you would use—for example, music, lighting, or camera angles—if you were making a movie of the story.

WRITE ABOUT READING

Response "Coming Distractions" tells how filmmakers use techniques to influence how we experience movies. Write a paragraph about one of your favorite movies. What techniques described in "Coming Distractions" does the film use? How do these techniques help make the movie memorable? Include text evidence from the selection. Conclude by restating your opinion.

Writing Tip

Use precise, domain-specific words. Make sure that verbs are in the correct tense and agree with the subjects in the sentences.

COMMON CORE **ELACC4RL2** determine theme from details/summarize; **ELACC4RI1** refer to details and examples when explaining what the text says explicitly and when drawing inferences; **ELACC4W1b** provide reasons supported by facts and details; **ELACC4W1d** provide a concluding statement or section; **ELACC4W9b** apply grade 4 Reading standards to informational texts; **ELACC4SL1a** come to discussions prepared/explicitly draw on preparation and other information about the topic

Lesson 7

INFORMATIONAL TEXT

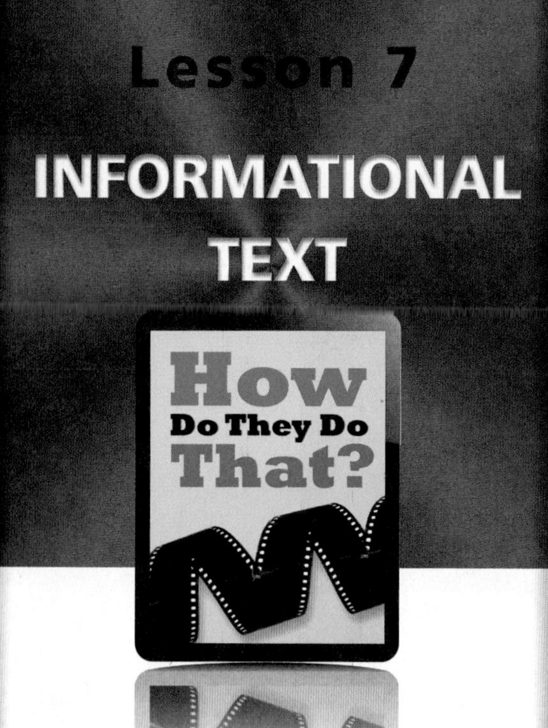

GENRE

Informational text, such as this magazine article, gives facts and examples about a topic.

TEXT FOCUS

Photographs and Captions Informational text generally includes photographs. A caption explains what an individual photograph shows and often includes additional information about the topic.

ELACC4RI7 interpret information presented visually, orally, or quantitatively

How Do They Do That?

by Allan Giles

Today's movies contain all sorts of make-believe characters and dangerous or seemingly impossible sequences. How do moviemakers create such characters and actions? How do they make them look believable? They use special effects.

There are many different kinds of special effects used in movies. Some examples include computer animation, blue-screen or green-screen filming, and model making. Others are makeup effects, stunt effects, and sound effects. The whole movie industry changes as new special-effects techniques are developed. New techniques lead to more exciting possibilities!

The movie *Jurassic Park* won awards for special effects. Director Steven Spielberg and his team of special-effects artists needed to make a variety of dinosaurs seem to come to life. They worked for three years to update old special-effects technologies and to develop new ones for the film.

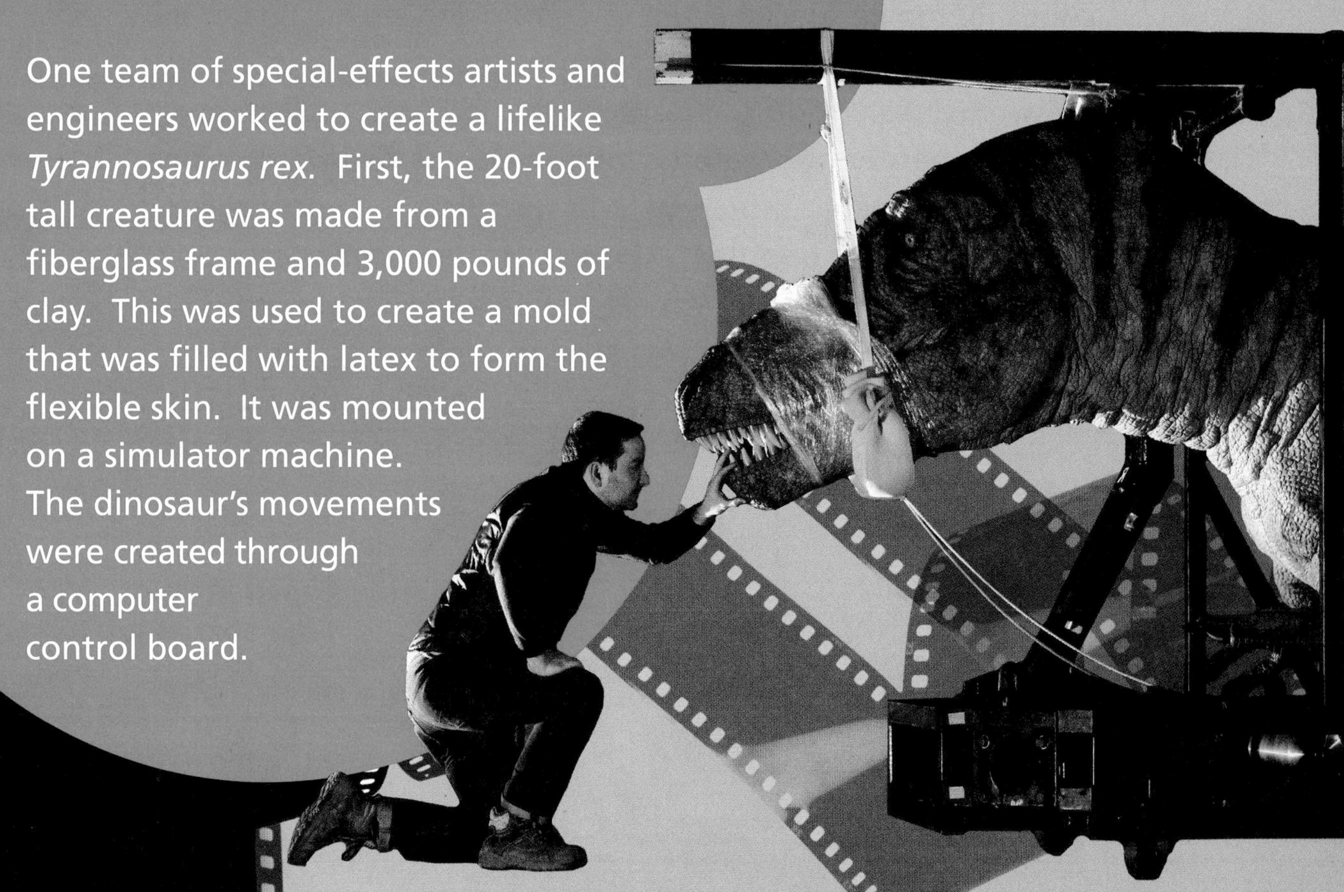

One team of special-effects artists and engineers worked to create a lifelike *Tyrannosaurus rex.* First, the 20-foot tall creature was made from a fiberglass frame and 3,000 pounds of clay. This was used to create a mold that was filled with latex to form the flexible skin. It was mounted on a simulator machine. The dinosaur's movements were created through a computer control board.

Imagine you are a movie director. The movie calls for an actress to hang from the side of a skyscraper. You don't want to risk the actress's life by asking her to dangle hundreds of feet in the air. So how do you film this in a way that looks realistic? You use a blue screen or green screen.

Filmmakers first film the background scene. In this case, they film the side of a skyscraper. Then, in the movie studio, they film the actress hanging from a rope in front of a blue or green screen. So now there are two pieces of film. One has the background scene of the skyscraper. One has the actress.

Then the special-effects department uses special filters to block out the green background to create a silhouette of the actress. This silhouette is then placed on the skyscraper background. Finally, they add the film of the actress in her silhouette.

◀ **If you've ever seen a weather map on the news, you've seen the result of the green-screen process.**

Another movie special effect is Computer-Generated Imagery (or CGI). This technology has seen great advancements in the past twenty years. Some films, such as the *Shrek* movies, are entirely computer generated. Others, such as *Avatar*, combine computer-generated effects with live actors.

One of the most popular CGI effects is the motion-capture technique used in *Avatar*. An actor wears special equipment with sensors placed at various points around the body. The actor's movements are captured, or copied, by special software. These movements are transformed into realistic computer simulations.

The red lights on this special suit help the computer record what the actor does. The movements of the robot on the screen are exactly the same as the actor's movements.

All these special-effects technologies allow filmmakers to create movies that never could have been created before. Filmmakers can now produce an unlimited variety of characters, landscapes, and even virtual worlds through the use of special effects. As special-effects techniques continue to advance, so will the ability of movies to make the impossible seem possible.

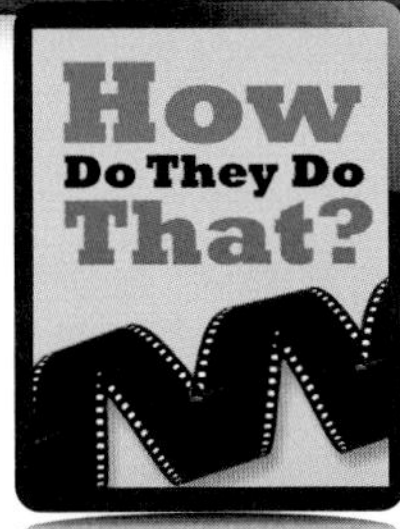

Compare Texts

TEXT TO TEXT

Compare a Radio Play and a Movie With a partner, discuss the special effects described in "Coming Distractions" and "How Do They Do That?" Then think back to the radio play "Invasion from Mars." How would the play be different if it were a movie with special effects? Write a paragraph that describes what special effects could be used in a movie of "Invasion from Mars."

TEXT TO SELF

Analyze Advertising Think of an advertisement you have seen recently for sodas or snack foods. What effect are these ads supposed to have on viewers? How do you know? Discuss with a partner whether you think this effect is positive or negative and why you think so.

TEXT TO WORLD

Compare Special Effects Compare and contrast the information presented in "Coming Distractions" with that of "How Do They Do That?" What are some other special effects that you have seen in movies? Discuss with your partner how these special effects might have affected the audience. Use text evidence to support your thoughts.

ELACC4RL7 make connections between the text and a visual or oral presentation of it; **ELACC4RI1** refer to details and examples when explaining what the text says explicitly and when drawing inferences; **ELACC4RI9** integrate information from two texts on the same topic; **ELACC4SL1a** come to discussions prepared/explicitly draw on preparation and other information about the topic

Grammar

What Are Verb Tenses? A verb in the **present tense** tells about action that is happening now or that happens over and over. A verb in the **past tense** tells about action that happened in the past. A verb in the **future tense** tells about what will happen in the future.

To form the past tense of a **regular verb,** add *-ed* to its present form. This is called the **past participle.** Verbs that do not add *-ed* to show past action are called **irregular verbs.** Another way to form the past tense is by using a helping verb, such as *have* or *has*, with the past participle. Verbs in the future tense use the helping verb *will*.

Sentence	Tense of Verb
Filmmakers include exciting scenes.	present tense
The director filmed a car chase.	past tense, regular verb
Millions of people have seen the movie.	past tense, irregular verb
You will see this chase in an ad.	future tense

Try This! **Copy these sentences onto another sheet of paper. Circle the verb in each sentence. Label each as *present tense, past tense,* or *future tense*.**

1. Marla will write about the film on her blog.
2. Jerome began the movie yesterday.
3. She started her blog last month.
4. He likes action movies.

When you write, be careful to use verb tenses correctly to show when events happened. Change tense only to show a change in time. Make sure your verbs agree with the subject and that you have formed the past tense correctly.

Incorrect Verb Agreement	Correct Verb Agreement

Hayley and I went to the movies. We watch *The Robot That Ate Chicago.* We knowed it would be scary, but we see it again tomorrow!	Hayley and I went to the movies. We watched *The Robot That Ate Chicago.* We knew it would be scary, but we will see it again tomorrow!

Connect Grammar to Writing

As you revise your informational paragraph, look carefully at verb tenses. Make sure that subjects and verbs agree and that you have spelled irregular past-tense verbs correctly.

ELACC4W2a introduce a topic and group related information/include formatting, illustrations, and multimedia; **ELACC4W2b** develop the topic with facts, definitions, details, quotations, or other information and examples; **ELACC4W2d** use precise language and domain-specific vocabulary; **ELACC4L3a** choose words and phrases to convey ideas precisely

Informative Writing

Word Choice "Coming Distractions" is an informational text about making movies. When you write an informational paragraph, use precise language to explain your topic. Define any words that your readers might not know. Develop your topic by providing facts, concrete details, and examples.

Marcela drafted an informational paragraph about how a movie director can create a scary mood. She added two sentences near the beginning of the paragraph to state her topic clearly. Later, she replaced vague words with precise ones.

Writing Traits Checklist

- **Ideas** Did I use concrete details and examples to explain my ideas?
- **Organization** Did I state my topic at the beginning?
- **Word Choice** Did I use precise language and define topic-specific words?
- **Voice** Did I express ideas in my own way?
- **Sentence Fluency** Did I change verb tense when needed?
- **Conventions** Did I use correct spelling and grammar?

Revised Draft

Think about the last scary movie you saw. You were sitting in the theater and ~~holding~~ gripping the armrests as your heart ~~beat~~ pounded. You probably didn't stop to think about how the movie director ~~creates~~ created that feeling of fear. Movie directors use many tricks to frighten audiences. These include special uses of lighting, ~~visuals~~ camera angles, and sound.

Final Copy

Making It Scary

by Marcela Cabral

Think about the last scary movie you saw. You were sitting in the theater and gripping the armrests as your heart pounded. You probably didn't stop to think about how the movie director created that feeling of fear. Movie directors use many tricks to frighten audiences. These include special uses of lighting, camera angles, and sound. For example, imagine a scene of a man alone in a room at night. The light flickers and goes out. The sound of footsteps gets louder and louder, and the door slowly creaks open. The camera zooms in on, or gets a close-up of, the man's terrified face. Are you scared yet? You bet you are! The director used lighting, sounds, and camera angles to create a spooky, scary mood. Your emotions were being influenced, and you didn't even know it! The next time you see a scary movie, don't just sit there. Try to figure out how the director made it scary.

Reading as a Writer

Find the sentence in Marcela's paragraph that states the topic. Does it help you understand what her writing is about? Does she use precise words?

In my final paper, I defined words specific to movie making that my readers might not know. I also made sure not to change verb tenses without a reason.

Lesson 8

Vocabulary in Context

TARGET VOCABULARY

glorious
studio
model
concerned
smeared
ruined
yanked
streak
schedule
feast

Vocabulary Reader

Context Cards

ELACC4L6 acquire/use vocabulary, including academic and domain-specific

1 glorious

Fine arts, such as collage and painting, are stunning, glorious forms of expression.

2 studio

A studio is an artist's workshop. Painters paint and potters make pots there.

3 model

As they design a building, architects may create a small, model version.

4 concerned

This photographer is concerned, or worried, that the penguin will move.

- Study each Context Card.
- Use context clues to determine the meanings of these words.

5 smeared

Paint may be lightly dabbed or thickly smeared onto a surface.

6 ruined

This handmade pot was perfect at first, but then it collapsed and became ruined.

7 yanked

This girl must have accidentally yanked, or pulled, the base from the vase.

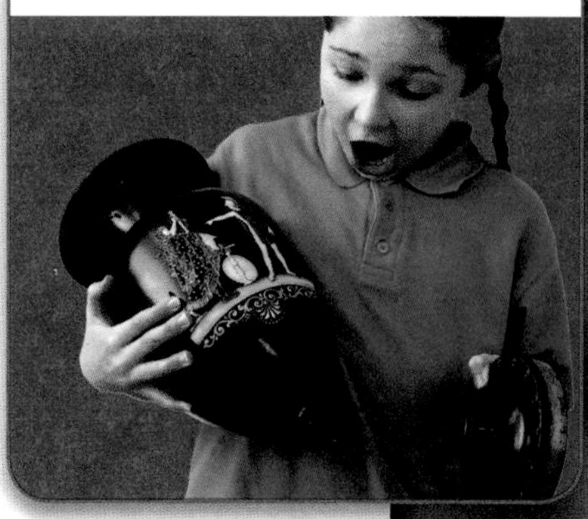

8 streak

In this lively artwork, some colors seem to streak across the painting.

9 schedule

Some artists stick to a regular schedule, or timetable, as they work.

10 feast

A photographer took a picture of this delicious feast full of food.

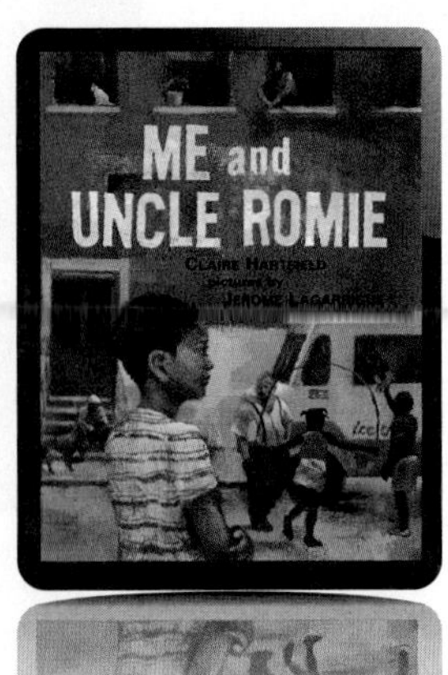

Read and Comprehend

TARGET SKILL

Understanding Characters As you read "Me and Uncle Romie," look for text evidence that helps you understand what the main **characters** are like. Pay attention to what they think, how they act, and what they say. Also, think about how you might react in a similar situation. To describe a character, use a graphic organizer to list text evidence of the character's **thoughts, actions**, and **words.**

Thoughts	Actions	Words

TARGET STRATEGY

Visualize To **visualize,** use details from the text to form a picture in your mind. As you read "Me and Uncle Romie," use details in the text to help you picture the characters, the places they go, and the things they do. Visualizing characters, settings, and events can help you better understand the story.

ELACC4RL1 refer to details and examples when explaining what the text says explicitly and when drawing inferences; **ELACC4RL3** describe a character, setting, or event, drawing on details

PREVIEW THE TOPIC

Visual Arts

Visual arts, such as paintings, collage, and sculpture, appeal mostly to our sense of sight. A collage combines many different materials in a single image. A collage may include paint, bits of cloth, photographs, ticket stubs, and anything else the artist wishes to use.

In "Me and Uncle Romie," the character of Uncle Romie is based on a well-known visual artist named Romare Bearden. His work portrays African American culture in the United States, especially in the American South and in Harlem, a neighborhood in New York City.

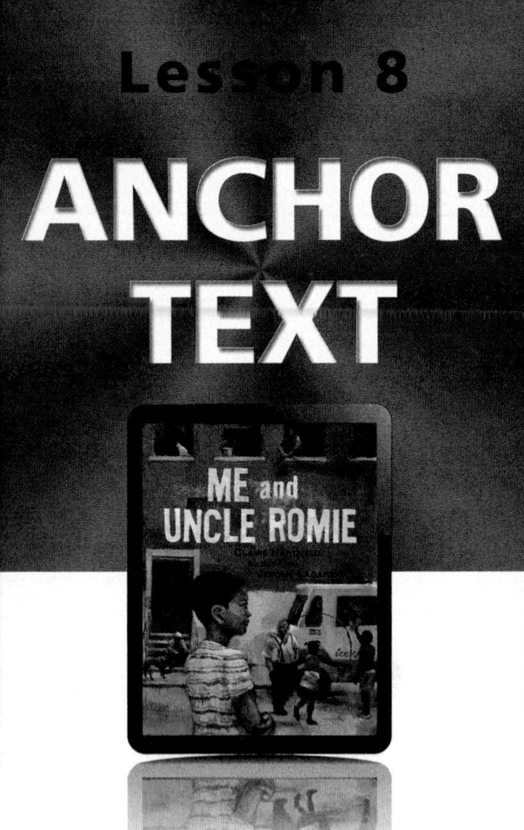

TARGET SKILL

Understanding Characters
Look for details to understand the characters.

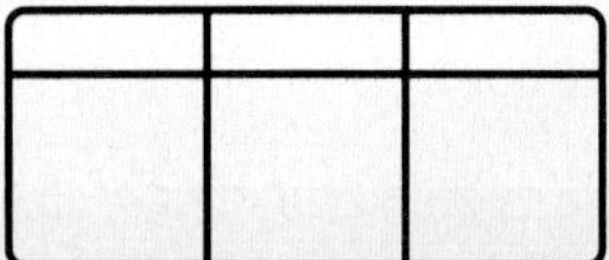

GENRE

Realistic fiction has characters and events that are like people and events in real life. As you read, look for:

- realistic characters and events
- characters who have feelings and actions just like real people
- details that help the reader picture the setting

ELACC4RL2 determine theme from details/ summarize; **ELACC4RL3** describe a character, setting, or event, drawing on details; **ELACC4RL6** compare and contrast the point of view from which stories are narrated; **ELACC4RL10** read and comprehend literature

MEET THE AUTHOR

Claire Hartfield

Claire Hartfield was born in Chicago. Her personal mission is to foster a better world for children, and she works diligently to make schools fairer and more equal for everyone. Today she pursues this goal as a lawyer. But for many years, as a dance teacher, she guided students to express themselves through movement. She became interested in the painter and collagist Romare Bearden because of his ability to tell stories with his art. In this story, the character of Uncle Romie is based on Bearden.

MEET THE ILLUSTRATOR

Jerome Lagarrigue

Born in Paris, France, Jerome Lagarrigue was inspired at a remarkably young age to express his ideas and emotions through creative art. He has won multiple awards and critical praise for his illustrations in children's books like *Freedom Summer*. In addition to his well-known work as an illustrator, Lagarrigue spends much of his time as a painter. He has even exhibited oil paintings in Italy. Look closely at the illustrations in "Me and Uncle Romie" to find the various printed materials Lagarrigue used to create unique collages that mimic the style of artist Romare Bearden.

ME and UNCLE ROMIE

by CLAIRE HARTFIELD
illustrated by JEROME LAGARRIGUE

ESSENTIAL QUESTION

How do an artist's experiences affect his or her art?

James waits nervously on a passenger train bound for New York City to visit his Aunt Nanette and Uncle Romie. He's never met them before, and he's a little concerned. James has left behind his home in North Carolina, and though he misses his friend B. J., his dad, and his mom (who will soon have twin babies), James hopes he will have fun on this summer vacation, especially since his birthday is coming up.

Then I saw it . . . New York City. Buildings stretching up to the sky. So close together. Not like North Carolina at all.

"Penn Station! Watch your step," the conductor said, helping me down to the platform. I did like Daddy said and found a spot for myself close to the train. Swarms of people rushed by. Soon I heard a silvery voice call my name. This had to be Aunt Nanette. I turned and saw her big smile reaching out to welcome me.

She took my hand and guided me through the rushing crowds onto an underground train called the subway. "This will take us right home," she explained.

ANALYZE THE TEXT

Point of View From what point of view is this story told? How is this similar to the point of view in "Because of Winn-Dixie"? How is it different?

Home was like nothing I'd ever seen before. No regular houses anywhere. Just big buildings and stores of all kinds—in the windows I saw paints, fabrics, radios, and TVs.

We turned into the corner building and climbed the stairs to the apartment—five whole flights up. *Whew!* I tried to catch my breath while Aunt Nanette flicked on the lights.

"Uncle Romie's out talking to some people about his big art show that's coming up. He'll be home soon," Aunt Nanette said. She set some milk and a plate of cookies for me on the table. "Your uncle's working very hard, so we won't see much of him for a while. His workroom—we call it his studio—is in the front of our apartment. That's where he keeps all the things he needs to make his art."

"Doesn't he just paint?" I asked.

"Uncle Romie is a collage artist," Aunt Nanette explained. "He uses paints, yes. But also photographs, newspapers, cloth. He cuts and pastes them onto a board to make his paintings."

"That sounds kinda easy," I said.

Aunt Nanette laughed.

"Well, there's a little more to it than that, James. When you see the paintings, you'll understand. Come, let's get you to bed."

Lying in the dark, I heard heavy footsteps in the hall. A giant stared at me from the doorway. "Hello there, James." Uncle Romie's voice was deep and loud, like thunder. "Thanks for the pepper jelly," he boomed. "You have a good sleep, now." Then he disappeared down the hall.

The next morning the door to Uncle Romie's studio was closed. But Aunt Nanette had plans for both of us. "Today we're going to a neighborhood called Harlem," she said. "It's where Uncle Romie lived as a boy."

Harlem was full of people walking, working, shopping, eating. Some were watching the goings-on from fire escapes. Others were sitting out on stoops greeting folks who passed by—just like the people back home calling out hellos from their front porches. Most everybody seemed to know Aunt Nanette. A lot of them asked after Uncle Romie too.

We bought peaches at the market, then stopped to visit awhile. I watched some kids playing stickball. "Go on, get in that game," Aunt Nanette said, gently pushing me over to join them. When I was all hot and sweaty, we cooled off with double chocolate scoops from the ice cream man. Later we shared some barbecue on a rooftop way up high. I felt like I was on top of the world.

As the days went by, Aunt Nanette took me all over the city—we rode a ferry boat to the Statue of Liberty . . . zoomed 102 floors up at the Empire State Building . . . window-shopped the fancy stores on Fifth Avenue . . . gobbled hot dogs in Central Park.

But it was Harlem that I liked best. I played stickball with the kids again . . . and on a really hot day a whole bunch of us ran through the icy cold water that sprayed out hard from the fire hydrant. In the evenings Aunt Nanette and I sat outside listening to the street musicians playing their saxophone songs.

On rainy days I wrote postcards and helped out around the apartment. I told Aunt Nanette about the things I liked to do back home—about baseball games, train-watching, my birthday. She told me about the special Caribbean lemon and mango cake she was going to make.

My uncle Romie stayed hidden away in his studio. But I wasn't worried anymore. Aunt Nanette would make my birthday special.

4 . . . 3 . . . 2 . . . 1 . . . My birthday was almost here!

And then Aunt Nanette got a phone call.

"An old aunt has died, James. I have to go away for her funeral. But don't you worry. Uncle Romie will spend your birthday with you. It'll be just fine."

That night Aunt Nanette kissed me good-bye. I knew it would not be fine at all. Uncle Romie didn't know about cakes or baseball games or anything except his dumb old paintings. My birthday was ruined.

When the sky turned black, I tucked myself into bed. I missed Mama and Daddy so much. I listened to the birds on the rooftop—their songs continued into the night.

The next morning everything was quiet. I crept out of bed and into the hall. For the first time the door to Uncle Romie's studio stood wide open. What a glorious mess! There were paints and scraps all over the floor, and around the edges were huge paintings with all sorts of pieces pasted together.

I saw saxophones, birds, fire escapes, and brown faces. *It's Harlem*, I thought. *The people, the music, the rooftops, and the stoops.* Looking at Uncle Romie's paintings, I could *feel* Harlem—its beat and bounce.

ANALYZE THE TEXT

Understanding Characters How does James's opinion of Uncle Romie change throughout the story? What thoughts and words does James use that show his change of opinion?

Then there was one that was different. Smaller houses, flowers, and trains. "That's home!" I shouted.

"Yep," Uncle Romie said, smiling, from the doorway. "That's the Carolina I remember."

"Mama says you visited your grandparents there most every summer when you were a kid," I said.

"I sure did, James. *Mmm.* Now that's the place for pepper jelly. Smeared thick on biscuits. And when Grandma wasn't looking . . . I'd sneak some on a spoon."

"Daddy and I do that too!" I told him.

We laughed together, then walked to the kitchen for a breakfast feast—eggs, bacon, grits, and biscuits.

"James, you've got me remembering the pepper jelly lady. People used to line up down the block to buy her preserves."

"Could you put someone like that in one of your paintings?" I asked.

"I guess I could." Uncle Romie nodded. "Yes, that's a memory just right for sharing. What a good idea, James. Now let's get this birthday going!"

He brought out two presents from home. I tore into the packages while he got down the pepper jelly and two huge spoons. Mama and Daddy had picked out just what I wanted—a special case for my baseball cards, and a model train for me to build.

"Pretty cool," said Uncle Romie. "I used to watch the trains down in North Carolina, you know."

How funny to picture big Uncle Romie lying on his belly!

"B. J. and me, we have contests to see who can hear the trains first."

"Hey, I did that too. You know, it's a funny thing, James. People live in all sorts of different places and families. But the things we care about are pretty much the same. Like favorite foods, special songs, games, stories . . . and like birthdays." Uncle Romie held up two tickets to a baseball game!

It turns out Uncle Romie knows all about baseball—he was even a star pitcher in college. We got our mitts and set off for the game.

Way up in the bleachers, we shared a bag of peanuts, cracking the shells with our teeth and keeping our mitts ready in case a home run ball came our way. That didn't happen—but we sure had fun.

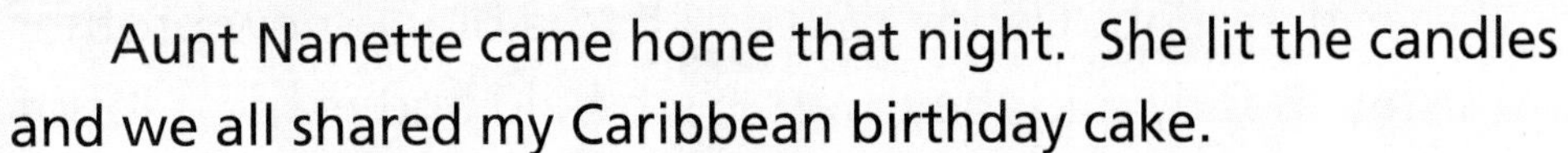

Aunt Nanette came home that night. She lit the candles and we all shared my Caribbean birthday cake.

After that, Uncle Romie had to work a lot again. But at the end of each day he let me sit with him in his studio and talk. Daddy was right. Uncle Romie is a good man.

The day of the big art show finally came. I watched the people laughing and talking, walking slowly around the room from painting to painting. I walked around myself, listening to their conversations.

"Remember our first train ride from Chicago to New York?" one lady asked her husband.

"That guitar-playing man reminds me of my uncle Joe," said another.

All these strangers talking to each other about their families and friends and special times, and all because of how my uncle Romie's paintings reminded them of these things.

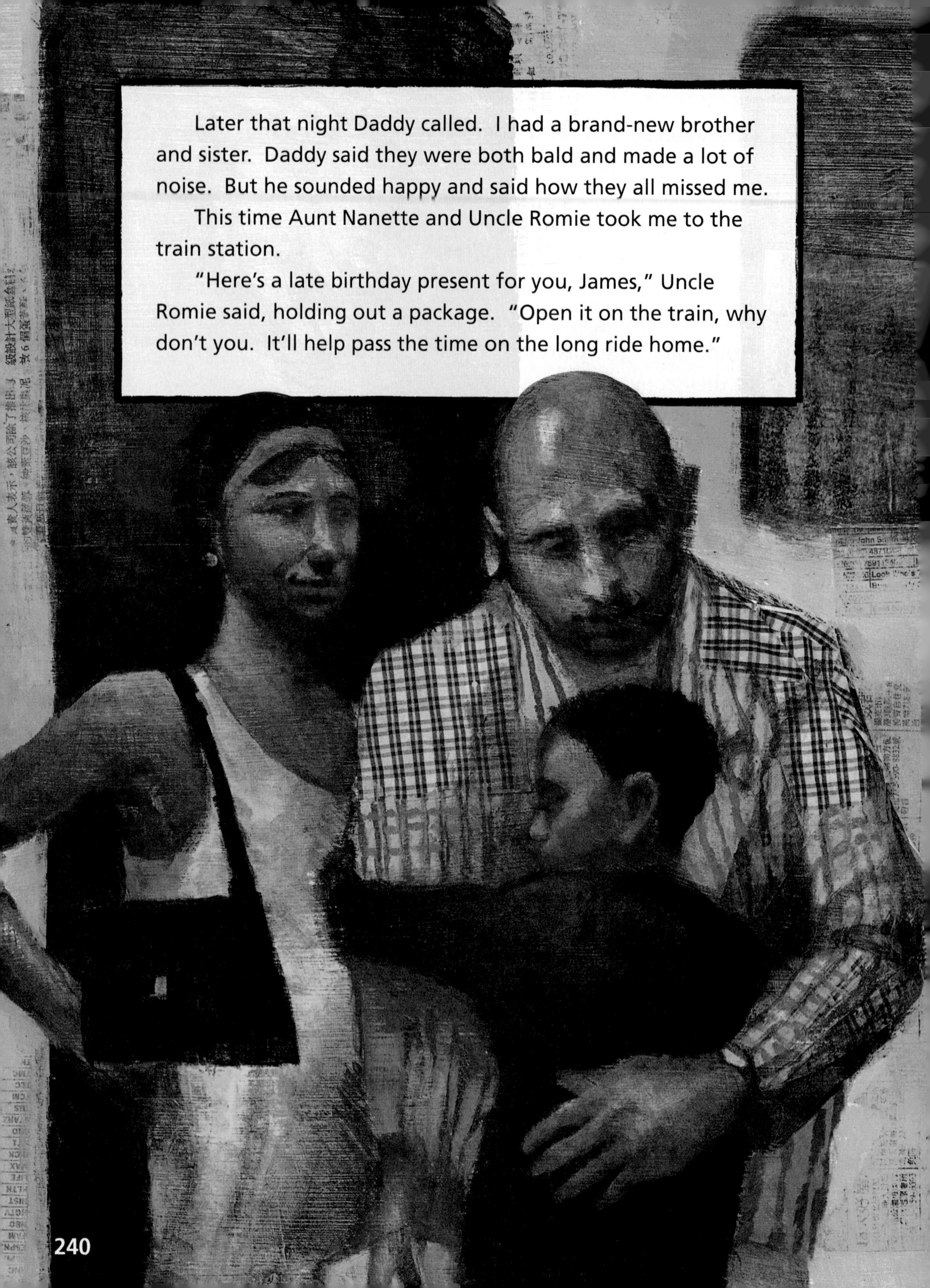

Later that night Daddy called. I had a brand-new brother and sister. Daddy said they were both bald and made a lot of noise. But he sounded happy and said how they all missed me.

This time Aunt Nanette and Uncle Romie took me to the train station.

"Here's a late birthday present for you, James," Uncle Romie said, holding out a package. "Open it on the train, why don't you. It'll help pass the time on the long ride home."

I waved out the window to Uncle Romie and Aunt Nanette until I couldn't see them anymore. Then I ripped off the wrappings!

And there was my summer in New York. Bright sky in one corner, city lights at night in another. Tall buildings. Baseball ticket stubs. The label from the pepper jelly jar. And trains. One going toward the skyscrapers. Another going away.

Back home, I lay in the soft North Carolina grass. It was the first of September, almost Uncle Romie's birthday. I watched the birds streak across the sky.

Rooftop birds, I thought. *Back home from their summer in New York, just like me.* Watching them, I could still feel the city's beat inside my head.

A feather drifted down from the sky. In the garden tiger lilies bent in the wind. *Uncle Romie's favorite flowers.* I yanked off a few blossoms. And then I was off on a treasure hunt, collecting things that reminded me of Uncle Romie.

I painted and pasted them together on a big piece of cardboard. Right in the middle I put the train schedule. And at the top I wrote:

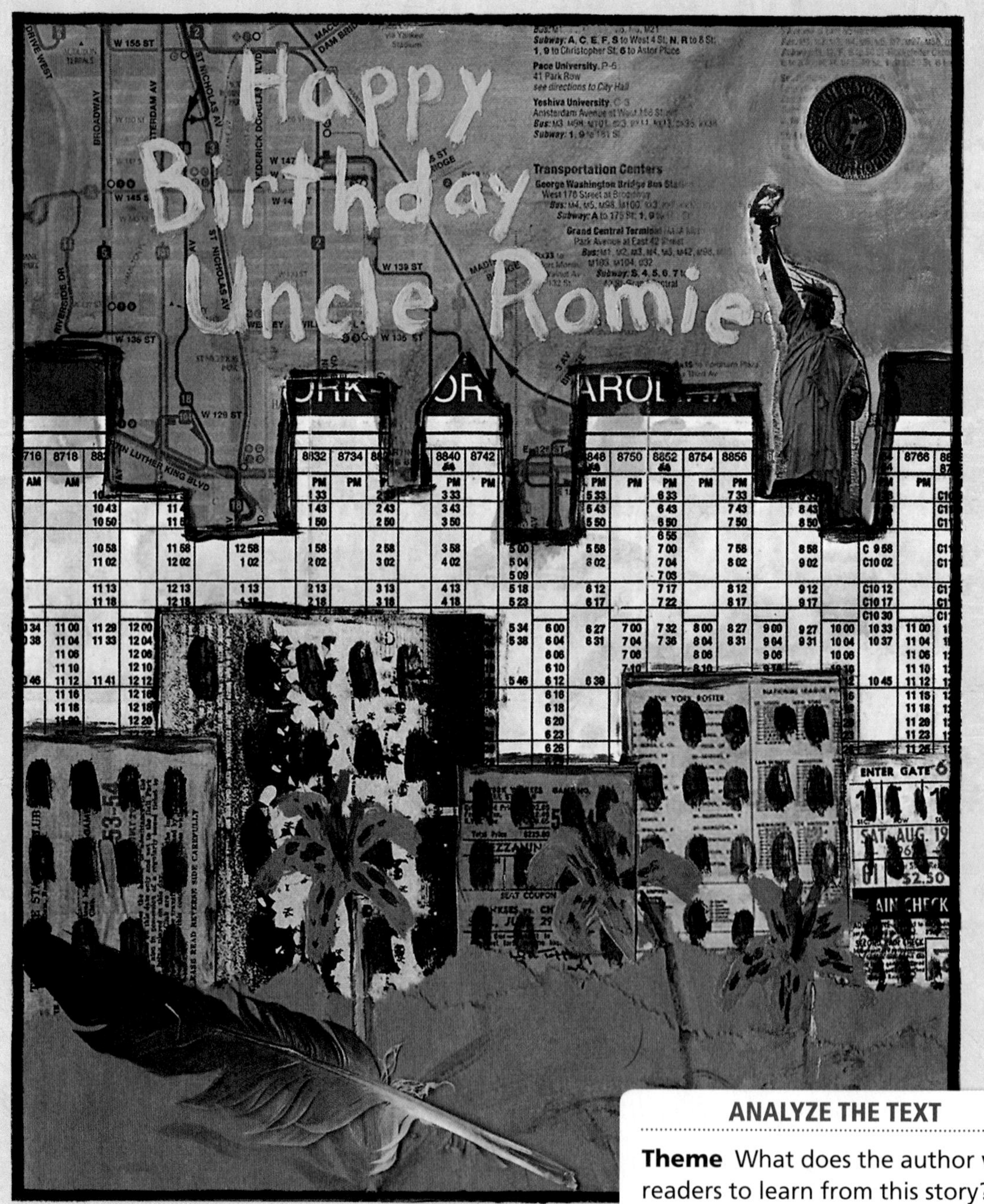

ANALYZE THE TEXT

Theme What does the author want readers to learn from this story? How does what happens to James help you understand this message?

Author's Note

This story, which is fictional, was inspired by the storytelling quality of Romare Bearden's art and has incorporated many of the basic facts of his life.

Romare Bearden was born in Charlotte, North Carolina, on September 2, 1911. He spent his early childhood in Charlotte and even after he moved north spent many summers there. When he was still a child, his family moved to Harlem in New York City. This was during the 1920s, a period called the Harlem Renaissance, when many famous African American writers, musicians, and artists lived and worked in Harlem. Bearden often sat out on the stoop of his apartment building, listening to music, getting to know his neighbors, and taking in the scene. In 1954, Bearden married Nanette Rohan, whose family is from the Caribbean island of St. Martin.

As Bearden grew to be a young man, he chose painting to express the African American experience as he knew it. He experimented with many different ways of painting, finally deciding that collage was the best form for expressing his ideas. Many of his paintings are on exhibit in museums and galleries across the Untied States. His work has also appeared in several children's books. In 1987 Romare Bearden was awarded the National Medal of Arts by President Ronald Reagan.

Bearden died on March 12, 1988.

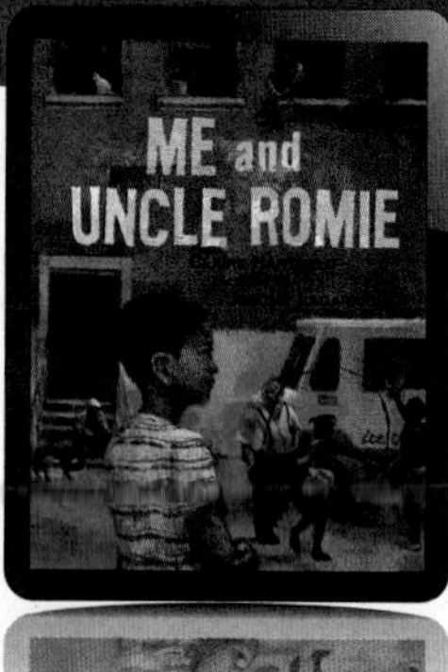

COMPREHENSION

Dig Deeper

How to Analyze the Text

Use these pages to learn about Understanding Characters, Theme, and Point of View. Then read "Me and Uncle Romie" again to apply what you learned.

Understanding Characters

"Me and Uncle Romie" is a **realistic fiction** story about a boy named James who visits his aunt and uncle in New York City. What the three **characters** do and what they learn is what makes the story interesting for readers. The author shows what the characters are like by describing what they think, what they do, and what they say.

Reread pages 236–237. Notice what James thinks, does, and says on the morning of his birthday. What can you tell about James, based on these details?

Thoughts	Actions	Words

ELACC4RL1 refer to details and examples when explaining what the text says explicitly and when drawing inferences; **ELACC4RL2** determine theme from details/summarize; **ELACC4RL3** describe a character, setting, or event, drawing on details; **ELACC4RL6** compare and contrast the point of view from which stories are narrated

Theme

The **theme** of a story is the main message about life the author wants readers to understand. You can figure out a story's theme by thinking about what happens in the story and what the characters learn. How does James feel about Uncle Romie at first? How do his feelings change throughout the story, and why? Using **events** and **details** from the text can help you figure out the theme the author wants to share.

Point of View

Authors tell stories from different **points of view.** When a story is told from the **first-person point of view,** the **narrator** is part of the story. Readers know what the narrator thinks but learn about other characters through what the characters say and do. When a story is told from the **third-person point of view**, the narrator is outside of the story. Readers learn what all the characters think, say, and do.

Your Turn

RETURN TO THE ESSENTIAL QUESTION

Turn and Talk Review the selection with a partner to prepare to discuss this question: *How do an artist's experiences affect his or her art?* Review key ideas with a partner. As you discuss the question, make sure you understand your partner's comments before you add your own comments.

"I understand
what you're saying.
Here's what I think."

Classroom Conversation

Continue your discussion of "Me and Uncle Romie" by explaining your answers with text evidence:

1. What causes James to change his opinion of New York City and begin to feel at home there?
2. Why does James begin to feel more comfortable with Uncle Romie?
3. What do you think is the most important thing James learns?

MAKE CONNECTIONS

Match It Up With a partner, review the illustrations in "Me and Uncle Romie." How do the illustrations connect to the words of the text? How do they show the characters and settings? Choose one illustration and find the matching description in the text. What is the effect of this illustration on the reader?

WRITE ABOUT READING

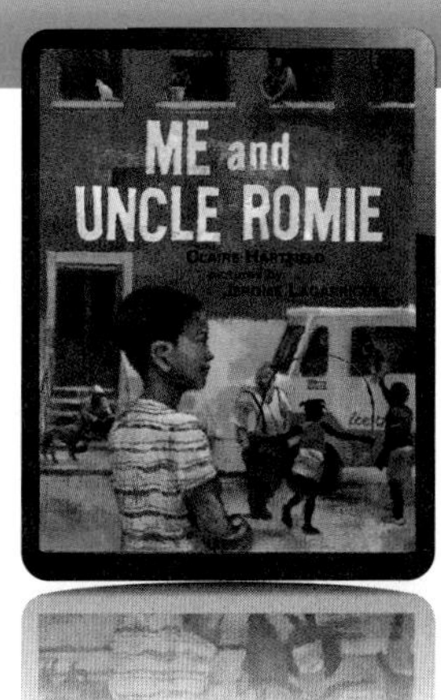

Response In the story, Uncle Romie gives James a special birthday gift: a picture collage to remind him of his summer in New York City. If Uncle Romie created a collage for you, what memories would you like the picture to show? Write a description of the collage you would like Uncle Romie to create.

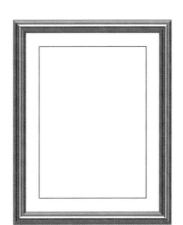

Writing Tip

Use vivid adjectives and specific nouns in your description. Be sure to use verb tenses correctly.

ELACC4RL7 make connections between the text and a visual or oral presentation of it; **ELACC4W10** write routinely over extended time frames and shorter time frames; **ELACC4SL1c** pose and respond to questions and make comments that contribute to the discussion and link to others' remarks; **ELACC4SL1d** review key ideas expressed and explain own ideas and understanding; **ELACC4L3a** choose words and phrases to convey ideas precisely

Lesson 8

READERS' THEATER

 GENRE

Readers' theater is a text that has been formatted for readers to read aloud.

 TEXT FOCUS

Directions A text may include a set of instructions telling how to do something, often instructing the reader to follow a series of steps. Review the steps presented in the text to create sidewalk art.

ELACC4RL5 explain major differences between poems, drama, and prose/refer to their structural elements; **ELACC4RL10** read and comprehend literature; **ELACC4RF4a** read on-level text with purpose and understanding

Sidewalk Artists

by Sam Rabe

Cast of Characters

Narrator, Kayla, Ms. Lee, Zack

Narrator: On a sunny day in southern Texas, Ms. Lee's students gathered in the school playground.

Ms. Lee: Tomorrow is the day of the sidewalk chalk-art festival. The principal has given us permission to practice our wet-chalk drawing on the playground pavement, which will be our studio. Remember, whenever you want to draw on a sidewalk, always ask an adult in charge for permission before you draw. Now let's review the steps of wet-chalk drawing. What do we do first?

Go Digital

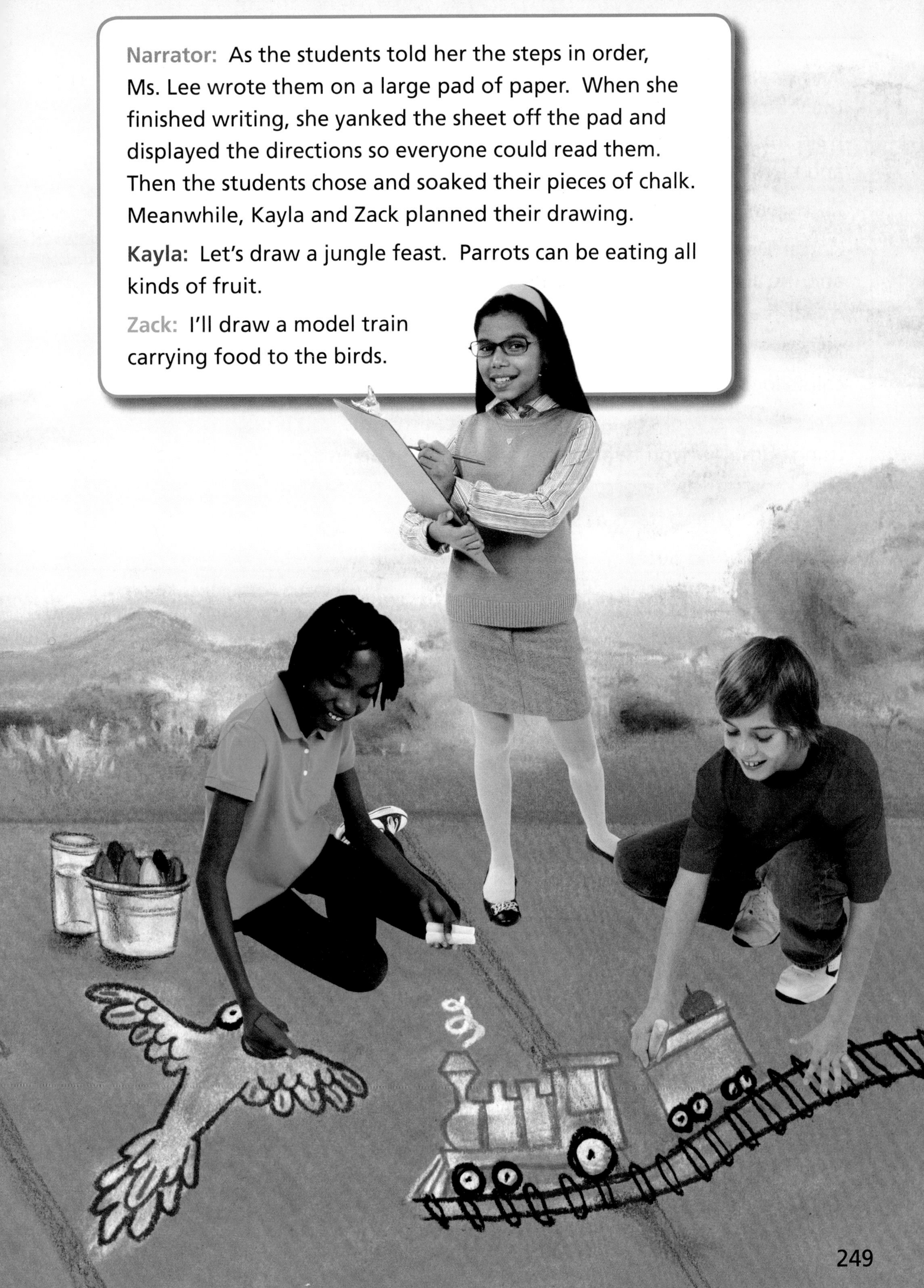

Narrator: As the students told her the steps in order, Ms. Lee wrote them on a large pad of paper. When she finished writing, she yanked the sheet off the pad and displayed the directions so everyone could read them. Then the students chose and soaked their pieces of chalk. Meanwhile, Kayla and Zack planned their drawing.

Kayla: Let's draw a jungle feast. Parrots can be eating all kinds of fruit.

Zack: I'll draw a model train carrying food to the birds.

Narrator: The students removed their pieces of chalk from the water and drew. As Zack drew a sweeping curve of train track, his hand knocked over the jar of water. He and Kayla watched water streak across their drawing.

Zack: Our drawing is ruined!

Kayla: Don't be so concerned! Quick, blend the water and the chalk together! Now let's layer on more chalk and smear it around.

Narrator: Kayla and Zack worked quickly. The smeared colors looked glorious, like rich, thick frosting on a cake.

Ms. Lee: That looks great! That's a neat technique you're using, kids. Are you two interested in taking part in the chalk-art festival tomorrow? The schedule for the festival says that drawing starts at 9:00 A.M.

Kayla and Zack: Sure!

Kayla: Tomorrow we'll spill water on our drawing on purpose.

Zack: Then we'll know just what to do!

Making Wet Chalk Drawings

1. Choose your pieces of chalk, and put them in a jar.
2. Fill the jar with water to cover three quarters of the length of the chalk. Let the chalk soak for a few minutes, but don't let it dissolve.
3. Remove the wet chalk from the jar.
4. Draw!
5. Let your drawing dry.

Compare Texts

TEXT TO TEXT

Compare Points of View "Stormalong" and "Me and Uncle Romie" are told from different points of view. With a partner, discuss the two stories. How are the main characters, Stormalong and James, alike and different? How does the point of view in each story affect what we know about these two characters?

TEXT TO SELF

Write a Description Think of an adult who is important to you. What items would you include in a collage about that person? Write a paragraph describing the collage you would make. Tell how each item reminds you of the person.

TEXT TO WORLD

Biography and Fiction "Me and Uncle Romie" is a fictional story based on a real artist. Read an online biography of the artist Romare Bearden. Then identify the things that were the same in both his real life and in this story. Share your findings with a partner.

ELACC4RL6 compare and contrast the point of view from which stories are narrated; **ELACC4W2b** develop the topic with facts, definitions, details, quotations, or other information and examples; **ELACC4W8** recall information from experiences or gather information from print and digital sources/take notes, categorize information, and provide a list of sources

ELACC4L1b use progressive verb tenses/aspects

Grammar

What Are Progressive Forms of Verbs? Verb phrases such as *is talking* and *were listening* tell about actions that happen over a period of time. These verb forms are called **progressive verb tenses.** Progressive verb tenses can tell about actions that happened in the past, are happening in the present, or will happen in the future.

Progressive Verb Tenses

To form the **present progressive,** use the present-tense form of the verb *be* and add *-ing* to the verb:

James and Uncle Romie are eating cake.

To form the **past progressive,** use the past-tense form of the verb *be* and add *-ing* to the verb:

They were watching the ball game.

To form the **future progressive,** use *will be* and add *-ing* to the verb:

Uncle Romie will be showing his work at the art show.

Try This! **Work with a partner to find the progressive-tense verb in each sentence. Tell whether the verb is present progressive, past progressive, or future progressive.**

1. Aunt Nanette was waiting for James at the train station.
2. Uncle Romie is showing James his artwork.
3. James will be thinking about Uncle Romie during his art show at school.

Use verb tenses and forms correctly to help readers keep track of when actions take place. Make sure to use the same verb tense or form in each sentence that tells about actions happening at the same time.

Inconsistent Verb Forms	Consistent Verb Forms
The people are looking at the art. They walked from room to room. They will talk about the paintings	The people are looking at the art. They are walking from room to room. They are talking about the paintings.

Connect Grammar to Writing

As you revise your book report, make sure that all the verb forms and tenses agree. This will help you to clearly communicate your ideas.

ELACC4W2a introduce a topic and group related information/include formatting, illustrations, and multimedia; **ELACC4W2e** provide a concluding statement or section; **ELACC4W9a** apply grade 4 Reading standards to literature; **ELACC4W10** write routinely over extended time frames and shorter time frames

Informative Writing

Organization In a **book report,** good writers organize their ideas so that related information is grouped together in a logical way. Begin your book report by stating the topic, including the book's title. Then summarize the story's most important events. End with a concluding statement or paragraph that sums up the main point of your report.

Davey drafted a book report about "Me and Uncle Romie." Then he revised the beginning so that it clearly stated his topic.

Writing Traits Checklist

- **Ideas** Is my topic clear?
- **Organization** Did I arrange my ideas in a clear way?
- **Word Choice** Did I choose words to clearly describe characters and events?
- **Voice** Did I express my ideas in my own way?
- **Sentence Fluency** Do my verb tenses agree?
- **Conventions** Did I use verb forms correctly?

Revised Draft

I read the book Me and Uncle Romie by Claire Hartfield and loved the characters.

~~This book~~ It is about a boy who visits his aunt and uncle in New York City for the summer. At first, James is worried he won't have a good time, but his feelings change.

James does lots of fun things with Aunt Nanette, but he doesn't see much of Uncle Romie. When his aunt has to go out of town, James spends time with his uncle.

Final Copy

A Book Report on Me and Uncle Romie

by Davey Watson

I read the book Me and Uncle Romie by Claire Hartfield and loved the characters. It is about a boy who visits his aunt and uncle in New York City for the summer. At first, James is worried he won't have a good time, but his feelings change.

James does lots of fun things with Aunt Nanette, but he doesn't see much of Uncle Romie. When his aunt has to go out of town, James spends time with his uncle. They have a great time together, and James learns all about Uncle Romie's amazing art. James says, "Looking at Uncle Romie's paintings, I could *feel* Harlem—its beat and bounce."

I really liked how the author created interesting, realistic characters and a great story!

Reading as a Writer

Davey summarized the story in his own words. Did you summarize the main events? In his conclusion, Davey told how he felt about the book. Did you sum up your feelings in your conclusion?

I introduced the topic by stating the book's title and the author's name. I included a quotation to explain how James felt about his uncle's art.

Lesson 9

When I Went to the Library

FIELD GUIDE to Snakes of the Southwest

Vocabulary in Context

TARGET VOCABULARY

fault
borrow
reference
fainted
genuine
local
apologize
proof
slimy
insisted

Vocabulary Reader

Context Cards

ELACC4L6 acquire/use vocabulary, including academic and domain-specific

1 fault

A misunderstanding between friends is often no one's fault, or responsibility.

2 borrow

If you borrow an item from someone, make sure to return it soon.

3 reference

A reference book is a good source of information. It can explain things clearly.

4 fainted

This person has not fainted. She is just taking a short nap.

- Study each Context Card.
- Use a dictionary to help you understand the meanings of these words.

5 genuine

If you say something that is not genuine, or sincere, someone's feelings could be hurt.

6 local

Visitors from another region may not understand local practices and customs.

7 apologize

If you do something wrong, it's best to apologize by saying you're sorry.

8 proof

Your parents might want proof that you really have done your homework.

9 slimy

These boys didn't mind that the soccer field had patches of slimy mud!

10 insisted

This boy's mom demanded, or insisted, that he fix the mess he made.

Read and Comprehend

TARGET SKILL

Conclusions and Generalizations Sometimes an author expects readers to draw a **conclusion,** or figure out a story detail that is not stated, on their own. A **generalization** is a kind of conclusion that is true about something *most* of the time, but not always. As you read "Dear Mr. Winston," notice details and text evidence that can help you draw a reasonable conclusion about the story. Use a graphic organizer like this one to help you use details to draw a conclusion or support a generalization.

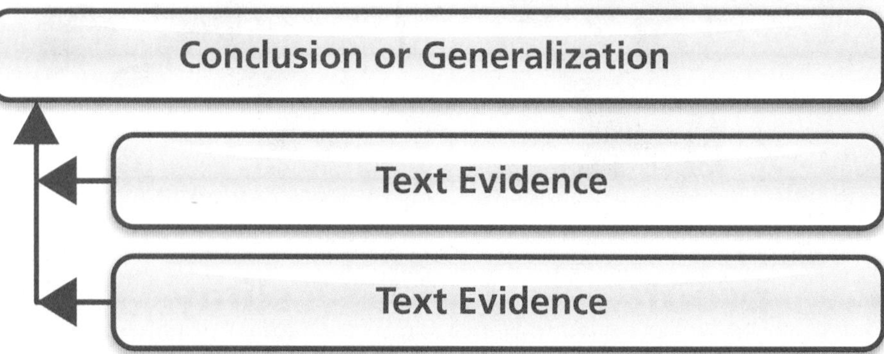

TARGET STRATEGY

Question Asking yourself **questions** such as *How did this happen?* or *Why did this happen?* can help you understand a story. You can ask questions before you read, as you read, and after you read. As you read "Dear Mr. Winston," use the question strategy to draw conclusions about the narrator's attitude and feelings.

ELACC4RL1 refer to details and examples when explaining what the text says explicitly and when drawing inferences

PREVIEW THE TOPIC

Research

When you do research, you look for information about a topic that interests you. You can look for information in nonfiction books, in newspapers, and on the Internet. Many students begin a research project by visiting the library. Interviewing experts on a subject is another good way to learn about a topic.

Sometimes research doesn't go as planned, however. In "Dear Mr. Winston," a student's research takes an unexpected turn.

Lesson 9

ANCHOR TEXT

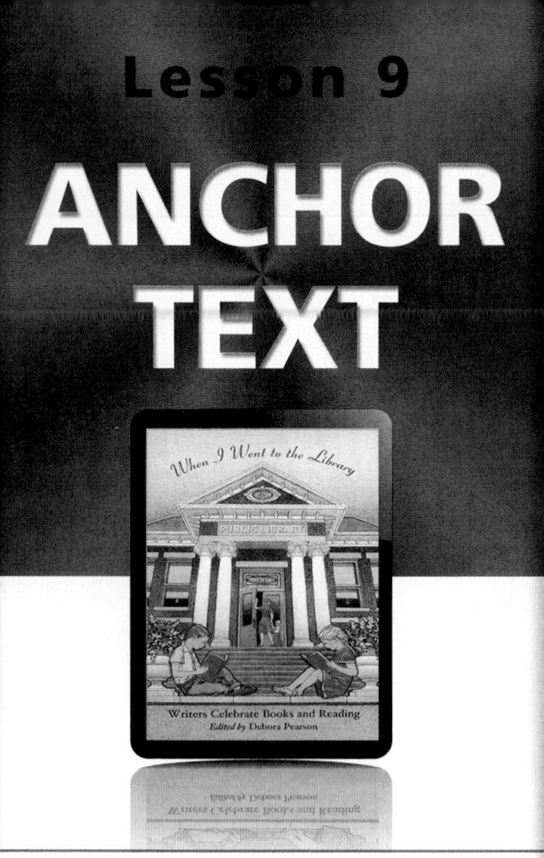

TARGET SKILL

Conclusions and Generalizations Figure out unstated or broad ideas.

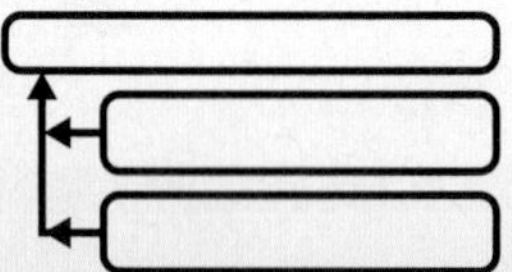

GENRE

Realistic fiction has characters and events that are like people and events in real life. As you read, look for:

- a setting that is familiar to most readers
- characters who have feelings that real people have
- challenges and problems that might happen in real life

ELACC4RL1 refer to details and examples when explaining what the text says explicitly and when drawing inferences; **ELACC4RL3** describe a character, setting, or event, drawing on details; **ELACC4RL10** read and comprehend literature

MEET THE AUTHOR

KEN ROBERTS

Like Mr. Winston, Ken Roberts is a librarian. He also writes books and plays and is a storyteller. "I am good at many things," he says, "but a master at none, really." Sometimes he works on many projects at once. At other times he reads quietly by the fireside.

MEET THE ILLUSTRATOR

ANDY HAMMOND

Andy Hammond has been a busy cartoonist for more than thirty years. He works in pen and ink and watercolor, often finishing his work on the computer. His favorite cartooning jobs are the ones that let him use his own style and allow his sense of humor to run free.

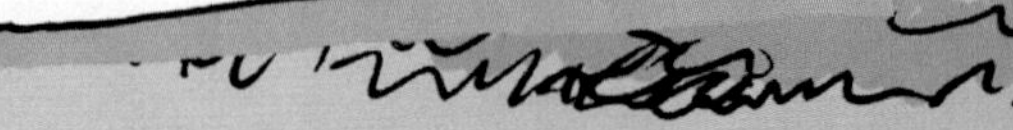

Dear Mr. Winston

from When I Went to the Library

by Ken Roberts

selection illustrated by Andy Hammond

ESSENTIAL QUESTION

What are some different ways to do research?

Dear Mr. Winston,

My parents said that I have to write and apologize. Dad says he is going to read this letter before it's sent and that I'd better make sure my apology sounds truly genuine. So, I am truly, genuinely sorry for bringing that snake into the library yesterday.

My parents say that what I did was wrong, even though the cardboard box was shut, most of the time, and there was no way that snake could have escaped if you hadn't opened the box and dropped it on the floor.

My parents say it's my fault for having brought that snake into the library and I truly, genuinely apologize but I still don't know how I was supposed to find out what kind of snake I had inside that box without bringing the snake right into the library so I could look at snake pictures and then look at the snake and try to find a picture that matched the snake.

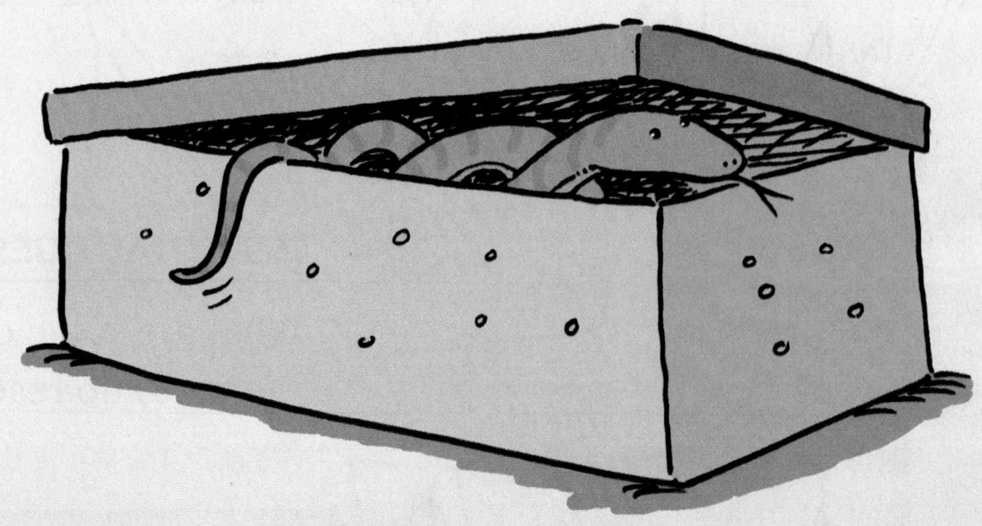

ANALYZE THE TEXT

Understanding Characters Does Cara seem "truly, genuinely sorry"? What words and actions of hers indicate her feelings?

I told my parents something that I didn't get a chance to remind you about before the ambulance took you away. I did come into the library without the snake, first. I left the box outside, hidden under a bush and tried to borrow a thick green book with lots of snake pictures. You told me that the big green book was a reference book which meant that it had to stay inside the library and I couldn't take it out, even for ten minutes.

My parents say I still shouldn't have brought that snake into the library and that I have to be truly, genuinely sorry if I ever hope to watch *Galactic Patrol* on television again. My parents picked *Galactic Patrol* because it's my favorite show, although I'm not sure what not watching a television program has to do with bringing a snake into the library.

The people at the library say you hate snakes so much that you won't even touch a book with a picture of snakes on the cover and that is why you won't be back at the library for a few more weeks. If you want, you could watch *Galactic Patrol*. It's on at 4:00 P.M. weekdays, on channel 7. There are no snakes on the show because it takes place in space.

Did the flowers arrive? Dad picked them out but I have to pay for them with my allowance for the next two months. The flowers are proof that I am truly, genuinely sorry for having brought that snake into the library. I hope the people who work at the library find that snake soon! Did they look under all the chairs?

WILD FLOWERS

That snake isn't dangerous. It is a local snake, and there are no poisonous snakes in Manitoba. The people at the library say you know that too because that was one of the reasons you decided to move here. I bought that snake from a friend. I paid one month's allowance for it, which means that snake has cost me a total of three months' allowance and I only owned it for one hour!

Mom says I don't have to tell who sold me that snake so I won't tell you either because Dad says he is going to read this letter. Besides, I don't want you to be mad at anyone else when I am the one who brought that snake into the library yesterday. I am truly, genuinely sorry.

I want you to know that I didn't plan to show you that snake. I didn't mean to scare you at all. I knew where the big green snake book was kept. I put the box on a table close to the book and tried to find the right picture. I looked at a picture, then at the snake, at another picture, and then the snake. I did that five times and can tell you that the snake inside the library is not a python, a rattlesnake, an anaconda, an asp, or a cobra.

Anyway, I was surprised when you wanted to see what was inside the box because I didn't ask for any help and there were plenty of people in the library who did need help.

Dad says that the fact that I said, "Nothing," instead of "A snake," is proof that I knew I was doing something wrong when I brought that snake into the library. I am truly, genuinely sorry even though my friend Jake Lambert promised me that the snake I bought from him is perfectly harmless.

ANALYZE THE TEXT

Humor Who does Cara blame for what happened to Mr. Winston? What words and phrases does the author use to tell us how she feels?

I did tell you that I didn't need any help and I did have a snake book open in front of me, so I don't know why you insisted on looking inside the box if you are so afraid of snakes and everything. I don't know why you picked up that box before opening a flap, either. If you had left the box on the table and maybe even sat down next to it, then maybe the box would have been all right when you screamed and fainted. You wouldn't have fallen so far, either, if you were sitting down.

Did you know that you broke out in a rash after you fainted? I thought a person had to touch something like poison ivy to get a rash. I didn't know it was possible to get a rash by just thinking about something but my parents say it really can happen. I think maybe you did touch something. Maybe, when you were lying on the floor, that snake slithered over to you and touched you! Did you know that snake skin feels dry, not wet and slimy at all?

I just thought of something. Maybe everyone's looking in the library for that snake but it's not in the library. Maybe it crawled into one of your pockets or up your sleeve and rode with you to the hospital! Wouldn't that be funny? Why don't you get one of the nurses to check? If it's not in your clothes, it might have crawled out and might be hiding inside the hospital someplace. I think people should be looking there, too.

ANALYZE THE TEXT

Conclusions and Generalizations Look at the first paragraph. What conclusion can you draw about the letter writer's attitude from her suggestions to Mr. Winston? What details and examples lead you to this conclusion?

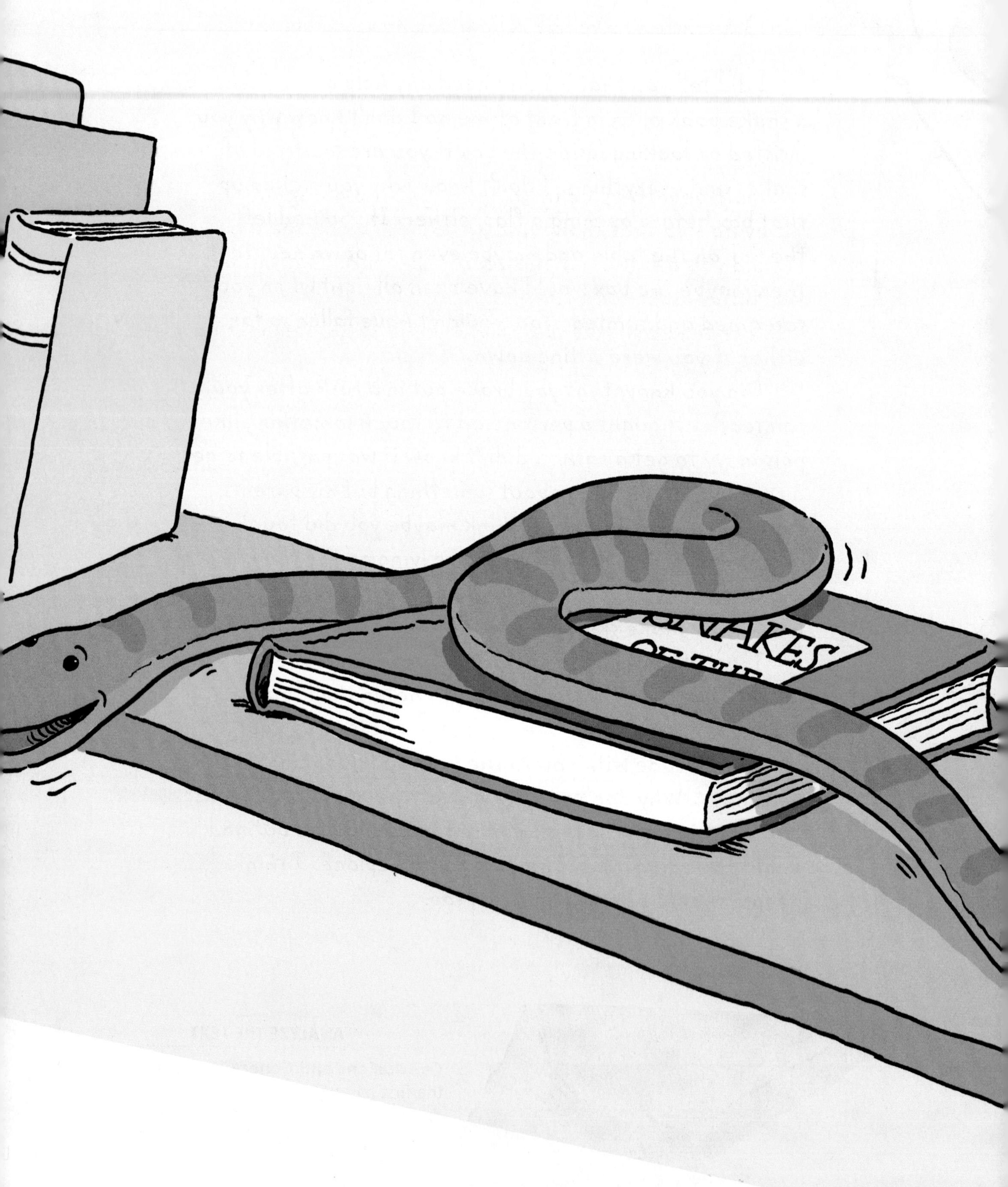
SNAKES

I am sure you will be talking to the people in the library, to make sure they find that snake before you go back to work. I hope they do find it, even though my parents say that I can't keep it. If that snake is found, could you ask the people at the library to give me a call? I would be interested in knowing that it is all right. And if they do find that snake and do decide to give me a call, could you ask them if they could compare that snake with the snake pictures in that big green reference book before they call me? I would still like to know what kind of snake I owned for an hour.

I am truly, genuinely sorry.

Your friend,

Cara

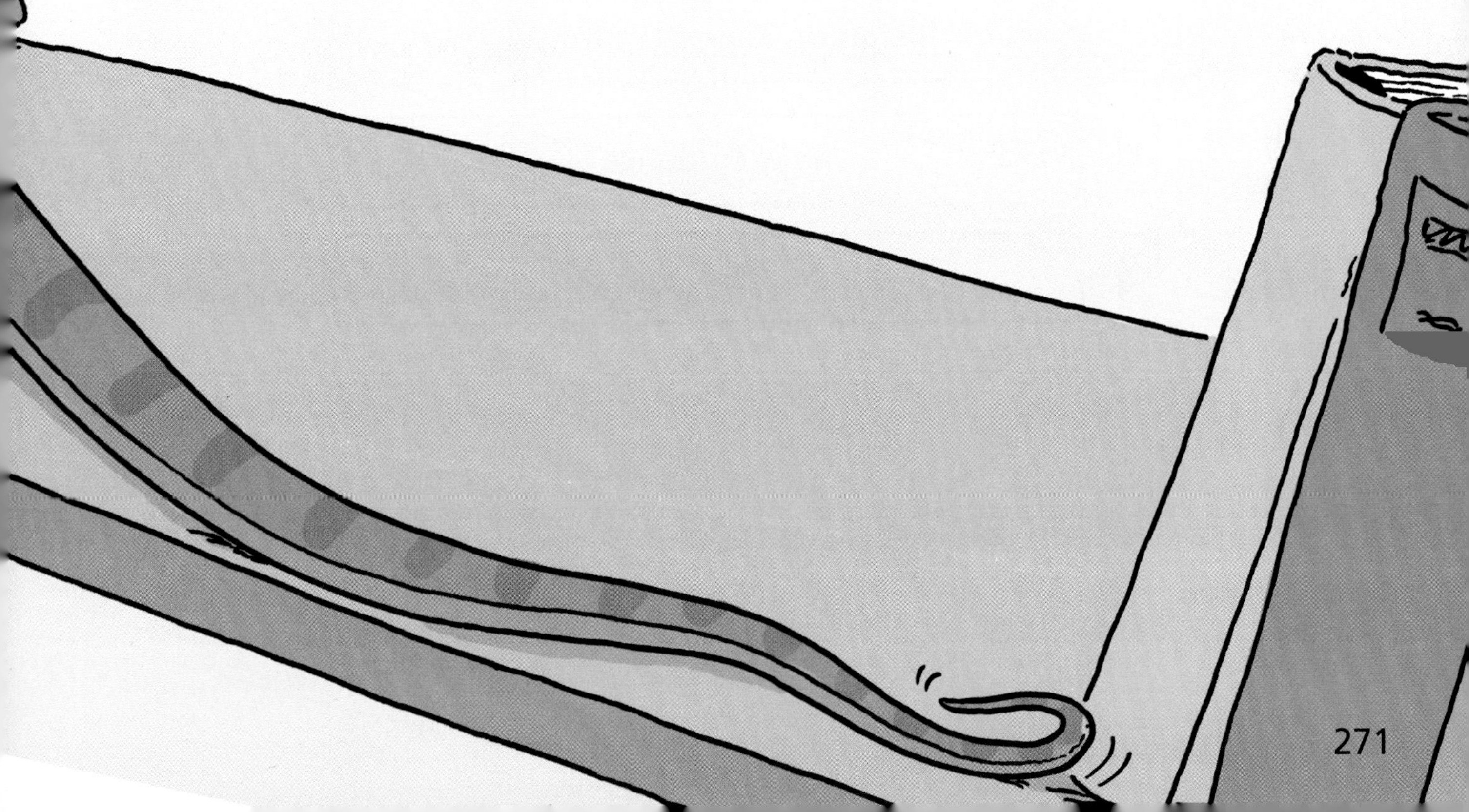

COMPREHENSION

Dig Deeper

How to Analyze the Text

Use these pages to learn about Conclusions and Generalizations, Understanding Characters, and Humor. Then read "Dear Mr. Winston" again to apply what you learned.

Conclusions and Generalizations

Realistic fiction like "Dear Mr. Winston" includes characters who have feelings that real people have. They face problems that might happen in real life.

Sometimes an author expects readers to figure out something on their own. This is called drawing a **conclusion** or making an **inference**. A **generalization** is a kind of conclusion that is true about something *most* of the time, but not always. In "Dear Mr. Winston," you can use text evidence such as details and examples to help you draw a conclusion about what Cara is thinking and feeling. Reread the beginning of Cara's letter. What conclusion can you draw about Cara?

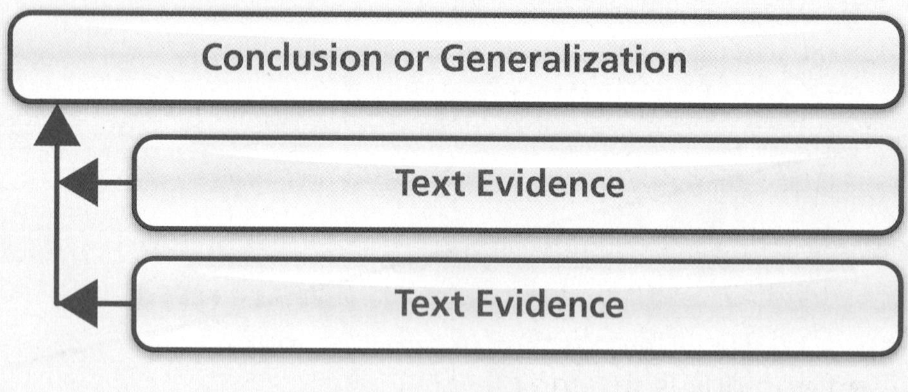

ELACC4RL1 refer to details and examples when explaining what the text says explicitly and when drawing inferences; **ELACC4RL3** describe a character, setting, or event, drawing on details; **ELACC4RL4** determine the meaning of words and phrases, including those that allude to characters in mythology

Understanding Characters

How can you determine what kind of person Cara is? You can understand what a **character** is like by paying attention to the character's **thoughts, words,** and **actions.** Cara begins her letter by saying that her parents are making her write to apologize and that her parents say that what she did was wrong. Her thoughts do not make her sound sorry.

Humor

Authors sometimes use **humor** to entertain their readers. Having Cara repeat the phrase "I am truly, genuinely sorry," though she means the opposite, is funny. The repetition of this sentence adds to the humor. Note how Cara presents her parents' view of the snake incident while also giving her own view. That's one reason why her letter of apology is so funny. What else makes her letter humorous?

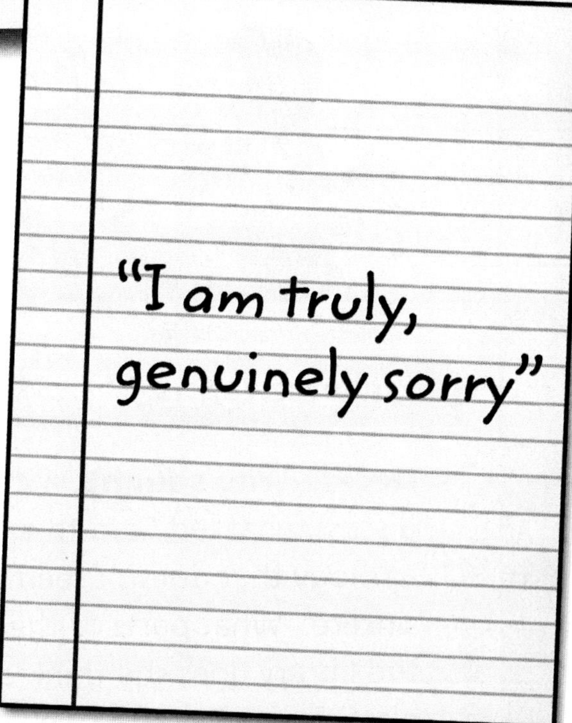
"I am truly, genuinely sorry"

Your Turn

RETURN TO THE ESSENTIAL QUESTION

Review the selection with a partner and prepare to discuss this question: *What are some different ways to do research?* As you discuss, take turns reviewing and explaining the key ideas in your discussion. Include text evidence in your responses.

Classroom Conversation

Continue your discussion of "Dear Mr. Winston" by explaining your answers to these questions:

1. Why do you think the author wrote the story in the form of a letter from Cara to Mr. Winston?
2. Does Cara show kindness and understanding toward Mr. Winston? Tell why or why not.
3. What lesson could Cara have learned from the incident in the library?

WHO'S TO BLAME?

Decide Who's Right With a group, discuss what led Cara to make an apology that doesn't seem completely sincere. What parts of the incident in the library does she think are someone else's fault? Do you think most people would feel the same way? Use text evidence to support your opinion.

WRITE ABOUT READING

Response How do you think Mr. Winston will react to Cara's apology? Imagine you are Mr. Winston, and write a reply to Cara's letter. Tell whether you accept her apology, and explain why or why not. Remember to use correct letter form, capitalization, and punctuation.

Dear Cara,

Cara

Writing Tip

Include facts and details when explaining your reasons for accepting or rejecting Cara's apology. Also, make sure your verb tenses are correct.

ELACC4RL1 refer to details and examples when explaining what the text says explicitly and when drawing inferences; **ELACC4W10** write routinely over extended time frames and shorter time frames; **ELACC4SL1d** review key ideas expressed and explain own ideas and understanding; **ELACC4L2a** use correct capitalization

Lesson 9

INFORMATIONAL TEXT

 GENRE

Informational text, such as this field guide, gives facts and examples about a topic.

TEXT FOCUS

Chart Informational text may include a chart, which organizes related information about a topic. How does the information in the chart on page 278 relate to the text?

COMMON CORE **ELACC4RI7** interpret information presented visually, orally, or quantitatively; **ELACC4RI10** read and comprehend informational texts; **ELACC4RF4a** read on-level text with purpose and understanding

FIELD GUIDE to Snakes of the Southwest

by Patrick Sutter

Snakes are amazing. They have no arms or legs, but they move quickly. They have no ears, but heat-sensing organs help them find their prey. Snakes survive in almost every ecosystem on Earth.

Many people fear snakes. Some individuals have even fainted at the sight of these reptiles, but this is no one's fault. It's true that some snakes are dangerous. Yet many are not. In fact, most snakes help local farmers by eating pests. People imagine a snake's skin is slimy, but it is made of dry scales.

This reference guide gives information about three snakes from the Southwest.

Common name: Mountain King Snake
Scientific name: *Lampropeltis zonata*
Size: 20–40 inches
Habitat: mountains, damp woods
Nonvenomous

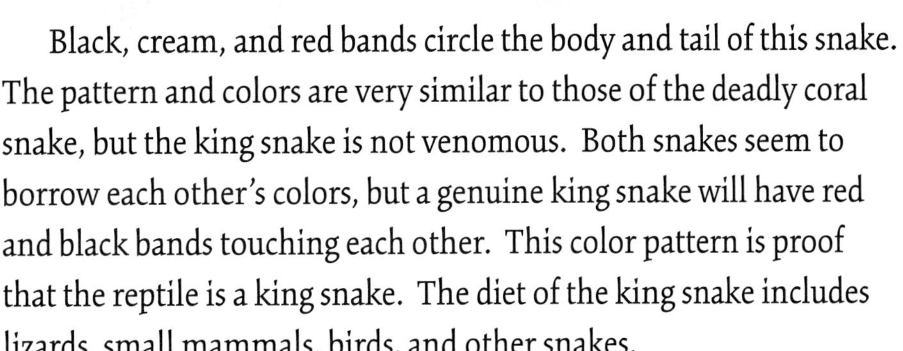

Black, cream, and red bands circle the body and tail of this snake. The pattern and colors are very similar to those of the deadly coral snake, but the king snake is not venomous. Both snakes seem to borrow each other's colors, but a genuine king snake will have red and black bands touching each other. This color pattern is proof that the reptile is a king snake. The diet of the king snake includes lizards, small mammals, birds, and other snakes.

Common name: Western Diamond-Backed Rattlesnake
Scientific name: *Crotalus atrox*
Size: 30–90 inches
Habitat: dry areas, such as deserts and rocky foothills
Venomous

This is the largest snake in the West. It eats small mammals, birds, and reptiles. People fear this snake because it is very dangerous. Even a dead rattlesnake can bite! Its jaws can still open when touched and can still inject venom. Scientists do not apologize for trying to protect rattlesnakes, though. They have insisted that in spite of the danger, rattlesnakes are important. This snake will not attack, but it will defend itself. First, it shakes its tail to make a rattling sound. This is a signal to back off!

Common names: Desert Threadsnake or Western Blind Snake
Scientific name: *Leptotyphlops humilis*
Size: 6–13 inches
Habitat: mountain slopes, deserts, rocky foothills
Nonvenomous

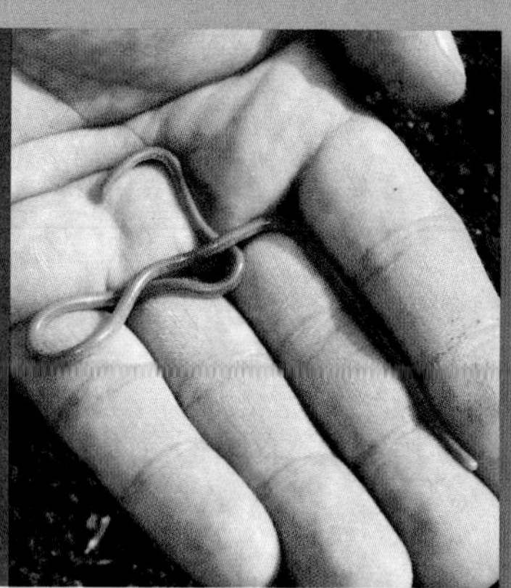

This tiny, harmless snake can be brown, purple, or pink in color. One of its two common names refers to its thin, wormlike body. The other refers to its lack of eyes. Instead of eyes that see, this snake has two black spots on its face. The threadsnake burrows for its food under plant roots and rocks and in ant nests. It eats ants and other small insects.

Traits of Southwestern Snakes

TRAITS	MOUNTAIN KING SNAKE	DIAMOND-BACKED RATTLESNAKE	DESERT THREADSNAKE
venomous		🐍	
nonvenomous	🐍		🐍
desert habitat		🐍	🐍
mountain habitat	🐍		🐍
large size	🐍	🐍	
small size			🐍

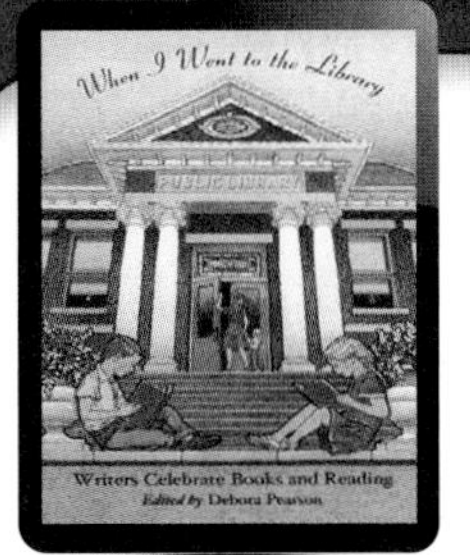

Compare Texts

TEXT TO TEXT

Compare and Contrast Choose one snake from"Field Guide to Snakes of the Southwest" and complete a Venn diagram to compare and contrast that snake with Cara's snake. Use details that Cara gives about her snake as well as the information in "Field Guide" to guess what kind of snake Cara might have had. Discuss your ideas with a partner. Then work together to write a paragraph explaining what kind of snake Cara might have. Use evidence from the text to support your thoughts.

Mountain King Snake
Both
Cara's Snake

TEXT TO SELF

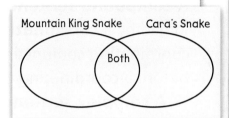

Write a Letter Everyone makes mistakes sometimes. Write a short letter of apology to a friend you should have said "I'm sorry" to but didn't. Include a date, a salutation, and a closing.

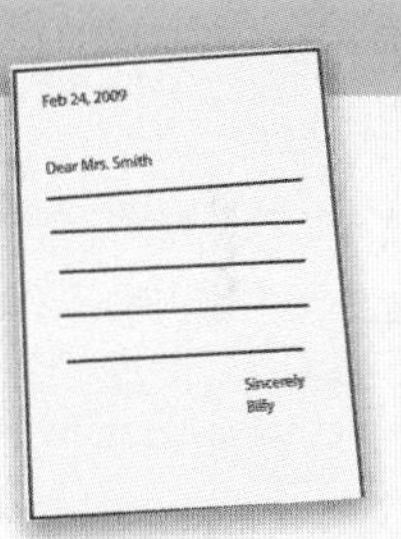

TEXT TO WORLD

Research Snakes Research a snake that lives somewhere other than the Southwest. Make a chart with facts such as where the snake lives, what it eats, how long it is, and whether or not it is venomous. Present your chart to the class.

ELACC4RL1 refer to details and examples when explaining what the text says explicitly and when drawing inferences; **ELACC4RI1** refer to details and examples when explaining what the text says explicitly and when drawing inferences; **ELACC4RI9** integrate information from two texts on the same topic; **ELACC4W7** conduct short research projects that build knowledge through investigation

ELACC4L2c use a comma before a coordinating conjunction in a compound sentence

Grammar

What Are Compound and Complex Sentences?
A **compound sentence** is made up of two simple sentences joined by a **coordinating conjunction.** The most common coordinating conjunctions are *and*, *but*, and *or*. Use a comma before a coordinating conjunction in a compound sentence.

A **complex sentence** is made up of a simple sentence and a clause with a **subordinating conjunction.** Subordinating conjunctions include *because*, *although*, *until*, *if*, and *since*. Do not use a comma if the subordinating conjunction is in the middle of the sentence.

Compound Sentence

complete sentence / complete sentence

Cara put the snake in a box, and she brought it to the library.

Comma / Conjunction

Complex Sentence

The snake got out because Mr. Winston peeked under the lid.

Subordinating Conjunction

Find the errors in these compound and complex sentences. Write the sentences correctly on a sheet of paper. Add commas where they belong.

1. Cara was curious about her snake And she took it to the library.
2. She left the snake outside. Because snakes are not allowed in the library.
3. She found a book about snakes but she couldn't check it out.

In your writing, you might find short sentences that are related in some way. Try combining these sentences. Use a comma and the conjunction *or*, *but*, or *and* to form a compound sentence. Use *because*, *although*, *until*, *if*, or *since* to form a complex sentence.

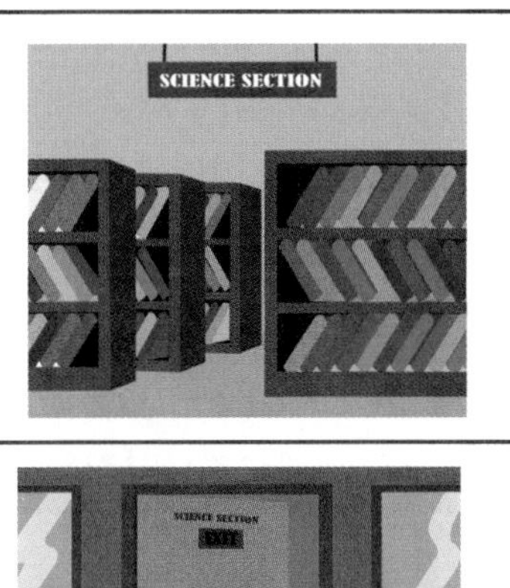

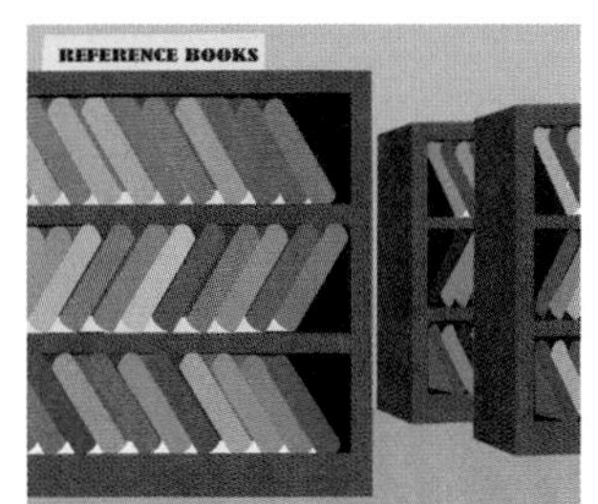

Related Sentences	Combined Sentence
Libraries have books on snakes. Only some books can be checked out.	Libraries have books on snakes, but only some books can be checked out.
I'll read it in the library. This book can't be checked out.	I'll read it in the library because this book can't be checked out.

 Connect Grammar to Writing

As you edit your explanatory essay next week, look for related sentences that you can combine into a compound or complex sentence. Don't forget to add a comma before the conjunctions *and*, *but*, and *or*.

ELACC4W2a introduce a topic and group related information/include formatting, illustrations, and multimedia; **ELACC4W2c** link ideas within categories of information using words and phrases; **ELACC4W2e** provide a concluding statement or section

Informative Writing

Reading-Writing Workshop: Prewrite

✓ Organization In "Dear Mr. Winston," Cara explains to Mr. Winston why she brought a pet snake into the library. In an **explanatory essay,** a writer explains *what* something is or *how* or *why* something happens.

Trudy decided that she wanted to explain to her classmates how to care for another kind of special pet—a canary she received as a gift from her grandmother. She listed her ideas, did some research, and then organized her ideas into an introduction, a body, and a conclusion.

Writing Process Checklist

▶ **Prewrite**

- ✓ Did I consider my audience and purpose?
- ✓ Did I think about what I want to explain?
- ✓ Did I find details to support my main ideas?
- ✓ Did I put my ideas in an order that makes sense?

Draft

Revise

Edit

Publish

Share

Exploring a Topic

Audience

Classmates

Purpose

Tell about pet canaries and explain how to care for them

What do I know about canaries?

Yellow, green, or orange

Sing songs, are gentle

Different kinds? Check resources.

How should canaries be cared for?

Water for drinking, bathing

Flying for exercise

Organization Chart

Introduction
Main idea: Canaries are small pets that are easy to care for.
Body
What are canaries? Details: • Small songbirds that range in color from yellow to orange. • Different kinds include Rollers, French canaries, and Belgian canaries.
How do you take care of canaries? Details: • Clean, roomy cages • Water for bathing, drinking • Seeds and greens for food
Conclusion
Why have canaries as pets? Small, sing songs, cheerful Easy to care for

Reading as a Writer

What other details could Trudy add to explain her main idea? What details could you add to your own chart?

In my chart, I detailed what I will include, including information to explain what, how, and why. I organized all the details so they will make sense to my audience.

Lesson

10

Vocabulary in Context

TARGET VOCABULARY

debut
stubborn
permission
hauling
mournful
towered
triumph
discouraged
toured
border

Vocabulary Reader

Context Cards

ELACC4L6 acquire/use vocabulary, including academic and domain-specific

1 debut

A performing artist is always excited at his or her debut, or first public show.

2 stubborn

Performers with a stubborn desire to succeed will continue to work hard.

3 permission

This musician is allowed to play in the subway. She was given permission.

4 hauling

When a band is traveling, workers are hauling equipment from city to city.

- Study each Context Card.
- Use a dictionary to help you pronounce these words.

5 mournful

The mournful songs of some singers are more memorable than their happy ones.

6 towered

Performers on stilts have always towered above their audiences.

7 triumph

Becoming a star is a triumph, or victory, most performing artists long for.

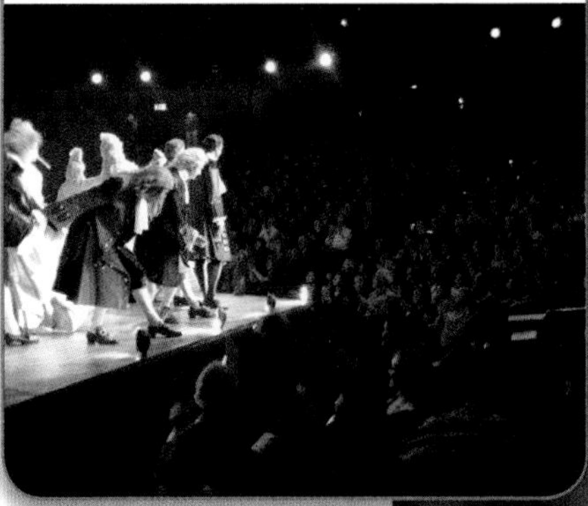

8 discouraged

Some musicians become discouraged, or disappointed, after a poor performance.

9 toured

A performer who has toured, or traveled, has gained new fans in every location.

10 border

Touring performers often cross an international border such as this one.

Read and Comprehend

TARGET SKILL

Author's Purpose As you read "José! Born to Dance," think about the author's reason, or **purpose,** for writing. Does she want to entertain, to inform, to persuade, or to describe? For clues, focus on the way the author describes the characters, events, and setting. Use a graphic organizer like this one to record text evidence that helps you identify the author's purpose.

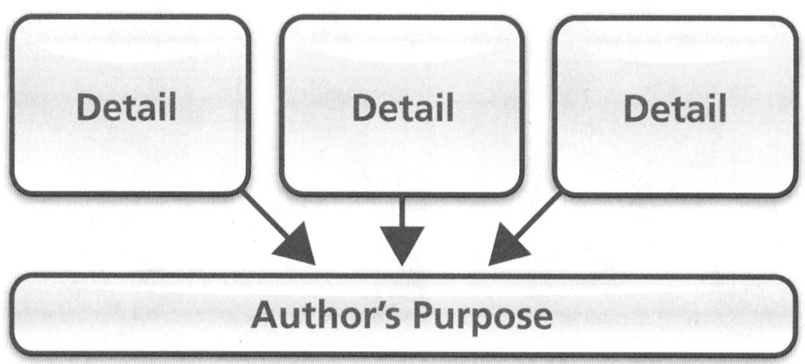

TARGET STRATEGY

Analyze/Evaluate As you read "José! Born to Dance," use the **analyze** and **evaluate** strategy to help you understand the author's purpose. Ask yourself why José worked so hard to become a dancer and why this is important to the author.

COMMON CORE **ELACC4RI8** explain how an author uses reasons and evidence to support points

PREVIEW THE TOPIC

Performance Arts

Performance arts are performed for a live audience. They include dance, drama, and music. Many people must work together to create a successful live performance, both on the stage and behind the scenes. For example, a great dance performance needs more than just great dancers. Set designers, costume designers, and choreographers, people who create the dances, are also key.

As you read "José! Born to Dance," you'll discover how a boy from Mexico became one of the most famous dancers and choreographers in the world.

Lesson 10

ANCHOR TEXT

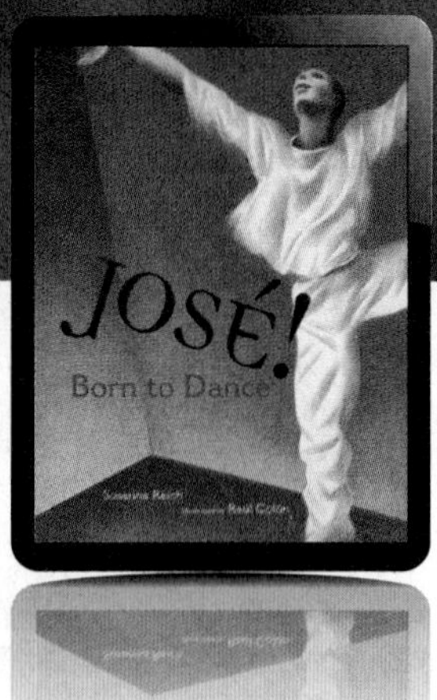

 TARGET SKILL

Author's Purpose Use text evidence to explain the author's reasons for writing.

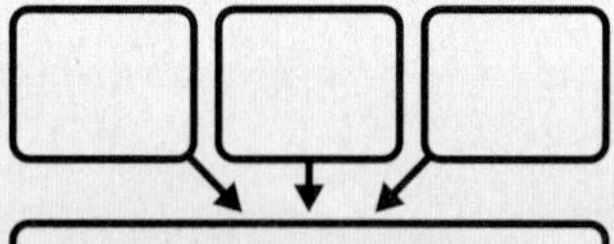

 GENRE

A **biography** tells about a person's life and is written by another person. As you read, look for:

- information about why the person is important
- events in time order
- reasons why the author might have written the biography

ELACC4RI5 describe the overall structure of a text or part of a text; **ELACC4RI8** explain how an author uses reasons and evidence to support points; **ELACC4RI10** read and comprehend informational texts; **ELACC4L5a** explain the meaning of similes and metaphors in context

 Go Digital

MEET THE AUTHOR

Susanna Reich

A former professional dancer, Susanna Reich is the author of *Clara Schumann: Piano Virtuoso*, an NCTE Orbis Pictus Honor Book, an ALA Notable, and a School Library Journal Best Book of the Year. Her other books include *Painting the Wild Frontier: The Art and Adventures of George Catlin* and *Penelope Bailey Takes the Stage*, a historical novel.

MEET THE ILLUSTRATOR

Raúl Colón

Because he had asthma as a boy, Raúl Colón was often kept inside, and he filled the time by drawing in his notebooks. "So my illness as a child," he recalls, "which kept me from going outside to play, became a blessing." He even created his own comic book. He began his official art training in the tenth grade and has since illustrated many children's books.

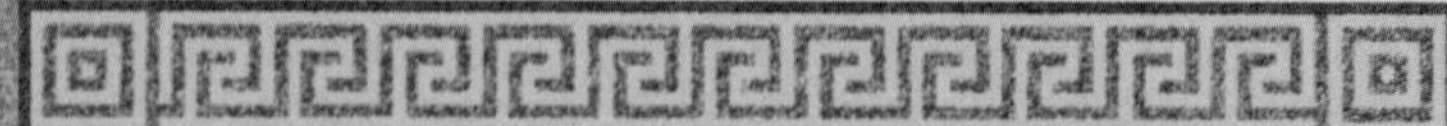

JOSÉ!

Born to Dance

by Susanna Reich
illustrated by Raúl Colón

ESSENTIAL QUESTION

What does it take to be a great performer?

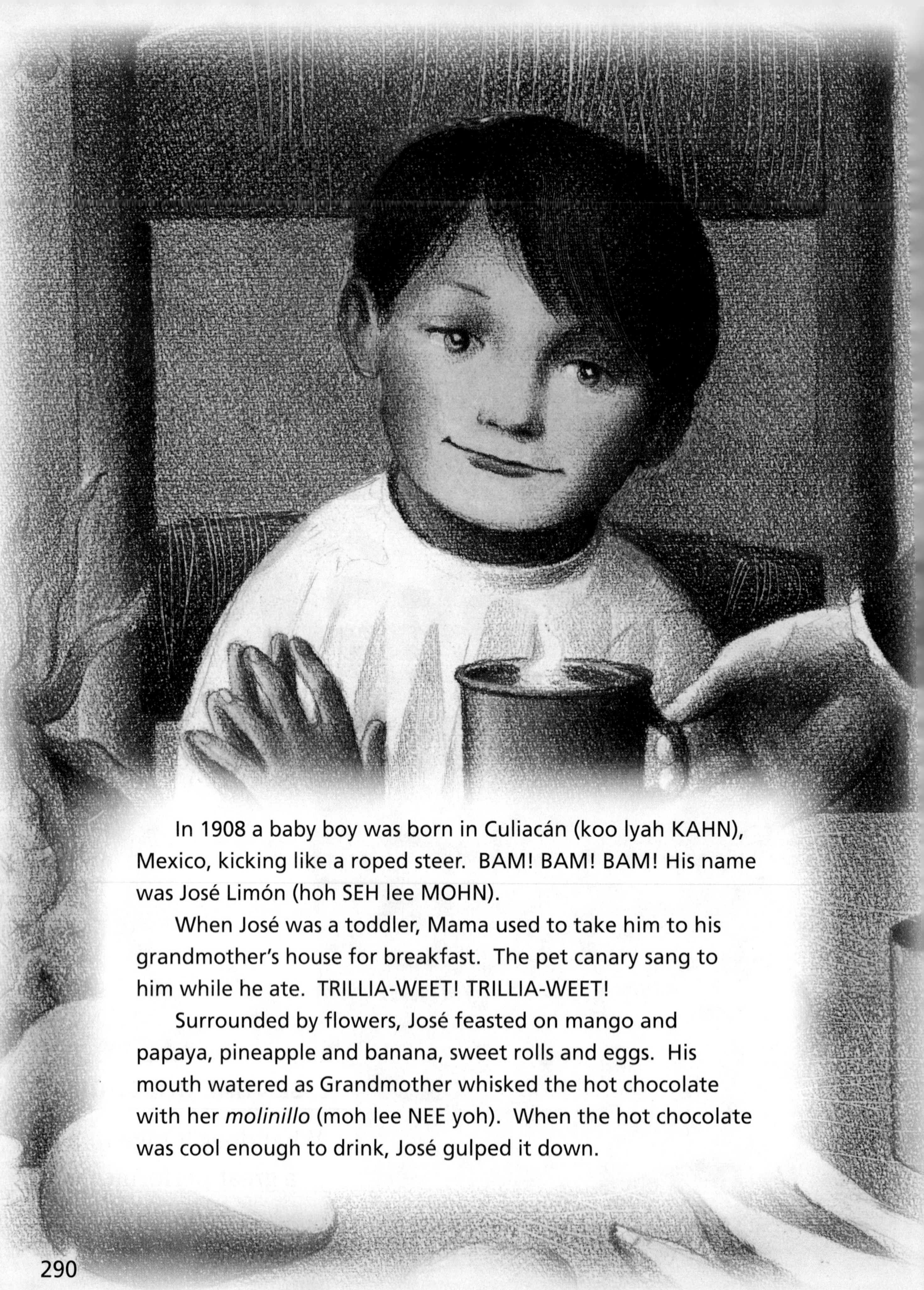

In 1908 a baby boy was born in Culiacán (koo lyah KAHN), Mexico, kicking like a roped steer. BAM! BAM! BAM! His name was José Limón (hoh SEH lee MOHN).

When José was a toddler, Mama used to take him to his grandmother's house for breakfast. The pet canary sang to him while he ate. TRILLIA-WEET! TRILLIA-WEET!

Surrounded by flowers, José feasted on mango and papaya, pineapple and banana, sweet rolls and eggs. His mouth watered as Grandmother whisked the hot chocolate with her *molinillo* (moh lee NEE yoh). When the hot chocolate was cool enough to drink, José gulped it down.

Sometimes Papa took José to the theater where Papa worked as a musician. José loved to watch the dancers on the stage. The cancan dancers lifted their petticoats and kicked their legs. OH LA LA!

The flamenco dancers flipped their skirts and clicked their heels. *¡Sí* (see)*! ¡Sí! ¡Sí!*

The ballet dancers leapt into the air. Raising their arms high above their heads, they seemed to fly. AHHHHH!

One afternoon Papa took José to the *corrida de toros* (koh REE dah deh TOH rohs). In the bullfight ring a torero swirled his red cloak to anger the black bull. *¡Olé* (oh LEH)! *¡Olé! ¡Olé!* The bull pawed the ground. It ran straight toward the bullfighter, its head down and its eyes ablaze. José gripped Papa's hand.

Later that night, when Mama tucked José into bed, her sweet voice echoed in the darkness. SORA-SORA-SO, SORA-SO. That night José dreamed of the bullfight.

One spring day when José was five, he saw government soldiers marching in the street. A civil war had broken out in Mexico. José slung a stick over his shoulder and marched through the house. *¡Uno* (OO noh)! *¡Dos* (dohs)! *¡Uno! ¡Dos!*

The next day at breakfast, shots rang out. The rebels had attacked their town. Surrounded by fighting, José's family hid in the cellar for three days and three nights.

Months passed and the war raged on. Safety lay across the border—in the United States. Perhaps Papa could find a job there.

José's family took a train to Nogales (noh GAH lehs), close to the border. Soldiers sat on top of the train, their guns at the ready. The train crawled through the hot desert. As the sun set, José heard the sound of an accordion—a slow, mournful song. *"O, soñador . . ."* (oh so nyah DOHR)

For two years José and his family lived in Nogales, waiting and waiting for permission to enter the United States. Finally Papa's work permit arrived, stamped with an official seal. They packed their bags and set out across the northern frontier. *Adiós* (ah DYOHS), Mexico.

At José's new school the children gathered around the teacher to read aloud from their books. When José read, the other children laughed at his poor English. At first José cried. Then he stamped his foot in fierce determination. PUM!

I will learn this language better than any of you, he said to himself—though it seemed nearly impossible.

But within three years José could speak English with confidence. He was quick to learn new words and translated for Mama wherever she went. *Carmesí* (kahr meh SEE). *Radiante* (rah DYAHN teh). *Liberación* (lee beh rah SYON). Crimson. Radiant. Liberation.

By sixth grade José had become known for his colorful drawings. Among his many younger brothers and sisters he was famous for his pictures of trains. Everyone thought he would become an artist.

But José loved music, too. As a teenager he practiced the piano at all hours of the day and night. When his fingers flew, his spirit soared. AHH!

After José finished high school in Los Angeles, Mama became very sick. When she died, sadness lay on José's heart.

He went to work in a factory. All day long he took tiles from one wheelbarrow and loaded them into another. At night he dreamed of painting and drawing. He dreamed of living in New York among the artists. But he didn't know if Papa could manage without him.

José waited, and brooded, and argued with himself. Finally, after a year, he made up his mind. "Papa," he announced, "I'm going."

Adiós, José. Farewell.

He headed east across the continent, two thousand four hundred and sixty-two miles.

When José reached New York, the shimmering city towered above him: marble, stone, brick, and steel. José floated down the sidewalk. He would become a great artist, *un artista grandioso y magnífico*. He would fill his sketchbooks with drawings like none the world had ever seen.

He took a job as a janitor, scooping ashes out of a coal furnace and hauling garbage cans to the curb. But as winter wore on, a cold loneliness settled over José. He missed his family, far away in sunny California.

Discouraged, he wandered the halls of the great museums. *Manet* (muh NAY), *Renoir* (ruhn WAHR), *and Picasso* (pih KAH soh), he thought. Perhaps they had already painted everything. His drawings would never compare. The music in his heart fell silent.

"New York is a cemetery," he said. "A jungle of stone."

José put away his drawings. He felt sad and lost. How could he be an artist without an art? He wanted to give a gift to the world, but he didn't know what it could be.

One day José's friend Charlotte invited him to a dance concert. The dancer twisted his body and leapt into the air. AIEEEEE!

ANALYZE THE TEXT

Simile and Metaphor A **simile** and a **metaphor** both compare one thing to something entirely different. A simile uses the words *like* or *as***.** One example of a metaphor is *New York is a jungle of stone*. Find another one on this page and explain what it means.

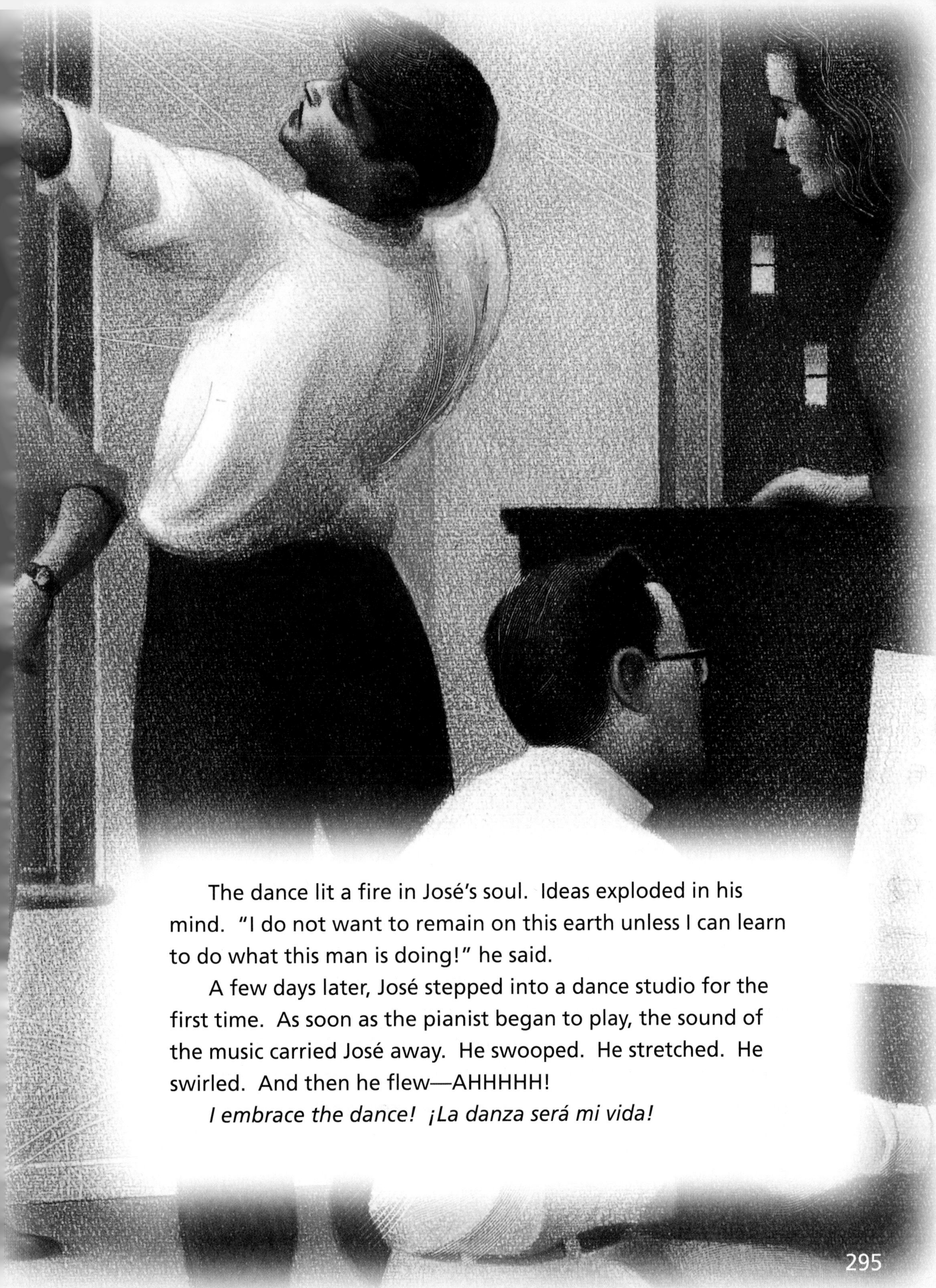

The dance lit a fire in José's soul. Ideas exploded in his mind. "I do not want to remain on this earth unless I can learn to do what this man is doing!" he said.

A few days later, José stepped into a dance studio for the first time. As soon as the pianist began to play, the sound of the music carried José away. He swooped. He stretched. He swirled. And then he flew—AHHHHH!

I embrace the dance! ¡La danza será mi vida!

From then on, José took classes from teachers Doris Humphrey and Charles Weidman (WYD muhn) nearly every day. Dripping with sweat, he struggled with his stiff and stubborn body. And at night he hobbled home, his muscles sore and aching.

Six weeks later, he made his debut (day BYOO), performing for the first time. As he waited to go onstage, he felt shy and nervous. All those people in the audience would be watching him.

But once he heard the thundering applause, his spirits lifted. "That night I tasted undreamed-of exaltation, humility, and triumph," he said.

Ankles and feet, knees and hips, chest and arms, head and neck, up and down and back and forth and in and out, José Limón became a dancer.

For eleven years José studied and danced with Doris and Charles. He learned to make his muscles sing. He learned to move his bones every which way. He learned to flow and float and fly through space with steps smooth as silk. He learned to be fierce like a bullfighter—*¡Olé!* Strong like a soldier—*¡Uno! ¡Dos! ¡Uno! ¡Dos!* And proud like a king—PUM!

He learned to make dances sweet as birdsong—TRILLIA-WEET! Hot as the desert sun—*¡Sí! ¡Sí!* Sad as broken dreams—*O, soñador . . .* Loving as a mother's lullaby floating on a Mexican breeze—SORA-SORA-SO, SORA-SO.

In time José became a world-famous choreographer and toured the globe with his own dance company. For forty years, with bare feet and broad shoulders, he graced the concert stage. From New York to Mexico City and London to Buenos Aires (BWEH nohs EYE rehs), he danced for presidents and princesses, builders and bricklayers, bankers and bus drivers, fiddlers and firemen.

ANALYZE THE TEXT

Biography In what order are the events of José's life told? What signal words indicate this structure?

And each night before the curtain rose, he whispered to himself, "Make me strong so I can give."

BRAVO! BRAVO! BRAVO!

ANALYZE THE TEXT

Author's Purpose Explain what the author wants you to learn from José's story. What is her perspective? What reasons and evidence does the author provide to support her perspective?

COMPREHENSION

Dig Deeper

How to Analyze the Text

Use these pages to learn about Author's Purpose, Biography, and Simile and Metaphor. Then read "José! Born to Dance" again to apply what you learned.

Author's Purpose

"José! Born to Dance" is about a famous dancer and choreographer. What do you think the **author's purpose,** or reason, was for writing this biography? Does she want to entertain, to inform, or to persuade? To answer these questions, think about how the author seems to feel about José Limón. Note the particular points the author makes about José and how he reacts to what happens to him. Notice the **reasons** and **evidence** the author uses to support her ideas.

You can use text evidence to help you identify the author's purpose and how the author supports it. Look back at pages 294–295. What details does the author use to describe the dancer and to tell what José thought?

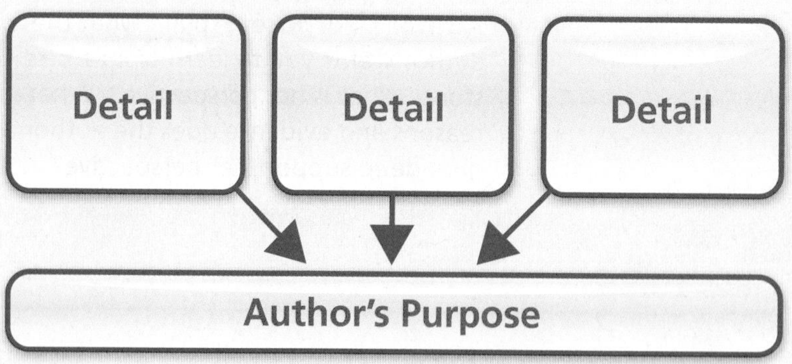

ELACC4RI5 describe the overall structure of a text or part of a text; **ELACC4RI8** explain how an author uses reasons and evidence to support points; **ELACC4L5a** explain the meaning of similes and metaphors in context

Biography

The way in which an author organizes a text is its **overall structure.** In a **biography,** the events that make up a person's life are usually told in the order they happened. Authors use dates and **signal words** to help readers follow the **sequence of events.** For example, on page 291 the author uses the phrases *One afternoon, Later that night,* and *One spring day*. These phrases help explain when events take place.

Simile and Metaphor

A **simile** is a kind of **figurative language** that compares two things that are different, using the word *like* or *as*. *The baby kicked like a wild horse* is a simile. A **metaphor** compares one thing to something entirely different without using *like* or *as*. *The dancer was a painted butterfly* is a metaphor. Authors use similes and metaphors to create vivid pictures and help readers see things in new ways.

Your Turn

RETURN TO THE ESSENTIAL QUESTION

Turn and Talk Review the selection with a partner to prepare to discuss this question: *What does it take to be a great performer?* Include text evidence and other reasons to support your ideas. Be sure not to interrupt your partner.

Classroom Conversation

Continue your discussion of "José! Born to Dance" by explaining your answers to these questions:

1. What do you think made José finally tell Papa that he was leaving?
2. What character traits help José become a success? Explain.
3. Before each performance José says, "Make me strong so that I can give." What is he giving?

MAKING COMPARISONS

Analyze Similes and Metaphors Authors use figurative language such as similes and metaphors to create vivid pictures in readers' minds. With a partner, page through the biography and find examples of figurative language. List three similes and three metaphors the author uses to describe José and his dancing. Discuss the meaning of each example.

WRITE ABOUT READING

Response Write a list of questions that you would like to ask José Limón about his life. Then search the text for clues about what José might tell a young person, based on his own experience. Write a short note explaining what he might say. Include a reason based on the text for each piece of advice.

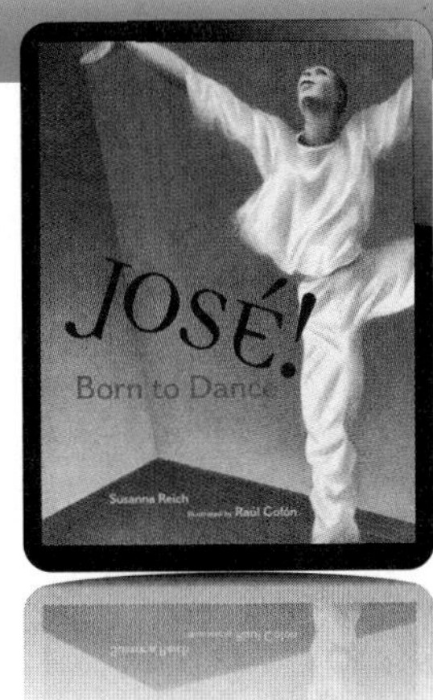

Writing Tip

Be sure to end your note with a strong concluding statement that summarizes the advice. Correct any sentence fragments you may have written in your note.

COMMON CORE **ELACC4RI8** explain how an author uses reasons and evidence to support points; **ELACC4W1b** provide reasons supported by facts and details; **ELACC4W9b** apply grade 4 Reading standards to informational texts; **ELACC4SL1b** follow rules for discussions; **ELACC4L1f** produce complete sentences, recognizing and connecting fragments and run-ons; **ELACC4L5a** explain the meaning of similes and metaphors in context

Lesson 10

POETRY

 GENRE

Poetry uses the sound and rhythm of words to suggest images and express feelings.

 TEXT FOCUS

Structure of a Poem
Poems are arranged in lines. The lines are often grouped into verses or stanzas. Which poems have verses? Rhythm, the regular pattern of stress in words, is part of the sound and tone of poems. As you read, note how the rhythm is different in each poem. How does the rhythm affect each poem?

ELACC4RL5 explain major differences between poems, drama, and prose/refer to their structural elements; **ELACC4RL10** read and comprehend literature

dance to the beat

by Adam Fogelberg

Dancers move their bodies to the beat, or rhythm, of music. Poems are like music and dance: They, too, have rhythm. As you read the following three poems about dancing, listen for their rhythm.

The Song of the Night

I dance to the tune
of the stars and the moon.
I dance to the song of the night.

I dance to the strains
of a cricket's refrain.
I dance to the fireflies' light.

I dance to the breeze
and the whispering trees.
I dance to the meteor's flight.

I dance to the beat
of the summertime heat.
I dance to the pulse of the night.

by Leslie D. Perkins

from Lines Written for Gene Kelly to Dance To

Can you dance a question mark?
Can you dance an exclamation point?
Can you dance a couple of commas?
And bring it to a finish with a period?

Can you dance like the wind is pushing you?
Can you dance like you are pushing the wind?
Can you dance with slow wooden heels
  and then change to bright and singing silver heels?
Such nice feet, such good feet.

by Carl Sandburg

Gene Kelly (1912–1996)

Gene Kelly was a famous actor, dancer, and director. He was born in Pittsburgh, Pennsylvania, in 1912. As a child he was small, and his peers towered above him. He wanted to become a professional athlete, but his mother would not give him permission. Instead of being discouraged, Kelly became a dancer. He ran a dancing school and toured with shows.

In 1938, he crossed the Pennsylvania border and headed to New York City. That year he made his Broadway debut.

During his career, Kelly enjoyed one triumph after another. He starred and danced in many movies.

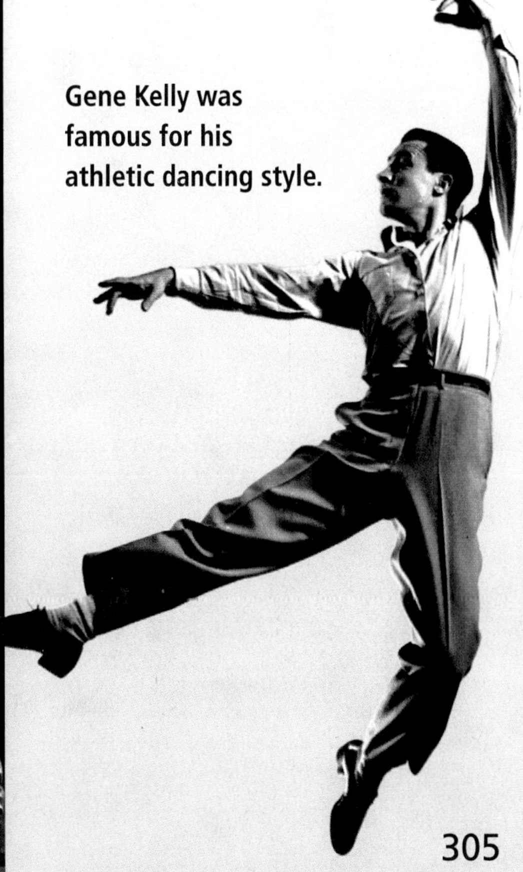

Gene Kelly was famous for his athletic dancing style.

Adapted from Three/Quarters Time

Dance with me . . . dance with me . . . we are the song . . . we are the music . . .
Dance with me . . .
Dance with me . . . dance with me . . . all night long . . .
We are the music . . . we are the song . . .

by Nikki Giovanni

Write a **Dance Poem**

How do you dance? Does your body feel like it is hauling a ton of bricks? Are your feet stubborn? Do they refuse to move, or do they glide across the floor? How does the music make you feel? Are you mournful or overjoyed? Express your feelings about dance in a poem.

Compare Texts

TEXT TO TEXT

Compare Dance Texts Each poem in "Dance to the Beat" talks about dancing in a different way. Reread each poem carefully. Find one that makes you think of José Limón. Then write a paragraph that explains why this poem reminds you of José Limón. Remember to state your opinion in the beginning. Include text evidence from both pieces to support your opinion.

TEXT TO SELF

Creative Interests José Limón drew, painted, and played piano before discovering dance. Write a paragraph about *your* main creative interest. Explain why you enjoy that activity.

TEXT TO WORLD

The World of Dance There are many different styles of dance, such as ballroom, ballet, tap, and jazz. With a partner, use online sources or reference texts to make a list of dance styles. Then write a brief description of one dance style.

ELACC4W1b provide reasons supported by facts and details; **ELACC4W2a** introduce a topic and group related information/include formatting, illustrations, and multimedia; **ELACC4W8** recall information from experiences or gather information from print and digital sources/take notes, categorize information, and provide a list of sources

Grammar

What Is a Pronoun? A **pronoun** is a word, such as *he* or *they*, that takes the place of one or more nouns. An **antecedent** is the noun or nouns that the pronoun replaces. A pronoun should agree with its antecedent in number and gender. A **reflexive pronoun's** antecedent is the subject of the sentence. It ends with *-self* or *-selves*. *This*, *that*, *these*, and *those* are **demonstrative pronouns**. *This* is used to talk about one thing that is nearby. *That* is for one thing that is far away. *These* and *those* are for more than one thing.

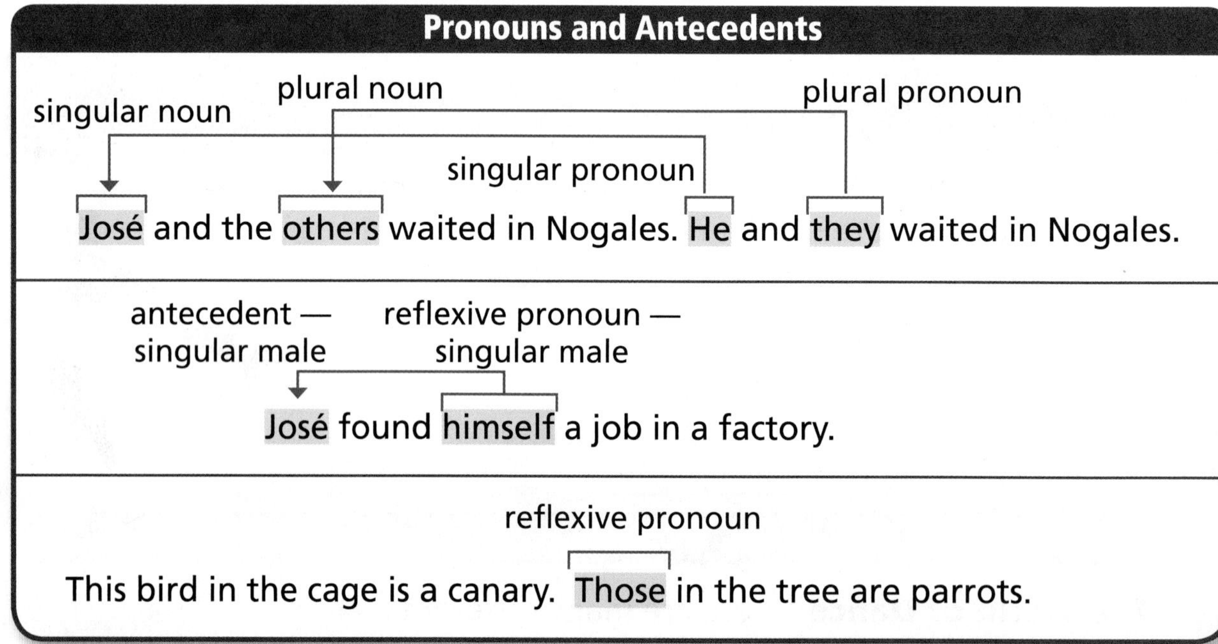

Pronouns and Antecedents
singular noun
plural noun
plural pronoun
singular pronoun
José and the others waited in Nogales. He and they waited in Nogales.
antecedent — singular male
reflexive pronoun — singular male
José found himself a job in a factory.
reflexive pronoun
This bird in the cage is a canary. Those in the tree are parrots.

Try This! **With a partner, find the pronoun and antecedent in each sentence. Is the pronoun reflexive? Is it demonstrative?**

1. José made himself a promise in New York.
2. Charlotte pleased José when she invited him to a show.
3. This dancer lit a fire in José's soul.

To make your writing flow smoothly, you can use pronouns to help combine sentences. If two choppy sentences tell about the same noun, try replacing one of the nouns with a pronoun. Then you can combine the two sentences without repeating the noun.

Separate Sentences

The ballet dancers twirled.

The ballet dancers raised their arms above their heads.

Complex Sentence

When the ballet dancers twirled, they raised their arms above their heads.

Separate sentences:	Michael twisted his body. Then Michael jumped into the air.
Complex Sentence:	After Michael twisted his body, he jumped into the air.

Connect Grammar to Writing

As you revise your explanatory essay, look for short, choppy sentences that repeat a noun. Try combining these sentences and replacing the noun with a pronoun.

ELACC4W2a introduce a topic and group related information/include formatting, illustrations, and multimedia; **ELACC4W2b** develop the topic with facts, definitions, details, quotations, or other information and examples; **ELACC4W2d** use precise language and domain-specific vocabulary; **ELACC4W2e** provide a concluding statement or section; **ELACC4L3a** choose words and phrases to convey ideas precisely

Informative Writing

Reading-Writing Workshop: Revise

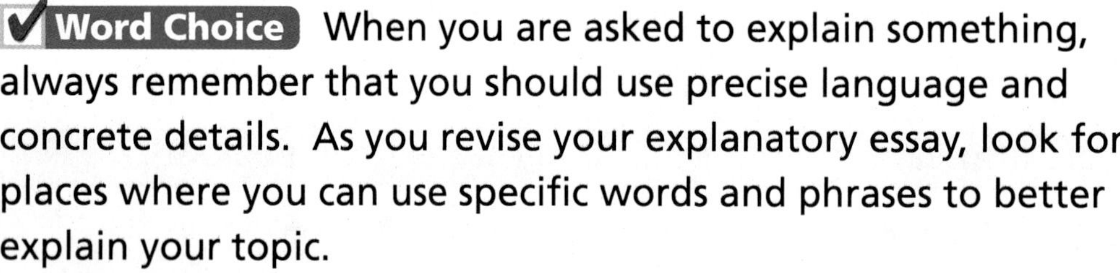

Word Choice When you are asked to explain something, always remember that you should use precise language and concrete details. As you revise your explanatory essay, look for places where you can use specific words and phrases to better explain your topic.

Trudy drafted her essay to include facts and details to clearly explain how to care for canaries. Later, she added a beginning sentence to get her readers' attention. Use the Writing Process Checklist as you revise your own writing.

Writing Process Checklist

- Prewrite
- Draft
- ▶ **Revise**
  - ✔ **Do I have an introduction, body, and conclusion?**
  - ✔ **Does my essay address my audience and purpose?**
  - ✔ **Does my introduction get my readers' attention?**
  - ✔ **Do I provide facts and details as support?**
- Edit
- Publish and Share

Revised Draft

Have you ever considered having a canary as a pet? These small, gentle birds are famous for their beautiful singing voices. ~~It is also~~ They are also easy to care for and make great companions.

According to World Book Online, canaries are one of the most popular kinds of birds that people choose as pets. Many people love their colors, ranging from pale yellow to bright yellow or green.

Final Copy

Caring for Pet Canaries

by Trudy Delgado

Have you ever considered having a canary as a pet? These small, gentle birds are famous for their beautiful singing voices. They are also easy to care for and make great companions.

According to World Book Online, canaries are one of the most popular kinds of birds that people choose as pets. Many people love their colors, ranging from pale yellow to bright yellow or green. If the canaries are fed red peppers, they tend to be bright orange.

One kind of canary, called a roller, produces a long, rolling musical sound. Other kinds of canaries are named for the different sounds they produce or for their unusual appearance. French canaries are covered with curly feathers.

When they are happy, canaries will produce some new songs and can live as long as ten years or more. Cages should be cleaned regularly. In addition, they need water for drinking and bathing as well as canary seed and greens to eat.

Many people have canaries as pets because they enjoy the birds' songs and cheerful personalities. Their tiny size, easy care, and gentleness can make them ideal pets.

Reading as a Writer

Why did Trudy need to add a sentence at the beginning? What will you say at the beginning of your explanation?

I used a question to get my reader's attention. I used concrete details to clearly explain my topic.

Read the passage "Ethan and the Finches." As you read, stop and answer each question using text evidence.

Ethan and the Finches

Mr. Wooster gave Ethan's class a new science assignment. "First, each of you needs to find a bird's nest and describe it in your science journals. Then draw a picture of the bird that built the nest. Use the picture to help you research the bird so you can identify it. Finally, you need to go back to the nest every day for two weeks to observe what is happening in the nest. You will take notes on your observations."

"What a fun assignment!" thought Ethan.

"Remember what we mean by an observation in science," Mr. Wooster said. "In everyday life, you might observe that your friend is crossing the street. When you make an observation in science, you should note details. For a scientific observation, you would tell exactly what your friend looks like and describe the clothes your friend is wearing. You would observe in which direction your friend is crossing the street, how much traffic there is, and whether there are other people around. You might also make notes about the weather and anything else you think is important. In other words, pay close attention and include details!"

1 What is the setting at the beginning of this passage? What is the first event?

Ethan eagerly began looking for a nest as soon as he got off the bus. There were only a few trees growing near the sidewalk, and none of them had nests in them. As Ethan walked along the path to his apartment building, he looked carefully at each tree and shrub. He still had no luck, though, and his eagerness about the assignment was beginning to fade a bit.

COMMON CORE **ELACC4RL1** refer to details and examples when explaining what the text says explicitly and when drawing inferences; **ELACC4RL2** determine theme from details/summarize; **ELACC4RL3** describe a character, setting, or event, drawing on details

He could hear plenty of birds, but he couldn't see them. They were chirping and twittering in the park across the street. Ethan guessed he'd have to go there to find a nest. Since he and his family had moved here a few months ago, Ethan had gone to the park only a few times. It was nice there, but he didn't know any of the kids. He'd just stood and watched while other kids were shooting baskets or playing games with their friends. They were having fun, but Ethan wasn't. He hadn't been back to the park lately.

Inside, Ethan went straight to his bedroom and threw down his backpack. He thought maybe he would put off until tomorrow going to the park to look for a nest. But then he decided he might as well go now and get it over with. He sighed and took his science journal out of his backpack.

 How does Ethan feel about going to the park, and why? Use details from the passage to support your response.

Ethan followed the dirt paths in the park. He had been looking for a while, and had seen several birds. He still hadn't found a nest, though, and he was getting discouraged. Nearby, he could hear and see a baseball game going on. The players were joking with each other and laughing a lot. Ethan loved baseball, but you couldn't play baseball all by yourself.

As Ethan turned to continue along the path, a small movement caught his eye. He moved in that direction for a closer look. Soon he came to a small, sturdy tree with a low-hanging branch. And on the branch Ethan spotted a bird's nest. He began to scribble notes in his science journal.

The oval-shaped nest was made of dried grass and twigs. Ethan could see a tiny egg inside it. The egg was very light blue, almost white, with a few black specks on it. There was no sign of the bird that had laid the egg. Ethan waited and watched until it was time to go home for dinner. Even though he hadn't seen an actual bird yet, he was excited about his discovery.

After school the next day, Ethan hurried to the park to check on the nest. He found a small brown bird sitting in it and a second bird perched beside it. The two birds looked very similar, except that one had a black streak on its white throat. Ethan wrote a description and drew pictures of the birds in his science journal.

 What conclusions can you draw about how and why Ethan's feelings have changed since the beginning of the passage?

"Hi," said a voice behind him. "What are you doing?" Ethan turned and saw a boy about his age watching him. He explained about his assignment and pointed out the nest. The boy told Ethan his name was Henry. "Those birds are house finches," he said. When Ethan got home, he looked up *house finch* in an online encyclopedia, and Henry was right. The bird with the black streak on its throat was the male, and the other bird was a female.

Ethan continued to watch the nest and record his observations. Sometimes Henry stopped by to watch, too. One day, as Ethan came near the nest, he heard a high-pitched chirp. A tiny bill was sticking out of the nest, and a baby bird's mouth was wide open. Ethan couldn't wait to tell Henry!

Ethan continued watching the nest even after he turned in his assignment. He watched the baby bird grow and begin to make small flights to nearby branches. Then one day it leapt into the air and flew away from the tree into the sky. Just then Ethan heard Henry calling him to come and play ball with him and some of his friends. Many of Henry's friends had become Ethan's friends, too, over the weeks he'd been watching the nest. Ethan knew the young finch would fly away to a new home one day soon. He hoped the bird would make friends and be happy in his new place in the world.

 What lesson has Ethan learned at the end of the passage?

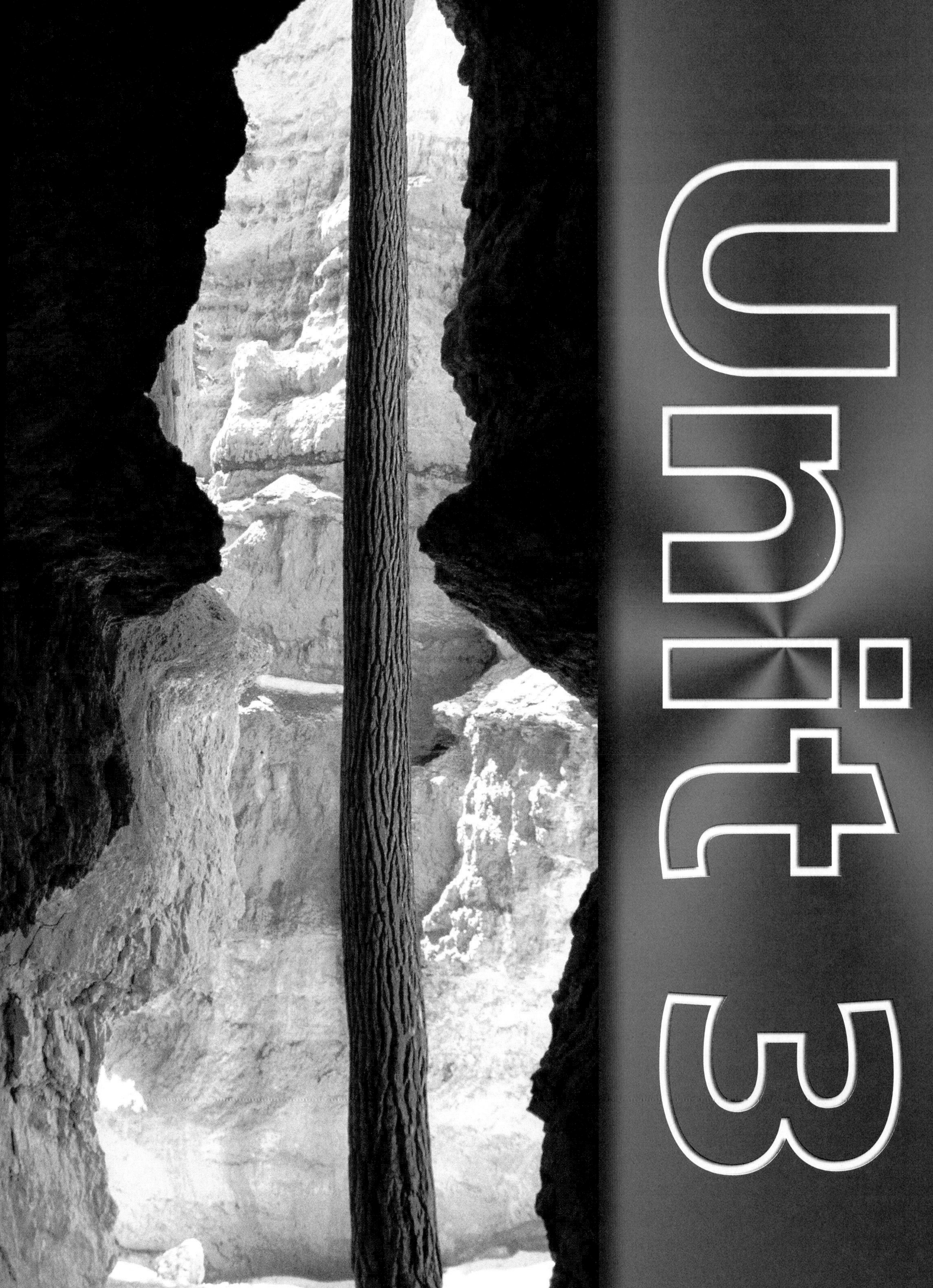
Unit 3

Lesson

11

HURRICANES

Earth's Mightiest Storms

Recovering from KATRINA

Vocabulary in Context

☑ TARGET VOCABULARY

whirling
rapidly
condense
source
rotating
rage
experience
ancient
predict
registered

Vocabulary Reader

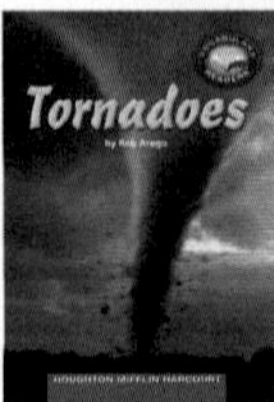

Context Cards

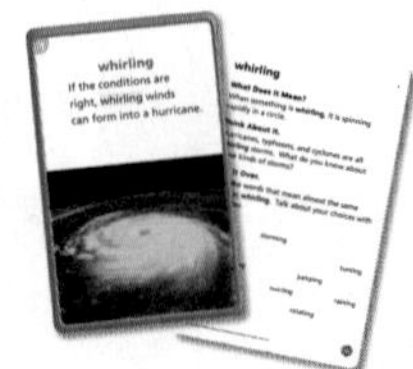

ELACC4L6 acquire/use vocabulary, including academic and domain-specific

1 whirling

If the conditions are right, whirling winds can form into a hurricane.

2 rapidly

The hot air balloon rose rapidly, or very fast, into the air.

3 condense

Water droplets will condense on the outside of a cold glass on a hot day.

4 source

Tiny water droplets are the source for forming clouds.

- Study each Context Card.
- Use context clues to determine the meanings of these words.

5 rotating

The Earth is always rotating. It never stops turning.

6 rage

Winds rage during a hurricane. They never seem to stop.

7 experience

Some places experience a lot of damage from hurricanes.

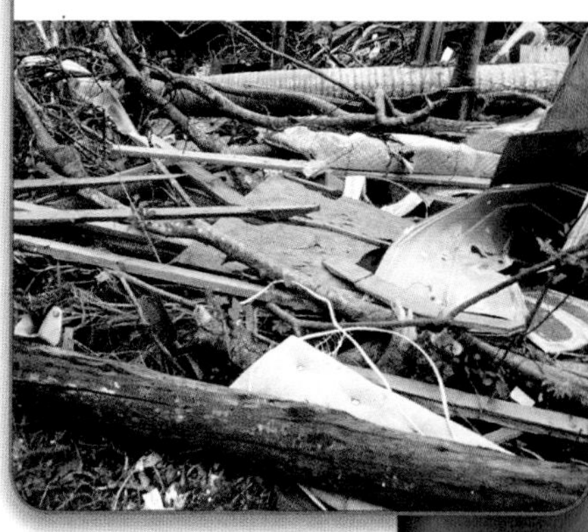

8 ancient

The ancient Greeks, who lived long ago, had storms during the summer and fall.

9 predict

People try to predict the weather, but often it is hard to know what the weather will do.

10 registered

This anemometer recorded wind speeds near a tornado. It registered high winds.

Read and Comprehend

TARGET SKILL

Text and Graphic Features As you read "Hurricanes: Earth's Mightiest Storms," look for **text features**, such as headings and captions, and for **graphic features** such as charts and diagrams. These features help you better understand the text's topic and provide factual information to add to your knowledge. Use a graphic organizer like the one below to record each text or graphic feature, where it is located, and the information it provides.

Text or Graphic Feature	Page Number	Information
•	•	•
•	•	•
•	•	•

TARGET STRATEGY

Infer/Predict When you make an **inference** or a **prediction**, you use text evidence and information from graphic features to figure out something the author does not state directly. Use facts and details in "Hurricanes" to help you make inferences and predictions about these ferocious storms and their effects.

COMMON CORE

ELACC4RI1 refer to details and examples when explaining what the text says explicitly and when drawing inferences;
ELACC4RI7 interpret information presented visually, orally, or quantitatively

PREVIEW THE TOPIC

Hurricanes

Hurricanes, which feature raging winds and pounding rain, are the biggest and deadliest storms on earth. The study of weather, including hurricanes, is part of earth science. Earth scientists study our planet's origin and features, including air, water, and weather.

As you read "Hurricanes: Earth's Mightiest Storms," you'll learn how wind, air temperature, and moisture interact to create one of the world's most awesome weather events.

Lesson 11

ANCHOR TEXT

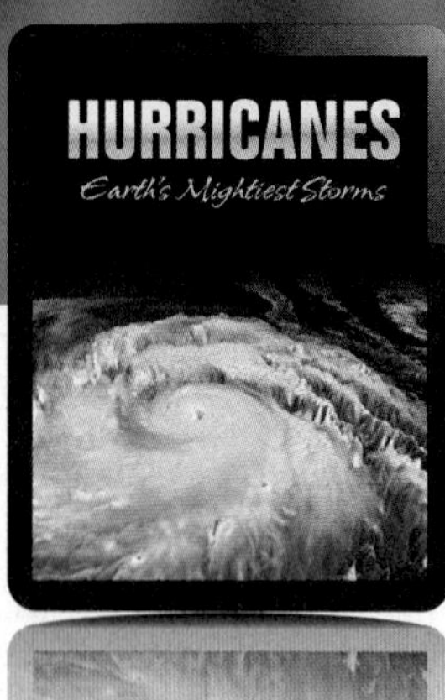

 TARGET SKILL

Text and Graphic Features
Identify text and graphic features. Explain how they help you understand the topic and what new information they add.

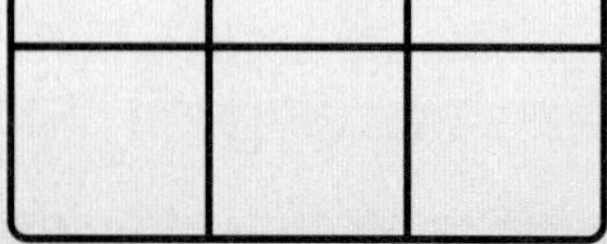

 GENRE

Informational text gives facts and examples about a topic. As you read, look for:

- headings that begin sections of related information
- features that give specific information about the topic, such as maps, diagrams, and charts

ELACC4RI3 explain events/procedures/concepts in a text; **ELACC4RI5** describe the overall structure of a text or part of a text; **ELACC4RI7** interpret information presented visually, orally, or quantitatively

 Go Digital

MEET THE AUTHOR

Patricia Lauber

Patricia Lauber said, "I was born wanting to write." And write she did! Patricia wrote over 125 children's books, many of them nonfiction texts on topics ranging from volcanoes to the history of eating utensils. Asked why she wrote so many science books, she said she believed that everyone, not just scientists, should know about the world around them.

HURRICANES

Earth's Mightiest Storms

by Patricia Lauber

ESSENTIAL QUESTION

What are the benefits of studying weather?

The Making of a Hurricane

Great whirling storms roar out of the oceans in many parts of the world. They are called by several names—hurricane, typhoon, and cyclone are the three most familiar ones. But no matter what they are called, they are all the same sort of storm. They are born the same way, in tropical waters. They develop the same way, feeding on warm, moist air. And they do the same kind of damage, both ashore and at sea. Other storms may cover a bigger area or have higher winds, but none can match both the size and the fury of hurricanes. They are earth's mightiest storms.

Like all storms, they take place in the atmosphere, the envelope of air that surrounds the earth and presses on its surface. The pressure at any one place is always changing. There are days when air is sinking and the atmosphere presses harder on the surface. These are times of high pressure. There are days when a lot of air is rising and the atmosphere does not press down as hard. These are times of low pressure. Low-pressure areas over warm oceans give birth to hurricanes.

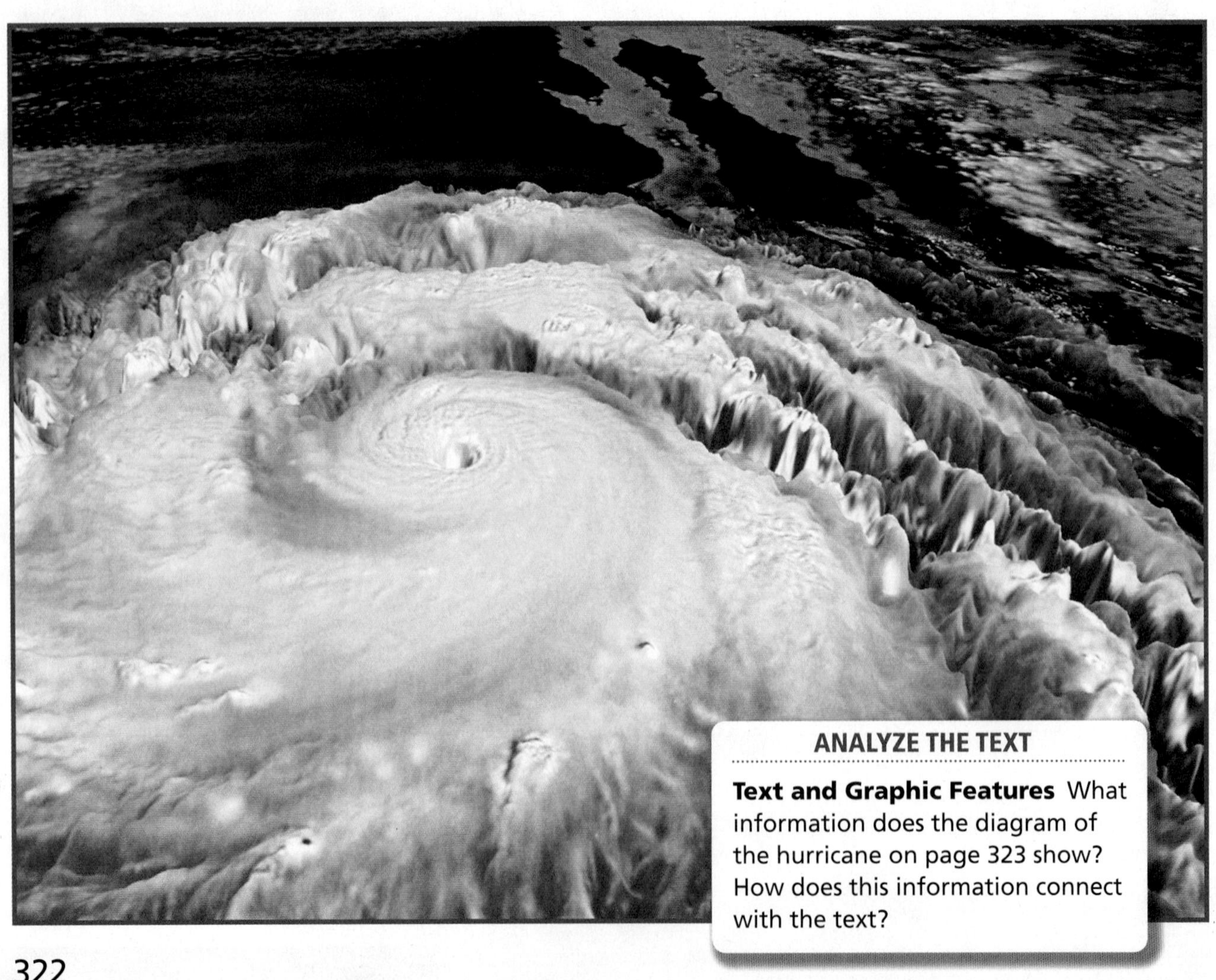

ANALYZE THE TEXT

Text and Graphic Features What information does the diagram of the hurricane on page 323 show? How does this information connect with the text?

No one knows exactly what happens to start these storms. But when conditions are right, warm, moist air is set in motion. It begins to rise rapidly from the surface of the ocean in a low-pressure area.

Like water in a hose, air flows from where there is more pressure to where there is less pressure. And so air over the surface of the ocean flows into the low-pressure area, picking up moisture as it travels. This warm, moist air soars upward.

As the air rises above the earth, it cools. The cooling causes moisture to condense into tiny droplets of water that form clouds. As the moisture condenses, it gives off heat. Heat is one kind of energy. It is the energy that powers the storm. The clouds are the source of the storm's rain.

BIRTH OF A HURRICANE: Warm, moist air flows into a low-pressure area. As the air rises and condenses into clouds, more warm air is drawn over the surface of the ocean. It spirals upwards, traveling counterclockwise. Clusters of thunderstorms form.

The low-pressure area acts like a chimney—warm air is drawn in at the bottom, rises in a column, cools, and spreads out. As the air inside rises and more air is drawn in, the storm grows.

The air being drawn in, however, does not travel in a straight line. The earth's surface is rotating, and the rotation causes the path to curve. The air travels in a spiral within the storm. In the Northern Hemisphere, the spiraling winds travel counterclockwise—the opposite of the way the hands on a clock move. In the Southern Hemisphere, they travel clockwise.

Most of these storms die out within hours or days of their birth. Only about one out of ten grows into a hurricane.

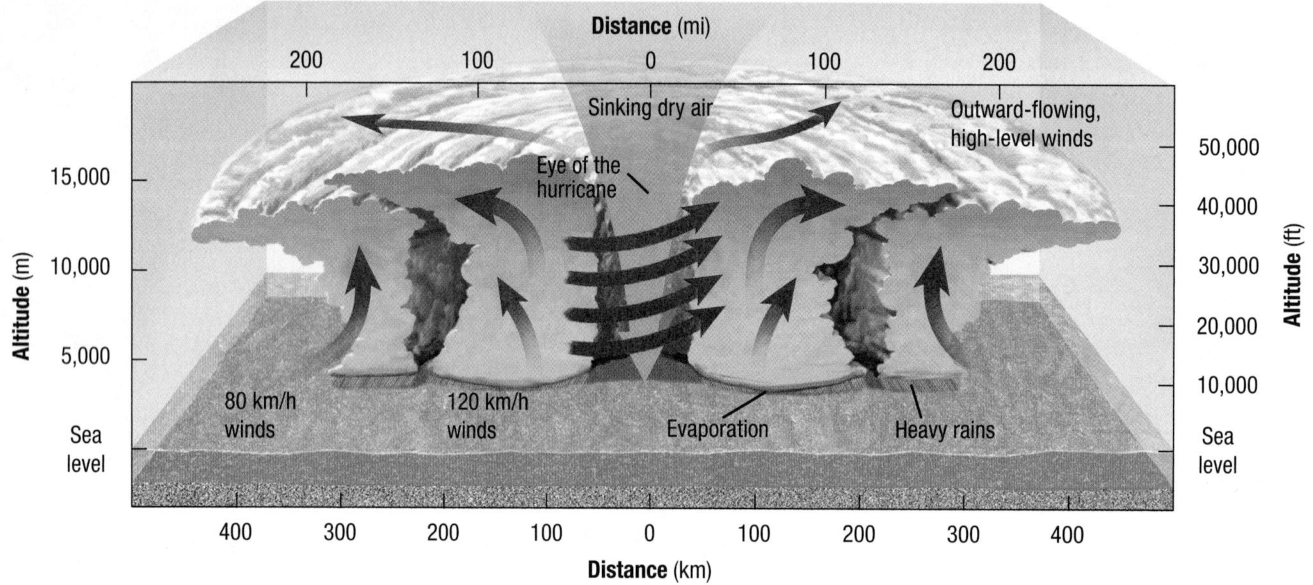

INSIDE A HURRICANE: High winds spiral around the eye, but within the eye all is calm. Air pressure within the eye is extremely low. Because there is less pressure on it than on surrounding areas, the sea under the hurricane rises in a bulge, or dome.

ANALYZE THE TEXT

Text Structure What causes a hurricane to grow? How does the structure of the text help you understand how a hurricane is born and how it grows?

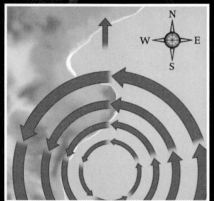

If hurricane winds first blow from the east, they will blow from the west after the eye has passed.

As high winds develop, air pressure falls rapidly at the center of the storm. This low-pressure area is called the eye, and it may be ten to 20 miles across. The eye is a hole that reaches from bottom to top of the storm. Winds rage around the hole, but within it all is calm. Winds are light. The air is clear, with blue sky or scattered clouds and sunshine above. People caught in a hurricane may suddenly experience calm air and dry skies. Sometimes they make the mistake of thinking the storm has ended, but it hasn't. The eye moves on and the second half of the storm arrives, with winds blowing from the opposite direction.

Some Weather Instruments

Ancient peoples lived through great storms. They looked for signs that would help them predict the weather. They tried to explain the weather they experienced. But no one can really study weather without measuring what is happening. The instruments to make such measurements were invented three to four hundred years ago. Modern versions of them are still used today.

BAROMETER

A barometer measures air pressure. Rising air pressure tells of fair weather, while falling air pressure tells of stormy weather. This kind of barometer is often seen in homes and schools.

HYGROMETER

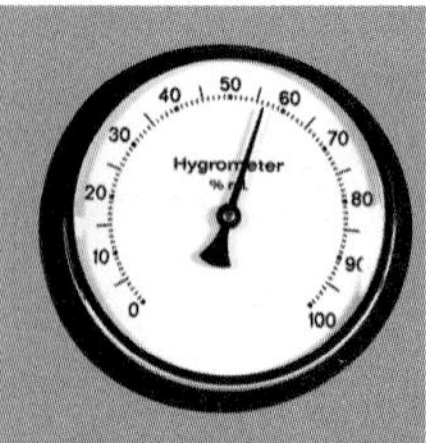

A hygrometer measures the amount of moisture in the air: the humidity. Warm air can hold more moisture, or water vapor, than cool or cold air. When warm, moist air is cooled, water vapor condenses, changing from a gas to a liquid. That is why a glass of ice-cold soda seems to sweat in the summer—warm air around the glass is chilled and water vapor condenses out of it onto the glass.

ANEMOMETER

An anemometer measures wind speed. The rate at which its blades spin outdoors is registered on a dial indoors. In the 1938 hurricane and other violent storms, anemometers have blown away, making it hard to tell what the highest wind speeds were.

THERMOMETER

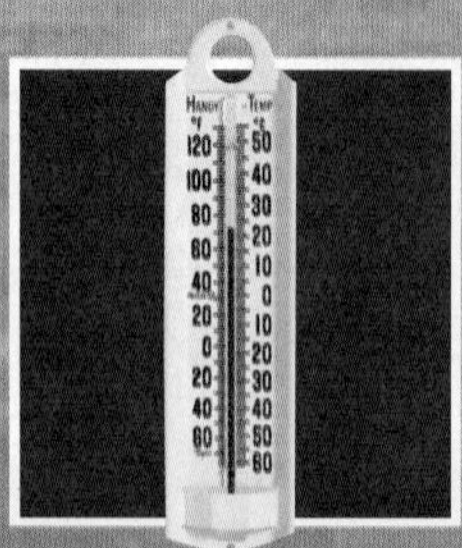

A thermometer measures temperature.

World Names

In the Caribbean Sea and North Atlantic, earth's mightiest storms are called *hurricanes*, after a Carib Indian word for "big wind." In the Pacific they are also called hurricanes if they occur east of the international dateline. West of the dateline they are called *typhoons*, from Chinese words for "great wind." In the Indian Ocean they are called *cyclones*, an English name based on a Greek word meaning "coil," as in "coil of a snake," because of the winds that spiral within them. The storms also have a number of local names. Many Australians, for example, call them *willy-willies*. The name probably began as "whirlwind," which became "whirly-whirly," which became "willy-willy."

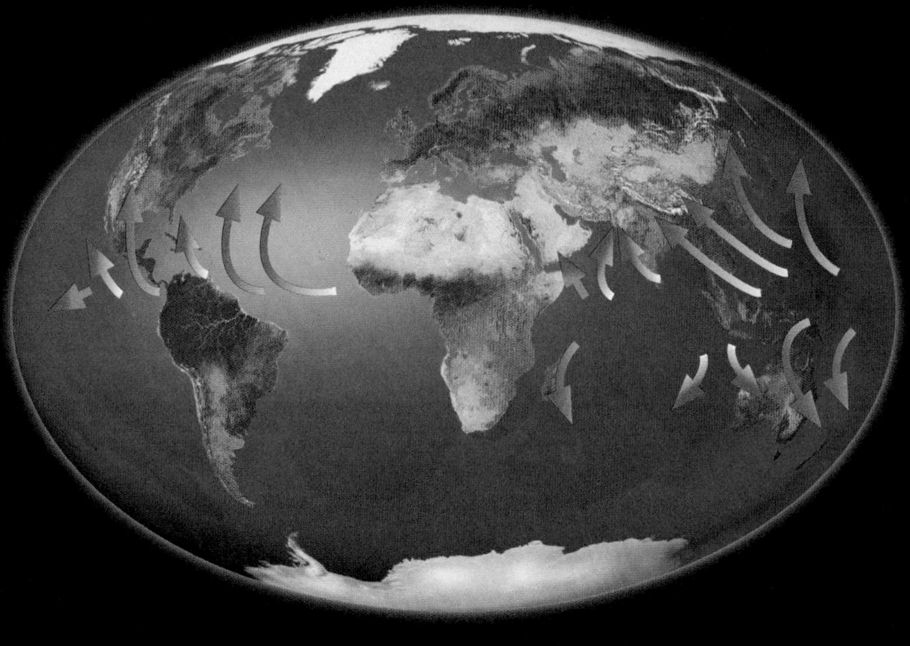

Earth's mightiest storms take shape over tropical waters. All move westward at first, then either die out over land or turn eastward, losing power over cooler ocean waters. For some reason, these storms do not form in the South Atlantic or southeast Pacific oceans.

Into the Eye of the Storm

Today rugged planes carry many instruments into hurricanes as they near land. The instruments measure winds, temperatures, and humidity. They measure the water content of clouds. They photograph the inside of hurricanes. They record radar images of the storms.

In April 1960, the first weather satellite rocketed into orbit. Now scientists hoped to find and track tropical storms before they neared land. They were rewarded almost at once. A few days after its launching, the satellite discovered a typhoon in the South Pacific.

Satellite instruments do not see into the heart of a hurricane—that work is still done by planes. Satellites show the size of the storm and its growth. They show changes in the size of the eye: if the eye is growing bigger, the storm is weakening; if it is growing smaller, the storm is strengthening. Most important, satellites can pinpoint the location of a storm, record its speed, and track it closely.

ANALYZE THE TEXT

Explain Scientific Ideas How have satellites changed scientists' understanding of and ability to predict hurricanes?

Information from ground stations and ships, from hurricane-hunting planes and satellites—forecasters have more information than the human mind can grasp. But since the 1960s, they have been able to feed all this information into computers. Now they can create computer models of hurricanes. They can compare a hurricane with similar ones that occurred years earlier. Forecasting just one storm may involve several million bits of data and several billion mathematical calculations. Huge computers do the work.

Today no one who reads a newspaper, listens to radio, or watches television can be taken by surprise when a hurricane strikes. Although forecasters cannot say exactly where a hurricane will come ashore, they do know which areas will feel the storm. They can warn people in its path, as they did with Andrew in the summer of 1992.

This satellite image shows Tropical Storm Dolly on July 21, 2008.

COMPREHENSION

Dig Deeper

How to Analyze the Text

Use these pages to learn about Text and Graphic Features, Explaining Scientific Ideas, and Text Structure. Then read "Hurricanes: Earth's Mightiest Storms" again to apply what you learned.

Text and Graphic Features

Informational texts such as "Hurricanes: Earth's Mightiest Storms" often contain text and graphic features to help readers understand complex ideas. **Text features** include headings, captions, and special kinds of type such as boldfaced words. **Graphic features** include diagrams, charts, and maps. Diagrams are pictures that explain how things work. Charts are often lists of facts and details. Maps show where places are and where events occur.

In "Hurricanes," the author includes a diagram in the middle of page 324. The diagram details how air moves inside a hurricane. How do winds move in relation to the eye of the hurricane? How does the diagram add to your understanding of the topic?

Text or Graphic Feature	Page Number	Information
•	•	•
•	•	•
•	•	•

ELACC4RI3 explain events/procedures/ideas/concepts in a text; **ELACC4RI5** describe the overall structure of a text or part of a text; **ELACC4RI7** interpret information presented visually, orally, or quantitatively

Explain Scientific Ideas

If you wanted to explain a **scientific idea** that you read about in a text, how would you begin? Start by rereading the explanation the author gives. Pay attention to the facts and details. Make sure you understand each scientific term. Then check your understanding by silently explaining the idea to yourself. Finally, explain the idea to someone else using your own words.

Text Structure

One way authors organize informational texts is by focusing on causes and effects. An author may state a **cause,** or why something happens. Then the author describes the **effect,** or what happens as a result of that cause. On page 326, the author says no one can study weather without measuring what is happening. Then she explains what happened as a result: people invented instruments to help them measure wind speed, temperature, and humidity.

Your Turn

RETURN TO THE ESSENTIAL QUESTION

Review the selection with a partner to prepare to discuss this question: *What are the benefits of studying weather?* Use evidence from both the text and the graphic features to form your answer. As you discuss your thoughts, take turns summarizing key ideas.

Classroom Conversation

Continue your discussion of "Hurricanes" by explaining your answers with text evidence:

1. The author calls hurricanes "earth's mightiest storms." Do you agree? Why or why not?
2. How has hurricane prediction changed over the years?
3. How does a better understanding of hurricanes benefit society?

ROLE-PLAY A SCIENTIST

Report on Hurricanes Imagine that you are a weather scientist appearing on TV. Work with a partner to outline key information and details that explain how hurricanes form. Then take turns role-playing a weather scientist explaining that process.

WRITE ABOUT READING

Response Write a short summary of "Hurricanes." Begin by stating the title and the author's name. Then use facts and important details as well as text evidence to tell readers about the scientific ideas in the selection.

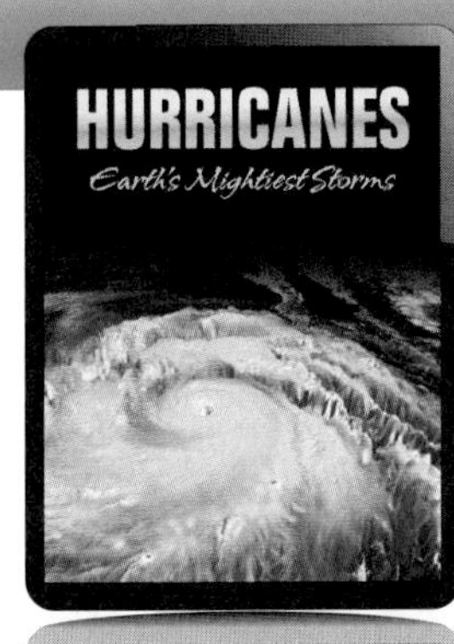

Writing Tip

Begin your summary by stating the topic of the selection. Check to make sure that you have used pronouns correctly.

COMMON CORE **ELACC4RI2** determine the main idea and explain how it is supported by details/summarize; **ELACC4RI3** explain events/procedures/ideas/concepts in a text; **ELACC4RI7** interpret information presented visually, orally, or quantitatively; **ELACC4W9b** apply grade 4 Reading standards to informational texts; **ELACC4SL1a** come to discussions prepared/explicitly draw on preparation and other information about the topic; **ELACC4SL1d** review key ideas expressed and explain own ideas and understanding

Lesson 11

INFORMATIONAL TEXT

 GENRE

Informational text, such as this newspaper article, gives information about a topic and usually includes visuals, such as maps and photographs with captions.

TEXT FOCUS

Events in Historical Text
A newspaper article can tell about events that happened in the past. Often the reporter will tell about the events in the order they happened. The reporter may compare and contrast the particular incident with a similar incident. What events are compared in this article?

ELACC4RI5 describe the overall structure of a text or part of a text; **ELACC4RI10** read and comprehend informational texts

Go Digital

THE DAILY NEWS August 2006

Recovering from KATRINA

by Alice Young ***Daily News Reporter***

Life has changed along the Gulf Coast in the past year. One year ago, Hurricane Katrina was churning in the warm, moist air of the Gulf of Mexico as a Category 5 storm. This is the strongest and most destructive rating for a hurricane. All along the Gulf Coast, residents were bracing for the impact of this mighty storm.

She was now a Category 3 hurricane with winds near 125 miles per hour.

On the morning of August 29, Hurricane Katrina made landfall in southern Louisiana. She was now a Category 3 hurricane with winds near 125 miles per hour. She left behind a path of destruction in Louisiana, Mississippi, and Alabama. Damages in New Orleans and along the Gulf Coast totaled $108 billion. This made Katrina the costliest and most destructive natural disaster in U.S. history. Most Atlantic hurricanes move north as they approach the Atlantic coast of the United States and do not land. Some storms hit Florida, and a few move into the Gulf of Mexico as Katrina did.

Even with warning, Hurricane Katrina still caused massive damage.

Before Katrina, Hurricane Andrew had been the costliest storm in U.S. history. Hurricane Andrew hit southern Florida on August 24, 1992, as a Category 5 storm. Violent winds and storm surges destroyed many homes and businesses.

Nearly 250,000 people were left homeless. Hurricane Andrew moved across Florida. Then it moved into the Gulf of Mexico. It struck south-central Louisiana as a Category 3 storm on August 26, 1992.

This infrared photo shows Hurricane Andrew hitting southern Florida in 1992.

A hurricane pulls up a dome of seawater that travels with the hurricane. The high water dome creates the storm surge. Strong winds create giant waves. The storm surge often causes the greatest damage in a hurricane.

Flooding caused much of the damage from Hurricane Katrina. Levees that separate New Orleans from surrounding lakes broke. These breaks caused most of New Orleans to lie under floodwater. Some parts of the city were covered by twenty feet of water. Huge twenty- to thirty-foot storm surges from Katrina also caused massive flooding in coastal cities of Mississippi and Alabama.

After Hurricane Katrina, hundreds of thousands of people were left homeless. They had to find temporary housing in hotels, homes of friends or family, or in shelters. Thousands of shelters were set up in schools, community centers, and various other buildings.

The Red Cross, government agencies, and other relief groups set up the shelters. One large shelter was set up at the Astrodome in Houston, Texas. In early September 2005, it housed more than 11,000 hurricane victims.

Compare this photograph of New Orleans before Hurricane Katrina with the photograph on the next page. Look for the large brown building in the center of each photo.

A year after Hurricane Katrina, many homes and other buildings still need repair. About one third of New Orleans's schools, hospitals, and libraries are still closed. Thousands of people whose homes were destroyed continue to live in trailers provided by FEMA, the Federal Emergency Management Agency. Relief agencies, such as FEMA and the Red Cross, continue to help rebuild damaged homes. They continue to relocate people whose homes were destroyed.

Recovering from such widespread destruction has been a huge task. Some people have been able to repair or rebuild their homes and businesses during the past year. Many residents have chosen to remain in the region where they grew up. They are determined to rebuild their homes, their communities, and their lives.

Recovering from such widespread destruction has been a huge task.

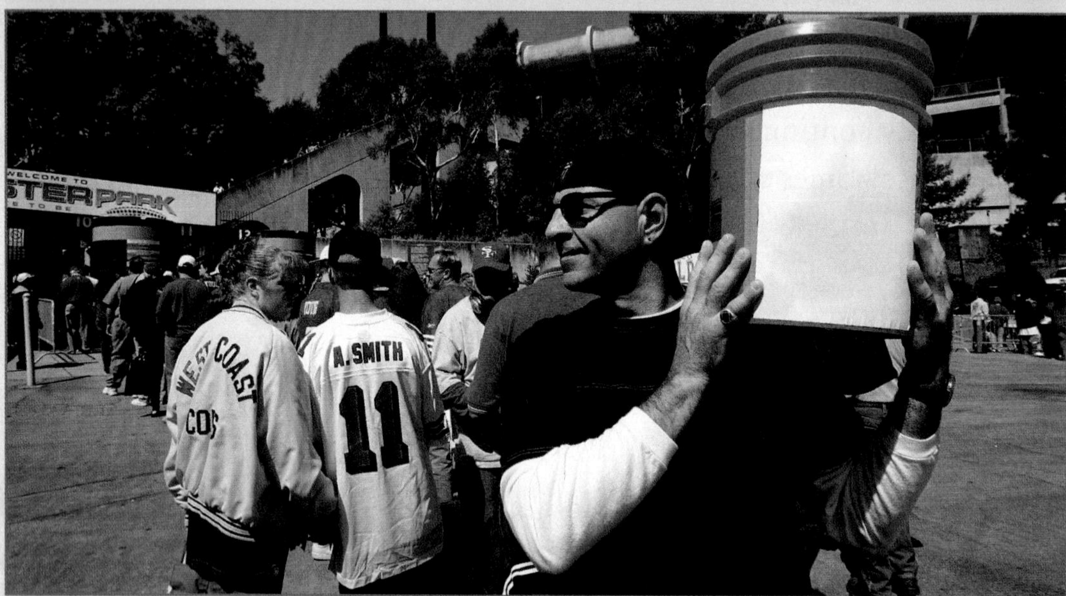

People from all over the United States came together to help rebuild New Orleans after Hurricane Katrina.

The volunteer response to Hurricane Katrina has been the largest in U.S. history. Hundreds of thousands of people across the country have stepped in to help in any way they can. Some come to the Gulf Coast region and volunteer for a weekend. Others stay for months at a time to help in the rebuilding effort. Much has been accomplished in the past year to rebuild the Gulf Coast. Yet much remains to be done.

Much has been accomplished in the past year to rebuild the Gulf Coast.

Compare Texts

TEXT TO TEXT

Compare Storm Texts Talk with a partner about the similarities and differences between "Hurricanes" and "Recovering from Katrina." Answer these questions: *What information does each text provide about the creation of hurricanes? What facts does each author give about what happens during and after a hurricane?* After discussing your ideas, work together to write a paragraph that explains the life of a hurricane. Include text evidence from both selections in your response.

TEXT TO SELF

Write a Report Write a newspaper report about a storm or another weather-related event you have experienced. Describe what you saw, heard, and felt. Also explain what effects the event had on your family, friends, and community.

TEXT TO WORLD

Compare Perspectives Think about the authors' perspectives in "Hurricanes" and "Recovering from Katrina." What does each author focus on? Which text seems more scientific? Which author tells about the effects of hurricane damage? Discuss your ideas with a partner.

ELACC4RI6 compare and contrast a firsthand and secondhand account of the same event or topic; **ELACC4RI9** integrate information from two texts on the same topic; **ELACC4W10** write routinely over extended time frames and shorter time frames

COMMON CORE **ELACC4L1g** correctly use frequently confused words

Grammar

What Words Are Frequently Confused? Many words in English sound alike but have different spellings and meanings. For example, the words *there, their,* and *they're* sound the same, but they have very different meanings. Words such as these are frequently confused. It's important to use frequently confused words properly so that your ideas are clear.

Frequently Confused Words

Word	Meaning	Example
there	"in that place"	Weather scientists expect flooding **there.**
they're	contraction of *they are*	**They're** warning us to stay home.
their	"belonging to them"	**Their** basement is full of water.
its	"belonging to it"	The storm's wind is scarier than **its** rain.
it's	contraction of *it is*	**It's** hard to hear over the wind.
to	"in the direction of"	Winds are blowing **to** the north.
two	number	We've had **two** inches of rain.
too	"also"; "in addition"	It will probably rain tomorrow, **too!**

Try This! **Copy each sentence. Fill in the blank with the correct word in parentheses.**

1. __________ saying the hurricane will reach us tonight. (They're / There)
2. __________ winds have been clocked at over 100 mph! (It's / Its)
3. Heavy rain is expected, __________. (to / too)
4. People on the coast have left __________ homes. (their / there)

Using an incorrect word can confuse your readers. When you proofread your writing, look for words that sound like other words but have different meanings and spellings. Make sure you're using the correct word. If you're not sure, look up the word in a dictionary.

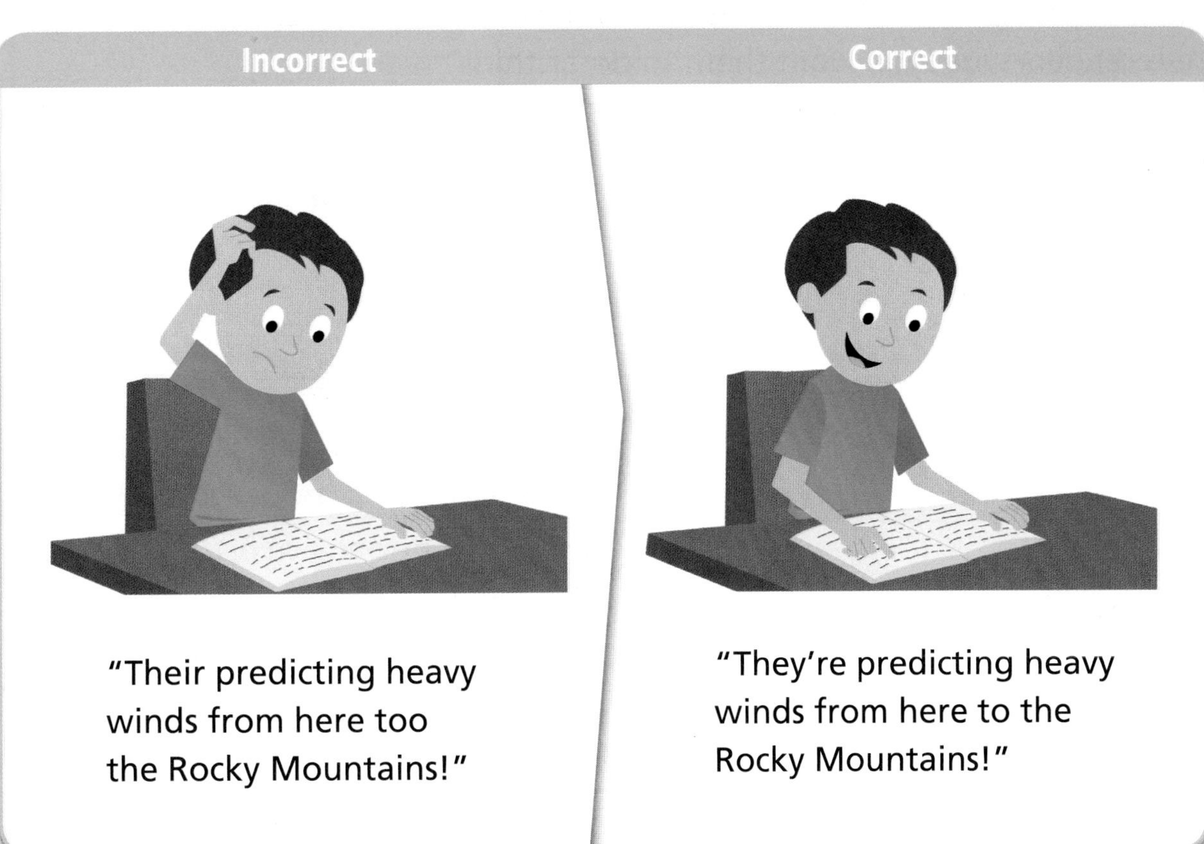

Incorrect
Correct
"Their predicting heavy winds from here too the Rocky Mountains!"
"They're predicting heavy winds from here to the Rocky Mountains!"

Connect Grammar to Writing

As you edit your persuasive paragraph, check to see that you have used the correct form of frequently confused words. Rewrite any incorrect words so that your sentences make sense.

ELACC4W1a introduce a topic, state an opinion, and create an organizational structure; **ELACC4W1b** provide reasons supported by facts and details; **ELACC4W1c** link opinion and reasons using words and phrases; **ELACC4W1d** provide a concluding statement or section; **ELACC4L1g** correctly use frequently confused words

Opinion Writing

Ideas A **persuasive paragraph** states your opinion and gives strong **reasons** to support it. It should include **facts and examples** to explain your reasons. Link your opinions and reasons with words or phrases such as *for example* and *another reason*. The paragraph should end with a call to action that tells readers what you want them to do or think.

Grace wrote a persuasive paragraph explaining the importance of hurricane preparedness. Later, she added words and phrases to link opinions and reasons. She also added an introduction to clearly state her opinion.

Writing Traits Checklist

Ideas
Did I state a clear opinion and support it with facts and details?

Organization
Did I organize my ideas in a way that makes sense?

Word Choice
Did I use words and phrases to link opinions and reasons?

Voice
Did I express my opinion convincingly?

Sentence Fluency
Do my sentences vary in length?

Conventions
Did I spell frequently confused words correctly?

Revised Draft

People who live in areas where hurricanes occur always need to be prepared. Every year, many people are affected by hurricanes. If you live in hurricane country, you need a disaster plan. This plan includes creating a disaster kit that contains things necessary for survival. For example, ~~W~~when water service is cut off and stores are boarded up, you'll be unable to get fresh water. So, your disaster kit needs plenty of bottled water.

Final Copy

Be Prepared!

by Grace Martin

People who live in areas where hurricanes occur always need to be prepared. Every year, many people are affected by hurricanes. If you live in hurricane country, you need a disaster plan. This plan includes creating a disaster kit that contains things necessary for survival. For example, when water service is cut off and stores are boarded up, you'll be unable to get fresh water. So, your disaster kit needs plenty of bottled water. Another reason you need a plan is so that you will know where you will go if your family must leave your home. For instance, if your home is flooded or the roof blows off, you'll need to find shelter. It's a good idea to know about nearby places that offer shelter during hurricanes. That way, when disaster strikes, you'll know exactly where to go. Making a disaster plan and a survival kit may seem like work, but in the end, your safety is worth the trouble!

Reading as a Writer

Which words and phrases did Grace use to link her opinions and reasons? What words and phrases can you use to link your ideas more clearly?

In my final paper, I added a conclusion that restated my opinion. I also made sure that I used the correct form of easily confused words, such as *your*.

Lesson

12

THE EARTH DRAGON AWAKES

The San Francisco Earthquake of 1906

LAURENCE YEP

TWISTERS

Vocabulary in Context

TARGET VOCABULARY

trembles
wreckage
slab
possessions
tenement
crushing
rubble
debris
timbers
constructed

Vocabulary Reader

Context Cards

ELACC4L6 acquire/use vocabulary, including academic and domain-specific

1 trembles

People sense an earthquake when everything nearby shakes and trembles.

2 wreckage

Even an earthquake shorter than one minute can leave a lot of wreckage.

3 slab

A falling concrete slab, or flat and thick piece, can destroy everything under it.

4 possessions

A quake can damage people's possessions. The things people own might be ruined.

- Study each Context Card.
- Use a dictionary to help you understand the meaning of these words.

5 tenement

A tenement, or poorly built apartment building, is especially at risk in a quake.

6 crushing

If falling structures are crushing everything inside them, the street is the safest place.

7 rubble

It can take a lot of time and effort to clean up broken bits of rubble.

8 debris

After a quake, the debris from a badly damaged road can be dangerous.

9 timbers

Houses made of timbers, or wooden beams, can collapse like toothpick toys.

10 constructed

Buildings now can be constructed in a way that helps them survive quakes.

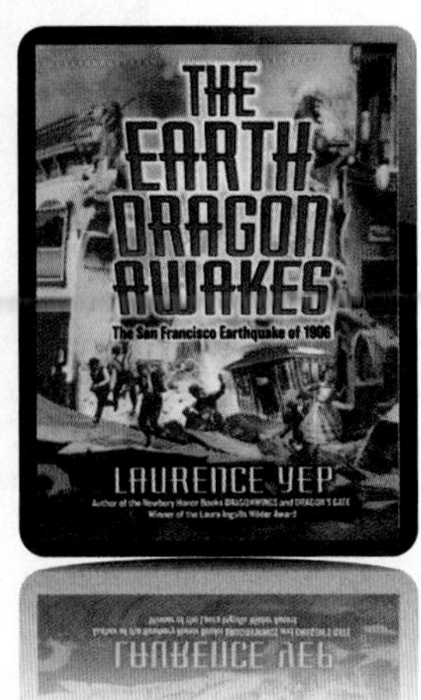

Read and Comprehend

TARGET SKILL

Sequence of Events As you read "The Earth Dragon Awakes," notice the **sequence,** or order, in which events take place. Notice also that the main sequence of events is interrupted once to tell the story from another point of view. To keep track of the sequence, look for details including dates and times of day as well as signal words such as *when*, *now*, *then*, and *again*. Use a graphic organizer like this one to help you keep track of the order in which events happen.

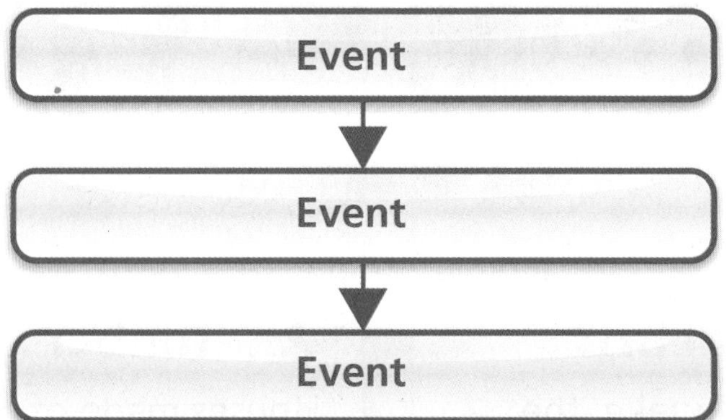

TARGET STRATEGY

Visualize When you visualize, you use details in a text to form a clear mental picture of characters, settings, and events. As you read "The Earth Dragon Awakes," use the **visualize** strategy to help you follow Chin and Ah Sing's story. Using text details to form pictures in your mind of the important events will help you remember the sequence of those events.

ELACC4RL1 refer to details and examples when explaining what the text says explicitly and when drawing inferences; **ELACC4RL3** describe a character, setting, or event, drawing on details

PREVIEW THE TOPIC

Forces of Nature

Geology is the study of the earth and how it changes over time. Many geologic changes happen slowly—over millions of years. Other changes happen suddenly. Earthquakes occur without warning, when huge plates of rock beneath earth's surface suddenly shift. Powerful earthquakes can cause buildings to crumble and bridges to fall.

In "The Earth Dragon Awakes," you will read about the devastating earthquake that shook San Francisco, California, in April 1906.

Lesson 12

ANCHOR TEXT

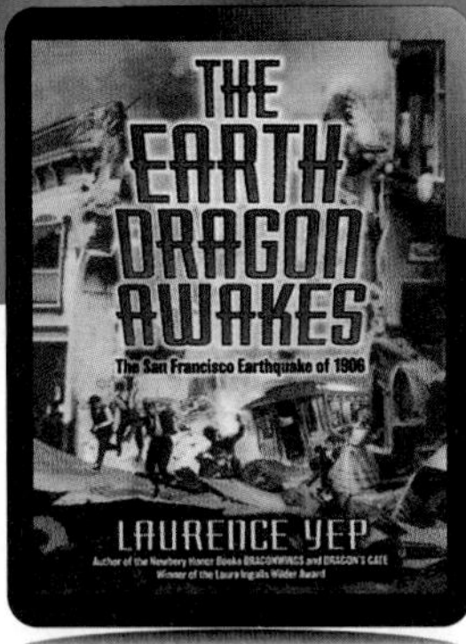

 TARGET SKILL

Sequence of Events
Examine the time order in which events take place.

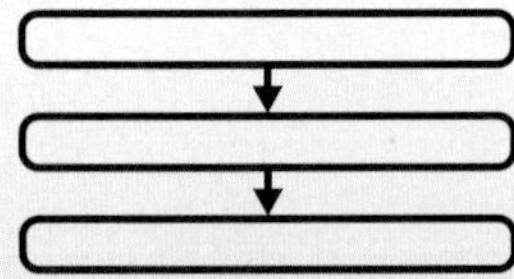

 GENRE

Historical fiction is a story that is set in the past and tells about people, places, and events that did happen or could have happened. As you read, look for:

- a setting that is a real time and place in the past
- realistic characters and events
- some made-up events and details

ELACC4RL1 refer to details and examples when explaining what the text says explicitly and when drawing inferences; **ELACC4RL3** describe a character, setting, or event, drawing on details; **ELACC4L3a** choose words and phrases for effect

MEET THE AUTHOR

LAURENCE YEP

During his childhood in San Francisco, Laurence Yep went to school in Chinatown but did not live there. As a young adult, Yep became increasingly interested in his Chinese-American heritage. He began his writing career during high school, when he was paid one cent per word to write science-fiction stories for a magazine. Now he is the author of many award-winning books, including *Dragonwings,* which also tells about Chinese immigrants living in San Francisco.

MEET THE ILLUSTRATOR

YUAN LEE

Yuan Lee has created artwork for advertisements, posters, and magazines. He designed a series of stamps for the United Nations showing the endangered species of the world. Yuan also illustrated *The Parthenon,* a book showing the construction of an ancient Greek temple.

The EARTH DRAGON AWAKES

The San Francisco Earthquake of 1906

by **Laurence Yep**

selection illustrated by **Yuan Lee**

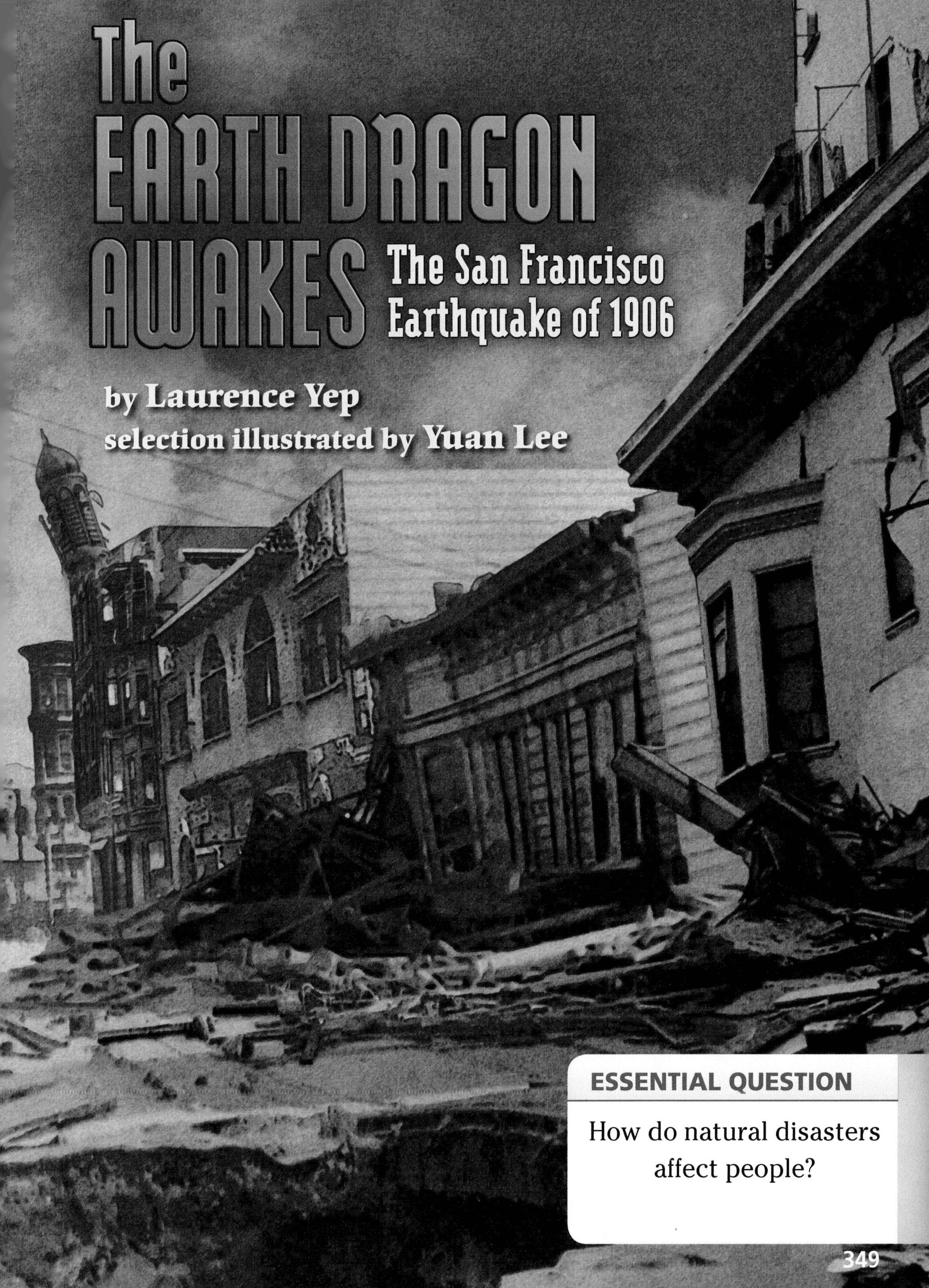

ESSENTIAL QUESTION

How do natural disasters affect people?

It is 5:12 A.M. on Wednesday, April 18, 1906. In San Francisco's Chinatown, Chin and his father, Ah Sing, are in their apartment. They are washing up, getting ready to go to the Travises' house, where Ah Sing works to send money to his wife in China. Their friend Ah Quon (kwahn) lives nearby.

Suddenly everything trembles. The bowl creeps across the table. Then even the table crawls away. Chin spills water everywhere.

"You can write your mother about your first earthquake," his father says unworriedly.

The floor rolls under them like a wooden sea. The bowl slips over the edge and crashes. Boxes tumble from the stack. Their possessions scatter across the boards. Chin and his father drop to their knees.

Ah Sing tries to sound brave. "The Earth Dragon must be scratching," he laughs.

Chin tries to be just as fearless. When the room stills, he tries to joke like his father. "He must really have an itch."

Before his father can answer, the trembling begins again.

Chin waits for it to stop. But it goes on and on. The tenement creaks and groans like an old giant. Their bed and bureau prowl like hungry animals.

Ah Sing crawls over. He puts his arms around Chin. "Don't be scared," he says. Ah Sing's voice sounds funny because he is shaking with the room.

Beneath them, unseen timbers crack like sticks. The next instant, one side of the room tilts upward. They slide helplessly with all the furniture toward the opposite wall. Chin feels like a doll. Their belongings crash and thump as they pile up.

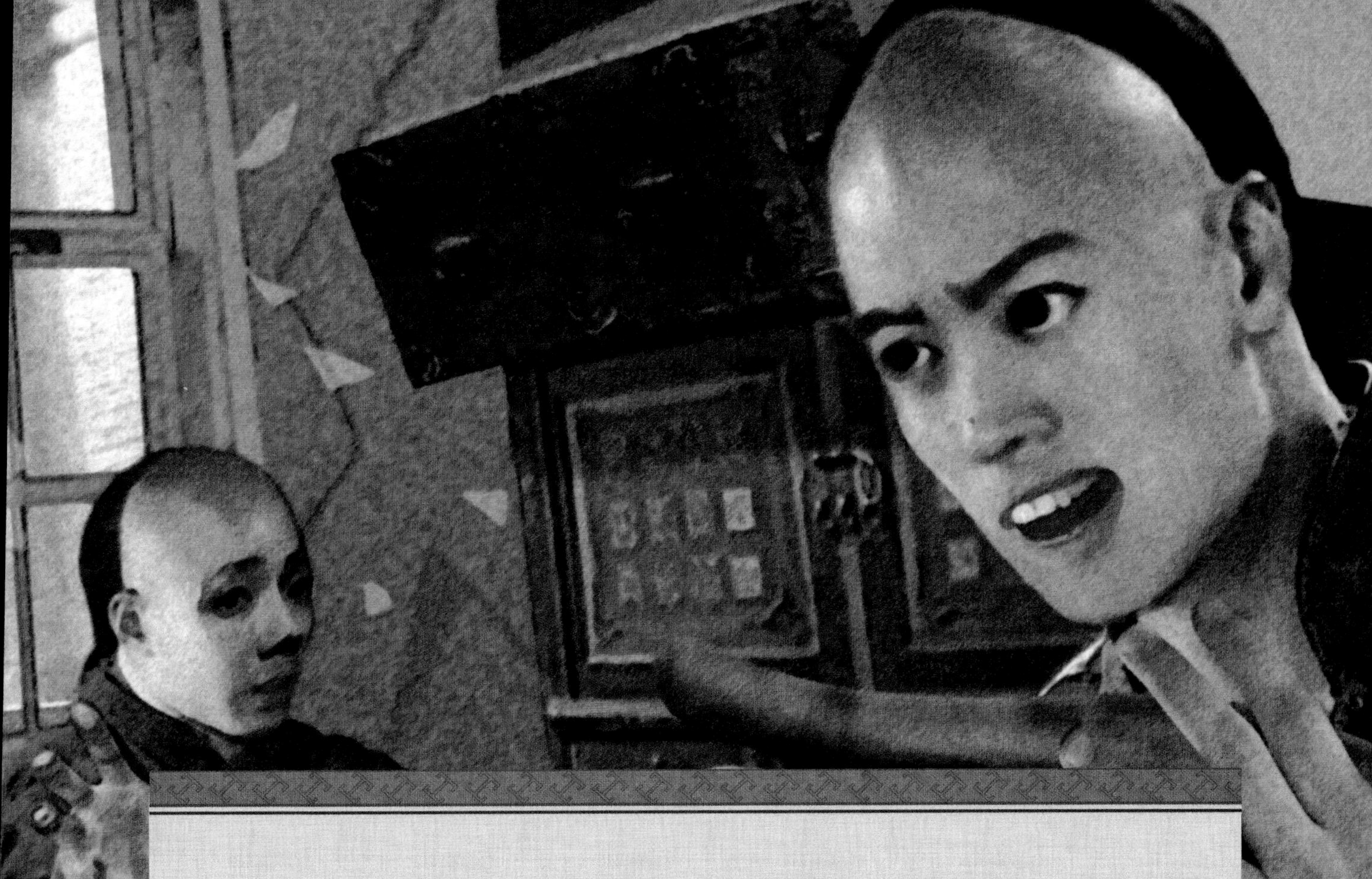

His father forces him under the table.

"The tenement is falling!" his father shouts.

Walls crack and crumble. Windows shatter. Broken glass sprays like little daggers.

Chin's stomach feels funny when the room itself drops. They bounce against the floor as it stops with a jerk. For a moment, they lie there. Their neighbors scream from the middle level. Ah Sing and Chin's room is crushing them.

Then the floor twitches. It plunges again. There are more screams. This time it is the ground level that is smashed.

Their floor gives one final thump and stops.

Dazed, Chin peeks out from beneath the table. He sees cracks. They spread like a crazy spiderweb around all the walls. Spurts of powdery plaster puff out. The walls crumble like paper. The ceiling drops down on them.

ANALYZE THE TEXT

Author's Word Choice What words or phrases clearly communicate what is happening to Chin and Ah Sing?

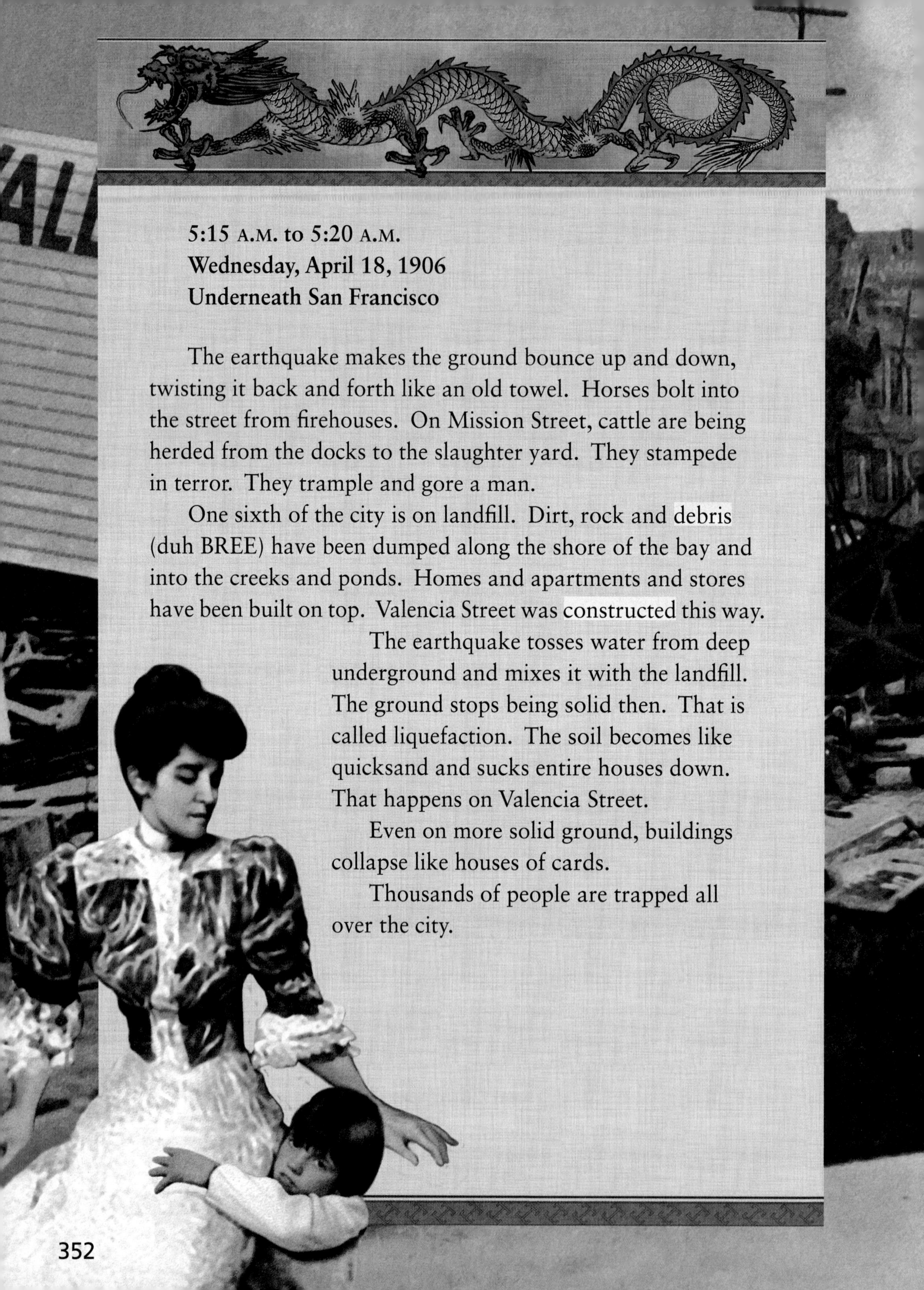

5:15 A.M. to 5:20 A.M.
Wednesday, April 18, 1906
Underneath San Francisco

The earthquake makes the ground bounce up and down, twisting it back and forth like an old towel. Horses bolt into the street from firehouses. On Mission Street, cattle are being herded from the docks to the slaughter yard. They stampede in terror. They trample and gore a man.

One sixth of the city is on landfill. Dirt, rock and debris (duh BREE) have been dumped along the shore of the bay and into the creeks and ponds. Homes and apartments and stores have been built on top. Valencia Street was constructed this way.

The earthquake tosses water from deep underground and mixes it with the landfill. The ground stops being solid then. That is called liquefaction. The soil becomes like quicksand and sucks entire houses down. That happens on Valencia Street.

Even on more solid ground, buildings collapse like houses of cards.

Thousands of people are trapped all over the city.

5:20 A.M.
Wednesday, April 18, 1906
Chin and Ah Sing's tenement
Chinatown

Chin cannot see. He cannot move. He can barely breathe.

In the darkness, he hears his father cough. "Are you all right, Chin?"

His father is holding him tight. Chin tries to answer. But dust fills his mouth and throat. So he simply nods. Since his father can't see him, Chin squeezes his arm.

Then he shifts around so he can raise one hand. He can feel the tabletop, but its legs have collapsed. Fallen pieces of ceiling and wall have turned the space into a tiny cave.

His father pushes at the wreckage around him. "It won't budge," he grunts.

Chin shoves with him. "The whole ceiling fell on us." If his father hadn't pulled him under the table, he would have been crushed.

But now they are buried alive.

Overhead, they hear footsteps.

"The Earth Dragon's mad," a man screeches in fear.

"Here!" cries Ah Sing.

"Help us!" Chin yells, too.

From nearby, someone hollers, "Fire!"

The footsteps run away.

Chin and his father shout until they are hoarse.

No one hears them though.

Trapped under the rubble, they will be buried alive.

"We'll have to rescue ourselves," his father says. "Try to find a loose section." They squirm and wriggle. There is a big slab of plaster near Chin's head. He gropes with his hands until they feel the plaster. Powdery chunks crumble into his hands.

He hears his father digging. Chin claws at the broken boards and plaster. Dust chokes their noses and throats. Still they scrabble away like wild animals.

ANALYZE THE TEXT

Sequence of Events Chin and Ah Sing realize that they will have to save themselves. What events lead them to this realization?

6:00 A.M.
Wednesday, April 18, 1906
Chin and Ah Sing's tenement
Chinatown

Chin and his father dig in the darkness. He just hopes they are digging out of the rubble. His arms ache. He is covered with cuts and bruises. Dust chokes his mouth and throat. He feels as if he cannot even breathe. The earth has swallowed them up.

"Fire!" people cry from above. He feels the thumping of running feet.

He screams, "Let me out!"

His father stops digging and wraps his arms around him. "Don't panic!"

But fear twists inside Chin like a snake. He is so dry he cannot even cry. He just lies there. His fingernails are broken. His fingers are bleeding.

They will never escape. He thinks about his mother. She won't know how they died.

Suddenly a breeze brushes his face like a soft hand. He smells fresh air.

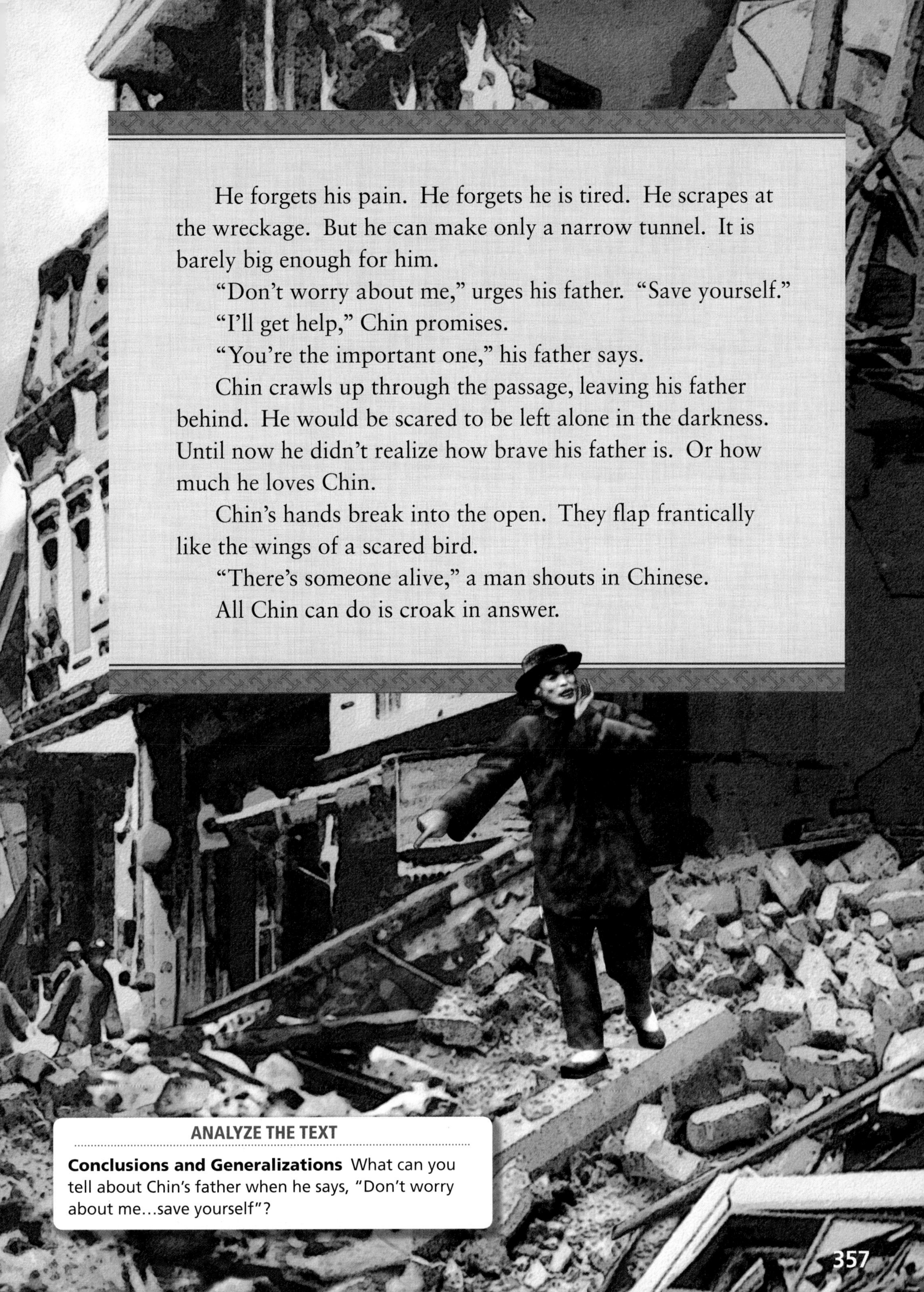

He forgets his pain. He forgets he is tired. He scrapes at the wreckage. But he can make only a narrow tunnel. It is barely big enough for him.

"Don't worry about me," urges his father. "Save yourself."

"I'll get help," Chin promises.

"You're the important one," his father says.

Chin crawls up through the passage, leaving his father behind. He would be scared to be left alone in the darkness. Until now he didn't realize how brave his father is. Or how much he loves Chin.

Chin's hands break into the open. They flap frantically like the wings of a scared bird.

"There's someone alive," a man shouts in Chinese.

All Chin can do is croak in answer.

ANALYZE THE TEXT

Conclusions and Generalizations What can you tell about Chin's father when he says, "Don't worry about me...save yourself"?

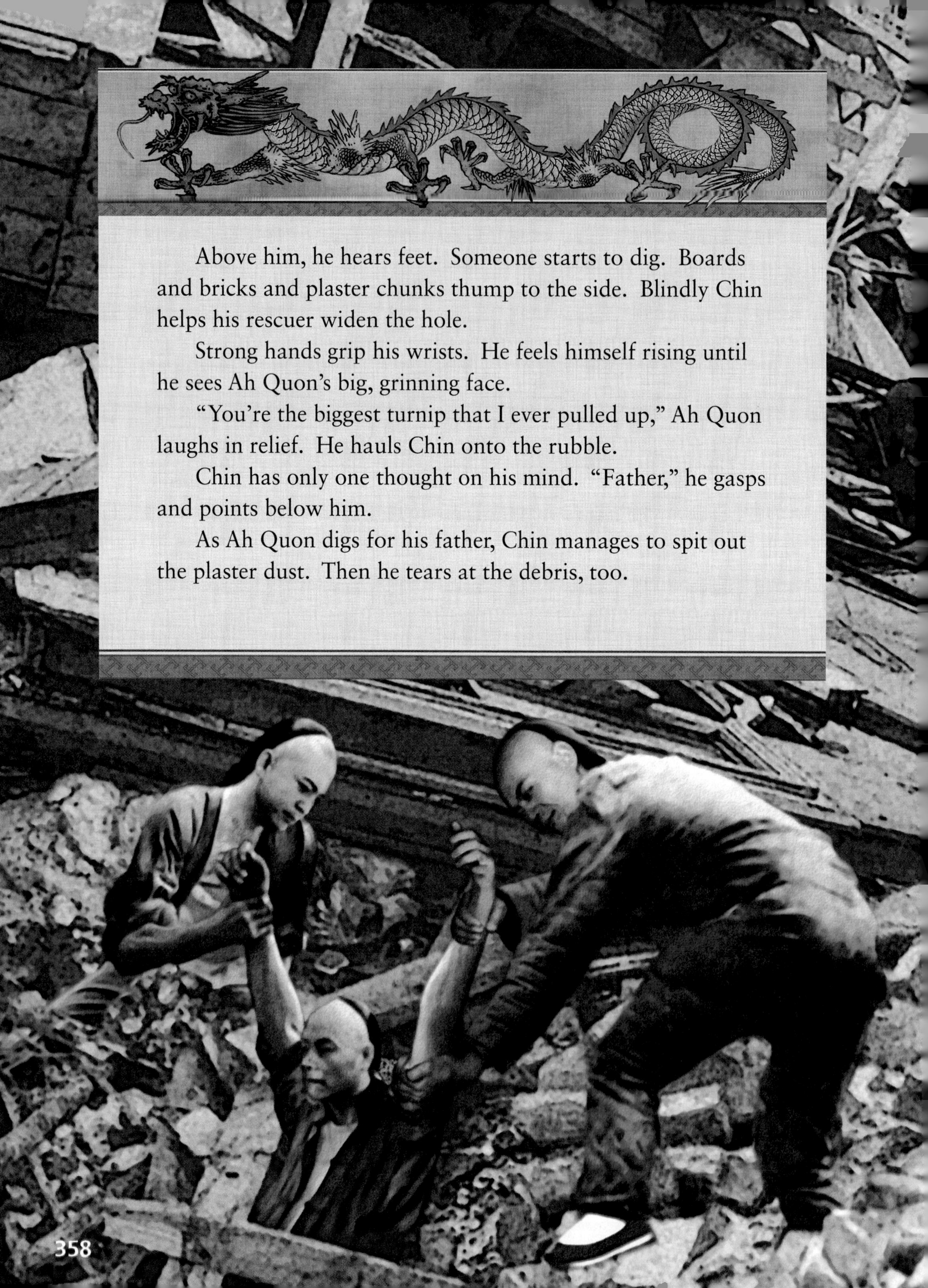

Above him, he hears feet. Someone starts to dig. Boards and bricks and plaster chunks thump to the side. Blindly Chin helps his rescuer widen the hole.

Strong hands grip his wrists. He feels himself rising until he sees Ah Quon's big, grinning face.

"You're the biggest turnip that I ever pulled up," Ah Quon laughs in relief. He hauls Chin onto the rubble.

Chin has only one thought on his mind. "Father," he gasps and points below him.

As Ah Quon digs for his father, Chin manages to spit out the plaster dust. Then he tears at the debris, too.

A LOOK BACK IN TIME:

San Francisco Earthquake

The epicenter of the earthquake of April 18, 1906, was near San Francisco, but the quake ruptured 296 miles along the San Andreas fault. The shaking of the ground was experienced by people in Oregon to the north, in Los Angeles to the south, east into Nevada, and likely continued west under the Pacific Ocean. The earthquake foreshock occurred at 5:12 A.M., and 20–25 seconds later, the full earthquake began and lasted for 45–60 seconds, followed by several aftershocks.

The earthquake toppled chimneys and damaged buildings in San Francisco, San Jose, Salinas, and Santa Rosa. It twisted pavement and bent streetcar tracks making some roads impassable. It broke water, sewer, and gas lines in the whole area. The breaking gas lines and toppled stoves in San Francisco are thought to have started the fire in the central business district. The fire department had no water to use in fighting the fire since the water mains were broken. The fire raged for 74 hours, even though the Navy began pumping water from the sea for the fire department. It was eventually extinguished completely by rain.

After the earthquake and fire, half the population of San Francisco was homeless. Everyone was in need of clean water and food. The newly-formed Red Cross and various government agencies moved into action to help the people displaced by the earthquake and fire.

Today, land-use guidelines direct hospitals, schools, and power plants to be built away from areas likely to be worst-affected in a future earthquake. Strict building codes ensure that buildings and structures are constructed to withstand the shaking and trembling of most earthquakes.

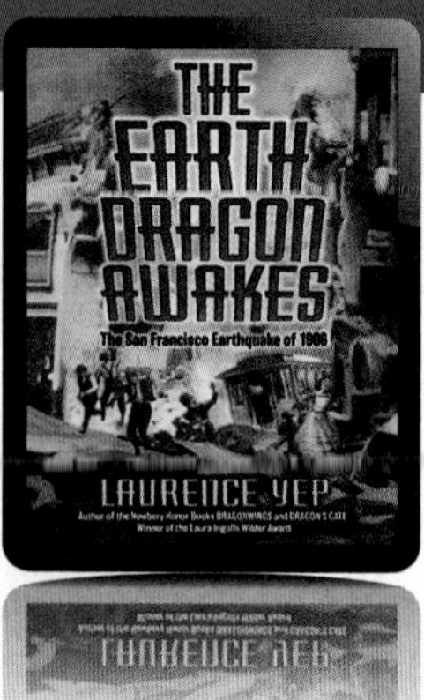

COMPREHENSION

Dig Deeper

How to Analyze the Text

Use these pages to learn about Sequence of Events, Conclusions and Generalizations, and Author's Word Choice. Then read "The Earth Dragon Awakes" again to apply what you learned.

Sequence of Events

Each section of "The Earth Dragon Awakes" begins with a time of day and a date. The time and date tell when the story events take place. However, in order to fully understand the **sequence of events,** you must pay attention to **details** in the text. Signal words such as *then, again, now,* and *when* help show the sequence. These words show how events are related to one another.

The introduction on page 350 tells you that the quake struck San Francisco at 5:12 A.M. on April 18, 1906. To understand exactly what happened in the moments that followed, you need to draw on specific text evidence. What happened in Chin's building right after the earthquake hit? What happened after Chin's father pulled him under the table?

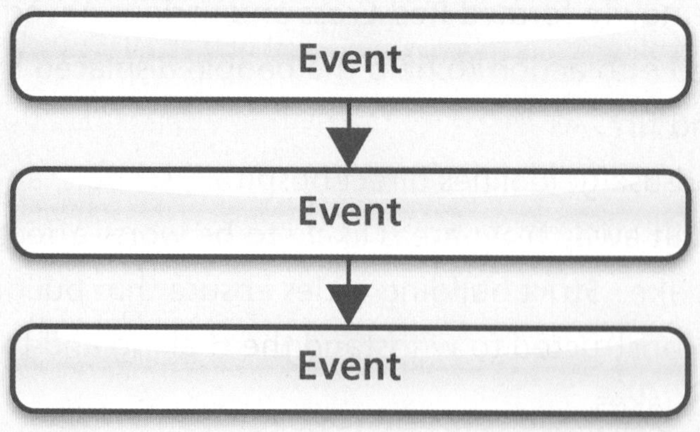

ELACC4RL1 refer to details and examples when explaining what the text says explicitly and when drawing inferences; **ELACC4RL3** describe a character, setting, or event, drawing on details; **ELACC4L3a** choose words and phrases for effect

Conclusions and Generalizations

As you read, you can draw **conclusions** about characters by thinking about their words, actions, and thoughts to figure out something the author doesn't tell you. A **generalization** is a type of conclusion that is true most of the time, but not always. Based on the rescuers' actions in this story, you can make the generalization that people often help each other during a disaster.

Author's Word Choice

Authors choose precise words and phrases to express their ideas clearly and to have a particular effect on readers. An author's **word choice** helps readers imagine how characters feel and what events are like. For example, when Chin is buried in the rubble, the author says that fear "twists inside Chin like a snake" to show how frightened he is.

Your Turn

RETURN TO THE ESSENTIAL QUESTION

Review the selection with a partner to prepare to discuss this question: *How do natural disasters affect people?* As you discuss, take turns reviewing the key ideas in the discussion and make comments that contribute to these ideas. Be sure to use text evidence to explain your thoughts.

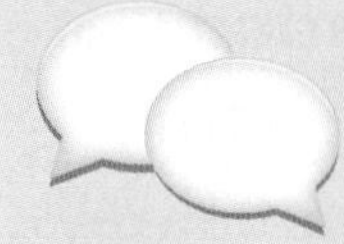

Classroom Conversation

Continue your discussion of "The Earth Dragon Awakes" by explaining your answers with text evidence:

1. What might have been the purpose for writing this story?
2. Why did Ah Sing encourage Chin to save himself? What traits does this reveal about Ah Sing?
3. How would the story be different if it were told from Chin's point of view?

EARTH DRAGON ALERT

Research Earthquakes Chin and Ah Sing refer to the "Earth Dragon" as the cause of the earthquake. With a partner, research the causes of earthquakes. Search the Internet for information to build your knowledge about this topic. Then discuss why an earthquake might be compared to an angry dragon in the earth.

WRITE ABOUT READING

Response Write a one-paragraph review of "The Earth Dragon Awakes." Begin by stating the title and the author's name. Then tell whether you liked the story, and explain why or why not. Conclude your review by telling whether you would recommend this story or others by the same author. Be sure to support your opinions with text evidence from the story.

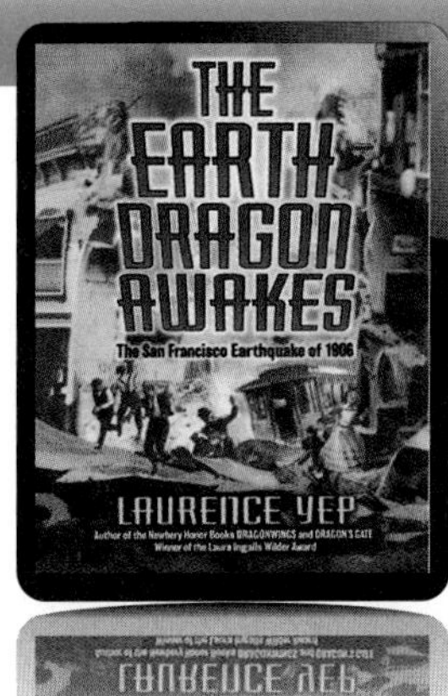

Writing Tip

Give two or three reasons for your opinion of the story. Check to make sure you have used the correct form of commonly confused words such as *to*, *too*, and *two*.

COMMON CORE **ELACC4RL3** describe a character, setting, or event, drawing on details; **ELACC4W1a** introduce a topic, state an opinion, and create an organizational structure; **ELACC4W1d** provide a concluding statement or section; **ELACC4W8** recall information from experiences or gather information from print and digital sources/take notes, categorize information, and provide a list of sources; **ELACC4SL1a** come to discussions prepared/explicitly draw on preparation and other information about the topic; **ELACC4L1g** correctly use frequently confused words

Lesson 12

INFORMATIONAL TEXT

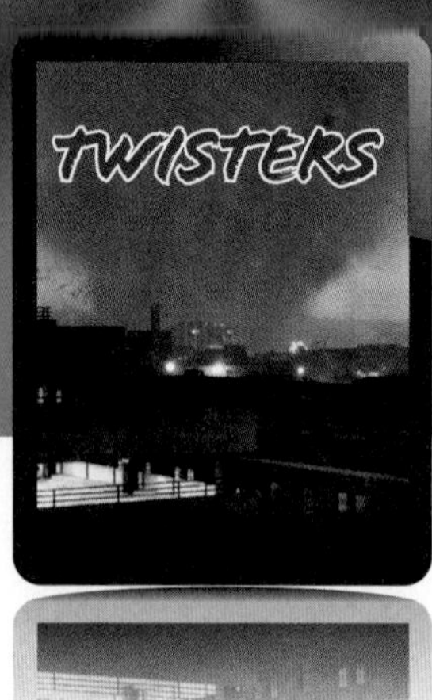

GENRE

Informational text, such as this magazine article, gives facts and examples about a topic.

TEXT FOCUS

Diagrams Informational text may include a diagram, a picture that explains how something works or how parts relate to each other. How does the diagram on page 365 support the information in the text?

ELACC4RI7 interpret information presented visually, orally, or quantitatively; **ELACC4RI10** read and comprehend informational texts

Go Digital

TWISTERS

by Laura Dameron

On March 28, 2000, a tornado passed through downtown Fort Worth, Texas. In about ten minutes, the tornado's crushing force left the city littered with debris. Right behind it, a second tornado damaged buildings in nearby towns. Each fallen slab added to the wreckage and rubble.

Around one thousand tornadoes form in the United States every year. Of all the states, Texas has the most tornadoes. It has an average of 153 twisters each year. Texas is an ideal setting for tornadoes. This is because it is located between the warm air of the Gulf of Mexico and the cool air of the Rocky Mountains.

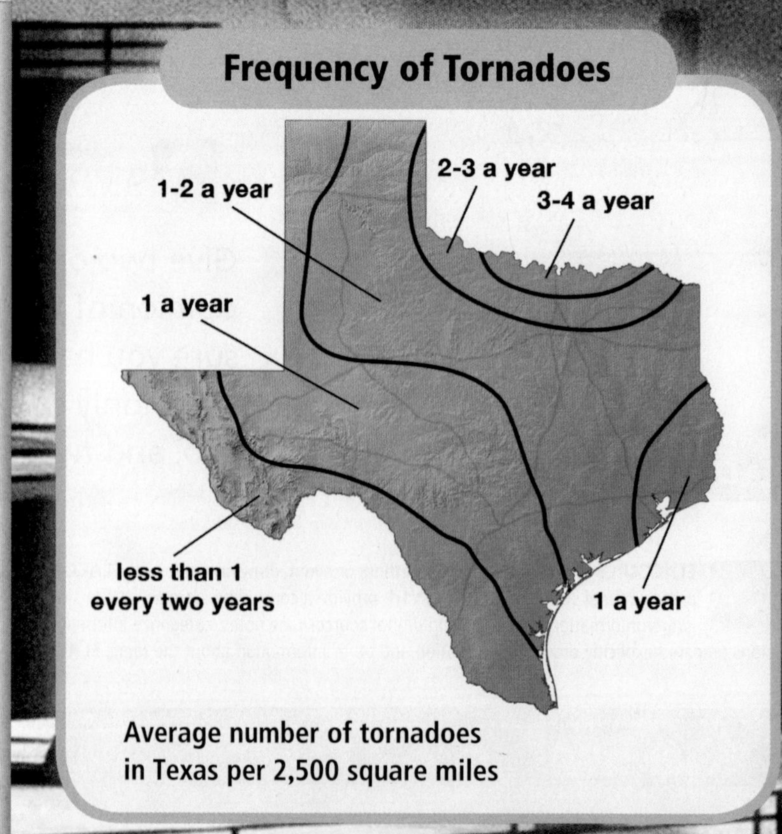

Average number of tornadoes in Texas per 2,500 square miles

Supercells and Funnel Clouds

Tornadoes form when warm air moving in different directions rises and cools. If the air keeps rising and spinning, it can develop into a thunderstorm called a supercell. It can then turn into a tornado.

Meteorologists, scientists who study the weather, can't predict exactly when a tornado will strike. But, they can use radar to track storms. When a supercell grows stronger, the radar measures its rotation for changes in speed. Meteorologists can also spot tornadoes by studying jet streams. They do this by looking at computer models and satellite pictures for signs of thunderstorms.

Fort Worth braces for a tornado on March 28, 2000.

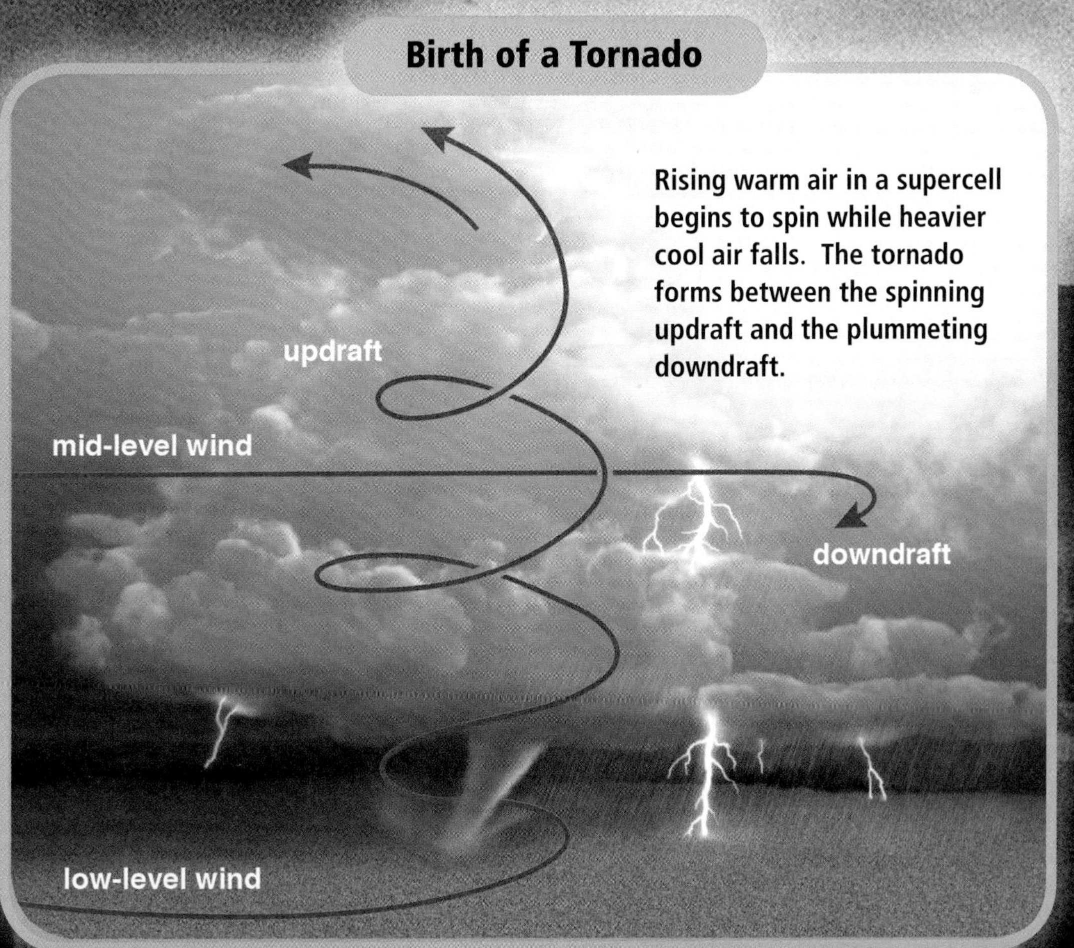
Birth of a Tornado
Rising warm air in a supercell begins to spin while heavier cool air falls. The tornado forms between the spinning updraft and the plummeting downdraft.
updraft
mid-level wind
downdraft
low-level wind

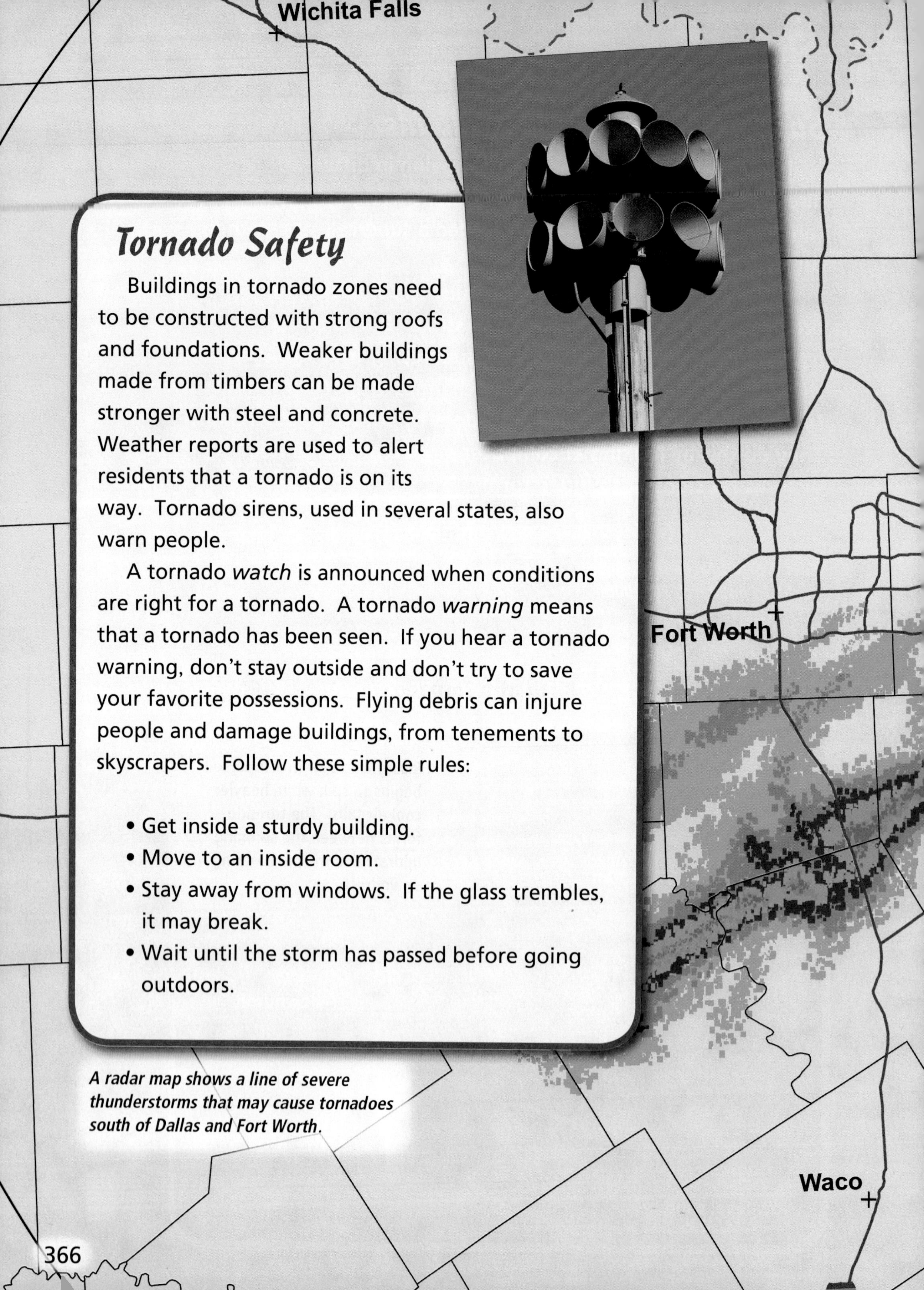

Tornado Safety

Buildings in tornado zones need to be constructed with strong roofs and foundations. Weaker buildings made from timbers can be made stronger with steel and concrete. Weather reports are used to alert residents that a tornado is on its way. Tornado sirens, used in several states, also warn people.

A tornado *watch* is announced when conditions are right for a tornado. A tornado *warning* means that a tornado has been seen. If you hear a tornado warning, don't stay outside and don't try to save your favorite possessions. Flying debris can injure people and damage buildings, from tenements to skyscrapers. Follow these simple rules:

- Get inside a sturdy building.
- Move to an inside room.
- Stay away from windows. If the glass trembles, it may break.
- Wait until the storm has passed before going outdoors.

A radar map shows a line of severe thunderstorms that may cause tornadoes south of Dallas and Fort Worth.

Compare Texts

TEXT TO TEXT

Compare Texts Talk with a partner about the similarities and differences between "The Earth Dragon Awakes" and "Twisters." Discuss these questions: *What might Chin and Ah Sing do if they were caught in a tornado? Are these actions similar to or different from what they did during the earthquake?* After you have discussed your ideas, work together to write an answer to each question. Use text evidence to explain your ideas.

TEXT TO SELF

Write a Disaster Plan What is one kind of natural disaster that happens where you live? What are the dangers associated with it? Write a step-by-step plan telling what people can do to be prepared for this kind of disaster. Then, with a group, take turns giving your instructions orally. After each person speaks, restate the instructions in your own words.

TEXT TO WORLD

Connect to Technology Use print and digital sources to research what a seismograph is and what is does. Take notes from your research and use them to write a paragraph about the seismograph.

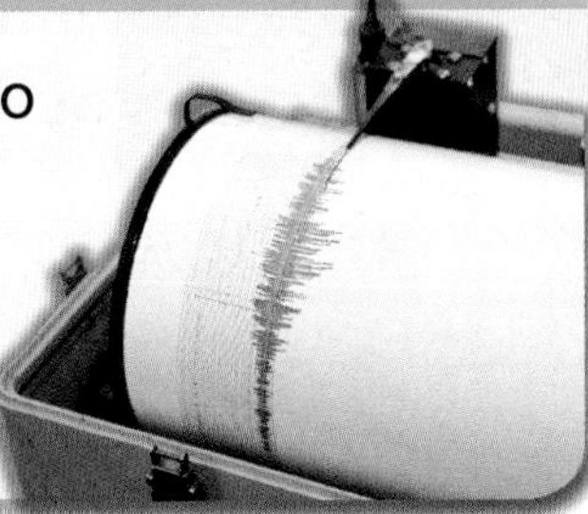

ELACC4RL1 refer to details and examples when explaining what the text says explicitly and when drawing inferences; **ELACC4W8** recall information from experiences or gather information from print and digital sources/take notes, categorize information, and provide a list of sources; **ELACC4SL2** paraphrase portions of a text read aloud or information presented in diverse media and formats

Grammar

What Is a Possessive Noun? A noun that shows ownership is a **possessive noun.** Add an **apostrophe** and an *-s* (*'s*) to a singular noun to make it possessive. When a plural noun ends with *-s*, add an apostrophe to make it possessive (*s'*). When a plural noun does not end with *-s*, add an apostrophe and an *-s* to make it possessive.

Possessive Nouns
singular possessive noun The boy's stomach felt odd during the quake.
plural possessive noun The fire trucks' sirens wailed and screamed.
plural possessive noun The children's pets ran away in fright.

Try This! **Rewrite each sentence on a sheet of paper. Change the underlined phrase to a possessive noun. Exchange papers with a partner and discuss your changes.**

1. The father of the girl holds her tight.
2. They can hear the voices of the rescuers.
3. The shovels of the men dig into the dirt.
4. The efforts of the diggers free the father and daughter.

When you write, you can sometimes make a sentence clearer by adding a possessive noun to indicate ownership. Showing possession helps the reader better understand what is happening.

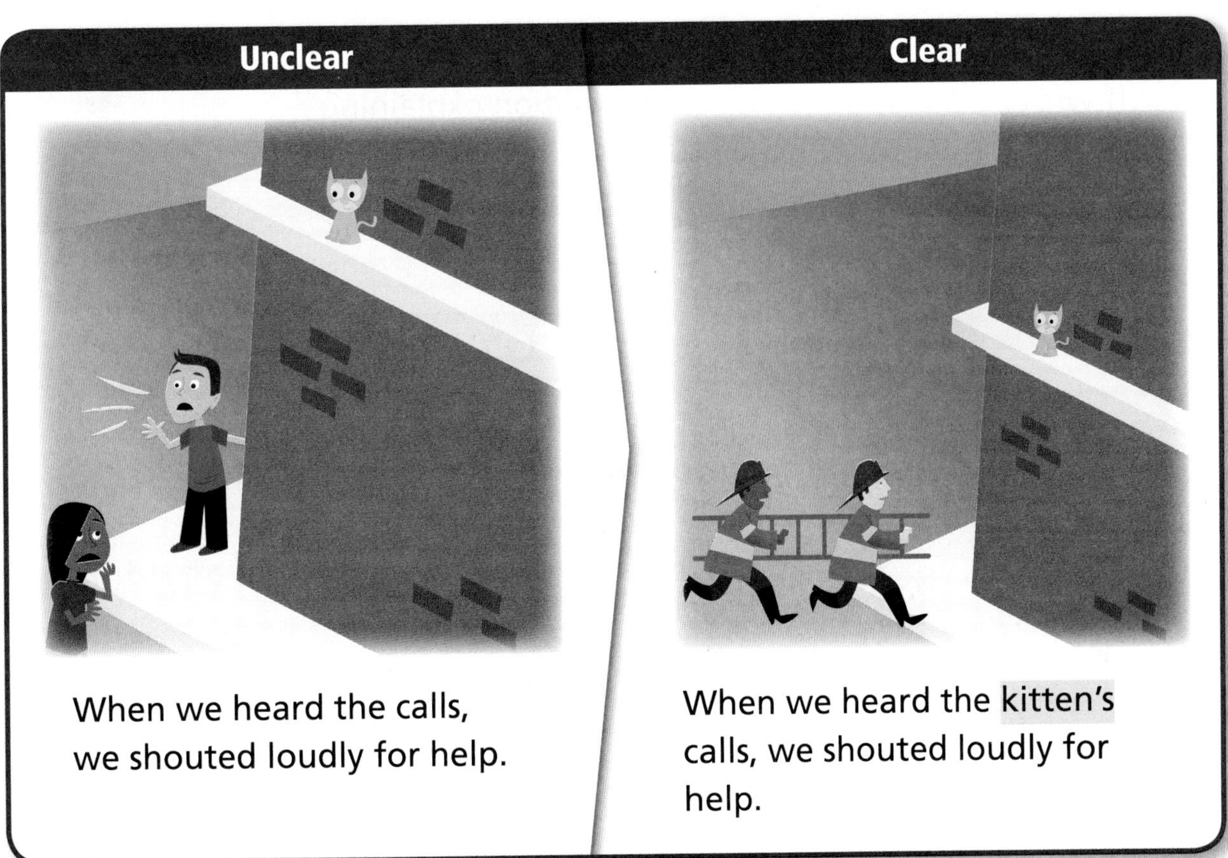

Unclear	Clear
When we heard the calls, we shouted loudly for help.	When we heard the kitten's calls, we shouted loudly for help.

Connect Grammar to Writing

As you revise your problem-solution composition, make your sentences clearer by adding possessive nouns to indicate ownership.

ELACC4W1a introduce a topic, state an opinion, and create an organizational structure; **ELACC4W1b** provide reasons supported by facts and details; **ELACC4W1c** link opinion and reasons using words and phrases; **ELACC4W1d** provide a concluding statement or section

Opinion Writing

Ideas A **problem-solution composition** first describes a problem and then explains how to solve it. As you write, include reasons and details to support your main idea. Try to be as persuasive as you can in order to convince a reader to agree with your solution. Use the Writing Traits Checklist below as you revise your writing.

Jeff wrote a problem-solution composition explaining why people should wear bicycle helmets. Later, he added persuasive details to make his points stronger.

Writing Traits Checklist

Ideas
Did I clearly explain the problem and the solution?

Organization
Do transition words make my ideas easy to follow?

Word Choice
Did I use words that made my points in a positive way?

Voice
Did I use a confident-sounding voice?

Sentence Fluency
Did I use possessive nouns correctly?

Conventions
Did I use correct spelling, grammar, and punctuation?

Revised Draft

Riding a bike is great exercise. It's a good way to get places, too. But riding your bike can be dangerous if you don't wear a helmet. Every year, more than 500,000 bicyclists go to emergency rooms with injuries. Many of the bicyclists' injuries happen to the brain. Experts say that ~~many~~ up to 85 percent of these brain injuries could have been prevented by helmets.

Final Copy

Wear Your Helmet

by Jeff Kowalski

Riding a bike is great exercise. It's a good way to get places, too. But riding your bike can be dangerous if you don't wear a helmet. Every year, more than 500,000 bicyclists go to emergency rooms with injuries. Many of the bicyclists' injuries happen to the brain. Experts say that up to 85 percent of these brain injuries could have been prevented by helmets.

How can we make sure that people wear helmets? First, helmets should be made available to all bicyclists. Second, people who make helmets should make them fit better and look cooler. Third, schools should have bicycle-safety classes. Finally, we all need to wear our helmets and tell our friends to wear theirs. If we do, we will save lives!

Reading as a Writer

Which persuasive details did Jeff add to strengthen his points? What details could you include to show how serious your safety problem or hazard is?

I added facts to make my points stronger and more persuasive to readers. I used words such as *first* and *second* to link my ideas. I also used a possessive noun.

Lesson 13

Jennifer Owings Dewey

Antarctic Journal

Four Months at the Bottom of the World

Cold, Cold Science

Vocabulary in Context

✓ TARGET VOCABULARY

display
alert
weariness
fractured
standards
vision
huddle
graceful
stranded
concluded

Vocabulary Reader

Context Cards

ELACC4L6 acquire/use vocabulary, including academic and domain-specific

1 display

The natural world is full of glorious scenes, such as this display of wildlife.

2 alert

These animals are alert. They are wide awake and ready to take action.

3 weariness

This bird can fly many miles. It may get tired, but it isn't stopped by its weariness.

4 fractured

In Antarctica, chunks of fractured, or broken, ice float through the icy sea.

- Study each Context Card.
- Use a dictionary to help you pronounce these words.

5 standards

By these polar bears' standards, or ways of measuring, cold air might be comfortable.

6 vision

Artists can have a vision, or mental image, of how to paint a scene from nature.

7 huddle

Baby goslings often huddle, or crowd together, to stay warm while they nap.

8 graceful

The delicate design of a spider's web is graceful and pleasing to see.

9 stranded

This fawn may seem stranded, or left helpless. Its mother is nearby, though.

10 concluded

Many people have concluded, or decided, that nature is full of beauty.

Read and Comprehend

TARGET SKILL

Sequence of Events As you read "Antarctic Journal: Four Months at the Bottom of the World," notice the **sequence**, or order, in which events take place. The author explains events through separate journal entries organized in time order. To keep track of the sequence, look for dates and times of day as well as signal words such as *when*, *now*, *then*, and *again*. Use a graphic organizer like the one below to help you keep track of the overall structure of the text.

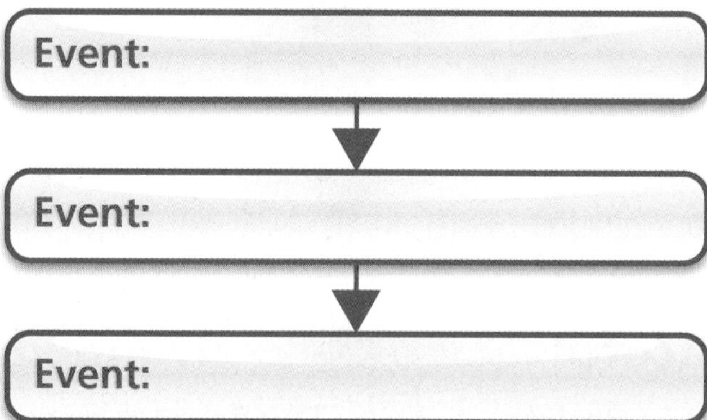

TARGET STRATEGY

Summarize When you summarize a section of text, you briefly retell the main ideas in your own words. As you read "Antarctic Journal," pause at the end of each page to briefly **summarize** what you have just read to make sure you understand it.

COMMON CORE **ELACC4RI2** determine the main idea and explain how it is supported by details/summarize; **ELACC4RI5** describe the overall structure of a text or part of a text

PREVIEW THE TOPIC

Interdependence

Life science is the study of living things and the environment in which they live. One of the things life scientists study is how plants and animals depend on one other and on their habitat.

In "Antarctic Journal," you'll join an expedition to one of the most extreme environments on Earth—the Antarctic. This frozen land near the South Pole is Earth's last true wilderness. As you read, you'll find out about some of the creatures that live in a sub-zero climate.

Lesson 13

ANCHOR TEXT

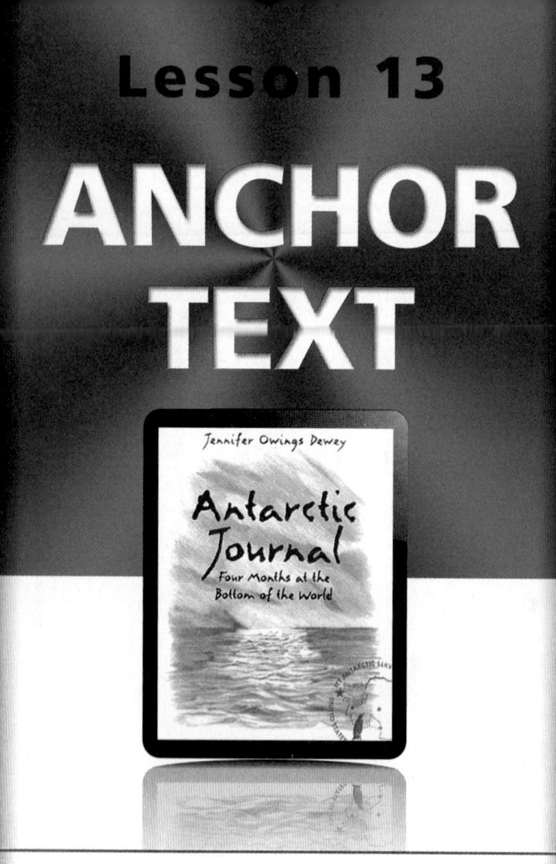

TARGET SKILL

Sequence of Events
Notice the overall structure of the text. Examine the order in which events take place.

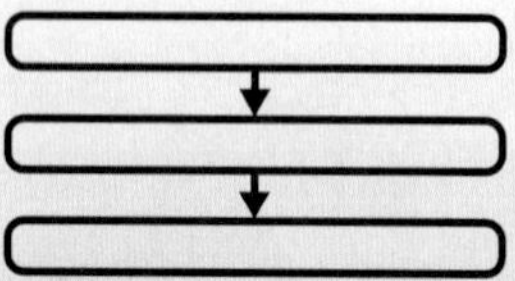

GENRE

Narrative nonfiction tells about people, things, events, or places that are real. A journal is a form of narrative nonfiction. As you read, look for:

- factual information that tells a story
- events in time order
- dates that tell when each journal entry was written

ELACC4RI4 determine the meaning of general academic and domain-specific words and phrases; **ELACC4RI5** describe the overall structure of a text or part of a text

 Go Digital

MEET THE AUTHOR AND ILLUSTRATOR

Jennifer Owings Dewey

When Jennifer Owings Dewey was ten, she wrote an illustrated autobiography. She doubted her ability to draw human figures, so she drew all the people as pieces of fruit. Since then she has gone on to illustrate not only people, but all kinds of creatures in dozens of her children's books.

Most of Dewey's books reflect her passion for nature and describe wild places and the animals that inhabit them. "Over the years. . . I've come to understand how much we think we know and how much we do not know," says Dewey of her nature writing. She adds that she will never stop writing for children because, like herself, they "want to know the why of things."

Antarctic Journal

Four Months at the Bottom of the World

written and illustrated by
Jennifer Owings Dewey

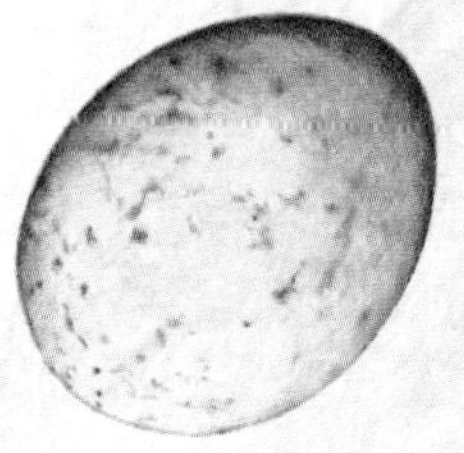

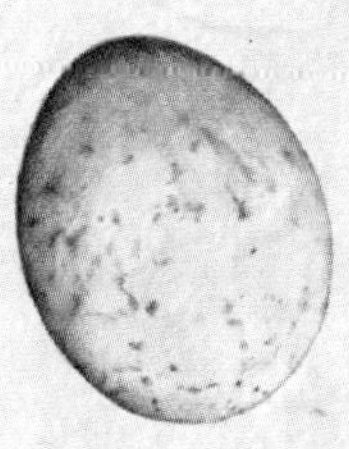

ESSENTIAL QUESTION

How are the different parts of an ecosystem connected?

The author has long had a vision of herself exploring Antarctica, what she calls "the windiest, coldest, most forbidding region on Earth." She has recently traveled by plane and ship to this icy continent. Her first exciting encounter was with humpback whales, when her ship stopped to let them pass. Now she has settled in at Palmer Station, where she'll be living for four months. During her visit to Antarctica, she plans to sketch, photograph, and write about this fascinating place.

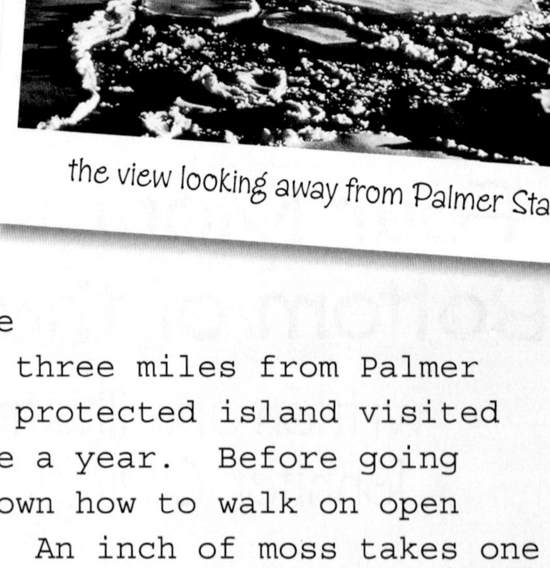
the view looking away from Palmer Station

November 27th Litchfield Island

In fair weather I go to Litchfield Island and spend the day, sometimes the night. Litchfield is three miles from Palmer by inflatable boat, a protected island visited by two or three people a year. Before going to Litchfield, I'm shown how to walk on open ground in Antarctica. An inch of moss takes one hundred years to grow. The careless scuff of a boot heel could rip out two hundred years of growth in seconds.

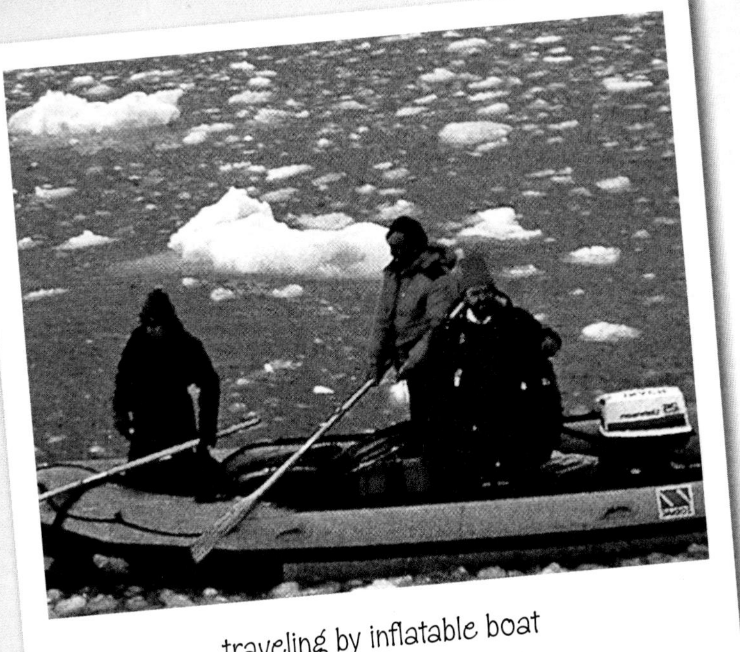

traveling by inflatable boat

I pack my food and extra clothes in a waterproof sea bag. A day pack holds pencils, pens, and paper for drawing and writing. There is no fresh water on the island. I carry two one-gallon canteens.

Each island has an emergency cache of food and supplies, marked with a flag, available if a person gets stranded during a storm.

Alone after being dropped on the island, I hear birds call, the whine of the wind, the waves pounding gravel shores, and no human sounds except my breathing.

Twilight falls and I crawl into my tent, alert and unable to sleep for a long time, listening to the sounds of the Antarctic night.

ANALYZE THE TEXT

Sequence of Events What signal words and phrases on pages 378–379 give you clues about the text's overall structure?

December 3rd
Litchfield Island

One of the larger islands offshore, Litchfield has a penguin rookery, or nesting area, on the gently sloping western edge. The ground is rocky but flat enough for penguins to build nests, with a beach close by for gathering small gray nest stones.

The rookery is occupied by two or three hundred penguins. It's small by penguin standards. The penguins are nearly all Adélies (uh DAY leez), named in 1838 by Dumont d'Urville (dur VEEL) after his wife. I wonder, did they look like her, act like her, or was he just missing her?

Pairs greet each other at the nest with calls like braying donkeys. They rub chests and bellies, flap wings, stretch necks, and reach for the sky with their bills—behavior called "ecstatic display."

I find a sheltered perch by the rookery and put my six-pound metal typewriter on a flat rock. The penguins begin to wander over.

They huddle close, smelling of guano (GWAH noh) and salt water, gently tugging at my clothing with their bills. One bold bird takes my hat and goes off with it.

They are curious about the tap-tap-tapping noise of the typewriter. They walk up and across it, tugging at the paper tucked into the roller. I let them have their way. Human visitors may not touch penguins, or any wildlife, but the penguins can take their time checking us out.

I follow penguins stone collecting, real work for an Adélie. They carry one stone at a time in their bills. It requires hundreds of trips to complete a nest.

Adélie penguin

Placing a stone takes time. With the stone in its bill, the penguin circles the nest, bowing like a butler. Finally deciding where the stone is needed most, the bird drops it and shuffles away to the beach for another. If one penguin steals a stone from another, a noisy argument erupts. Frustrated birds shriek like squabbling children, but they never come to blows.

ANALYZE THE TEXT

Domain-Specific Vocabulary What are some of the science-specific words and terms on pages 380–381? What do they mean, and how do you know?

December 20th
Palmer Station

I have learned that the largest animal on Earth, the hundred-ton blue whale, eats only one of the smallest animals on Earth: krill. There are more krill in the seas than there are stars in the visible universe.

Krill is one link in a simple food chain. Penguins, seals, and whales eat krill. In turn the tiny shrimplike krill eat phytoplankton, one-celled plants that bloom in the sea in spring and summer.

My new friend, Carl, an oceanographer, said we ought to try eating krill since so many animals thrive on it.

In the bio lab we scooped krill into a jar.

We got a small fry pan, then melted butter and cooked up the krill.

Someone said, "Add garlic."

Somebody said, "How about pepper and salt?"

These were added. When the mixture looked ready, we ate it.

"Tastes like butter," one person said.

"More like garlic," another said.

"Tastes like butter *and* garlic," Carl said.

"Krill don't have their own taste," I concluded.

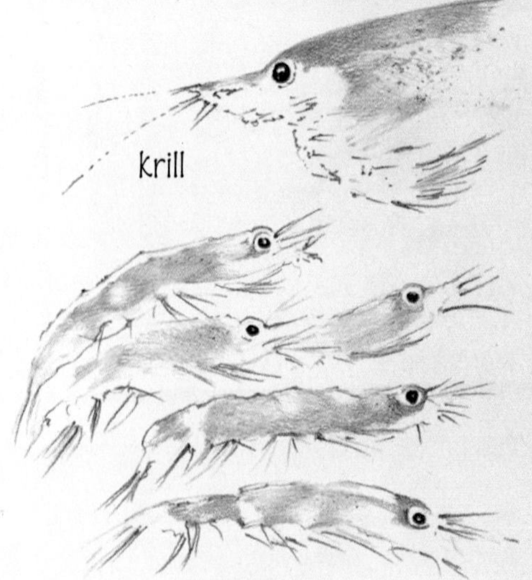

December 24th
Palmer Station

It was three in the morning, bright outside, and I couldn't sleep. I crept downstairs, signed out, and took the flagged trail up the glacier.

Dressed in a watchman's cap, three layers under my parka, and boots, I climbed in a stillness broken only by the noise of snow crunching under my soles. Greenish-purple clouds covered the sky from edge to edge. The sea was the color of pewter.

Near the top I heard a cracking sound, a slap magnified a million times in my ear. Another followed, then another. Echoes of sound, aftershocks, sizzled in the air. The sky began to glow with an eerie luminescence, as if someone in the heavens had switched on a neon light in place of the sun.

I felt myself dropping straight down. A crack had appeared under me, a crevasse (krih VAS) in the glacier.

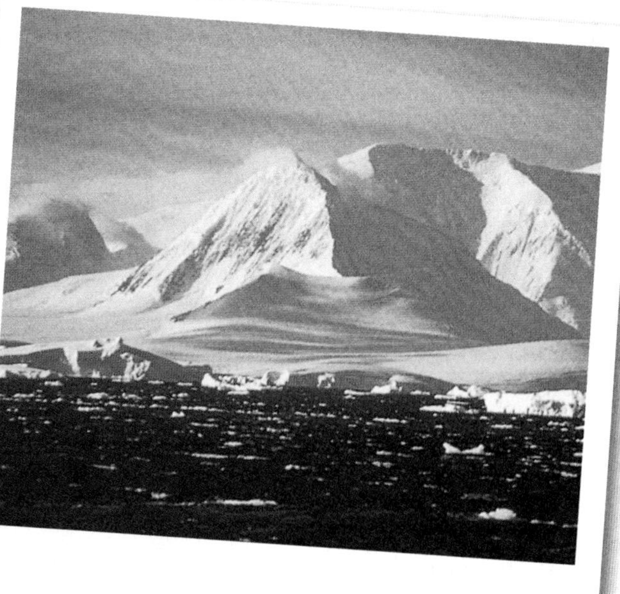

ANALYZE THE TEXT

Simile and Metaphor The author uses **similes** and **metaphors** in the text to compare one thing to something entirely different. A simile uses the words *like* or *as*, but a metaphor does not. One example of a metaphor is the comparison of the cracking sound to a slap. Find another example on page 383.

I'm alive because the crack was narrow. I fell to my shoulders, my boot soles too wide to fit through the bottom of the crack. I stared below into a blue-green hole cut with facets like a diamond.

After a few deep breaths, I began to scramble out. Terrified the crack would keep growing, I moved slowly. It was an hour before I was on firm ice.

The color of the sky shifted to blue-gray with streaks of yellow along the western horizon. To my horror, I saw a pattern of cracks zig-zagging, like fractured window glass, across the glacier surface.

I checked my watch. I'd been gone three hours. I don't know why, but I didn't want anyone rescuing me. I decided to crawl down the glacier on hands and knees.

I felt my way inch by inch, rubbing the surface of the snow with my palms before making a move.

I have a new weariness tonight, born of having been frightened out of my wits while watching one of the most beautiful skies I'll ever see.

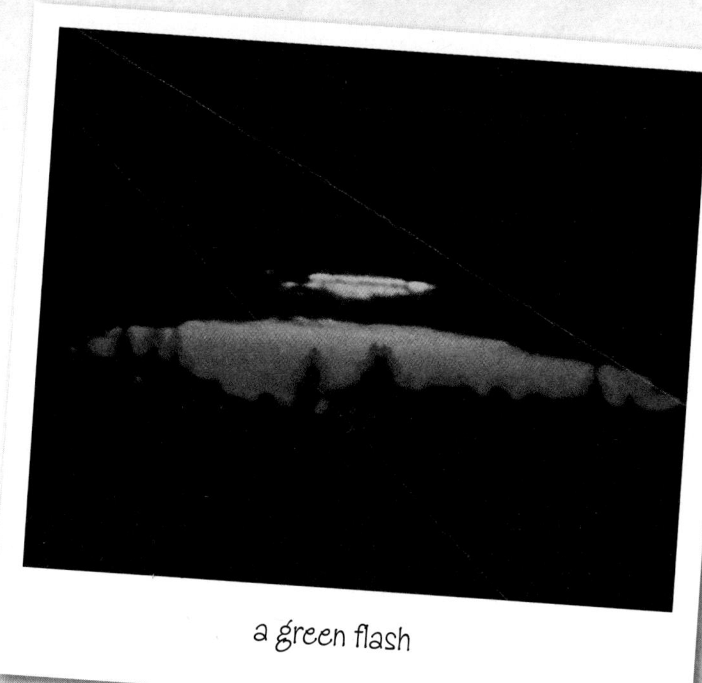
a green flash

January 6th
Palmer Station

Earlier today my friend Carl, the ocean scientist, came to my room and said, "Let's go see the green flash."

"The what?" I asked.

"Come on. You'll see. Hurry or we'll miss it."

We headed up the glacier, and at the top we sat facing west. The sun slipped slowly toward the horizon. As it fell, its orb glowed a deep orange. The shape of it was fat, like a squashed pumpkin. Near the end of the drop the light on top of the orb flashed green—the green flash.

"There it is," I said. "I saw it!"

The green flash is a rare, fleeting event in the Earth's atmosphere. To catch it with the naked eye, there must be a clear horizon at sunset, as often seen over water. The green flash comes with certain conditions in the sky having to do with the way light bends. It lasts less than a twentieth of a second.

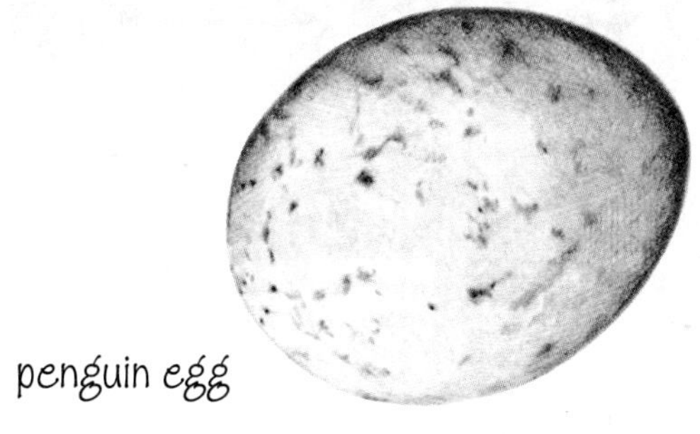
penguin egg

March 12th
Winging Home

Before leaving, I collected (with permission) a sterile penguin egg that would never hatch. I made room for it in my suitcase by giving a lot of my clothes away.

The airline lost my bag in Miami. I told the airline people that I had to have it back, pleading, begging. "It has a penguin egg in it," I said. They glanced at each other and eyed me funny.

Fortunately for me, and them, they found the bag.

The egg reminds me of my trip to the place where penguins raise downy chicks, krill swarm in numbers greater than stars in the sky, whales have rights, and icebergs drift in graceful arcs across Southern Ocean swells. At home, I'll look out at the desert landscape and remember the Antarctic desert, the last great wilderness on Earth.

COMPREHENSION

Dig Deeper

How to Analyze the Text

Use these pages to learn about Sequence of Events, Domain-Specific Vocabulary, and Simile and Metaphor. Then read "Antarctic Journal" again to apply what you learned.

Sequence of Events

"Antarctic Journal: Four Months at the Bottom of the World" is written as a collection of journal entries. In journals, authors share experiences from their own lives—as they happen. Each entry in a journal usually begins with a date. The dates help readers follow the **sequence of events** and know how much time passed between entries. Clue words such as *after* and *tonight* also show the sequence of events.

Using a graphic organizer like the one below can help you describe the overall structure of a text organized by sequence of events. What is the first date and event in "Antarctic Journal"?

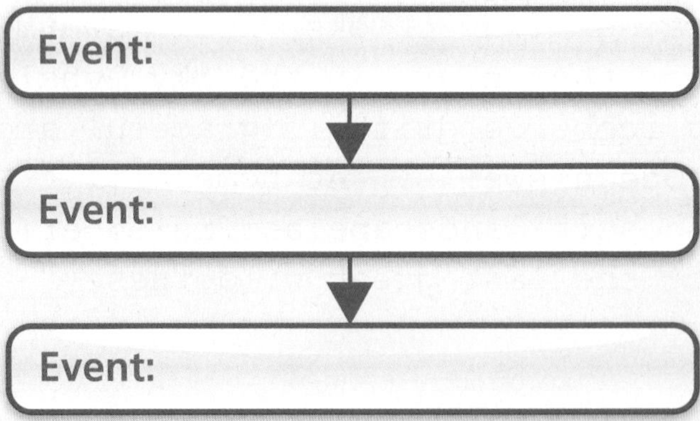

ELACC4RI3 explain events/procedures/ideas/concepts in a text; **ELACC4RI4** determine the meaning of general academic and domain-specific words and phrases; **ELACC4RI5** describe the overall structure of a text or part of a text; **ELACC4L5a** explain the meaning of similes and metaphors in context; **ELACC4L6** acquire/use vocabulary, including academic and domain-specific

Domain-Specific Vocabulary

Nonfiction often focuses on specific topics. Areas of knowledge are called **domains.** Every domain has its own set of words. For example, the words *krill* and *phytoplankton* are important to the subject of the ocean ecosystem. When you come across **domain-specific words,** look for **clues** to the meaning. On page 382, the words *tiny* and *shrimplike* are clues for *krill*.

Simile and Metaphor

Similes and **metaphors** are kinds of **figurative language** that compare one thing to something entirely different. A simile uses the word *like* or *as*, but a metaphor does not. *The penguins are men dressed in tuxedos* is a metaphor. This comparison helps you picture the black-and-white pattern of a penguin. When you read a simile or metaphor, think about what is being compared and what the comparison helps you picture.

Your Turn

RETURN TO THE ESSENTIAL QUESTION

Review the selection with a partner to prepare to discuss this question: *How are the different parts of an ecosystem connected?* As you discuss, take turns reviewing text evidence and explaining the key ideas.

Classroom Conversation

Continue your discussion of "Antarctic Journal" by explaining your answers to these questions:

1. Why are there so many rules when visiting Antarctica?
2. What are three things you'd take on a trip to Antarctica?
3. What do you think the author means when she calls the Antarctic the "last great wilderness on Earth"?

KNOWING THE FACTS

Follow the Food Chain Draw an Antarctic food chain showing whales, krill, and phytoplankton. Then discuss this question with a partner: *What effects might the disappearance of the krill have on whales and other animals and on oceanic ecosystems?* Use text evidence from "Antarctic Journal" to explain your answers.

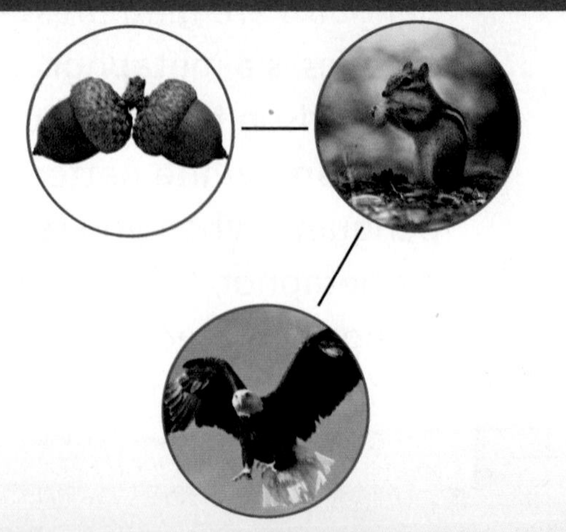

WRITE ABOUT READING

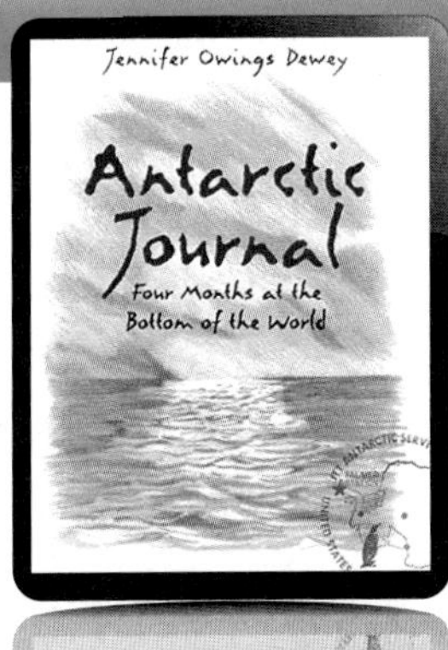

Response The author chose to share information about her Antarctic adventure by writing a journal. Do you think that reading a journal about the Antarctic is more interesting than reading about it in a typical informational text? Why or why not? Write a paragraph expressing your opinion. Give reasons for your opinion, and support them with text evidence, facts, and details. Restate your opinion in the conclusion.

Writing Tip

As you write your response, remember to use verb tenses correctly. Make sure your subjects and verbs agree.

COMMON CORE **ELACC4RI1** refer to details and examples when explaining what the text says explicitly and when drawing inferences; **ELACC4RI5** describe the overall structure of a text or part of a text; **ELACC4W1a** introduce a topic, state an opinion, and create an organizational structure; **ELACC4W1b** provide reasons supported by facts and details; **ELACC4W1d** provide a concluding statement or section; **ELACC4W9b** apply grade 4 Reading standards to informational texts; **ELACC4SL1d** review key ideas expressed and explain own ideas and understanding

Lesson 13

INFORMATIONAL TEXT

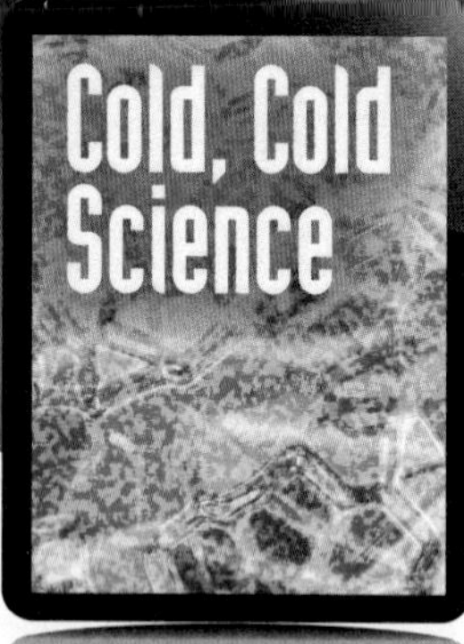

 GENRE

Informational text, such as this article, gives information about a topic. Each topic is often organized under a heading. Informational text usually includes photographs with captions or labels.

 TEXT FOCUS

Secondhand Account A secondhand account gives information that the author did not learn through his or her own experience. The author did research in books, on the Internet, and perhaps talked to people who had experienced the events included in the article. A secondhand account is written in third-person point of view.

ELACC4RI6 compare and contrast a firsthand and secondhand account of the same event or topic; **ELACC4RI9** integrate information from two texts on the same topic

Go Digital

Cold, Cold Science

by Dewey Badeaux

At Palmer Station in Antarctica, scientists live and work in a world of ice. A giant ice sheet that covers the continent helps scientists at Palmer Station understand an environment that doesn't exist anywhere else on Earth.

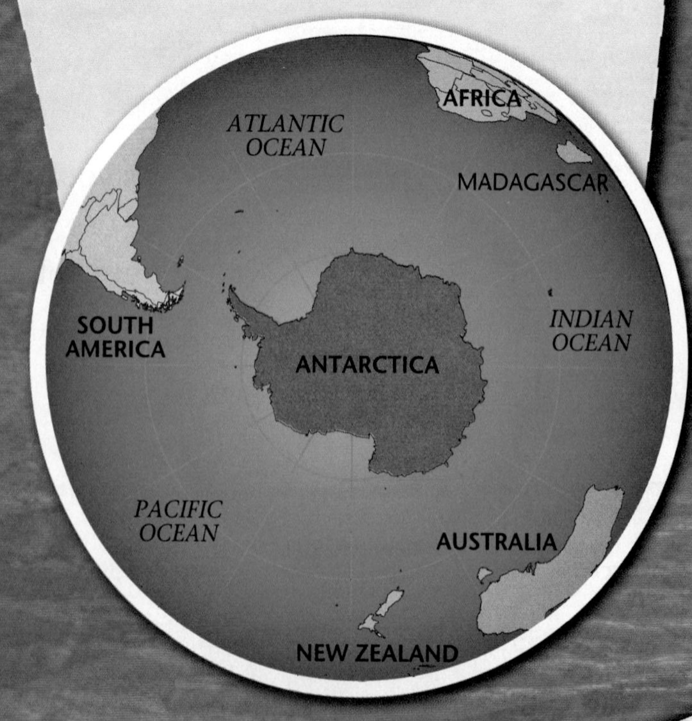

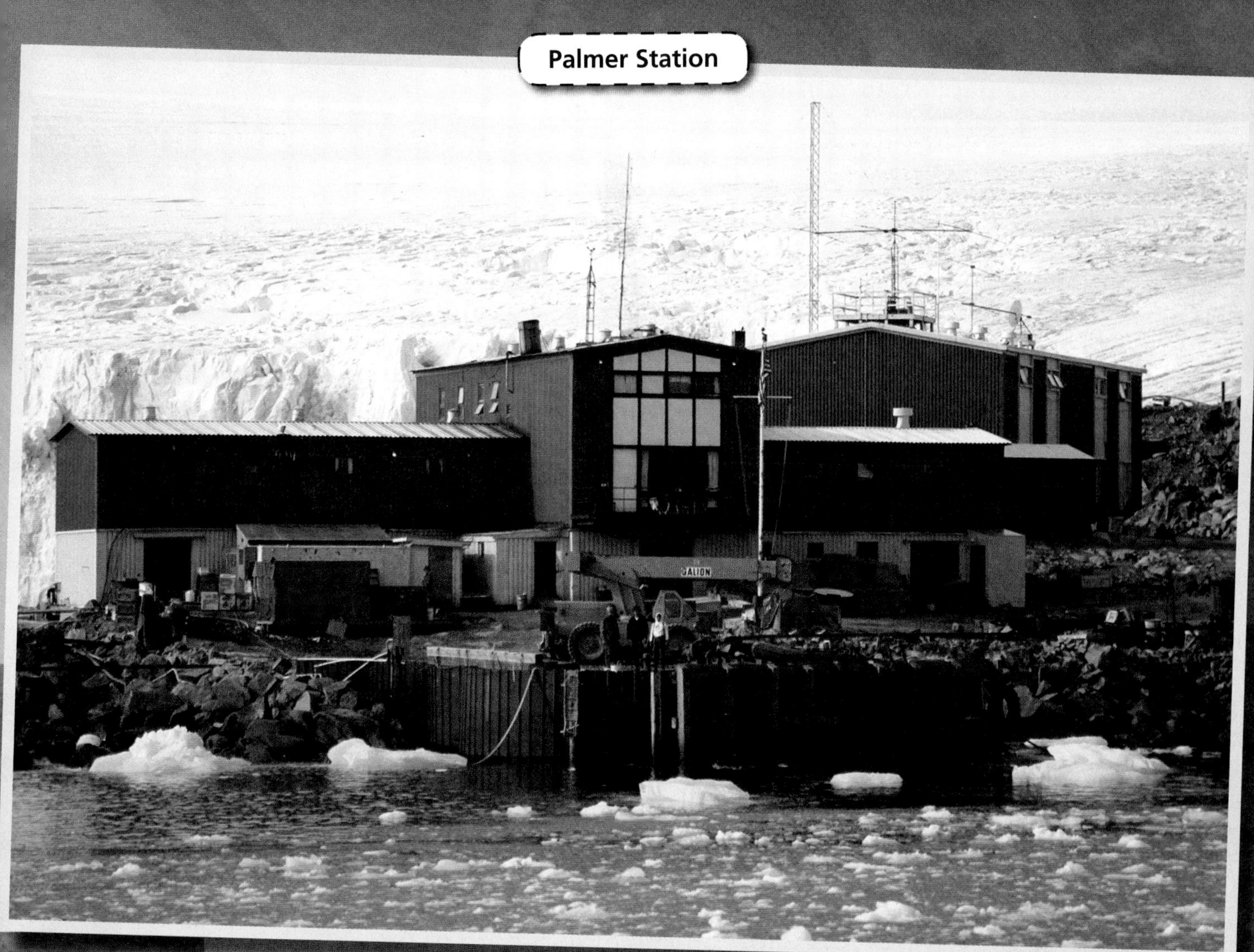
Palmer Station

Home Away from Home

Palmer Station is one of three bases in Antarctica operated by the United States. It is located on Anvers Island, just west of the Antarctic Peninsula in the northwestern part of the continent. Scientists at Palmer Station live at the base year-round and perform field studies in the surrounding environment. One visiting writer, Kate Madin, said, "This town has a single purpose, and everyone here is a part of it: scientific research on the Antarctic coastal ecosystem."

Ninety percent of our planet's ice is found in Antarctica.

Frozen Sculptures

The unique features of the Antarctic landscape give the scientists at Palmer Station many frozen clues to use in their research. Antarctica is glacier country. A glacier is a mass of ice and snow formed on land over thousands of years. A glacier slowly moves across land due to gravity and its great weight. The Antarctic ice sheet, an enormous glacier, covers 98 percent of the continent and contains approximately 5 million square miles of ice, averaging 7,000 feet thick. The Antarctic ice sheet is the largest single mass of ice on Earth, and it contains about 70 percent of Earth's freshwater.

Nearly half of Antarctica's coastline is made up of thick, floating ice called ice shelves. Ice shelves result from the Antarctic ice sheet's movement towards the coastline. They form where the ice sheet meets the water. Palmer Station is located near the Larsen Ice Shelf.

Icebergs can be seen in the frigid waters near Antarctica's coast. An iceberg is a large mass of floating ice broken off from a glacier or ice shelf. Icebergs can be the size of an automobile or a small country! An iceberg's movement is influenced by ocean currents and winds. Eventually, icebergs melt and disappear.

Scientists at Palmer Station study how the Antarctic ice sheet moves and how the temperature of the ocean changes over time. They learn how changes to the ice sheet and ice shelves affect animals that live in Antarctica. The scientists' work also helps them understand how changes in Earth's climate can impact the rest of the world.

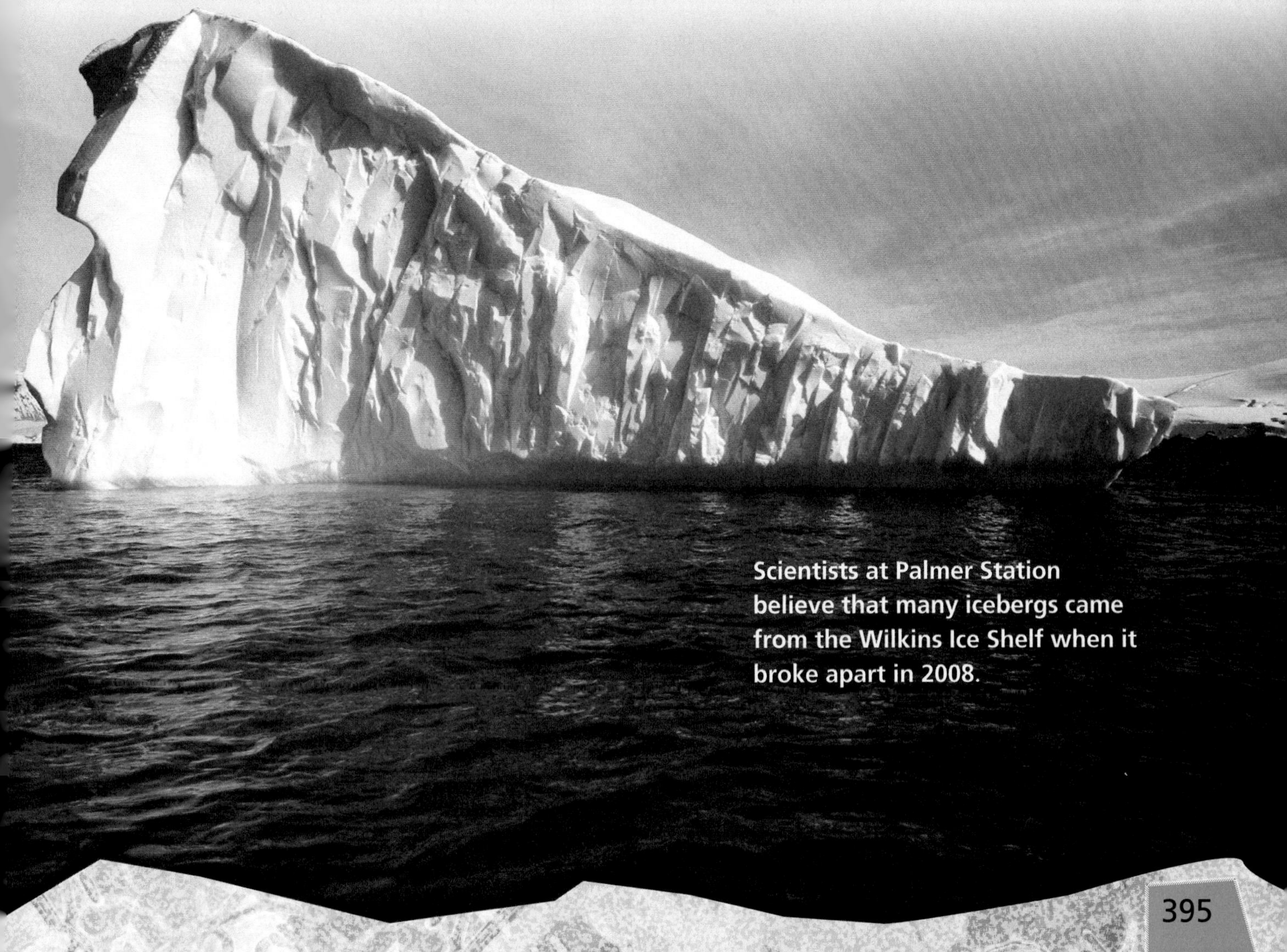

Scientists at Palmer Station believe that many icebergs came from the Wilkins Ice Shelf when it broke apart in 2008.

Antarctic winds can reach speeds of 185 miles per hour!

Windiest, Driest, Coldest

Antarctica is a place of climate extremes. Did you know that it is the windiest place on Earth? During a blizzard, the wind in Antarctica is so strong that it can change the shape of ice and rocks. The strongest winds are found along the coast of the continent and on the Antarctic Peninsula.

Antarctica may not be hot, but much of the continent is the driest place on Earth. It is a desert! Because the air is so cold and dry, it is hard for clouds to form and make rain or snow in the central part of the continent. Not only is Antarctica the world's driest desert, it's also the largest!

The temperature in Antarctica's interior during the winter can get as cold as –94° F. However, in summer, the temperature along the Antarctic Peninsula can climb to almost 60° F. Because the conditions in Antarctica can be so harsh, scientists are very busy there during the warmer summer season. During certain weeks in summer, the sun does not set at all—there is daylight 24 hours a day! The warm temperatures cause the ice along the coast to melt and can impact Antarctica's wildlife.

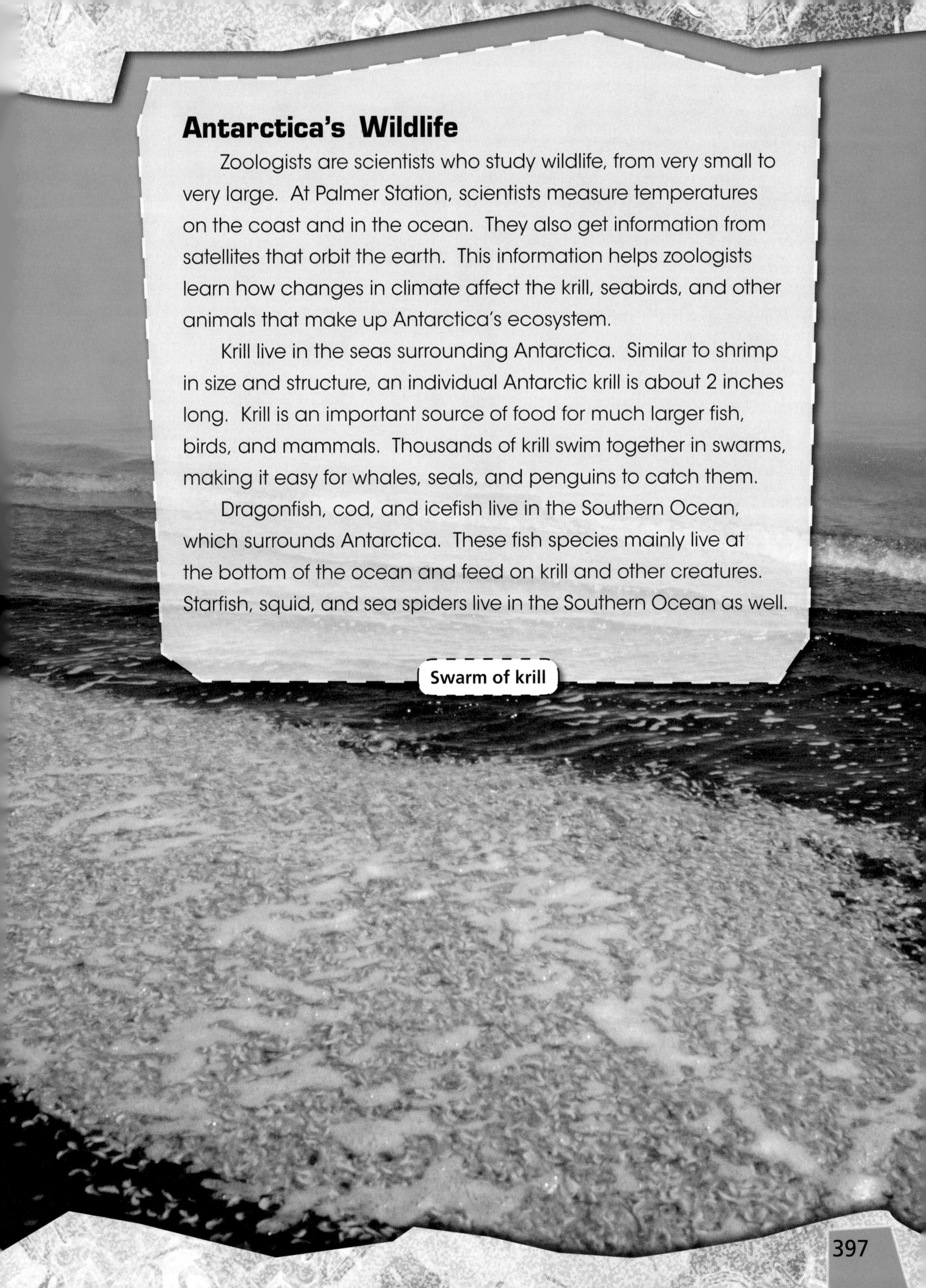

Antarctica's Wildlife

Zoologists are scientists who study wildlife, from very small to very large. At Palmer Station, scientists measure temperatures on the coast and in the ocean. They also get information from satellites that orbit the earth. This information helps zoologists learn how changes in climate affect the krill, seabirds, and other animals that make up Antarctica's ecosystem.

Krill live in the seas surrounding Antarctica. Similar to shrimp in size and structure, an individual Antarctic krill is about 2 inches long. Krill is an important source of food for much larger fish, birds, and mammals. Thousands of krill swim together in swarms, making it easy for whales, seals, and penguins to catch them.

Dragonfish, cod, and icefish live in the Southern Ocean, which surrounds Antarctica. These fish species mainly live at the bottom of the ocean and feed on krill and other creatures. Starfish, squid, and sea spiders live in the Southern Ocean as well.

Swarm of krill

Seals can be found relaxing in the cold waters of Antarctica. Of the many different types of seals in Antarctica, the elephant seal is the largest. A male elephant seal can weigh up to 8,000 lbs. Many scientists believe that seals are most similar to otters and skunks. On the other hand, other scientists believe seals are more closely related to bears!

Seals are able to hold their breath for a long time while swimming underwater. Some seals can swim up to 50 miles a day when they are hunting for krill, fish, and penguins.

Enormous whales live in the Southern Ocean, too. Like other mammals, whales need air to live. Most mammals, such as seals, breathe through their noses and mouths. Whales, however, breathe through an opening on the top of their heads. Humpbacks, orcas, and many other types of whales can be seen in the icy seas of Antarctica.

Elephant seal

Humpback whale

Different kinds of seabirds call Antarctica home. They live and nest on Antarctica's shores and look for food in the water. The albatross is one kind of seabird that lives in Antarctica. It has a wingspan of 11 feet, making it the largest flying bird in the world.

Penguins, another kind of seabird, live and nest in large groups. Unlike other seabirds, these black and white birds cannot fly. Penguins walk on land and swim in the Southern Ocean to look for food.

At Palmer Station, scientists are very interested in penguins. These scientists study how the sun, atmosphere, ocean, and food supply cause the penguin population to rise or fall. Because Antarctica is so isolated, scientists can focus on a single species and learn a lot about how that species survives.

Emperor penguins

Looking Back and to the Future

Fossils discovered on the islands near the Antarctic Peninsula have led many scientists to believe that Antarctica was once a much warmer place, where small, bird-like dinosaurs roamed the land. Fossils of ancient trees also suggest it was warm enough for flowers to bloom. Can you imagine Antarctica warm and sunny?

Too much sun, of course, is a problem. Scientists have discovered a hole in the ozone layer in the atmosphere above Antarctica. The ozone layer is a gaseous shield that protects us from the sun's powerful rays. Without this protection, most life on Earth could not survive. To help shrink the ozone hole, governments in many countries are teaming up to decrease pollution. In time, scientists believe this will help solve the problem.

The work that scientists do at Palmer Station allows people around the world to learn about our planet's climate, oceans, and animal life. By studying clues from the past and what is happening today, they also uncover information that helps us make important predictions about the future.

Scientists take an ice sample for their research.

Compare Texts

TEXT TO TEXT

Compare Firsthand and Secondhand Accounts "Antarctic Journal" is a firsthand account of Antarctica, written by someone who actually visited it. "Cold, Cold Science" is a secondhand account, written by an outside observer. How are the two accounts the same? How are they different? Discuss these questions with a partner. To speak knowledgeably, cite text evidence from both selections in your discussion.

TEXT TO SELF

Extreme Vacation The Antarctic is an environment of extremes. Would you want to visit or work in Antarctica? Why or why not? Write a paragraph and provide reasons supported by facts and details. Make sure to clearly state your opinion.

TEXT TO WORLD

Understanding the Antarctic Discuss with a group what information you learned from "Antarctic Journal" that was not in "Cold, Cold Science." How did "Cold, Cold Science" add to your understanding of Jennifer Owings Dewey's experience?

ELACC4RI6 compare and contrast a firsthand and secondhand account of the same event or topic; **ELACC4RI9** integrate information from two texts on the same topic; **ELACC4W1a** introduce a topic, state an opinion, and create an organizational structure; **ELACC4W1b** provide reasons supported by facts and details; **ELACC4W10** write routinely over extended time frames and shorter time frames

ELACC4L1c use modal auxiliaries to convey various conditions

Grammar

What Are Modal Auxiliaries? Helping verbs are verbs that work with a **main verb** but do not show action themselves. For example, in the sentence *I am running, am* is a helping verb that shows when the action is happening. Another type of helping verb, called the **modal auxiliary**, shows how things could be or should be. Modal auxiliaries include *may, might, can, could*, and *must*.

Modal Auxiliary	Example	Meaning
may, might	You may get lost in the Antarctic wilderness.	The action could take place but is not likely to.
can	People can get frostbite in the freezing cold.	It is possible that the action will take place.
could	Dr. Ernst could arrive as early as tomorrow.	It is unknown how likely or unlikely the action is to happen.
must	You must wear layers of clothes in this bitterly cold climate.	The action absolutely has to take place.

Try This! Work with a partner. Point out the main verb and modal auxiliary in each sentence. Then discuss the meaning of each modal auxiliary.

1. People can become lonely in Antarctica.
2. The scientist might fly home early.
3. The other group members could stay for several weeks.
4. The scientist must make up his mind by tomorrow.

You can use helping verbs to make the meaning of your sentences even clearer to your readers. Modal auxiliaries, such as *can*, *may*, *might*, *must*, and *could,* let your readers know how likely it is that an action or event will happen.

Action could take place, but isn't likely to	Action absolutely has to take place
 Shauna **might** go to Antarctica someday.	 Dr. Patillo **must** fly to Antarctica today.

Connect Grammar to Writing

As you revise your persuasive letter, look for places where modal auxiliaries could make your meaning clearer. If you have used any helping verbs, make sure that you have used them correctly.

ELACC4W1a introduce a topic, state an opinion, and create an organizational structure; ELACC4W1b provide reasons supported by facts and details; ELACC4W4 produce writing in which development and organization are appropriate to task, purpose, and audience; ELACC4L1c use modal auxiliaries to convey various conditions

Opinion Writing

Voice One way of convincing people to do or believe something is by writing a **persuasive letter**. Start a persuasive letter by introducing your topic and clearly stating your opinion. Include reasons for your opinion, along with facts and details to support those reasons. Your letter should include a heading, salutation, closing, and signature.

Jenna wrote a persuasive letter asking her teacher to approve a class field trip. She revised her introduction to clearly introduce her topic and state her opinion and added reasons to support her opinion.

Writing Traits Checklist

- **Ideas** Did I give reasons and support them with facts and details?
- **Organization** Did I use all parts of the letter correctly?
- **Word Choice** Did I choose words that were convincing?
- **Voice** Is the tone of my letter friendly and positive?
- **Sentence Fluency** Did I use modal auxiliaries correctly?
- **Conventions** Did I use correct spelling, grammar, and mechanics?

Revised Draft

I believe that going to the New England Aquarium would be the perfect field trip for our class.

~~Our class never gets to go anywhere exciting!~~ As you know, we have read about penguins in Antarctica. Now we want to learn more about them. Going on a ~~So instead~~ field trip to the aquarium would make ~~we would like to go to the New England~~ learning fun and exciting for the whole class! ~~Aquarium.~~

Final Copy

4680 Pine Avenue
Boston, MA 02101
November 8, 2013

Dear Ms. Beal,

I believe that going to the New England Aquarium would be the perfect field trip for our class. As you know, we have read about penguins in Antarctica. Now we want to learn more about them. Going on a field trip to the aquarium would make learning fun and exciting for the whole class! We would see the three different kinds of penguins that live there. We could learn more about their habitats. The trip would be almost as good as visiting Antarctica.

In conclusion, I hope you will consider my idea for a field trip. I think a trip to the New England Aquarium would be awesome for everyone!

Sincerely,
Jenna Morgan

Reading as a Writer

How did Jenna change her first sentence? As you write your letter, revise your introduction so that it clearly states your opinion on the topic.

In my final paper, I revised my first sentence with a new introduction that tells the reader my feelings. Then I checked that I used helping verbs correctly.

Lesson

14

TARGET VOCABULARY

social
exchanges
excess
reinforce
storage
transport
chamber
scarce
obstacles
transfers

Vocabulary Reader

Context Cards

ELACC4L6 acquire/use vocabulary, including academic and domain-specific

Vocabulary in Context

1 social

Many animals are social. They live together in organized groups.

2 exchanges

Some people have seen exchanges in which dolphins give and receive food.

3 excess

People harvest only excess honey from a beehive. The bees need the rest to live.

4 reinforce

Elephants reinforce, or strengthen, their bond as they protect their young.

- Study each Context Card.
- Use context clues to determine the meanings of these words.

5 storage

Squirrels save food in storage. They can get food from that place later.

6 transport

Working together is handy when a group has to transport, or move, a big object.

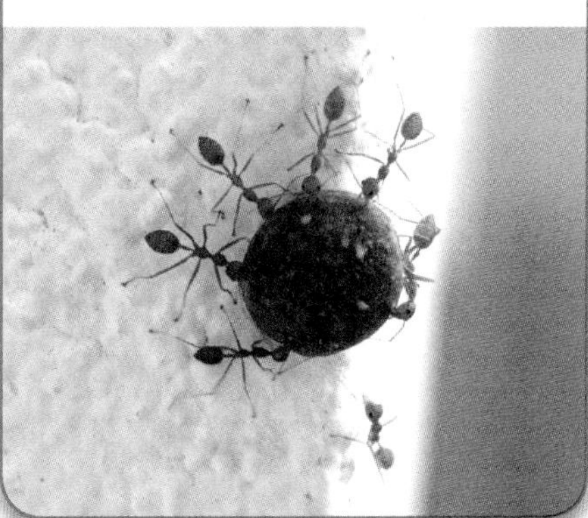

7 chamber

This wasp is working in a hollow chamber of its hive's nest.

8 scarce

Drinking water for wild animals is sometimes scarce, or hard to find.

9 obstacles

There are no obstacles blocking the entry to this rabbit's home.

10 transfers

Humankind transfers, or passes along, information through teaching.

Read and Comprehend

TARGET SKILL

Text and Graphic Features As you read "The Life and Times of the Ant," notice the text and graphic features. **Text features** include headings and captions. **Graphic features** include diagrams, timelines, and other visuals. Graphic features often add information that is not included in the text. As you read, think about how each feature adds to your understanding of the text. Use a graphic organizer like this one to list the selection's text and graphic features and the information each feature provides.

Text or Graphic Feature	Page Number	Information

TARGET STRATEGY

Question Asking yourself questions before, during, and after reading will help you monitor your understanding of the selection. As you read "The Life and Times of the Ant," pause to ask yourself questions, such as *Why do ants do this?* Look for text evidence to answer your questions.

ELACC4RI1 refer to details and examples when explaining what the text says explicitly and when drawing inferences;
ELACC4RI7 interpret information presented visually, orally, or quantitatively

PREVIEW THE TOPIC

Insects

Scientists believe that there are more than eight million species of insects in the world today. Many species have been scurrying around since the time of dinosaurs. Insects may be tiny, but they are very important to our environment. For example, they fertilize soil and pollinate flowers and trees.

In "The Life and Times of the Ant," you will learn about the amazing and complicated life of ants. You'll find out why they are one of the world's most important insects.

Lesson 14

ANCHOR TEXT

TARGET SKILL

Text and Graphic Features Examine how text and graphics work together.

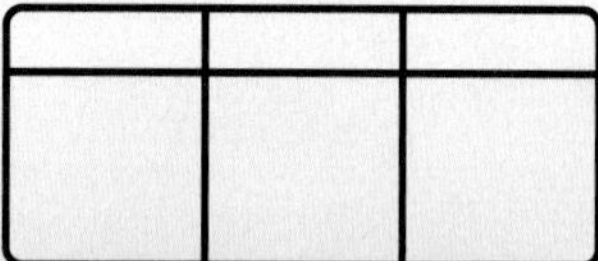

GENRE

Informational text gives facts and information about a topic. As you read, look for:

- headings that begin sections of related information
- graphics to help explain the topic, such as maps, diagrams, or charts
- text structure—the ways the ideas and information are organized

ELACC4RI3 explain events/procedures/ ideas/ concepts in a text; **ELACC4RI7** interpret information presented visually, orally, or quantitatively; **ELACC4RI8** explain how an author uses reasons and evidence to support points

MEET THE AUTHOR AND ILLUSTRATOR

Charles Micucci

Charles Micucci takes a hands-on approach to his work. To research "The Life and Times of the Ant," he built his own ant farm and observed the ants' behavior. Micucci's other books in this series include "The Life and Times of the Apple," "The Life and Times of the Honeybee," and "The Life and Times of the Peanut." For the apple book, he planted twenty-three apple seeds and grew the plants in his apartment. Two of those plants were later relocated to Central Park in New York City. Micucci has also illustrated several books written by other authors.

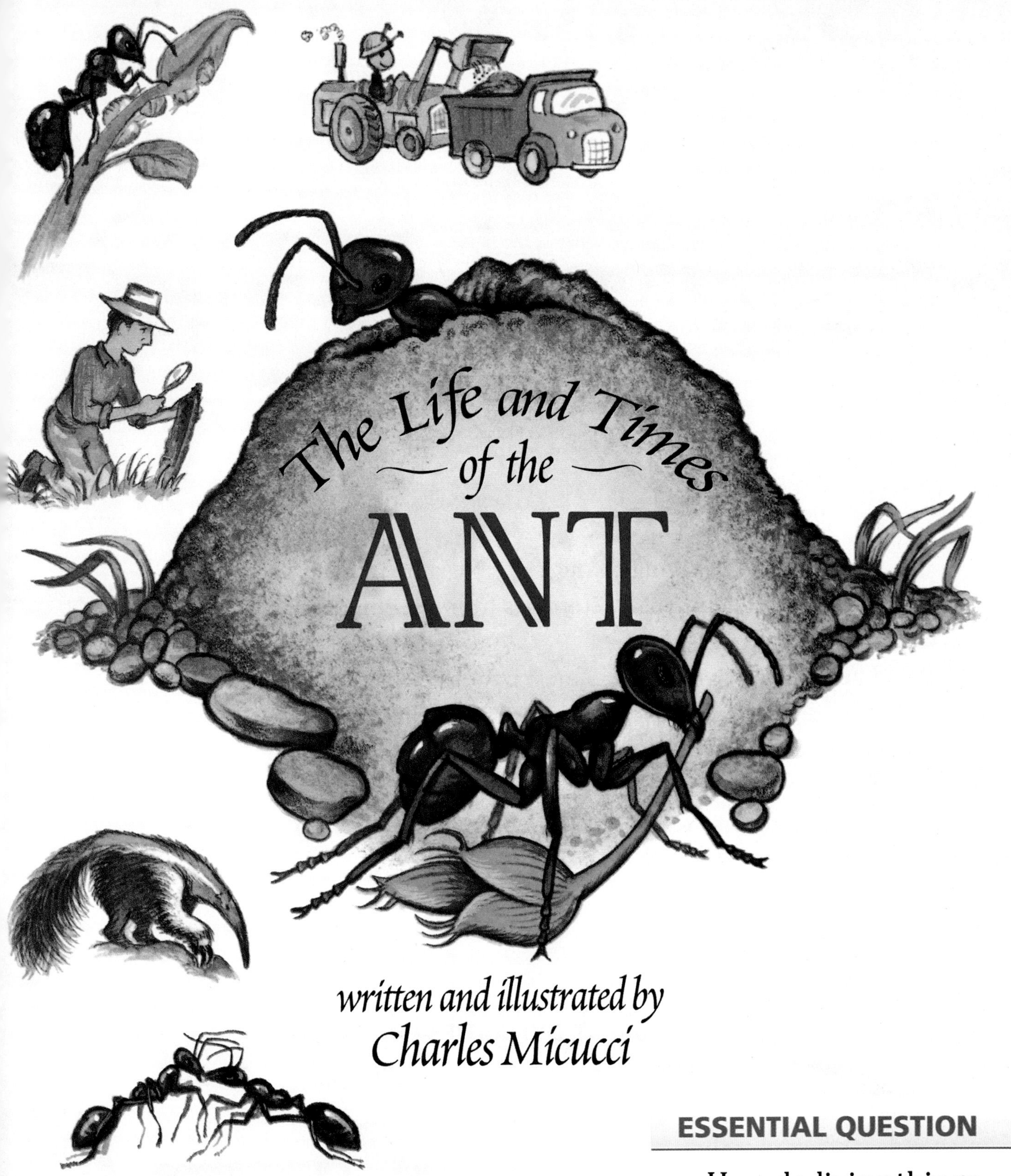

The Life and Times of the ANT

written and illustrated by
Charles Micucci

ESSENTIAL QUESTION

How do living things each have an important role in the world?

Masters of the Earth

Ants have been digging through dirt for more than 100 million years. Their dynasty stretches from the time of dinosaurs to today.

They are one of the world's most important insects. They plow more soil than beetles, eat more bugs than praying mantises, and outnumber many insects by 7 million to 1.

Tunneling out of jungles and forests and into back yards on every continent except Antarctica, ants ramble on as if they own the Earth. Perhaps they do.

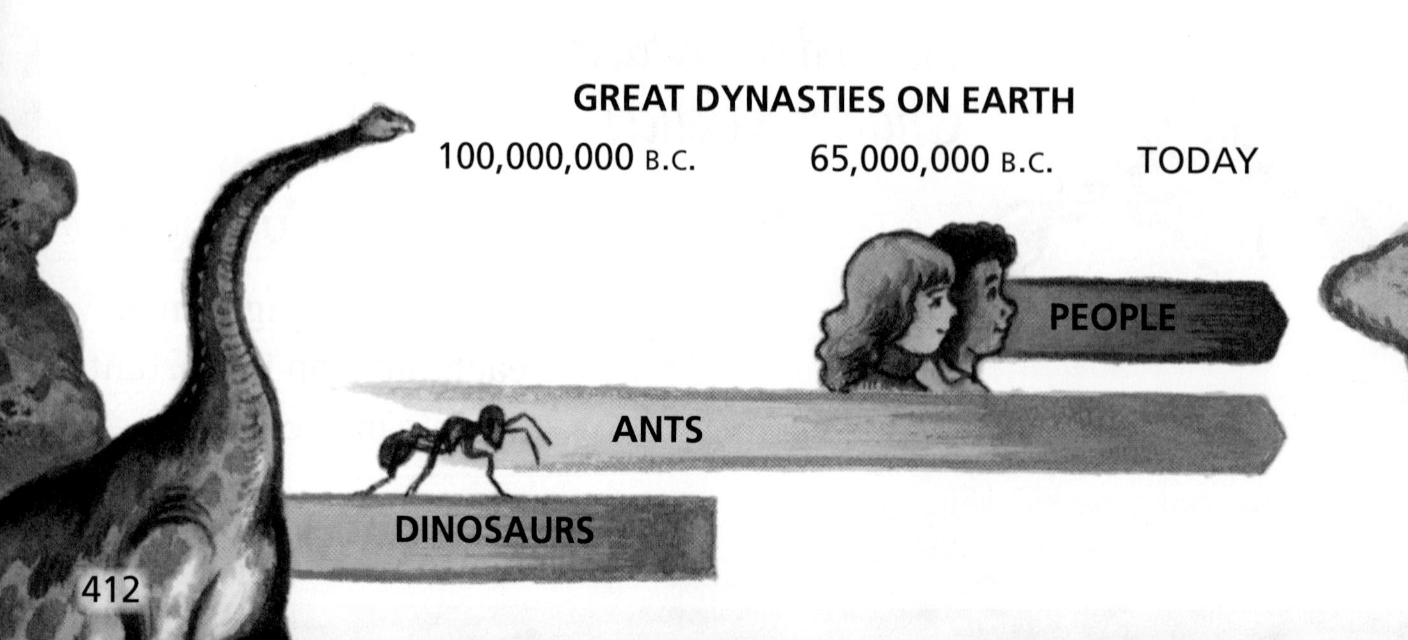

Ounce for ounce, an ant is one of the strongest animals on earth. An ant can lift a seed five times its weight, while an elephant can lift a log only one fifth of its weight.

Each year, the world's ants dig up more than 16 billion tons of dirt—enough to fill 3 billion dump trucks.

Ants are frequently compared with people because they live in social communities and work together to solve their problems.

Inside an Ant Hill

Most ants build their homes underground. Ants dig by scooping dirt with their mandibles (jaws). As they chew the dirt, it mixes with their saliva to form little bricks. Then they pack the little bricks together to reinforce the tunnels. Finally, the ants carry the excess dirt outside with their mandibles, and it gradually forms an anthill.

Beneath the anthill lies the ant nest. Small nests have only one chamber just inches below the surface, while large nests may have thousands of chambers and may be as deep as twenty feet. All nests provide shelter from the weather and a safe environment for the queen ant to lay eggs.

An anthill absorbs the sun's rays and transfers the heat down into the nest. An anthill can be ten degrees warmer than the surrounding area.

Ants often nest beneath a rock or log, which protects the nest and traps moisture in the dirt. Ants require moisture so that their bodies do not dry out.

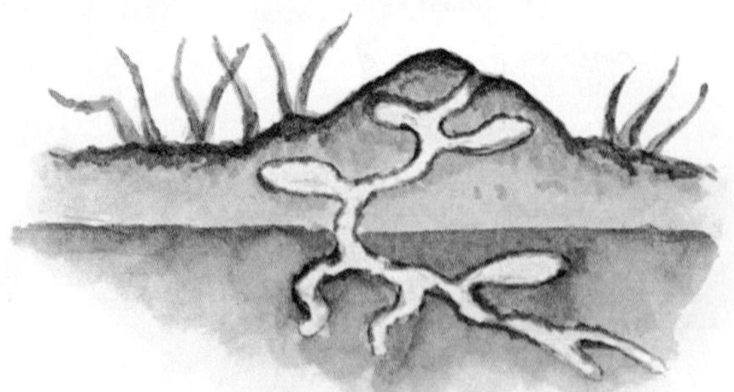

Ants dig their nests deep enough to reach damp dirt. As air dries out the nest, they dig new tunnels into the damp dirt.

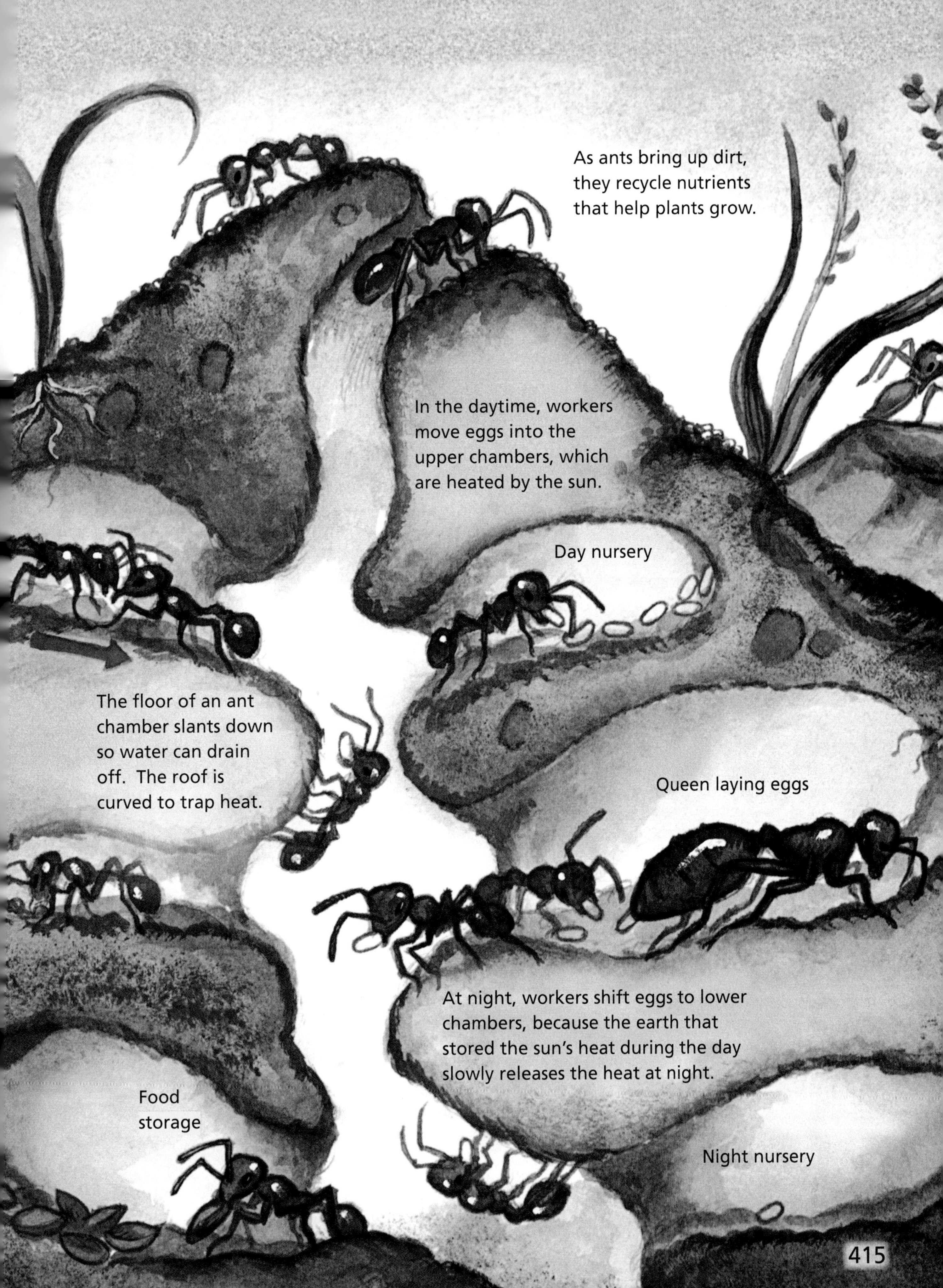
As ants bring up dirt, they recycle nutrients that help plants grow.
In the daytime, workers move eggs into the upper chambers, which are heated by the sun.
Day nursery
The floor of an ant chamber slants down so water can drain off. The roof is curved to trap heat.
Queen laying eggs
At night, workers shift eggs to lower chambers, because the earth that stored the sun's heat during the day slowly releases the heat at night.
Food storage
Night nursery

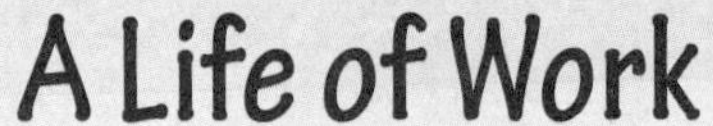

A Life of Work

Ants begin their working lives by cleaning themselves. In a couple of days they start sharing food and licking each other. These food exchanges bond the colony together. There is no boss ant, but active ants usually begin doing chores and then other ants join in.

Younger ants work in the nest—tending the queen ant, feeding larvae (LAHR vee), and digging tunnels. After a couple of months, the ants leave the nest to search for food. There is no retirement; worn out or battle-scarred, ants work until they die.

Queen Tender
Young ants help the queen deliver her eggs by grabbing the eggs with their mandibles.

Nurse Ant
Ants lick larvae so they do not dry out, and feed them so they grow.

ANALYZE THE TEXT

Author's Purpose What does the author want you to know on pages 416–417? What evidence does he provide to help you understand this?

Foragers
The oldest ants search for food. Most foragers search within fifty feet of the nest, but if food is scarce, they may travel thousands of feet.

Guard
When ants first leave the nest, they stand near the entrance, blocking strange ants from entering.

Tunnel Digger
As the population grows, ants dig more tunnels for the increased traffic and new chambers to store the eggs and larvae.

Digging holes can be hard work. To remove a pile of dirt 6 inches high, 6 inches wide, and 6 inches long requires 500,000 loads of dirt.

Grass Root Highways

Some ants connect their anthills to food sources by a system of ant trails. Unlike scent trails, which are invisible, these trails can be easily seen. Construction crews remove grass and twigs to form paths two to six inches wide that may stretch over six hundred feet. When food is plentiful, a thousand ants per foot crowd the trail. Established ant colonies may travel over the same grass root highways for many years.

ANALYZE THE TEXT

Text and Graphic Features What do the illustrations on pages 418–419 show? What does the chart on page 419 tell you? How does the information from each graphic feature connect to the text?

In forests, wood ants connect their anthills together by ant trails. Large wood ant colonies transport thousands of caterpillars and insects a day over their trails.

Harvester ants construct their trails to wildflowers, where they collect seeds. Surrounding their anthills, discarded seeds sprout into new plants.

Some ant trails are so well preserved that larger animals such as deer and even people may use them as footpaths.

Army ants form living bridges to cross streams by linking themselves together.

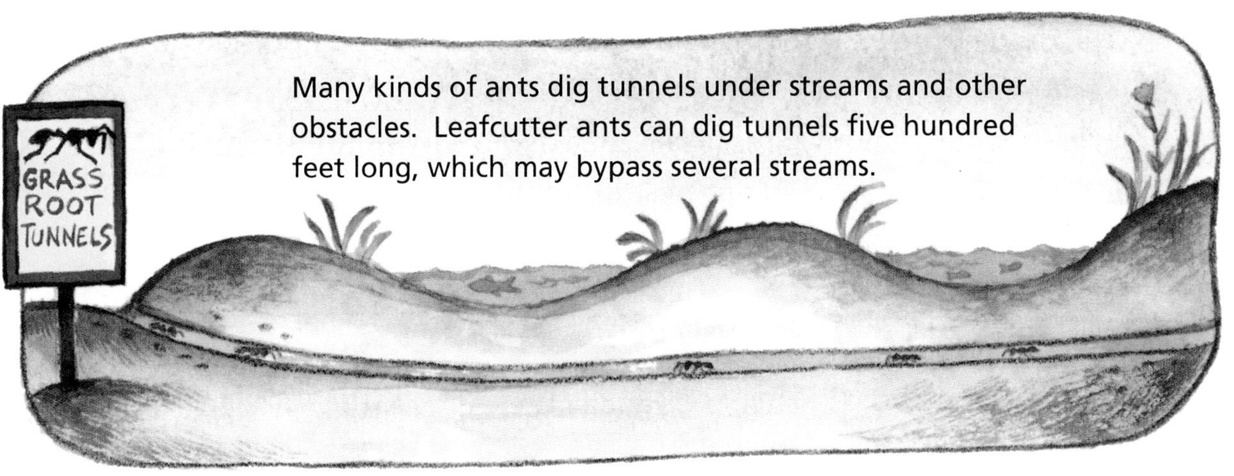

Many kinds of ants dig tunnels under streams and other obstacles. Leafcutter ants can dig tunnels five hundred feet long, which may bypass several streams.

GRASS ROOT SPEED LIMITS

Harlow Shapley, an astronomer whose hobby was ants, tested their speed. He discovered that they run faster on hot days.

TEMPERATURE	78 °F	85 °F	92 °F
SPEED* (inches per second)	1	$1\frac{3}{8}$	$1\frac{5}{8}$

*Speeds are for the Argentine ant

A Dangerous World

When you are only a quarter-inch tall, the world can be a dangerous place. Every time an ant leaves home, there is a risk that she will not return. Horned lizards lap up ants as they exit the nest, woodpeckers pick them off as they climb trees, and ant lions ambush them in sand pits.

Sometimes ants are not safe even in their own homes. Armadillos feast on burrowing ants, as does the biggest home wrecker of all: the giant anteater of Central and South America. Seven feet long and weighing as much as seventy pounds, a giant anteater can tear open an ant nest in minutes and devour twenty thousand ants in one meal.

Sand Trap of No Return

The ant lion digs a circular sand pit and waits at the bottom.

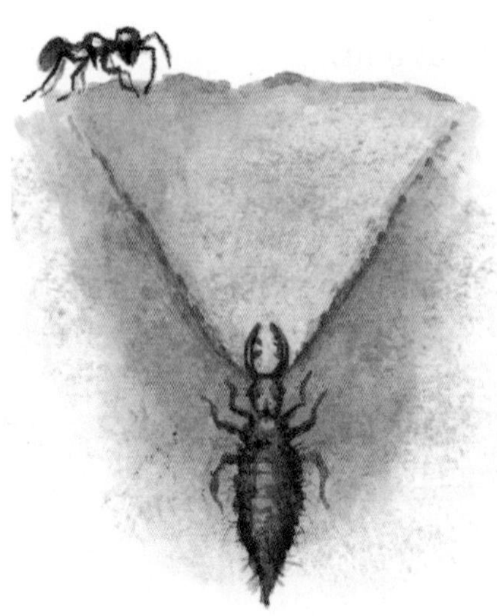

When an ant looks into the pit, the ant lion tosses sand into the air to trip up the ant.

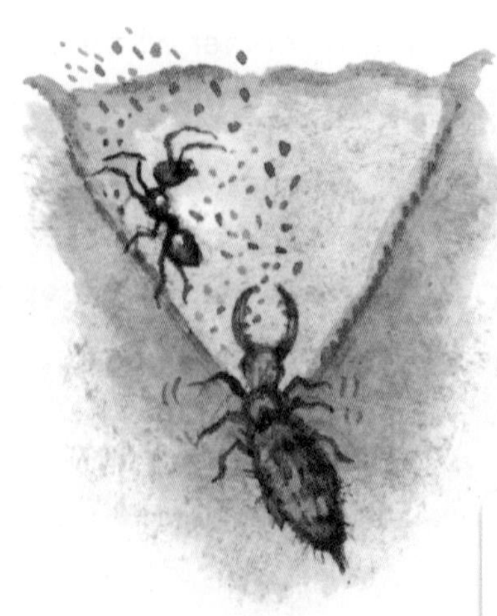

The ant stumbles into the pit, and the ant lion grabs it with its large pincers.

ANALYZE THE TEXT

Explain Scientific Concepts and Ideas What is the main idea the author wants you to know in this section?

The Giant Anteater

The giant anteater is a slow, nearsighted, toothless animal that has escaped extinction for one reason only: it specializes in eating ants and termites.

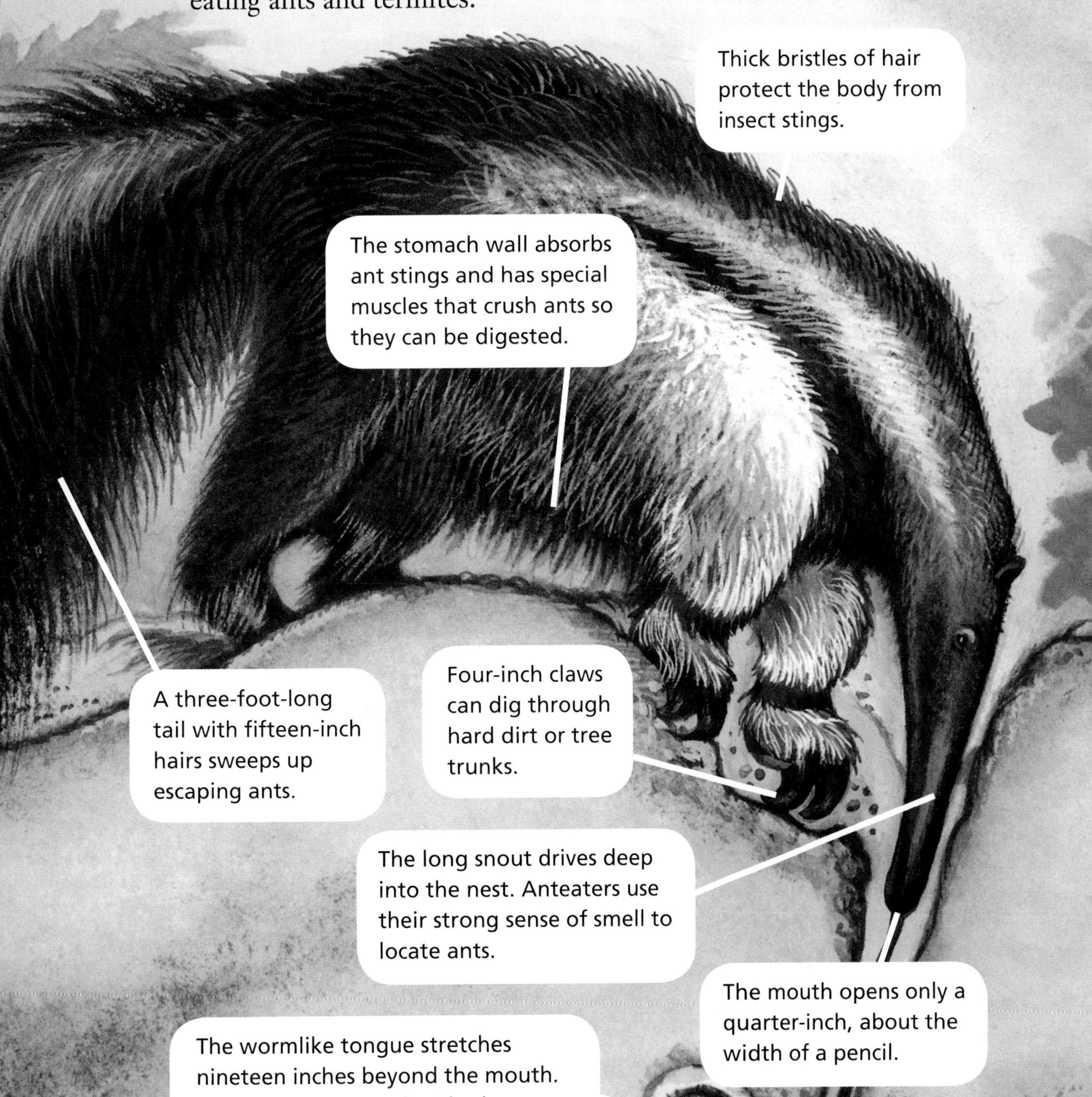

Thick bristles of hair protect the body from insect stings.
The stomach wall absorbs ant stings and has special muscles that crush ants so they can be digested.
A three-foot-long tail with fifteen-inch hairs sweeps up escaping ants.
Four-inch claws can dig through hard dirt or tree trunks.
The long snout drives deep into the nest. Anteaters use their strong sense of smell to locate ants.
The mouth opens only a quarter-inch, about the width of a pencil.
The wormlike tongue stretches nineteen inches beyond the mouth. The tongue is coated with gluey saliva, which causes ants to stick to it.

How Ants Recycle Leaves

Leafcutter ants harvest leaves and take them to the nest. In the process, they thin jungle overgrowth and return mulch from the crushed leaves to the soil.

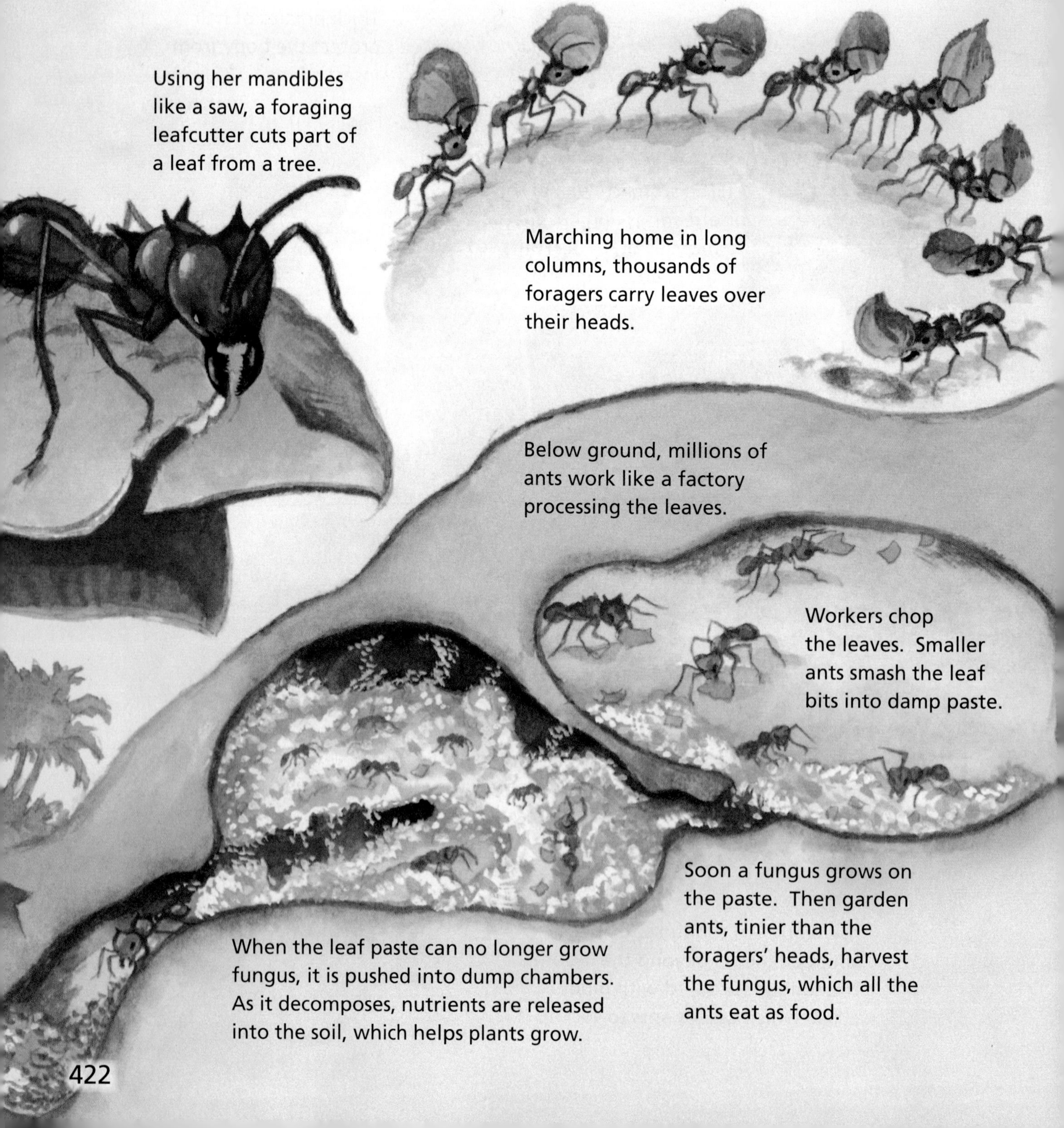

Using her mandibles like a saw, a foraging leafcutter cuts part of a leaf from a tree.

Marching home in long columns, thousands of foragers carry leaves over their heads.

Below ground, millions of ants work like a factory processing the leaves.

Workers chop the leaves. Smaller ants smash the leaf bits into damp paste.

Soon a fungus grows on the paste. Then garden ants, tinier than the foragers' heads, harvest the fungus, which all the ants eat as food.

When the leaf paste can no longer grow fungus, it is pushed into dump chambers. As it decomposes, nutrients are released into the soil, which helps plants grow.

Dig Deeper

How to Analyze the Text

Use these pages to learn about Text and Graphic Features, Scientific Concepts and Ideas, and Author's Purpose. Then read "The Life and Times of the Ant" again to apply what you learned.

Text and Graphic Features

"The Life and Times of the Ant" gives facts about ants. Like other informational texts, it includes **text features** such as headings and captions. It also includes **graphic features** such as pictures, diagrams, tables, and timelines. These features organize information and help readers understand the topic. Sometimes a graphic feature adds information that is not presented in the words of the text.

When you come to a text or graphic feature, pause to think about how the information helps you understand the topic or adds to your knowledge of the topic.

Look at *Sand Trap of No Return* on page 420. How do the illustrations help explain how an ant lion uses a trap?

Text or Graphic Feature	Page Number	Information

ELACC4RI3 explain events/procedures/ideas/concepts in a text; **ELACC4RI7** interpret information presented visually, orally, or quantitatively; **ELACC4RI8** explain how an author uses reasons and evidence to support points

Explain Scientific Concepts and Ideas

Authors of informational texts often describe complex **scientific concepts and ideas.** As you reread the selection, be sure you understand what happens during ants' lives and why. Explain the concepts by using details and information in the text.

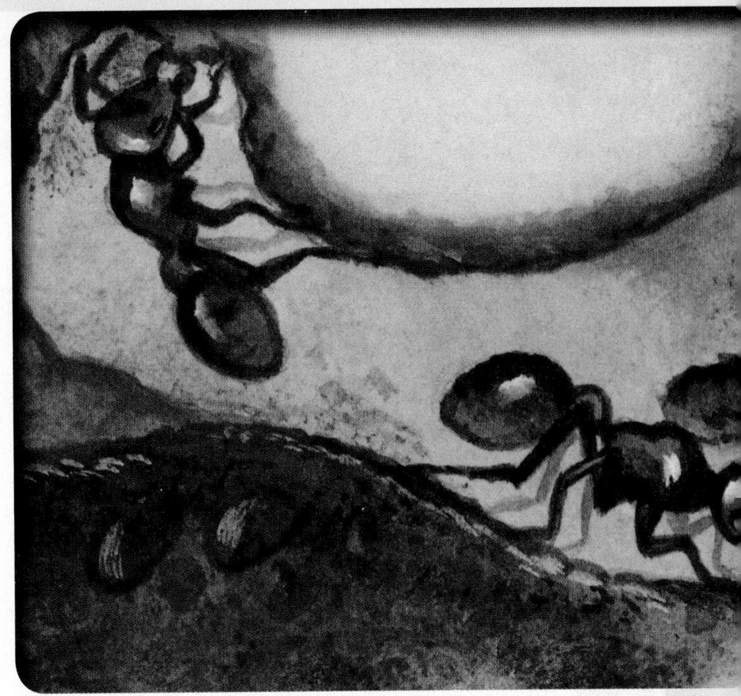

Author's Purpose

An **author's purpose** is his or her reason for writing. An author may have more than one purpose. You can determine the author's purpose by analyzing how reasons and evidence support his or her main points. Is the author trying to inform you, persuade you, or entertain you? For example, one of the author's purposes for writing "The Life and Times of the Ant" is to explain why ants are important on Earth. On pages 412–413, the author gives facts and details that support the view that ants are important creatures.

Your Turn

RETURN TO THE ESSENTIAL QUESTION

Review the selection with a partner to prepare to discuss this question: *How do living things each have an important role in the world?* Take turns reviewing and explaining the key ideas in your discussion. Ask and answer questions to clarify each others' ideas.

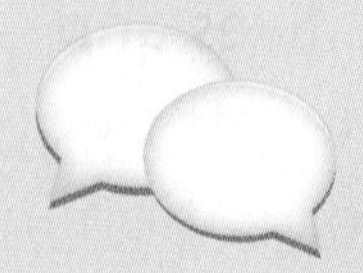

Classroom Conversation

Continue your discussion of "The Life and Times of the Ant" by explaining your answers to these questions with text evidence:

1. Why does the author call ants "masters of the Earth"?
2. How did your opinion of ants change after reading the text?
3. What do you think people can learn from ants about living and working together?

USING GRAPHIC FEATURES

Create a Diagram Look at the diagram on page 415. Draw your own anthill diagram. Use the information on page 414 to add details and captions to your diagram. Then discuss with a partner how the diagram in the book and your diagram help you understand how an anthill is built and functions.

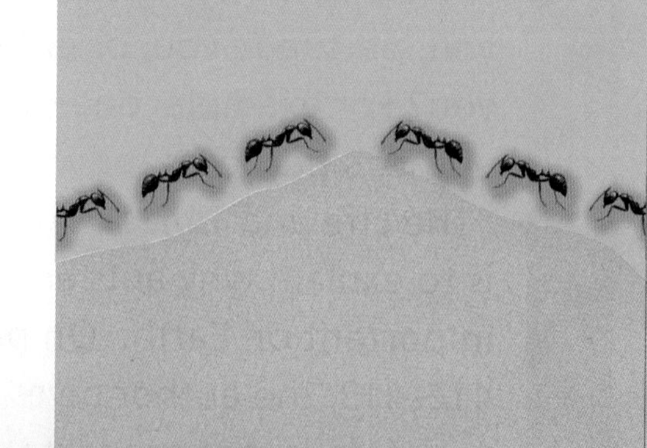

WRITE ABOUT READING

Response Think of the various ways that ants work together to create a society. Then write two paragraphs that compare and contrast ant colonies with human communities. In the first paragraph, tell how the two societies are alike. In the second paragraph, tell how they are different.

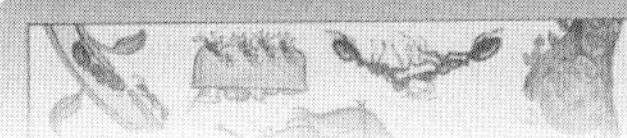

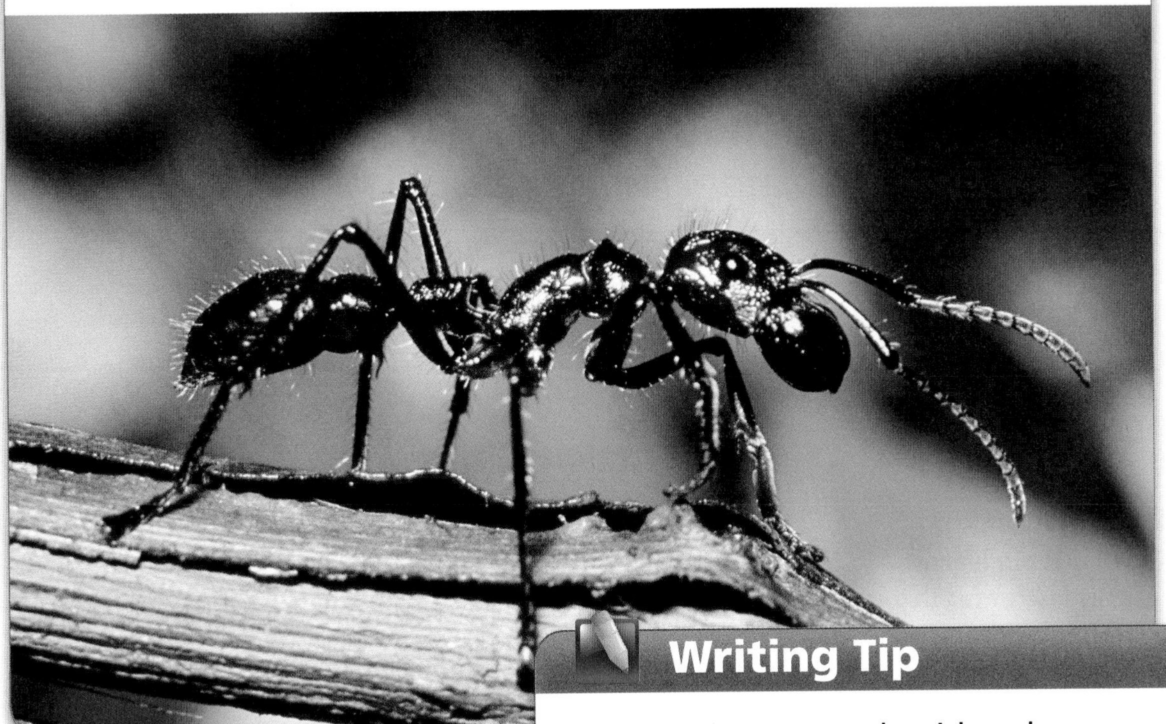

Writing Tip

Begin each paragraph with a clear statement about the similarities or differences. Use transition words and phrases such as *similarly* and *but* to signal how the societies are alike or different.

COMMON CORE **ELACC4RI1** refer to details and examples when explaining what the text says explicitly and when drawing inferences; **ELACC4RI7** interpret information presented visually, orally, or quantitatively; **ELACC4W2c** link ideas within categories of information using words and phrases; **ELACC4W9b** apply grade 4 Reading standards to informational texts; **ELACC4SL1c** pose and respond to questions and make comments that contribute to the discussion and link to others' remarks

Lesson 14

FABLE

GENRE

A **fable** is a short story in which a character, usually an animal, learns a lesson.

TEXT FOCUS

A **moral** is the lesson that a character in a fable learns. What does this lesson teach you about helping others?

ELACC4RL2 determine theme from details/summarize; **ELACC4RL10** read and comprehend literature

THE DOVE AND THE ANT

retold by Anne O'Brien

This retelling of an old fable is set on the island of Puerto Rico, where a wide river, the Rio de la Plata, flows from the mountains down to the sea. Near the river stands a large ausubo tree.

A Dove sat in the branches of the ausubo tree. He was a social creature who liked to meet other animals.

At the base of the tree was an anthill. There an Ant was working to transport food for storage. The Dove watched her reinforce the anthill and clear the central chamber. He saw her moving obstacles from the tunnels.

"What a hard worker!" remarked the Dove.

Not long after, he heard the Ant say in a tiny voice, "I'm so thirsty!"

The Dove wanted to help. He flew down to a lower branch. "The river is not far," he called out to the Ant. "It is just beyond that tall grass."

At the riverbank, the Ant had a long drink. Then suddenly a gust of wind blew her into the water.

"Help!" cried the Ant. Hearing the Ant's cry, the Dove grabbed a twig in his beak and dropped it into the water.

"Climb on and save yourself!" the Dove called. Clinging to the twig, the Ant was soon washed to shore.

"How can I ever thank you?" the Ant asked the Dove. "Life is hard and such kindness is scarce."

"It was my pleasure," the Dove replied. "I like to help my fellow creatures. There can never be excess kindness in this world."

Thinking over the Dove's words, the Ant returned to work.

Later that day, a hunter named Rafael appeared, carrying a large sack. He spotted the Dove in the ausubo tree. He set to work near the anthill, building a bird trap.

The Ant saw the sack and the trap. "When the hunter catches a bird, he transfers it into the sack and carries it away," the Ant thought.

Just then the Ant saw the Dove flying toward the trap. "Oh, no," said the Ant. "The Dove will be caught! I have to act quickly."

In a flash, the Ant crawled up Rafael's foot and bit his ankle. The hunter cried out in pain. Startled, the Dove flew higher up into the tree.

Rafael rubbed his ankle. "Too bad," he thought. "Now I will have to catch my dinner elsewhere."

When the hunter had gone, the Dove turned to his friend. "Now it is my turn to thank you," he said.

"It was my pleasure," the Ant replied.

The lesson of the tale is this: The best way to make friends is by exchanges of kind deeds.

Compare Texts

TEXT TO TEXT

Compare Texts Compare the fictional ant in "The Dove and the Ant" to the real ants in "The Life and Times of the Ant." In what ways does the Ant in "The Dove and the Ant" behave like a real ant? What do real ants do that he does not? Work with a partner to list ideas from text evidence. Then compare your list with that of other students.

TEXT TO SELF

Make a "Fun Facts" List "The Life and Times of the Ant" contains many facts about ants. Which facts were the most fun for you to learn about? Quickly skim the text again and make a list of five facts about ants that you found interesting or strange. Share your list with a partner.

TEXT TO WORLD

Compare Ants Use reference texts and Internet search engines to research and take notes on two kinds of ants. Then construct a chart to compare them. Include details that tell what they look like, where they live, and what their habits are. Present your findings to the class.

ELACC4RI1 refer to details and examples when explaining what the text says explicitly and when drawing inferences; **ELACC4W7** conduct short research projects that build knowledge through investigation; **ELACC4W8** recall information from experiences or gather information from print and digital sources/take notes, categorize information, and provide a list of sources

Grammar

What Are Participles? A **participle** is a verb form used as an adjective. Each verb has two forms that can be used as participles. The **present participle** form has *-ing* added to the verb. The **past participle** form usually has *-ed* added to the verb.

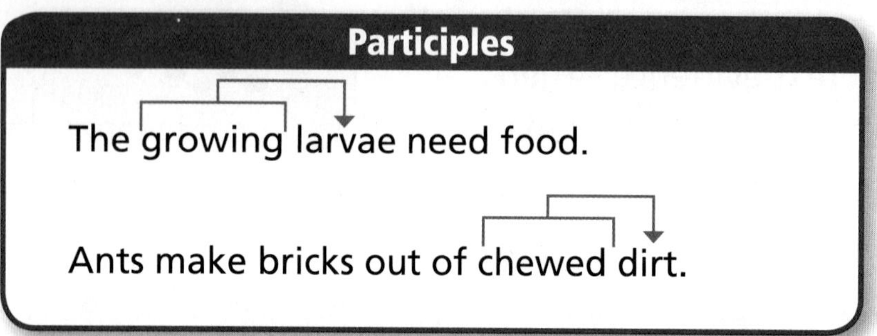

Participles
The growing larvae need food.
Ants make bricks out of chewed dirt.

A **participial phrase** begins with a participle and describes a noun.

participial phrase

The larvae growing in the ant nest need food.

participial phrase

The ants make bricks out of dirt mixed with saliva.

Try This! **Work with a partner. Identify the participle in each sentence. Tell whether it is a present participle or a past participle. If the participle begins a participial phrase, identify the phrase.**

1. The expanded ant nest has new chambers.
2. Day nurseries are warm chambers filled with eggs.
3. Workers must move stored eggs each day.
4. The ants tending the eggs are young.

In your writing, you can sometimes combine two related sentences by making one a participial phrase, which is made up of a participle and any accompanying words. The participial phrase in the new sentence tells more about the subject.

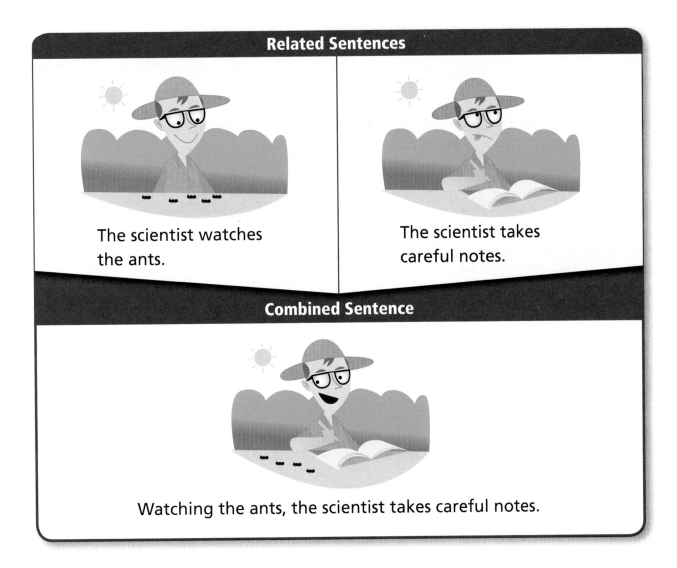

Related Sentences

The scientist watches the ants.	The scientist takes careful notes.

Combined Sentence

Watching the ants, the scientist takes careful notes.

Connect Grammar to Writing

As you revise your persuasive essay next week, look for places to use a participial phrase to describe someone, something, or an action, or to combine sentences.

ELACC4W1a introduce a topic, state an opinion, and create an organizational structure; **ELACC4W1b** provide reasons supported by facts and details; **ELACC4W5** develop and strengthen writing by planning, revising, and editing; **ELACC4W10** write routinely over extended time frames and shorter time frames

Opinion Writing

Reading-Writing Workshop: Prewrite

✔ **Organization** Good writers organize their ideas before writing their **persuasive essays**. Taking notes can help you identify reasons, facts, and details to support your opinion. Making a graphic organizer can help you organize them for your essay.

For his persuasive essay, Julio chose to write about classroom ant farms. First, he did some research and took notes. Then he used an idea-support map to organize his reasons, facts, and details. Later, he reordered his reasons in order of importance.

Writing Process Checklist

▶ **Prewrite**

- ✔ Did I state a clear opinion and goal?
- ✔ Did I list strong reasons that support my opinion?
- ✔ Did I include facts and details to support my reasons?
- ✔ If I did research, did I identify sources and take notes using my own words?

Draft

Revise

Edit

Publish and Share

Exploring a Topic

Why are ants interesting?

— stronger than elephants for their size

— build underground homes with many parts

— work together to care for queen, eggs

Micucci, Charles. The Life and Times of the Ant.

How do ant farms work?

— two types: gel; sand or soil

— get 25 ants; feed and water every day

"Setting Up a Classroom Ant Farm."
AllThingsAnt.com, 15 Nov. 2010.

Idea-Support Map

Opinion: The students in Room 6 should have an ant farm.

Reason: It would teach us responsibility.
Facts and details:
We would have to choose the farm (sand, soil, or gel). There would be 25 ants to start with. We would have to feed and water them regularly.

Reason: Ants are fascinating.
Facts and details:
Ants are stronger than elephants for their size. They have a complicated social structure.

Reason: We will be able to learn by observation.
Facts and details:
We could observe how the ants build their homes and take care of each other. We could watch the community develop and grow.

Reading as a Writer

How can Julio's idea-support map help him develop paragraphs? As you write your persuasive essay this week, look for ways that an idea-support map could help organize your thoughts.

I took notes about ants and ant farms. Then I used the notes to create an idea-support map. I listed reasons to support my opinion. I added facts and details to support my reasons. This helped me organize my ideas.

Lesson 15

Vocabulary in Context

Ecology for Kids

Wonderful Weather

TARGET VOCABULARY

organisms
directly
affect
traces
vast
habitats
variety
species
banned
radiation

Vocabulary Reader

Context Cards

ELACC4L6 acquire/use vocabulary, including academic and domain-specific

1 organisms

Biologists study the organisms, or living things, on Earth.

2 directly

You can directly help the environment by planting trees. You can see results quickly.

3 affect

Smog and smoke negatively affect the air by making it unhealthy to breathe.

4 traces

Wash your hands thoroughly, or else traces of dirt and germs may remain.

▶ Study each Context Card.

▶ Use a dictionary to help you understand the meanings of these words.

5 vast

The vast desert stretched for hundreds of miles in every direction.

6 habitats

Forests and oceans are types of habitats that support different plants and animals.

7 variety

The rain forest contains a wide variety of animals and plants.

8 species

There are many different species of sharks, such as the hammerhead.

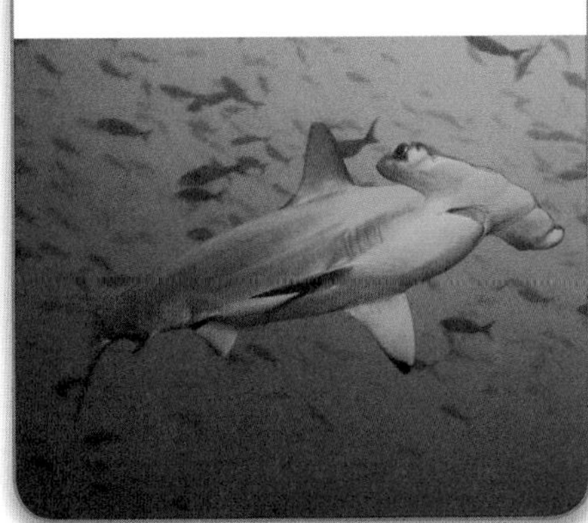

9 banned

Littering is banned in many public places. People should dispose of trash responsibly.

10 radiation

Invisible rays of energy called radiation are produced by the sun and other stars.

Read and Comprehend

TARGET SKILL

Main Ideas and Details As you read "Ecology for Kids," look for the **main ideas,** or the most important points the author makes. Look for supporting **details** that give facts or examples of the main ideas. Note how the details the author chooses to include support the main reason for writing. Use a graphic organizer like this one to help you.

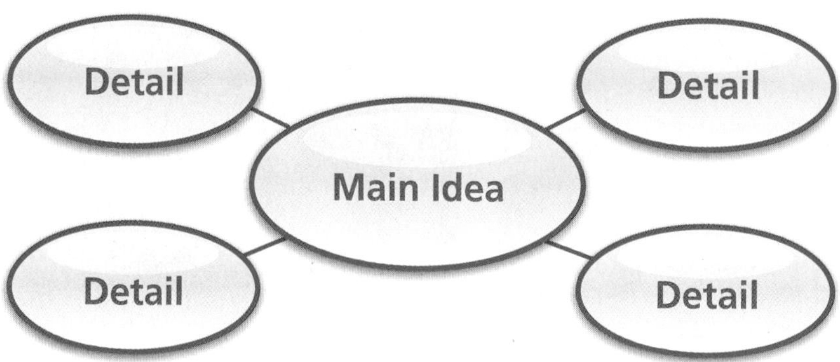

TARGET STRATEGY

Monitor/Clarify As you read "Ecology for Kids," **monitor,** or pay attention to, your understanding of the text. If something does not make sense, stop to **clarify** it, or make it clear.

ELACC4RI1 refer to details and examples when explaining what the text says explicitly and when drawing inferences; **ELACC4RI2** determine the main idea and explain how it is supported by details/summarize; **ELACC4RF4c** use context to confirm or self-correct word recognition and understanding

PREVIEW THE TOPIC

The Environment

Life science is the study of all living things. Did you know that living things can affect their environment? This is a topic that ecologists study. Ecologists are scientists who study living things and their environment.

The Earth seems so large that you may not think your actions can affect it. In fact, everyone's actions do affect the environment. In "Ecology for Kids," you'll learn about the many ways humans affect the environment. You'll also learn what we can do to protect the earth.

Lesson 15

ANCHOR TEXT

TARGET SKILL

Main Ideas and Details
Explain the main idea, or what the text is mostly about. Find details that support the main idea.

GENRE

Informational text gives facts and examples about a topic. As you read, look for:

- headings that begin sections of related information
- photographs and captions
- facts and details about a subject or topic

ELACC4RI2 determine the main idea and explain how it is supported by details/summarize; **ELACC4RI8** explain how an author uses reasons and evidence to support points; **ELACC4L3a** choose words and phrases to convey ideas precisely

MEET THE AUTHOR

Federico Arana

Federico Arana has spent his life studying the environment and, as a science teacher, knows all about ecology. He also spends his time painting and making music. Federico's paintings have been shown in Germany, Switzerland, the United States, and in his home country, Mexico. However, he knows that educating people about the dangers the environment faces is of great importance, and he has written numerous books to help people understand what they can do to save the planet.

Go Digital

Ecology for Kids

By Federico Arana

ESSENTIAL QUESTION

Why is it important to be informed about what is happening in our world?

Ecology

What does the word *ecology* mean? The term was invented by Ernst Haeckel (HEHK uhl), a German biologist. He joined two Greek words: *oikos*, meaning "house," and *logie*, meaning "the study of." Together they mean "the study of the house." The "house" Haeckel had in mind is our planet, Earth. Earth is home for all living things—humans, animals, plants, fungi, and even tiny microbes.

To study a house is to learn how its residents use it. An ecologist is a scientist who studies the relationships between organisms and their environment. The environment is an organism's surroundings. It may include water, gases, rocks, and temperature.

Ecologists also study the delicate balance of using the environment while protecting it.

An ecologist once asked a boy what he thought it meant to protect the environment.

The boy said, "You go into the forest and look for somebody who wants to cut down a tree. You take away his ax. You tell him about how important trees are. You say they are good for natural beauty, saving soil, putting oxygen into the air, and giving shelter to birds and other animals."

Trees give us resources and natural beauty.

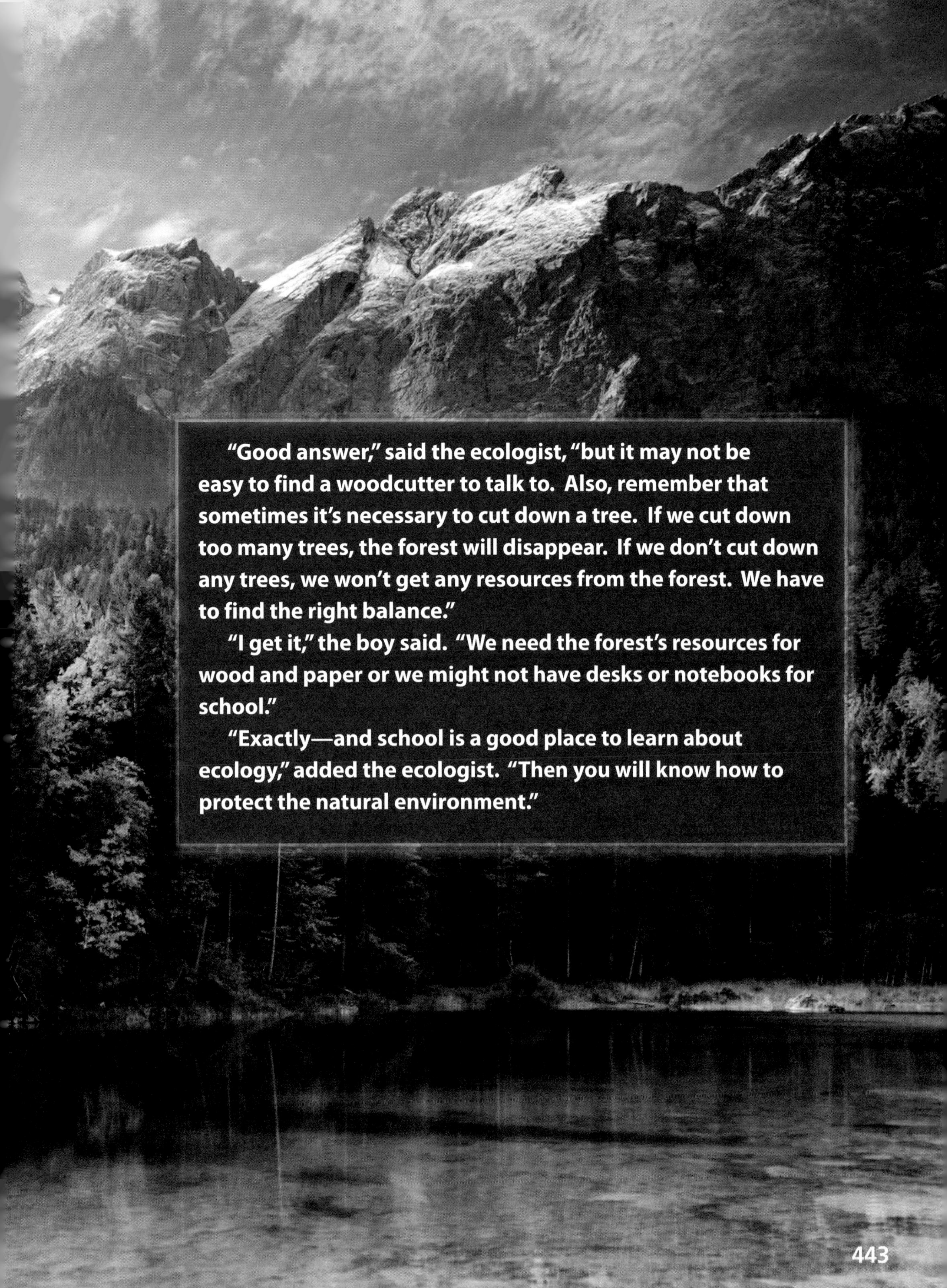

"Good answer," said the ecologist, "but it may not be easy to find a woodcutter to talk to. Also, remember that sometimes it's necessary to cut down a tree. If we cut down too many trees, the forest will disappear. If we don't cut down any trees, we won't get any resources from the forest. We have to find the right balance."

"I get it," the boy said. "We need the forest's resources for wood and paper or we might not have desks or notebooks for school."

"Exactly—and school is a good place to learn about ecology," added the ecologist. "Then you will know how to protect the natural environment."

Ecosystem

Scientists call Earth and its surrounding atmosphere the biosphere. To study it, they divide it into parts called ecosystems.

An ecosystem is a natural area where groups of living and nonliving things interact with their environment. Forests, lakes, swamps, and deserts are all examples of ecosystems.

One ecosystem and the organisms that live in it may depend on other ecosystems. For example, a bear that lives in a forest might use a lake to find fish to eat and water to drink.

In the same way, the problems of one ecosystem often directly affect the organisms of other ecosystems. Take, for example, the problems of the tropical rain forest.

This bear relies on two different ecosystems.

Destruction of the Forests

Four of Earth's seven continents have traces of what used to be vast tropical forests. Now, these forests are gone.

How did they disappear? A large part of the forests was cut down to clear lands for farming. This caused problems. The layer of soil upon which a forest rests is thin. Without deeply rooted trees, the soil is washed away by rain. Soon nothing remains but dry, sandy soil in which very little can grow.

Without plants to eat, animals must leave their habitats. Huge amounts of oxygen are also lost. The Amazon rain forest alone is thought to produce one-third of all the oxygen in Earth's atmosphere. In addition, many rain forest plants are used to produce medicines. Preserving the rain forest is important to all living things.

Clearing a tropical forest can create problems for the world.

ANALYZE THE TEXT

Author's Word Choice How does the author use precise, specific words to explain the problems in the rain forests?

An Ocean of Resources

The sea is another ecosystem to be both used and protected.

The sea covers four-fifths of Earth's surface. It is an amazing world filled with a huge variety of creatures. These creatures include fish, crabs, jellyfish, corals, sponges, clams, snails, and algae. Marine mammals, such as dolphins and whales, spend their whole lives in the sea. Other mammals, including seals, walruses, and polar bears, live near the sea and spend much of their time in it. The sea turtle and some birds, such as penguins, spend most of their lives at sea. Scientists are still discovering new species of sea life.

The sea is home to an amazing variety of creatures.

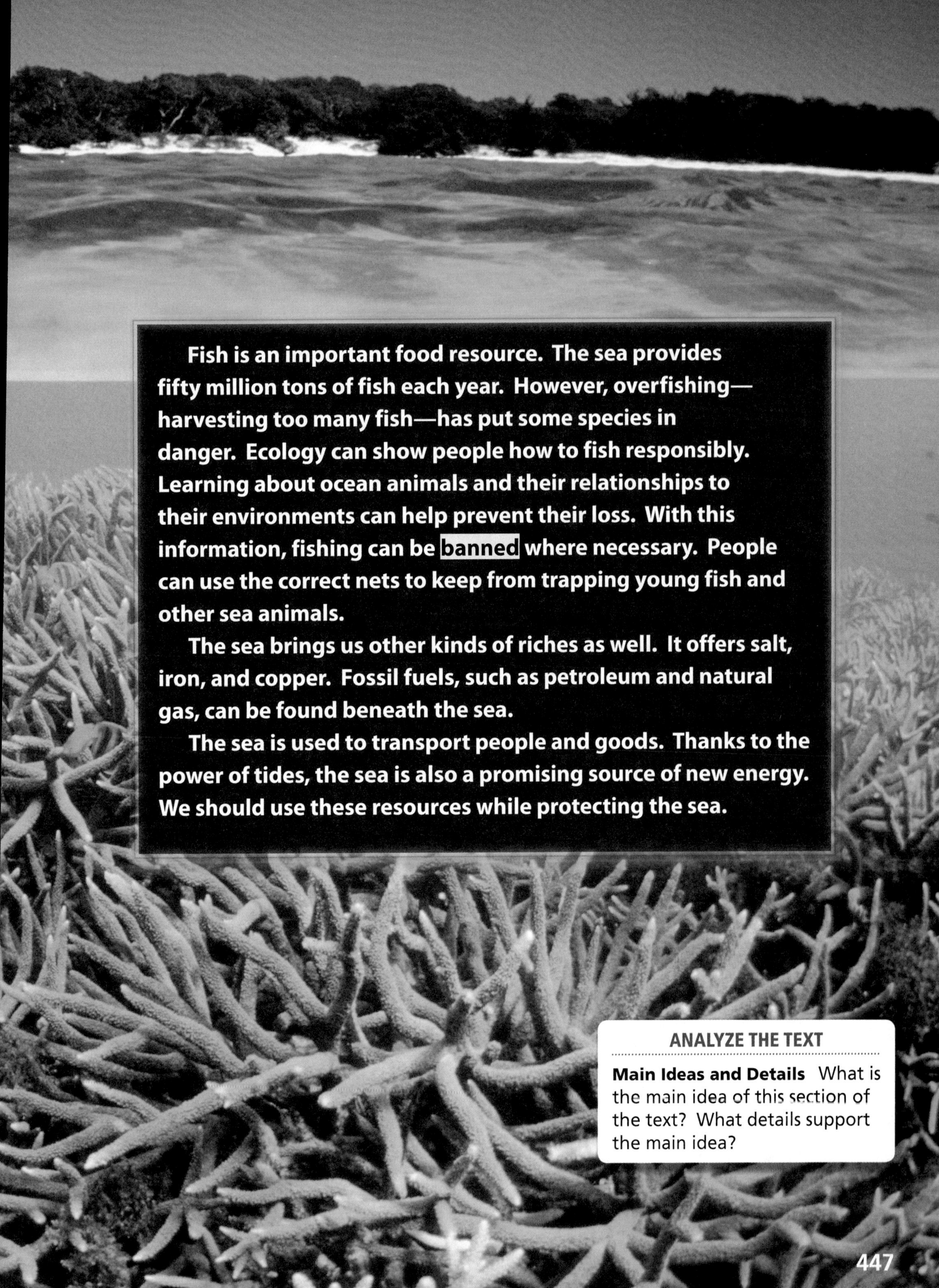

Fish is an important food resource. The sea provides fifty million tons of fish each year. However, overfishing—harvesting too many fish—has put some species in danger. Ecology can show people how to fish responsibly. Learning about ocean animals and their relationships to their environments can help prevent their loss. With this information, fishing can be banned where necessary. People can use the correct nets to keep from trapping young fish and other sea animals.

The sea brings us other kinds of riches as well. It offers salt, iron, and copper. Fossil fuels, such as petroleum and natural gas, can be found beneath the sea.

The sea is used to transport people and goods. Thanks to the power of tides, the sea is also a promising source of new energy. We should use these resources while protecting the sea.

ANALYZE THE TEXT

Main Ideas and Details What is the main idea of this section of the text? What details support the main idea?

The Protective Ozone Layer

Another important part of Earth's biosphere is the atmosphere. This is the blanket of air covering Earth. Part of the atmosphere is the ozone layer. It protects us from the sun.

The sun's light lets us see and is needed for growth. Its heat controls the temperature of Earth. All living things need the sun's light and heat to live and grow.

The sun also produces powerful **radiation**, including X rays, ultraviolet rays, and microwaves. If the ozone layer were to disappear, Earth would receive too many of these harmful rays. This would hurt all living things.

People have banned the use of chemicals that can weaken the ozone layer. By thinking ecologically, we can safely use the sun's resources.

The ozone layer protects the Earth from the sun's harmful rays.

How Can You Protect Biosphere Earth?

One important way to protect the environment is to help stop pollution. Here are a few ideas:

Put trash in its place. Trash does not belong in the streets, the rivers, or the oceans. Trash and other kinds of pollution harm all living things.

Use solar-powered clocks and calculators when you can. If you use battery-power, recycle used batteries.

When you leave a room, turn off the light. When you are not using televisions, radios, and computers, turn them off, too. That way, your family will use less electricity and will save money.

A clean environment is everyone's responsibility.

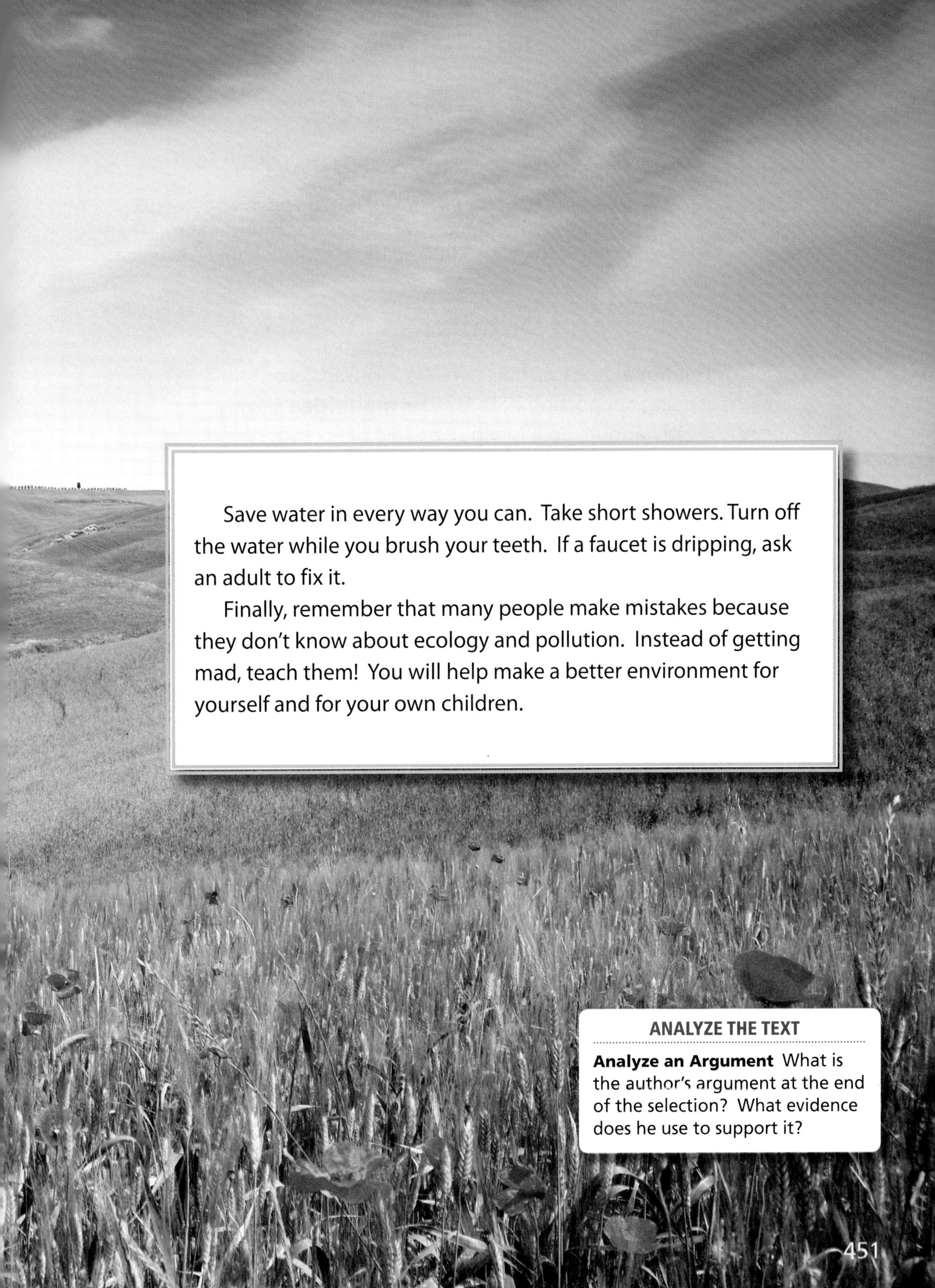

Save water in every way you can. Take short showers. Turn off the water while you brush your teeth. If a faucet is dripping, ask an adult to fix it.

Finally, remember that many people make mistakes because they don't know about ecology and pollution. Instead of getting mad, teach them! You will help make a better environment for yourself and for your own children.

ANALYZE THE TEXT

Analyze an Argument What is the author's argument at the end of the selection? What evidence does he use to support it?

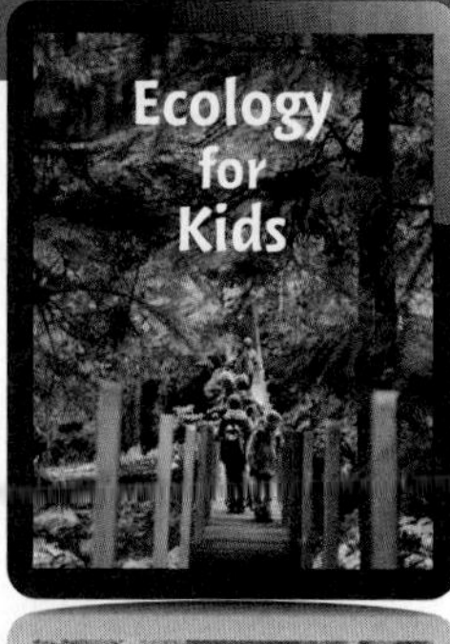

COMPREHENSION

Dig Deeper

How to Analyze the Text

Use these pages to learn about Main Ideas and Details, Author's Word Choice, and Analyzing an Argument. Then read "Ecology for Kids" again to apply what you learned.

Main Ideas and Details

Informational texts such as "Ecology for Kids" contain a main idea and supporting details. The **main idea** is what the text is mostly about. To explain the topic of ecology, the author uses **details** and evidence to support the main idea.

When a main idea is stated, it's as if the author is saying, "This is what I'm writing about, and here's how I support my ideas." If a main idea is implied, or suggested, the reader must use clues to figure it out.

Look back at page 444 in "Ecology for Kids." In this section of text, the main idea is stated. Which sentence states the main idea? Which sentences support the main idea?

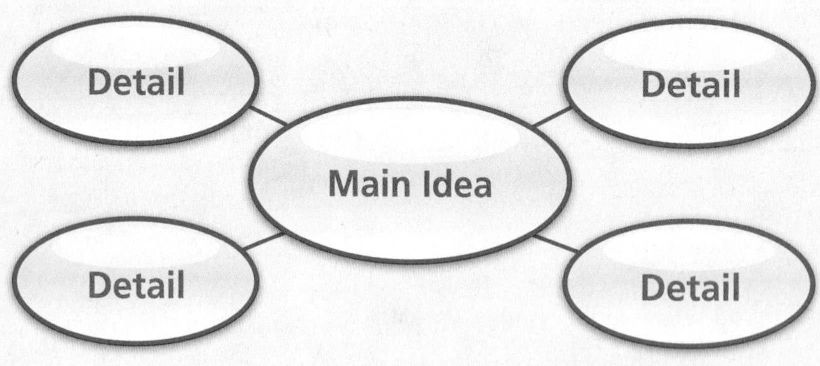

ELACC4RI2 determine the main idea and explain how it is supported by details/summarize; **ELACC4RI8** explain how an author uses reasons and evidence to support points; **ELACC4L3a** choose words and phrases to convey ideas precisely

Author's Word Choice

Authors of informational text carefully choose words to express their ideas clearly and precisely. Look back at 442. The author uses the phrase *delicate balance* to describe what an ecologist studies. One meaning of *delicate* is "tricky or complicated." The author's word choice shows readers that an ecologist's job can be challenging.

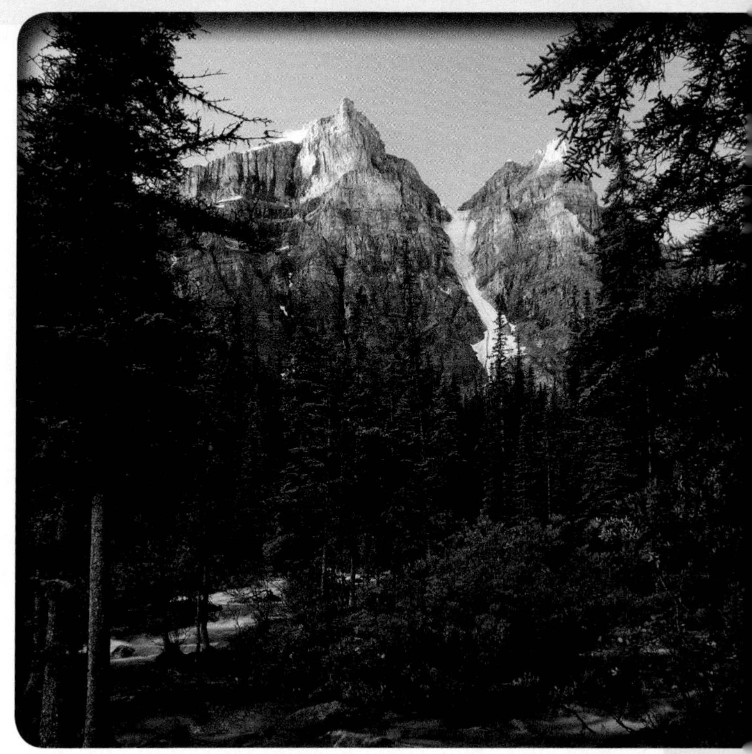

Analyze an Argument

When authors include **argument** in a piece of writing, they build a case for something they want readers to believe or do. The last section of "Ecology for Kids" makes an argument. Read the heading on page 450. How does the heading help you know what to expect from the author's argument?

Your Turn

RETURN TO THE ESSENTIAL QUESTION

Turn and Talk Review the selection with a partner to prepare to discuss this question: *Why is it important to be informed about what is happening in our world?* As you discuss, take turns reviewing text evidence to explain the key ideas.

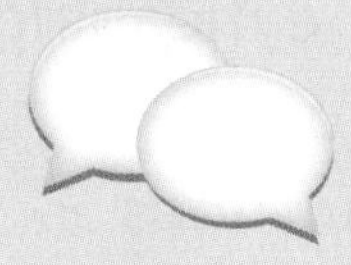

Classroom Conversation

Continue your discussion of "Ecology for Kids" by explaining your answers to these questions:

1. What is the most important idea the author wants you to understand about ecology?
2. How does information in the text connect to things that you do every day?
3. What actions can you take to help protect the environment?

WHAT DOES IT MEAN?

Use Reference Sources Choose four of these words from the selection: *environment, resources, biosphere, atmosphere, ecosystem, pollution.* Find each word in the selection. Then look up each word in a print or digital dictionary. Write a new sentence for each word that includes a definition. Share your sentences with a partner.

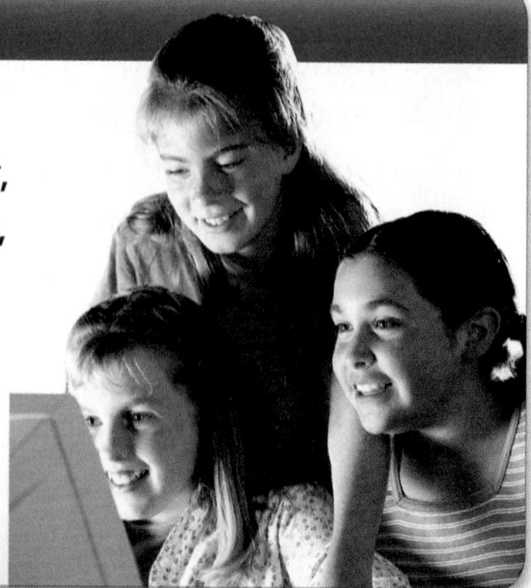

WRITE ABOUT READING

Response Do you agree or disagree with the author of "Ecology for Kids" that we need to balance our use of natural resources with protecting the environment? What reasons and evidence does the author use to support his ideas? Write a paragraph to explain why you agree or disagree with the author. Use facts and text evidence from the selection to support your ideas.

Writing Tip

State your opinion at the beginning of your response. Use transition words and phrases to link the different reasons and evidence for your opinion.

COMMON CORE **ELACC4RI2** determine the main idea and explain how it is supported by details/summarize; **ELACC4W1b** provide reasons supported by facts and details; **ELACC4W1c** link opinion and reasons using words and phrases; **ELACC4W9b** apply grade 4 Reading standards to informational texts; **ELACC4SL1c** pose and respond to questions and make comments that contribute to the discussion and link to others' remarks; **ELACC4SL1d** review key ideas expressed and explain own ideas and understanding; **ELACC4L4c** consult reference materials, both print and digital, to find pronunciation and determine or clarify meaning

Lesson 15

POETRY

GENRE

Poetry uses the sound and rhythm of words to suggest images and express feelings.

TEXT FOCUS

Rhyme is the repeated sounds at the end of two or more words. It helps give a poem rhythm and form.

COMMON CORE **ELACC4RL5** explain major differences between poems, drama, and prose/refer to their structural elements; **ELACC4RL10** read and comprehend literature

Wonderful Weather

Get ready for a variety of weather and poems. "Fog" uses a metaphor to form a picture in your mind. In the haiku "Spring Rain," and in "Umbrella," you may feel traces of a shower. Listen for the sounds in "Weather," and step into "Weatherbee's Diner" for weather that suits all kinds of habitats.

Fog

The fog comes
on little cat feet.

It sits looking
over harbor and city
on silent haunches
and then moves on.

by Carl Sandburg

Spring Rain

In the rains of spring,
An umbrella and raincoat
Pass by, conversing.

by Buson

Umbrella

Out there — wet
In here — dry
Cozy little roof
Between me and the sky

by Rob Hale

Weather

Weather is full
of the nicest sounds:
it sings
and rustles
and pings
and pounds
and hums
and tinkles
and strums
and twangs
and whishes
and sprinkles
and splishes
and bangs
and mumbles
and grumbles
and rumbles
and flashes
and CRASHES.

by Aileen Fisher

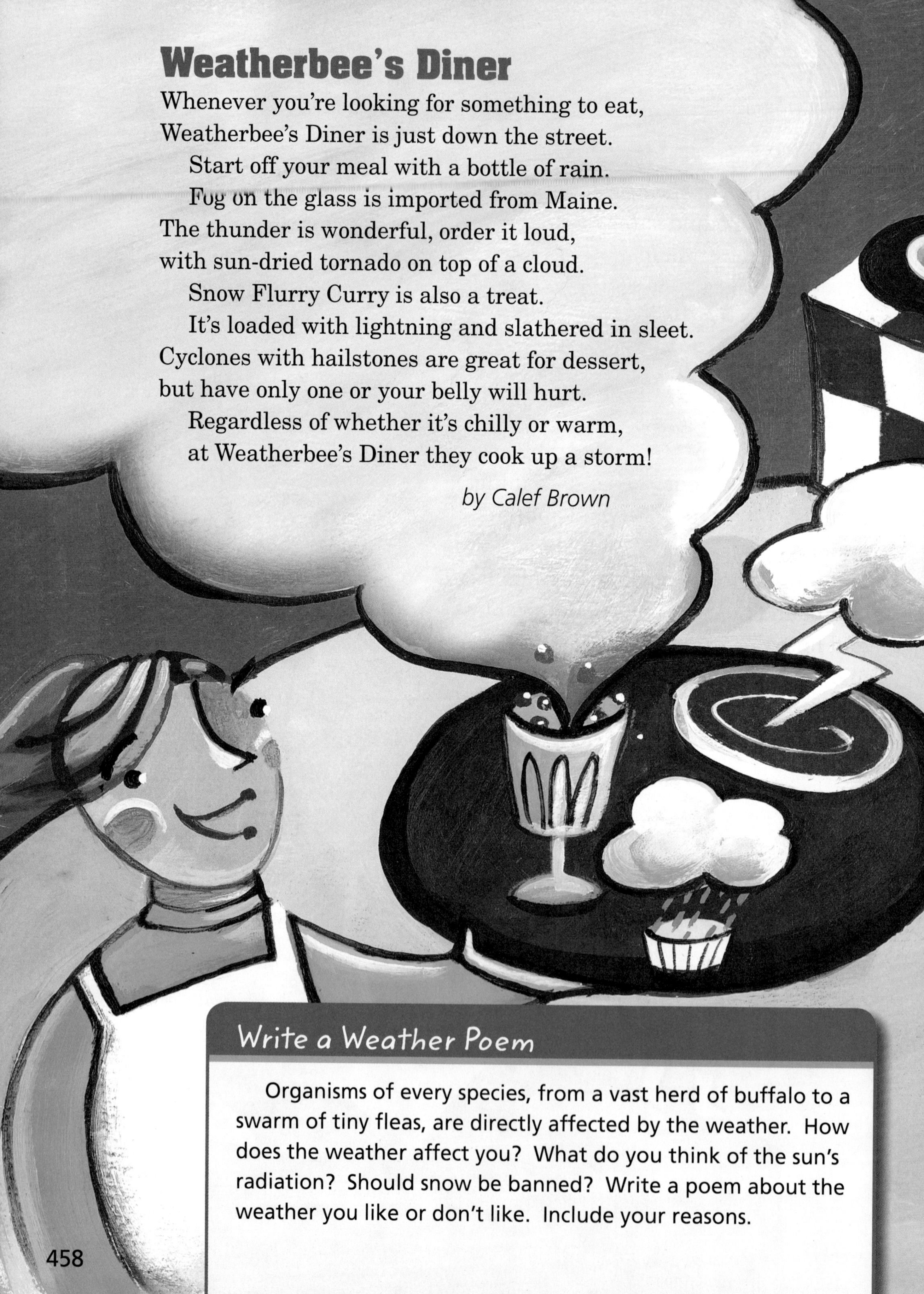

Weatherbee's Diner

Whenever you're looking for something to eat,
Weatherbee's Diner is just down the street.
  Start off your meal with a bottle of rain.
  Fog on the glass is imported from Maine.
The thunder is wonderful, order it loud,
with sun-dried tornado on top of a cloud.
  Snow Flurry Curry is also a treat.
  It's loaded with lightning and slathered in sleet.
Cyclones with hailstones are great for dessert,
but have only one or your belly will hurt.
  Regardless of whether it's chilly or warm,
  at Weatherbee's Diner they cook up a storm!

by Calef Brown

Write a Weather Poem

Organisms of every species, from a vast herd of buffalo to a swarm of tiny fleas, are directly affected by the weather. How does the weather affect you? What do you think of the sun's radiation? Should snow be banned? Write a poem about the weather you like or don't like. Include your reasons.

Compare Texts

TEXT TO TEXT

Compare Nature Texts Talk with a partner about "Ecology for Kids" and "Wonderful Weather." Discuss these questions: *Which text is about how the environment affects you? Which text is about how you can affect the environment? Which text is about both?* After you have discussed your ideas, work together to write an answer to each question. Use text evidence from each selection to support your answers.

TEXT TO SELF

List Habits Reread the last page of "Ecology for Kids." Identify the five things you can do to help protect the environment. Then make a list of the things you already do to protect the planet. Make a second list of what you would like to begin doing.

What I Do to Help the Earth	What I Want to Start Doing

TEXT TO WORLD

Chart Rainfall Water is an important resource. Research the amount of rain that falls in your community or state in a typical year. Record the information in a chart.

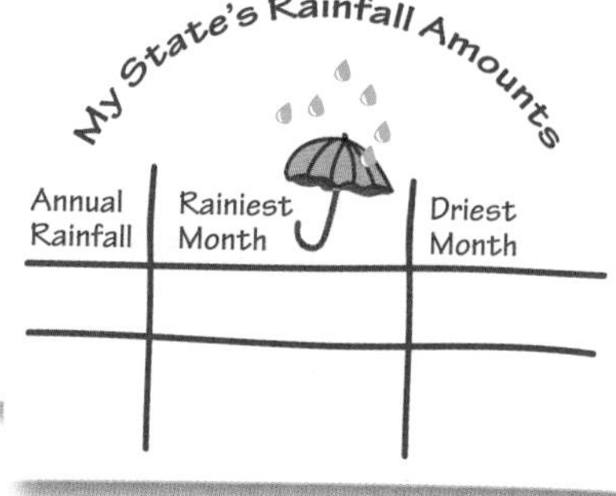

My State's Rainfall Amounts
Annual Rainfall
Rainiest Month
Driest Month

ELACC4RI1 refer to details and examples when explaining what the text says explicitly and when drawing inferences; **ELACC4RI2** determine the main idea and explain how it is supported by details/summarize; **ELACC4RI9** integrate information from two texts on the same topic; **ELACC4W7** conduct short research projects that build knowledge through investigation; **ELACC4W9b** apply grade 4 Reading standards to informational texts

Grammar

What Is an Irregular Verb? Verbs that do not add *-ed* to show past action are called **irregular verbs.** The spellings of irregular verbs can change in many different ways from present-tense to past-tense forms, so you must remember the spelling of each form.

I **give** now. I **gave** earlier. I **have given** already.

Present	Past	Past with Helping Verb
break	broke	(has, have, had) broken
bring	brought	(has, have, had) brought
come	came	(has, have, had) come
begin	began	(has, have, had) begun
eat	ate	(has, have, had) eaten
give	gave	(has, have, had) given
grow	grew	(has, have, had) grown
know	knew	(has, have, had) known
make	made	(has, have, had) made
say	said	(has, have, had) said
take	took	(has, have, had) taken
tell	told	(has, have, had) told

Try This! **Copy each sentence. Fill in the blank with the correct form of the verb in parentheses.**

1. Our field trip _________ at 8 A.M. yesterday. (begin)
2. Our teacher had _________ maps of the county park. (bring)
3. The bus _________ us to the park. (take)
4. A ranger _________ a talk about the park's ecology. (give)

The use of an incorrect verb form can confuse your readers. When you proofread your writing, be sure you have used the correct forms of irregular verbs to show past action. Also be sure that you have used correct forms of the helping verbs *has*, *have*, and *had*.

Incorrect Verb Form	Correct Verb Form
The science teacher has brung a poster of a typical food web. Yesterday I maked a drawing of a food web for our pond.	The science teacher has brought a poster of a typical food web. Yesterday I made a drawing of a food web for our pond.

Connect Grammar to Writing

As you edit your persuasive essay, look closely at each irregular verb form you use. Correct any errors you notice. Using verb forms correctly is an important part of good writing.

ELACC4W1a introduce a topic, state an opinion, and create an organizational structure; **ELACC4W1b** provide reasons supported by facts and details; **ELACC4W1c** link opinion and reasons using words and phrases; **ELACC4W1d** provide a concluding statement or section; **ELACC4L3a** choose words and phrases to convey ideas precisely

Opinion Writing

Reading-Writing Workshop: Revise

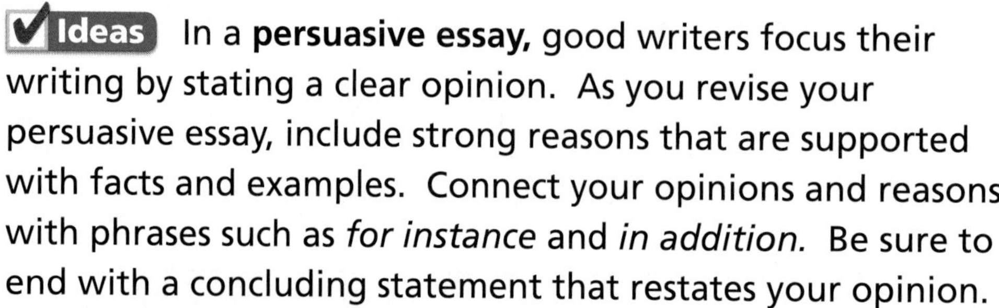

Ideas In a **persuasive essay,** good writers focus their writing by stating a clear opinion. As you revise your persuasive essay, include strong reasons that are supported with facts and examples. Connect your opinions and reasons with phrases such as *for instance* and *in addition.* Be sure to end with a concluding statement that restates your opinion.

Julio replaced vague words with specific ones. Then he added phrases to connect opinions and reasons. He also added a strong concluding sentence.

Writing Process Checklist

Prewrite

Draft

▶ **Revise**

- ✔ Did I state my opinion clearly?
- ✔ Did I support it with reasons, facts, and examples?
- ✔ Did I use strong, specific words to make my points persuasive?
- ✔ Did I use irregular verbs correctly?

Edit

Publish and Share

Revised Draft

One reason why we ~~Our class~~ should get an ant farm is that ~~because~~ ants are fascinating ~~cool!~~ For instance, ~~A~~ants are stronger than elephants for their size. In addition, ~~T~~they have a complex social structure. The ants work together to build homes and forage ~~look~~ for food. They also take care of the queen. A classroom ant farm is a great idea because we would learn about ants and teamwork!

Final Copy

Why Room 6 Needs an Ant Farm

by Julio Cordoza

Chadbourne Elementary has a "no pets in the classroom" rule. This makes sense. A lot of people are allergic to animals such as hamsters and rabbits. But wouldn't it be great if we could have classroom pets no one is allergic to? The students in Room 6 think so. That's why we want to have a classroom ant farm.

One reason why we should get an ant farm is that ants are fascinating. For instance, ants are stronger than elephants for their size. In addition, they have a complex social structure. The ants work together to build homes and forage for food. They also take care of the queen. A classroom ant farm is a great idea because we would learn about ants and teamwork!

Reading as a Writer

Which words and phrases did Julio use to link his opinion with the reasons for his opinion? How can you link your opinions with reasons?

In my final paper, I replaced weak and vague words with stronger, more specific words. I also made sure I used irregular verbs correctly.

Read the article "Wildfires!" As you read, stop and answer each question using text evidence.

Wildfires!

Wildfires are large fires that sweep out of control across the land. They often occur in wilderness areas. Each year there are about 100,000 wildfires in the United States.

What does the word *wilderness* mean, and how is it related to the word *wildfires*?

A Scary Summer

In the summer of 1988, wildfires swept through Yellowstone National Park. In four months, the fires scorched over 793,000 acres of land, 36% of the park.

Why were the fires of 1988 so damaging? For one thing, that summer was very dry. In fact, it was the driest summer in Yellowstone's recorded history. To make things worse, the weather was hot and windy. These conditions cause fire to spread quickly.

The Yellowstone fires began in June with a few small fires. At first, there was no danger to people or buildings, so park officials decided to let the fires burn themselves out.

Allowing a small fire to burn can be good for the land. Fires clear away dead plants so new plants can grow. Lodgepole pine trees cover nearly 80% of Yellowstone's wooded land. This tree needs the high heat of fires to burst open its cones, releasing the seeds. Only then can new trees begin to grow. The roots of grasses and flowers under the ground are not usually harmed by wildfires. The plants grow back again quickly.

COMMON CORE **ELACC4RI4** determine the meaning of general academic and domain-specific words and phrases; **ELACC4RI3** explain events/procedures/ideas/concepts in a text; **ELACC4RI5** describe the overall structure of a text or part of a text; **ELACC4RI8** explain how an author uses reasons and evidence to support points

Over time, though, the fires in Yellowstone that summer grew too large. Forty-two new fires were started by lightning strikes. People who were careless with matches or campfires caused nine more. Not all of the fires began inside the park, but they all raced through it. Fires spread out over the land, and smaller fires joined to form larger ones. A change in the direction of the wind could quickly change the direction in which the fire was moving.

Smoke from the Yellowstone fires billowed thousands of feet into the air. Ash rained down for miles around. In nearby Cooke City, someone with a good sense of humor added the letter "d" to the end of "Cooke" on the town sign. But the overall situation was not funny at all.

Local firefighters were not able to put out so many fires by themselves. Fire-fighting teams from across the country came to help, but it was still an impossible task. In the end, 25,000 people took part in the effort and $120 million was spent. But it was rain and snow that finally brought the fires to an end in September.

How did the author structure this section of the article? List some words and phrases that show the structure.

Wilderness Firefighters

You may have seen photos or videos of city firefighters racing into burning buildings. These firefighters wear heavy clothing that protects them from flames and falling rubble. Wilderness firefighters do not wear the same kind of gear as city firefighters. They have a different wardrobe and different equipment.

Wilderness firefighting is hard work. Firefighters have to chop down trees and clear brush. They dig ditches to keep fires from spreading. If they wore hot, heavy clothing, their body temperatures would rise to a dangerous level.

To solve this problem, scientists have invented special gear for wilderness firefighters. Their clothing is made from a special lightweight fabric. They also carry tents made of a special foil that reflects heat away from the tent. A firefighter who is covered by this emergency shelter can survive a fire with temperatures of more than 1,000° F.

 What new types of gear did scientists develop for wilderness firefighters, and why?

Smokejumpers are special firefighters who work in remote areas. A Forest Service smokejumper base is located in West Yellowstone. Smokejumpers travel quickly to wildfire locations by plane, helicopter, ground vehicle, and on foot. They are well-trained and must be in excellent condition. They have to be brave, too. That's because their job is to parachute out of planes and land close to wildfires.

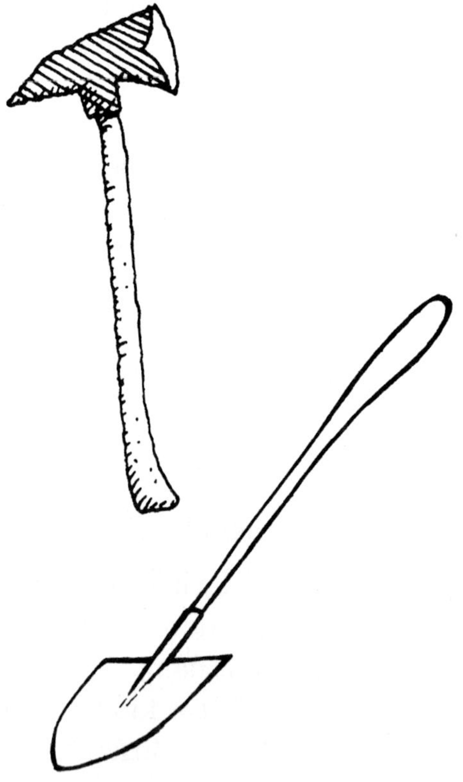

After the firefighters have landed, the tools, food, and water they will need are also dropped by parachute. Then the smokejumpers travel quickly across rough terrain, each packing up to 115 pounds of gear. They face long periods of smoke, fire, and heat. They carry enough food and water with them to last two days. Sometimes they run short before they have finished their work.

Fighting wildfires is an important and challenging job. The men and women who do it risk their lives to save our lands. We should all be grateful to these brave people.

 What evidence does the author present in this article to support the statement that fighting wildfires is a challenging job?

Unit 4

Lesson 16

Vocabulary in Context

TARGET VOCABULARY

escorted
swelled
relied
reputation
worthy
churning
situation
deserve
defended
satisfied

Vocabulary Reader

Context Cards

ELACC4L6 acquire/use vocabulary, including academic and domain-specific

1 escorted

Guides who knew the western trails well often escorted, or led, travelers.

2 swelled

The number of wagons heading west swelled, or grew, in the 1850s.

3 relied

This family built a house of sod. They relied, or depended, on materials they found.

4 reputation

When customers were happy about a shop, its owner earned a good reputation.

- Study each Context Card.
- Break the longer words into syllables. Use a dictionary to confirm.

5 worthy

This plot of land was worthy, or valuable. It had rich soil and access to water.

6 churning

Dark clouds and churning winds over the plains could signal a tornado.

7 situation

Mail carriers were prepared for any situation, or event, as they rode alone.

8 deserve

Kids who worked hard on the farm would deserve an occasional treat.

9 defended

Westward travelers defended themselves from harm by circling their wagons.

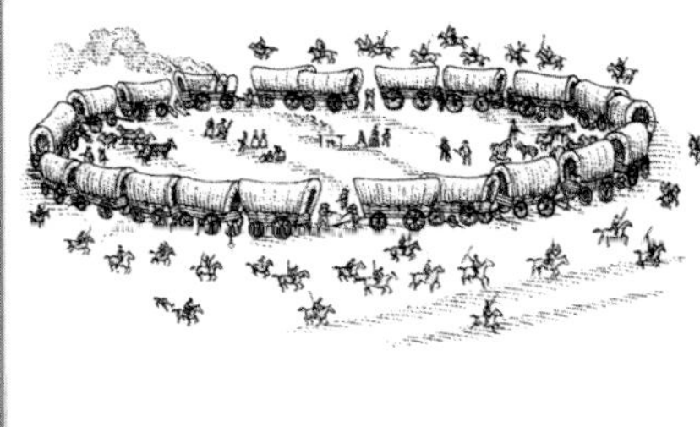

10 satisfied

Despite the hard work and danger, some settlers were satisfied with life in the West.

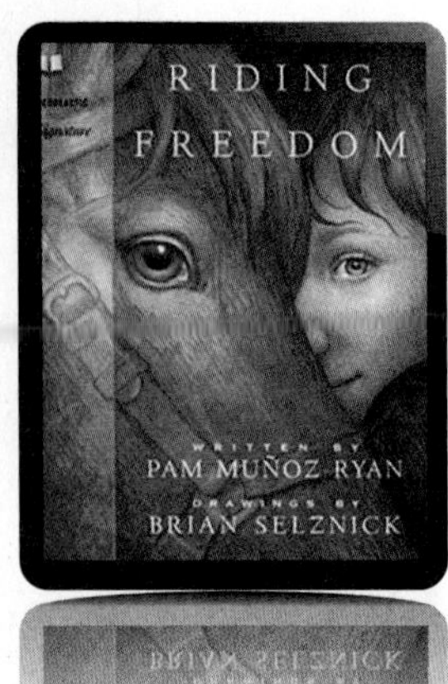

Read and Comprehend

TARGET SKILL

Compare and Contrast To help you understand a story, it can be useful to **compare** and **contrast** the characters' words, actions, and thoughts. As you read "Riding Freedom," compare and contrast the different characters. Look for ways in which they are alike and different. Pay careful attention to text evidence showing what each character says, does, and thinks at different points in the story. Use a graphic organizer like the one below to help you compare and contrast these characters.

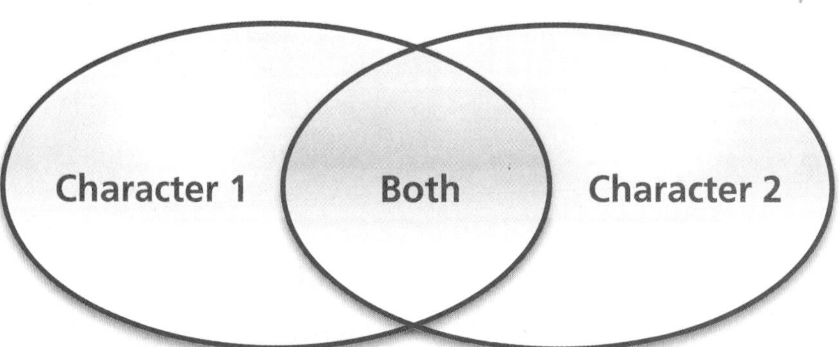

TARGET STRATEGY

Monitor/Clarify As you read "Riding Freedom," remember to **monitor,** or look for, words or ideas that do not make sense. If something is confusing, pause to **clarify** the text, or make it clear. For example, you might try rereading the part of the text that confused you.

ELACC4RL3 describe a character, setting, or event, drawing on details; **ELACC4RF4c** use context to confirm or self-correct word recognition and understanding

PREVIEW THE TOPIC

Individual Contributions

Throughout our history, individuals have made important contributions to our nation. Some, like Abraham Lincoln, are famous. Others are everyday people who helped the United States grow through hard work and determination. Stagecoach drivers, for instance, helped people travel long distances over dangerous land in the 1800s. Before railroads and cars were invented, stagecoach drivers took people safely over bumpy dirt roads and rickety bridges.

"Riding Freedom" is a story about Charlotte Parkhurst, a determined young woman who drives a stagecoach in the mid-1800s. You'll find out how she works against the odds to be successful in a job that only men had done before.

Lesson 16

ANCHOR TEXT

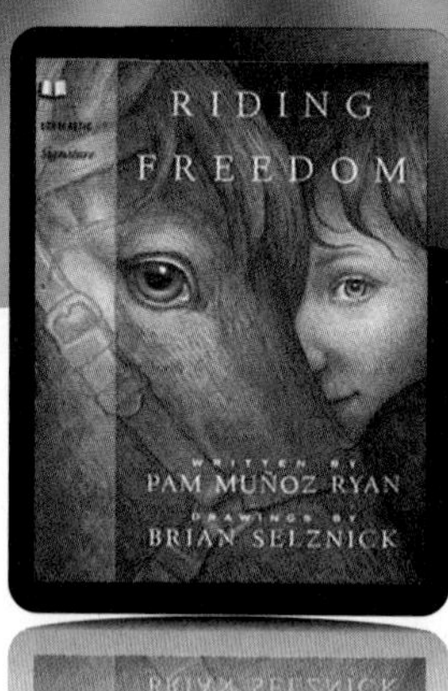

 TARGET SKILL

Compare and Contrast
Examine how characters are alike and different.

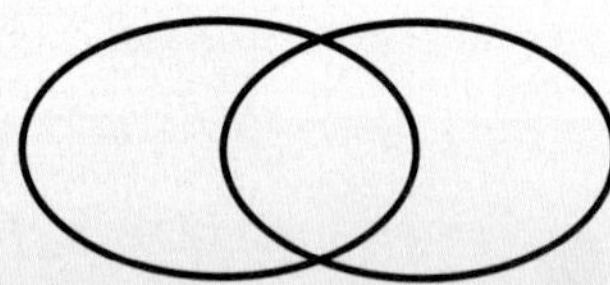

 GENRE

Historical fiction is a story that is set in the past and portrays people, places, and events that did happen or could have happened. As you read, look for:

- a setting that is a real time and place in the past
- details that show the story took place in the past

ELACC4RL3 describe a character, setting, or event, drawing on details; **ELACC4RL4** determine the meaning of words and phrases, including those that allude to characters in mythology; **ELACC4RL10** read and comprehend literature

MEET THE AUTHOR

Pam Muñoz Ryan

To research "Riding Freedom," Pam Muñoz Ryan recalls, "I wanted to travel on a dusty trail over rolling hills in a rutted-out road." She found an amusement park that offered rides in old stagecoaches. There she rode a coach, sat in the box seat, and even held the horses' reins. "Riding Freedom" is a winner of the national Willa Cather Award.

MEET THE ILLUSTRATOR

Marc Scott

Marc Scott knows a lot about illustrating an action-packed scene. In addition to working on books about whaling and mining, he has provided art for video games based on World Series baseball, trick skiing, and the movie *Star Wars*.

Riding Freedom

by Pam Muñoz Ryan

selection illustrated by Marc Scott

ESSENTIAL QUESTION

What traits do successful people have?

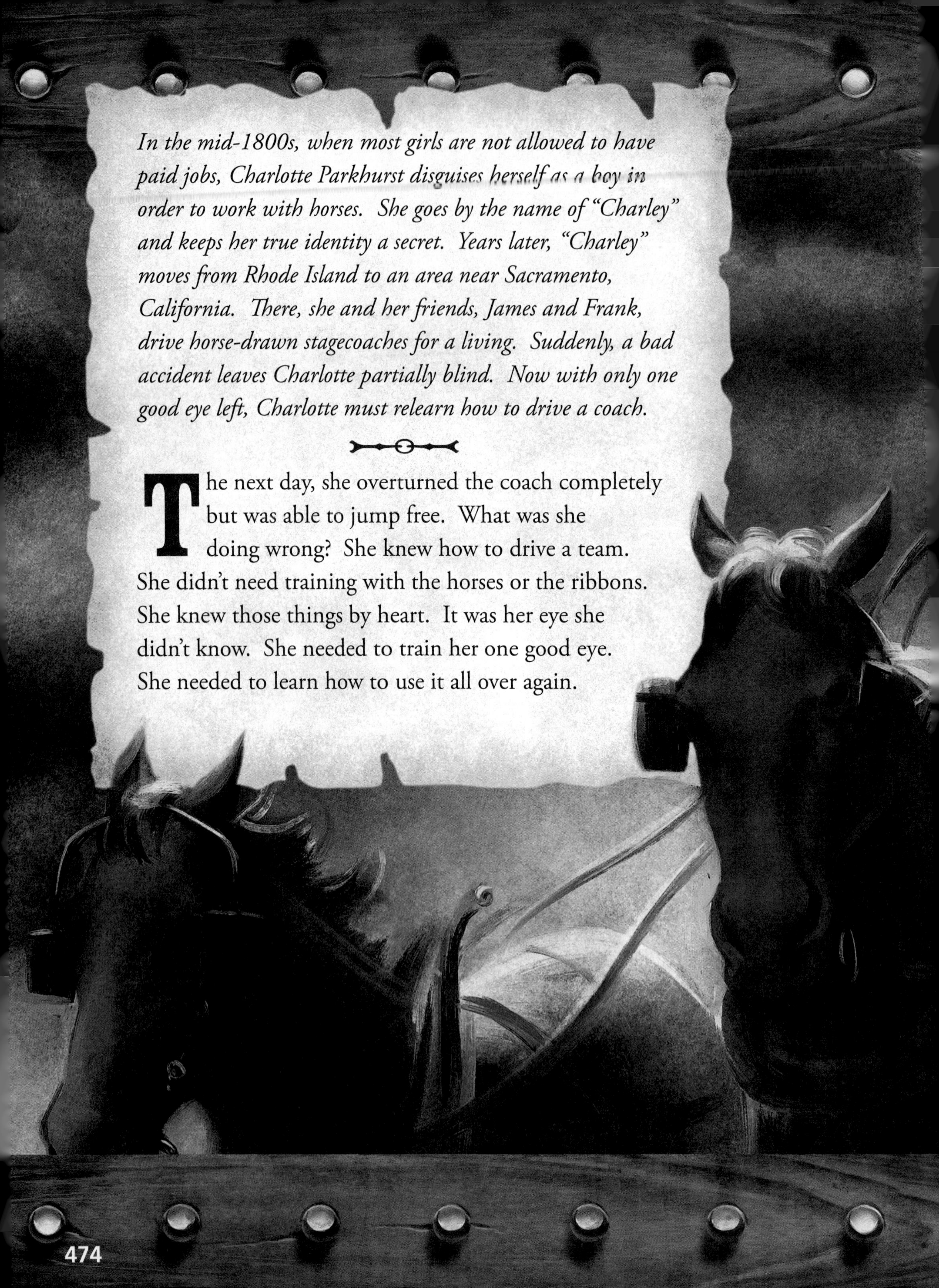

In the mid-1800s, when most girls are not allowed to have paid jobs, Charlotte Parkhurst disguises herself as a boy in order to work with horses. She goes by the name of "Charley" and keeps her true identity a secret. Years later, "Charley" moves from Rhode Island to an area near Sacramento, California. There, she and her friends, James and Frank, drive horse-drawn stagecoaches for a living. Suddenly, a bad accident leaves Charlotte partially blind. Now with only one good eye left, Charlotte must relearn how to drive a coach.

The next day, she overturned the coach completely but was able to jump free. What was she doing wrong? She knew how to drive a team. She didn't need training with the horses or the ribbons. She knew those things by heart. It was her eye she didn't know. She needed to train her one good eye. She needed to learn how to use it all over again.

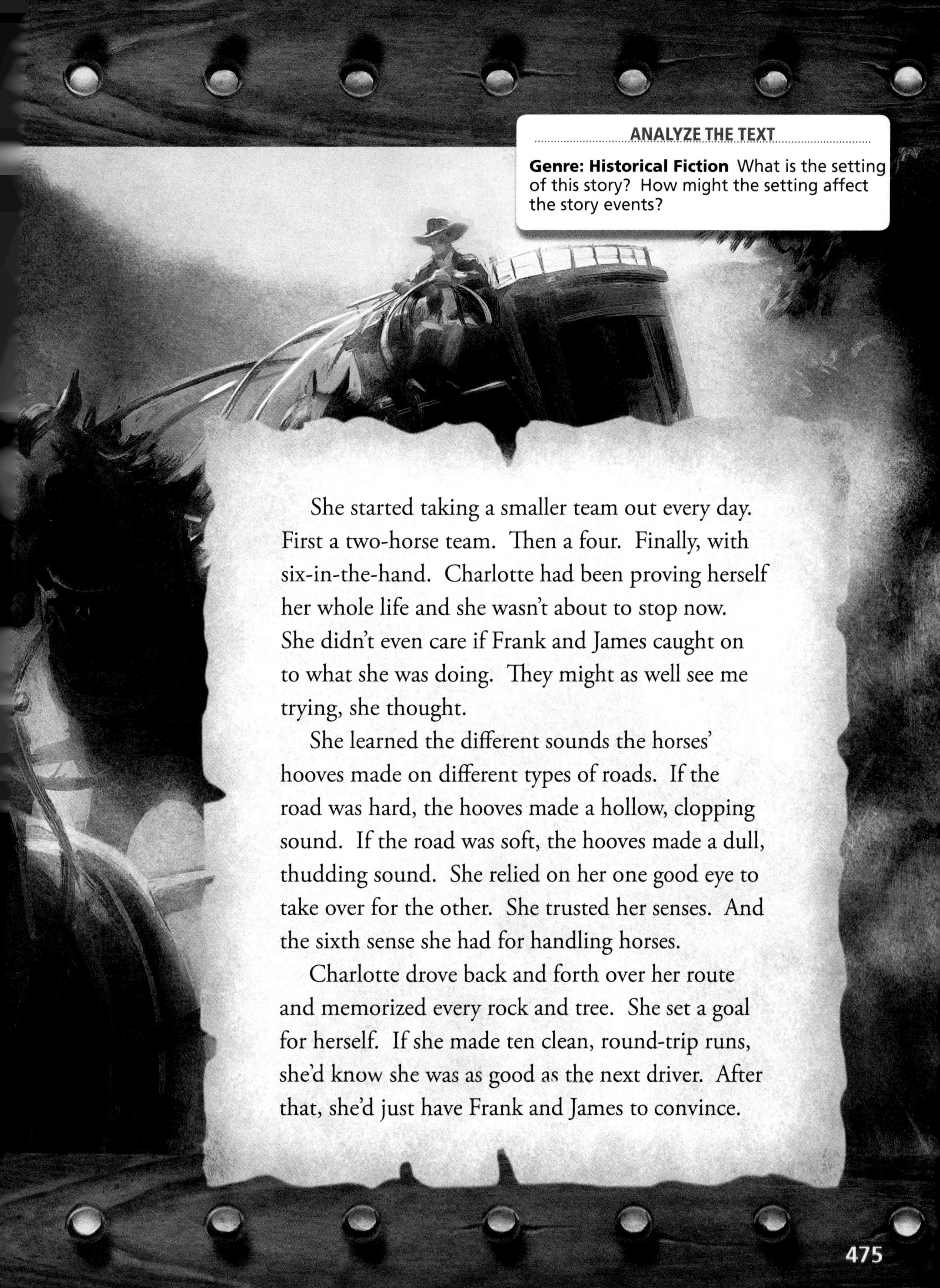

ANALYZE THE TEXT

Genre: Historical Fiction What is the setting of this story? How might the setting affect the story events?

She started taking a smaller team out every day. First a two-horse team. Then a four. Finally, with six-in-the-hand. Charlotte had been proving herself her whole life and she wasn't about to stop now. She didn't even care if Frank and James caught on to what she was doing. *They might as well see me trying,* she thought.

She learned the different sounds the horses' hooves made on different types of roads. If the road was hard, the hooves made a hollow, clopping sound. If the road was soft, the hooves made a dull, thudding sound. She relied on her one good eye to take over for the other. She trusted her senses. And the sixth sense she had for handling horses.

Charlotte drove back and forth over her route and memorized every rock and tree. She set a goal for herself. If she made ten clean, round-trip runs, she'd know she was as good as the next driver. After that, she'd just have Frank and James to convince.

After the tenth clean run, Charlotte went to James. "I want to drive the stage run over the river."

"Now, Charley, we've been over all that. Me and Frank think . . ."

"You ride with me, and if you don't think I'm fit, then I won't bother you again," said Charlotte.

"What will the passengers say about your eye patch?" said James.

"Just tell them it's to frighten off bandits. They won't know any different."

"I don't know . . ."

Charlotte defended herself. "You know my reputation. I traveled all this way. Riding coaches is the whole reason I came to California. And I came because you asked me to come. You know I been practicin'. Go by my past drivin'. That's all I'm askin', and I wouldn't be askin' if I didn't know I could drive."

Reluctantly, James said, "The first sign that you can't handle the situation, I take the reins."

"I'll tell you if I need help. Don't go steppin' in unless I ask."

"Fair enough," said James.

"Tomorrow?"

"Tomorrow, if the weather holds."

"I ain't going to be a fair-weather driver," said Charlotte. "I want to drive, same as usual, like all the other drivers."

"Well, I guess you deserve that much. Tomorrow, rain or shine."

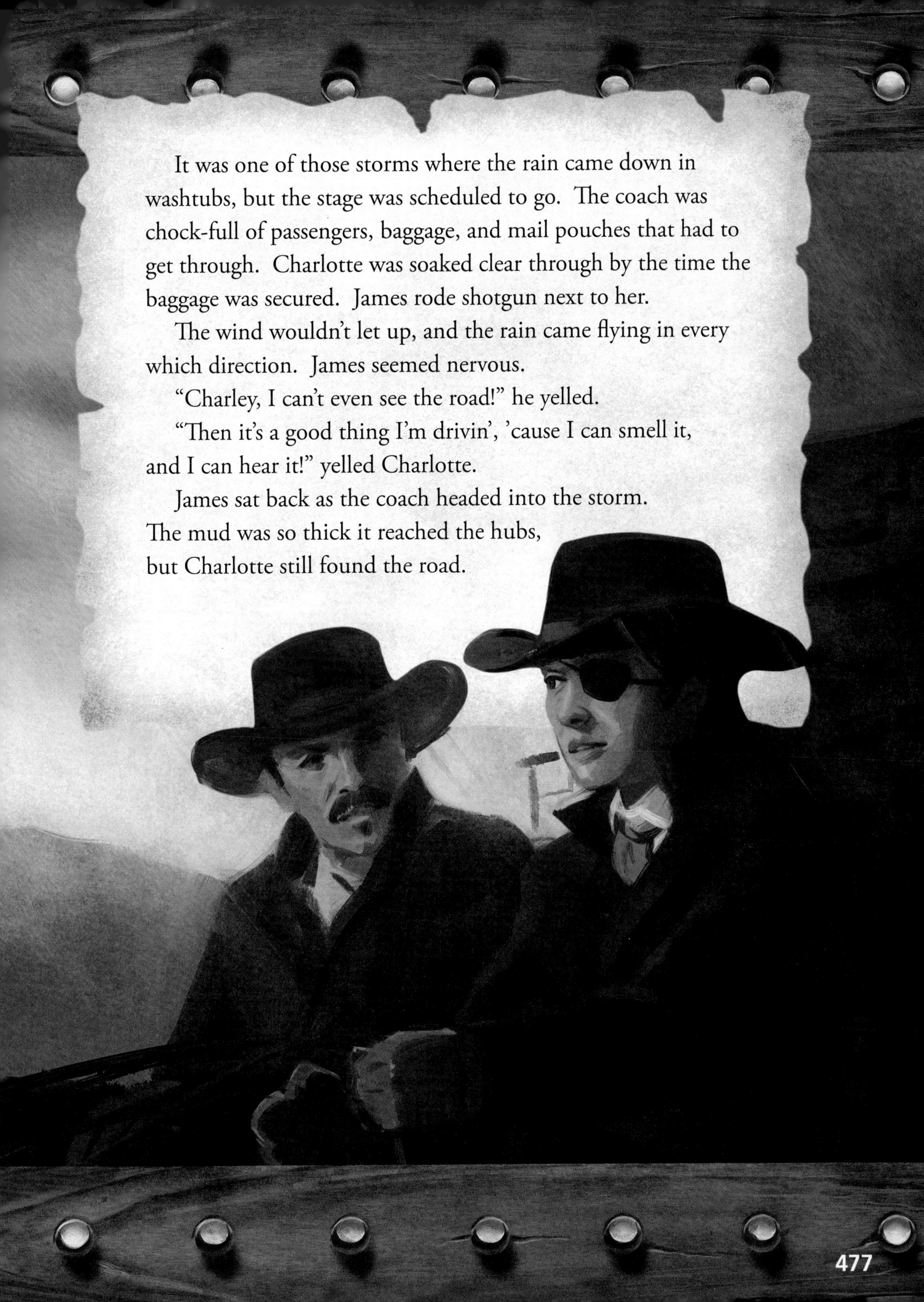

It was one of those storms where the rain came down in washtubs, but the stage was scheduled to go. The coach was chock-full of passengers, baggage, and mail pouches that had to get through. Charlotte was soaked clear through by the time the baggage was secured. James rode shotgun next to her.

The wind wouldn't let up, and the rain came flying in every which direction. James seemed nervous.

"Charley, I can't even see the road!" he yelled.

"Then it's a good thing I'm drivin', 'cause I can smell it, and I can hear it!" yelled Charlotte.

James sat back as the coach headed into the storm. The mud was so thick it reached the hubs, but Charlotte still found the road.

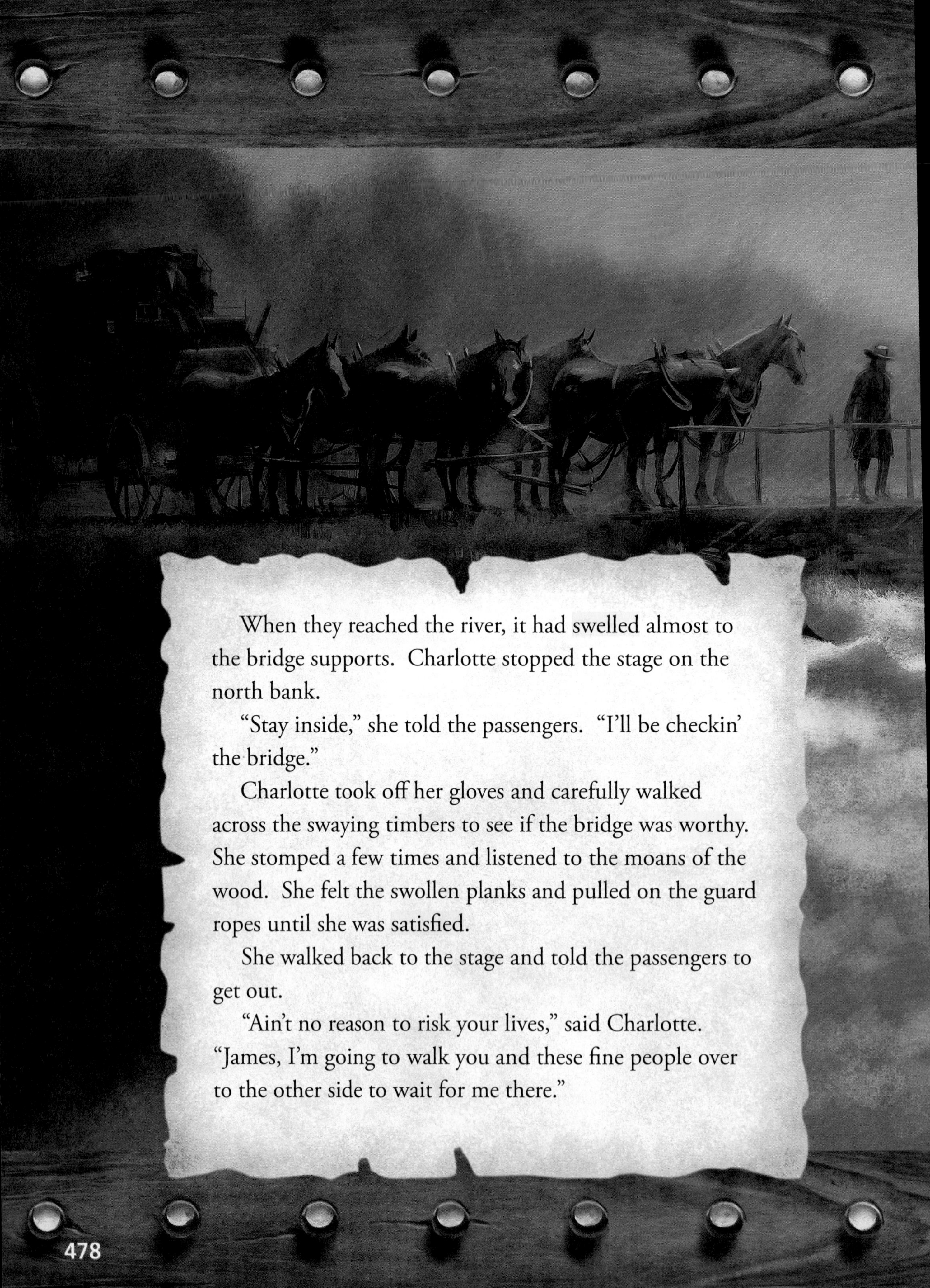

When they reached the river, it had swelled almost to the bridge supports. Charlotte stopped the stage on the north bank.

"Stay inside," she told the passengers. "I'll be checkin' the bridge."

Charlotte took off her gloves and carefully walked across the swaying timbers to see if the bridge was worthy. She stomped a few times and listened to the moans of the wood. She felt the swollen planks and pulled on the guard ropes until she was satisfied.

She walked back to the stage and told the passengers to get out.

"Ain't no reason to risk your lives," said Charlotte. "James, I'm going to walk you and these fine people over to the other side to wait for me there."

But a portly gentleman refused to budge.

"I'll take my chances inside the coach," he said.

"Not on my coach," said Charlotte.

"I'm familiar with adventure, young man," he argued.

"The bridge can't take any extra weight, and I'm not about to lose my first passenger to that river. Now, step out or I'll help you step out."

Still grumbling, the man reluctantly climbed down.

In the blinding rain, Charlotte escorted the group, a few at a time, across the bridge. When they were safely settled on the other side, she walked back for the stage.

ANALYZE THE TEXT

Personification Authors sometimes use a type of metaphor called **personification**. Personification gives human characteristics to nonliving objects. Find an example of personification on pages 478–479 and explain what it means.

She got back in the box. Thunder growled nearby. She knew what was coming next. She held tight to the ribbons and waited for the lightning. It hit within a mile but she kept the horses reined. Trusting her instincts, she inched the horses and the stage across the bridge. The timbers groaned as the iron-capped wheels clacked across the wooden planks. Ahead, the passengers huddled together and watched anxiously from the other side. The river raced a few feet beneath the wheels.

The bridge rocked and the horses reared and whinnied. The coach was smack in the middle of the bridge.

Charlotte kept her sights on the far bank.

She heard the splintering and cracking of weathered wood that meant the bridge was coming apart.

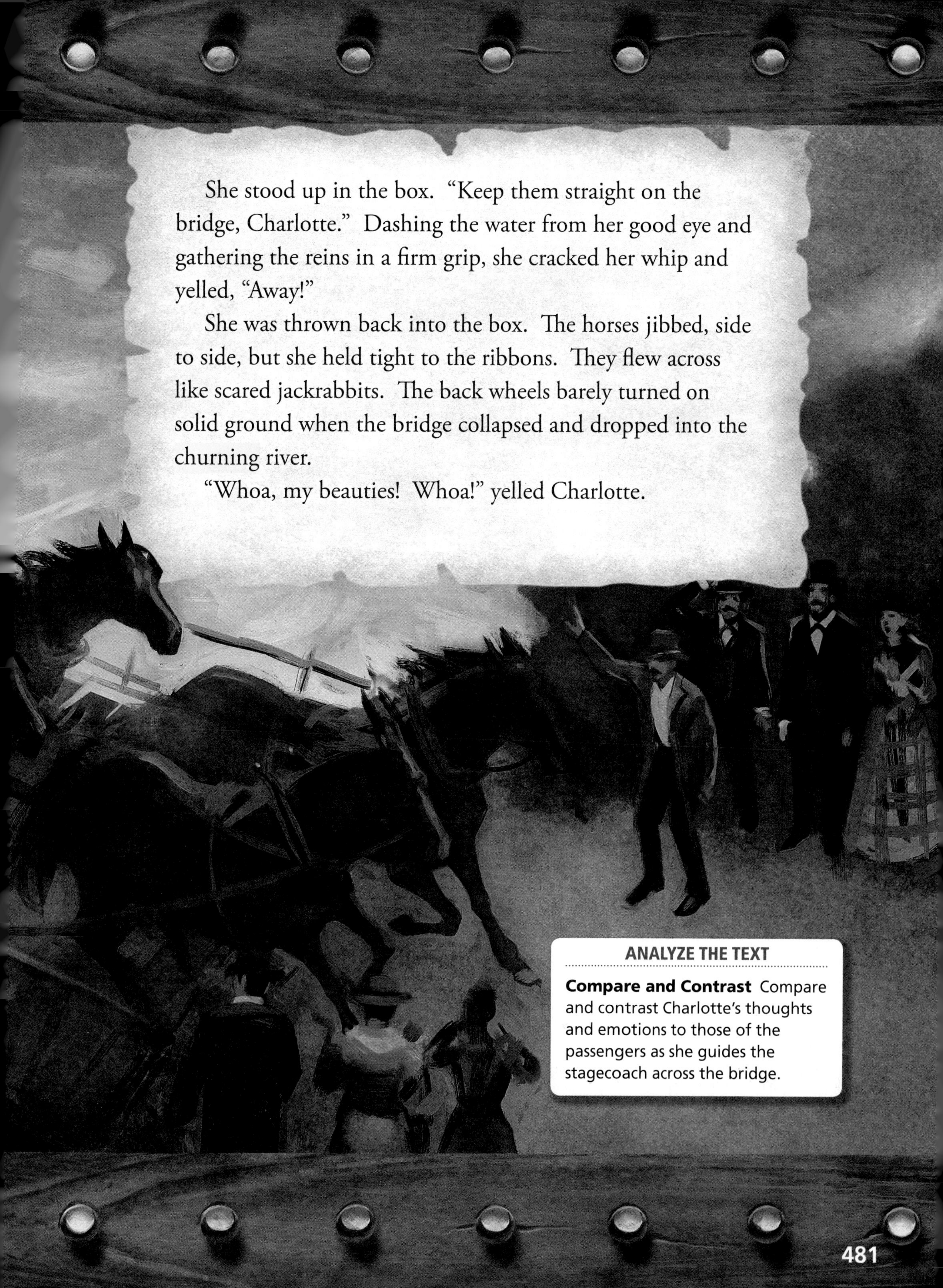

She stood up in the box. "Keep them straight on the bridge, Charlotte." Dashing the water from her good eye and gathering the reins in a firm grip, she cracked her whip and yelled, "Away!"

She was thrown back into the box. The horses jibbed, side to side, but she held tight to the ribbons. They flew across like scared jackrabbits. The back wheels barely turned on solid ground when the bridge collapsed and dropped into the churning river.

"Whoa, my beauties! Whoa!" yelled Charlotte.

ANALYZE THE TEXT

Compare and Contrast Compare and contrast Charlotte's thoughts and emotions to those of the passengers as she guides the stagecoach across the bridge.

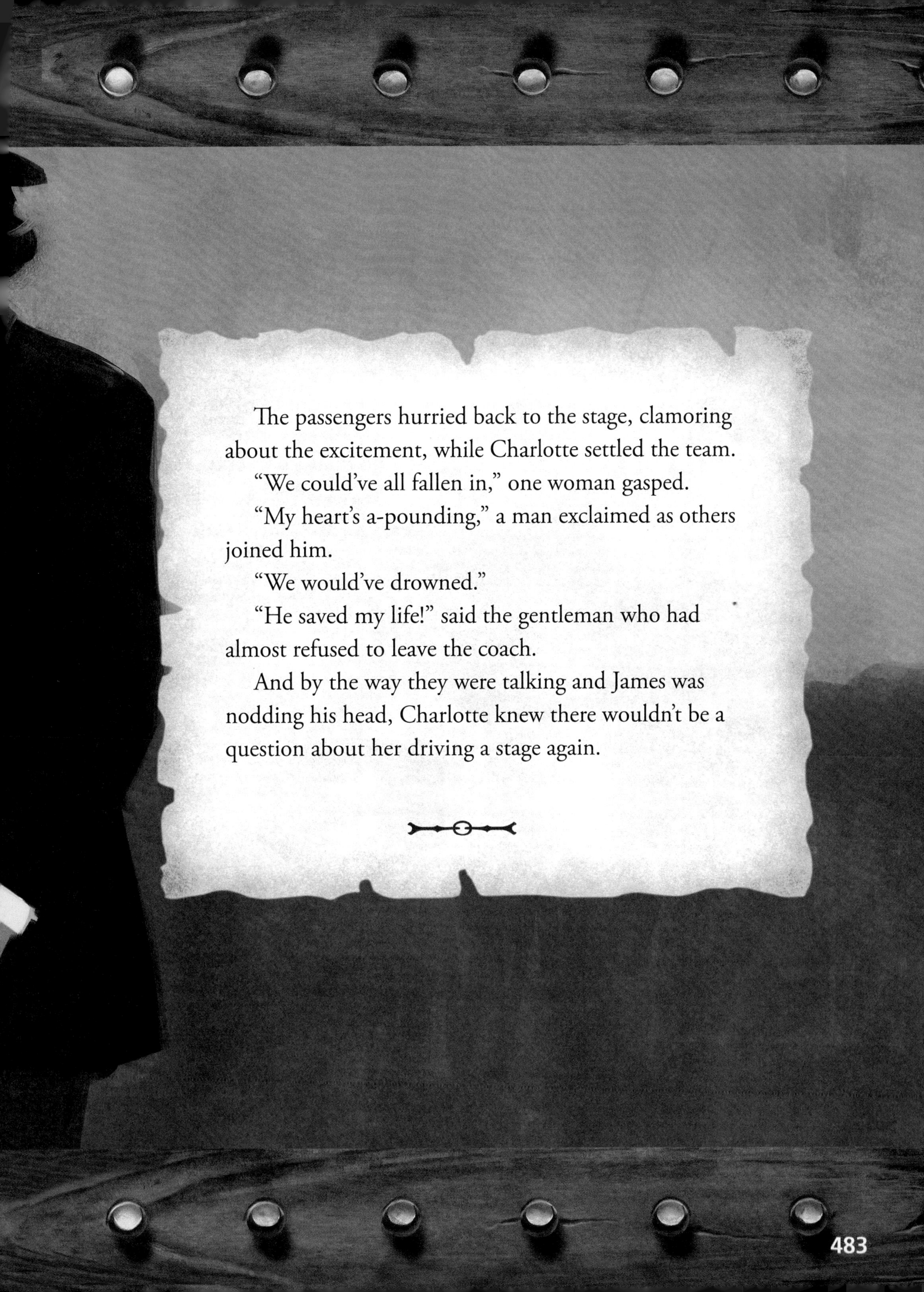

The passengers hurried back to the stage, clamoring about the excitement, while Charlotte settled the team.

"We could've all fallen in," one woman gasped.

"My heart's a-pounding," a man exclaimed as others joined him.

"We would've drowned."

"He saved my life!" said the gentleman who had almost refused to leave the coach.

And by the way they were talking and James was nodding his head, Charlotte knew there wouldn't be a question about her driving a stage again.

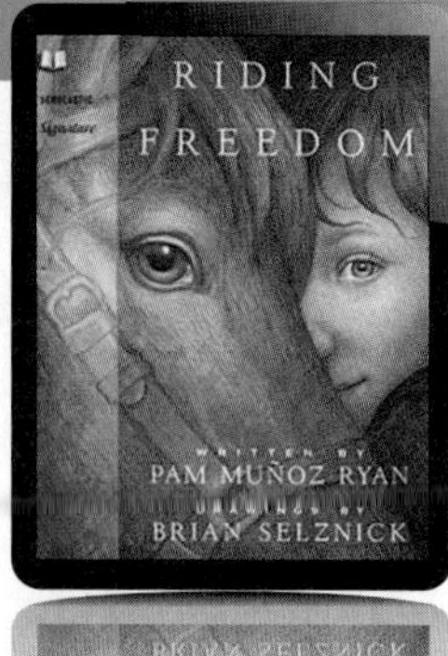

COMPREHENSION

Dig Deeper

How to Analyze the Text

Use these pages to learn about Comparing and Contrasting, Historical Fiction, and Personification. Then read "Riding Freedom" again to apply what you learned.

Compare and Contrast

"Riding Freedom" is a historical fiction story about a young woman who overcomes many challenges in order to reach her goal of becoming a stagecoach driver. To better understand the story, **compare** and **contrast** the two main characters, Charlotte and James. Think about what each character is like. Pay attention to text evidence, such as what the characters think, say, and do.

Using a graphic organizer like the one below can help you describe how the characters are alike and different. What traits do Charlotte and James share? What traits of theirs are different?

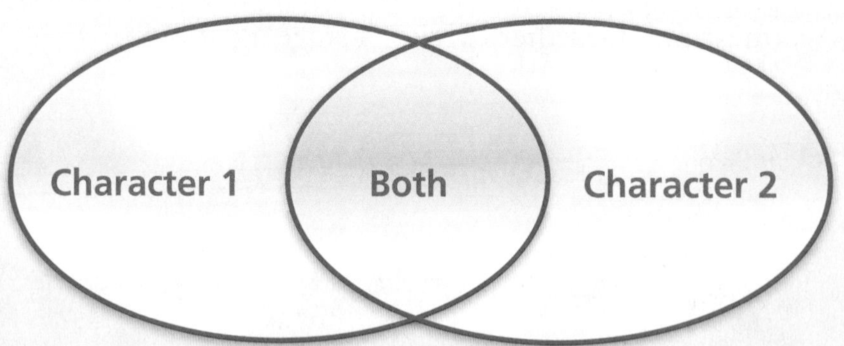

ELACC4RL3 describe a character, setting, or event, drawing on details; **ELACC4RL4** determine the meaning of words and phrases, including those that allude to characters in mythology; **ELACC4L5a** explain the meaning of similes and metaphors in context

Genre: Historical Fiction

A good **historical fiction** story gives readers a vivid picture of the time and place in which the story is set. Authors of historical fiction must carefully describe the characters, events, and setting so that they are believable. In "Riding Freedom," look for details about stagecoaches and other things unique to the time period to help you describe the setting.

Personification

A **metaphor** is a colorful comparison that describes one thing as if it were something else. For example, *the wind was a monster* is a metaphor. **Personification** is a type of metaphor. It gives a human characteristic to a nonliving object. If an author writes *the rain did a tap dance on the roof*, the author isn't actually saying that the rain is the dancer. Rather, the author is using personification to help readers "hear" the loud splatters of rain that beat down loudly on the roof.

Your Turn

RETURN TO THE ESSENTIAL QUESTION

Review "Riding Freedom" with a partner to prepare to discuss this question: *What traits do successful people have?* Be sure to support your answers with text evidence from the selection about characters' thoughts, words, and actions.

Classroom Conversation

Continue your discussion of "Riding Freedom" by explaining your answers to these questions:

1. What do you learn about Charlotte from the way she solves the problem of her eye?
2. Do you think Charlotte is right to hide her true identity?
3. What advice might Charlotte give other people about reaching their goals in life?

STEAL THE SCENE

Compare a Performance and Text
With a small group, select a scene from the story. Rehearse the scene and then perform it for classmates. Afterward, compare the performance with the print version of the story. Discuss how the actors portrayed specific details and events described in the selection.

WRITE ABOUT READING

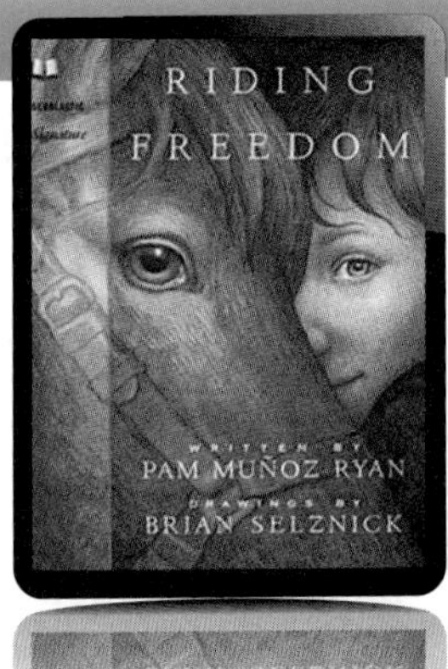

Response In order to drive a stagecoach, Charlotte must keep her identity as a woman a secret. What does this tell you about people's attitudes toward women in the mid-1800s? Write a paragraph comparing attitudes toward what women could do in the mid-1800s to attitudes toward what women can do today. Use text evidence to support your ideas.

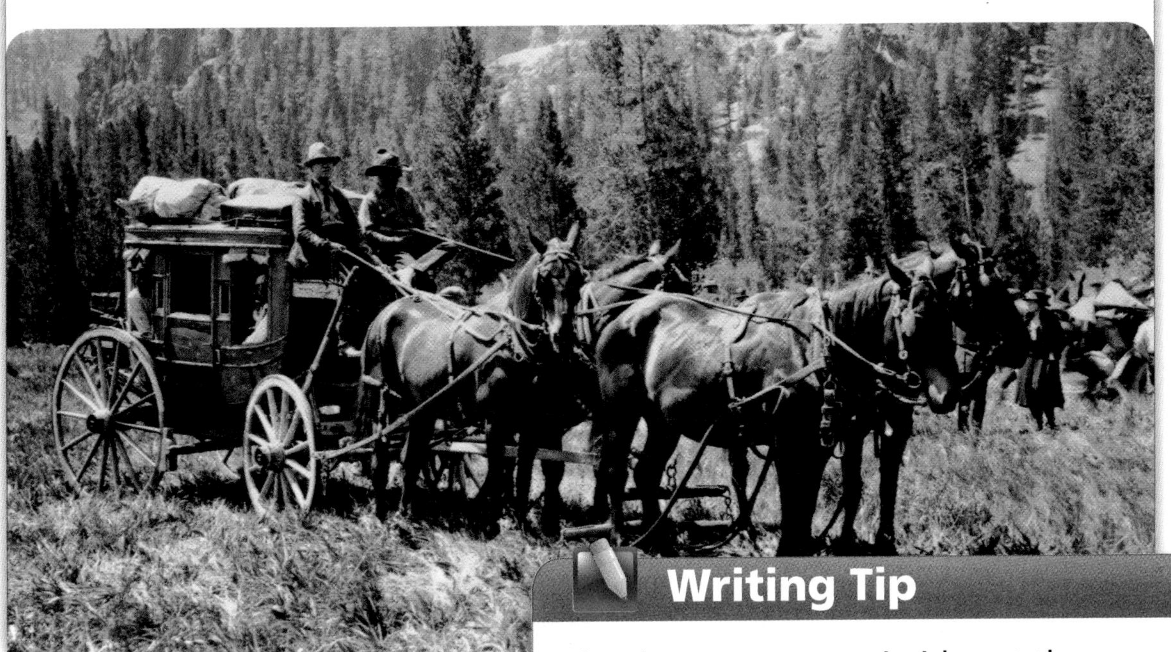

Writing Tip

Clearly state your main idea at the beginning of your paragraph. Use details from the text and your own knowledge about life today to support your idea.

COMMON CORE **ELACC4RL3** describe a character, setting or event, drawing on details; **ELACC4RL7** make connections between the text and a visual or oral presentation of it; **ELACC4W9a** apply grade 4 Reading standards to literature; **ELACC4W10** write routinely over extended time frames and shorter time frames; **ELACC4SL1a** come to discussions prepared/explicitly draw on preparation and other information about the topic

Lesson 16

INFORMATIONAL TEXT

GENRE

Informational text, such as this **Internet encyclopedia entry**, gives factual information about a topic.

TEXT FOCUS

Digital Media The Internet provides access to many different kinds of media, including Internet articles such as this one. Many websites have options that permit you to see video clips, hear what is being described, ask questions, give feedback, or add information. What is the purpose of the e-mail on page 490?

ELACC4RI7 interpret information presented visually, orally, or quantitatively; **ELACC4RI10** read and comprehend informational texts; **ELACC4RF4a** read on-level text with purpose and understanding

TEXAS HISTORY: Online

Spindletop

News • Publications • Education • Events

In the 1890s Texas produced only small amounts of oil. But one risk-taker thought that east Texas was worthy of further study. In 1892, Pattillo (puh TIH loh) Higgins, a self-taught geologist, began drilling for oil. He drilled near Beaumont, Texas, in an area called Spindletop Hill. Spindletop was a salt dome, a hill formed by rising underground mineral salts. Higgins's first drills found nothing. His financial situation was looking bad. So he hired Captain Anthony F. Lucas to take over.

Tools Help

search

OIL: Spindletop

The Lucas Geyser

Lucas was a leading geologist with a reputation as an expert on salt domes. He began drilling at Spindletop in 1899. At first, he, too, had no luck. The money he relied on was running out. Lucas escorted businessmen to Beaumont, hoping that they would invest in the well. Most of them felt that he did not deserve their help. But Lucas defended his ideas about salt domes and oil. Finally, his investors were satisfied that his project was worthwhile, and the funds came in.

On the morning of January 10, 1901, Lucas's team drilled down 1,139 feet—and found oil. "The Lucas Geyser," as it came to be called, blew oil more than 150 feet in the air. In time, it would produce 100,000 barrels per day. Until then, few oil fields in Texas had produced more than 25 barrels per day!

The Spindletop Gusher, 1901

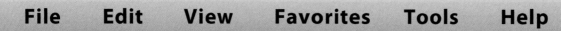

OIL: Industry

Birth of an Industry

Spindletop was the largest oil well the world had ever seen. Nearby Beaumont became one of the first oil-fueled boomtowns. Its population of 10,000 tripled in three months, and eventually swelled to 50,000. Spindletop is now known as the birthplace of the modern oil industry.

We welcome input from our readers. Please e-mail us your comments!

From: TCastillo@beaumont.net
To: webmaster@texashistoryonline.com
CC:

Subject: Spindletop

Dear Texas History Online,

Here's an interesting fact I learned. In just two years after the Spindletop gusher, there were more than 600 oil companies with 285 churning oil wells in the Beaumont area. Some of those oil companies are still around!

Thanks for the article.

Taylor Castillo
Grade 4
Beaumont Hill School

Compare Texts

TEXT TO TEXT

Compare and Contrast Charlotte Parkhurst, Pattillo Higgins, and Anthony Lucas all faced challenges. How are the challenges Charlotte faced similar to those faced by Pattillo Higgins (right) and Anthony Lucas in Texas? How are they different? Use text evidence from each selection.

TEXT TO SELF

Write a Letter Imagine that you have traveled back in time to the mid-1800s. What differences do you notice between your neighborhood now and in the past? Write a letter to a friend in which you compare and contrast the two settings.

TEXT TO WORLD

Connect to Social Studies In "Riding Freedom," Charlotte Parkhurst overcomes a physical challenge in order to continue doing what she loves. Work in a group to identify a famous person you have heard or read about who has done something similar, and discuss his or her experiences.

ELACC4RL1 refer to details and examples when explaining what the text says explicitly and when drawing inferences; **ELACC4RI1** refer to details and examples when explaining what the text says explicitly and when drawing inferences; **ELACC4W10** write routinely over extended time frames and shorter time frames; **ELACC4SL1a** come to discussions prepared/explicitly draw on preparation and other information about the topic

ELACC4L1d order adjectives within sentences according to conventional patterns

Grammar

What Is an Adjective? An **adjective** is a word that gives information about a noun. An adjective of purpose tells what a noun is used for. If two or more adjectives are used to describe something, they appear in a particular order. The adjective telling about number is first, followed by adjectives telling opinion, size, shape, color, and purpose.

number	opinion	size	shape	color	purpose	noun

Adjective of Purpose	Order of Adjectives
The campers slept in sleeping bags.	number opinion color Six strong black horses pulled the carriage.

Try This! **With a partner, find the adjectives that tell about the underlined nouns. If two or more adjectives are used to describe one noun, what is the correct order?**

1. The brave two drivers looked at the muddy road.
2. She tied one brown tired horse to a hitching post.
3. She left large three black horses with her young partner.
4. She stepped into a waiting crowded room.
5. She wanted the doctor to look at her bad one eye.

To make your writing flow smoothly, you can move adjectives to combine sentences. If two choppy sentences tell about the same noun, combine the sentences by moving the adjectives from one sentence and placing them before the noun in the other. Make sure the adjectives are in the correct order.

Short, Choppy Sentences

The horses trotted along the dusty road.

There were five colorful horses.

Longer, Smoother Sentence

The five colorful horses trotted along the dusty road.

Connect Grammar to Writing

As you revise your descriptive paragraph, look for short, choppy sentences that may repeat a noun. Try combining these sentences by moving the adjectives. Be sure to put the adjectives in the correct order.

ELACC4W3a orient the reader by establishing a situation and introducing a narrator or characters/organize an event sequence; **ELACC4W3b** use dialogue and description to develop experiences and events or show characters' responses; **ELACC4W3c** use transitional words and phrases to manage the sequence of events; **ELACC4W3d** use concrete words and phrases and sensory details

Narrative Writing

Ideas In "Riding Freedom," the author uses **concrete words** and **sensory details** to make her descriptions clear and lively. As you revise your **descriptive paragraph,** include clear, colorful language to make your descriptions more vivid. Add transition words to make the sequence of events clear.

Claire drafted a descriptive paragraph about a bus ride during a rainstorm. Then she reread her draft and added some concrete words and sensory details. She also clarified the situation she was writing about and added some transition words.

Writing Traits Checklist

Ideas
Did I clearly establish the situation in which my scene took place?

Organization
Are all my details about one main event?

Word Choice
Have I used concrete words and sensory details?

Voice
Did I show how it feels to be in the place I describe?

Sentence Fluency
Did I combine short, choppy sentences and use transition words?

Conventions
Did I use correct spelling, grammar, and mechanics?

Revised Draft

Bang! The thunder ~~was really loud.~~ sounded like dynamite exploding. Everyone on the school bus shrieked, and then the older kids started laughing. Next, some ~~Some~~ kindergartners burst out crying. ~~They were~~ scared. All of a sudden, ~~water~~ gigantic raindrops began hammering on the roof. The rain grew as loud as a drum roll.

Final Copy

A Ride to Remember

by Claire Amaral

Bang! The thunder sounded like dynamite exploding. Everyone on the school bus shrieked, and then the older kids started laughing. Next, some scared kindergartners burst out crying. All of a sudden, gigantic raindrops began hammering on the roof. The rain grew as loud as a drum roll. Soon my window fogged up. In the front of the bus, the windshield wipers were jerking back and forth like a conductor keeping time to some super-fast music.

When the bus finally stopped and the door opened, the water in the street was up to the curb. The kids who got off at the first couple stops had to leap over the water to the sidewalk. For once, I was glad my stop was last!

Reading as a Writer

What does Claire's writing help you see and hear? Where can you add descriptive words in your own writing? Where can you add transition words to make the sequence of events clearer?

In my final paper, I clarified where my story takes place. I combined two short sentences by moving an adjective. I replaced some vague words with specific, colorful words.

Lesson 17

TARGET VOCABULARY

reward
graduate
symbol
foster
disobey
confidence
patiently
confesses
ceremony
performs

Vocabulary Reader

Context Cards

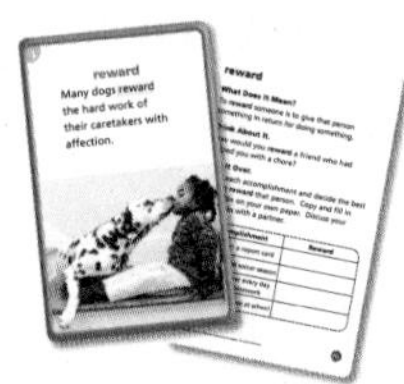

ELACC4L6 acquire/use vocabulary, including academic and domain-specific

Vocabulary in Context

1 reward

Many dogs reward the hard work of their caretakers with affection.

2 graduate

Some dogs graduate to show they have completed obedience school.

3 symbol

For some dogs, a leash is a symbol, or sign, of outdoor fun.

4 foster

Some service dogs live with foster caretakers for a short time.

- Study each Context Card.
- Use context clues to determine the meanings of these words.

5 disobey

Well-trained dogs don't disobey, or ignore, their owners' commands.

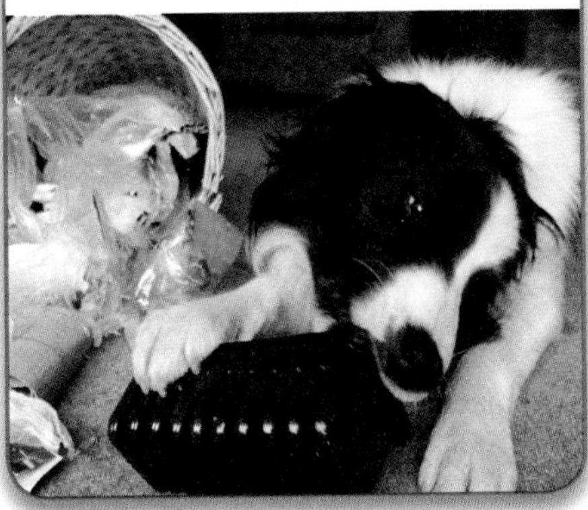

6 confidence

Praising a dog helps it gain confidence that it is learning well.

7 patiently

Show dogs must remain calm and wait patiently for long periods.

8 confesses

This girl confesses, or admits, that daily care of a dog is hard work.

9 ceremony

Dogs who win awards may be honored in a special event known as a ceremony.

10 performs

This working dog performs its job by herding sheep.

Read and Comprehend

TARGET SKILL

Sequence of Events As you read "The Right Dog for the Job," notice the **sequence**, or order, in which events are organized. Some events may happen at the same time, but others follow one another. Look for dates as well as clue words such as *next*, *then*, and *now* to help you. Use a graphic organizer like the one below to help you describe the text's overall structure.

Event

↓

Event

↓

Event

TARGET STRATEGY

Summarize As you read, use the sequence of events to help you **summarize**, or briefly restate, the most important events. You should use your own words in the summary to help make sure you understand the ideas and events.

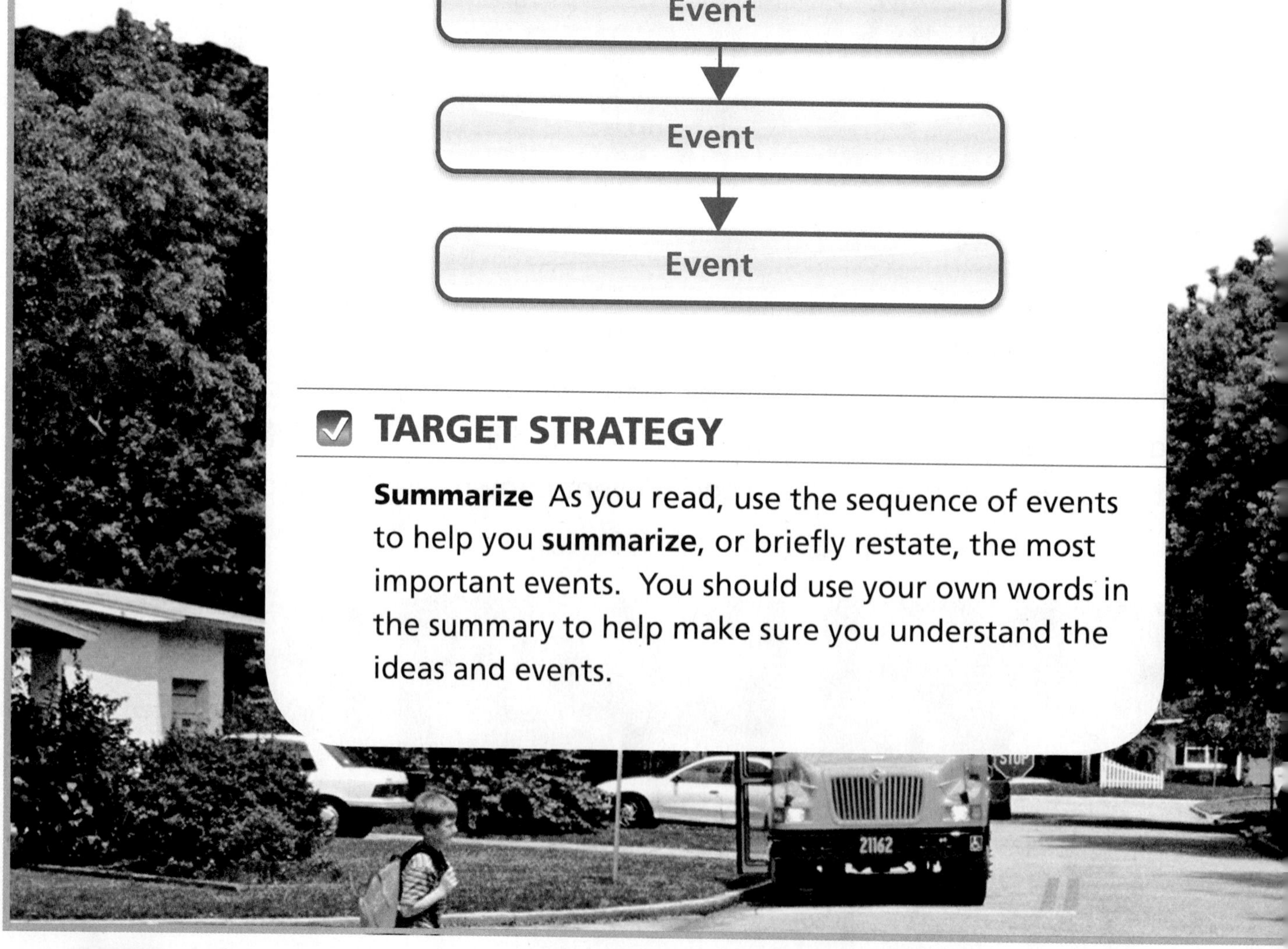

ELACC4RI2 determine the main idea and explain how it is supported by details/summarize; **ELACC4RI5** describe the overall structure of a text or part of a text

PREVIEW THE TOPIC

Service Animals

Think about the many things you do each day to stay safe, such as looking both ways before crossing the street. For people with disabilities, staying safe can be a challenge. Imagine how difficult it is for a person who cannot see to safely cross a busy street.

Some animals can be trained to help people with disabilities do many things. "The Right Dog for the Job" tells the story of a service dog named Ira. As you read, you'll find out how Ira learned the many things that a service dog needs to know.

Lesson 17

ANCHOR TEXT

THE RIGHT DOG FOR THE JOB
Ira's Path from Service Dog to Guide Dog

TARGET SKILL

Sequence of Events
Examine the time order in which events take place.

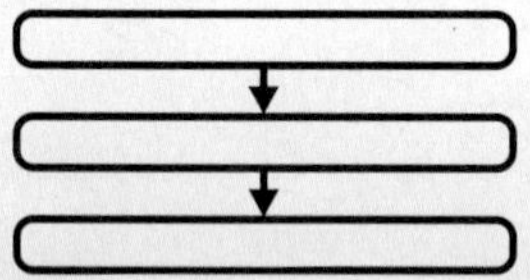

GENRE

Narrative nonfiction tells about people, things, events, or places that are real. As you read, look for:

- factual information that tells a story
- text features such as photographs and captions
- events that are told in time order

COMMON CORE **ELACC4RI2** determine the main idea and explain how it is supported by details/summarize; **ELACC4RI4** determine the meaning of general academic and domain-specific words and phrases; **ELACC4RI5** describe the overall structure of a text or part of a text

MEET THE AUTHOR

Dorothy Hinshaw Patent

Dorothy Hinshaw Patent has always loved animals and the outdoors. As a child she kept snakes, frogs, and fish in her bedroom. She studied science in college and wanted to teach others to love nature. Like *The Right Dog for the Job*, her book *The Buffalo and the Indians* describes a close relationship between people and animals.

MEET THE PHOTOGRAPHER

William Muñoz

William Muñoz has traveled around the United States, closely studying animals and the environment with his camera. Some of the animals he has photographed include grizzly bears, ospreys, and bald eagles. He and Dorothy Hinshaw Patent have worked together on more than sixty books.

THE RIGHT DOG FOR THE JOB

Ira's Path from Service Dog to Guide Dog

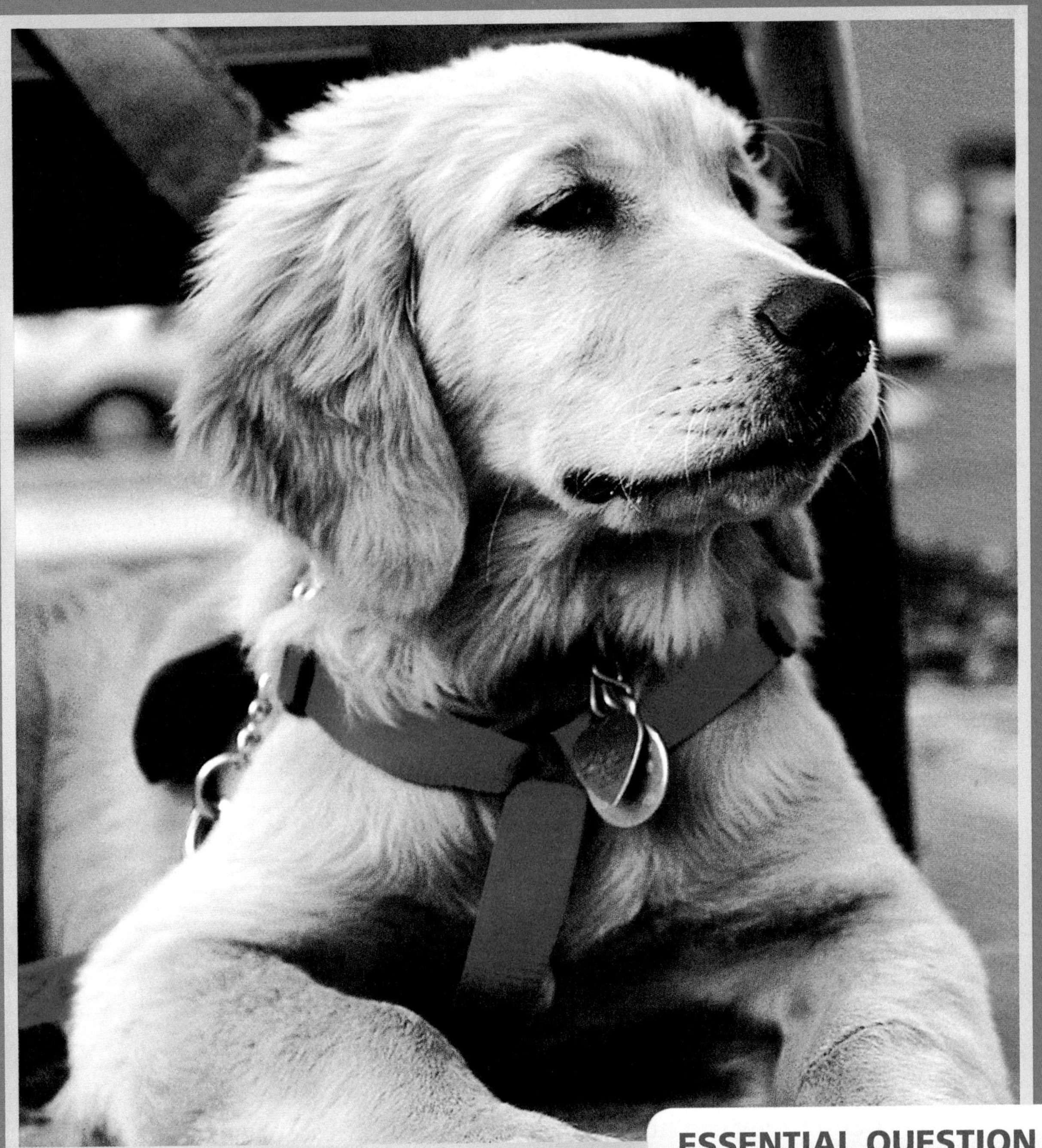

by Dorothy Hinshaw Patent
photographs by William Muñoz

ESSENTIAL QUESTION

How do people and animals benefit each other?

Ira was born on Shy Bear Farm in Montana, along with his sister, Ivy, and his brother, Ike. Like all newborn puppies, the three young golden retrievers have closed eyes, velvety ears, and very soft fur. But unlike most puppies, these three were born for a special purpose. By the time they are two years old, each is expected to have become a service dog, helping a person who has difficulty moving around on his or her own to lead a fuller life. Ira, Ivy, and Ike are part of PawsAbilities, Canine Partners for People with Disabilities.

Brea, the puppies' mother, and Kathleen Decker, PawsAbilities' foster puppy coordinator, take good care of the puppies. They grow bigger and stronger. Their eyes and ears open so they can take in the world around them. Soon they are romping and playing together, getting bolder each day. Kathleen begins to feed them puppy food when they are four weeks old. By the age of six weeks, they no longer need their mother's milk. Soon it will be time to leave home.

Before they can help people with disabilities, service dogs need to learn to deal confidently with the world and whatever it might present to them—loud noises, smelly buses, crowds of people.

Each puppy goes to live with a special person called a foster puppy raiser. The puppy becomes a member of the family, where it gets plenty of love, attention, and praise as the puppy raiser introduces it to the world.

When they are about eight weeks old, Ira, Ivy, and Ike meet their puppy raisers. Ira goes home with Sandy Welch, a sixth-grade teacher in Lolo, Montana. Sandy already has her own beautiful golden retriever, Laddy Griz. Laddy and Ira quickly become friends. Kathleen visits Ira and Sandy a month later. She wants to see how Ira is doing and check on his service-dog skills.

One of the most important tasks a service dog performs is retrieving things such as dropped keys. Sandy has already been working on this skill with Ira, so Kathleen throws her keys and tells Ira to fetch them. He runs over, picks them up in his mouth, and brings them back to Kathleen. Good news—Ira is already on his way to becoming a service dog!

ANALYZE THE TEXT

Sequence of Events Explain, in order, the events that happen to Ira on this page.

Ira retrieves Kathleen's keys.

All along, the puppy raisers meet as a group to learn how to teach the young dogs what they need to know. The puppies have to learn how to come or to sit on command and how to walk at heel on a leash.

Kathleen also shows them how to teach the puppies to press a wheelchair-access sign with their paw. The symbol appears on buttons that open doors automatically when pressed. Kathleen uses a plastic lid attached to a stick with a strip of cloth. On the lid is the wheelchair-access sign. She puts a dog treat on the deck and covers it with the lid. One by one, the puppies sniff and push the lid with their noses, trying to get at the treat. But only when they scratch at it with a foot does Kathleen lift the stick so the puppy is rewarded.

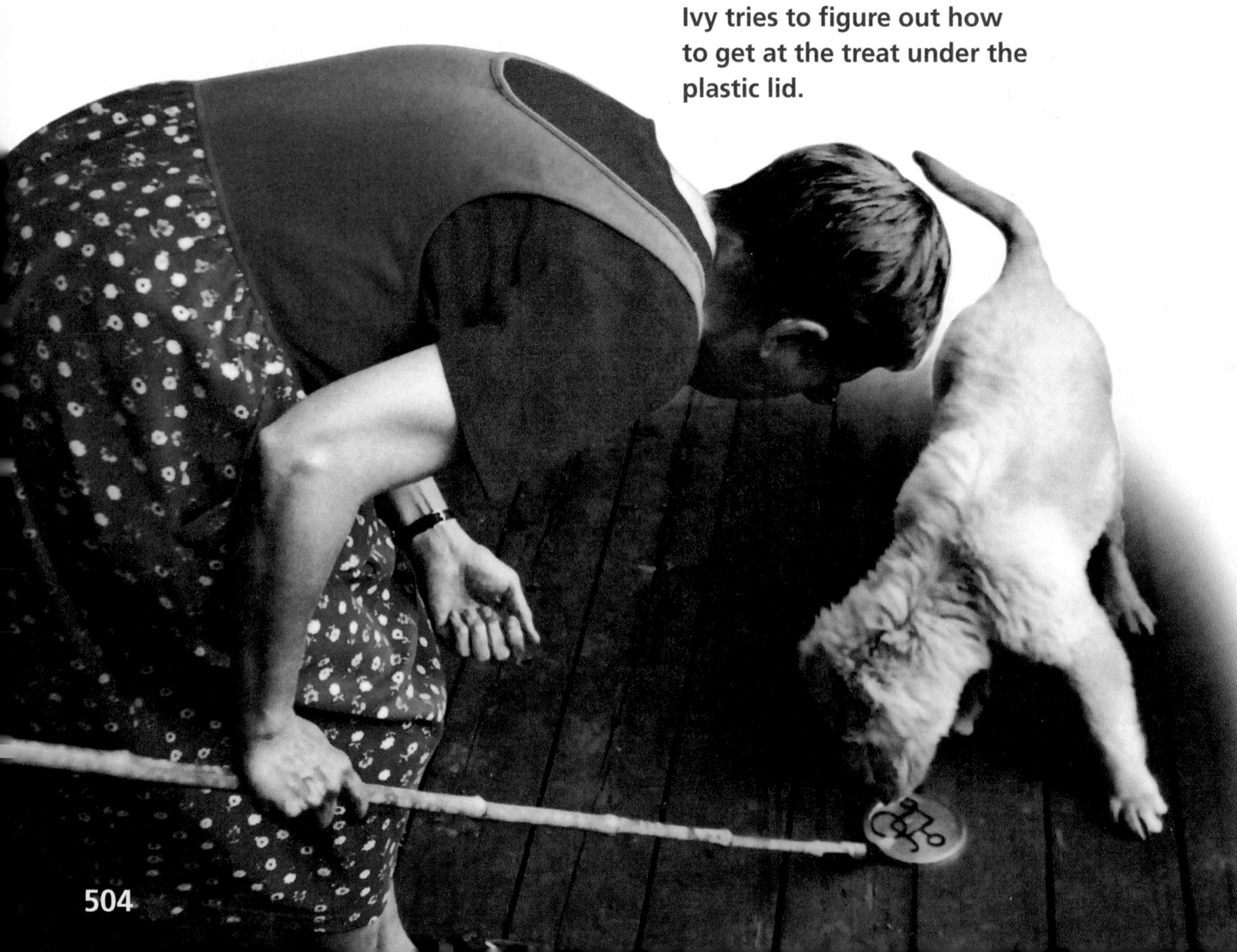

Ivy tries to figure out how to get at the treat under the plastic lid.

Ira gets off the bus.

Next, the group goes to the bus station. The bus company loans PawsAbilities a bus and driver. The puppies practice getting on and off over and over again. They ride around town and learn to stay calm on the bus as it stops and starts. By the end of the day, riding the bus has become as natural as a trip in the car.

The puppy raisers take the dogs wherever they can, such as to sporting events and the farmers' market. Every two weeks, the group meets at a different place somewhere in town. At the mall, the puppies learn not to be distracted at the pet store or by the crowds of people walking by. They also practice pushing the button with the wheelchair sign to open the door. At the university, they learn how to pull open a door using a tug made of rope tied to the knob. At the library, they learn to lie quietly under the table while the puppy raisers look through books. They also learn how to enter the elevator correctly, walking right beside the puppy raiser instead of going in front or behind. It would be dangerous if the elevator door closed on the leash.

Sandy brings Ira to her classroom two days a week. She explains to her students the importance of training Ira correctly.

"Ira needs to learn to lie down by himself and stay there, even if he gets bored," she says. "You have to leave him alone, even if he wants to be petted, so he doesn't get distracted from his job. You can also help teach the other children not to pet a service dog in training."

Ira has his own corner of the room, where he must lie quietly on his rug. If he gets up and wanders around, Sandy says in a firm voice, "Rug!" Then she tells Ira to sit, lie down, or stay. He must also learn to always stay close to the person he is helping.

When Sandy and the students work with Ira, they form a circle and bring Ira into the center. Then one of the children calls him. He knows he'll get a treat if he lays his head in the child's lap. The children take turns calling him, helping him learn to come reliably every time he is called. Then they help teach him to use his nose to push a light switch, another important job for a service dog to learn.

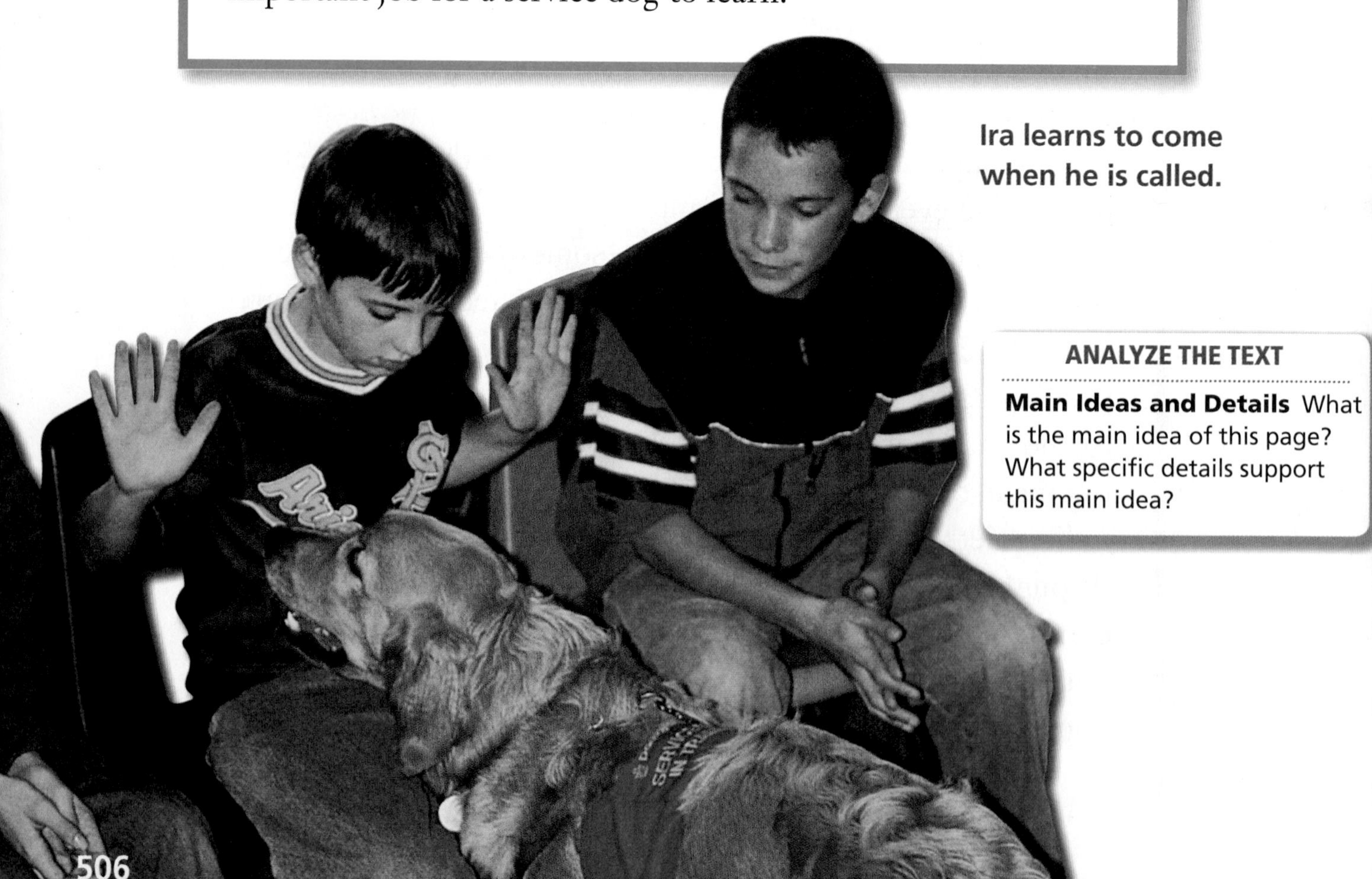

Ira learns to come when he is called.

ANALYZE THE TEXT

Main Ideas and Details What is the main idea of this page? What specific details support this main idea?

It takes lots of practice for Ira to learn to flip a light switch with his nose instead of his mouth.

Ira goes all over the school, so he gets used to noisy places like the cafeteria and the gym during pep rallies. Sandy also takes him to other classrooms and tells the other students about service dogs.

As summer approaches, Sandy's students must say good-bye to Ira. Each child gets a chance to say what having Ira in the classroom meant to her or him.

"I feel special because I got to help train Ira," says one.

"I never liked dogs before Ira came, but now I like having him around," confesses another.

"Having Ira in the classroom has made me feel beyond wonderful," says a third.

To reward the children for their help, Sandy arranges a field trip to Shy Bear Farm. The students take turns making dog toys, working on scrapbooks for Ira's new companion, touring the farm, and playing with the six-week-old puppies. They also get to say one last good-bye to Ira.

As summer starts it's time for Ira to leave Sandy and go for more detailed service-dog training. But his assigned training facility isn't ready yet. Glenn Martyn, director of PawsAbilities, can't find another service-dog group that can use Ira. Everyone worries. What will happen? Can Ira learn a new career?

Though they rarely take dogs raised and trained elsewhere, Guide Dogs for the Blind in San Rafael, California, steps in. "Ira has lots of confidence, which is very important in a guide dog, so we'll give Ira a chance," says their coordinator. "But we'll have to change his name. Each dog we train has a different name, and we already have one called Ira. We'll just change the spelling to 'Irah' so he won't have to learn a new name."

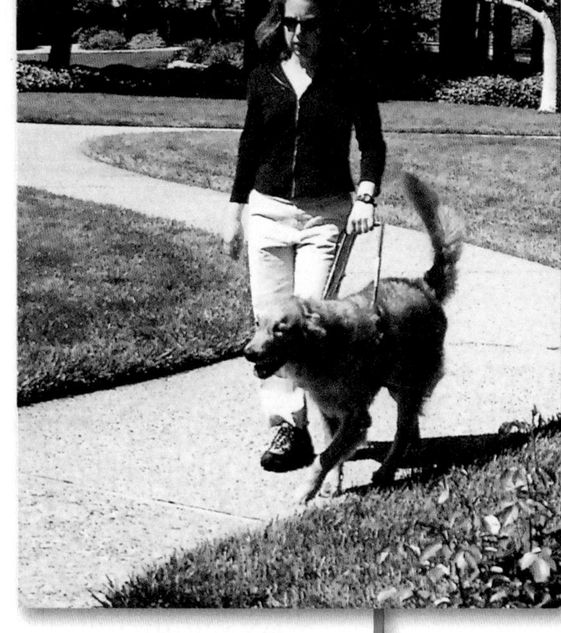

Stacy works with Irah on the Guide Dogs for the Blind campus.

Now Irah needs to learn a whole new set of skills, which takes four to five months. He has to get used to wearing a guide-dog harness. Trainer Stacy Burrow helps him learn many things, such as stopping at street corners and crossing only when the way is clear.

The most important thing a guide dog must learn is intelligent disobedience. Knowing when to disobey can enable a guide dog to save its owner's life. For example, if the blind person tells the dog to go forward when a car is running a red light, the dog must refuse to obey. Irah is smart. He passes the program with flying colors.

ANALYZE THE TEXT

Domain-Specific Vocabulary What do the terms *guide dog, training facility, guide-dog harness,* and *intelligent disobedience* mean? How can you use context clues to figure out the meanings of these terms?

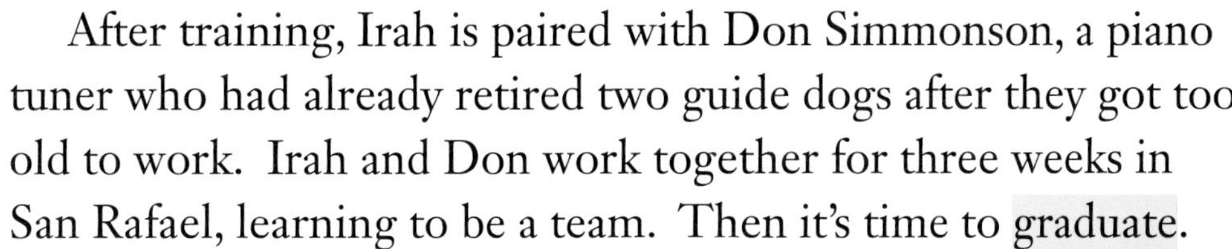

After training, Irah is paired with Don Simmonson, a piano tuner who had already retired two guide dogs after they got too old to work. Irah and Don work together for three weeks in San Rafael, learning to be a team. Then it's time to graduate.

Sandy comes from Montana for the graduation. She gets to see Irah and meet Don before the ceremony. Irah and Sandy are delighted to be together again, but Irah clearly knows his place is now with Don.

During the graduation ceremony, Don's name is announced when his turn comes. Sandy hands Irah over to Don. Irah is Don's dog now, and the two will be loving, giving partners. Sandy will miss Irah, but she is happy that he has found a home with someone like Don.

At home in Kennewick, Washington, Don and Irah continue to learn to work together. Grayson, Don's retired guide dog, also lives with them. Grayson and Irah become fast friends, playing together just like Irah and Laddy did.

Stacy, Sandy, and Irah stand by as Don speaks at the graduation.

Joey escorts Don and Irah to the stage for their big moment.

When Don goes to work, Irah guides him. Once they enter the room with the piano, Don says, "Irah, find the piano," and Irah leads him to it. Then Don gets to work and Irah lies down nearby, waiting patiently, as he learned to do in Sandy's classroom. He is there for Don whenever he is needed.

"I'm so glad Irah and I found each other," Don says. "He's just the right dog for me."

Sandy and Don become friends, and, as a surprise, Sandy invites Don to the eighth-grade graduation of the children who helped train Irah.

Don's wife, Robbie, drives their motor home to Montana for the graduation. After Sandy talks to the audience about Irah and Don, she shows a movie of their graduation from Guide Dogs for the Blind. Then she announces that Don and Irah are in the auditorium, and Joey, Irah's favorite student, escorts them to the stage. The surprised students are delighted to see the results of their hard work and the hard work of so many others. Their own canine student, Irah, is now a working guide dog!

COMPREHENSION

Dig Deeper

How to Analyze the Text

Use these pages to learn about Sequence of Events, Main Idea and Details, and Domain-Specific Vocabulary. Then read "The Right Dog for the Job" again to apply what you learned.

Sequence of Events

Narrative nonfiction selections such as "The Right Dog for the Job" tell a story about something that happened in real life. The events are usually told in the **sequence,** or order, in which they happen. The way a text is organized is called its **structure.** Dates, numbers, and signal words such as *next*, *then*, and *after training* are clues that a text is organized by the sequence of events.

You can better understand "The Right Dog for the Job" by describing its structure. Turn to pages 502–503. What signal words do you see? What is the order of events on these pages?

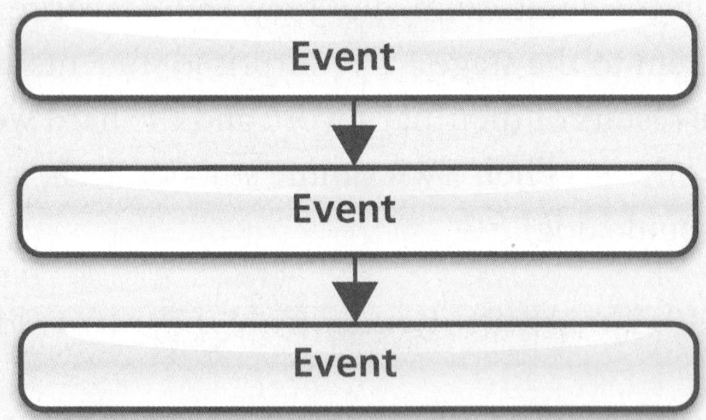

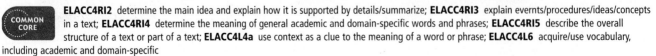

COMMON CORE **ELACC4RI2** determine the main idea and explain how it is supported by details/summarize; **ELACC4RI3** explain evernts/procedures/ideas/concepts in a text; **ELACC4RI4** determine the meaning of general academic and domain-specific words and phrases; **ELACC4RI5** describe the overall structure of a text or part of a text; **ELACC4L4a** use context as a clue to the meaning of a word or phrase; **ELACC4L6** acquire/use vocabulary, including academic and domain-specific

Main Ideas and Details

Authors support their **main ideas,** what a text is mostly about, by providing **details,** such as facts and examples. The main idea on pages 504–505 is that puppy raisers must teach puppies important skills. Details explain what the author means:

- pressing a wheelchair-access button
- pulling doors open
- getting on and off of elevators and buses

Domain-Specific Vocabulary

Nonfiction texts often focus on specific topics. These specific areas of knowledge are called **domains.** Every domain includes words that are important to know when learning about that subject. For example, the words *service dog*, *canine*, and *on command* are important to the subject of guide dogs. When you see a **domain-specific word** that you are not familiar with, use context clues or a dictionary to understand its meaning.

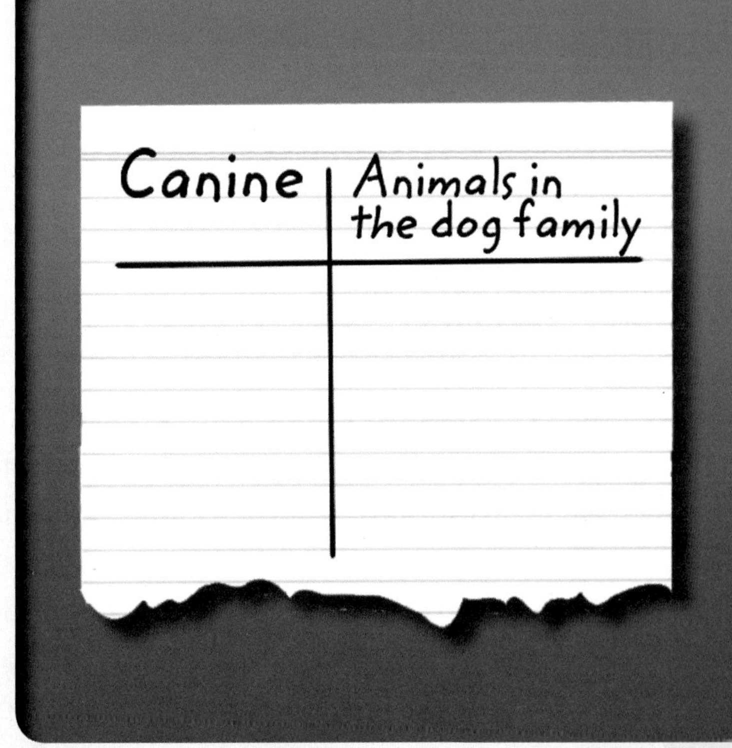

Your Turn

RETURN TO THE ESSENTIAL QUESTION

Turn and Talk Review the selection with a partner to prepare to discuss this question: *How do people and animals benefit each other?* Support your ideas with text evidence. Take turns reviewing and explaining key ideas in your discussion with your partner. Follow agreed-upon rules such as not interrupting each other and listening carefully to each other.

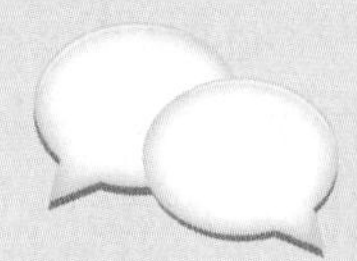

Classroom Conversation

Continue your discussion of "The Right Dog for the Job" by discussing these questions:

1. Why might it be difficult for puppy trainers such as Sandy to say goodbye to each puppy?
2. What is the most important trait a good guide dog should have? Explain.
3. What skills or traits do puppy trainers need to do their jobs?

WANTED: PUPPY RAISERS

Make a Flyer With a partner, make a flyer inviting people to raise foster puppies. Briefly summarize what puppy raisers do. Use headings to organize your ideas, and include important details in each section. Be sure to include drawings or photos of puppies as well.

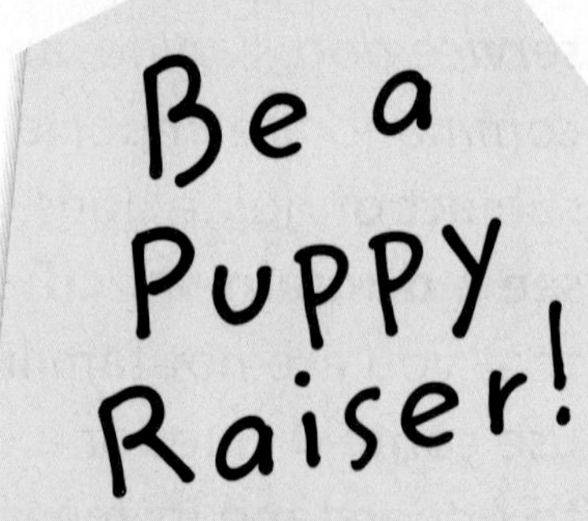

WRITE ABOUT READING

THE RIGHT DOG FOR THE JOB
Ira's Path from Service Dog to Guide Dog

Response Think about what puppy raisers do to teach young dogs the skills needed to become good service dogs. Would you want to train a service dog? Why or why not? Write a paragraph explaining your opinion. Include reasons and support them with facts, details, and evidence from the selection.

Writing Tip

Use transition words and phrases such as *also* and *another reason* to link your opinions and reasons. Also look for short, choppy sentences that you can combine to make your writing smoother.

COMMON CORE **ELACC4RI1** refer to details and examples when explaining what the text says explicitly and when drawing inferences; **ELACC4RI2** determine the main idea and explain how it is supported by details/summarize; **ELACC4RI5** describe the overall structure of a text or part of a text; **ELACC4W1b** provide reasons supported by facts and details; **ELACC4W1c** link opinion and reasons using words and phrases; **ELACC4SL1a** come to discussions prepared/explicitly draw on preparation and other information about the topic

Lesson 17

INFORMATIONAL TEXT

GENRE

Informational text, such as this magazine article, gives factual information about a topic by presenting main ideas and supporting details.

TEXT FOCUS

Headings Identify the main ideas of sections of a text, such as chapters, paragraphs, and sidebars. Before you begin reading, scan the headings and topic sentences to gain an overview of the text.

ELACC4RI2 determine the main idea and explain how it is supported by details/ summarize; **ELACC4RI10** read and comprehend informational texts

KNOWING NOSES SEARCH-AND-RESCUE DOGS

by Ellen Gold

Search-and-rescue dogs are trained to perform some very special jobs. They often assist in finding someone who is lost. Sometimes they help police officers solve crimes such as burglaries. These hard-working dogs are also known as SAR dogs. SAR stands for "Search And Rescue."

Noses to the Rescue!

Dogs have a great sense of smell. They have about twenty-five times more smell receptors than people have. This makes them good at search-and-rescue work. SAR dogs are trained to follow scents in the air, on the ground, and even underwater!

Air-scent dogs are the most common type of SAR dog. They can find a lost person by smelling the scent that person has left behind. The dogs follow the scent as it gets stronger. Then, they lead the rescuers to the lost person.

Qualities of a Good SAR Dog

SAR dog trainers look for certain qualities in dogs prior to teaching them SAR skills. They look for dogs that like to play and like to please their trainers. Dogs with these qualities will respond to rewards when being trained. SAR dogs should also be friendly, healthy, and smart. They should not be afraid of strangers. Certain types of dogs have a natural talent for search-and-rescue work. These are usually bloodhounds, German shepherds, and golden retrievers.

SPECIAL FEATURE

The SAR Dog and the Lost Boy: A Happy Ending

In March of 2007, a twelve-year-old Boy Scout wandered away from his troop's campsite in North Carolina. He misjudged the seriousness of being alone in the wilderness and soon found himself lost.

The boy survived for four days by drinking stream water and finding safe places to sleep. His father speculated that the boy was trying to live out his favorite story. It is about a boy who survives in the wilderness on his own.

Meanwhile, a search-and-rescue team with dogs was looking for the boy. One of the dogs, named Gandalf, picked up the boy's scent and found him. What a great favor Gandalf did for the boy and his family!

SAR Training and Work

Training SAR dogs is a big job. It can take more than a year to get a dog ready for a search-and-rescue mission. Regrettably, some dogs that go through training don't have what it takes to be SAR dogs.

Those that do become SAR dogs deal with different types of jobs. Sometimes they search for a suspect who is part of a crime scheme. Often their searches help innocent people. They might search for someone lost in the wilderness or trapped in fallen buildings.

Whatever their mission might be, SAR dogs are a big help to their human teams.

Compare Texts

TEXT TO TEXT

Compare Actions Do you think Ira would be a good search-and-rescue dog? Why or why not? Discuss your thoughts with a partner. Use text evidence from each selection to support your ideas.

TEXT TO SELF

Working with Animals Have you ever trained a pet or observed someone else training a pet? Write a paragraph detailing the lessons someone might learn from training an animal.

TEXT TO WORLD

Research Service Dogs Ira was first trained as a service dog and then as a guide dog. Some dogs are trained as search-and-rescue dogs. What other jobs and services can dogs be trained to do? Work with a group to research other ways dogs are trained to help humans. As you research, take notes and categorize the information. Present your findings to the class.

ELACC4RI1 refer to details and examples when explaining what the text says explicitly and when drawing inferences; **ELACC4RI9** integrate information from two texts on the same topic; **ELACC4W7** conduct short research projects that build knowledge through investigation; **ELACC4SL4** report on a topic or text, tell a story, or recount an experience/speak clearly at an understandable pace

ELACC4L3a choose words and phrases to convey ideas precisely

Grammar

What Is an Adverb? An **adverb** is a word that describes a verb. Adverbs give more information about an action verb or a form of the verb *be*. They tell *how, when,* or *where*. Most adverbs telling *how* end with *-ly*.

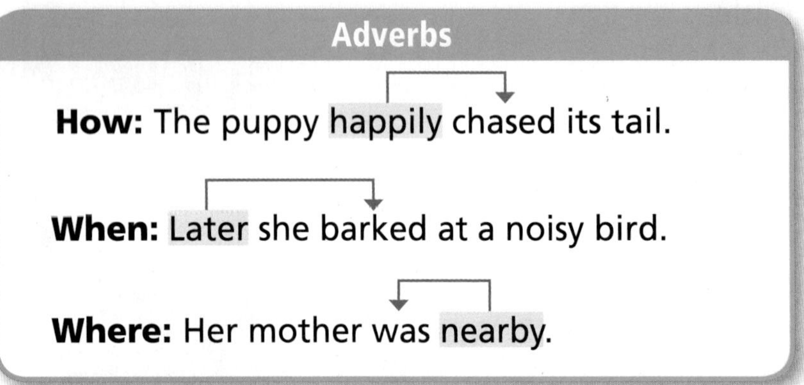

Adverbs

How: The puppy happily chased its tail.

When: Later she barked at a noisy bird.

Where: Her mother was nearby.

An **adverb of frequency** tells how often something happens. **Adverbs of intensity** tell to what degree or how much something happens.

Adverb of Frequency: Puppies usually love walks.

Adverb of Intensity: Our puppy almost caught a squirrel.

Try This! **Write the following sentences on a sheet of paper and identify the adverbs. Note whether they tell about intensity or frequency.**

1. A cat visits our yard often.
2. Our dog barks loudly.
3. She nearly jumps through the window.

When you write, use precise adverbs to create clear pictures of how, when, and where things happen. Precise adverbs also help make your writing more interesting and easier to understand.

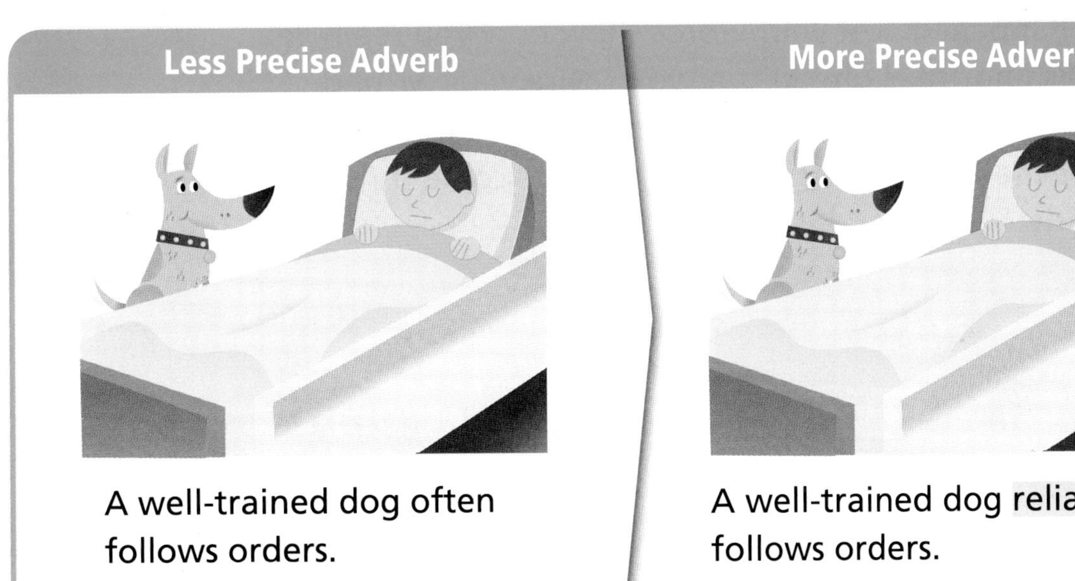

Less Precise Adverb	More Precise Adverb
A well-trained dog often follows orders.	A well-trained dog reliably follows orders.

Less Precise Adverb	More Precise Adverb
A service dog does not get distracted.	A service dog rarely gets distracted.
My dog doesn't leave my side.	My dog never leaves my side!

Connect Grammar to Writing

As you revise your friendly letter, look for opportunities to use precise adverbs. Use descriptive language to help readers create clear pictures in their minds.

ELACC4W3a orient the reader by establishing a situation and introducing a narrator or characters/organize an event sequence; **ELACC4W3b** use dialogue and description to develop experiences and events or show characters' responses; **ELACC4W3e** provide a conclusion; **ELACC4W4** produce writing in which development and organization are appropriate to task, purpose, and audience

Narrative Writing

Voice In "The Right Dog for the Job," Don lets his feelings come through when he says, "I'm so glad Irah and I found each other." When you revise your **friendly letter,** don't just tell what happened. Let your words show how you really feel. Use the Writing Traits Checklist as you revise your writing.

Anthony drafted a letter to his aunt about getting a dog. Then he revised some parts to let his feelings come through more clearly.

Writing Traits Checklist

- **Ideas**
  Does my ending wrap up my purpose for writing?
- **Organization**
  Did I tell the events in chronological order?
- **Sentence Fluency**
  Did I combine short, choppy sentences so they read smoothly?
- **Word Choice**
  Did I choose vivid, interesting words?
- **Voice**
  Did I sound like myself and show my feelings?
- **Conventions**
  Did I use correct spelling, grammar, and mechanics?

Revised Draft

Dear Aunt Brenda,

Guess what! Last week I got the ~~Last week I got a dog. She is a very~~ smartest, most adorable dog. ~~good dog.~~ At the animal shelter, I immediately noticed a little brown and white dog named Patsy. ~~I noticed her immediately.~~ She came right to me, wagging her tail. When I petted her, she licked my face. After that, there was no way I was leaving ~~So I decided that I wanted her.~~ the shelter without her.

Final Copy

14 West Orchard Street
Nashville, Tennessee 37215
June 30, 2014

Dear Aunt Brenda,

Guess what! Last week I got the smartest, most adorable dog. At the animal shelter, I immediately noticed a little brown and white dog named Patsy. She came right to me, wagging her tail. When I petted her, she licked my face. After that, there was no way I was leaving the shelter without her. When we got home, I started teaching her, and she quickly learned to sit and stay. Now I'm teaching her to shake hands. I can't wait until you meet Patsy. Please visit us soon!

Love,
Anthony

Reading as a Writer

Which parts show how Anthony feels about his dog Patsy? Where can you show more feeling in your letter?

In my final letter, I made changes to better show how I feel. I also combined two short sentences by moving an adverb.

Lesson 18

HERCULES' QUEST

ZOMO'S FRIENDS

TARGET VOCABULARY

acquire
unfortunate
coerce
boasted
beamed
glared
ceased
declared
devised
resourceful

Vocabulary Reader

Context Cards

ELACC4L6 acquire/use vocabulary, including academic and domain-specific

Vocabulary in Context

1 acquire

To acquire more strength, this woman works out at a gym.

2 unfortunate

It is unfortunate when an accident happens. It makes us feel unlucky.

3 coerce

Never use threats to coerce a classmate to give you something you want.

4 boasted

The boy boasted about the fish he caught. He was proud about how big it was.

- Study each Context Card.
- Use a dictionary to help you understand the meanings of these words.

5 beamed

The student beamed at her good grade. Her smile showed how proud she was.

6 glared

The boy glared. He stared in anger because he had done the wrong homework.

7 ceased

The rain ceased at noon. It stopped in time for the baseball game.

8 declared

The student declared what she would do as class president. She stated it strongly.

9 devised

The boy devised a plan to both do his chores and play basketball.

10 resourceful

People who are resourceful can deal well with difficult situations.

Read and Comprehend

 TARGET SKILL

Story Structure As you read "Hercules' Quest," keep track of text evidence that shows the **story's structure.** Pay attention to new characters as they are introduced. Look for details that help you picture the setting, or where and when the story takes place. Also look for the most important events in the story's plot. Use a graphic organizer like this one to record the text evidence you find.

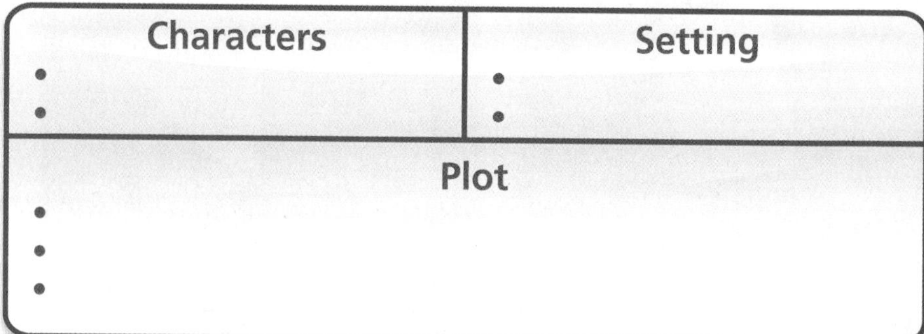

TARGET STRATEGY

Question As you read "Hercules' Quest," ask important **questions** about each character's behavior and personality. For example, you might ask why a character acts a certain way or says certain things. In addition to asking questions while reading, ask yourself questions about a story before and after reading, too.

ELACC4RL3 describe a character, setting, or event, drawing on details

PREVIEW THE TOPIC

Traditional Tales

A traditional tale is a story that gets passed along through the years by word of mouth. Each culture has stories that people tell and retell. A myth is one kind of traditional tale. Myths often include gods, goddesses, heroes, and monsters. The heroes of myths demonstrate the strength, cleverness, and courage needed to meet challenges. Myths reflect the beliefs of a culture.

"Hercules' Quest" is a Greek myth that tells about the adventures of the mighty Hercules, the son of the god Zeus.

Lesson 18

ANCHOR TEXT

TARGET SKILL

Story Structure Explain the elements that make up the story: characters, a setting, and a plot, or series of events.

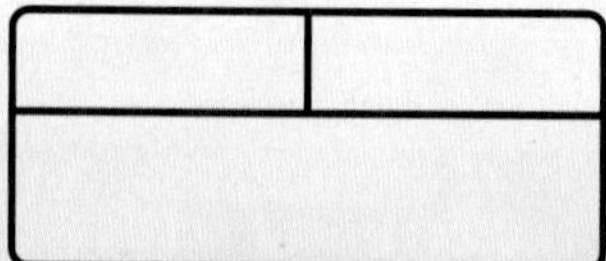

GENRE

Myths are imaginative stories that show what a group of people in the past believed. As you read, look for:

- an explanation of how people and places came to be
- larger-than-life or supernatural characters
- events that cannot happen in real life

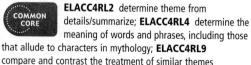

COMMON CORE **ELACC4RL2** determine theme from details/summarize; **ELACC4RL4** determine the meaning of words and phrases, including those that allude to characters in mythology; **ELACC4RL9** compare and contrast the treatment of similar themes and topics

MEET THE ILLUSTRATOR

David Harrington

David Harrington's earliest memories are of drawing pictures. He drew on anything that didn't move: floors, walls, furniture, and even the back of his homework! For David, the process for creating his characters starts with imagination. He thinks about what they are like—their personalities, attitudes, and motivations—until they become real to him. Once he knows his characters, then he begins to see them and can start to draw them. David loves to illustrate children's books. He says, "They open a door to a new world."

HERCULES' QUEST

retold by Martina Melendez illustrated by David Harrington

ESSENTIAL QUESTION

What makes a character memorable?

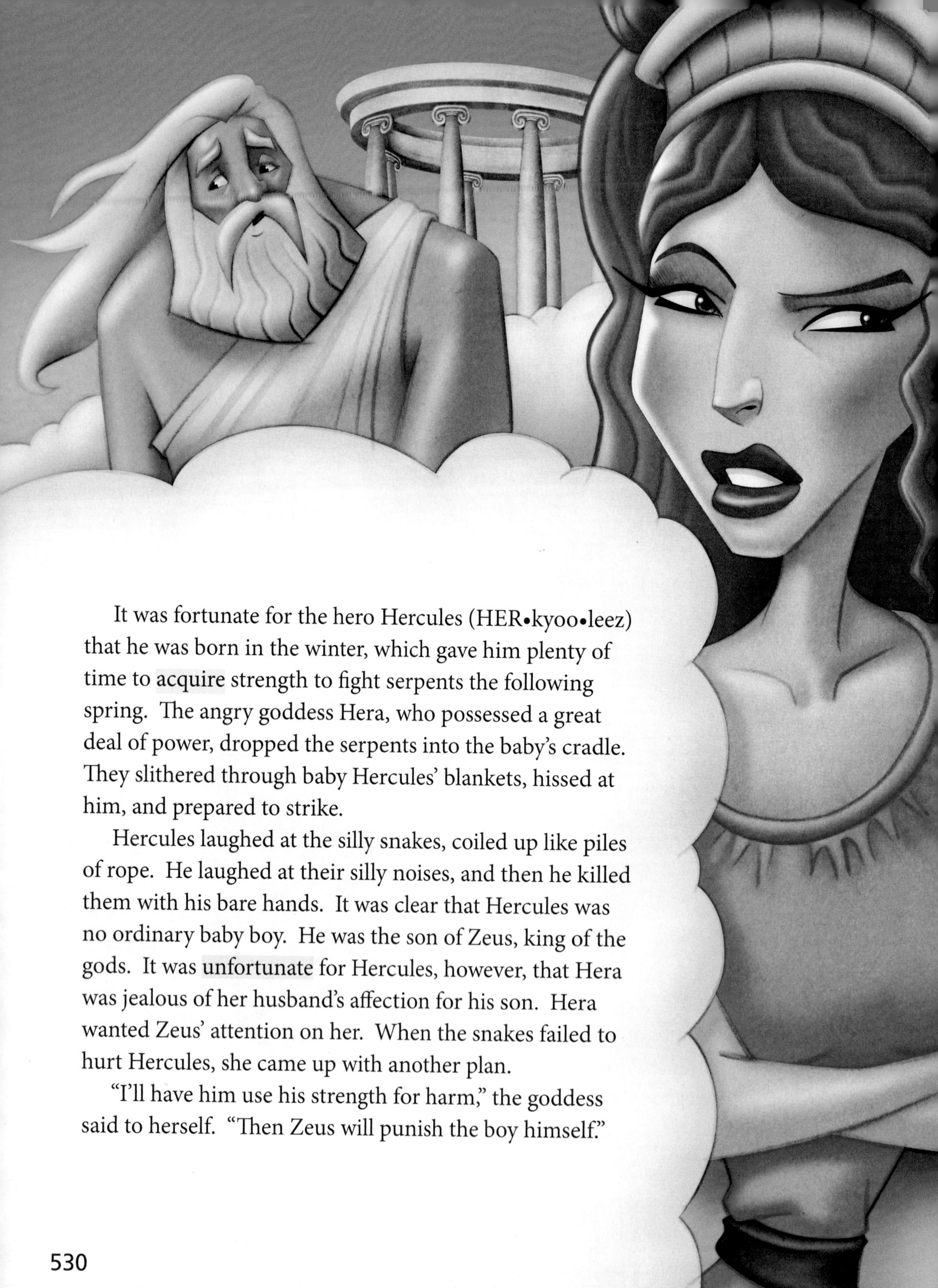

It was fortunate for the hero Hercules (HER•kyoo•leez) that he was born in the winter, which gave him plenty of time to acquire strength to fight serpents the following spring. The angry goddess Hera, who possessed a great deal of power, dropped the serpents into the baby's cradle. They slithered through baby Hercules' blankets, hissed at him, and prepared to strike.

Hercules laughed at the silly snakes, coiled up like piles of rope. He laughed at their silly noises, and then he killed them with his bare hands. It was clear that Hercules was no ordinary baby boy. He was the son of Zeus, king of the gods. It was unfortunate for Hercules, however, that Hera was jealous of her husband's affection for his son. Hera wanted Zeus' attention on her. When the snakes failed to hurt Hercules, she came up with another plan.

"I'll have him use his strength for harm," the goddess said to herself. "Then Zeus will punish the boy himself."

Hera used her power to coerce Hercules into doing dangerous and dishonorable things. Zeus was disappointed at his son's behavior, and so he decided that Hercules would have to earn back his honor and prove worthy of the gift of strength.

Zeus ordered Hercules to serve King Eurystheus (yoo•RIS•thee•us). Many dangerous enemies lived near Eurystheus' kingdom, and Zeus knew that a strong boy like Hercules could keep Eurystheus' people safe.

However, Hera had other things in mind for Hercules. To be sure that Hercules would be out of the way for a long time, she gave Eurystheus a detailed list of tasks that Hercules could never complete. Hercules went to live among the herdsmen and cattle in Eurystheus' kingdom. A fierce, evil lion lived nearby in the valley of Nemea (NEE•me•uh).

"Your first task," said King Eurystheus, "is to kill the Nemean lion."

The impossible mission was Hera's idea, of course. The lion had claws like gleaming swords and teeth even sharper. It could eat a herd of antelope for breakfast and a small boy in a single bite.

After accepting the challenge, Hercules watched and waited for the lion to come out of the forest. "The lion may be strong, but I am stronger," Hercules boasted, "I fought serpents when I was a baby; I killed them with my hands."

When the lion emerged, Hercules first tried to kill the lion with his mighty club, but that failed and so he tried to kill the lion with razor-sharp spears. When no weapon Hercules possessed would harm the beast, the boy wrapped his arms around the lion's neck. Hercules had killed serpents barehhanded, and he killed the lion with his bare hands, too.

Hercules beamed with pride as the lion lay dead at his feet. He lifted the heavy body and paraded it through the land. The people cheered and hollered, and they praised Hercules for his strength. Zeus smiled from his throne on Olympus, while Hera just glared.

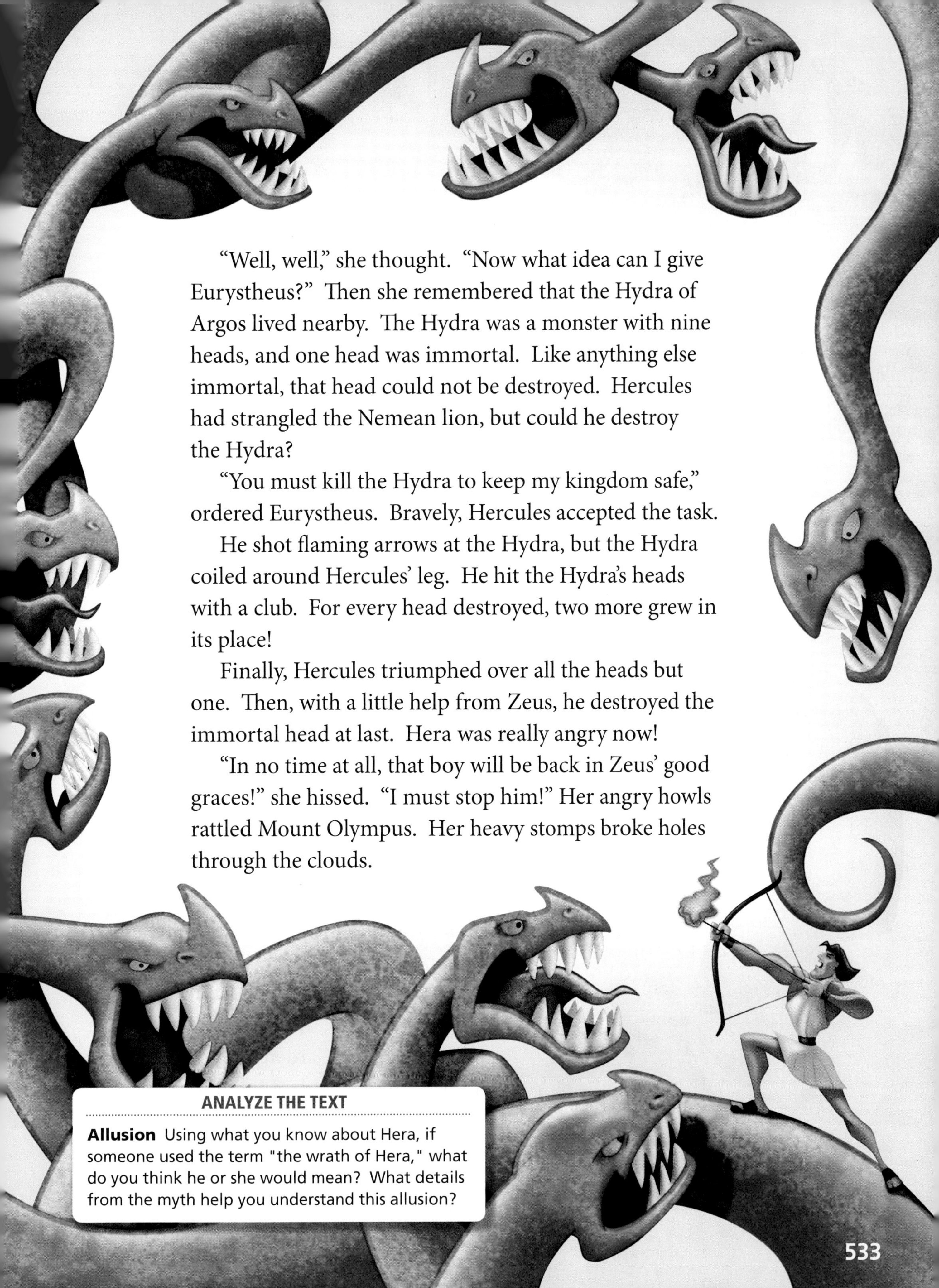

"Well, well," she thought. "Now what idea can I give Eurystheus?" Then she remembered that the Hydra of Argos lived nearby. The Hydra was a monster with nine heads, and one head was immortal. Like anything else immortal, that head could not be destroyed. Hercules had strangled the Nemean lion, but could he destroy the Hydra?

"You must kill the Hydra to keep my kingdom safe," ordered Eurystheus. Bravely, Hercules accepted the task.

He shot flaming arrows at the Hydra, but the Hydra coiled around Hercules' leg. He hit the Hydra's heads with a club. For every head destroyed, two more grew in its place!

Finally, Hercules triumphed over all the heads but one. Then, with a little help from Zeus, he destroyed the immortal head at last. Hera was really angry now!

"In no time at all, that boy will be back in Zeus' good graces!" she hissed. "I must stop him!" Her angry howls rattled Mount Olympus. Her heavy stomps broke holes through the clouds.

ANALYZE THE TEXT

Allusion Using what you know about Hera, if someone used the term "the wrath of Hera," what do you think he or she would mean? What details from the myth help you understand this allusion?

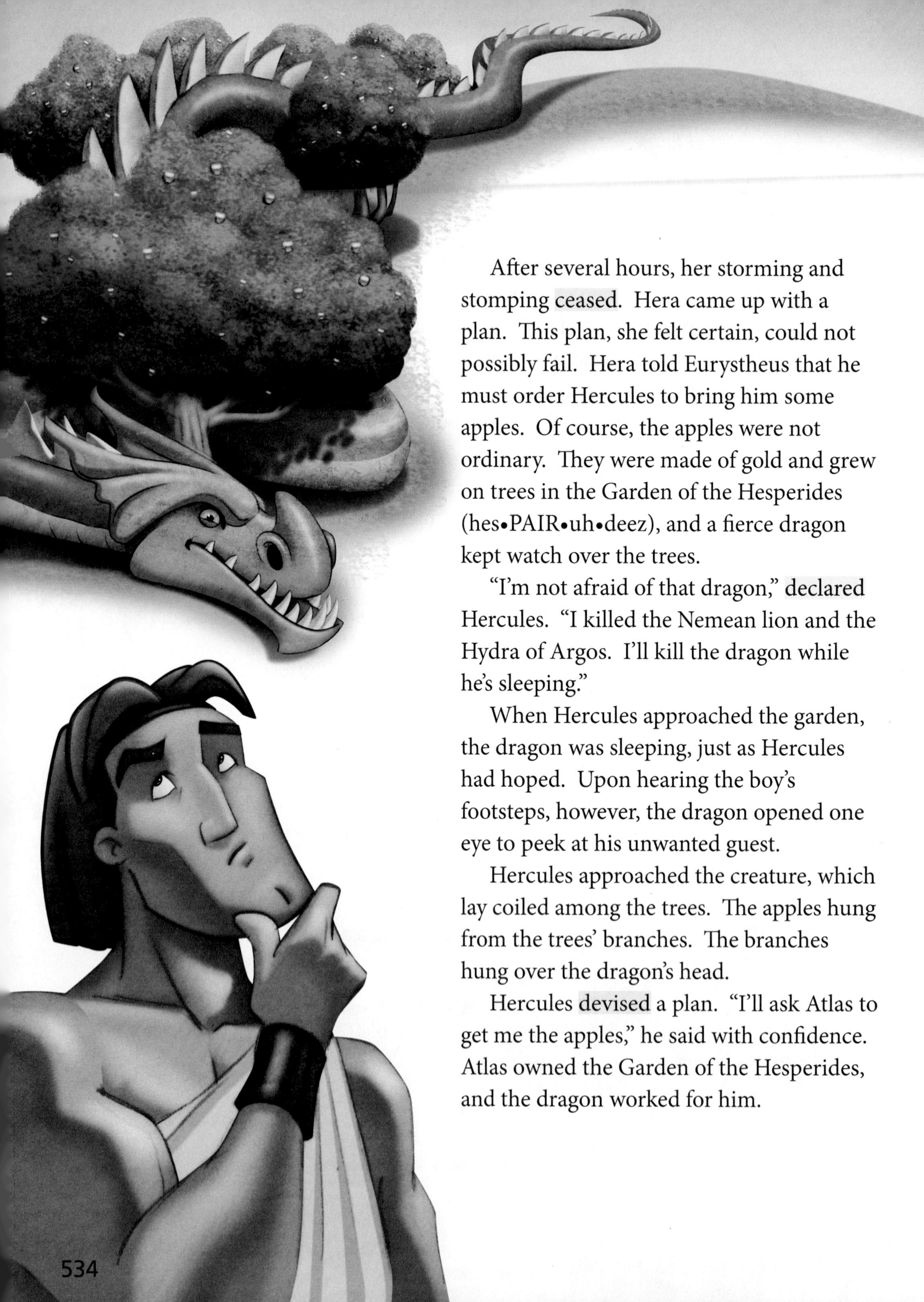

After several hours, her storming and stomping ceased. Hera came up with a plan. This plan, she felt certain, could not possibly fail. Hera told Eurystheus that he must order Hercules to bring him some apples. Of course, the apples were not ordinary. They were made of gold and grew on trees in the Garden of the Hesperides (hes•PAIR•uh•deez), and a fierce dragon kept watch over the trees.

"I'm not afraid of that dragon," declared Hercules. "I killed the Nemean lion and the Hydra of Argos. I'll kill the dragon while he's sleeping."

When Hercules approached the garden, the dragon was sleeping, just as Hercules had hoped. Upon hearing the boy's footsteps, however, the dragon opened one eye to peek at his unwanted guest.

Hercules approached the creature, which lay coiled among the trees. The apples hung from the trees' branches. The branches hung over the dragon's head.

Hercules devised a plan. "I'll ask Atlas to get me the apples," he said with confidence. Atlas owned the Garden of the Hesperides, and the dragon worked for him.

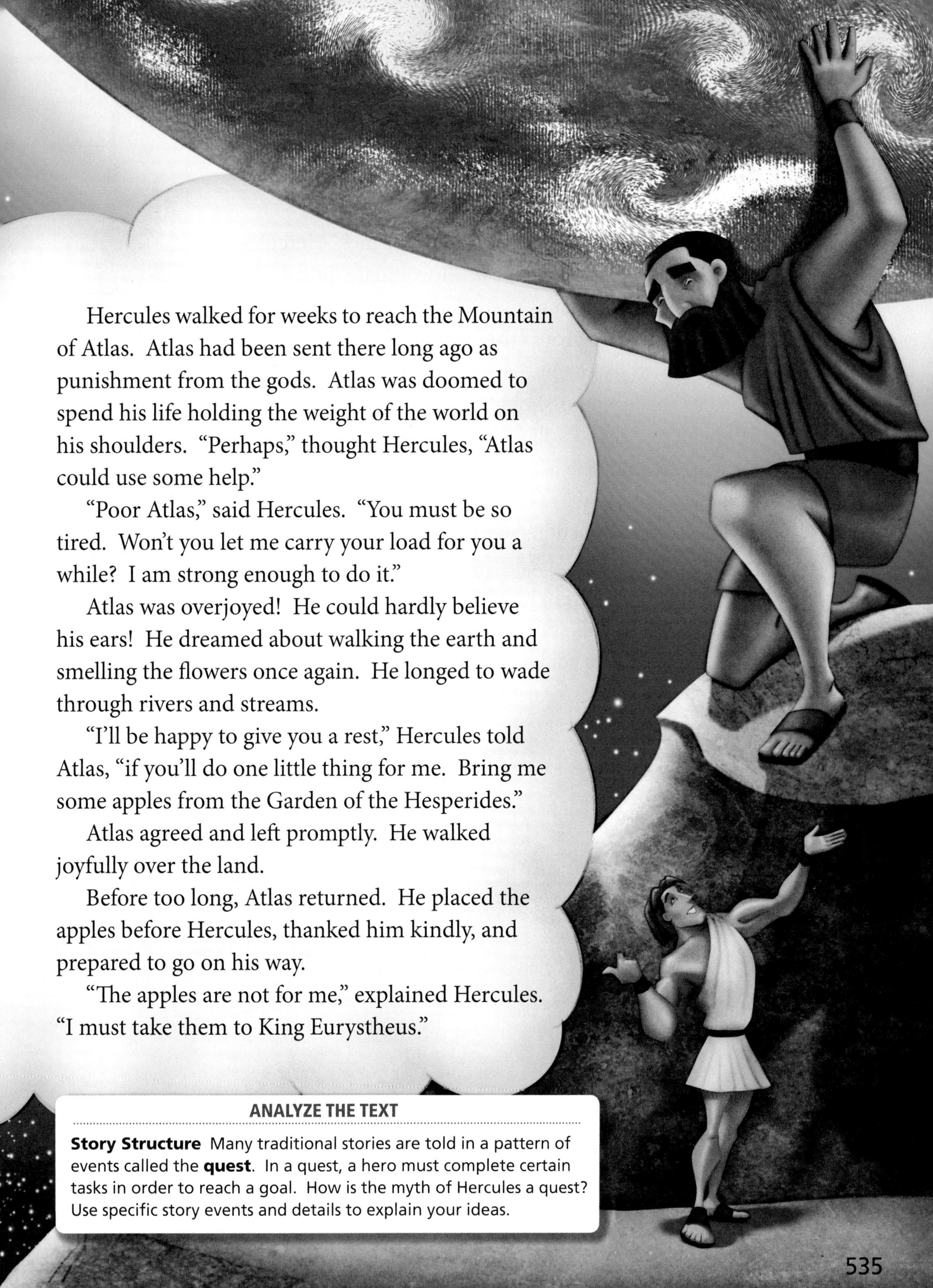

Hercules walked for weeks to reach the Mountain of Atlas. Atlas had been sent there long ago as punishment from the gods. Atlas was doomed to spend his life holding the weight of the world on his shoulders. "Perhaps," thought Hercules, "Atlas could use some help."

"Poor Atlas," said Hercules. "You must be so tired. Won't you let me carry your load for you a while? I am strong enough to do it."

Atlas was overjoyed! He could hardly believe his ears! He dreamed about walking the earth and smelling the flowers once again. He longed to wade through rivers and streams.

"I'll be happy to give you a rest," Hercules told Atlas, "if you'll do one little thing for me. Bring me some apples from the Garden of the Hesperides."

Atlas agreed and left promptly. He walked joyfully over the land.

Before too long, Atlas returned. He placed the apples before Hercules, thanked him kindly, and prepared to go on his way.

"The apples are not for me," explained Hercules. "I must take them to King Eurystheus."

ANALYZE THE TEXT

Story Structure Many traditional stories are told in a pattern of events called the **quest**. In a quest, a hero must complete certain tasks in order to reach a goal. How is the myth of Hercules a quest? Use specific story events and details to explain your ideas.

"I'll take the apples to him for you," said Atlas, who had tasted freedom and wanted more of it. Hercules was sure he would never return.

"Oh, would you please take them for me?" Hercules begged without missing a beat. "I would be forever grateful. But I am not as used to this load as you are, and my arms have grown tired and stiff. Would you relieve me for just a minute while I take a little rest?"

Atlas shrugged his shoulders. "Okay, just for a moment, and then I will personally deliver your apples for you," he said. He handed Hercules the apples and took back the weight of the world.

Hercules stretched his weary shoulders. He stretched his arms and legs. Then he bid Atlas a fond farewell and left for Eurystheus' palace.

"Well, well," said Eurystheus when Hercules gave him the golden apples. "You are not only strong, but resourceful. You've accomplished yet another impossible task."

Now, Eurystheus was a powerful king, but Zeus was a powerful god. Zeus had the power to grant the gift of strength, and he had the power to take it away. From that day on, Hercules promised to use his strength only to help others. He treated people respectfully and acted kindly at all times.

Zeus was pleased with his son Hercules and rewarded him. He brought his son to Mount Olympus to live among the gods. Hercules was now immortal and lived forever on Olympus with a duty to protect the mortals below.

ANALYZE THE TEXT

Theme What lesson do you learn from how Hercules handled each task? Use details from the myth to support your ideas.

COMPREHENSION

Dig Deeper

How to Analyze the Text

Use these pages to learn about Story Structure, Theme, and Allusion. Then read "Hercules' Quest" again to apply what you learned.

Story Structure

Myths such as "Hercules' Quest" contain characters, a setting, and a plot. **Characters** are often gods and goddesses with supernatural powers. The **setting** is the time and place in which the story occurs. In myths, the **plot**—or series of events—is typically made up of tests that the main character must pass while on a journey, or **quest**. These tests often come in a pattern of three.

Look for text evidence in the story to help you describe the characters, setting, and plot. Turn to pages 530–531. How does the author describe the setting of the story? What do these details tell you about what could happen in the myth?

Characters	Setting
• •	• •
Plot • • •	

ELACC4RL2 determine theme from details/summarize; **ELACC4RL3** describe a character, setting, or event, drawing on details; **ELACC4RL4** determine the meaning of words and phrases, including those that allude to characters in mythology; **ELACC4RL9** compare and contrast the treatment of similar themes and topics

Theme

"Hercules' Quest" is a Greek myth from long ago. Like many myths, it sends its hero on a quest. At the end of the quest, the hero learns an important lesson about life. This life lesson is the story's **theme.** Details about characters, events, and setting help you figure out the theme. For example, the detail that Hercules beamed with pride after killing the lion gives a hint about the theme.

Allusion

When an author makes a reference to a famous person, place, or event, the author is using an **allusion.** Often authors refer to characters from myths to help them describe a character's personality traits. For example, if an author writes, "Paolo had Herculean strength," the author means that Paolo is very strong, like Hercules.

When you come across an allusion to a person not in the story, ask yourself, "Who is this person and what is this person known for?"

Your Turn

RETURN TO THE ESSENTIAL QUESTION

Review the selection with a partner to prepare to discuss this question: *What makes a character memorable?* As you discuss, use text evidence to explain the key ideas. Also, make comments on your partner's ideas and opinions.

Classroom Conversation

Continue your discussion of "Hercules' Quest" by explaining your answers to these questions:

1. Do you think that Hera and Zeus make good use of their power? Why or why not?
2. Do you think Hercules should have tricked Atlas into holding up the world again? Explain.
3. What lesson did you learn from the myth?

HERCULES: THE PERFORMANCE

Make Connections Between a Performance and a Text With a small group, select a scene from the myth. Rehearse the scene and then perform it for classmates. In a discussion with classmates, compare how the actors portrayed specific details and events and how the details and events were described in the myth.

WRITE ABOUT READING

Response Imagine you are a TV interviewer. What questions would you ask Hercules? Write a list of these questions, leaving space below each to record the answers. With a partner, take turns asking and answering each other's questions. Jot down notes about each answer.

Writing Tip

Use specific nouns and precise verbs in your questions to make them clear and easy to understand. Be sure to use correct punctuation at the end of each question.

COMMON CORE **ELACC4RL2** determine theme from details/summarize; **ELACC4RL7** make connections between the text and a visual or oral presentation of it; **ELACC4W10** write routinely over extended time frames and shorter time frames; **ELACC4SL1c** pose and respond to questions and make comments that contribute to the discussion and link to others' remarks; **ELACC4SL1d** review key ideas expressed and explain own ideas and understanding; **ELACC4L3a** choose words and phrases to convey ideas precisely

Lesson 18

FOLKTALE

GENRE

A **folktale** is a story that has been handed down from one generation to the next. The characters are often animals who learn a lesson about life.

TEXT FOCUS

Adages and proverbs are short sayings that tell a basic truth. You have probably heard the saying, "The early bird catches the worm."

ELACC4RL10 read and comprehend literature; **ELACC4L5b** recognize and explain the meaning of idioms, adages, and proverbs

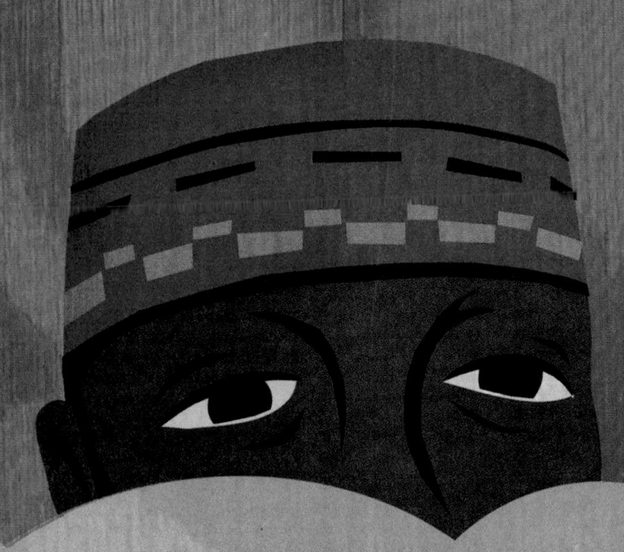

ZOMO'S FRIENDS

retold by Tamara Andrews
illustrated by Benjamin Bay

The best way to have a friend is to be one. Zomo the Rabbit didn't know that—he had to learn it for himself. Many animals lived in the jungle, and many were good friends to one another. Zomo thought he was better than all the other animals, and he certainly thought he was more clever. He was the cleverest animal in the jungle. He was the cleverest animal in the land.

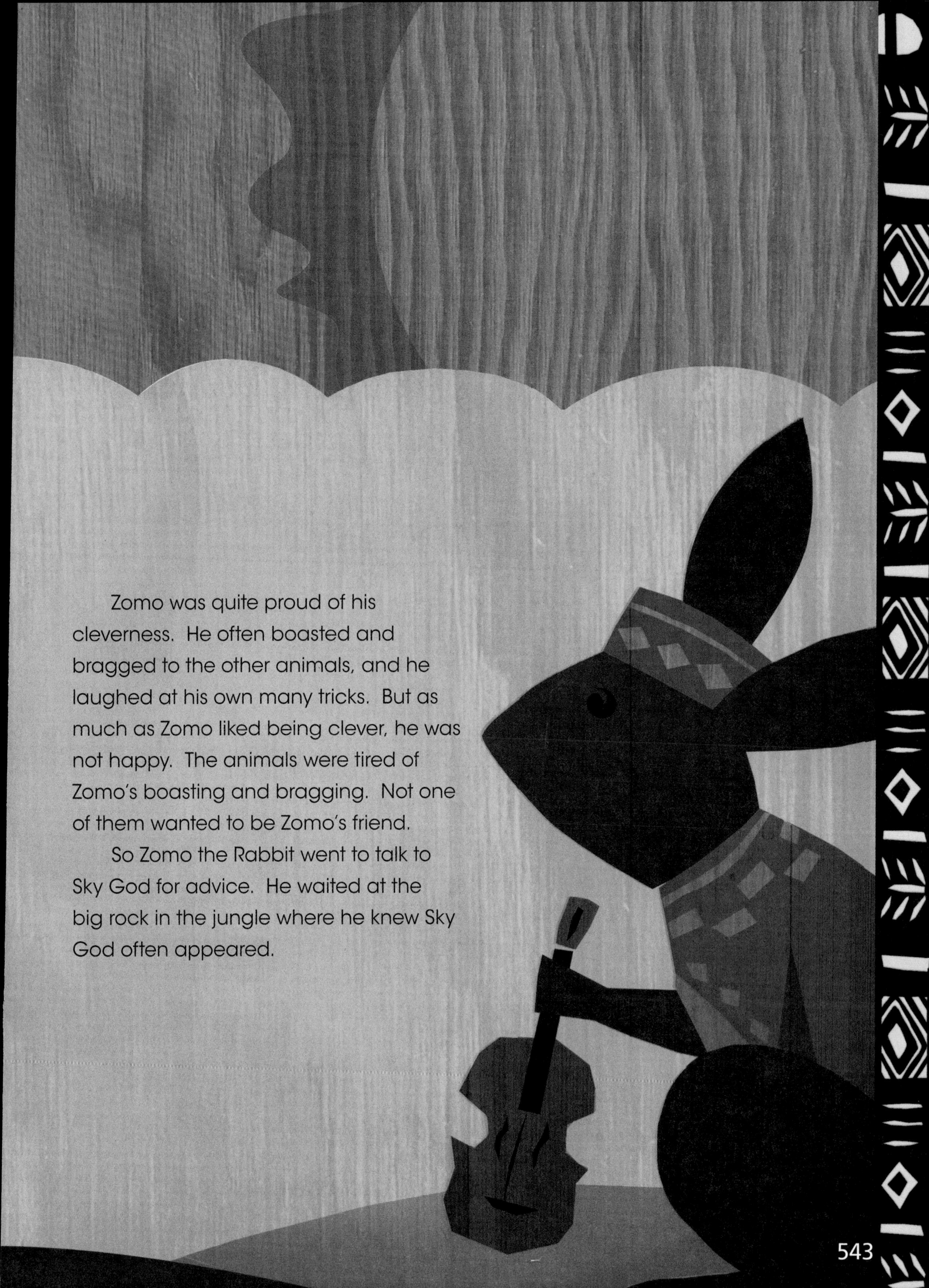

Zomo was quite proud of his cleverness. He often boasted and bragged to the other animals, and he laughed at his own many tricks. But as much as Zomo liked being clever, he was not happy. The animals were tired of Zomo's boasting and bragging. Not one of them wanted to be Zomo's friend.

So Zomo the Rabbit went to talk to Sky God for advice. He waited at the big rock in the jungle where he knew Sky God often appeared.

"The animals don't trust you," Sky God told Zomo. "They have all been victims of your tricks, and you have lost their respect. If it's friendship you seek, you must earn it. The only way to have friends is to be one yourself."

"What can I do to earn friendship?" Zomo asked Sky God. "How can I earn the animals' trust?"

"Show them you can be trusted," said Sky God. "Bring me the tail of the Zebra," ordered Sky God. Zebra lived in the grasslands far away.

"Remember," warned Sky God, "cleverness is a gift, but you must learn to use it wisely. Trickery can be used for good, but trickery can also make others angry. You must always do unto others as you would have others do unto you."

Zomo was eager to start on his journey. He barely heard Sky God's words. Zomo hopped off to find Zebra in the grasslands to the west.

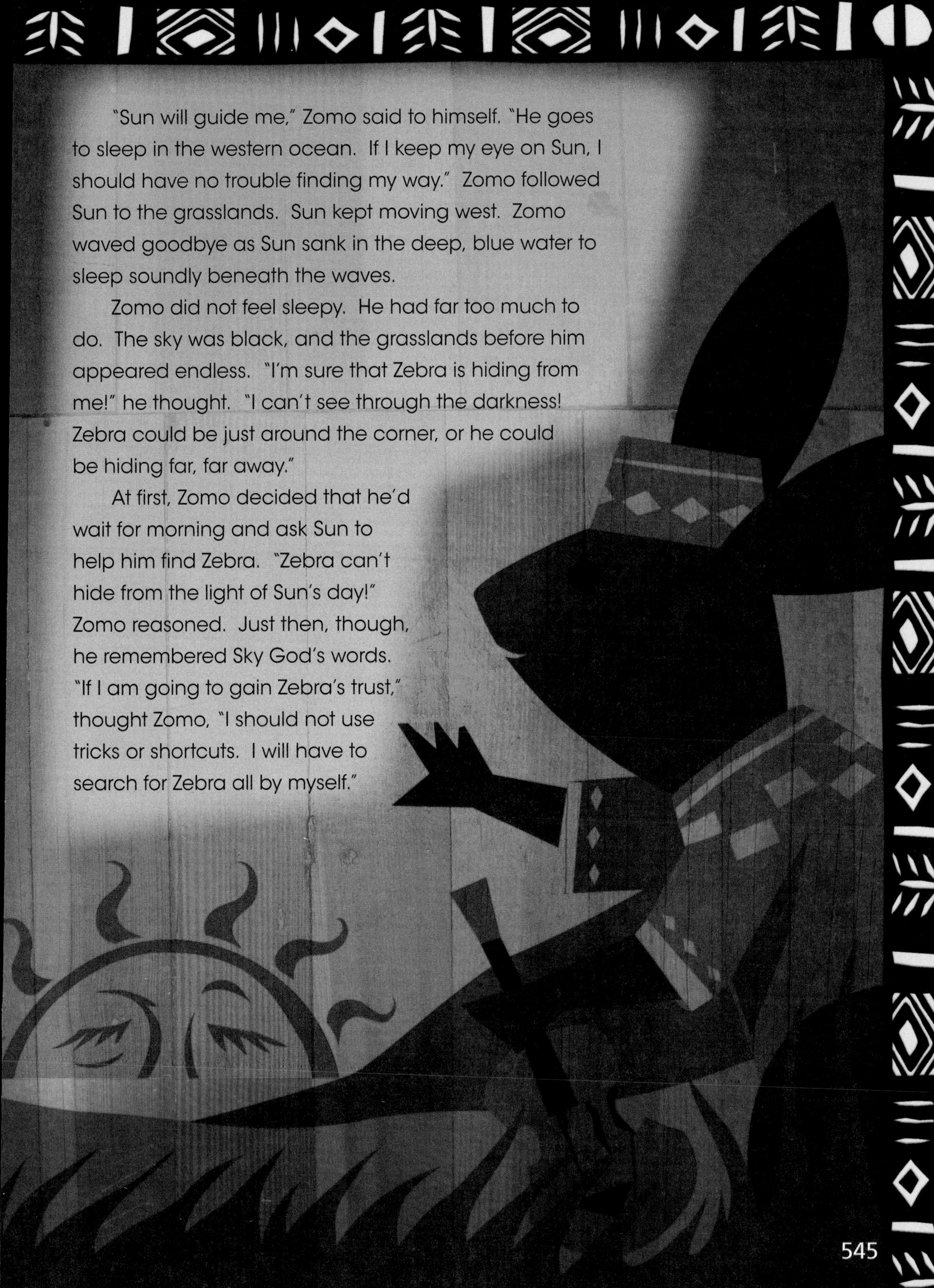

"Sun will guide me," Zomo said to himself. "He goes to sleep in the western ocean. If I keep my eye on Sun, I should have no trouble finding my way." Zomo followed Sun to the grasslands. Sun kept moving west. Zomo waved goodbye as Sun sank in the deep, blue water to sleep soundly beneath the waves.

Zomo did not feel sleepy. He had far too much to do. The sky was black, and the grasslands before him appeared endless. "I'm sure that Zebra is hiding from me!" he thought. "I can't see through the darkness! Zebra could be just around the corner, or he could be hiding far, far away."

At first, Zomo decided that he'd wait for morning and ask Sun to help him find Zebra. "Zebra can't hide from the light of Sun's day!" Zomo reasoned. Just then, though, he remembered Sky God's words. "If I am going to gain Zebra's trust," thought Zomo, "I should not use tricks or shortcuts. I will have to search for Zebra all by myself."

Zomo walked through the grasslands and began to play his violin. The music awakened Zebra, who listened and began to dance.

As he played, Zomo watched Zebra move with grace amid the tall grass. "Why Zebra!" Zomo called out. "How lovely! How did you learn to dance?"

Zebra stopped dancing. Zomo stopped playing.

"I learned to dance from my father," said Zebra. "He was the greatest dancer in the jungle and the greatest dancer in all the land. When my father danced, the rain fell softly from the sky." Zebra swayed this way and that way, gliding across the grasslands. He reached for Zomo's hand.

Together, they glided from left to right. Hand in hand, they danced until Sun appeared again. They smiled as a soft warm rain fell from the clouds and watered the land.

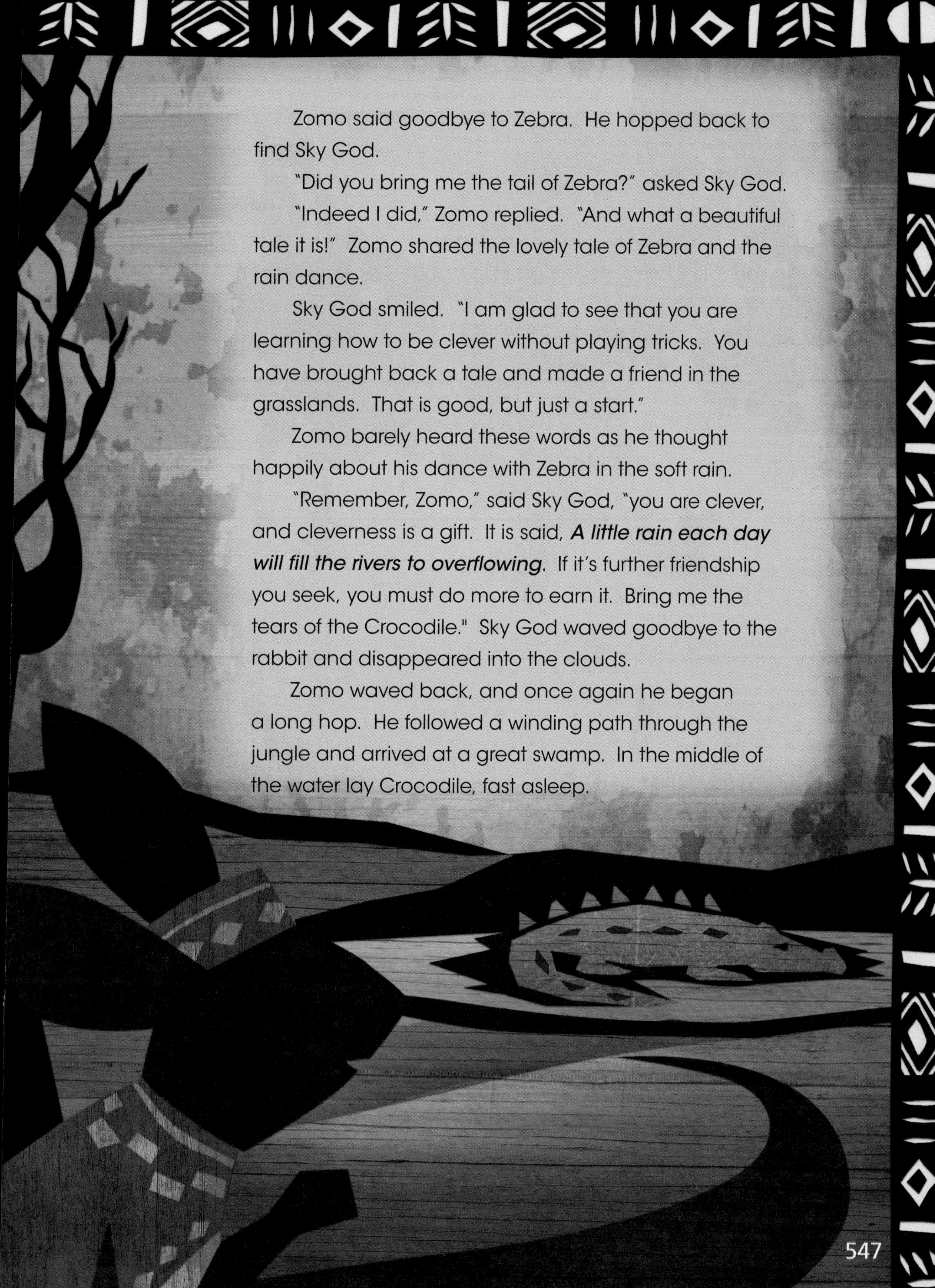

Zomo said goodbye to Zebra. He hopped back to find Sky God.

"Did you bring me the tail of Zebra?" asked Sky God.

"Indeed I did," Zomo replied. "And what a beautiful tale it is!" Zomo shared the lovely tale of Zebra and the rain dance.

Sky God smiled. "I am glad to see that you are learning how to be clever without playing tricks. You have brought back a tale and made a friend in the grasslands. That is good, but just a start."

Zomo barely heard these words as he thought happily about his dance with Zebra in the soft rain.

"Remember, Zomo," said Sky God, "you are clever, and cleverness is a gift. It is said, ***A little rain each day will fill the rivers to overflowing***. If it's further friendship you seek, you must do more to earn it. Bring me the tears of the Crocodile." Sky God waved goodbye to the rabbit and disappeared into the clouds.

Zomo waved back, and once again he began a long hop. He followed a winding path through the jungle and arrived at a great swamp. In the middle of the water lay Crocodile, fast asleep.

"Hey, Croc!" shouted Zomo. "It's morning! Don't you think it's time to wake up?" Crocodile opened his eyes angrily. The last thing he wanted to see was Zomo. He took one look and snapped his eyes shut.

"I have a story to tell you," said Zomo. "It's really a beautiful tale." He started talking, but Croc kept his eyes shut. Zomo shared the tale of Zebra and the rain dance. He told about how Zebra's dancing made the rain fall from the clouds. Finally, Croc began to listen, wide awake!

"Aha! I have your attention," said Zomo. "Now I can show you the dance." Zomo began to dance, but not like he danced with Zebra. He did not glide—he hopped. He did not sway—he fell. He fell into the water near Crocodile. His hat landed upside down.

Crocodile laughed and laughed. Zomo began laughing, too. Crocodile laughed so hard he cried big crocodile tears. The tears dripped from his eyes and fell into Zomo's hat.

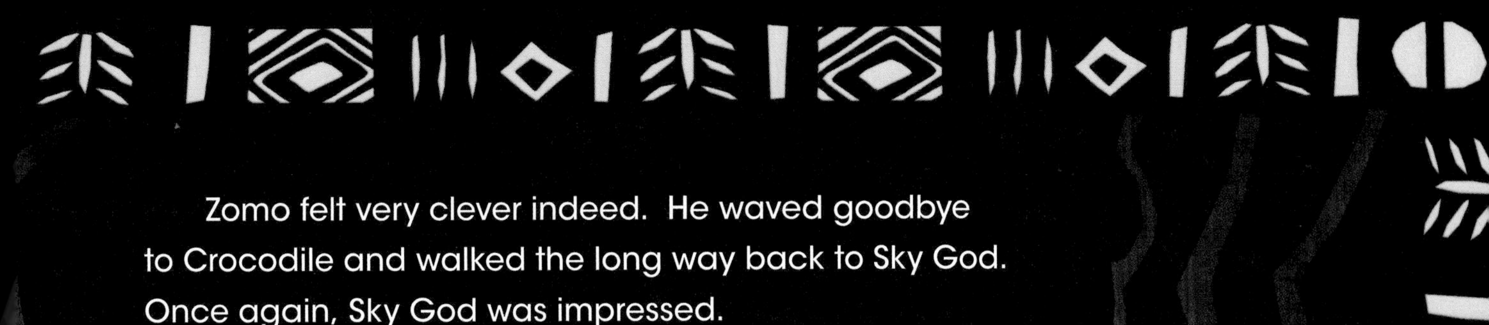

Zomo felt very clever indeed. He waved goodbye to Crocodile and walked the long way back to Sky God. Once again, Sky God was impressed.

"So now you have a friend in the grasslands," said Sky God. "You have Crocodile's friendship, too. You made them smile and laugh, but these animals are not happy. They won't be happy at all until someone brings back the Moon."

Zomo had forgotten about the Moon. The Moon had been stolen years ago, and the night sky had grown very dark. "I brought back the tale of Zebra," thought Zomo. "I brought back Crocodile's tears, too. I can bring back the Moon—I know it. I am the cleverest animal in the jungle. I am the cleverest animal in all the land."

Zomo set out once again, this time to look for the Moon. He walked deep into the jungle and searched for the deepest ditch. Before long, he found it. He peered inside, and just as he suspected, he saw a faint white ball glowing beneath the dirt.

Zomo wasted no time. He was sure he had found the Moon. He tipped over his hat, which was quite heavy with Croc's tears, and emptied it into the ditch. As the water in the ditch got higher and higher, the Moon floated to the surface. Zomo lifted it from the water and tossed it up in the sky.

The animals came out from their hidden homes in the jungle. One by one, they looked up at the sky. Suddenly, the animals began shouting! "Hooray for Zomo!" shouted Casey the Camel. "Friend to us all," said Glinda the Goat.

Zomo felt more clever than ever. He felt better than ever, too. It was great to be clever, but it was even better to have friends. It seemed all of the animals were now Zomo's friends. He remembered an old saying that was kind of clever: *You can never have enough friends.*

Compare Texts

TEXT TO TEXT

Compare Quests Complete a Venn diagram to compare and contrast the patterns of events in the myth "Hercules' Quest" and in the folktale "Zomo's Friends." In what way are Hercules' and Zomo's quests alike? How are they different? Think about the number and type of tasks each performs.

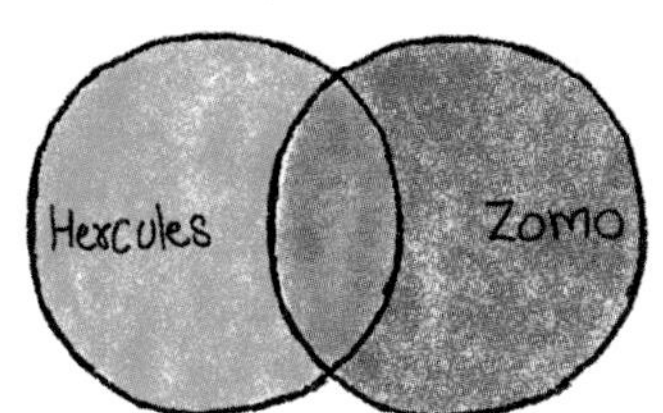

TEXT TO SELF

Write Sayings Think about the theme in "Hercules' Quest" and "Zomo's Friends." What lesson or new understanding did you learn from the myth and the folktale? Write an adage or proverb stating clearly what you learned from each story. An adage or proverb is a brief saying that teaches something in a memorable way.

TEXT TO WORLD

Compare Tales Think of other folktales you have read or heard from other cultures. Compare and contrast the pattern of events and themes of one of those tales with "Hercules' Quest" and "Zomo's Friends." With a partner, discuss the similarities and differences.

ELACC4RL2 determine theme from details/summarize; **ELACC4RL9** compare and contrast the treatment of similar themes and topics; **ELACC4L5b** recognize and explain the meaning of idioms, adages, and proverbs

Grammar

What Is a Preposition? What Is a Prepositional Phrase? A **preposition** is a word that shows a connection between other words in a sentence. A **prepositional phrase** begins with a preposition and ends with a noun or pronoun. Prepositions are used to convey location or time, or to provide other details.

Prepositions and Prepositional Phrases	
Convey location:	prepositional phrase preposition noun My hero traveled to the Lost Kingdom.
Convey time:	prepositional phrase preposition noun She stayed there for three days.
Provide details:	prepositional phrase preposition noun She learned many lessons about trust.

Try This! **Find the prepositions in the underlined prepositional phrases. Tell whether each prepositional phrase conveys location or time, or provides other details.**

1. A fierce lion lived in Nemea.
2. Hercules arrived before sundown.
3. Hercules hit the Hydra with a club.
4. The hero was tired after his adventures.

In your writing you can use prepositional phrases to add helpful and interesting information to your sentences. Adding details to your sentences helps the reader visualize what you are describing.

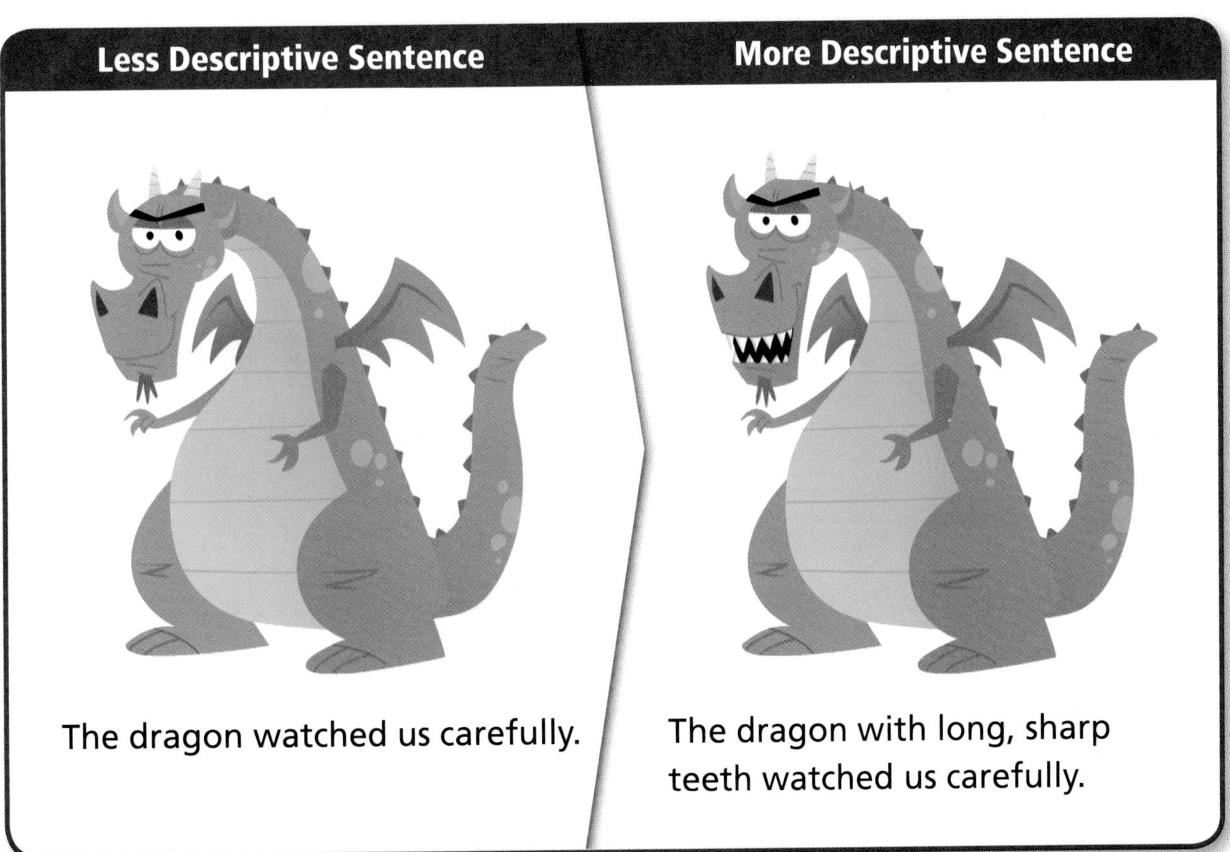

Less Descriptive Sentence	More Descriptive Sentence
The dragon watched us carefully.	The dragon with long, sharp teeth watched us carefully.

Connect Grammar to Writing

As you revise your story, look for sentences that you can make more descriptive by adding prepositional phrases.

ELACC4W3a orient the reader by establishing a situation and introducing a narrator or characters/organize an event sequence; **ELACC4W3b** use dialogue and description to develop experiences and events or show characters' responses; **ELACC4W3d** use concrete words and phrases and sensory details; **ELACC4W3e** provide a conclusion; **ELACC4L3a** choose words and phrases to convey ideas precisely

Narrative Writing

Word Choice In "Hercules' Quest," the author uses concrete words and synonyms to be specific and to avoid repeating words. For example, instead of repeating *strong,* she uses *fierce,* which makes the detail more vivid. When you revise your **story,** replace repeated words with more exact synonyms. As you revise, use the Writing Traits Checklist.

Tina drafted a story about a boy who went on a quest. Later, she replaced some words with synonyms.

Revised Draft

Balthazar was large and strong. No one had ever seen such a ~~strong~~ mighty kid. By the time he was eight, he had grown as tall as a coconut tree!

One day an ogre kidnapped the wisest woman in the village. Balthazar knew he had to rescue her. First, Balthazar encountered a giant serpent. ~~He~~ Using his brute strength, he crushed the ~~serpent~~ snake easily.

Writing Traits Checklist

- **Ideas** Did I include vivid details?
- **Organization** Did I write an interesting opening?
- **Word Choice** Did I use synonyms to avoid repeating words?
- **Voice** Did I use an appropriate tone?
- **Sentence Fluency** Did I vary the way my sentences begin?
- **Conventions** Did I use correct spelling, grammar, and mechanics?

Final Copy

Strength Plus

by Tina Herzog

Balthazar was large and strong. No one had ever seen such a mighty kid. By the time he was eight, he had grown as tall as a coconut tree!

One day an ogre kidnapped the wisest woman in the village. Balthazar knew he had to rescue her. First, Balthazar encountered a giant serpent. Using his brute strength, he crushed the snake easily. Then, he was stopped by a man leaning on a tree. He exclaimed, "I will let you pass if you solve this riddle." Balthazar worked for three days to figure out the answer, but at last, he solved the second task.

Finally, Balthazar reached the ogre's slimy swamp. His last task was to swim a mile through mud to the middle of the swamp! He found the woman in a cage made of reeds. He set her free and brought her home. The villagers burst into a song of praise when they saw Balthazar and the wise woman approaching.

Reading as a Writer

What repeated words in your story can you replace with synonyms? How can you make your conclusion stronger?

In my final story, I replaced some repeated words. I also varied the sentence types by moving a phrase to the beginning.

Lesson 19

Vocabulary in Context

☑ TARGET VOCABULARY

overcome
association
capitol
drought
dedicate
publicity
violence
conflicts
horizon
brilliant

Vocabulary Reader

Context Cards

ELACC4L6 acquire/use vocabulary, including academic and domain-specific

1 **overcome**

Cesar Chavez worked hard to overcome, or conquer, hardships.

2 **association**

These kids have formed a group, or association, that cleans up beaches.

3 **capitol**

A state capitol is a building where lawmakers can make and change laws.

4 **drought**

In the 1930s, a drought, or lack of rain, made life hard for many farmers.

- Study each Context Card.
- Use a dictionary to help you pronounce these words.

5 dedicate

Martin Luther King Jr. wanted to dedicate his life to equality. It was his life's work.

6 publicity

The media can spread publicity, or news, about events and causes.

7 violence

Many people believe change should come through peaceful ways, not violence.

8 conflicts

Most conflicts, or disagreements, can be solved by talking things over.

9 horizon

In the fields, Chavez often worked until the sun fell below the horizon.

10 brilliant

The bright, brilliant colors of the American flag symbolize freedom.

Read and Comprehend

TARGET SKILL

Conclusions and Generalizations Authors don't always state things directly. Sometimes you have to draw your own **conclusions**, or inferences. A conclusion is an understanding you come to yourself. A **generalization** is a kind of conclusion that is true about something *most* of the time, but not always. As you read "Harvesting Hope," use details and examples from the text to help you draw conclusions about Cesar Chavez and make generalizations about the challenges he faced. Record your conclusions and the text details that support them in a graphic organizer.

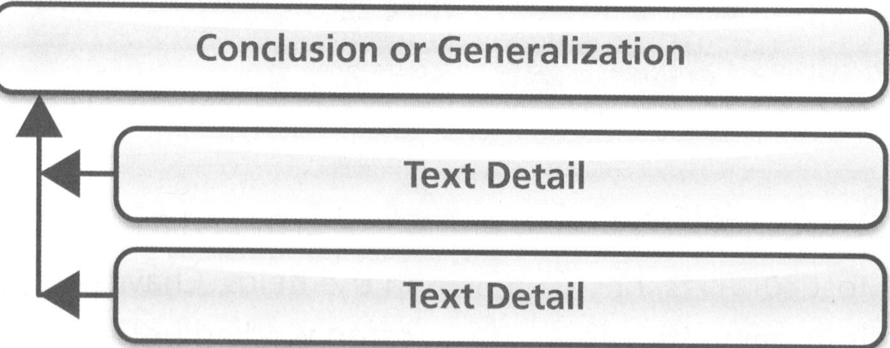

TARGET STRATEGY

Infer/Predict Sometimes an author's ideas are not stated directly in the text. As you read "Harvesting Hope," use details and evidence from the text to help you **infer** ideas that are not stated directly.

ELACC4RI1 refer to details and examples when explaining what the text says explicitly and when drawing inferences

PREVIEW THE TOPIC

Agriculture

While machines harvest some of the crops grown in the United States, much of this work is still done by human hands. Migrant farm workers travel from farm to farm, working long hours wherever their help is needed. Up until the 1960s, life was even harder for farm workers than it is today. They worked long hours for little pay. There were no laws to protect them from dangerous working conditions.

"Harvesting Hope" tells the story of Cesar Chavez, who fought for the rights of migrant farm workers in California. Because he fought for justice without using violence, many people continue to celebrate Chavez as a hero.

Lesson 19

ANCHOR TEXT

 TARGET SKILL

Conclusions and Generalizations Use text details to figure out unstated or broad ideas.

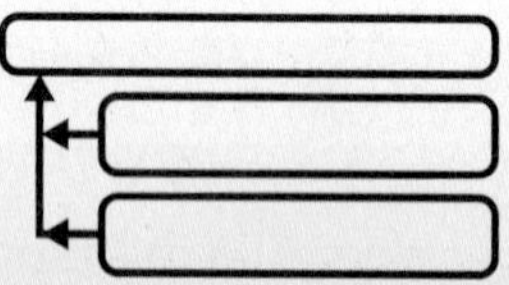

 GENRE

A **biography** tells about a person's life and is written by another person. As you read, look for:

- information about why the person is important
- opinions and personal judgments based on facts
- events in time order

ELACC4RI1 refer to details and examples when explaining what the text says explicitly and when drawing inferences; **ELACC4RI5** describe the overall structure of a text or part of a text; **ELACC4L5b** recognize and explain the meaning of idioms, adages, and proverbs

MEET THE AUTHOR

Kathleen Krull

As a teenager, Kathleen Krull was fired from her part-time job at the library for reading too much! When she went on to become an author, she found a job that would allow her to read as much as she wanted. Known for her history books and biographies, she has written about presidents, scientists, writers, musicians, and athletes.

MEET THE ILLUSTRATOR

Yuyi Morales

Yuyi Morales was born in Xalapa, Mexico. As a child she wanted to be an acrobat. Today she is a writer and an illustrator, and her books have been published in English and Spanish. Not all of her artwork is done on paper. She also makes puppets.

Harvesting Hope

The Story of Cesar Chavez

by Kathleen Krull illustrated by Yuyi Morales

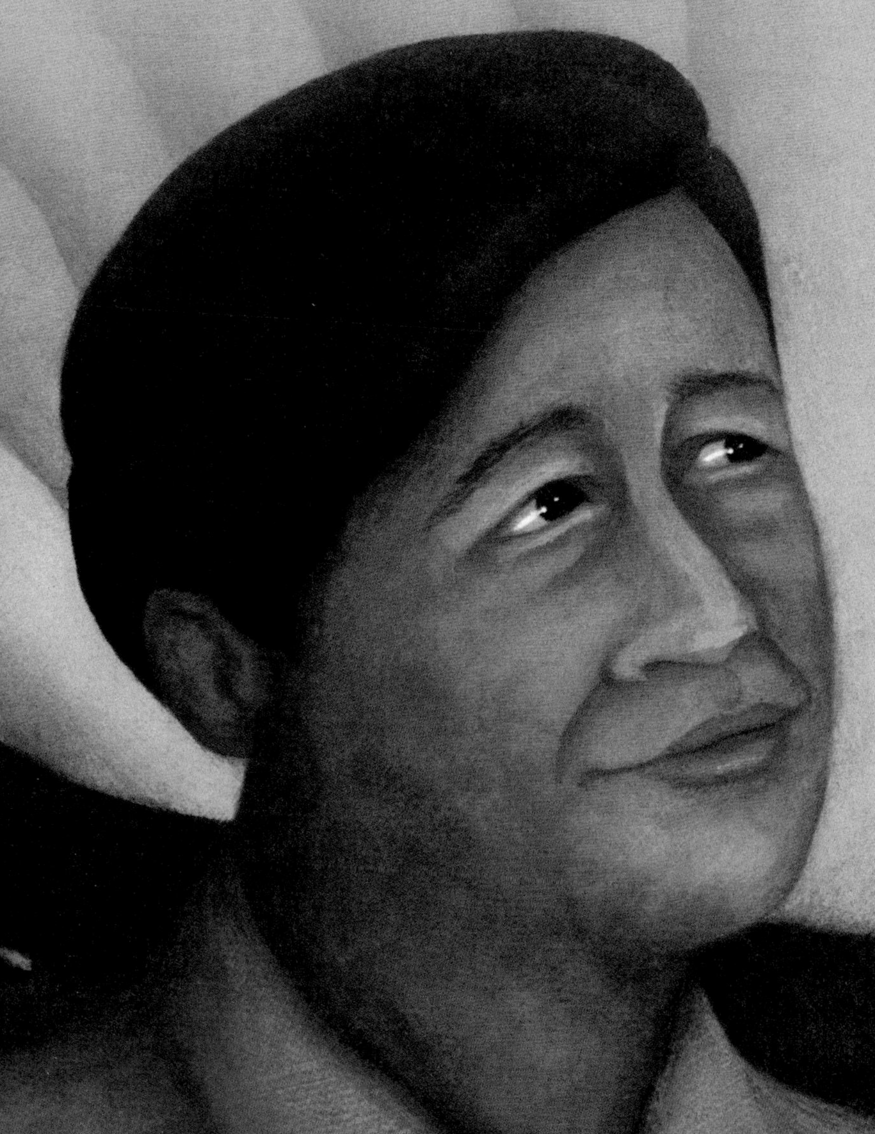

ESSENTIAL QUESTION

Why is farming important?

As a boy, Cesar Chavez (SEH sahr CHAH vehz) lived on his family's big ranch in Arizona. His family had a big house and all the food they could want. Cesar loved to play with his cousins and his brother Richard. He liked to listen to his relatives' tales of life back in Mexico.

Then, in 1937, the summer Cesar was ten, the trees around the ranch began to wilt. The sun baked the farm soil rock hard. A drought (drowt) was choking the life out of Arizona. Without water for the crops, the Chavez family couldn't make money to pay its bills.

There came a day when Cesar's mother couldn't stop crying. In a daze, Cesar watched his father strap their possessions onto the roof of their old car. After a long struggle, the family no longer owned the ranch. They had no choice but to join the hundreds of thousands of people fleeing to the green valleys of California to look for work.

Cesar's old life had vanished. Now he and his family were migrants—working on other people's farms, crisscrossing California, picking whatever fruits and vegetables were in season.

When the Chavez family arrived at the first of their new homes in California, they found a battered old shed. Its doors were missing and garbage covered the dirt floor. Cold, damp air seeped into their bedding and clothes. They shared water and outdoor toilets with a dozen other families, and overcrowding made everything filthy. The neighbors were constantly fighting, and the noise upset Cesar. He had no place to play games with Richard. Meals were sometimes made of dandelion greens gathered along the road.

Cesar swallowed his bitter homesickness and worked alongside his family. He was small and not very strong, but still a fierce worker. Nearly every crop caused torment. Yanking out beets broke the skin between his thumb and index finger. Grapevines sprayed with bug-killing chemicals made his eyes sting and his lungs wheeze. Lettuce had to be the worst. Thinning lettuce all day with a short-handled hoe would make hot spasms shoot through his back. Farm chores on someone else's farm instead of on his own felt like a form of slavery.

The Chavez family talked constantly of saving enough money to buy back their ranch. But by each sundown, the whole family had earned as little as thirty cents for the day's work. As the years blurred together, they spoke of the ranch less and less.

The towns weren't much better than the fields. WHITE TRADE ONLY signs were displayed in many stores and restaurants. None of the thirty-five schools Cesar attended over the years seemed like a safe place, either. Once, after Cesar broke the rule about speaking English at all times, a teacher hung a sign on him that read, I AM A CLOWN. I SPEAK SPANISH. He came to hate school because of the conflicts, though he liked to learn. Even he considered his eighth-grade graduation a miracle. After eighth grade he dropped out to work in the fields full-time.

His lack of schooling embarrassed Cesar for the rest of his life, but as a teenager he just wanted to put food on his family's table. As he worked, it disturbed him that landowners treated their workers more like farm tools than human beings. They provided no clean drinking water, rest periods, or access to bathrooms. Anyone who complained was fired, beaten up, or sometimes even murdered.

So, like other migrant workers, Cesar was afraid and suspicious whenever outsiders showed up to try to help. How could they know about feeling so powerless? Who could battle such odds?

Yet Cesar had never forgotten his old life in Arizona and the jolt he'd felt when it was turned upside down. Farmwork did not have to be this miserable.

Reluctantly, he started paying attention to the outsiders. He began to think that maybe there was hope. And in his early twenties, he decided to dedicate the rest of his life to fighting for change.

Again he crisscrossed California, this time to talk people into joining his fight. At first, out of every hundred workers he talked to, perhaps one would agree with him. One by one—this was how he started.

At the first meeting Cesar organized, a dozen women gathered. He sat quietly in a corner. After twenty minutes, everyone started wondering when the organizer would show up. Cesar thought he might die of embarrassment.

"Well, I'm the organizer," he said—and forced himself to keep talking, hoping to inspire respect with his new suit and the mustache he was trying to grow. The women listened politely, and he was sure they did so out of pity.

But despite his shyness, Cesar showed a knack for solving problems. People trusted him. With workers he was endlessly patient and compassionate. With landowners he was stubborn, demanding, and single-minded. He was learning to be a fighter.

In a fight for justice, he told everyone, truth was a better weapon than violence. "Nonviolence," he said, "takes more guts." It meant using imagination to find ways to overcome powerlessness.

More and more people listened.

One night, 150 people poured into an old abandoned theater in Fresno. At this first meeting of the National Farm Workers Association, Cesar unveiled its flag—a bold black eagle, the sacred bird of the Aztec Indians.

La Causa (lah KOW sah)—The Cause—was born.

It was time to rebel, and the place was Delano. Here, in the heart of the lush San Joaquin (hwah KEEN) Valley, brilliant green vineyards reached toward every horizon. Poorly paid workers hunched over grapevines for most of each year. Then, in 1965, the vineyard owners cut their pay even further.

Cesar chose to fight just one of the forty landowners, hopeful that others would get the message. As plump grapes drooped, thousands of workers walked off that company's fields in a strike, or *huelga* (WEHL gah).

Grapes, when ripe, do not last long.

ANALYZE THE TEXT

Idioms What does the idiom in the sentence "Nonviolence takes more guts" mean? How does this connect to what Cesar Chavez is trying to convince the others to do?

The company fought back with everything from punches to bullets. Cesar refused to respond with violence. Violence would only hurt *La Causa*.

Instead, he organized a march—a march of more than three hundred miles. He and his supporters would walk from Delano to the state capitol in Sacramento to ask for the government's help.

Cesar and sixty-seven others started out one morning. Their first obstacle was the Delano police force, thirty of whose members locked arms to prevent the group from crossing the street. After three hours of arguing—in public—the chief of police backed down. Joyous marchers headed north under the sizzling sun. Their rallying cry was *Sí Se Puede* (see seh PWEH deh), or "Yes, It Can Be Done."

The first night, they reached Ducor. The marchers slept outside the tiny cabin of the only person who would welcome them.

Single file they continued, covering an average of fifteen miles a day. They inched their way through the San Joaquin Valley, while the unharvested grapes in Delano turned white with mold. Cesar developed painful blisters right away. He and many others had blood seeping out of their shoes.

The word spread. Along the way, farmworkers offered food and drink as the marchers passed by. When the sun set, marchers lit candles and kept going.

Shelter was no longer a problem. Supporters began welcoming them each night with feasts. Every night was a rally. "Our pilgrimage is the match," one speaker shouted, "that will light our cause for all farmworkers to see what is happening here."

Eager supporters would keep the marchers up half the night talking about change. Every morning, the line of marchers swelled, Cesar always in the lead.

On the ninth day, hundreds marched through Fresno.

The long, peaceful march was a shock to people unaware of how California farmworkers had to live. Now students, public officials, religious leaders, and citizens from everywhere offered help. For the grape company, the publicity was becoming unbearable.

And on the vines, the grapes continued to rot.

In Modesto, on the fifteenth day, an exhilarated (ihg ZIHL uh ray tehd) crowd celebrated Cesar's thirty-eighth birthday. Two days later, five thousand people met the marchers in Stockton with flowers, guitars, and accordions.

ANALYZE THE TEXT

Conclusions and Generalizations By the end of the march, hundreds of people had joined. Why might these people have joined the march? From where might they have come?

That evening, Cesar received a message that he was sure was a prank. But in case it was true, he left the march and had someone drive him all through the night to a mansion in wealthy Beverly Hills. Officials from the grape company were waiting for him. They were ready to recognize the authority of the National Farm Workers Association, promising a contract with a pay raise and better conditions.

Cesar rushed back to join the march.

On Easter Sunday, when the marchers arrived in Sacramento, the parade was ten-thousand-people strong.

From the steps of the state capitol building, the joyous announcement was made to the public: Cesar Chavez had just signed the first contract for farmworkers in American history.

ANALYZE THE TEXT

Problem and Solution What did Cesar Chavez do when he encountered a problem? How did he solve the major problem of worker's rights?

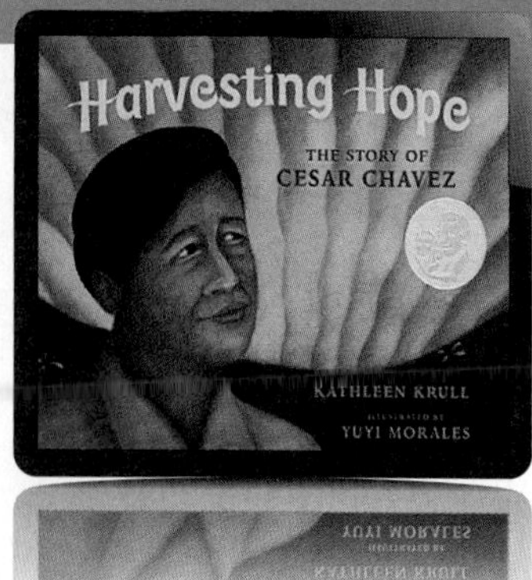

Dig Deeper

How to Analyze the Text

Use these pages to learn about Conclusions and Generalizations, Problem and Solution, and Idioms. Then read "Harvesting Hope" again to apply what you learned.

Conclusions and Generalizations

"Harvesting Hope" is a biography about the life of Cesar Chavez. The author gives many facts about Cesar, but she doesn't explain everything. She expects readers to figure some things out on their own. When readers do this, it is called drawing a **conclusion,** or inference. A **generalization** is a kind of conclusion that is true about something *most* of the time, but not always. You can use details and examples from "Harvesting Hope" to help you draw a conclusion about Cesar Chavez.

In "Harvesting Hope," we learn that Cesar Chavez was very good at organizing others. What details and text evidence help readers draw this conclusion?

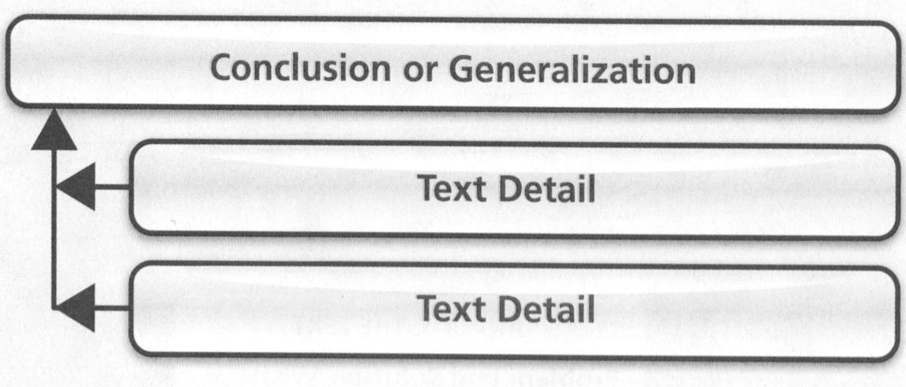

ELACC4RI1 refer to details and examples when explaining what the text says explicitly and when drawing inferences; **ELACC4RI5** describe the overall structure of a text or part of a text; **ELACC4L5b** recognize and explain the meaning of idioms, adages, and proverbs

Problem and Solution

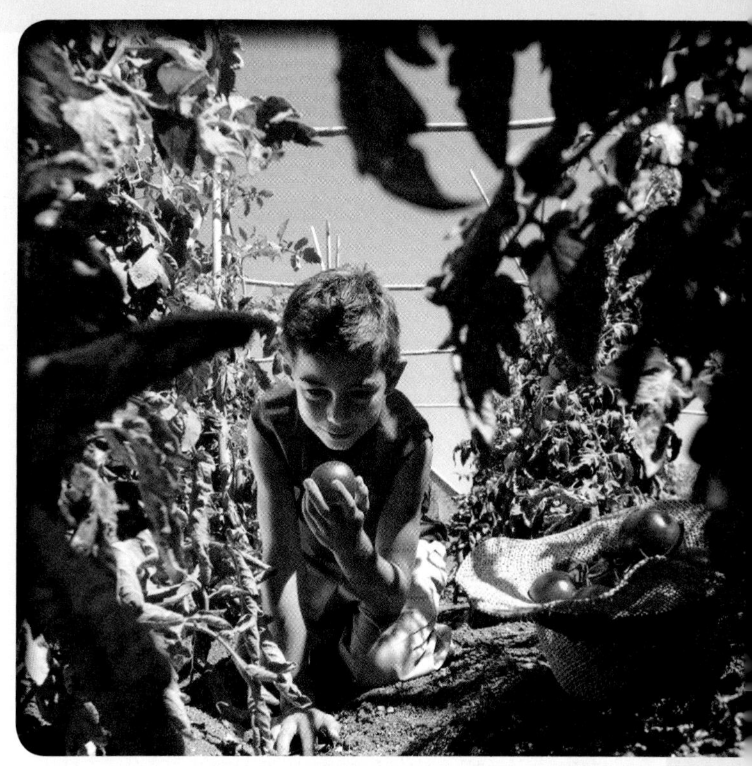

Problem and solution is a type of **text structure.** In "Harvesting Hope," the author organizes information about Cesar Chavez's life by first describing problems he had to face. Then the author explains Cesar's solutions to those problems. For example, when Cesar felt homesick after his family lost their land, he decided to try to forget his sadness and work hard alongside his family.

Idioms

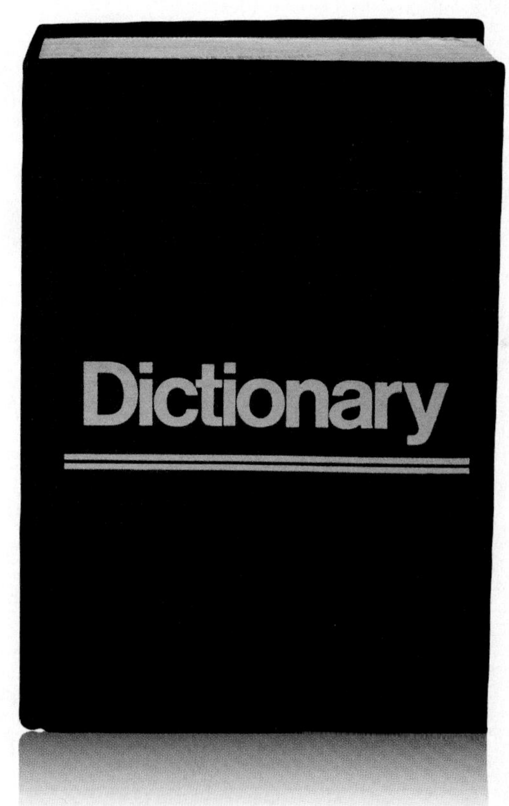

Authors sometimes use **idioms,** or phrases that mean something different than the meaning of the individual words. Authors use idioms to describe things in interesting ways. For example, the author writes that Cesar Chavez's life "was turned upside down" when describing Cesar's loss of his home in Arizona. The idiom *turned upside down* means that something changed completely in a confusing or upsetting way. You can often use a dictionary to check the meaning of an idiom.

Your Turn

RETURN TO THE ESSENTIAL QUESTION

Review the selection with a partner to prepare to discuss this question: *Why is farming important?* Include text evidence from the selection to support your inferences. As you discuss, take turns reviewing and explaining the key ideas in your discussion.

Classroom Conversation

Continue your discussion of "Harvesting Hope" by explaining your answers to these questions:

1. Why do you think Cesar Chavez was embarrassed about not having more of an education?
2. What did Cesar mean when he said that truth is a better weapon than violence?
3. What lessons can you learn from Cesar Chavez?

DON'T FIGHT—MARCH!

Discuss the Protest With a partner, discuss why you think Cesar Chavez used peaceful demonstrations instead of violence to get what the farmworkers wanted. What persuaded the grape growers to give in to his demands? Use details and text evidence from the selection to explain your ideas.

WRITE ABOUT READING

Response By the time he was in the eighth grade, Cesar Chavez had worked on his family's own ranch as well as on land owned by others. Write a paragraph explaining how these experiences prepared him to fight for farmworkers' rights. Include text evidence from the selection that helps to explain the effect his childhood experiences had on him.

Writing Tip

As you write your response, stay focused on the topic. Prepare to write by identifying relevant experiences from Cesar's childhood. Use prepositional phrases to add interesting informatio to your response.

COMMON CORE **ELACC4RI1** refer to details and examples when explaining what the text says explicitly and when drawing inferences; ...nd ...e topic; **ELACC4W9b** apply grade 4 Reading standards to informational texts; **ELACC4W10** write routinely over extended t... shorter time frames; **ELACC4SL1a** come to discussions prepared/explicitly draw on preparation and other informat... **ELACC4SL1d** review key ideas expressed and explain own ideas and understanding; **ELACC4L1e** form and use prepositional ph...

Lesson 19

INFORMATIONAL TEXT

GENRE

Informational text, such as this magazine article, gives facts and examples about a topic.

TEXT FOCUS

Pie Chart Informational text may include a pie chart, a type of chart that uses portions of a circle to show how amounts of something relate to one another. What does the pie chart on page 578 tell you about nutrition?

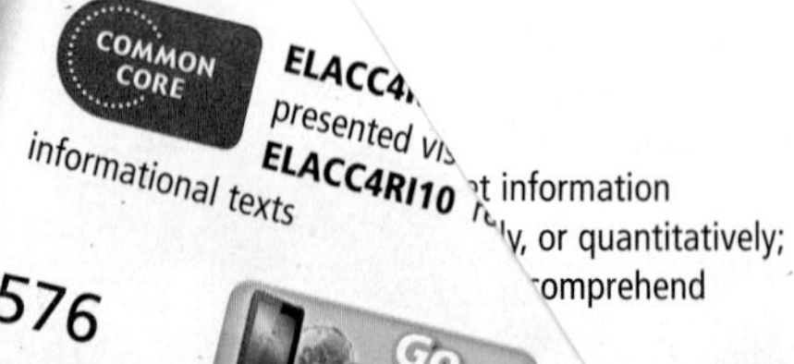

ELACC4R... presented vis... ...t information ...ly, or quantitatively; ELACC4RI10 ...comprehend informational texts

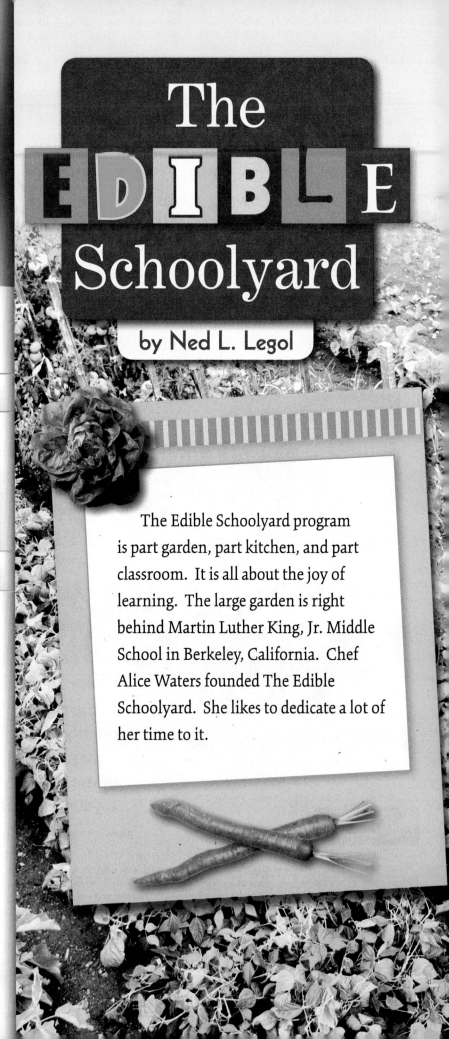

The EDIBLE Schoolyard

by Ned L. Legol

The Edible Schoolyard program is part garden, part kitchen, and part classroom. It is all about the joy of learning. The large garden is right behind Martin Luther King, Jr. Middle School in Berkeley, California. Chef Alice Waters founded The Edible Schoolyard. She likes to dedicate a lot of her time to it.

Inside the Edible Schoolyard

Every year, the school's sixth-grade students plant, tend, and harvest the crops from the garden. They learn about the effects that changing climate and weather have on the plants. During a drought, for example, they must water the garden more often. This keeps everything alive and healthy.

The students grow many types of fruits, vegetables, and herbs. Brilliant colors surround the kids as they work in the garden that stretches toward the horizon.

Time to Get Cooking

The students also learn how to cook healthy meals with the food they grow. The school houses many different students and cultures. So, the meals vary from Indian curries to Mediterranean grape leaves. Some of the kids learn to overcome their fear of unknown foods.

If there are conflicts in the kitchen or the garden, students must work to solve them. The program fits with Martin Luther King, Jr.'s vision of inclusion, equality, and peaceful growth without violence.

The Edible Schoolyard has inspired similar programs around the country. This Florida student is part of the Plant a Thousand Gardens program.

Tastes Great and Is Healthy Too

The Edible Schoolyard program has received good publicity for teaching students about healthy food. Everything grown in the garden is organic. All meals the kids prepare are good for them.

Many other groups, such as The American Dietetic Association, also teach kids and adults about eating healthy. Because it is so important, a healthy school lunch is something that is often talked about in every state capitol.

Healthy Eating

According to the U.S. government, people should eat the following kinds and amounts of food each day.

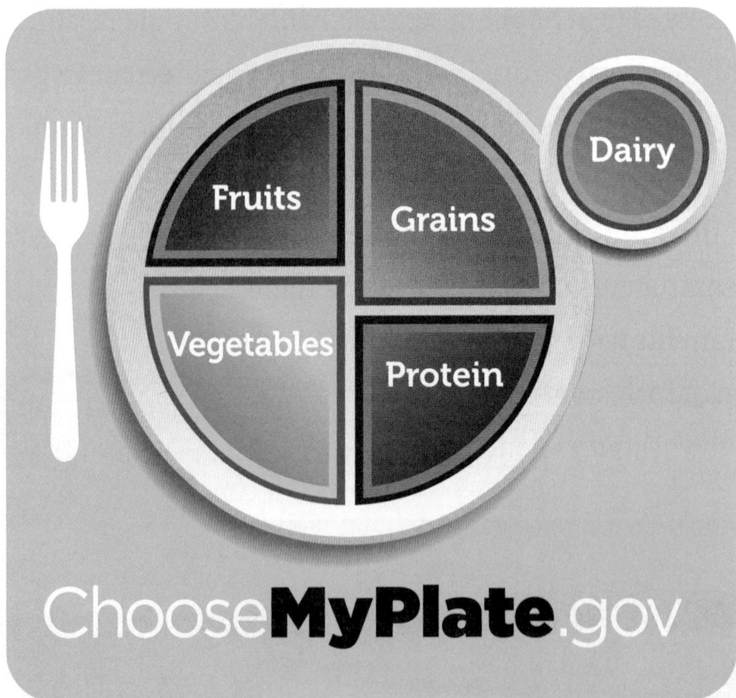

Grains	Vegetables	Fruits	Dairy	Protein
6 oz	2.5 cups	2 cups	3 cups	5.5 oz

Measurement: oz = ounces

Source: United States Department of Agriculture

Compare Texts

TEXT TO TEXT

What Would Cesar Think? Imagine that Cesar Chavez toured an edible garden run by an elementary school. What do you think he would say about the work being done there? Do you think he would approve? Explain your thoughts in a paragraph using text evidence.

TEXT TO SELF

Write a Narrative Think of a time when you had to be persistent to solve a problem. Describe that occasion. Explain the problem that you had to solve and how being persistent helped you solve it.

TEXT TO WORLD

Connect to Social Studies Farming is an important industry in many communities. Work with a partner to list the different agricultural products that are grown in or near your community. Discuss how the farming of these products affects your community. Share your findings with the class.

ELACC4RI1 refer to details and examples when explaining what the text says explicitly and when drawing inferences; **ELACC4RI9** integrate information from two texts on the same topic; **ELACC4W3a** orient the reader by establishing a situation and introducing a narrator or characters/organize an event sequence; **ELACC4W7** conduct short research projects that build knowledge through investigation

COMMON CORE **ELACC4L1a** use relative pronouns and relative adverbs

Grammar

What Are Relative Pronouns and Adverbs? A **clause** is a group of words that has a subject and a predicate but may or may not be a complete sentence. A **dependent clause** is a type of clause that cannot stand alone. An **independent clause** can stand alone because it is a complete sentence.

independent clause — dependent clause

My uncle cooks stew when the weather turns cold.

A dependent clause can be introduced by a **relative pronoun** such as *who*, *whom*, *which*, or *that*, or by a **relative aderb,** such as *where*, *when*, or *why*.

relative pronoun — dependent clause

My uncle, who is a chef, cooks stew.

relative adverb — dependent clause

My uncle cooks stew when the weather turns cold.

Try This! **With a partner, identify the dependent clauses in the sentences below. Note whether the sentence has a relative pronoun or relative adverb.**

1. The workers met when they were fed up with their working conditions.
2. Cesar, who organized the meeting, began the discussion.
3. The farmers, whose fields were not being picked, became frustrated.
4. When the growers gave up, they met with the workers.
5. Why do you think the union members were successful?

When you write, combine sentences using clauses to help clearly show how related ideas are connected. Use relative adverbs or pronouns, as appropriate.

Separate	Combined
 I began eating the sandwich. I took it out of the bag.	 I began eating the sandwich when I took it out of the bag.
My mom makes the best sandwiches. She is a chef.	My mom, who is a chef, makes the best sandwiches.

 Connect Grammar to Writing

As you revise your personal narrative next week, check to see that you have used relative pronouns and adverbs correctly. Also use clauses to combine sentences to make your writing less choppy.

ELACC4W3a orient the reader by establishing a situation and introducing a narrator or characters/organize an event sequence; **ELACC4W3b** use dialogue and description to develop experiences and events or show characters' responses; **ELACC4W4** produce writing in which development and organization are appropriate to task, purpose, and audience; **ELACC4W5** develop and strengthen writing by planning, revising, and editing

Narrative Writing

Reading-Writing Workshop: Prewrite

Organization Good writers organize their ideas before they draft. You can organize ideas for a **personal narrative** by using an events chart. In your chart, write the main events in order. Below each main event, write important or interesting details about it. Use the Writing Process Checklist below as you prewrite.

Steve decided to write about a class adventure. First he jotted down some notes. Then he organized them in a chart.

Writing Process Checklist

▶ Prewrite

- ✔ Did I think about my purpose for writing?
- ✔ Did I choose a topic that I will enjoy writing about?
- ✔ Did I explore my topic to remember the events and details?
- ✔ Did I organize the events in the order in which they happened?

Draft

Revise

Edit

Publish and Share

Exploring a Topic

Topic: my class went on the Walk to End Hunger

discuss project with class
- my idea—Walk to End Hunger
- help people
- 5-mile walk
- vote—my idea won!!!

collect pledges
- got people to donate money
- total—$425

day of Walk
- bus ride
- big crowd
- balloons, food
- walked 2 hours
- TIRED!
- band
- felt really proud

Events Chart

Event: My class discussed ideas for a community project.

Details: Some kids gave ideas. Mine was to go on the Walk to End Hunger to help people, walk 5 miles, and get free snacks. We voted and my idea won.

Event: We collected pledges from people.

Details: Friends and relatives pledged to donate money. We raised $425.

Event: Class rode bus to the Walk on May 6.

Details: At the starting place was a big crowd, balloons, free water, granola bars, caps.

Event: We walked for 2 hours.

Details: It was easy at first, but hard later—we were tired and had sore feet.

Event: We finished the Walk.

Details: A band was playing. I just wanted to go home. The next day I felt really proud.

Reading as a Writer

What kind of order did Steve use to arrange his events? Which parts of your events chart can you organize more clearly?

In my chart, I put the events and details in an order that makes sense. I added some descriptive details.

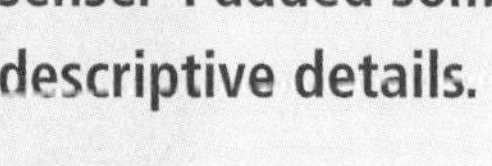

Lesson 20

Vocabulary in Context

☑ **TARGET VOCABULARY**

territory
accompany
proposed
interpreter
duty
supplies
route
corps
clumsy
landmark

Vocabulary Reader

Context Cards

ELACC4L6 acquire/use vocabulary, including academic and domain-specific

1 territory

To many people, polar lands are unfamiliar territory.

2 accompany

Explorers going into a cave should find others to accompany them.

3 proposed

Some scientists have proposed, or suggested, further exploration of Mars.

4 interpreter

An interpreter, or translator, is helpful when people use different languages.

- Study each Context Card.
- Use context clues to determine the meanings of these words.

5 duty

Divers have a duty. They are required not to harm a marine area or its creatures.

6 supplies

Hikers need to carry supplies, such as food and water.

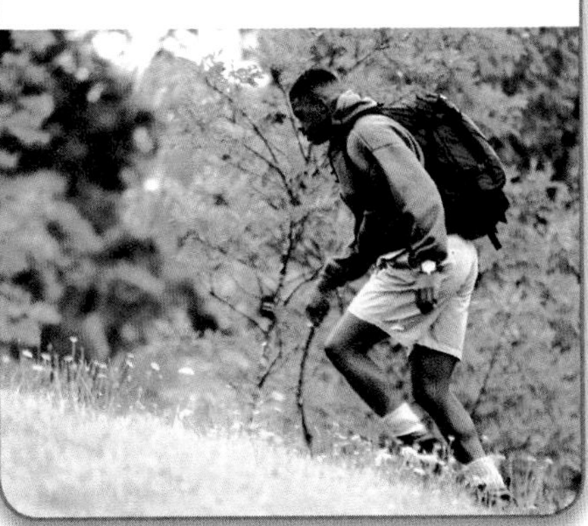

7 route

Backpackers should choose a safe route and stick to that path.

8 corps

On a research trip, every member of the corps, or team, must have valuable skills.

9 clumsy

A clumsy, or awkward, mistake can mean the loss of months of research.

10 landmark

Noting a landmark or other recognizable object makes the return trip easier.

Read and Comprehend

TARGET SKILL

Main Ideas and Details As you read "Sacagawea," look for the most important ideas the author presents. The most important ideas are called the **main ideas**. Also look for **supporting details** that tell more about the main ideas. Use a graphic organizer like the one below to help you see the relationship between main ideas and the details that support them. Then summarize the most important ideas.

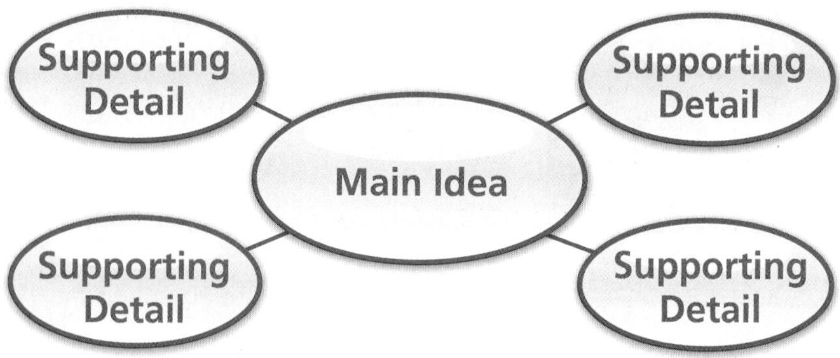

TARGET STRATEGY

Visualize You can **visualize** various stages of Sacagawea's journey to help you identify the main ideas and supporting details at each part of their journey. Descriptive details in the text will help you form clear mental pictures of the people and places Sacagawea and her companions visited.

ELACC4RI2 determine the main idea and explain how it is supported by details/summarize

PREVIEW THE TOPIC

Native American History

In the early 1800s, most of the American West was inhabited only by Native Americans. The Native Americans had deep knowledge of the lands where they lived. They were experts at locating food, making shelters, and finding their way in the wilderness.

In 1804, Captains Meriwether Lewis and William Clark led an expedition to explore the western half of North America. Along the way, a young Shoshone woman named Sacagawea joined the expedition as a guide and translator. As you read "Sacagawea," you'll learn about the many contributions she made to the expedition.

Lesson 20

ANCHOR TEXT

 TARGET SKILL

Main Ideas and Details
Summarize a topic's main ideas and supporting details.

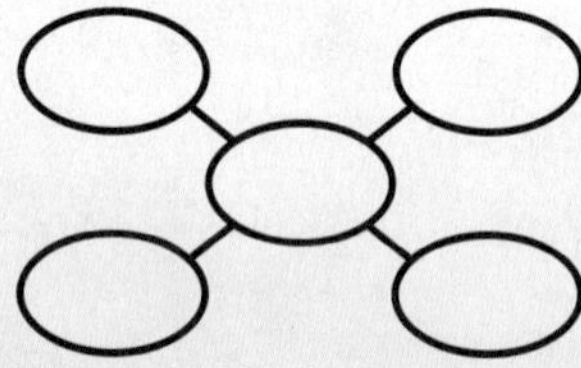

 GENRE

A **biography** tells about a person's life and is written by another person. As you read, look for:

- information about why the person is important
- opinions and personal judgments based on facts
- events in sequence

ELACC4RI2 determine the main idea and explain how it is supported by details/summarize; **ELACC4RI3** explain events/procedures/ideas/concepts in a text; **ELACC4RI5** describe the overall structure of a text or part of a text

MEET THE AUTHOR

Lise Erdrich

Lise Erdrich is part Native American and a member of the Turtle Mountain band of Plains-Ojibway. She was inspired to become a writer by her grandfather, who was always writing or telling stories. Her sister Louise is also a writer of books for children and adults.

MEET THE ILLUSTRATOR

Julie Buffalohead

Part Ponca Indian, Julie Buffalohead researched traditional Native American art while in college. She often depicts Native American legends and traditions in her painting. She sometimes uses her painting as a way to explore important topics, such as prejudices some people may have about Native Americans.

SACAGAWEA

by Lise Erdrich illustrated by Julie Buffalohead

ESSENTIAL QUESTION

How do people from different cultures contribute to American history?

It is the early 1800s. Teenaged Sacagawea (sak uh juh WEE uh) is a Shoshone (shoh SHOH nee) Indian living in the Knife River villages, in what is now North Dakota. When she was a child, Hidatsa (hee DAHT sah) Indians kidnapped her from her home in the Rocky Mountains. Since then, she has lived with them on the Great Plains, far from her family. Sacagawea has learned many things from the Hidatsa, including how to grow food. She is now married to a French Canadian fur trapper named Toussaint Charbonneau (too SAN shahr bohn OH).

Meanwhile, Captains Meriwether Lewis and William Clark have been preparing for the Corps (kohr) of Discovery. They and their team, which includes a large, black Newfoundland dog, are about to start a long journey of exploration, all the way to the Pacific Ocean.

On May 14, 1804, a crew of more than forty men set off against the Missouri River current in a keelboat and two large canoes called pirogues (pih ROHGZ). The Corps of Discovery was under way.

The expedition arrived at the Knife River villages at the end of October. They were greeted with great excitement. Sacagawea heard tales of a gigantic black dog that traveled with the explorers. She heard that a fierce and awesome "white man" with black skin was among the crew. This was York, the slave of Captain Clark.

The explorers built a fort and called it Fort Mandan. Then they settled in to spend the winter at the Knife River villages. Lewis and Clark soon learned they would need horses to cross the Rocky Mountains. The people of the villages told them they could get the horses from the Shoshone when the expedition reached the mountain passes.

The wily Charbonneau proposed that they hire him as a guide and interpreter. He did not speak Shoshone, but Sacagawea did. He told her they would be joining the Corps of Discovery in the spring. This was exciting news, but Sacagawea's mind was on other matters. She was soon to become a mother.

In February, the time came for Sacagawea to have her baby. It was a long, difficult birth. Captain Lewis wanted to help her. He gave a crew member two rattlesnake rattles to crush and mix with water. Just a few minutes after drinking the mixture, Sacagawea gave birth to a baby boy. He was named Jean-Baptiste (zhawn bap TEEST) Charbonneau, but Captain Clark called him Pompy. Before long, the boy was known to everyone as Pomp.

On April 7, 1805, the Corps of Discovery started west, struggling upstream on the mighty, muddy Missouri in two pirogues and six smaller canoes. Pomp was not yet two months old. As Sacagawea walked along the riverbank, she carried Pomp on her back, in a cradleboard or wrapped up snug in her shawl.

Every member of the Corps of Discovery was hired for a special skill—hunter, blacksmith, woodsman, sailor. As an interpreter, Charbonneau was paid much more than the other crew members. But his skills as a sailor, guide, and outdoorsman were very poor. The only thing he did well was cook buffalo sausage.

Sacagawea did what she could to help the expedition, even though she was paid nothing. As she walked along the shore with Captain Clark, Sacagawea looked for plants to keep the crew healthy. She gathered berries or dug for wild artichoke roots with her digging stick. Her Shoshone childhood had prepared her well for this journey.

The Corps had been traveling less than two months when near disaster struck. Charbonneau was steering a boat through choppy waters when a sudden high wind tipped it sideways. He lost his wits and dropped the rudder while the boat filled with water. The expedition's valuables were spilling overboard! Charbonneau was ordered to right the boat or be shot.

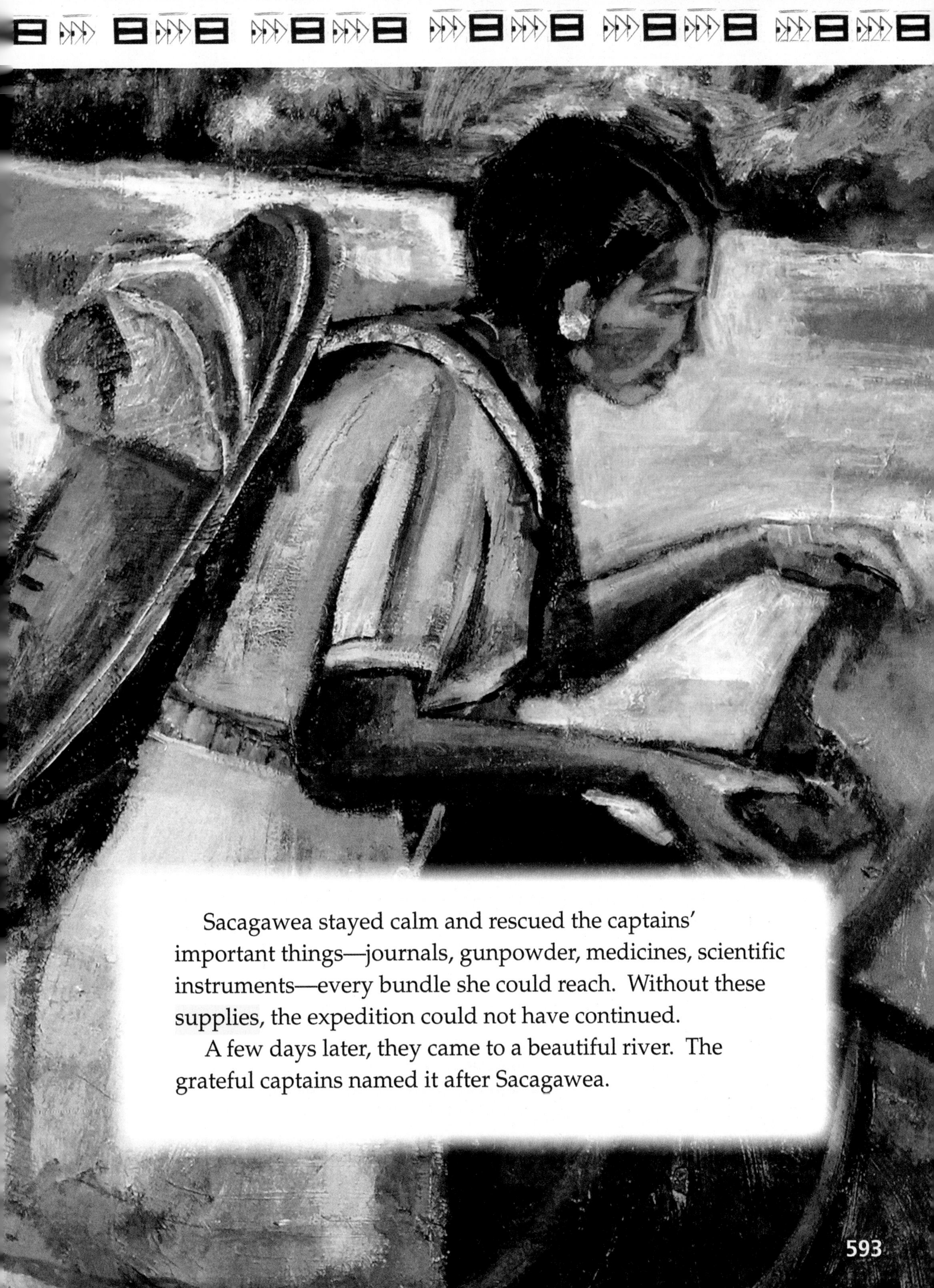

Sacagawea stayed calm and rescued the captains' important things—journals, gunpowder, medicines, scientific instruments—every bundle she could reach. Without these supplies, the expedition could not have continued.

A few days later, they came to a beautiful river. The grateful captains named it after Sacagawea.

By June, the corps was entering mountain country. Soon they could hear the distant roaring sound of the Great Falls of the Missouri. Captain Lewis thought the waterfall was the grandest sight he had ever seen. But there was no way to get past it by boat. It would take the corps nearly a month to get around the Great Falls and the four waterfalls they found just beyond it.

The crew built creaky, clumsy wagons to carry their boats and supplies. Battered by hail, rain, and wind, the men dragged the wagons over sharp rocks and prickly pear cactus that punctured their moccasins.

One day, a freak cloudburst caused a flash flood. Rocks, mud, and water came crashing down the canyon. Sacagawea held on to her son as tight as she could while Clark pushed and pulled them both to safety. Pomp's cradleboard, clothes, and bedding were swept away by the rushing water, but all three were unharmed.

By the middle of July, the corps was once again paddling up the Missouri. They reached a valley where three rivers came together, a place Sacagawea knew well. If she was upset to see it again, she did not show it. The captains learned how Sacagawea had been captured and her people killed.

Sacagawea recognized a landmark that her people called the Beaver Head Mountain. She knew they must be nearing the summer camp of the Shoshone.

ANALYZE THE TEXT

Onomatopoeia In the first paragraph on this page is the word *roaring*. *Roar* is an example of **onomatopoeia**. That is, the sound and meaning of the word are similar. Find another example of onomatopoeia in the second paragraph on this page.

Nearly two weeks later, Sacagawea walked along the river, scanning the familiar territory. She spotted some men on horseback far ahead of them. Suddenly, Captain Clark saw Sacagawea dance up and down with happiness, sucking her fingers. He knew this sign meant that these were her people, the Shoshone.

An excited crowd greeted the explorers at the Shoshone camp. Although years had passed since Sacagawea had been captured, a Shoshone woman recognized her. She rushed up to Sacagawea and threw her arms around her.

Lewis and Clark had discovered that their need for Shoshone horses was even greater than they thought. There was far more mountain country between the Missouri River and a water route to the Pacific than they expected. A grand council was called to discuss the matter. Sacagawea was to be one of the translators.

Interpreting for the men at the chief's council was a serious responsibility. Sacagawea wanted to do her best. But when she looked at the face of the Shoshone chief, she burst into tears. He was her brother, Cameahwait (kah mah WAY uht)! Sacagawea jumped up, threw her blanket over her brother, and wept.

Cameahwait was moved, too. But the council had to continue. Though tears kept flooding back, Sacagawea kept to her duty until the council ended.

Sacagawea spent the last days of August with her people. The time passed too quickly. Before long, the expedition had to mount Shoshone horses and continue across the mountains, leaving their boats behind.

The next part of their journey almost killed them. The mountain paths were narrow and dangerous, especially once it started to snow. Their feet froze, they didn't have enough to eat, and the mountains seemed without end.

Finally, the expedition emerged on the Pacific side of the Rockies. There Nez Perce (nehz purs) Indians helped them make new boats and agreed to keep the horses in case they returned that way in the spring.

With great relief, the crew dropped their boats into the Clearwater River and let the current carry the expedition toward the ocean.

At the beginning of November, the explorers noticed a sound that could only be the crashing of waves. They had finally reached the Pacific Ocean!

The crew voted on where to make winter camp. Sacagawea was allowed to vote, too. She wanted to stay where she could find plenty of wapato roots for winter food. They set up camp not far from the ocean, in case a ship came to take them back home. But by now, people back east were sure the whole corps was long dead. No ship came for them.

A cold rain soaked the crew as they cut logs and built Fort Clatsop. The hunters went to find game, while Sacagawea dug for wapato roots in the soggy ground.

ANALYZE THE TEXT

Text Structure Briefly summarize what has happened thus far in the text. Why did they set up a winter camp? How is the text organized?

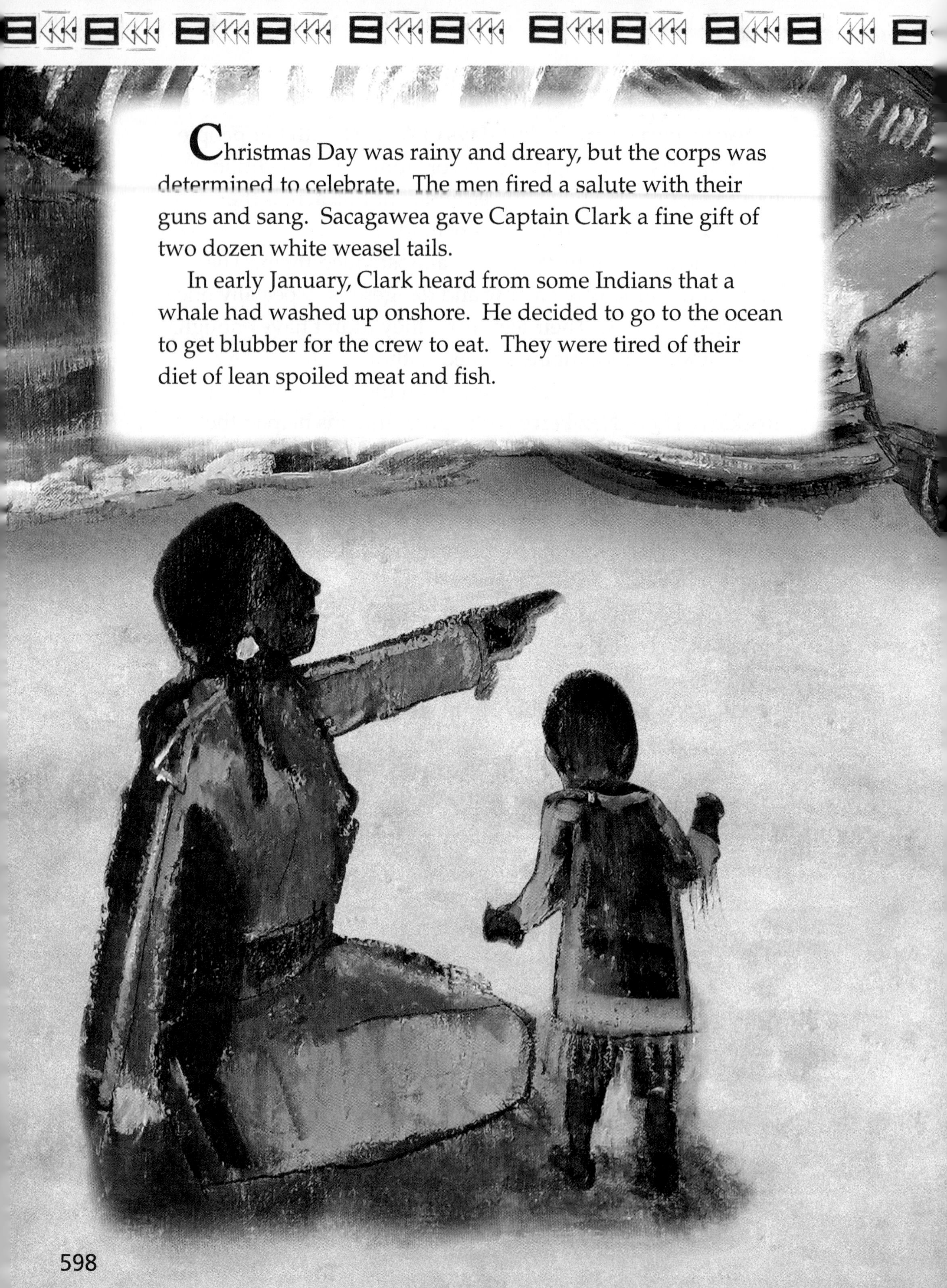

Christmas Day was rainy and dreary, but the corps was determined to celebrate. The men fired a salute with their guns and sang. Sacagawea gave Captain Clark a fine gift of two dozen white weasel tails.

In early January, Clark heard from some Indians that a whale had washed up onshore. He decided to go to the ocean to get blubber for the crew to eat. They were tired of their diet of lean spoiled meat and fish.

Sacagawea gathered up her courage and insisted that she be allowed to accompany Clark. She hadn't traveled so far to leave without ever seeing the ocean! And she wanted to see that monstrous creature. The captains agreed to let her go.

At last, Sacagawea saw the Pacific Ocean. She stood and stared at the great waters stretching endlessly in front of her. On the beach was the great skeleton of the whale. It was an amazing sight, nearly as long as twenty men lying end to end. The whale had been picked clean, but Clark was able to buy some blubber from the Indians to feed his men.

The crew stayed busy all winter, hunting, sewing moccasins, and making repairs on their equipment. Clark made maps, while Lewis worked on his report to President Jefferson.

Sacagawea watched over Pomp as he began to walk. Captain Clark called him "my little dancing boy." He had become very attached to Sacagawea and her son. When the time came, it would be hard for them to part.

Spring arrived, and it was time to go back the way they had come. In late March, the Corps of Discovery headed up the Columbia River to retrieve their horses from the Nez Perce.

At a place called Travelers' Rest, the expedition divided into two groups. Sacagawea would help guide Clark's group south to the Yellowstone River. Lewis's group would head northeast to explore the Marias River.

At the end of July, Clark's group came across an enormous rock tower on the banks of the Yellowstone. Clark named it Pompy's Tower in honor of his beloved little friend. In the side of the rock, he carved:

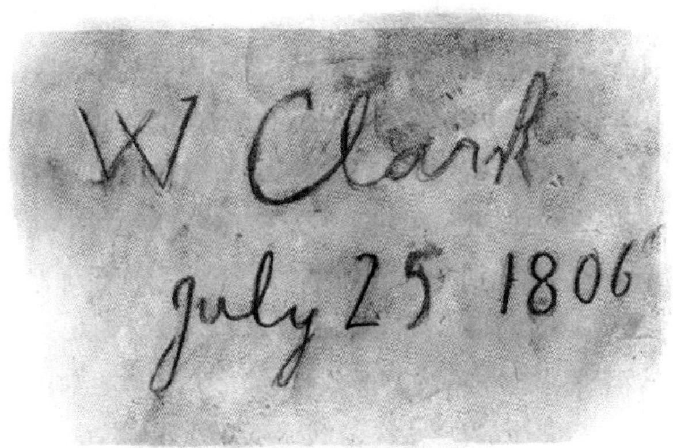

The two groups met up on August 12. Two days later, Sacagawea gazed once again upon the round earth lodges of the Knife River villages. She had been gone a year and four months.

Lewis and Clark prepared to return to St. Louis. Before they left, Captain Clark came to talk to Sacagawea and Charbonneau. He offered to take Pomp back to St. Louis with him. He would see that the boy had a good education and would raise him as his own son.

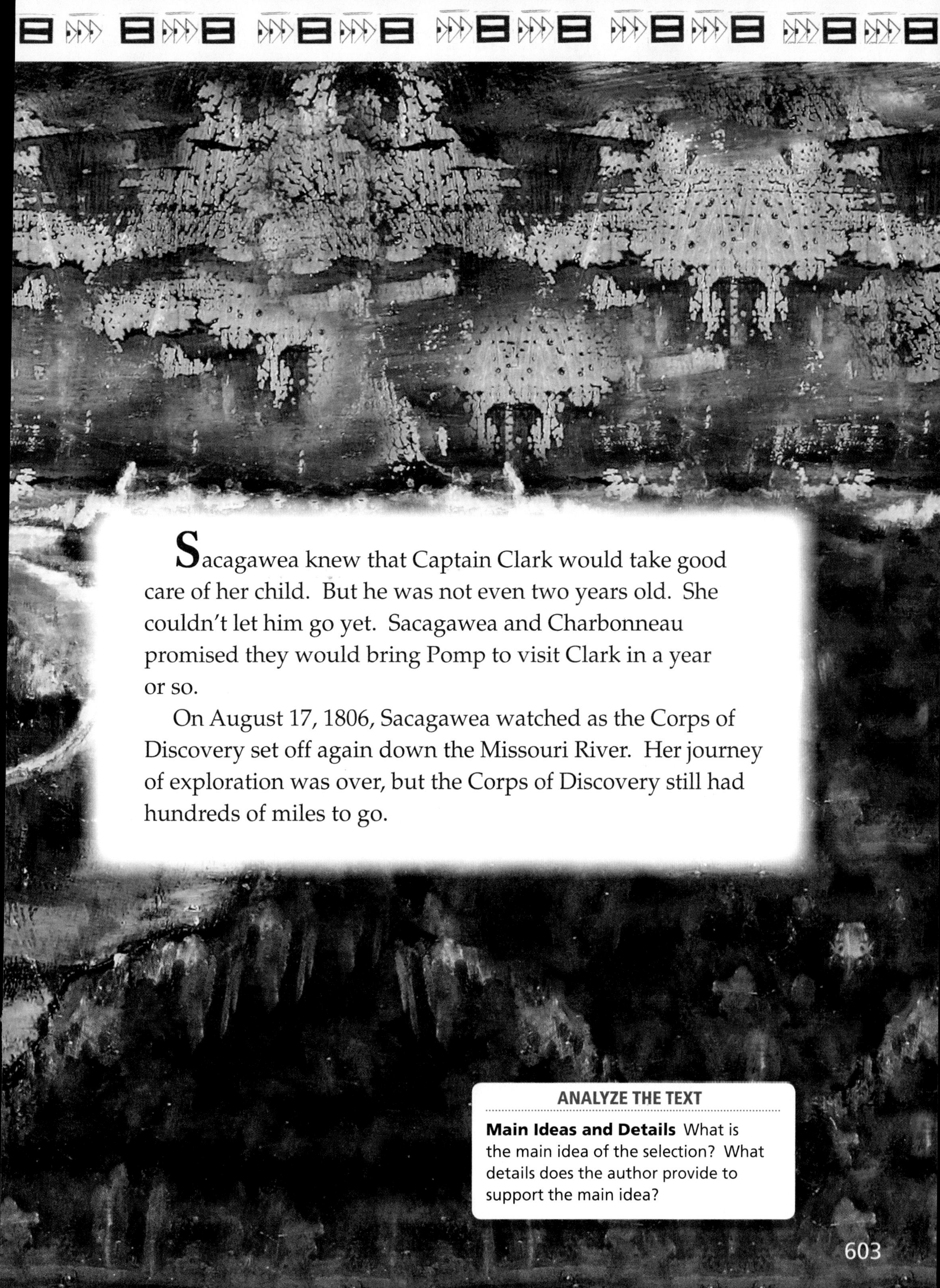

Sacagawea knew that Captain Clark would take good care of her child. But he was not even two years old. She couldn't let him go yet. Sacagawea and Charbonneau promised they would bring Pomp to visit Clark in a year or so.

On August 17, 1806, Sacagawea watched as the Corps of Discovery set off again down the Missouri River. Her journey of exploration was over, but the Corps of Discovery still had hundreds of miles to go.

ANALYZE THE TEXT

Main Ideas and Details What is the main idea of the selection? What details does the author provide to support the main idea?

COMPREHENSION

Dig Deeper

How to Analyze the Text

Use these pages to learn about Main Ideas and Details, Text Structure, and Onomatopoeia. Then read "Sacagawea" again to apply what you learned.

Main Ideas and Details

"Sacagawea" is a biography of a young Shoshone Indian named Sacagawea who helped captains Lewis and Clark explore the West. Throughout the selection, the author presents **main ideas,** or important ideas, about Sacagawea and her experience. The author explains these main ideas by giving **details.** Details include facts and examples that tell more about the main ideas.

In "Sacagawea," you learned that Sacagawea was a very important part of the Corps of Discovery. What details from the text support this main idea?

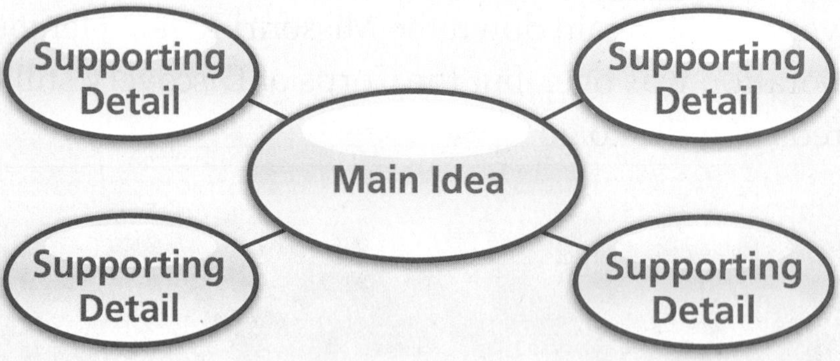

ELACC4RI2 determine the main idea and explain how it is supported by details/summarize; **ELACC4RI3** explain events/procedures/ideas/concepts in a text; **ELACC4RI5** describe the overall structure of a text or part of a text

Text Structure

Text structure is the way in which an author organizes ideas in a text or part of a text. Authors of historical texts usually explain events in the **sequence** in which they happened. For example, "Sacagawea" begins on the day the expedition set out in May of 1804. Next, the author describes their arrival at the Knife River villages at the end of October. Think about how each event fits into the text's overall structure.

MAY

S	M	T	W	T	F	S
		1	2	3	4	5
6	7	8	9	10	11	12
13	14	15	16	17	18	19
20	21	22	23	24	25	26
27	28	29	30	31		

Onomatopoeia

Onomatopoeia is a literary device authors sometimes use to help readers imagine what something sounds like. When authors use **onomatopoeia,** they choose a word that sounds like what it means. For example, the word *buzz* sounds like a flying bee, and the word *whoosh* sounds like a waterfall.

Your Turn

RETURN TO THE ESSENTIAL QUESTION

Review the selection to prepare to discuss this question with a partner: *How do people from different cultures contribute to American history?* As you talk, take turns reviewing key ideas and explaining your own. Discuss rules, such as "Do not interrupt each other."

Classroom Conversation

Continue your discussion of "Sacagawea" by explaining your answers to these questions:

1. Why do you think Sacagawea helped the Corps of Discovery?
2. What can you learn from Clark about how to be a good leader? Use ideas from the selection.
3. What do you think was Sacagawea's most important contribution? Why?

TEAM PLAYERS

Discuss Success With a partner, discuss what made the Corps of Discovery team successful. Think about the challenges they faced and how they worked together to meet those challenges. How important was Sacagawea as a member of this team? Use text evidence from the selection to support your ideas.

WRITE ABOUT READING

Response Suppose that you had been invited to go on Lewis and Clark's expedition. Think about the qualities or skills that you would bring to the team. Also decide what you would have enjoyed most about the trip and what you would have found most difficult. Write two paragraphs explaining your ideas based on text evidence.

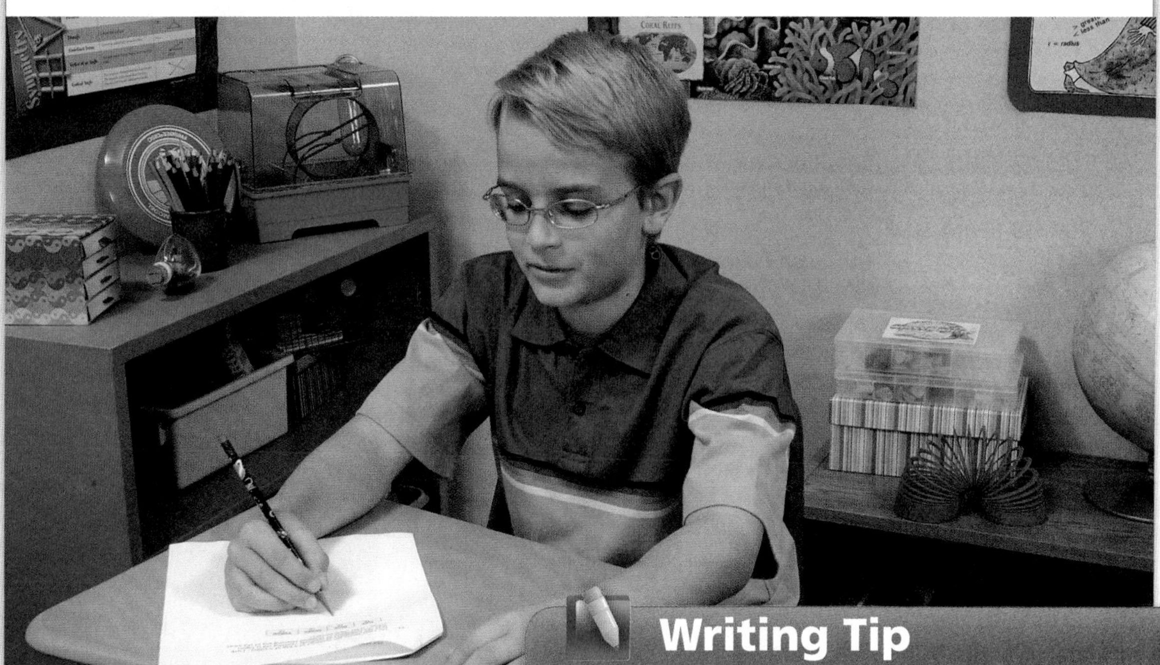

Writing Tip

To make your writing more interesting and precise, include colorful adjectives. End your paragraph with a strong conclusion that summarizes your skills.

COMMON CORE **ELACC4RI1** refer to details and examples when explaining what the text says explicitly and when drawing inferences; **ELACC4RI2** determine the main idea and explain how it is supported by details/summarize; **ELACC4W2d** use precise language and domain-specific vocabulary; **ELACC4W2e** provide a concluding statement or section; **ELACC4W9b** apply grade 4 Reading standards to informational texts; **ELACC4SL1b** follow rules for discussions; **ELACC4SL1d** review key ideas expressed and explain own ideas and understanding

Lesson 20

POETRY

GENRE

Poetry uses the sound and rhythm of words to suggest images and express feelings.

TEXT FOCUS

Free verse is poetry without a regular rhyme or regular rhythm. As you read "The Wind," note how the poem does not have rhyme or rhythm like other poems you have read. How do the line breaks help create the poem's feeling of wind movement?

ELACC4RL5 explain major differences between poems, drama, and prose/refer to their structural elements; **ELACC4RL10** read and comprehend literature

Native American NATURE POETRY

Nature and a person's relationship to nature are two important themes in Native American poetry. A poem might include details that describe a common place, such as a forest with wind rustling through the trees. It might personify an object, giving human characteristics to it. Then again, a poem might tell what is important in life.

Here am I
Behold me
It said as it rose,
I am the moon
Behold me.
Teton Sioux

The Wind

At night,
The wind keeps us awake,
Rustling through the trees.
We don't know how we'll get to sleep,
Until we do—
Dropping off as suddenly
As the wind dying down.
Crow

PRESERVING ORAL TRADITIONS

For centuries Native Americans passed their poems, songs, and stories orally from one generation to the next. People who did not speak Native American languages needed an interpreter to help them understand and write down these stories.

By the late 1800s, people could use cylinder recorders to record and play sounds. Compared to today's small electronic recorders, cylinder recorders were clumsy to use. Yet they preserved sounds exactly. In 1890 this recorder became important to scientist Jesse Fewkes, who was asked to accompany a corps of researchers to the southwestern United States. The cylinder recorder was among Fewkes's supplies. He used it to record and preserve Native American oral stories.

A cylinder recorder

You, whose day it is,
Make it beautiful.
Get out your rainbow colors,
So it will be beautiful.

Nootka

I Think Over Again My Small Adventures

I think over again my small adventures,
My fears,
Those small ones that seemed so big,
For all the vital things
I had to get and to reach;
And yet there is only one great thing,
The only thing,
To live to see the great day that dawns
And the light that fills the world.

Anonymous
(North American Indian;
nineteenth century)

Write a Poem About Beauty

The poem "You, whose day it is" suggests that it is one's duty to make the day beautiful. How would you make your day beautiful? Would you help someone you care about? Would you take a special route to visit a favorite landmark? Would you make a picture or admire a sunset? Have friends proposed ideas to you in the past? Write a poem that tells what you would do.

Compare Texts

TEXT TO TEXT

Compare Poems Sacagawea saw many wonderful natural sights during her journey. Which of the poems from "Native American Nature Poetry" might she have used to describe what she saw? Discuss with a partner which you think she would choose and why. Then write a poem about one of the sights Sacagawea saw. Use onomatopoeia, similes, and metaphors to help readers picture the scene. When you have finished, share your poem with a partner. Explain the similes and metaphors you have used.

TEXT TO SELF

Write a Journal Entry We know details of the Corps of Discovery expedition because Lewis and Clark kept journals. Recall an interesting trip you have taken. Write a journal entry about it. Explain why the trip was important to you.

TEXT TO WORLD

Research Native Americans Choose a Native American group that lived in your state in the past. Find at least three interesting facts about this group, and list them on a poster, along with drawings or photographs that help explain your facts.

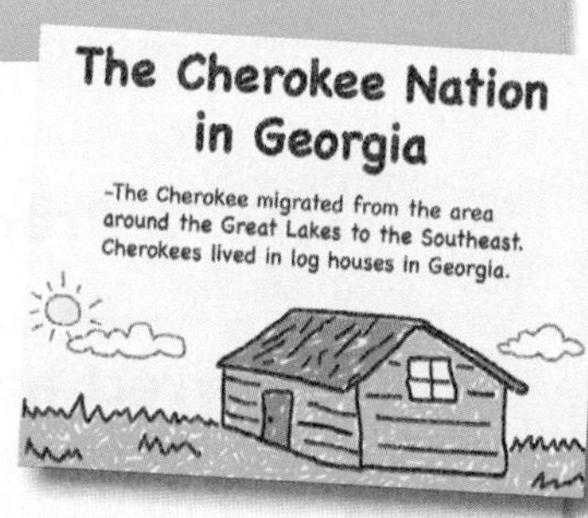

The Cherokee Nation in Georgia
-The Cherokee migrated from the area around the Great Lakes to the Southeast. Cherokees lived in log houses in Georgia.

ELACC4W7 conduct short research projects that build knowledge through investigation; **ELACC4W10** write routinely over extended time frames and shorter time frames; **ELACC4L3a** choose words and phrases to convey ideas precisely; **ELACC4L5a** explain the meaning of similes and metaphors in context

COMMON CORE **ELACC4L2a** use correct capitalization

Grammar

What Is an Abbreviation? How Are Abbreviations Written? Some words have a shortened form called an **abbreviation.** An abbreviation stands for a whole word. Most abbreviations begin with a capital letter and end with a period. Use them only in special kinds of writing, such as addresses and lists.

Some Common Abbreviations			
Titles	Mr. → Mister Jr. → Junior	Capt. → Captain Dr. → Doctor	Mrs. → married woman Ms. → any woman
Addresses	Rd. → Road St. → Street	Ave. → Avenue Blvd. → Boulevard	Ct. → Court P.O. → Post Office
Months	Feb. → February	Aug. → August	Oct. → October
Days	Mon. → Monday	Wed. → Wednesday	Thurs. → Thursday
Measurements	in. → inch/inches	ft. → foot/feet	mi. → mile/miles

Try This! **Proofread the items below. On a sheet of paper, rewrite each group of words, using the correct abbreviations.**

1. Andrew Perkins
   438 Groat Avenue
   Grapevine, TEX 76051
2. 5,280 feet = 1 mile
3. Thursday, Feb'y 8, 2010
4. Doctor Linda Martinez
   4195 Buffalo Street
   Chadron, Nebraska 69337

Good writers use abbreviations only in special kinds of writing, such as addresses and lists. When you use abbreviations, make sure you write them correctly.

Incorrect Abbreviations	Correct Abbreviations

Doct. James Sekiguchi The Bradley Comp 127 Saratoga Boul. Montgomery, Ala. 36104 Weds, Sep. 18 4 ft, 7 in	Dr. James Sekiguchi The Bradley Co. 127 Saratoga Blvd. Montgomery, AL 36104 Wed., Sept. 18 4 ft., 7 in.

Connect Grammar to Writing

As you edit your personal narrative, correct any errors in capitalization or punctuation that you discover. If you used any abbreviations, make sure you used proper capitalization and punctuation.

ELACC4W3a orient the reader by establishing a situation and introducing a narrator or characters/organize an event sequence; **ELACC4W3b** use dialogue and description to develop experiences and events or show characters' responses; **ELACC4W3c** use transitional words and phrases to manage the sequence of events; **ELACC4W3d** use concrete words and phrases and sensory details; **ELACC4W3e** provide a conclusion

Narrative Writing

Reading-Writing Workshop: Revise

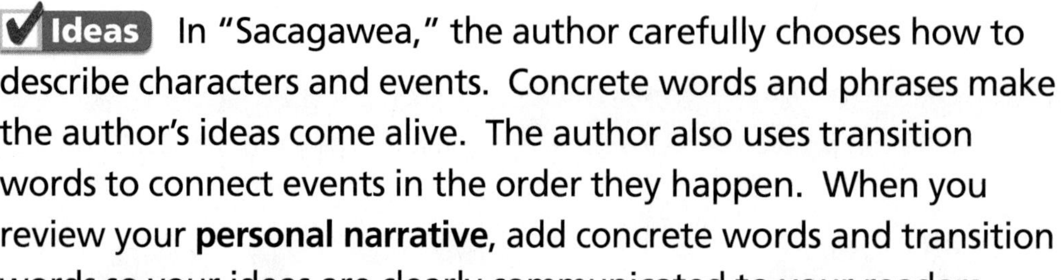

Ideas In "Sacagawea," the author carefully chooses how to describe characters and events. Concrete words and phrases make the author's ideas come alive. The author also uses transition words to connect events in the order they happen. When you review your **personal narrative**, add concrete words and transition words so your ideas are clearly communicated to your readers. Use the Writing Process Checklist below as you revise your writing.

Steve drafted his narrative about a class adventure. When he revised it, he added concrete words and transition words.

Writing Process Checklist

Prewrite

Draft

▶ **Revise**

- ✔ Did I begin with an attention grabber?
- ✔ Did I organize events in a logical order?
- ✔ Did I use transition words to clearly show the order of events?
- ✔ Did I include detailed descriptions with concrete words and phrases?
- ✔ Does my ending show how the events worked out?

Edit

Publish and Share

Revised Draft

When our teacher, Mrs. Kay, asked, "What kind of ^community project should our class do?" my hand ~~went~~ ^shot up.

"Let's go on the Walk to End Hunger," I said. "We'll raise money to help people. It will be awesome to walk for ^five miles ^through our hilly city."

^First, Mrs. Kay listed our project ideas. ^Then We voted. The walk won ^by ten votes!

Final Copy

Our Walk to End Hunger

by Steve Jones

When our teacher, Mrs. Kay, asked, "What kind of community project should our class do?" my hand shot up.

"Let's go on the Walk to End Hunger," I said. "We'll raise money to help people. It will be awesome to walk for five miles through our hilly city."

First, Mrs. Kay listed our project ideas. Then we voted. The walk won by ten votes!

People were really eager to help, including our principal, Mr. Desmond. "I'm so proud of you kids for doing this," he said, and then he made a generous pledge. The day before the walk, our pledges totaled $425!

The next day, May 6, we went by bus to where the walk would begin. There were colorful balloons, huge banners, and long tables with juice and granola bars. We walked for two hours. When we crossed the finish line, the crowd cheered wildly. I felt proud.

Reading as a Writer

How did Steve keep his narrative interesting? Where in your writing can you add descriptive details and concrete words and phrases?

I added a conclusion that tells how the event turned out. I also made sure to use correct punctuation.

Read the passages "The Stonecutter" and "Changing His Tune." As you read, stop and answer each question using text evidence.

The Stonecutter

a Japanese folktale

Once there was a stonecutter who lived in a small but comfortable cottage in the country. He was content with his quiet life until one winter day when he paid a visit to the nearby city. There he saw a magnificent dwelling far more splendid than his own. "My greatest wish is to have a magnificent house like this!" the stonecutter cried.

When the stonecutter returned home, his cozy cottage was gone. In its place stood an enormous palace. For a time, the stonecutter was delighted with his fine new home. Before long, however, summer arrived. The sun burned hotter each day. Even in his fine palace, the stonecutter could not bear the ferocious heat. "I may be wealthy, but the sun is even more powerful than I am!" he cried. "My greatest wish is to become the mighty sun!"

Instantly, the stonecutter was transformed into the sun, mighty and powerful. His rays shone on Earth until the rice crops dried up in the fields, and he burned the faces of rich and poor people alike.

Then one day, a dark cloud covered the face of the sun. The sun cried, "I am powerful, but this cloud is even mightier than I am! My greatest wish is to become a cloud!"

 How would you describe the character of the stonecutter and how he has changed? Give examples from the passage to support your response.

So the stonecutter was transformed into a cloud, just as he had wished. He rained on Earth for days, and it grew green again. Then he continued pouring down rain until huge floods destroyed vast rice fields and entire villages. Only the great mountain stood firm and strong amid the floods.

COMMON CORE **ELACC4RL2** determine theme from details/summarize; **ELACC4RL3** describe a character, setting, or event, drawing on details; **ELACC4RL4** determine the meaning of words and phrases, including those that allude to characters in mythology; **ELACC4RL9** compare and contrast the treatment of similar themes and topics

Seeing this, the cloud cried, "I am powerful, but the mountain is even mightier than I am! My greatest wish is to become the mountain!" Suddenly the stonecutter was transformed into the mountain. He stood tall and proud, not bothered by sun or rain. The days turned into weeks, the weeks into months, and the months into years. All this time, the mountain stood silent and alone, growing more and more lonely.

Finally, the mountain sighed gloomily, "My greatest wish now is to be a simple stonecutter again." So the stonecutter became a man once more, living in his own little cottage in the country. And never again did he wish to be anyone or anything but what he was.

 What lesson does the stonecutter learn? Use details from the passage to support your response.

Changing His Tune

a fable

Once there was a small bird named Twitter who took such great pleasure in singing that he sang all day long. He had a very unusual voice, unlike any of the other birds. "T-t-t-witt! T-t-t-witt!" he warbled in a sweet and pleasing tone.

One day, Twitter stopped singing for a while and listened to the songs of the other birds. It seemed to him that their music sounded better to him than his own little song. Right then, he decided he would change his song and sing just like the other birds.

Twitter sat high in a tree listening to another bird's song until he could repeat it exactly. "Ta-weee! Ta-weee!" he sang out loudly.

A moment later, his friend Skye the blue jay landed on the branch beside him. Skye peered at him and asked, "Is that really you, Twitter? You don't sound like yourself at all today. I thought it must be someone else singing."

“That’s because I decided to sing like my friend Kiwi today,” answered Twitter. “Tomorrow I intend to sing like Dove. The next day I’ll sing like Marcella.” Twitter paused for breath and chirped, “Listen, Skye, I can even sing like you!” Twitter gave a harsh, jeering call like a blue jay’s. It hurt his throat and made him cough, but it *did* sound like Skye.

“That was a good imitation!” squawked Skye. “But why are you imitating other birds, Twitter, instead of just singing like yourself?”

“The other birds sing such wonderful songs,” Twitter replied. Then he added sadly, “Their songs sound so much more musical than mine.”

“I’m very sorry you feel that way,” Skye said with a frown. “I’ve always thought your song was the most melodious one of all.”

 What is the meaning of the word *melodious* as it is used in the passage? Explain how the way the word is used in the passage makes its meaning clear.

“Really?” Twitter asked in disbelief. Skye nodded. Twitter wondered whether what Skye had said could be true. He thought about how imitating other birds bothered his throat and made him feel uncomfortable. He stretched out a wing to Skye and said, “Thank you, my friend. I’ve decided to change my tune—back to my old song!”

And from that moment on, Twitter always sang in his own lovely warble, “T-t-t-witt! T-t-t-witt!” And once again he took such great pleasure in his singing that he sang all day long.

 How are the themes of these two passages similar, and how are they different?

unit 5

Lesson 21

The World According to Humphrey

Make the Switch

TARGET VOCABULARY

appreciate
blaring
combination
promptly
introduce
nocturnal
feats
effort
suggest
racket

Vocabulary Reader

Context Cards

ELACC4L6 acquire/use vocabulary, including academic and domain-specific

Vocabulary in Context

1 appreciate

Many people highly value, or appreciate, their pets.

2 blaring

If a dog barks at loud, blaring noises, it should be trained not to do that.

3 combination

People may feel a combination of love for and frustration with their pets.

4 promptly

If a dog needs to go out, it should be taken out promptly, or right away.

▶ Study each Context Card.

▶ Use a dictionary to help you understand the meanings of these words.

5 introduce

You should carefully introduce a new pet to the other pets in your house.

6 nocturnal

Some pets, such as cats and hamsters, are nocturnal. They're most active at night.

7 feats

Many people enjoy teaching their pets to perform tricks and other feats of skill.

8 effort

It takes effort, or hard work, to care for a pet, no matter what kind of animal it is.

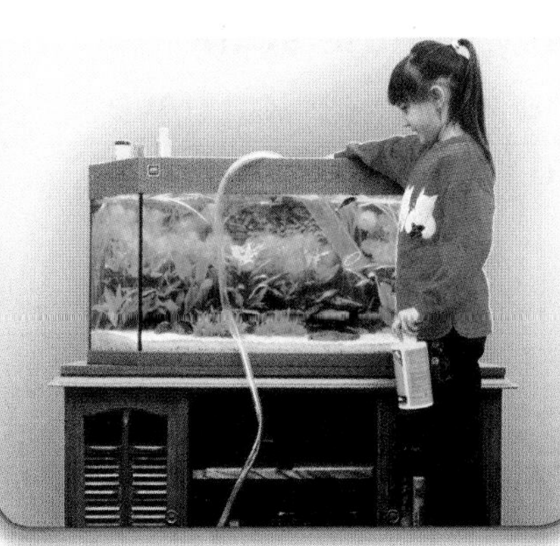

9 suggest

Experts suggest, or recommend, that people remain calm when training a pet.

10 racket

Some pet birds can talk, but they can also create a loud racket by screaming.

Read and Comprehend

TARGET SKILL

Theme As you read "The World According to Humphrey," ask yourself what important lesson the main characters learn over the course of the story. This lesson is the story's **theme**. Use a graphic organizer like the one below to record text evidence of the characters' thoughts and actions, as well as the ways in which they change and grow. This will help you figure out the story's theme.

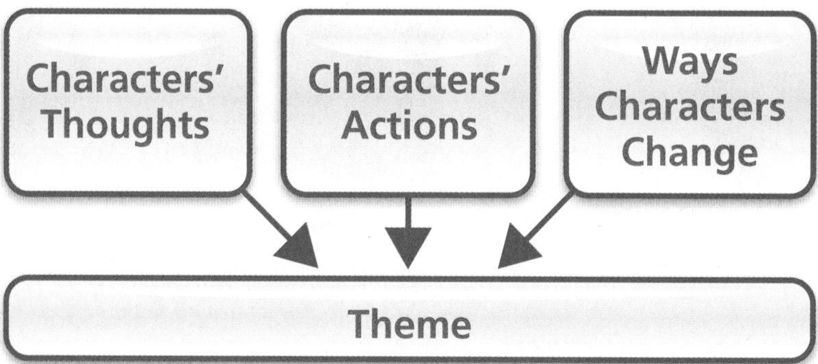

TARGET STRATEGY

Summarize When you summarize a story, you briefly retell the main events in your own words. As you read "The World According to Humphrey," pause at the end of each page to briefly summarize what you have read to make sure you understand it.

COMMON CORE **ELACC4RL1** refer to details and examples when explaining what the text says explicitly and when drawing inferences; **ELACC4RL2** determine theme from details/summarize

PREVIEW THE TOPIC

Media

Media such as television, magazines, and the Internet are powerful communication tools. But is it possible to have too much of a good thing? Today, many Americans spend hours each day watching television and playing and working on computers. How did we spend our time before media took up most of our attention?

"The World According to Humphrey" is the story of a family that learns a valuable lesson about media.

Lesson 21

ANCHOR TEXT

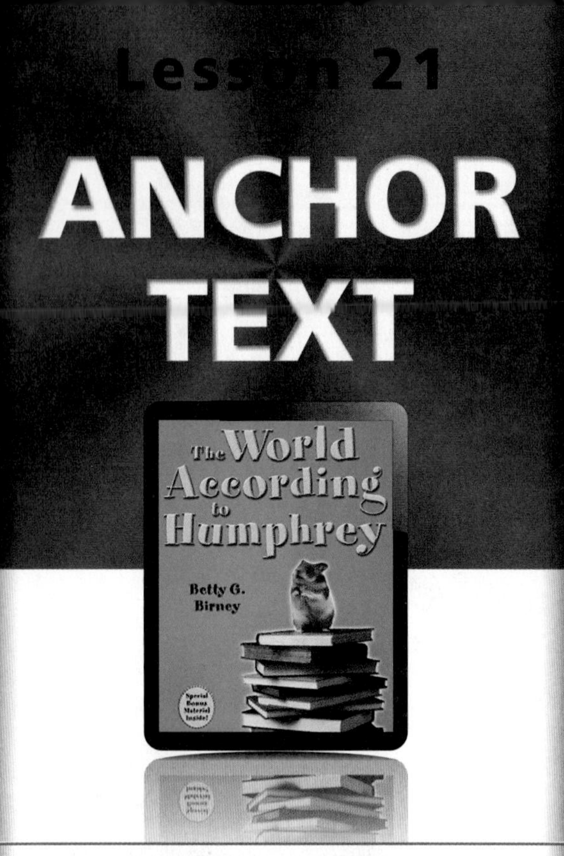

TARGET SKILL

Theme Explain the lesson or message in a work of fiction.

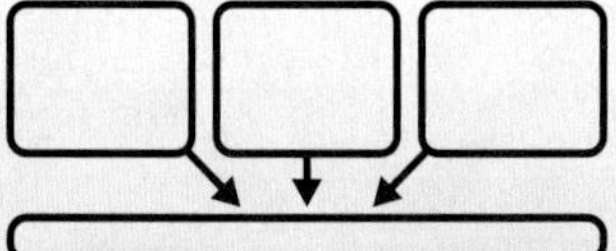

GENRE

A **fantasy** is an imaginative story that may have unrealistic characters and events. As you read, look for:

- story events or settings that could not happen in real life
- characters who behave in unrealistic ways

ELACC4RL2 determine theme from details/summarize; **ELACC4RL6** compare and contrast the point of view from which stories are narrated; **ELACC4RL10** read and comprehend literature; **ELACC4L5b** recognize and explain the meaning of idioms, adages, and proverbs

MEET THE AUTHOR

Betty G. Birney

Betty G. Birney wrote her first "book," titled *The Teddy Bear in the Woods*, when she was seven years old. It was soon followed by a sequel, and she has been writing ever since, authoring more than twenty-five children's books including several others in the *Humphrey* series. Although Birney criticizes television in this selection, she has contributed to that medium, too, having written more than two hundred episodes of popular TV programs, such as *Madeline* and *Fraggle Rock*.

MEET THE ILLUSTRATOR

Teri Farrell-Gittins

Teri Farrell-Gittins might never have achieved her dream of becoming an artist if she had watched as much TV as the family in this selection does. She often didn't even have a TV in the house when she was growing up, so she spent her time in more creative pursuits such as sketching and drawing. Illustrating this selection reminded her of how important it is to unplug from distractions, tune in to her imagination, and look out on the beauty of the world around her.

THE WORLD ACCORDING TO HUMPHREY

by Betty G. Birney

selection illustrated by Teri Farrell-Gittins

ESSENTIAL QUESTION

How can media be a distraction?

The kids in Mrs. Brisbane's class love taking care of their hamster, Humphrey. The weekends are especially fun because one of them takes Humphrey home. This weekend, the lucky student is A. J.

The bus let us off close to A. J.'s house. It was a two-story old house with a big porch. As soon as I entered, I got a warm welcome from A. J.'s mom, his younger brother, Ty, his little sister, DeeLee, and his baby brother, Beau.

"Anthony James, introduce us to your little friend," his mom said, greeting us.

Anthony James? Everybody at school called A. J. by his initials or just "Aje."

"This is Humphrey," he answered.

"Hello, Humphrey," said Mrs. Thomas. "So how was your day, Anthony?"

"Lousy. Garth kept shooting rubber bands at me. He won't leave me alone."

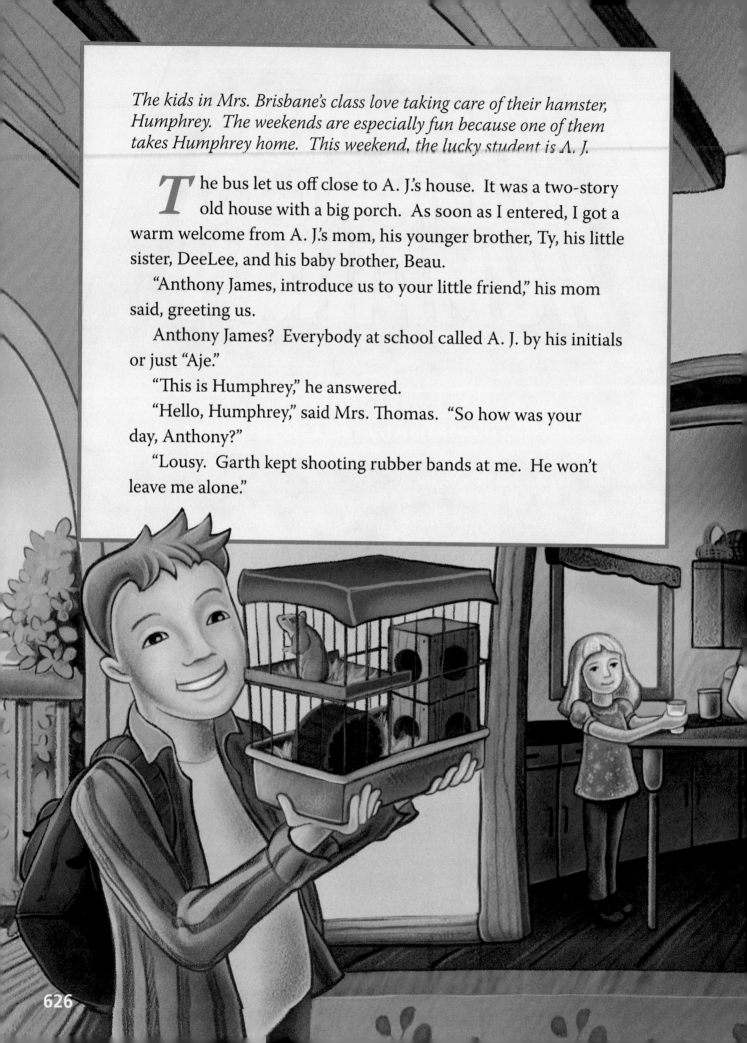

"But you two used to be friends," his mother said.

"Used to be," said A. J. "Until he turned into a JERK."

Mom patted her son on the shoulder. "Well, you've got the whole weekend to get over it. Now take Humphrey into the den and get him settled."

Mrs. Brisbane called him Lower-Your-Voice-A. J. because A. J. always talked extra loud in class. I soon noticed that everybody at A. J.'s house talked extra loud. They had to, because in the background the TV was always blaring.

Now, every house I've been in so far has had a TV, and I've enjoyed some of the shows I've seen.

There's one channel that has nothing but the most frightening shows about wild animals attacking one another. I mean *wild,* like tigers and bears and hippopotamuses. (Gee, I hope that's not on our vocabulary test in the near future.) Those shows make me appreciate the protection of a nice cage. As long as the lock doesn't quite lock.

There's another channel that only has people in funny-looking clothes dancing and singing in very strange places. It makes me glad that I have a fur coat and don't have to figure out what to wear every day.

Mostly, I like the cartoon shows. Sometimes they have mice and rabbits and other interesting rodents, although I've never seen a hamster show. Yet.

Anyway, the difference at the Thomases' house is that the television is on *all the time.* There's a TV on a table across from a big comfy couch and a big comfy chair and someone's almost always sitting there watching. I know because they put my cage down on the floor next to the couch. I had a very good view of the TV.

I couldn't always hear the TV, though, because A. J.'s mother had a radio in the kitchen, which was blaring most of the time while she cooked or did crossword puzzles or talked on the phone. No matter what she did, the radio was always on.

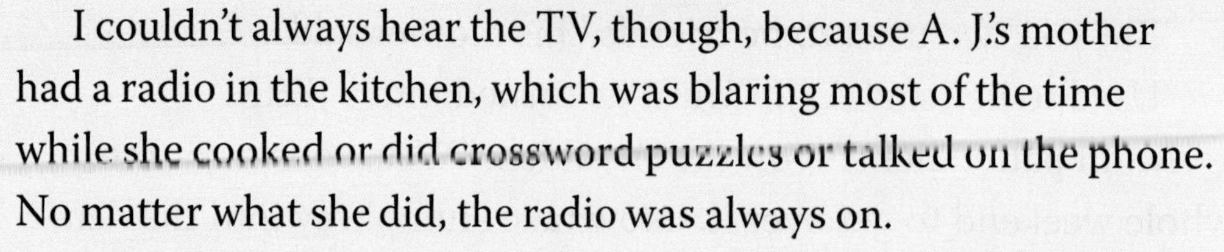

When A. J.'s dad came home from work, he plopped down on the couch and watched TV while he played with the baby. Then A. J. and Ty plugged in some video games and played while Dad watched. DeeLee listened to the radio with her mom and danced around the kitchen.

When it was time for dinner, the whole family took plates and sat in the den so they could watch TV while they ate.

Then they watched TV some more. They made popcorn and kept watching.

Finally, the kids went to bed. The baby first, then DeeLee and later Ty and A. J.

After they were all in their rooms, Mr. and Mrs. Thomas kept watching TV and ate some ice cream.

Later, Mrs. Thomas yawned loudly. "I've had it, Charlie. I'm going to bed and I suggest you do, too," she said.

But Mr. Thomas just kept on watching. Or at least he kept on sitting there until he fell asleep on the couch. I ended up watching the rest of the wrestling match without him.

ANALYZE THE TEXT

Idioms What does Mrs. Thomas mean when she says, "I've had it"? How does the use of this idiom affect the story?

Unfortunately, the wrestler I was rooting for, Thor of Glore, lost. Finally, Mr. Thomas woke up, yawned, flicked off the TV and went upstairs to bed. Peace at last.

But the quiet only lasted about ten minutes. Soon Mom brought Beau downstairs and gave him a bottle while she watched TV. When Beau finally fell asleep, Mrs. Thomas yawned and flicked off the TV. Blessed relief.

Five minutes later, Mr. Thomas returned. "Sorry, hamster. Can't sleep," he mumbled to me as he flicked on the remote. He watched and watched and then dozed off again. But the TV stayed on, leaving me no choice but to watch a string of commercials for car waxes, weight-reducing programs, exercise machines and "Red-Hot Harmonica Classics."

The combination of being nocturnal and being bombarded with sight and sound kept me wide-awake.

At the crack of dawn, DeeLee tiptoed into the room, dragging her doll by its hair, and switched to a cartoon show about princesses.

She watched another show about cats and dogs. (Scary!) Then Mr. Thomas woke up and wanted to check some sports scores. Mrs. Thomas handed him the baby and his bottle and soon the older boys switched over to video games and their parents watched them play.

It was LOUD-LOUD-LOUD. But the Thomases didn't seem to notice.

"What do you want for breakfast?" Mom shouted.

"What?" Dad shouted louder.

"WHAT DO YOU WANT FOR BREAKFAST?" Mom yelled.

"TOASTER WAFFLES!" Dad yelled louder.

"I CAN'T HEAR THE TV!" Ty hollered, turning up the volume.

"DO YOU WANT JUICE?" Mom screamed.

"CAN'T HEAR YOU!" Dad responded.

And so it went. With each new question, the sound on the TV would be turned up higher and higher until it was positively deafening.

Then Mom switched on her radio.

The Thomases were a perfectly nice family, but I could tell it was going to be a very long and noisy weekend unless I came up with a Plan.

So, I spun on my wheel for a while to help me think. And I thought and thought and thought some more. And then it came: the Big Idea. I probably would have come up with it sooner if I could have heard myself think!

Around noon, the Thomases were all watching the football game on TV. Or rather, Mr. Thomas was watching the football game on TV while A. J. and Ty shouted questions at him. Mrs. Thomas was in the kitchen listening to the radio and talking on the phone. DeeLee played peekaboo with the baby in the cozy chair.

No one was watching me, so I carefully opened the lock-that-doesn't-lock on my cage and made a quick exit.

Naturally, no one could hear me skittering across the floor as I made my way around the outside of the room, over to the space behind the TV cabinet. Then, with Great Effort, I managed to pull out the plug: one of the most difficult feats of my life.

ANALYZE THE TEXT

Point of View Who is telling this story? How does that affect what you know about the events?

The TV went silent. Beautifully, blissfully, silently silent. So silent, I was afraid to move. I waited behind the cabinet, frozen.

The Thomases stared at the TV screen as the picture slowly went dark.

"Ty, did you hit that remote?" Mr. Thomas asked.

"Naw. It's under the table."

"Anthony, go turn that thing on again," Mr. Thomas said. A. J. jumped up and hit the power button on the TV.

Nothing happened.

"It's broken!" he exclaimed.

Mrs. Thomas rushed in from the kitchen. "What happened?"

Mr. Thomas explained that the TV had gone off and they discussed how old it was (five years), whether it had a guarantee (no one knew) and if Mr. Thomas could fix it (he couldn't).

"Everything was fine and it went off—just like that. I guess we'd better take it in to get fixed," Mr. Thomas said.

"How long will it take?" DeeLee asked in a whiny voice.

"I don't know," her dad replied.

"How much will it cost?" Mrs. Thomas asked.

"Oh. Yeah," her husband said. "I forgot. We're a little low on funds right now."

The baby began to cry. I thought the rest of the family might start crying, too.

"Well, I get paid next Friday," Dad said.

A. J. jumped up and waved his hands. "That's a whole week away!"

"I'm going to Grandma's house. Her TV works," said Ty.

"Me, too," DeeLee chimed in.

"Grandma's got her bridge club over there tonight," Mom said.

"I know," said Dad. "Let's go to a movie."

"Do you know how much it costs to go to a movie?" Mom asked. "Besides, we can't take the baby."

"Oh."

They whined and bickered for quite a while. They got so loud, I managed to scamper back to my cage, unnoticed. Then I guess I dozed off. Remember, I had hardly had a wink of sleep since I'd arrived. The bickering was a nice, soothing background after all that racket.

I was only half-asleep when the squabbling changed.

"But there's nothing to do," DeeLee whined.

Her father chuckled. "Nothing to do! Girl, my brothers and I used to spend weekends at my grandma's house and she never had a TV. Wouldn't allow it!"

"What did you do?" A. J. asked.

"Oh, we were busy every minute," he recalled. "We played cards and board games and word games. And we dug in her garden and played tag." He chuckled again. "A lot of times we just sat on the porch and talked. My grandma . . . she could *talk.*"

"What'd you talk about?" Ty wondered.

"Oh, she'd tell us stories about her growing up. About funny things, like the time her uncle was walking in his sleep and went to church in his pajamas."

Mrs. Thomas gasped. "Oh, go on now, Charlie."

"I'm just telling you what she told us. He woke up in the middle of the service, looked down and there he was, in his blue-and-white striped pajamas."

I let out a squeak of surprise and the kids all giggled.

Then Mrs. Thomas told a story about a girl in her class who came to school in her slippers by accident one day. "Yes, the fuzzy kind," she explained with a big smile.

They talked and talked and Dad got out some cards and they played a game called Crazy Eights and another one called Pig where they put their fingers on their noses and laughed like hyenas. When Beau fussed, they took turns jiggling him on their knees.

After a while, Mrs. Thomas gasped. "Goodness' sakes! It's an hour past your bedtimes."

The children all groaned and asked if they could play cards tomorrow and in a few minutes all the Thomases had gone to bed and it was QUIET-QUIET-QUIET for the first time since I'd arrived.

Early in the morning, Ty, DeeLee and A. J. raced downstairs and played Crazy Eights. Later, they ran outside and threw a football around the yard.

The Thomases were having breakfast with Beau when the phone rang. Mr. Thomas talked for a few minutes, mostly saying "Uh-huh, that's fine." When he hung up, he told Mrs. Thomas, "We're going to have a visitor. But don't tell Anthony James."

Oooh, a mystery. I like mysteries because they're fun to solve. Then again I don't like mysteries because I don't like not knowing what's going on. So I waited and waited.

A few hours later, the doorbell rang.

The visitor turned out to be Garth Tugwell and his father! "I really appreciate this," Mr. Tugwell told the Thomases. "It was Mrs. Brisbane's idea. Since Garth can't have Humphrey at our house right now, she suggested that he could help A. J. take care of him over here."

Sounds like Mrs. Brisbane. As if I'm trouble to take care of.

But Garth had been crying because he couldn't have me. So maybe—maybe—she was trying to be nice.

After Mr. Tugwell left, Mr. Thomas called A. J. in.

A. J. ran into the room and practically backed out again when he saw Garth.

"We have a guest," said Mr. Thomas. "Shake hands, Anthony. Garth is here to help you take care of Humphrey."

A. J. and Garth reluctantly shook hands.

"How come?" asked A. J.

Garth shrugged his shoulders. "Mrs. Brisbane said to."

"Well, come on. We'll clean his cage and get it over with," A. J. said.

The boys didn't talk much while they cleaned the cage. But they started giggling when they cleaned up my potty corner. (I don't know why that makes everybody giggle.)

After they stopped giggling, they started talking and kidding around. They decided to let me out of the cage, so they took a set of old blocks from DeeLee's room and built me a huge maze. Oh, I love mazes!

ANALYZE THE TEXT

Theme A. J. learns a lesson when Garth comes to his house. What is this lesson? How does this lesson relate to the theme of the story?

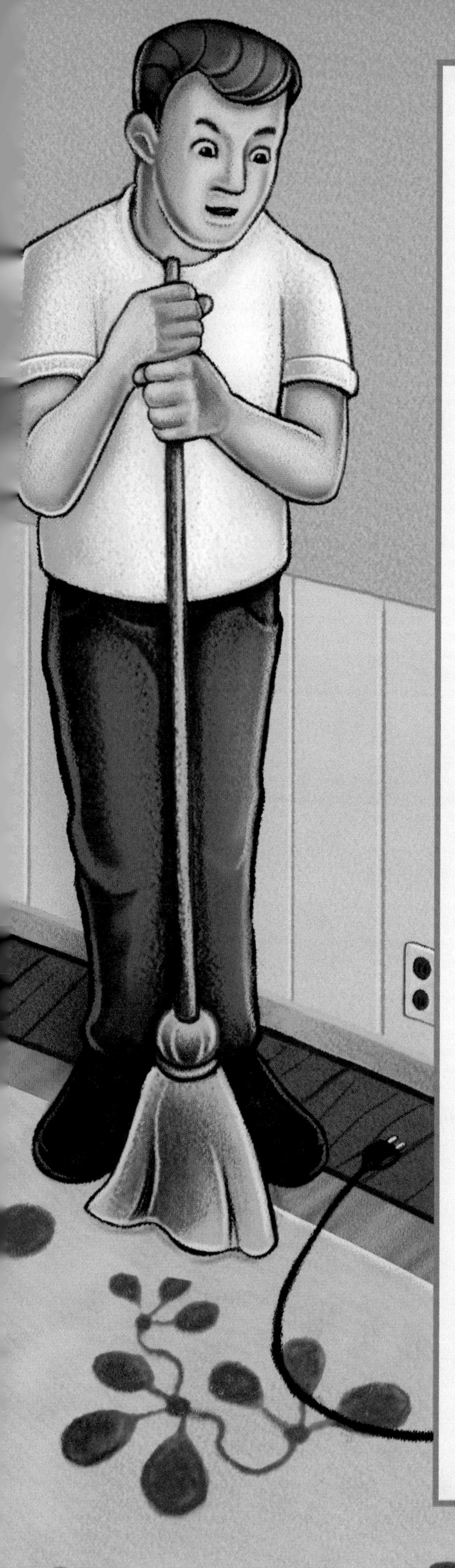

When we were all tired of that game, A. J. offered to teach Garth to play Crazy Eights and then Ty and DeeLee joined them in a game of Go Fish.

Nobody mentioned the TV. Nobody shot any rubber bands.

Later in the afternoon, the kids were all outside playing football. I was fast asleep until Mrs. Thomas came into the den with a broom and started sweeping. A minute later, Mr. Thomas entered.

"What are you doing, hon?"

"What does it look like? I'm sweeping. You know, all the snacking we do in here makes a real mess on the floor," she said.

"Beau's asleep?" her husband asked.

"Uh-huh."

Mr. Thomas walked over to his wife and took the broom away from her. "Then you sit down and rest a spell, hon. I'll sweep. Go on, don't argue."

Mrs. Thomas smiled and thanked him and sat down on the couch. Mr. Thomas swept all around the outside of the room.

Even behind the TV. Uh-oh.

When he got there, he stopped sweeping and leaned down.

"Well, I'll be," he muttered.

"What's wrong?" asked Mrs. Thomas.

"The TV is unplugged," he said. "It's unplugged!" He came out from behind the TV, plug in hand and a very puzzled look on his face.

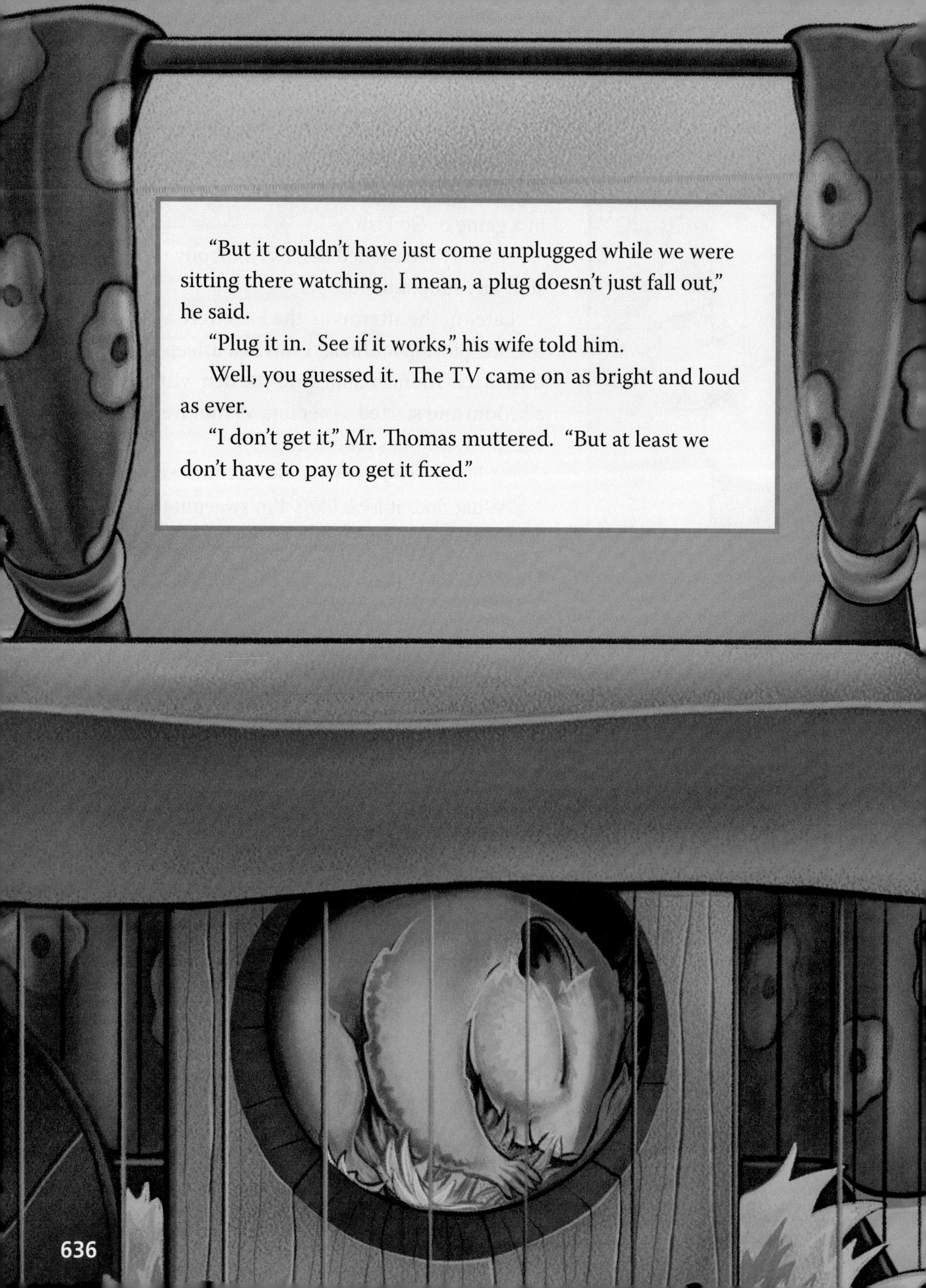

"But it couldn't have just come unplugged while we were sitting there watching. I mean, a plug doesn't just fall out," he said.

"Plug it in. See if it works," his wife told him.

Well, you guessed it. The TV came on as bright and loud as ever.

"I don't get it," Mr. Thomas muttered. "But at least we don't have to pay to get it fixed."

Mrs. Thomas stared at the screen for a few seconds, then glanced out the window at the kids playing happily outside.

"Charlie, what do you say we keep it unplugged for a couple more days?" she asked. "We just won't tell the kids."

Mr. Thomas grinned. Then he bent down and unplugged the TV. "Couldn't hurt," he said.

He put down the broom and sat on the couch near his wife and the two of them just sat there in the den, giggling like—well, like Stop-Giggling-Gail!

Suddenly, Mr. Thomas looked over at me.

"You don't mind a little peace and quiet, do you, Humphrey?"

"NO-NO-NO!" I squeaked. And I promptly fell asleep.

COMPREHENSION

Dig Deeper

How to Analyze the Text

Use these pages to learn about Theme, Point of View, and Idioms. Then read "The World According to Humphrey" again to apply what you learned.

Theme

"The World According to Humphrey" is a fantasy story. In it, a hamster helps a family learn an important lesson. The lesson the family learns over the course of the story is the story's **theme.**

Paying careful attention to the text evidence, including the characters' thoughts and actions, can help you figure out a story's theme. The ways in which characters grow and change also reveal the theme.

On page 637, Mr. and Mrs. Thomas decide not to plug in the TV. Why did they do this? What did the Thomas family learn about television viewing in the story?

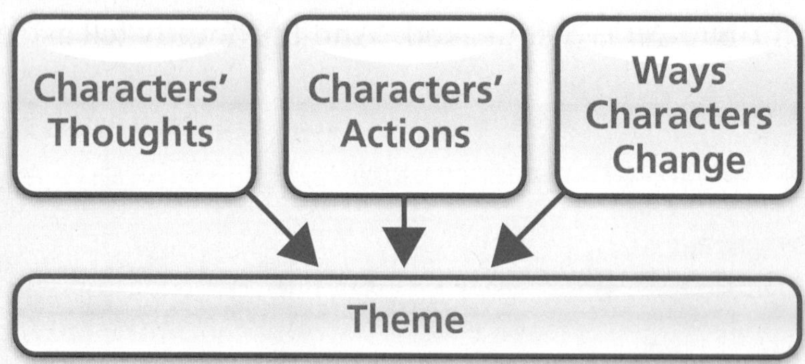

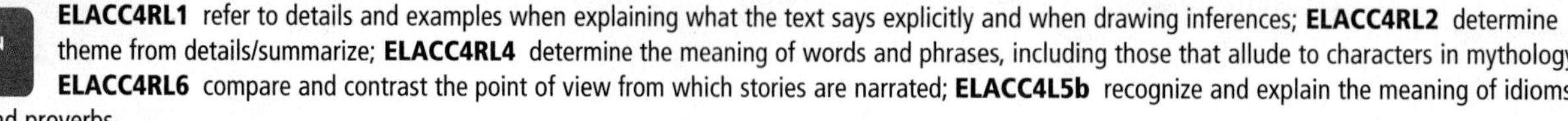

ELACC4RL1 refer to details and examples when explaining what the text says explicitly and when drawing inferences; **ELACC4RL2** determine theme from details/summarize; **ELACC4RL4** determine the meaning of words and phrases, including those that allude to characters in mythology; **ELACC4RL6** compare and contrast the point of view from which stories are narrated; **ELACC4L5b** recognize and explain the meaning of idioms, adages, and proverbs

Point of View

Point of view is the standpoint from which a story is written. When a story is told from the **first-person point of view,** the narrator is a character in the story. The narrator uses the pronoun *I* and tells about events and people the way he or she sees them. If an outside observer of the story events is the narrator, then the story is told from the **third-person point of view.** The narrator uses the words *he*, *she*, and *they* to tell about the characters.

Idioms

Authors often use **idioms,** phrases that mean something different from the literal meanings of the words themselves. In a story, if a character were to say she was "out of gas," what do you think she means? The literal meaning of this phrase is "out of fuel," but the expression can also mean "tired or lacking energy." Authors use idioms to say things in more imaginative ways.

Your Turn

RETURN TO THE ESSENTIAL QUESTION

Review the selection with a partner to prepare to discuss this question: *How can media be a distraction?* As you discuss, review the story's theme and other key ideas. Take turns commenting and using text evidence to contribute to the discussion.

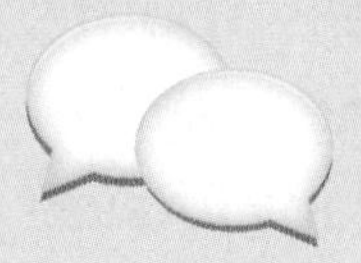

Classroom Conversation

Continue your discussion of "The World According to Humphrey" by answering these questions:

1. How does the author use humor in the story? Give examples.
2. Do you think Mr. and Mrs. Thomas should have told the children right away that the TV was working? Why or why not?
3. Which activities in the story would you like to do? Why?

THE WORLD ACCORDING TO A. J.

Retell a Scene Pretend you are A. J. Tell about the scene in which you and Garth clean the hamster cage and build a maze for Humphrey. Make sure to retell the story from A. J.'s point of view. Then discuss with a partner how A. J.'s telling of the scene is similar to and different from Humphrey's.

WRITE ABOUT READING

Response Do you think the lesson the Thomas family learns after Humphrey unplugs the TV is an important lesson? Write a paragraph expressing your opinion. Use text evidence from the story to support your ideas. End your paragraph with a concluding sentence that clearly restates your opinion.

Writing Tip

Be sure to describe in your paragraph the lesson that the family learns. Look for short, choppy sentences that you can combine.

COMMON CORE **ELACC4RL2** determine theme from details/summarize; **ELACC4RL6** compare and contrast the point of view from which stories are narrated; **ELACC4W1a** introduce a topic, state an opinion, and create an organizational structure; **ELACC4W1b** provide reasons supported by facts and details; **ELACC4W1d** provide a concluding statement or section; **ELACC4W9a** apply grade 4 Reading standards to literature; **ELACC4SL1c** pose and respond to questions and make comments that contribute to the discussion and link to others' remarks

Lesson 21

ADVERTISEMENTS

 GENRE

Advertisements, such as these posters, are short announcements designed to grab the attention of the public in order to get people to support an idea or action.

TEXT FOCUS

Persuasive techniques are the types of language and graphics an author uses to convince a reader to think or act in a certain way. How do the language and graphics work together to persuade the reader?

COMMON CORE **ELACC4RI7** interpret information presented visually, orally, or quantitatively; **ELACC4RI10** read and comprehend informational texts

How many ads do you see on an average day? Chances are you see hundreds of them. They may be on billboards, T-shirts, and buses, in stores and magazines, and, of course, on television.

Ads may be selling a product, a service, or an idea, but they all have one thing in common. Their goal is to influence you. Ads use a combination of techniques to do this. Often they introduce ideas not just with words but with pictures and colors.

Be aware of the persuasive techniques used in ads. Sometimes ads try to convince you to do things you were not aware of or even things that you didn't want to do at all! On the following pages are two posters for you to study. How do they try to influence your thoughts and behavior?

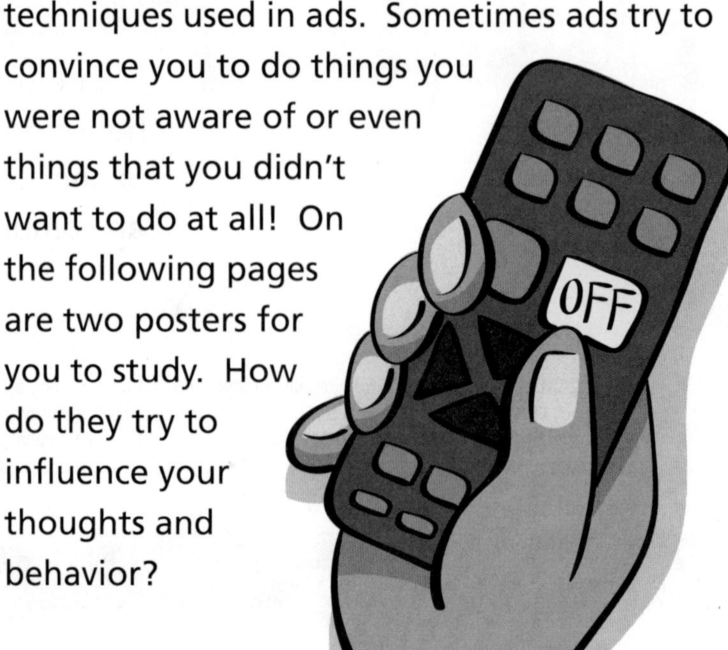

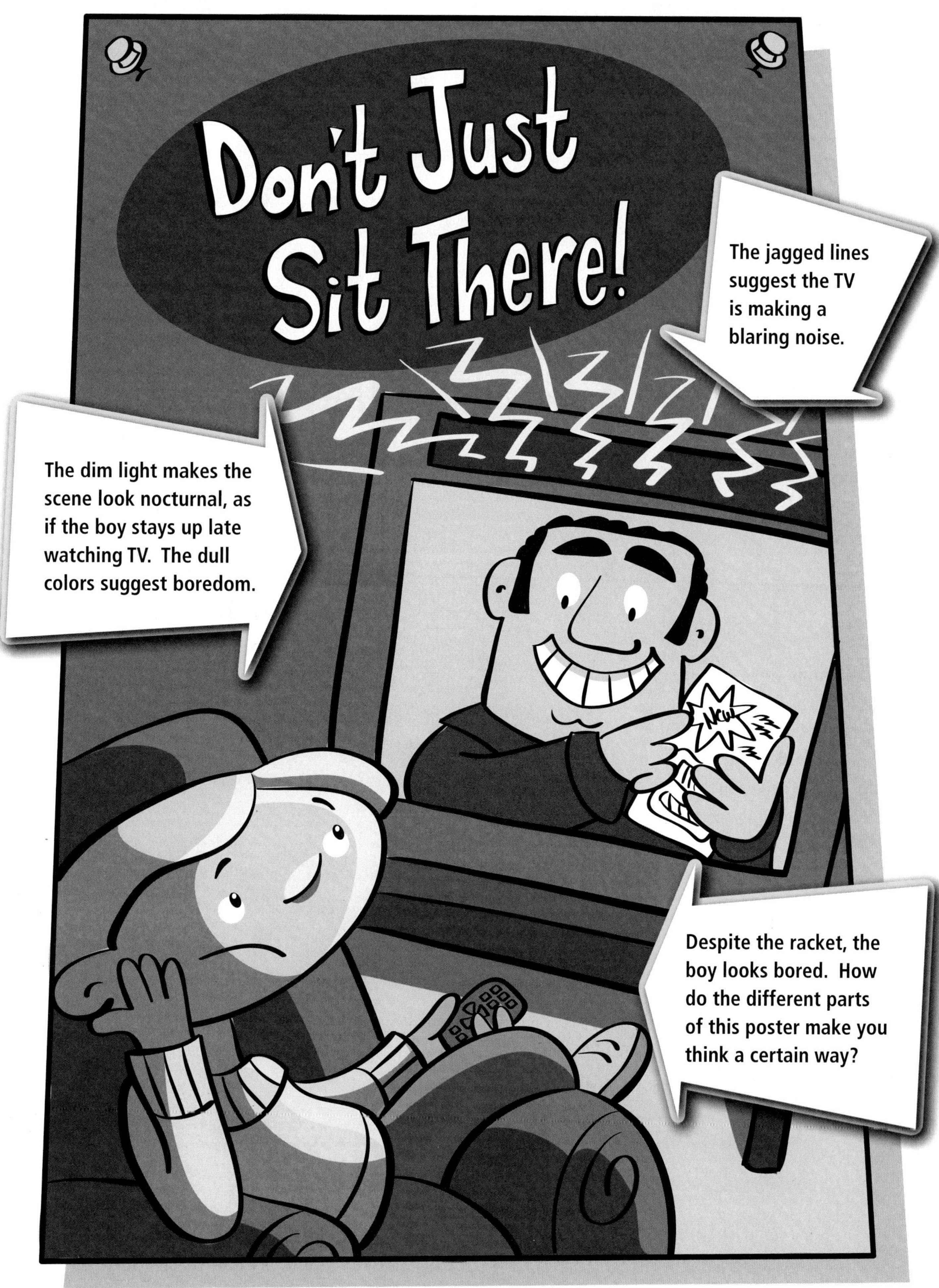
Don't Just Sit There!
The jagged lines suggest the TV is making a blaring noise.
The dim light makes the scene look nocturnal, as if the boy stays up late watching TV. The dull colors suggest boredom.
Despite the racket, the boy looks bored. How do the different parts of this poster make you think a certain way?

The colors in this poster are very bright. The colors can help turn ordinary activities into great feats of adventure.
The goal of this poster is to make you appreciate the joys of activity.
How do these children feel? How do you know?
The drawings show movement and look lively. They show that the effort of finding something else to do will be rewarding.
TV OFF! LIFE ON!
Five Fabulous Things to Do
Read a Book!
Ride a Bike!
Talk with a Friend!
Create!
Play a Game!

These posters want to influence you. They want you to turn off the television and promptly find something else to do. What positive and negative effects might they have on the audience?

Compare Texts

TEXT TO TEXT

Compare and Contrast Point of View What point of view is used to tell "The World According to Humphrey"? What point of view is used to tell "Hercules' Quest"? With a partner, discuss the difference between first- and third-person point of view. Discuss the effect of point of view on the stories. Use text evidence to support your ideas.

TEXT TO SELF

Express Your Opinion Would you rather watch TV in the evening or play games and tell stories like the Thomas family did when their TV was unplugged? Explain your thoughts in a paragraph. Support your reasons with facts and details from the story as well as your own experiences.

TEXT TO WORLD

Analyze Ads Find two print ads—one for a type of food and one for a game you enjoy. Then compare your ads with those of a partner. How do these ads try to convince you to buy or use their products? How do they make you feel? Discuss your responses with your partner.

COMMON CORE **ELACC4RL6** compare and contrast the point of view from which stories are narrated; **ELACC4RI1** refer to details and examples when explaining what the text says explicitly and when drawing inferences; **ELACC4W1a** introduce a topic, state an opinion, and create an organizational structure; **ELACC4W1b** provide reasons supported by facts and details; **ELACC4W10** write routinely over extended time frames and shorter time frames

ELACC4L1d order adjectives within sentences according to conventional patterns

Grammar

What Are Comparative and Superlative Adjectives? What Are Comparative and Superlative Adverbs? A **comparative adjective** compares two people, places, or things. Add *-er* to most adjectives to make their comparative forms. A **superlative adjective** compares more than two persons, places, or things. Add *-est* to most adjectives to make their superlative form. Remember to put adjectives in order.

adjective:	The kids played two annoying, noisy video games.
comparative adjective:	Next they played an even noisier one.
superlative adjective:	Then they played the noisiest video game of all.

Many **adverbs** also have comparative and superlative forms. To make the comparative form of most adverbs, put the word *more* in front of the adverb. To make the superlative form, use the word *most*.

adverb:	The family played Crazy Eights enthusiastically.
comparative adverb:	They told stories more enthusiastically.
superlative adverb:	The family played Pig the most enthusiastically of all.

Try This! **Work with a partner to identify whether each underlined word is an adjective or an adverb, and whether it is comparative or superlative.**

1. Our hamster is the smartest rodent in the world.
2. He nibbles his food the most happily of all our pets.
3. His fur is thicker than our mouse's fur was.
4. He watches us more frequently than the mouse did.

When you write, you can sometimes make a sentence clearer and more descriptive by adding a comparative or a superlative adjective or adverb.

Less Descriptive	More Descriptive
 Our new hamster is big.	 Our new hamster is bigger than our old hamster was.
 Our hamster runs quickly.	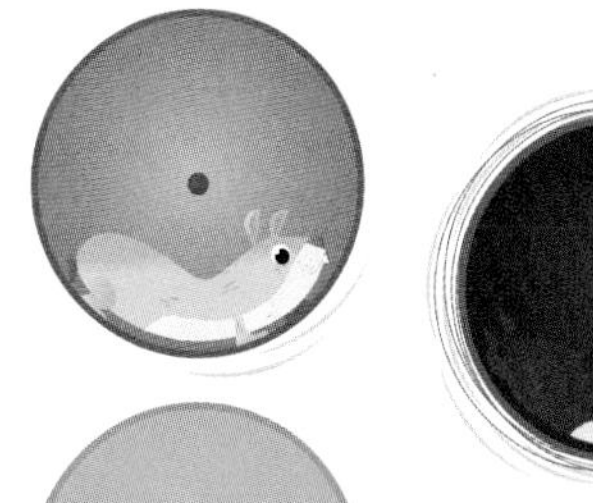 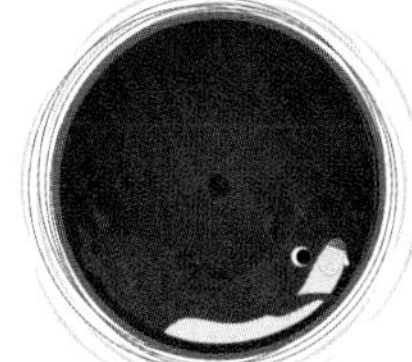 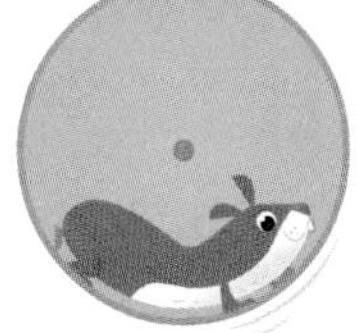 Our hamster runs the most quickly of all.

Connect Grammar to Writing

As you revise your summary, look for places to add more details and to make your sentences clearer by using comparative and superlative adjectives and adverbs. Remember to put two or more adjectives in the correct order.

ELACC4W2a introduce a topic and group related information/include formatting, illustrations, and multimedia; **ELACC4W2b** develop the topic with facts, definitions, details, quotations, or other information and examples; **ELACC4W2c** link ideas within categories of information using words and phrases; **ELACC4W9a** apply grade 4 Reading standards to literature

Informative Writing

Ideas "The World According to Humphrey" is a fiction story. A **summary** of a fiction story is a short retelling that informs readers about the story. A good story summary introduces the topic clearly. It describes the main characters and most important events. Examples from the story help explain the main events.

Amanda summarized part of "The World According to Humphrey." Later, she added a sentence to clearly introduce the topic. She took out unimportant details and added an example. She also added linking words and phrases to help connect ideas.

Writing Traits Checklist

Ideas
Did I develop the topic by including important details and examples?

Organization
Did I introduce the topic?

Sentence Fluency
Did I use words and phrases to link ideas?

Word Choice
Did I use my own words?

Voice
Did my summary sound interesting?

Conventions
Did I use comparative and superlative adjectives correctly?

Revised Draft

"The World According to Humphrey" is a fantasy story told by Humphrey, a hamster. Each weekend one of the students in Mrs. Brisbane's class takes Humphrey home. One weekend Humphrey goes home with A. J. ~~He has a little sister named DeeLee.~~ Humphrey doesn't like A. J.'s house because The television is on constantly. ~~One program is about animals.~~ The family is always watching TV, even during dinner.

Final Copy

Summary of "The World According to Humphrey"

by Amanda Farrell

"The World According to Humphrey" is a fantasy story told by Humphrey, a hamster. Each weekend one of the students in Mrs. Brisbane's class takes Humphrey home. One weekend Humphrey goes home with A. J. Humphrey doesn't like A. J.'s house because the television is on constantly. The family is always watching TV, even during dinner. Humphrey sneaks out of his cage and secretly unplugs the TV. The family is upset at first. Then they find other fun ways to spend time, for example, telling stories and playing card games. A. J.'s parents finally discover that the TV is unplugged. They keep it a secret because everyone seems much happier!

Reading as a Writer

Why did Amanda add examples? As you write your summary paragraph, make sure you include examples from the story that help readers understand your summary.

In my final summary, I added phrases to link information. I also included specific examples from the text to help explain the story's main events.

Lesson 22

I Could Do That! Esther Morris Gets Women the Vote

The Role of the Constitution

Vocabulary in Context

TARGET VOCABULARY

politics
intelligent
disorderly
approve
polls
legislature
amendment
candidates
informed
denied

Vocabulary Reader

Context Cards

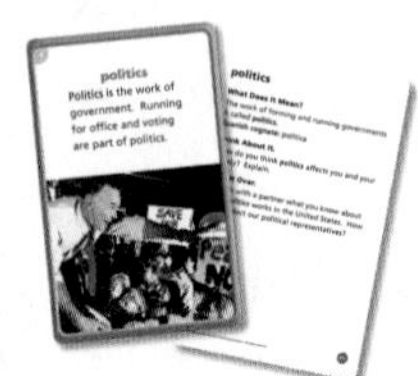

ELACC4L6 acquire/use vocabulary, including academic and domain-specific

1 politics

Politics is the work of government. Running for office and voting are part of politics.

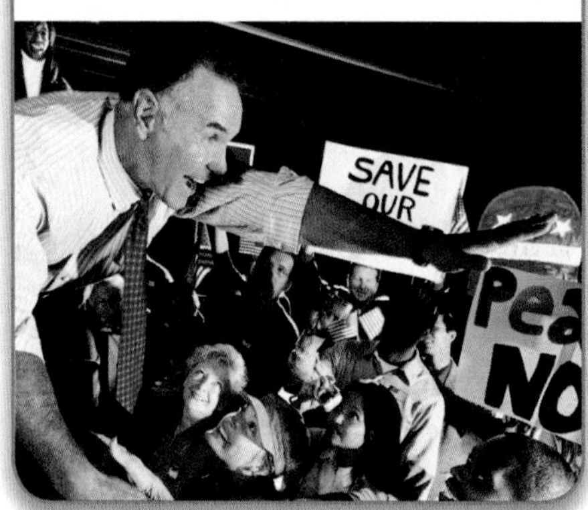

2 intelligent

Smart people make intelligent decisions when they vote.

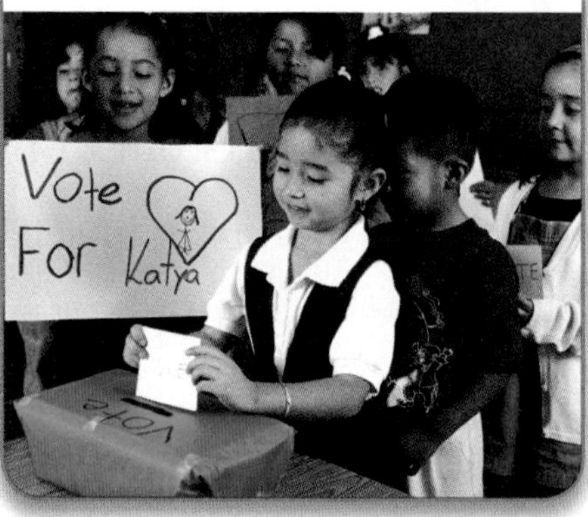

3 disorderly

Without a set of rules or laws, society might be disorderly, or disorganized.

4 approve

People who run for office hope voters will like and approve of them.

- Study each Context Card.
- Use a dictionary to help you pronounce these words.

5 polls

Voters go to the polls, or election locations, to place their votes on Election Day.

6 legislature

A legislature is a group of elected officials who make laws.

7 amendment

Only in 1920 did an amendment to the Constitution allow all U.S. women to vote.

8 candidates

Candidates, or people trying to get elected to office, sometimes have public debates.

9 informed

Informed voters have learned about issues in order to decide how they will vote.

10 denied

People should not be denied, or refused, meetings with their elected officials.

Read and Comprehend

TARGET SKILL

Cause and Effect As you read "I Could Do That!," note how some events lead to, or **cause,** other events. These events are called **effects.** Sometimes several causes have one effect. At other times, one cause may have several effects or start a whole series of events. A signal word such as *because*, *so*, or *when* may tell readers when an author has organized information by describing a cause-and-effect relationship. A cause or an effect could also be implied, or not stated directly in the text. A graphic organizer like the one below can be used to record text evidence of causes and effects.

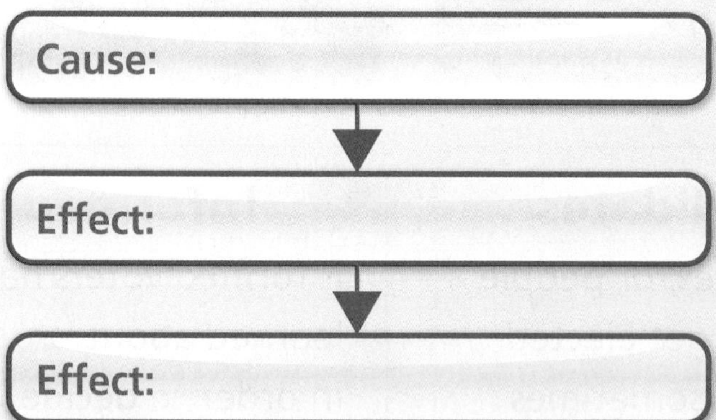

TARGET STRATEGY

Infer/Predict When you make **inferences,** you use text evidence to figure out what the author doesn't state directly. As you read, make inferences to help you understand the cause-and-effect relationships between events in "I Could Do That!"

ELACC4RI1 refer to details and examples when explaining what the text says explicitly and when drawing inferences; **ELACC4RI3** explain events/procedures/ideas/concepts in a text; **ELACC4RI5** describe the overall structure of a text or part of a text

PREVIEW THE TOPIC

Citizens' Rights

Civics is the study of government and the role individuals play in government. Citizens' rights are the things that people are allowed to do according to the law. For example, attending school is a right all citizens under the age of 18 have in the United States. Voting in elections is a right all adult citizens have.

"I Could Do That!" takes place during the 1800s. At this time, women were not allowed to vote in the United States. In the selection you'll meet Esther Morris, a woman who believed that all citizens should have the right to vote. You'll find out what she did to help women gain this right.

Lesson 22

ANCHOR TEXT

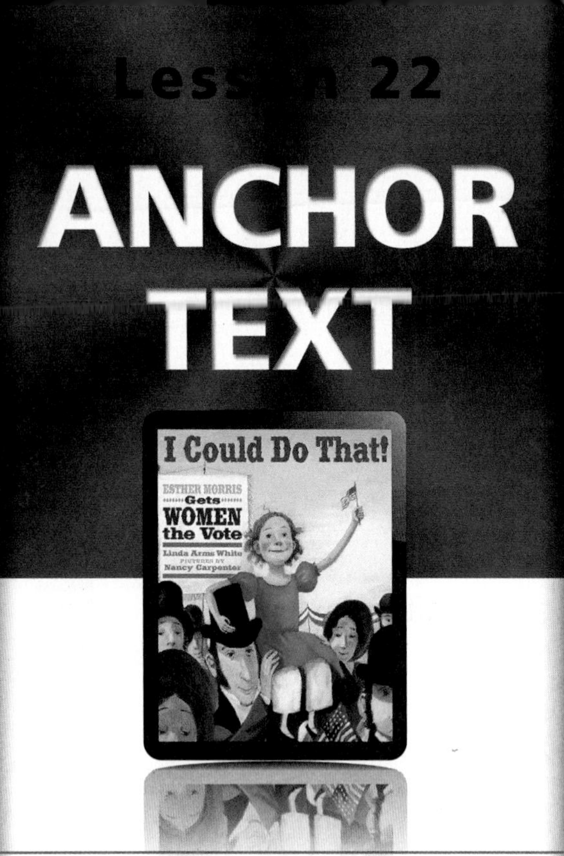

 TARGET SKILL

Cause and Effect Explain cause-and-effect relationships, or how one event leads to another. Find clue words that signal cause-and-effect relationships.

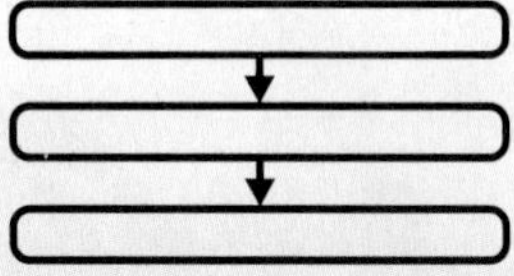

 GENRE

A **biography** tells about a person's life and is written by another person. As you read, look for:

- information about why the person is important
- opinions and personal judgments based on facts
- events told in time order

ELACC4RI3 explain events/procedures/ideas/concepts in a text; **ELACC4RI4** determine the meaning of general academic and domain-specific words and phrases; **ELACC4RI5** describe the overall structure of a text or part of a text; **ELACC4L4a** use context as a clue to the meaning of a word or phrase

Go Digital

MEET THE AUTHOR

Linda Arms White

Linda Arms White grew up in the wide open spaces of Wyoming, which is also known as the "Equality State." When she was a child, she heard inspiring stories about Esther Morris. As an adult, Linda began writing the day her youngest child was old enough to start school. Now her children are grown, and she has published many books for both children and adults, including *Too Many Pumpkins* and *Comes a Wind.*

MEET THE ILLUSTRATOR

Nancy Carpenter

Nancy Carpenter got her start in children's books when she handed in a cover drawing and the publisher spilled something on it. "So," she says, "I redid the job for free." The publisher soon gave her a whole book to illustrate. Ten more followed. She is the illustrator of *Apples to Oregon*, *Fannie in the Kitchen*, and *Abe Lincoln: The Boy Who Loved Books*.

I Could Do That!

Esther Morris Gets Women the Vote

Linda Arms White

Pictures by Nancy Carpenter

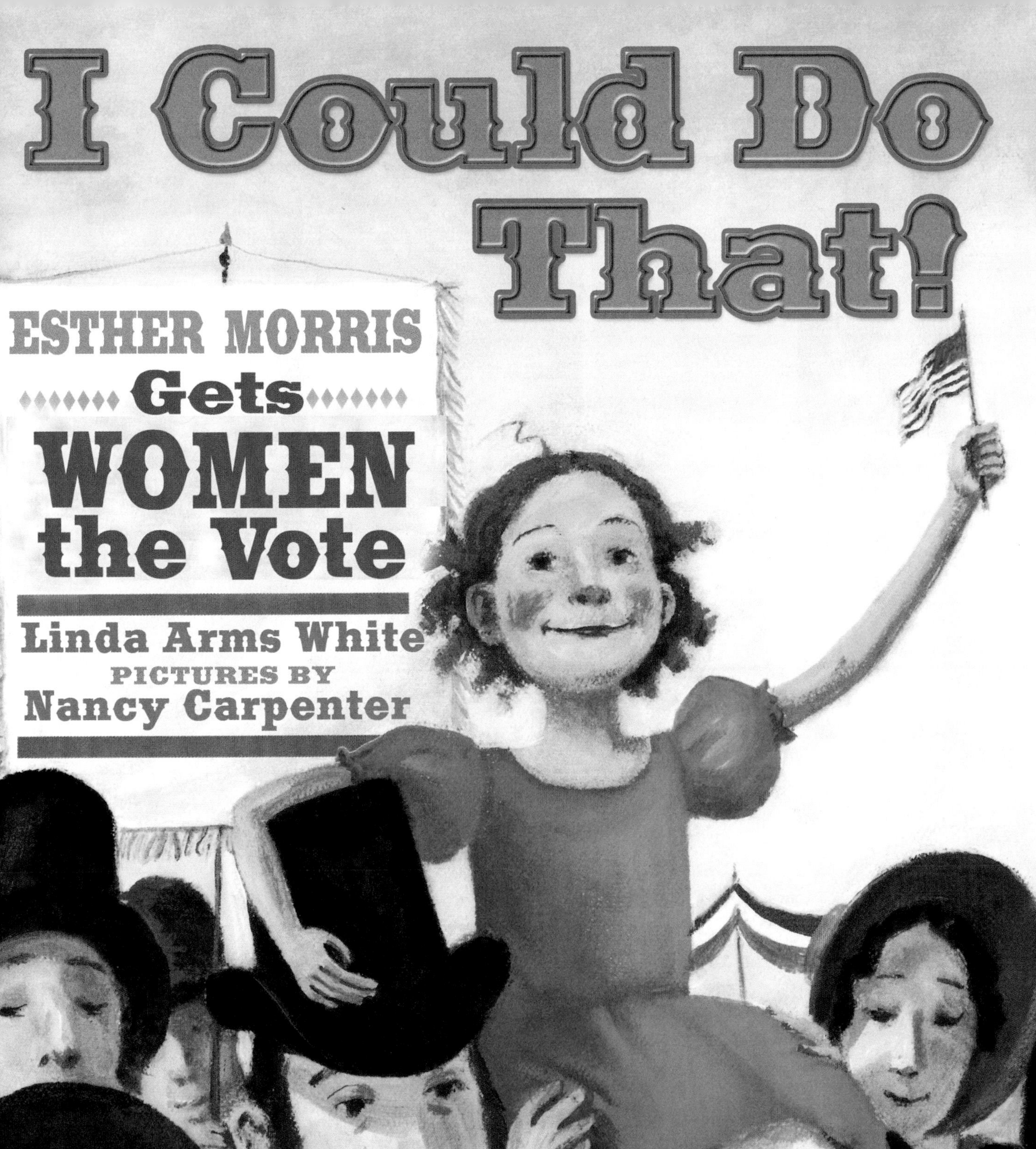

ESSENTIAL QUESTION

What causes change in a community?

In 1820, six-year-old Esther McQuigg studied her mother making tea. "I could do that," she said.

"Make tea?" asked Mama. "The older girls do that."

"But I want to learn," said Esther, and she did. She pumped water into the kettle and set it on the woodstove to boil. She scooped tea leaves into the teapot, then poured steaming water over them. Esther strained the tea into cups, one for her mother, one for herself.

As they sat near the window of their New York house, Esther saw men riding by in their best suits, some carrying flags.

"Where are those men going, Mama?" asked Esther.

"They are going to vote for the next president of the United States," Mama said.

"Will Papa vote?"

"Yes, Papa always votes."

"Will you vote, Mama?"

"No, dear, only men can vote."

When Esther was eight, she watched her mother sew a fine seam. The needle pulled thread in and out, in and out, tracking tiny, even stitches across the fabric. Esther felt her hands mimicking her mother's. "I could do that," she said. And she did.

She made clothes for her doll from scraps, and when her stitches became neat and straight, she sewed a shirt for Papa.

When Esther was eleven, her mother died, and for the first time she saw her father cry. He gathered his eleven children together. "I don't know what we'll do without your mama," he said. "I'm depending on each of you to be brave and to take care of one another." Esther, eighth of the eleven, cried, too. But then she said, "I can do that, Papa." And she did.

When Esther was nineteen, six feet tall, and on her own, she earned a living making dresses with leg-of-mutton sleeves for society ladies.

When the ladies wanted hats to match the dresses, Esther designed and made those, too. Soon, she thought of opening a millinery shop.

"You are much too young to run a business," she was told.

"I don't see why" was Esther's reply, and with that, she opened a hat shop in Owego, New York.

Esther started attending abolitionist meetings at her church. But a throng of people who believed in the right to own slaves threatened to stop the meetings even if they had to tear down the Baptist church where they were held.

"You can't do that," Esther said. "I'll stop anyone who tries."

When Esther was twenty-eight, she married Artemus Slack and, a few years later, had a son they called Archy.

But when Artemus died in an accident, Esther made a big decision. "I'm moving to Illinois," she told her friends. "I'll claim the land Artemus owned there and raise our son."

"You can't do that!" her friends cried. "Illinois is the very edge of civilization. It's full of dangerous people and wild animals."

"Yes," she said, "I can." And that was that.

In Illinois, she fought long and hard to claim Artemus's land, but was denied her inheritance because she was female. So Esther opened another hat shop.

Esther met and married John Morris, a merchant and immigrant from Poland, and in 1851 she gave birth to twin boys, Edward and Robert.

But John had a hard time making a living. So while Esther raised the children, cooked the meals, and washed the clothes, she helped earn the money, too.

When Esther was forty-six, she went with John to the presidential election polls and watched through the window while he voted.

"You know," she told him when he came out, "I could do that."

"Politics is the business of men, my dear," he said.

"Humph," said Esther. "It's our country, too."

When war broke out between the Northern and Southern states, Esther was proud that Archy joined the victorious fight of the North to end slavery. Soon after, an amendment to the Constitution granted African American men all rights of citizenship, including the right to vote.

When Esther heard Susan B. Anthony speaking out about women's rights, Esther began to hope that someday women might vote, too.

ANALYZE THE TEXT

Conclusions and Generalizations
What does Esther think of the place of women in the world? How do you know?

In 1869, when Esther was fifty-five, she and her eighteen-year-old sons moved to the newly formed Wyoming Territory, where John and Archy, who'd gone there the year before, waited.

Esther and the boys traveled by train across miles of prairie, then by stage over rocky hills to South Pass City, a dusty, hurriedly built town where gold had been found. Most of the two thousand people who lived there were rowdy young men.

The Morrises moved their belongings into a small log cabin, and South Pass City became home. John tried his hand at another business.

Archy bought a printing press and started a newspaper.

Esther opened another hat shop.

But with six men to every woman, there was always a need for someone to nurse the sick and wounded, sew clothes, help deliver babies, and give motherly advice to the few young women in town. "I could do that," Esther said.

And she did.

One day, Esther read a proclamation tacked to a wall: ALL MALE CITIZENS 21 AND OLDER ARE CALLED TO VOTE IN THE FIRST TERRITORIAL ELECTIONS. Esther looked around at the disorderly young men.

"It's time I did that," she said.

When Esther's sons watched her march toward home, they knew it was more likely that things were about to change than that things would stay the same.

Esther invited the two men running for the territorial legislature to her house to speak to the citizens. Then she sent out invitations to the most influential people in the territory: "Come for tea, and talk to the candidates."

She scrubbed her tiny home from top to bottom, washed the curtains, and ironed her best dress.

When the candidates and guests arrived, Esther served them tea. "One thing I like about Wyoming," she said, "is how everyone is important. It takes all of us to run the town, women as well as men."

"Yes," her guests agreed.

"And it's a place where people aren't afraid to try new things."

Her guests agreed again.

Esther smiled. She turned to the candidates. "Then, would you, if elected, introduce a bill in the legislature that would allow women to vote?"

Suddenly, in that tiny room full of people, not a sound was heard.

Finally, Colonel William Bright spoke. "Mrs. Morris, my wife would like to vote, too. She is intelligent and well educated. Truth be told, she would be a more informed voter than I. If I am elected, I will introduce that bill."

Not wanting to be outdone, the other candidate, Herman Nickerson, also agreed.

Applause broke out in that tiny cabin, and Esther dropped to her chair. "Thank you," she said.

People warned her that once the bill was introduced, the men of the legislature would have to approve it. And the governor would have to sign it. This had never happened anywhere. Why did she think it could happen here?

But Esther had seen that things that were not likely to happen, happened every day. She wrote letters and visited legislators to make sure this bill would happen, too.

And it did. On December 10, 1869, Governor John Campbell signed this bill into law! WYOMING WOMEN GOT THE VOTE!

Yee-haw!
Yippee!
Hurrah!
Hurrah!

ANALYZE THE TEXT

Domain-Specific Vocabulary What words related to government and citizenship are on pages 662–663? What do they mean?

Women across the country rejoiced for the women of Wyoming.

But some people didn't like it. Only eight days later, Judge James Stillman, the county's justice of the peace, turned in his resignation. He refused to administer justice in a place where women helped make the laws.

Word went out that a new justice of the peace was needed.

Esther's boys turned to her.

"Mama, you could do that," they said.

And so she applied.

Archy, then clerk of the court, proudly swore his mother in, making Judge Esther Morris the first woman in the country to hold public office.

But Judge Stillman refused to turn over the official court docket to Esther.

"Never mind," she said. "Archy, will you please go to the Mercantile and buy me a ledger? I'll start my own docket."

And, of course, she did.

On September 6, 1870, one year after her tea party, Judge Esther Morris put on her best dress and walked with her husband, John, and her sons down the dusty street to the polling place. She would be one of a thousand Wyoming women voting that day, the first ever given that right permanently by any governing body in the United States.

As they walked, John, who still didn't think women should vote, tried to coach her on which candidates and issues to vote for.

Esther held up her hand.

"I can do this," she said.

And she did.

ANALYZE THE TEXT

Cause and Effect What events led to Esther Morris becoming the first woman in the country to hold public office? What details from the text tell you this?

COMPREHENSION

Dig Deeper

How to Analyze the Text

Use these pages to learn about Cause and Effect, Conclusions and Generalizations, and Domain-Specific Vocabulary. Then read "I Could Do That!" again to apply what you learned.

Cause and Effect

"I Could Do That!" describes the important things Esther Morris did during her life. The biography is organized by **cause-and-effect** relationships. A cause-and-effect relationship exists when one event leads to another event. Sometimes several causes have one effect. At other times a single cause has many effects. **Signal words** such as *because*, *so*, or *when* may help you recognize a cause-and-effect relationship. A cause or an effect can also be implied, or not stated directly in the text.

On page 659 of "I Could Do That!," the author describes several cause-and-effect relationships. For example, Esther's husband, Artemus, dies in an accident. What are the effects of this event? Use text evidence in your answer.

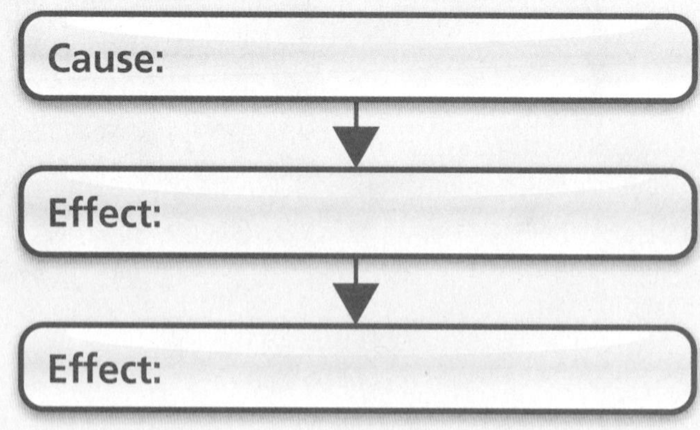

ELACC4RI1 refer to details and examples when explaining what the text says explicitly and when drawing inferences; **ELACC4RI3** explain events/procedures/ideas/concepts in a text; **ELACC4RI4** determine the meaning of general academic and domain-specific words and phrases; **ELACC4RI5** describe the overall structure of a text or part of a text; **ELACC4L4a** use context as a clue to the meaning of a word or phrase; **ELACC4L4c** consult reference materials, both print and digital, to find pronunciation and determine or clarify meaning

Conclusions and Generalizations

When Esther was six and wanted to make tea, Mama said, "The older girls do that." Mama's statement was a **generalization,** a **conclusion** that is often true but not always. During the 1800s, people made many unfair generalizations about what women could and couldn't do. Esther had a different view. You can evaluate a generalization by asking yourself if the statement is always true, sometimes true, or never true.

Domain-Specific Vocabulary

"I Could Do That!" focuses on the rights of women during the 1800s and one woman's efforts to change things. The author uses many words that are important in the **domain** of civics. These words include *citizenship* and *proclamation*. When you come to a **domain-specific word** that you do not know, look for context clues in the text or look it up in a print or an online dictionary.

Your Turn

RETURN TO THE ESSENTIAL QUESTION

Review the selection with a partner to prepare to discuss this question: *What causes change in a community?* Take turns using text evidence and examples from your experience to support your response. Answer questions your partner has and comment on his or her remarks.

Classroom Conversation

Continue your discussion of "I Could Do That!" by explaining your answers to these questions:

1. While Esther was growing up, how did she show that she was an independent thinker?
2. According to the text, why didn't Esther accept the idea that "politics is the business of men"?
3. What actions can individuals take to help citizens' rights?

ESTHER DID IT!

Make a Timeline Think about the many important things Esther did in her life. With a partner, create a timeline that shows her accomplishments, as described in "I Could Do That!" Make sure to include details about the people, places, and events from the text.

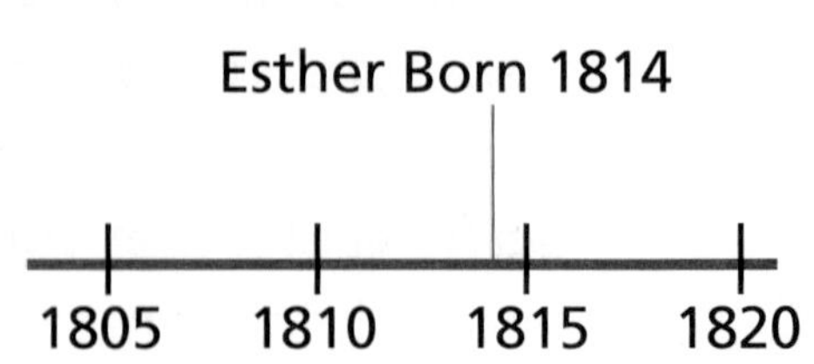

WRITE ABOUT READING

Response Do you think Esther improved her community of South Pass City, Wyoming? If so, how did she improve it? Write a paragraph that states your opinion. Support your opinion with facts and details from the text.

Writing Tip

When you write your response, use domain-specific vocabulary to make your meaning clearer. Include a concluding statement in your paragraph.

ELACC4RI1 refer to details and examples from the text when explaining what the text says explicitly and when drawing inferences; **ELACC4RI3** explain events/procedures/ideas/concepts in a text; **ELACC4W1b** provide reasons supported by facts and details; **ELACC4W1d** provide a concluding statement or section; **ELACC4W9b** apply grade 4 Reading standards to informational texts; **ELACC4SL1a** come to discussions prepared/explicitly draw on preparation and other information about the topic

Lesson 22

INFORMATIONAL TEXT

GENRE

Informational text, such as this article, gives information about a topic. Informational text usually includes photographs and other visuals, such as charts and graphs.

TEXT FOCUS

Graphs show numerical information in a visual format that allows comparisons to be made. Two common types of graphs are bar graphs and line graphs. What information does the bar graph in this article show?

ELACC4RI7 interpret information presented visually, orally, or quantitatively; **ELACC4RI10** read and comprehend informational texts

The Role of the Constitution

by Carl DeSoto

The Constitution

A constitution is a plan of government. A government is a system of leaders and laws by which a community, state, or nation is governed. The United States Constitution sets up the national government. It says that all citizens should be treated fairly by government. It says that their freedom should be protected.

The United States Constitution

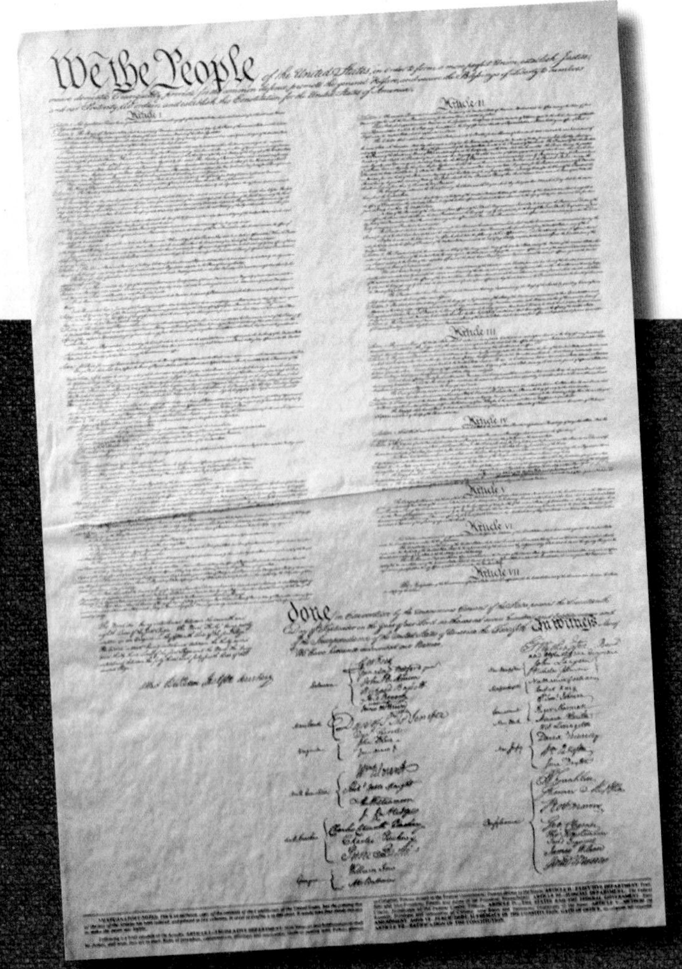

Go Digital

Each state has a state constitution that sets up the government for that state. A state constitution must obey the United States Constitution. It cannot take away rights granted by the United States Constitution.

The Constitution sets up the United States government as a democracy, which means that the people elect leaders to govern them. The government gets its power from the people, so it is a republic. Citizens elect leaders to represent them in government.

The Three Branches

The United States Constitution organizes the national government into three branches, or parts. These three branches are the legislative branch, the executive branch, and the judicial branch. Likewise, each state has a government divided into these three branches. The Constitution tells what each branch of the government can and cannot do.

The signing of the Constitution

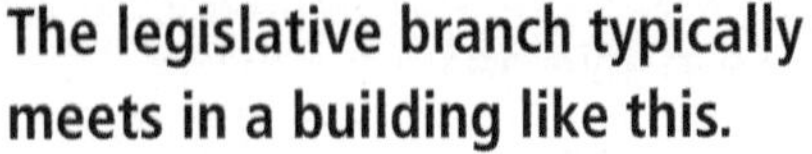
The legislative branch typically meets in a building like this.

The Legislative Branch

The legislative branch of government makes laws that the entire nation must follow. Congress is the main body of the legislative branch. Congress is made up of two parts: the Senate and the House of Representatives. The Senate has two senators elected from each state—one hundred in all. The number of representatives elected from each state depends on the state's population. The more residents a state has, the more representatives it is allowed to elect to the House of Representatives. All states, except Nebraska, also have a legislative branch made up of a state senate and a house of representatives. Nebraska has just one house.

The Executive Branch

The executive branch carries out the laws made by Congress. The President of the United States is the leader of the executive branch. When the President takes office, he or she promises to preserve, protect, and defend the Constitution of the United States. At the state level, the leader of the executive branch is the governor.

The Judicial Branch

The judicial branch is made up of the Supreme Court as well as other courts. The Supreme Court is the nation's highest court. It is made up of nine judges, called justices. The justices are chosen by the President and approved by Congress. The justices make sure laws agree with the Constitution and are carried out fairly. Similarly, each state has a judicial branch made up of a state supreme court and various other courts.

Branches of the Federal Government		
Legislative Branch	**Executive Branch**	**Judicial Branch**
• Makes national laws • Made up of Senate and House of Representatives	• Enforces national laws • Led by President of the United States	• Makes sure laws agree with the Constitution • Made up of Supreme Court and other courts

Rights and Freedoms

The United States Constitution provides rights and freedoms for American citizens. The Bill of Rights is a part of the Constitution. It lists the many rights and freedoms of American citizens. These freedoms include freedom of the press, freedom of speech, and freedom of religion. It also protects Americans accused of crimes by giving them the right to a trial by jury.

One important right is the right to choose leaders and make decisions by majority rule. Under the Constitution, each citizen who is at least 18 years old gets one vote in an election. The winner is the person or idea that gets the most votes.

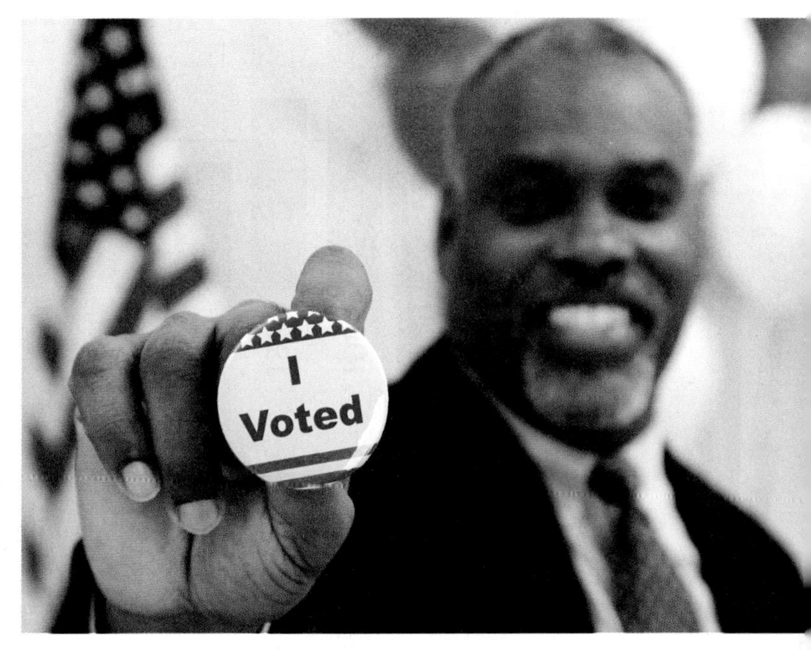

Every American citizen that is at least 18 years old has the right to vote.

Duties of Citizens

Americans' rights are balanced by duties. For example, the right to choose leaders is balanced by the duty to vote. The right to a jury trial is balanced by the duty to serve on a jury.

The government provides services for American citizens. It maintains the military to protect the country in times of war. It helps people rebuild their communities after natural disasters. In return, citizens have the duty to pay taxes. The money from taxes pays for the costs of running the government. The Constitution gives the government the right to collect taxes.

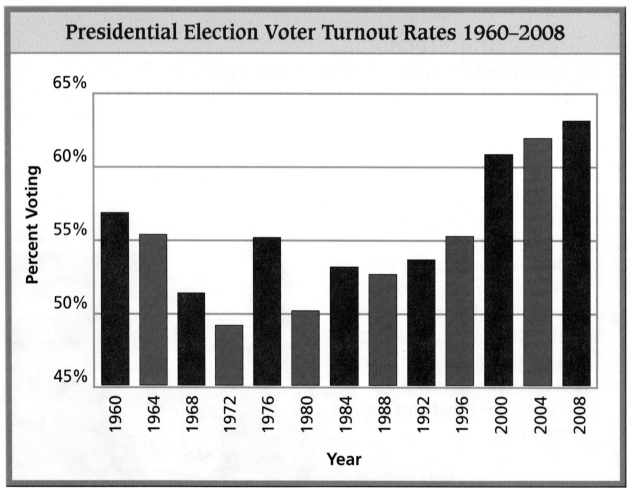

Presidential Election Voter Turnout Rates 1960–2008

Percent Voting

65%
60%
55%
50%
45%

1960 1964 1968 1972 1976 1980 1984 1988 1992 1996 2000 2004 2008

Year

The graph shows the percentage of people eligible to vote who actually voted in presidential elections from 1960 to 2008. In most years, more than half of eligible voters did their duty by voting to elect the President. In recent years, more than 60% of eligible voters cast ballots, or voted.

Compare Texts

TEXT TO TEXT

Compare Informational Texts Talk with a partner about how "The Role of the Constitution" relates to "I Could Do That!" Discuss these questions: *How did Esther Morris affect the constitution of Wyoming? How did she change the role that women played in Wyoming?* Use text evidence to support your answers during your discussion with your partner.

TEXT TO SELF

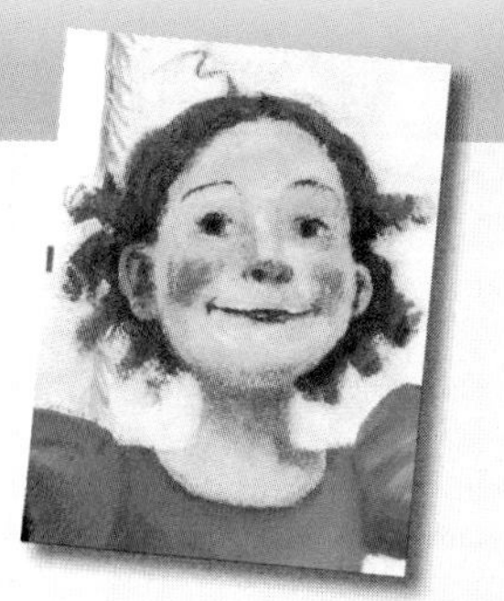

Write a Letter Imagine that you could talk to Esther Morris. What would you say to her? Write your thoughts in a short letter. Be sure to include a salutation, the date, and a closing.

TEXT TO WORLD

Connect to Social Studies Esther Morris worked hard to get women the right to vote because she thought it was very important. Work with a partner to research other elections that happen in your community and state. What is the role of the individual voter in these elections?

ELACC4RI9 integrate information from two texts on the same topic; **ELACC4W8** recall information from experiences or gather information from print and digital sources/take notes, categorize information, and provide a list of sources; **ELACC4W7** conduct short research projects that build knowledge through investigation; **ELACC4W10** write routinely over extended time frames and shorter time frames

Grammar

What Is a Negative? A word that makes a sentence mean "no" is called a **negative.** The words *no, no one, nobody, none, nothing, nowhere,* and *never* are negatives. The word *not* and contractions made with *not* are also negatives. Never use two negatives together in a sentence.

Incorrect	Correct
There weren't no states in which women could vote.	There weren't any states in which women could vote. *OR* There were no states in which women could vote.
Esther Morris wouldn't never give up hope.	Esther Morris wouldn't ever give up hope. *OR* Esther Morris would never give up hope.

Try This! **Work with a partner to read each sentence below and tell whether it has one or two negatives in it. If a sentence has two negatives, correct it by removing one negative and rephrasing the sentence if necessary. Say each corrected sentence aloud.**

1. Long ago, women couldn't own no property.
2. They generally weren't able to borrow money.
3. Many men didn't want nothing to change.
4. Many women were not happy with the situation.

Sometimes you can join a verb and the word *not* to make a contraction. As you edit your writing, make sure that you have not used two negatives in one sentence.

Sentence with Double Negative	Corrected Sentence
My aunt Leona hasn't let no one hold her back.	My aunt Leona hasn't let anyone hold her back.
No challenge isn't too big for her to accept.	No challenge is too big for her to accept.

Connect Grammar to Writing

As you edit your explanation, look for negatives. If you find two negatives in any sentence, rewrite the sentence to eliminate the double negative.

ELACC4W2a introduce a topic and group related information/include formatting, illustrations, and multimedia; ELACC4W2c link ideas within categories of information using words and phrases; ELACC4W2d use precise language and domain-specific vocabulary

Informative Writing

Sentence Fluency The biography "I Could Do That!" explains important events from Esther Morris's life. A good **explanation** clearly introduces the topic, puts related facts together, and uses **transition words** such as *for example*, *also*, and *because* to link ideas. As you revise your explanation, make sure you have included these elements.

Joel explained what led Esther Morris to open her first hat shop. He edited the introduction to make the topic clearer. Then he deleted a sentence that was out of place. Later, he added some transition words to link ideas and changed a word to a precise word.

Revised Draft

The events that led Esther Morris to open a hat shop began when she was only eight. ~~Esther Morris opened a hat shop. Her shop was successful.~~ Because Esther's mother was ~~good~~ skilled at sewing, Esther loved to watch her make clothes for the family. She wanted to try it herself. She began to practice sewing by making doll clothes. As a result, she learned to sew very well. ~~She practiced~~ Another way she practiced sewing was by making her father's shirts.

Writing Traits Checklist

- **Ideas** Did I use facts to explain?
- **Organization** Are the events or ideas in a logical order?
- **Word Choice** Did I use precise words and phrases?
- **Voice** Did I sound interested in the topic?
- **Sentence Fluency** Did I link my ideas with words and phrases?
- **Conventions** Did I use correct spelling, grammar, and mechanics?

Final Copy

A Hat Shop for Esther

by Joel Silver

The events that led Esther Morris to open a hat shop began when she was only eight. Because Esther's mother was skilled at sewing, Esther loved to watch her make clothes for the family. She wanted to try it herself. She began to practice sewing by making doll clothes. As a result, she learned to sew very well. Another way she practiced sewing was by making her father's shirts.

When Esther was nineteen, she earned money by making fancy dresses. Her wealthy customers wanted hats to go with their dresses, so Esther began making hats, too. This gave her a wonderful idea. Why not open a hat shop? Because of Esther's determination and customer demand, her hat shop was a huge success!

Reading as a Writer

Joel inserted transition words into several sentences to connect his ideas. What transition words can you add to your explanation to link ideas more clearly?

In my final paper, I linked my ideas with transition words. I used the precise word *skilled* instead of *good*. I was also careful to not use double negatives.

Lesson 23

The Ever-Living Tree: The Life and Times of a Coast Redwood

Towering Trees

☑ TARGET VOCABULARY

resources
dense
evaporate
shallow
moisture
civilized
continent
opportunities
customs
independent

Vocabulary Reader

Context Cards

ELACC4L6 acquire/use vocabulary, including academic and domain-specific

Vocabulary in Context

1 resources

Trees and forests are among the earth's valuable resources, or supplies.

2 dense

Roots grow from a banyan tree's branches like a thick, dense forest.

3 evaporate

The broad leaves of some trees let water evaporate easily into the air.

4 shallow

Some trees have shallow roots. The roots don't go deep into the ground.

- Study each Context Card.
- Use context clues to determine the meanings of these words.

5 moisture

Over half the world's species live in rain forests, helped by the moisture, or wetness.

6 civilized

Most civilized, or advanced, cities set aside places for trees to grow.

7 continent

The continent of North America has the world's tallest trees, coast redwoods.

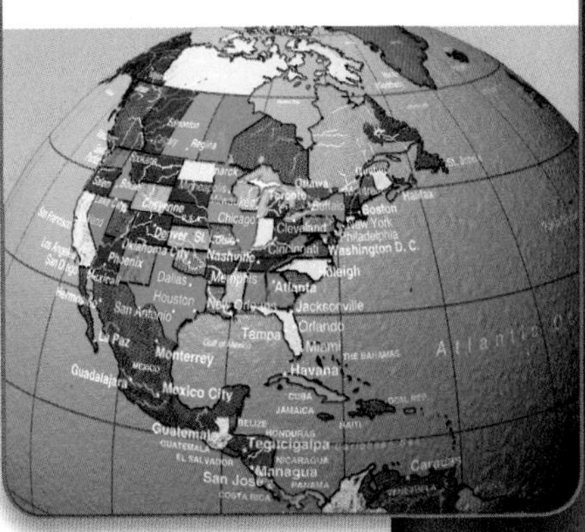

8 opportunities

A forest offers many opportunities, or chances, for a career or volunteer work.

9 customs

Some human customs, such as the practice of clearing trees, are ruining many forests.

10 independent

People cannot be independent from trees. We need the oxygen trees provide.

Read and Comprehend

TARGET SKILL

Text and Graphic Features As you read "The Ever-Living Tree," notice the **text and graphic features** in the selection. These features include icons, timelines, maps, diagrams, and italic type. A graphic feature often adds to information in the text. When you come to a text or graphic feature, ask yourself, *How does this help me understand the text? How does it add to my understanding of the topic?* Use a graphic organizer like the one below to list each text and graphic feature and tell what information it gives.

Text or Graphic Feature	Page Number	Information
•	•	•
•	•	•
•	•	•

TARGET STRATEGY

Monitor/Clarify "The Ever-Living Tree" covers a number of centuries and switches between natural and human history. As you read, **monitor** your comprehension of the events and the passage of time in the selection. If you don't understand something, pause to **clarify,** or clear up your confusion.

COMMON CORE **ELACC4RI7** interpret information presented visually, orally, or quantitatively; **ELACC4RF4c** use context to confirm or self-correct word recognition and understanding

PREVIEW THE TOPIC

Life Cycles

Every living thing has a life cycle. The life cycle begins with birth and ends with death. For most trees, life begins when a seed splits apart and a seedling, or tiny tree, begins to grow.

"The Ever-Living Tree" tells the story of a coast redwood's life cycle. Coast redwoods, native to California, are among earth's oldest and tallest living things. As you read this selection, you'll find out how long a coast redwood can live and what it must survive in order to become a "living giant."

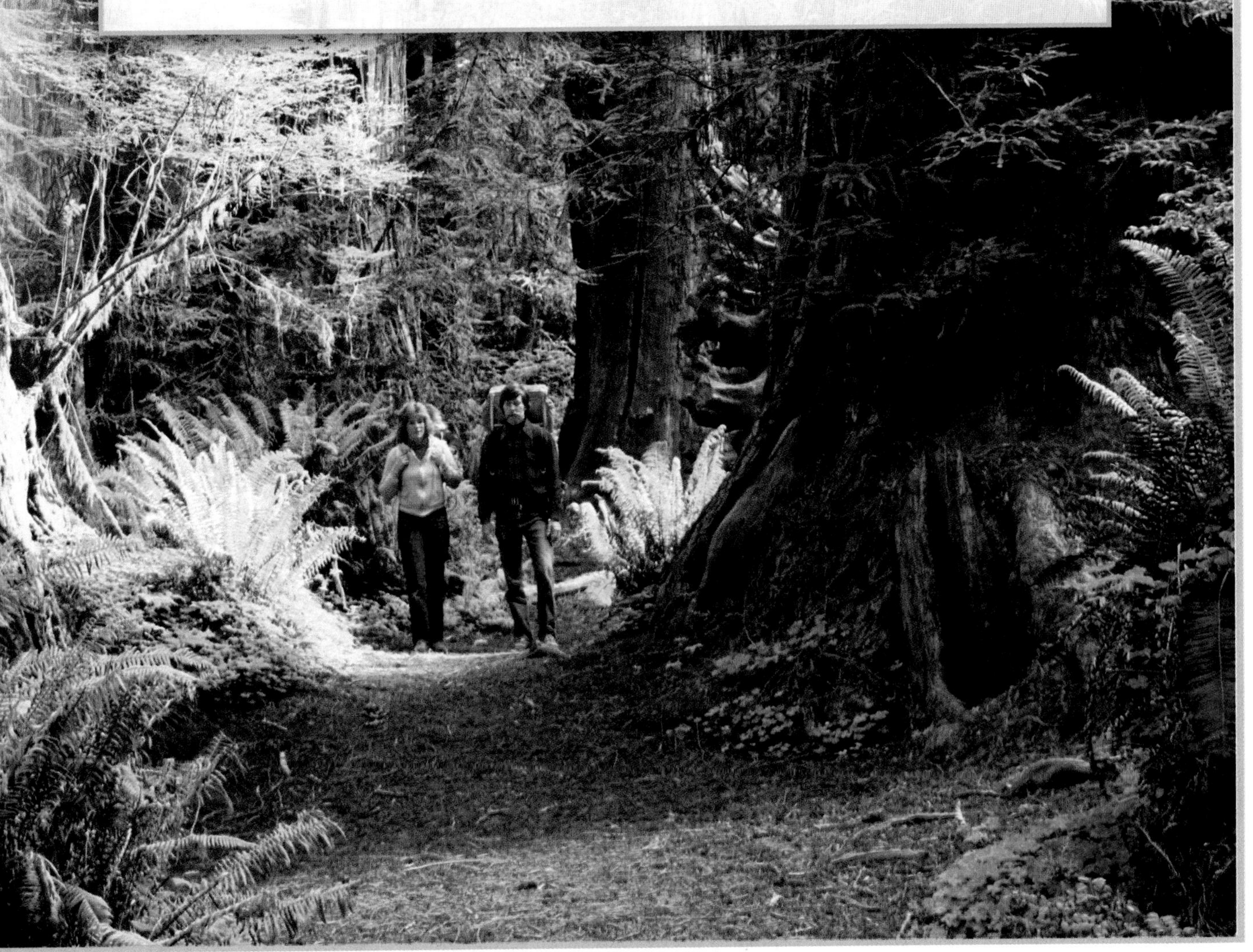

Lesson 23

ANCHOR TEXT

TARGET SKILL

Text and Graphic Features
Examine how text features help you understand and locate information.

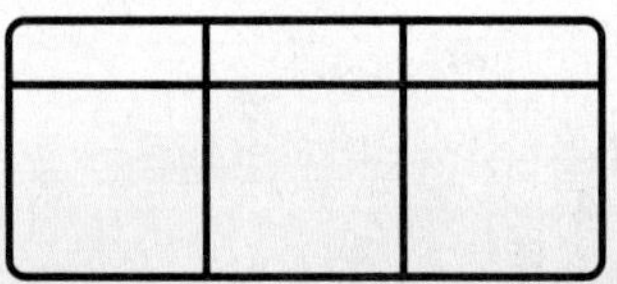

GENRE

Informational text gives facts and examples about a topic. As you read, look for:

- headings that begin sections of related information
- graphics to help explain the topic, such as maps, diagrams, charts, or icons
- text structure—the ways the ideas and information are organized

ELACC4RI5 describe the overall structure of a text or part of a text; **ELACC4RI7** interpret information presented visually, orally, or quantitatively

 Go Digital

MEET THE AUTHOR

Linda Vieira

Linda Vieira uses writing as a way to understand something. She "prewrites" in her head at dawn each morning while walking the dog. What if she can't begin writing immediately? "I trust myself and let the thinking happen for as long as it takes before starting," says Vieira.

MEET THE ILLUSTRATOR

Christopher Canyon

Can only talented people become artists? This illustrator says no. He believes working hard at your art is much more important. "Some people are naturally talented, but even if you are not, you should *never give up* on the things that you love or the dreams that you have."

The Ever-Living Tree

The Life and Times of a Coast Redwood

by Linda Vieira
illustrated by Christopher Canyon

ESSENTIAL QUESTION

How do forests and trees show change?

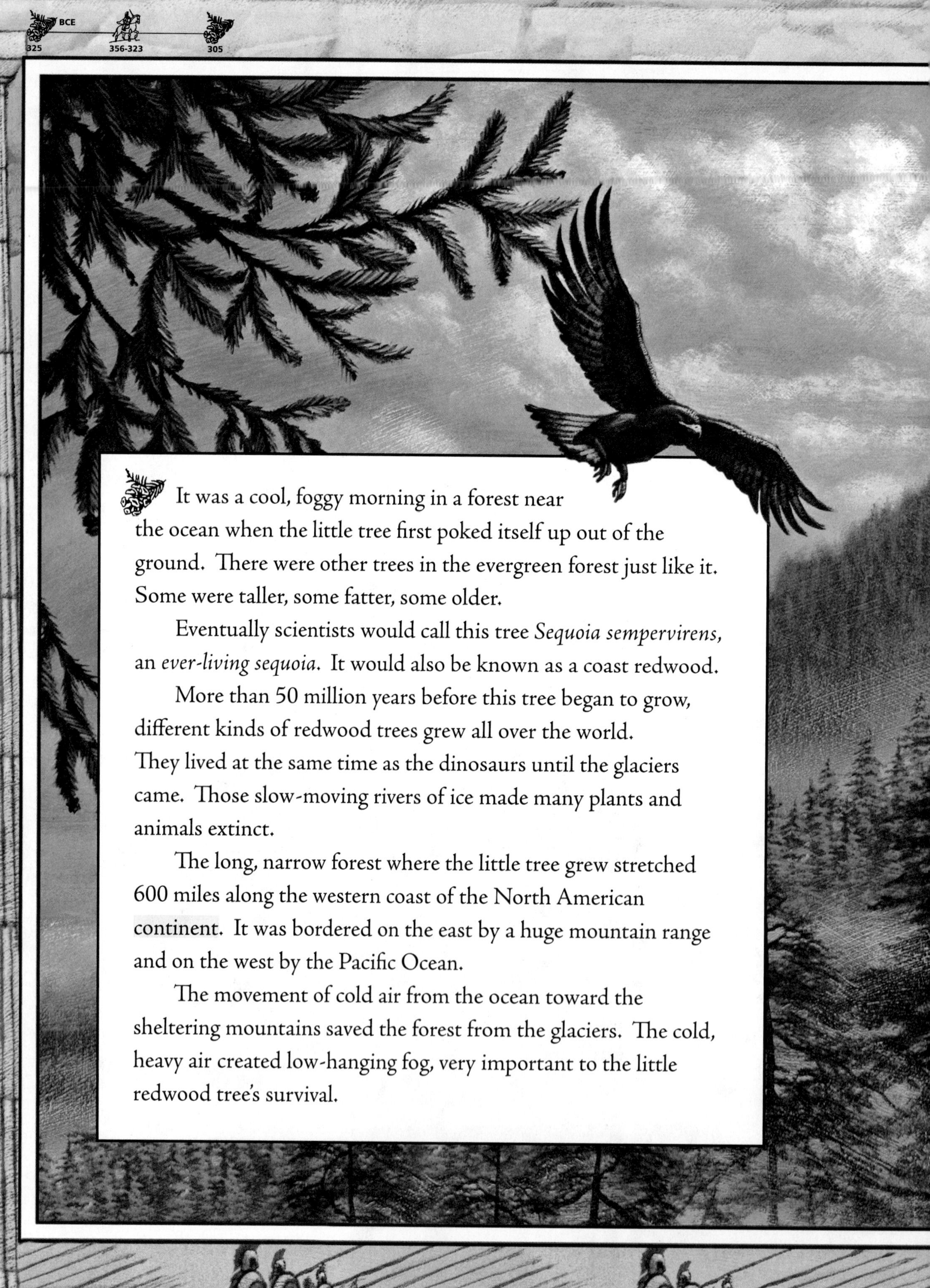

It was a cool, foggy morning in a forest near the ocean when the little tree first poked itself up out of the ground. There were other trees in the evergreen forest just like it. Some were taller, some fatter, some older.

Eventually scientists would call this tree *Sequoia sempervirens*, an *ever-living sequoia*. It would also be known as a coast redwood.

More than 50 million years before this tree began to grow, different kinds of redwood trees grew all over the world. They lived at the same time as the dinosaurs until the glaciers came. Those slow-moving rivers of ice made many plants and animals extinct.

The long, narrow forest where the little tree grew stretched 600 miles along the western coast of the North American continent. It was bordered on the east by a huge mountain range and on the west by the Pacific Ocean.

The movement of cold air from the ocean toward the sheltering mountains saved the forest from the glaciers. The cold, heavy air created low-hanging fog, very important to the little redwood tree's survival.

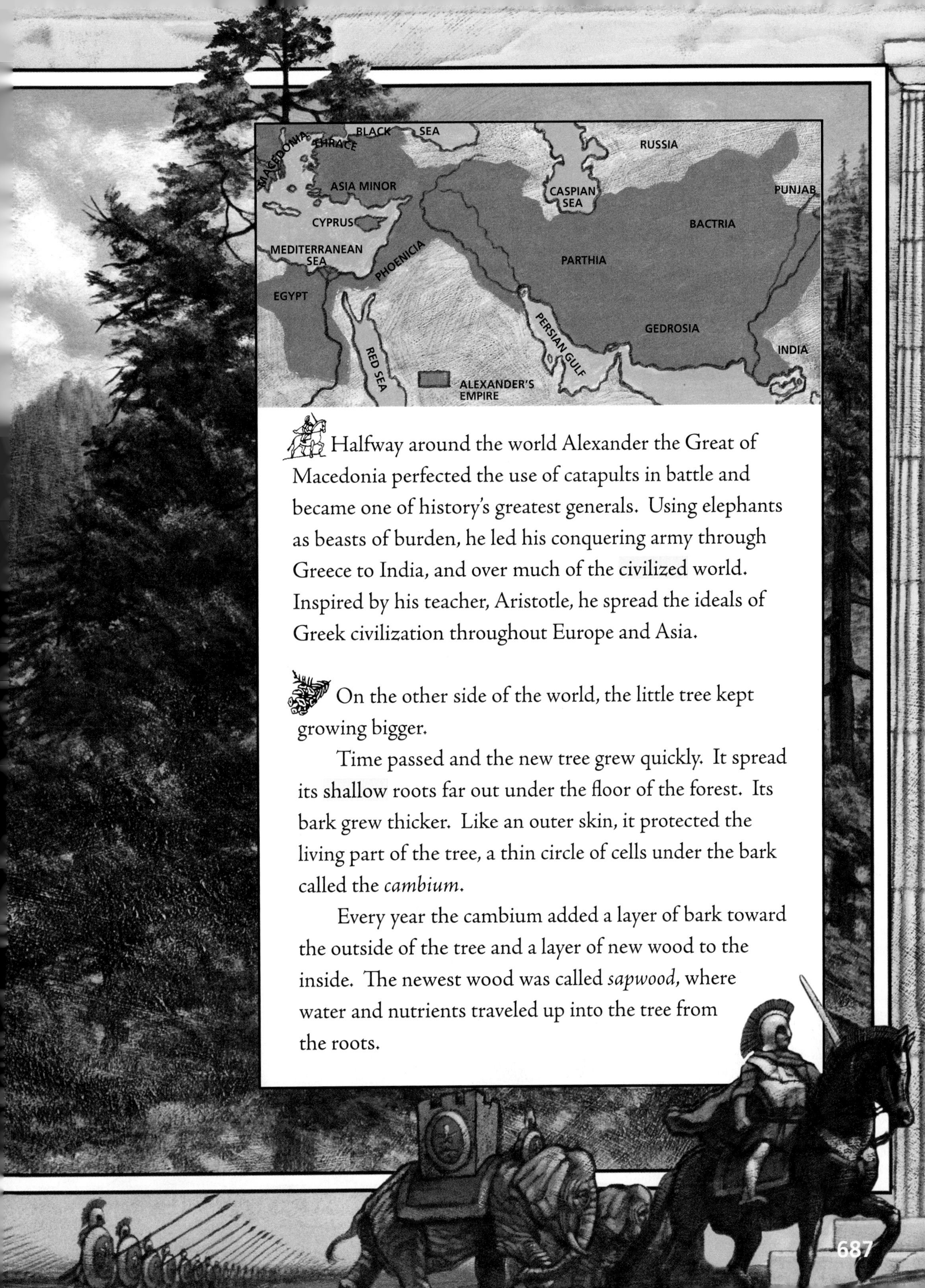

Halfway around the world Alexander the Great of Macedonia perfected the use of catapults in battle and became one of history's greatest generals. Using elephants as beasts of burden, he led his conquering army through Greece to India, and over much of the civilized world. Inspired by his teacher, Aristotle, he spread the ideals of Greek civilization throughout Europe and Asia.

On the other side of the world, the little tree kept growing bigger.

Time passed and the new tree grew quickly. It spread its shallow roots far out under the floor of the forest. Its bark grew thicker. Like an outer skin, it protected the living part of the tree, a thin circle of cells under the bark called the *cambium*.

Every year the cambium added a layer of bark toward the outside of the tree and a layer of new wood to the inside. The newest wood was called *sapwood*, where water and nutrients traveled up into the tree from the roots.

The cambium added more and more rings of sapwood to the inside of the tree closest to its bark. The older sapwood became the heartwood of the tree. Its fibrous chambers, clogged with wastes, were no longer used to carry food and water, but the tree still needed the heartwood to help it stand straight and tall.

Time went on. Dozens of trapping spiders looked for spaces up and down the thick, uneven bark of the tree. They stretched their webs wherever they could. The outside of the tree looked like an apartment house for spiders. The webs didn't hurt the tree at all. It just kept growing.

Across the ocean in China, men began building a great stone wall along their borders for protection against their enemies. Built entirely by hand of earth, brick, and stone, it took millions of workers hundreds of years to complete. The Great Wall eventually stretched more than 1,500 miles across mountains and valleys.

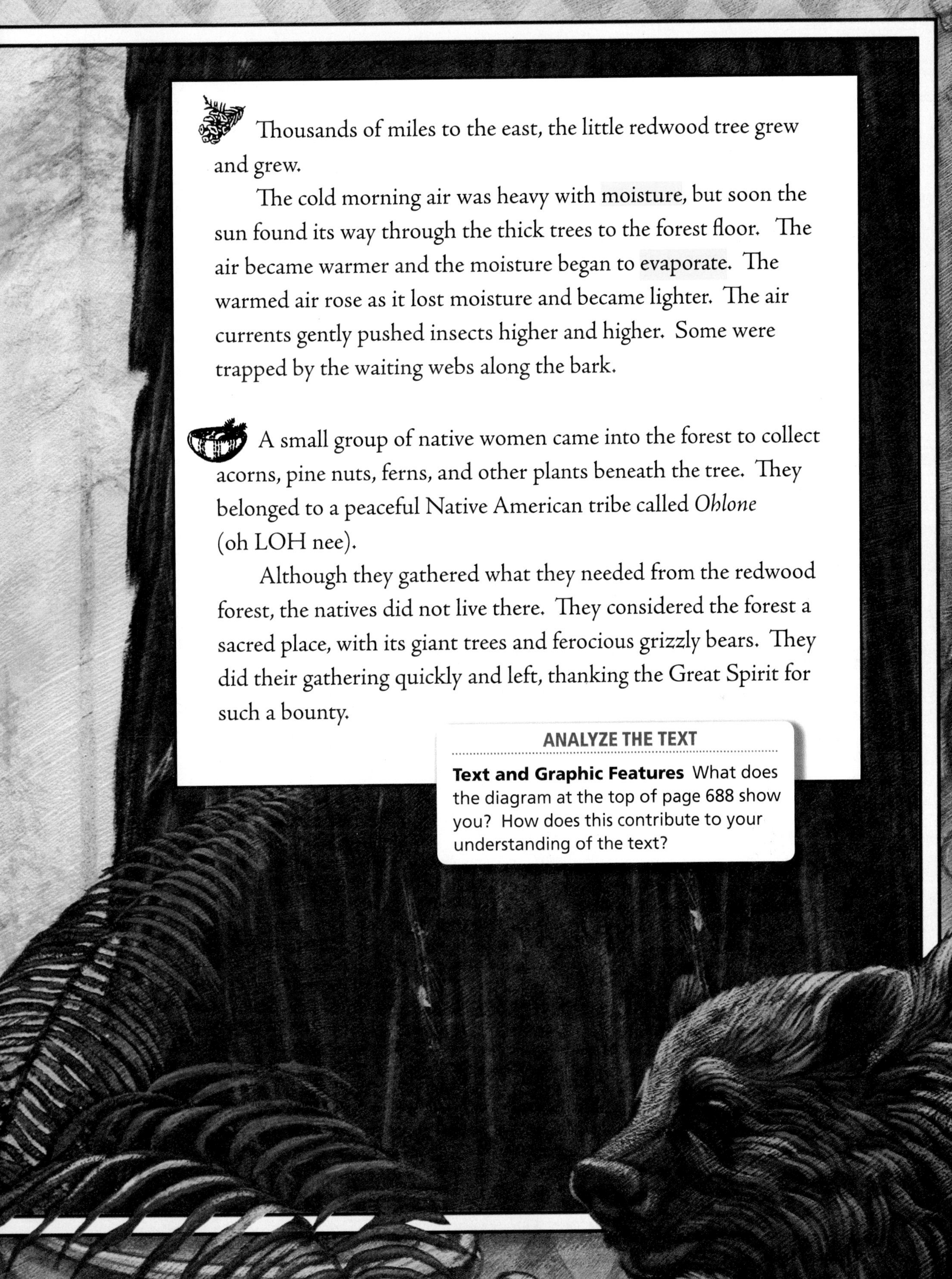

Thousands of miles to the east, the little redwood tree grew and grew.

The cold morning air was heavy with moisture, but soon the sun found its way through the thick trees to the forest floor. The air became warmer and the moisture began to evaporate. The warmed air rose as it lost moisture and became lighter. The air currents gently pushed insects higher and higher. Some were trapped by the waiting webs along the bark.

A small group of native women came into the forest to collect acorns, pine nuts, ferns, and other plants beneath the tree. They belonged to a peaceful Native American tribe called *Ohlone* (oh LOH nee).

Although they gathered what they needed from the redwood forest, the natives did not live there. They considered the forest a sacred place, with its giant trees and ferocious grizzly bears. They did their gathering quickly and left, thanking the Great Spirit for such a bounty.

ANALYZE THE TEXT

Text and Graphic Features What does the diagram at the top of page 688 show you? How does this contribute to your understanding of the text?

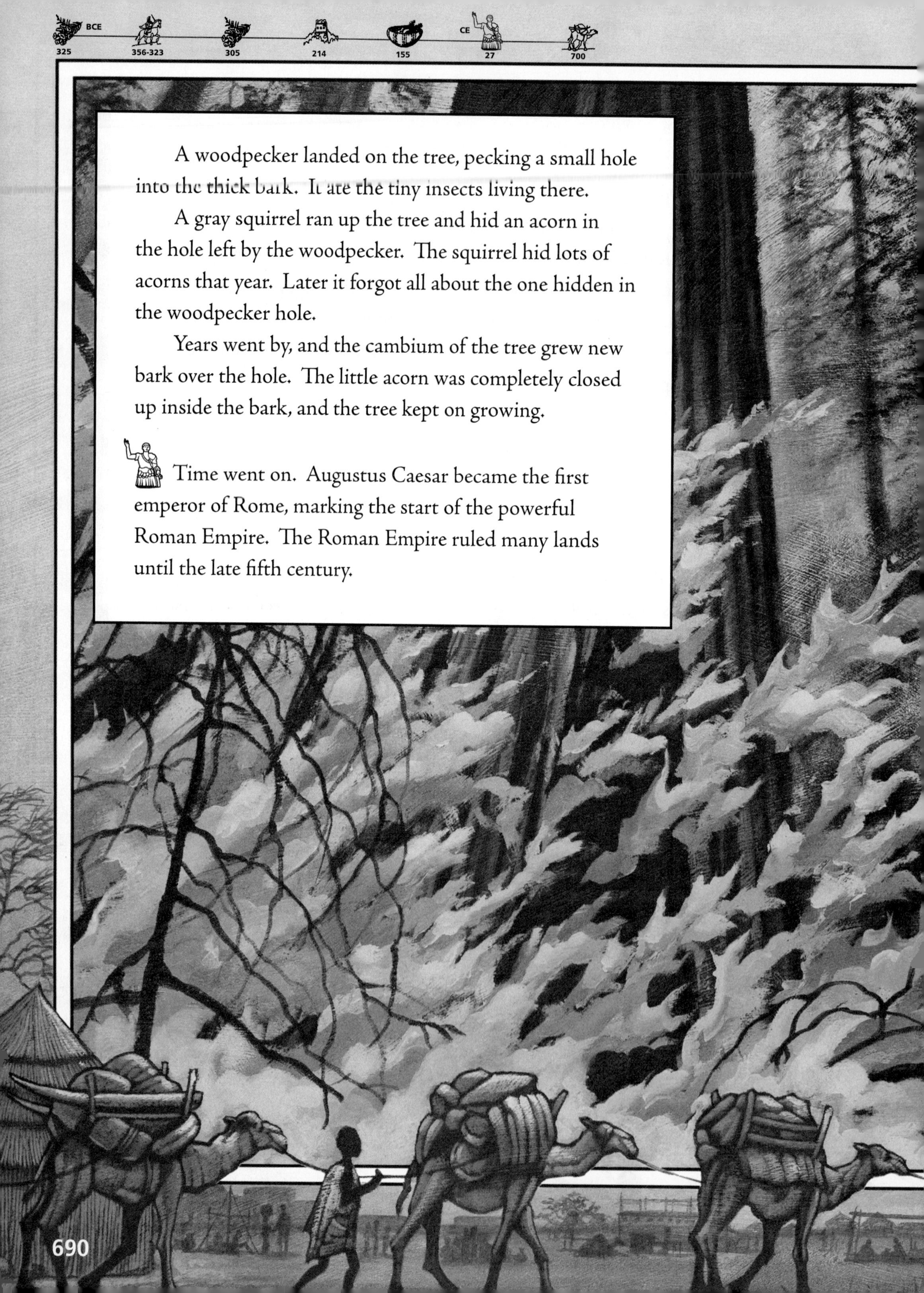

A woodpecker landed on the tree, pecking a small hole into the thick bark. It ate the tiny insects living there.

A gray squirrel ran up the tree and hid an acorn in the hole left by the woodpecker. The squirrel hid lots of acorns that year. Later it forgot all about the one hidden in the woodpecker hole.

Years went by, and the cambium of the tree grew new bark over the hole. The little acorn was completely closed up inside the bark, and the tree kept on growing.

Time went on. Augustus Caesar became the first emperor of Rome, marking the start of the powerful Roman Empire. The Roman Empire ruled many lands until the late fifth century.

The tree was over 300 years old by then, still young for an ever-living sequoia. It stood almost 200 feet tall and measured about 20 feet around its base.

One day there was a big fire in the forest and many trees burned. Flames ate into the redwood tree near the ground. Fire-resistant elements in the heartwood finally stopped the fire, leaving a low, hollowed-out cave inside.

The cambium of the tree was not hurt badly by the fire. It continued to grow new bark around the opening of the cave. Over many years, the new bark almost closed up the opening, while the inside stayed hollow. The tree grew on and on.

Almost nine thousand miles southeast of the forest lay the continent of Africa. In a grassy savanna at the edge of the vast Sahara desert, the kingdom of Kanem flourished as a major commercial center. Caravans brought metalware, horses, and salt from North Africa and Europe to trade there for ivory and kola nuts from the south.

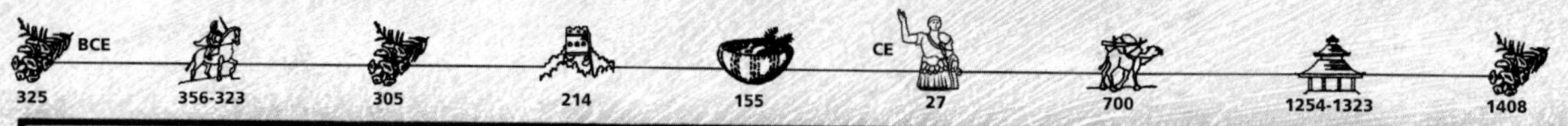

In the peaceful forest far away to the west, the redwood tree stood tall and strong.

Tiny striped chipmunks ran up and down the tree. They nestled on a branch that grew in a strange and different way. The branch had become a burl. Its wood was curled into a lump cozy enough for a chipmunk to rest upon. The burl didn't stop the tree from growing higher and wider. By now it was over 250 feet tall. It was more than 50 feet around the bottom. It grew and grew and grew.

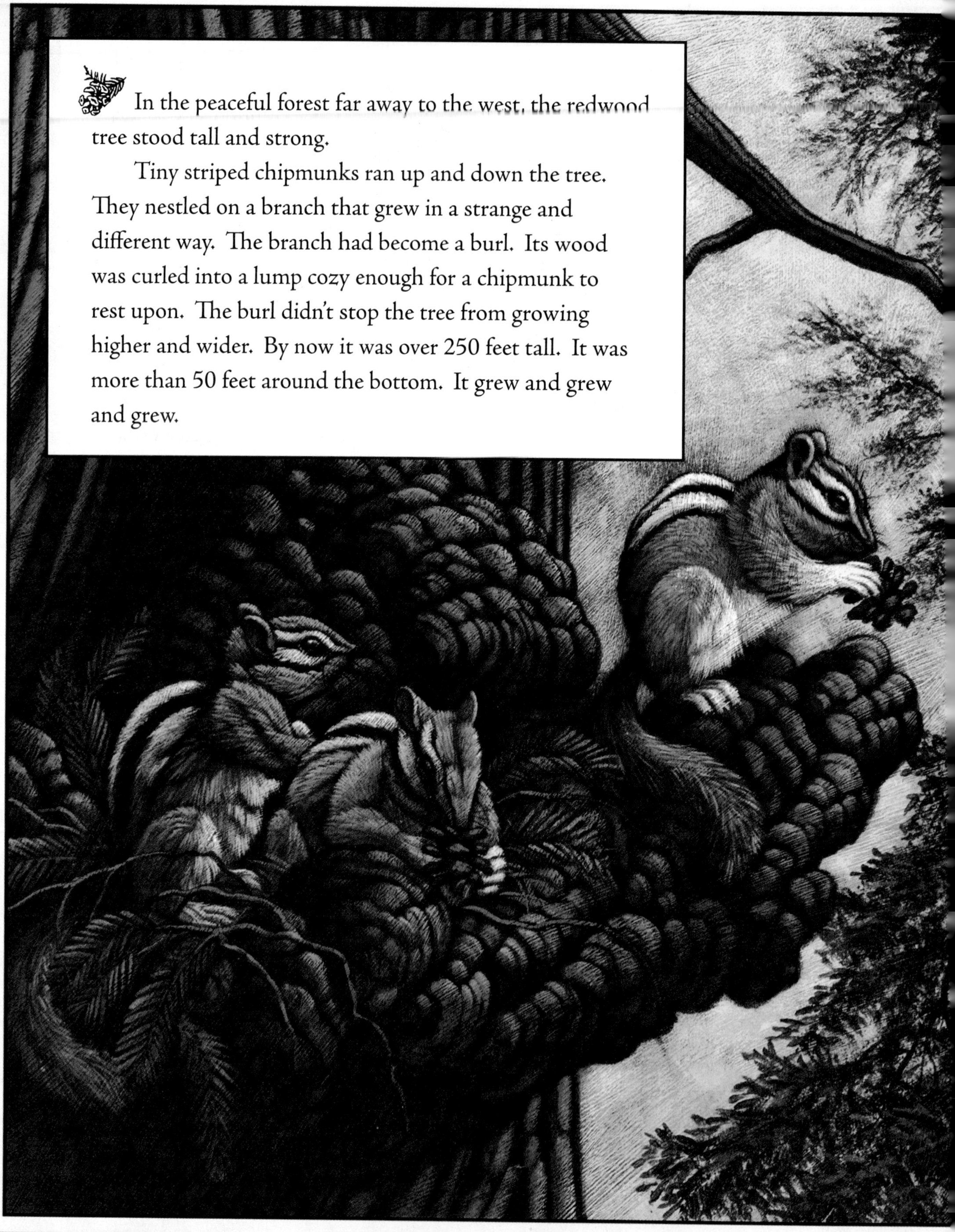

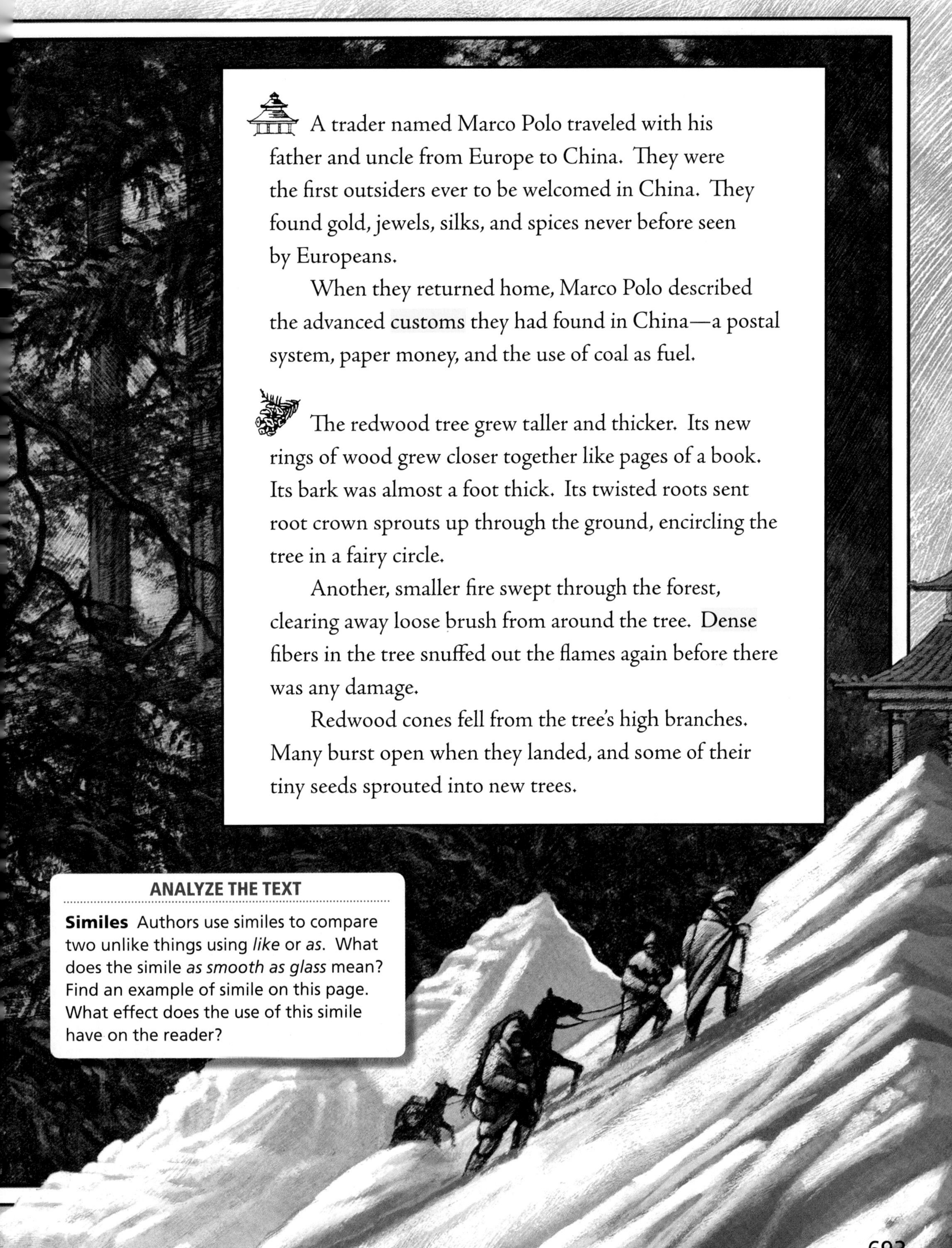

A trader named Marco Polo traveled with his father and uncle from Europe to China. They were the first outsiders ever to be welcomed in China. They found gold, jewels, silks, and spices never before seen by Europeans.

When they returned home, Marco Polo described the advanced customs they had found in China—a postal system, paper money, and the use of coal as fuel.

The redwood tree grew taller and thicker. Its new rings of wood grew closer together like pages of a book. Its bark was almost a foot thick. Its twisted roots sent root crown sprouts up through the ground, encircling the tree in a fairy circle.

Another, smaller fire swept through the forest, clearing away loose brush from around the tree. Dense fibers in the tree snuffed out the flames again before there was any damage.

Redwood cones fell from the tree's high branches. Many burst open when they landed, and some of their tiny seeds sprouted into new trees.

ANALYZE THE TEXT

Similes Authors use similes to compare two unlike things using *like* or *as*. What does the simile *as smooth as glass* mean? Find an example of simile on this page. What effect does the use of this simile have on the reader?

An Italian explorer named Christopher Columbus wanted to find a new route to China. Inspired by the explorations of Marco Polo, he persuaded the queen of Spain to finance his voyage through uncharted seas to the west. Although Columbus did not reach China, he landed at the southeastern part of North America and called it the New World.

The redwood tree was almost 3,000 miles away from where Columbus landed, still growing in its sheltered forest far to the west.

Deer walked the trails of the forest and found hidden areas to protect them from their enemies while they grazed on the lush vegetation.

Gray foxes lived in the forest, too. Some of their babies were born inside the tree's sheltered cave.

Birds nested in the topmost branches of the tallest, oldest trees. Mammals, birds, insects, and reptiles lived together, replenishing their species every year according to a natural balance.

ANALYZE THE TEXT

Text Structure How are the ideas in the text structured? How does the timeline along the top of the page support this structure?

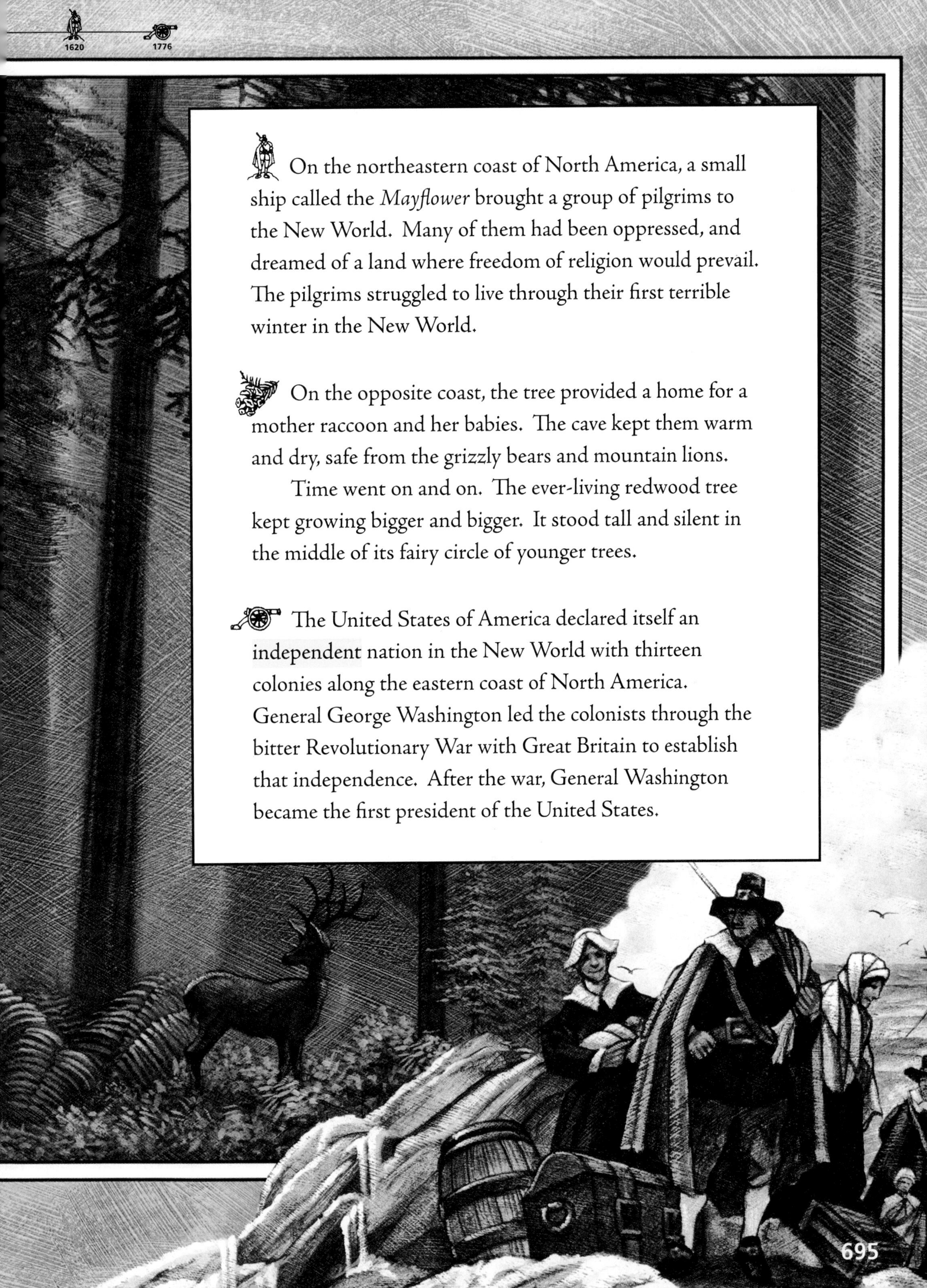

On the northeastern coast of North America, a small ship called the *Mayflower* brought a group of pilgrims to the New World. Many of them had been oppressed, and dreamed of a land where freedom of religion would prevail. The pilgrims struggled to live through their first terrible winter in the New World.

On the opposite coast, the tree provided a home for a mother raccoon and her babies. The cave kept them warm and dry, safe from the grizzly bears and mountain lions.

Time went on and on. The ever-living redwood tree kept growing bigger and bigger. It stood tall and silent in the middle of its fairy circle of younger trees.

The United States of America declared itself an independent nation in the New World with thirteen colonies along the eastern coast of North America. General George Washington led the colonists through the bitter Revolutionary War with Great Britain to establish that independence. After the war, General Washington became the first president of the United States.

The giant redwood tree was now more than 300 feet tall—one of the tallest living things on the face of the earth.

One day there was a terrible storm in the forest. Wind and rain lashed at the trees. Claps of thunder made the animals run and hide. A flashing bolt of lightning struck the base of the tree at its weakest part, near the cave. The tree fell over on its side with a tremendous crash. Its huge trunk broke into pieces when it hit the ground.

Gold was discovered in the western territories of North America. Thousands of people crossed the continent in horse-drawn wagons, dreaming of riches and new opportunities.

Boom towns and cities grew quickly. Hunters, loggers, tanners, and miners exploited the resources of the land. Soon a railroad reached across the continent from coast to coast. Trains carried settlers to places near the redwood forest, where the vigorous roots of the fallen tree kept growing.

Time went on. The life force of the ever-living sequoia would not die. Its roots gave life and strength to the smaller trees around it. Soon a new tree began to grow up from the broken trunk.

Millions of insects used the bark of the old tree for food. Over many years the wood began to change into a fine dust. Banana slugs changed the dust into organic elements, which went back into the soil as nutrients.

In outer space, a man walked on the moon for the first time. People watched him on television screens all over the world. Astronauts and cosmonauts from different countries traveled into space. Scientists planned to build a space station hundreds of miles from Earth.

Today people camp in the shelter of the tree, and children play games on its decomposing log. They are amazed at its length—longer than a football field.

In the narrow, ancient forest, the ever-living sequoias keep growing. They stand like giant statues as millions of visitors from all over the world come to marvel at their incredible height.

Tiny new trees poke themselves up out of the ground. Life in a coast redwood forest goes on and on.

Dig Deeper

How to Analyze the Text

Use these pages to learn about Text and Graphic Features, Text Structure, and Similes. Then read "The Ever-Living Tree" again to apply what you learned.

Text and Graphic Features

"The Ever-Living Tree" is an informational text about the growth of a coast redwood. The selection includes **text and graphic features** that give information that adds to the text. These features include italic type, timelines, maps, diagrams, and icons. Icons are small pictures that represent ideas.

In this selection, the map of Alexander's empire and the diagram of the layers of a redwood tree help explain ideas in the text. The icons at the beginning of each section are clues to what the author is describing there. The repeating redwood cone icon is a signal that tells you, "Now the author will discuss the redwood tree again."

Look back at page 687 in "The Ever-Living Tree." What graphic features are on that page? What do they tell you?

Text or Graphic Feature	Page Number	Information
•	•	•
•	•	•
•	•	•

ELACC4RI5 describe the overall structure of a text or part of a text; **ELACC4RI7** interpret information presented visually, orally, or quantitatively; **ELACC4L5a** explain the meaning of similes and metaphors in context

Text Structure

The way authors organize their facts in informational texts is called **text structure.** In "The Ever-Living Tree," the author presents two sets of events. One set of events describes the life of a tree. The other tells about human events that happened during the tree's lifetime. The redwood cone icon signals facts about the redwoods. Other icons signal human events. As you reread, look for clues to how the text is structured.

Similes

Authors use **similes** to compare two unlike things using *like* or *as*. Similes help readers get a clear picture in their minds of what an author is describing. In the sentence "The surface of the lake was as reflective as a mirror," *as reflective as a mirror* is a simile. The comparison shows that the water is still, smooth, and reflects images like a mirror.

Your Turn

RETURN TO THE ESSENTIAL QUESTION

Review the selection, including the graphic features, with a partner to prepare to discuss this question: *How do forests and trees show change?* Use text evidence and the graphic features to support your answers. Take turns reviewing and explaining the key ideas. Ask and answer questions to clarify ideas.

Classroom Conversation

Continue your discussion of "The Ever-Living Tree" by explaining your answers to these questions:

1. What does the author want you to know about redwood trees?
2. What have you learned about the history of the world from the events the author describes?
3. If a redwood could talk, what might it tell about the things it has seen since it sprouted?

TIME MARCHES ON

Recall Historical Events With a partner, think of two recent historical events to add to the timeline in "The Ever-Living Tree." Write a short description of each event you have chosen, and create a picture, or icon, to go with each event. Then compare your events with the events another pair of students chose for the timeline.

WRITE ABOUT READING

Response What did you enjoy most about the selection? Was the author's choice to tell the story of humans along with the story of the redwood a good one? Write two paragraphs that explain your opinions about the text. Include reasons for your opinions and details that support your reasons.

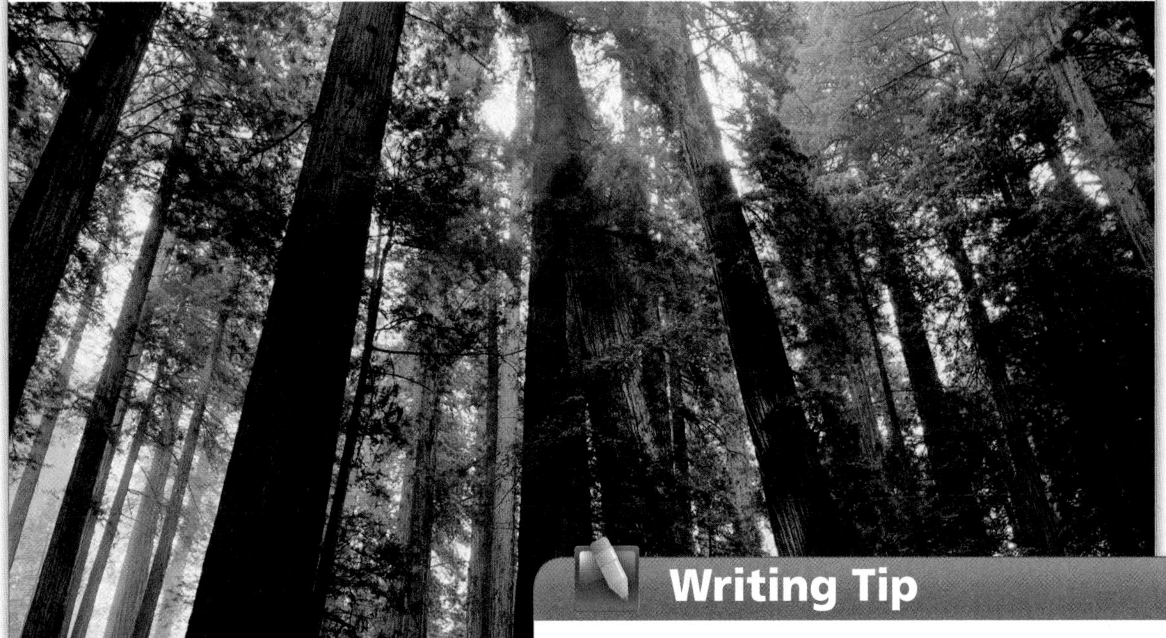

Writing Tip

In the first paragraph, state what you liked most about the selection. Give two reasons why. In the second paragraph, state your opinion about the structure of the selection. Give one or two reasons for your opinion.

COMMON CORE **ELACC4RI1** refer to details and examples when explaining what the text says explicitly and when drawing inferences; **ELACC4RI7** interpret information presented visually, orally, or quantitatively; **ELACC4W1a** introduce a topic, state an opinion, and create an organizational structure; **ELACC4W8** recall information from experiences or gather information from print and digital sources/take notes, categorize information, and provide a list of sources; **ELACC4W9b** apply grade 4 Reading standards to informational texts; **ELACC4SL1a** come to discussions prepared/explicitly draw on preparation and other information about the topic

Lesson 23

POETRY

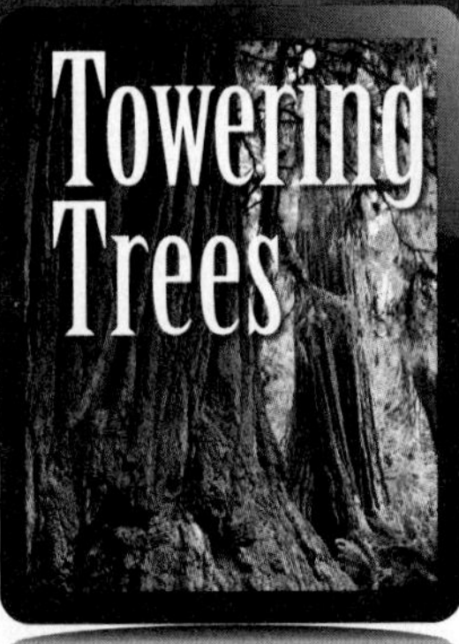

 GENRE

Poetry uses the sound and rhythm of words to suggest images and express feelings.

 TEXT FOCUS

Narrative poetry focuses on telling a story, often about a particular event. Narrative poetry is broken into lines, and a section of lines is called a **stanza** or **verse.** The way the verses and lines are structured is called the **meter.** As you read each poem, note how each stanza ties into the meaning of the entire poem.

ELACC4RL5 explain major differences between poems, drama, and prose/refer to their structural elements; **ELACC4RL10** read and comprehend literature

Towering Trees

The poems you will read next are about people and trees. "Ancestors of Tomorrow" compares children to growing trees, while "First Recorded 6,000-Year-Old Tree in America" and "Giant Sequoias" describe the majesty of towering trees.

Ancestors of Tomorrow

children are
the blooming
branches of trees

one day their seeds
will become
the roots

of other trees
bearing their own
blooming branches

by Francisco X. Alarcón

Go Digital

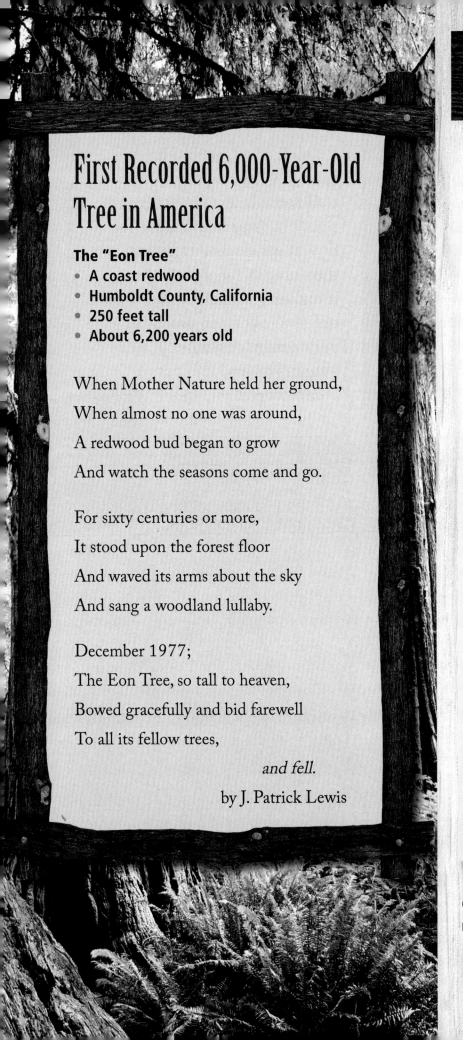

First Recorded 6,000-Year-Old Tree in America

The "Eon Tree"

- **A coast redwood**
- **Humboldt County, California**
- **250 feet tall**
- **About 6,200 years old**

When Mother Nature held her ground,
When almost no one was around,
A redwood bud began to grow
And watch the seasons come and go.

For sixty centuries or more,
It stood upon the forest floor
And waved its arms about the sky
And sang a woodland lullaby.

December 1977;
The Eon Tree, so tall to heaven,
Bowed gracefully and bid farewell
To all its fellow trees,
and fell.

by J. Patrick Lewis

Humboldt Redwoods State Park

Visitors to Humboldt Redwoods State Park in California have numerous opportunities to see redwoods. Redwoods are important natural resources on the continent of North America. Plentiful rain and dense fog provide redwoods with moisture to grow. The trees' shallow roots take in water from the soil.

Cars can drive through some redwoods near the state park.

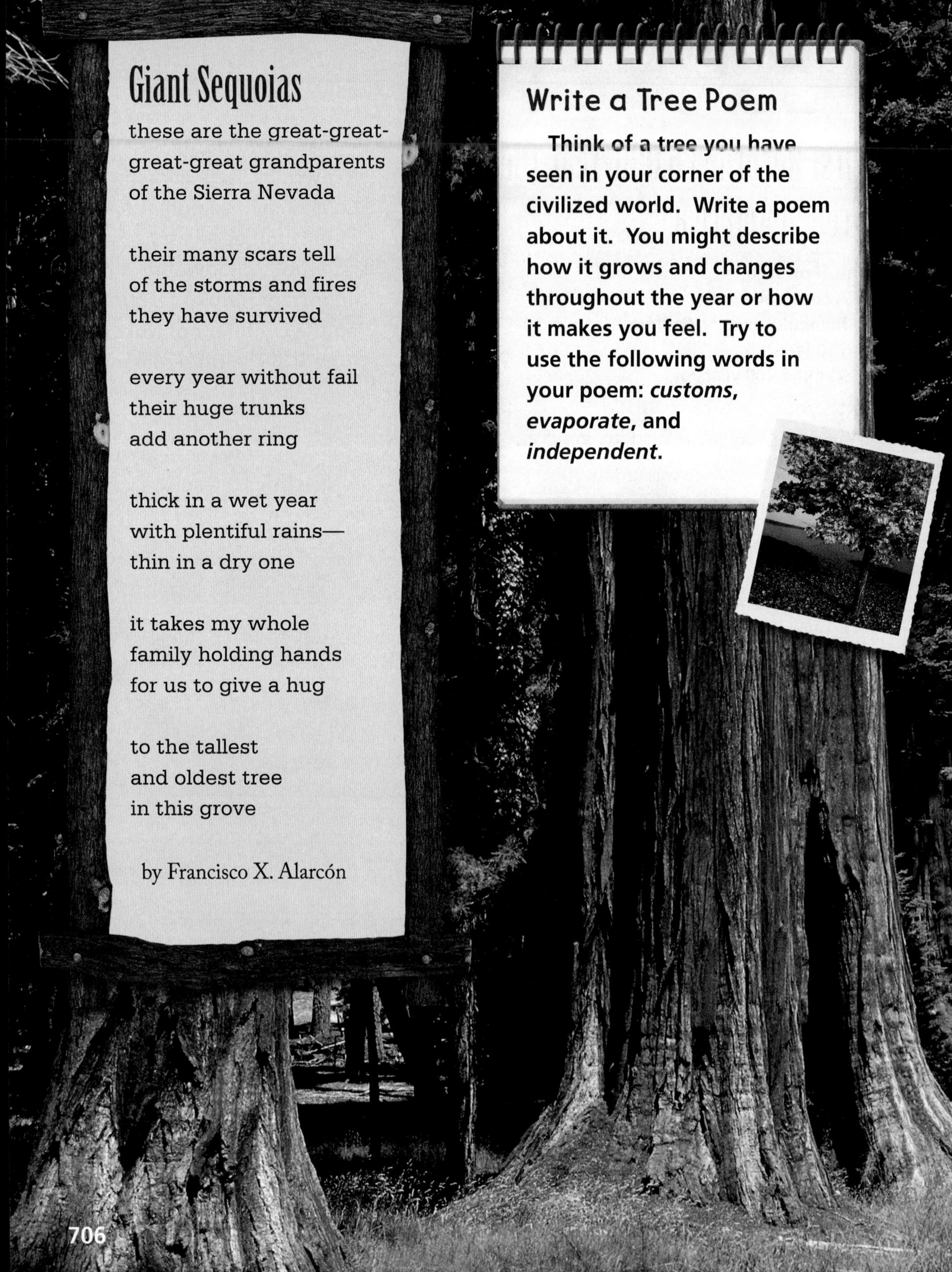

Giant Sequoias

these are the great-great-
great-great grandparents
of the Sierra Nevada

their many scars tell
of the storms and fires
they have survived

every year without fail
their huge trunks
add another ring

thick in a wet year
with plentiful rains—
thin in a dry one

it takes my whole
family holding hands
for us to give a hug

to the tallest
and oldest tree
in this grove

by Francisco X. Alarcón

Write a Tree Poem

Think of a tree you have seen in your corner of the civilized world. Write a poem about it. You might describe how it grows and changes throughout the year or how it makes you feel. Try to use the following words in your poem: *customs*, *evaporate*, and *independent*.

Compare Texts

TEXT TO TEXT

Compare Text and Poetry Compare the poems in "Towering Trees" with "The Ever-Living Tree." Discuss these questions with a partner: *What does each poem describe? What information in the poems is also found in the selection? Why?* Work with your partner to write answers to the questions. Include text evidence to support your ideas.

TEXT TO SELF

Write a Response Many animals depend on trees for survival and often stay with the same tree for many years. Do you have a favorite tree that you like to sit under or climb? Write a paragraph about how trees have had an impact on your life.

TEXT TO WORLD

Construct a Timeline Research the dates of the historical events mentioned in "The Ever-Living Tree." Then use those dates to construct a timeline of events that occurred throughout the redwood tree's life. Summarize the events in the selection to include on your timeline.

ELACC4RL1 refer to details and examples when explaining what the text says explicitly and when drawing inferences; **ELACC4RI1** refer to details and examples when explaining what the text says explicitly and when drawing inferences; **ELACC4RI9** integrate information from two texts on the same topic; **ELACC4W10** write routinely over extended time frames and shorter time frames

COMMON CORE **ELACC4L3b** choose punctuation for effect

Grammar

How Can Punctuation Affect Readers? Each type of punctuation in your writing has a different effect on your readers. An **exclamation point** shows excitement. An **ellipsis** creates tension and an ominous effect in a sentence. A **dash** can be used for emphasis. A **colon** introduces new but related information in a sentence. **Quotation marks** should be used to record a speaker's exact words. Put a **comma** before the quotation marks to introduce the quotation.

exclamation point	This coast redwood is over 100 years old!
ellipsis	Pedro was unsure what he would find in the shed as the door creaked open. . .
dash	Tanya knew one thing—she would save the forest.
colon	Chin reviewed everything he needed: a flashlight, a map, and a backpack.
comma, quotation marks	Marie asked Jeremy, "What time are we leaving?"

Write each of these sentences on a sheet of paper, using the correct punctuation.

1. Finally Joe and Laura were on summer vacation ______
2. Joe wanted to accomplish two things ______ visit a redwood forest and swim in the ocean.
3. Joe knew he was forgetting something ______
4. ______ This tree is sixty feet around ______ ______ Laura announced.
5. One thing was certain ______ that was a very, very tall tree.

Related sentences can often be combined using certain types of punctuation, such as an ellipsis or a colon. Combining sentences can make your sentences more fluid and have a greater impact on readers.

Separate	Combined
Jack said, "Shh. Don't scare the woodpecker in that redwood tree."	Jack said, "Shh . . . don't scare the woodpecker in that redwood tree."

Separate: We have what we need. We have binoculars, a bird identification book, and a notebook.

Combined: We have what we need: binoculars, a bird identification book, and a notebook.

Connect Grammar to Writing

As you revise your procedural composition, look for places you can use different types of punctuation to have a greater effect on the reader.

ELACC4W2a introduce a topic and group related information/include formatting, illustrations, and multimedia; **ELACC4W2b** develop the topic with facts, definitions, details, quotations, or other information and examples; **ELACC4W2c** link ideas within categories of information using words and phrases; **ELACC4W2d** use precise language and domain-specific vocabulary

Informative Writing

Organization In "The Ever-Living Tree," the author describes the events in the life of a redwood tree. In a **procedural composition,** you explain a process, or a series of events. Begin by introducing the topic, and then explain each step of the process in order. Use linking words such as *first* and *because* to make the process clearer. Group ideas together in a way that makes sense, and define domain-specific terms.

Erin wrote a draft of a procedural composition explaining how a redwood grows from a cone to a tree. Later, she reordered events and added transitions, or linking words, to clarify her ideas. She also added precise language.

Writing Traits Checklist

- **Ideas** Did I group together related ideas into paragraphs?
- **Organization** Did I use linking words to make the order of events clear?
- **Word Choice** Did I define domain-specific vocabulary?
- **Voice** Did I express my ideas clearly?
- **Sentence Fluency** Did I vary the length of my sentences?
- **Conventions** Did I punctuate my sentences correctly?

Revised Draft

The magnificent coast redwoods are fast-growing ~~trees~~ conifers. Conifers are plants that bear seeds in a cone—and that's how some redwoods get their start. First, ~~C~~cones on a redwood tree begin to open up. Next, the dry cones dry out. Then they shed their seeds. Not many of the seeds sprout. However, ~~W~~when they do, these tiny redwoods are called seedlings.

Final Copy

How a Young Redwood Grows

by Erin Casey

The magnificent coast redwoods are fast-growing conifers. Conifers are plants that bear seeds in a cone—and that's how some redwoods get their start. First, the cones on a redwood tree begin to dry out. Next, the dry cones open up. Then they shed their seeds. Not many of the seeds sprout. However, when they do, these tiny redwoods are called seedlings.

As a seedling grows taller, its roots spread outward. The roots get nutrients, or food, from the soil, and the seedling grows. Seedlings can grow more than a foot a year. The young strong trees are called saplings. Eventually those saplings become mighty redwoods.

Reading as a Writer

As you write your procedural composition, make sure that you group related ideas into paragraphs so that your ideas are well organized and easy to follow.

In my final paper, I reordered some steps in the process and used linking words. I made sure I punctuated sentences correctly.

Lesson

24

☑ TARGET VOCABULARY

bond
suffered
intruder
companion
enclosure
inseparable
charged
chief
exhausted
affection

Vocabulary Reader

Context Cards

ELACC4L6 acquire/use vocabulary, including academic and domain-specific

Vocabulary in Context

1 bond

Many people feel a very strong **bond**, or connection, with animals.

2 suffered

A veterinarian treats animals who have **suffered** injury or illness.

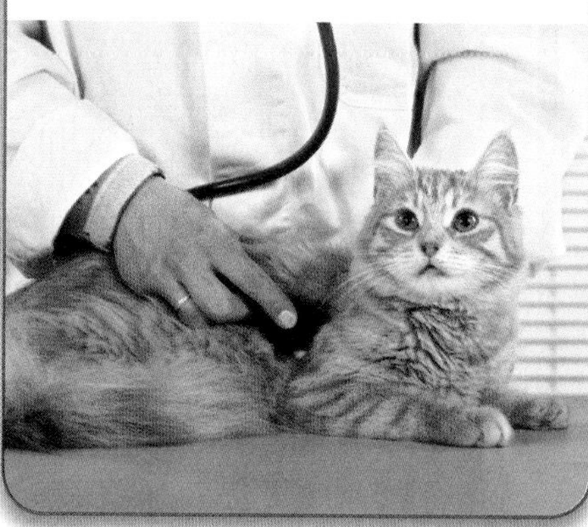

3 intruder

Animals are cautious when an **intruder** invades their territory.

4 companion

A pet is usually a **companion** of its owner. They spend a lot of time together.

▶ Study each Context Card.

▶ Use a dictionary to help you understand the meanings of these words.

5 enclosure

This ranch worker checks to be sure that an animal's enclosure is secure and safe.

6 inseparable

People and their service animals often become inseparable. They are never apart.

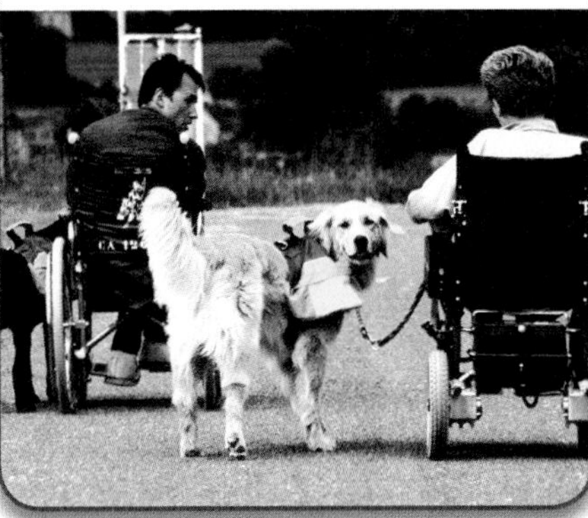

7 charged

This dog has charged, or rushed at, the ball that its owner has tossed.

8 chief

One of the chief jobs of an aquarium biologist is to educate visitors about sea life.

9 exhausted

This dog walker loves his job, but he will be exhausted, or worn out, by the day's end.

10 affection

This girl feels affection, or fondness, for the sheep on her family's farm.

Read and Comprehend

TARGET SKILL

Compare and Contrast The next selection is about two very different animals who find a common bond. As you read "Owen and Mzee," look for ways in which the authors organize information to show how the two animals are **alike** and **different**. Think about each animal's size, age, and situation. Use a graphic organizer like the one below to help you note their similarities and differences.

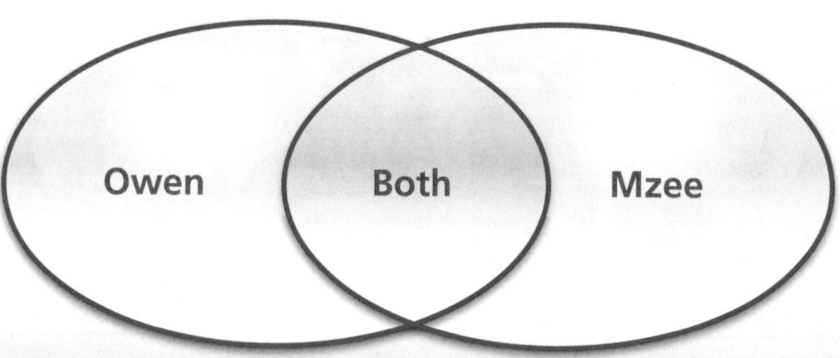

TARGET STRATEGY

Analyze/Evaluate When you **analyze** and **evaluate** a text, you think carefully about what you have read. You use text evidence to form your own opinion about the topic.

ELACC4RI1 refer to details and examples when explaining what the text says explicitly and when drawing inferences; **ELACC4RI5** describe the overall structure of a text or part of a text

PREVIEW THE TOPIC

Animal Behavior

By studying animal behavior, what do you think scientists are trying to find out? One thing they are trying to learn more about is how animals form social bonds, or close ties with each other. Most of the time, the bonds that form between animals are easy to predict. Sometimes, though, animals form bonds that shock even the experts.

"Owen and Mzee" is a true story about a baby hippo and an old tortoise that meet at an animal-rescue center. As you read, you'll find out why these two animals made headlines all over the world.

Lesson 24

ANCHOR TEXT

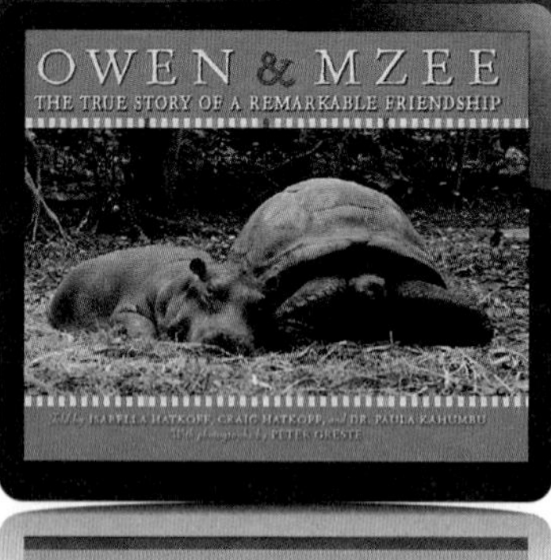

 TARGET SKILL

Compare and Contrast
Examine the similarities and differences between the animals.

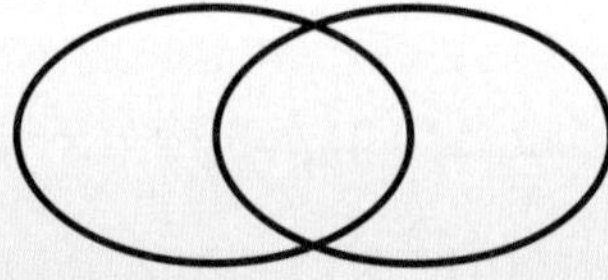

 GENRE

Narrative nonfiction tells about people, things, events, or places that are real. As you read, look for:

- ▶ factual information that tells a story
- ▶ text features such as photographs and captions

ELACC4RI5 describe the overall structure of a text or part of a text; **ELACC4RI8** explain how an author uses reasons and evidence to support points; **ELACC4RI10** read and comprehend informational texts; **ELACC4L3a** choose words and phrases to convey ideas precisely

MEET THE AUTHORS

Isabella Hatkoff

Craig Hatkoff

Dr. Paula Kahumbu

Isabella Hatkoff was six years old when she saw a photo of Owen and Mzee in the newspaper. She decided to write about them with the help of her father, Craig. Dr. Paula Kahumbu is an ecologist in Kenya. She's responsible for the health and safety of Owen and Mzee.

MEET THE PHOTOGRAPHER

Peter Greste

Peter Greste took the newspaper photo that led the Hatkoffs and Dr. Kahumbu to write "Owen and Mzee." Greste works not only as a photographer but also as a radio news reporter. He travels the world covering important events.

OWEN & MZEE

THE TRUE STORY OF A REMARKABLE FRIENDSHIP

by Isabella Hatkoff, Craig Hatkoff, *and* Dr. Paula Kahumbu
photographs by Peter Greste

ESSENTIAL QUESTION

How can animal behavior be like human behavior?

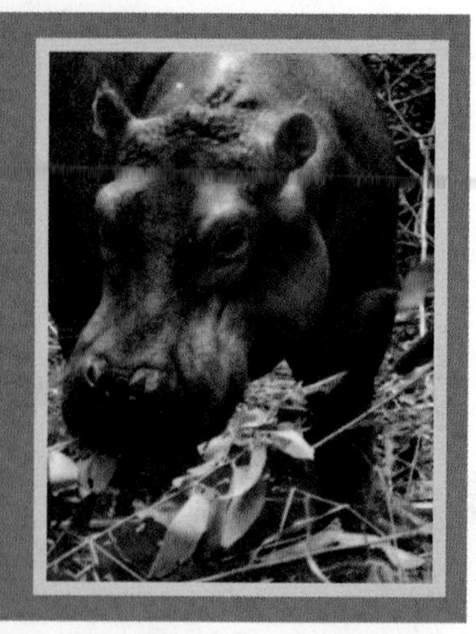

This story began in Malindi, Kenya, on the east coast of Africa, in December 2004. A pod of hippopotamuses was grazing along the shore of the Indian Ocean. Suddenly, giant, surging waves from a tsunami (tsu NAH mee) rushed high onto the beach. The powerful waves caused destruction for miles around. After the water went down, only one hippo remained, and it was stranded on a reef. Hundreds of villagers worked for hours to rescue the six-hundred-pound baby. Finally, a man named Owen caught the animal, which was later named after him. The rescuers wrapped the hippo in a net and placed him in a pickup truck.

People weren't sure where Owen should be taken next. They called Haller Park, an animal sanctuary about fifty miles away, near the city of Mombasa. Dr. Paula Kahumbu, the manager, immediately offered Owen a place to live there. She explained that he could never be returned to the wild. Since he was still a baby, he wouldn't have learned yet how to fend for himself. And he would never be welcomed into another hippo pod—he would be seen as an intruder and attacked. But they would take good care of him in Haller Park. Dr. Paula offered to drive to Malindi herself to bring Owen to his new home.

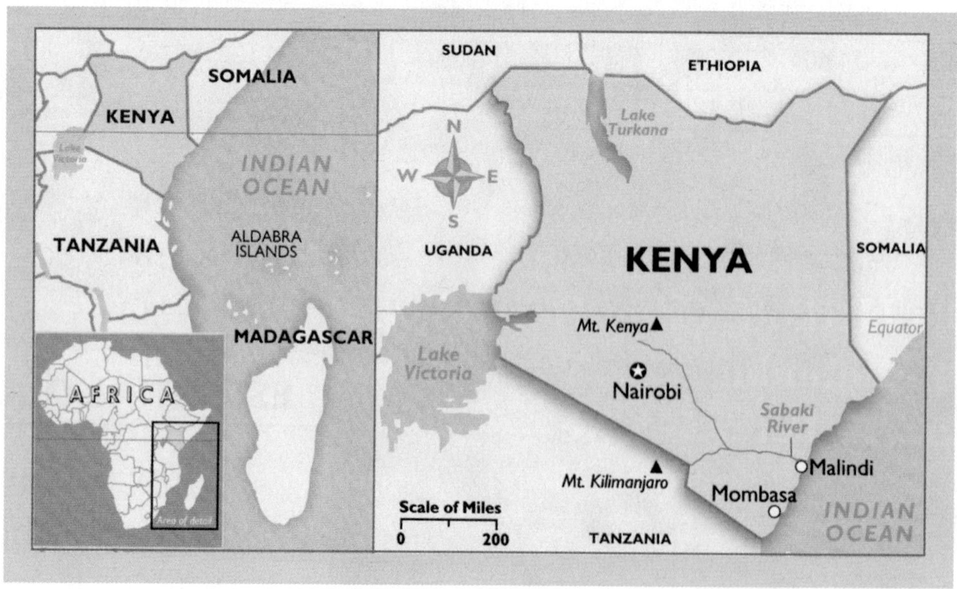

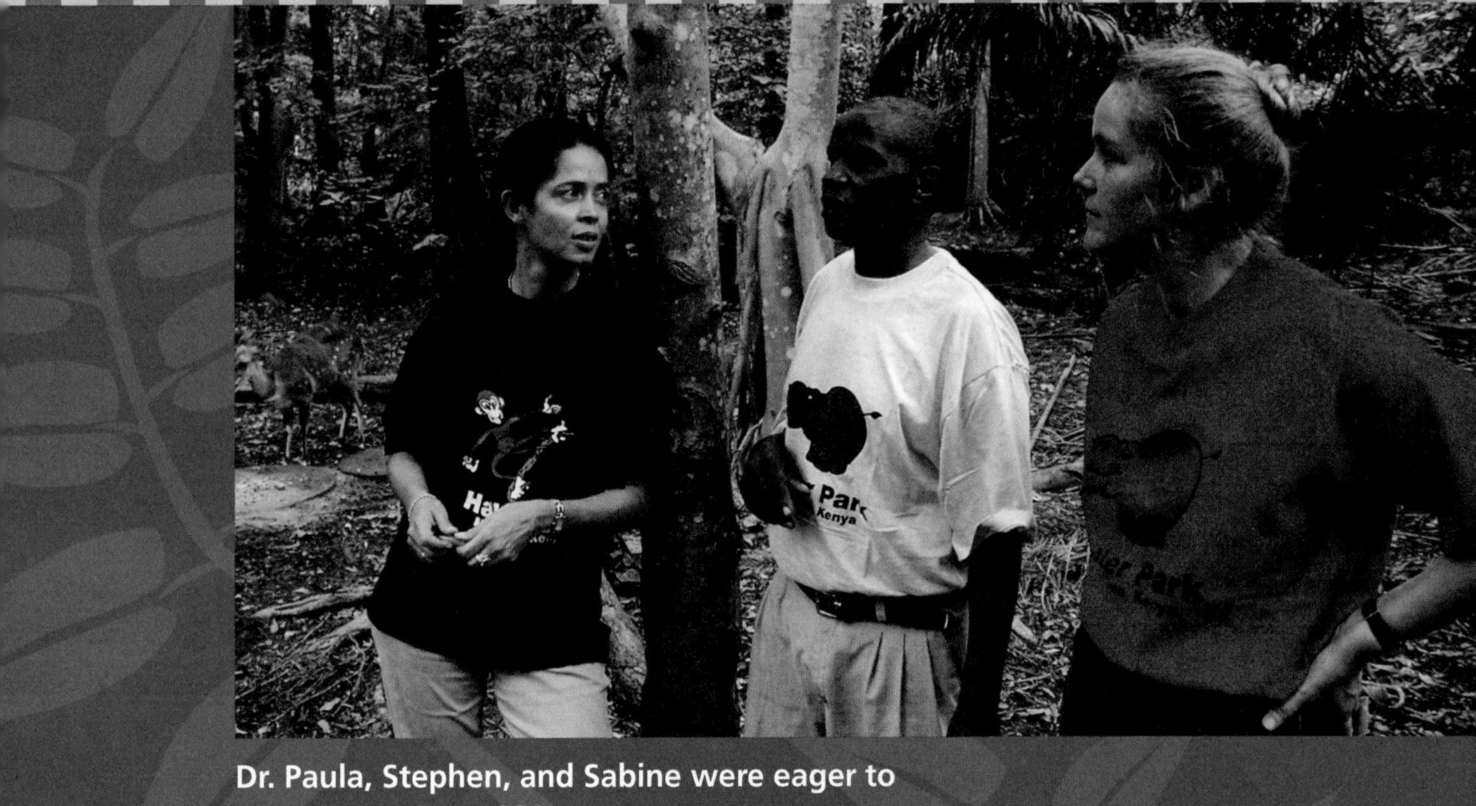

Dr. Paula, Stephen, and Sabine were eager to help the orphaned hippo.

Dr. Paula knew she would need help. She asked the chief animal caretaker, Stephen Tuei, to come along with her. She knew that Stephen had a special way with animals. Some people said he could even talk to them. Dr. Paula and Stephen quickly set off in her small truck to Malindi.

Meanwhile, ecologist Sabine Baer got to work with others at Haller Park to prepare for Owen's arrival.

When Dr. Paula and Stephen arrived in Malindi, they helped to remove the nets and lead Owen out of the pickup. But Owen became angrier than ever and charged at the people gathered around. They tried to help him calm down by wrapping a blanket around his head. That way, he wouldn't see the things that were upsetting him. But Owen was angry about that, too. After many hours, about a dozen rescuers managed to move Owen from the pickup into Dr. Paula's truck, tying him so that he would be safe during the long drive to Haller Park.

Stephen tickles Mzee.

Meanwhile, Sabine and other workers prepared a large enclosure for Owen. They chose a part of the park that had a pond and a mud wallow, as well as tall trees and brush—everything a hippo could want. The area was already home to a number of bushbucks, vervet monkeys, and a giant Aldabra tortoise called Mzee (mzay).

Mzee, whose name means "wise old man" in the Swahili (swah HEE lee) language, was the oldest creature in the park. At about 130 years of age, he had been alive since before Stephen's great-grandmother was born. He wasn't very friendly, except to Stephen, who seemed to know just what he liked, such as getting tickled under the chin. Otherwise, Mzee kept to himself.

No one could have guessed how Mzee's life was about to change.

Finally, Dr. Paula and Stephen arrived with Owen, who was now weak and exhausted. As soon as the ropes that held him were untied, Owen scrambled from the truck directly to Mzee, resting in a corner of the enclosure. Owen crouched behind Mzee, the way baby hippos often hide behind their mothers for protection. At first, Mzee wasn't happy about this attention. He hissed at Owen and crawled away. But Owen, who could easily keep up with the old tortoise, did not give up. Slowly, as the night went on, Mzee began to accept his new companion. When the park workers checked on them in the morning, Owen was snuggled up against Mzee. And Mzee didn't seem to mind at all.

At first, Mzee crawled away, but Owen wouldn't give up.

ANALYZE THE TEXT

Fact and Opinion Find one fact and one opinion on this page. How did you tell which was a fact and which was an opinion?

Over the next few days, Mzee continued to crawl away, and Owen continued to follow him. But sometimes it was Owen who would walk away from Mzee, and Mzee who would follow. Bit by bit, Mzee grew friendlier.

At first, Owen wouldn't eat any of the leaves left out for him. Stephen and the other caretakers were worried that he would weaken even more. Then they noticed Owen feeding right beside Mzee, as if Mzee were showing him how to eat. Or perhaps it was Mzee's protective presence that helped Owen feel calm enough to eat. No one will ever know. But it was clear that the bond between Owen and Mzee was helping the baby hippo to recover from being separated from his mother and stranded in the sea.

With Mzee by his side, Owen began to eat.

Both hippos and tortoises love the water.

As the weeks went on, Owen and Mzee spent more and more time together. Soon, they were inseparable. Their bond remains very strong to this day. They swim together, eat together, drink together, and sleep next to each other. They rub noses. Owen leads the way to different parts of the enclosure, then Mzee leads the way. Owen playfully nuzzles Mzee's neck, and Mzee stretches his neck forward asking for more, just as he does when Stephen tickles him under the chin. Though both animals could easily injure each other, they are gentle with one another. A sense of trust has grown between them.

ANALYZE THE TEXT

Author's Word Choice The authors use careful word choice to shape your opinion about Owen and Mzee's friendship. How do words such as *snuggled* and *inseparable* shape your opinion of the pair?

Owen nuzzles Mzee's ticklish neck.

Wildlife experts are still puzzled about how this unlikely friendship came to be. Most have never heard of a mammal, such as Owen, and a reptile, such as Mzee, forming such a strong bond.

Perhaps for Owen, it happened this way: Young hippos like Owen need their mothers in order to survive. An old, slow tortoise like Mzee can never protect Owen the way a fierce mother hippo could. But since Mzee's coloring and rounded shape are similar to a hippo's, it's possible that to Owen, Mzee looks like the hippo mother he needs.

Harder to explain is the affection that Mzee seems to show for Owen. Like most Aldabra tortoises, Mzee had always preferred to be alone. But sometimes these tortoises live in groups, and perhaps Mzee sees Owen as a fellow tortoise, the first tortoise he is willing to spend time with. Or perhaps Mzee knows that Owen isn't a tortoise, but likes him anyway.

The reasons are unclear. But science can't always explain what the heart already knows: Our most important friends are sometimes those we least expected.

News of Owen and Mzee's friendship quickly spread around the world. People all over have come to love Owen, who endured so much, yet never gave up, and Mzee, who became Owen's friend when he needed one most. Their photographs have appeared in countless newspaper and magazine articles. Television programs and even a film documentary have been made about them. Visitors come to Haller Park every day to meet the famous friends.

ANALYZE THE TEXT

Compare and Contrast How are Owen and Mzee alike? How are they different? Use details from the text to explain these similarities and differences.

Owen and Mzee look out for each other.

Owen's future is bright.

Owen suffered a great loss. But with the help of many caring people, and through his own extraordinary (ihk STROHR dn ehr ee) resilience, Owen has begun a new, happy life. Most remarkable is the role that Mzee has played. We'll never know for sure whether Owen sees Mzee as a mother, a father, or a very good friend. But it really doesn't matter. What matters is that Owen isn't alone—and neither is Mzee.

And that is the true story of Owen and Mzee, two great friends.

COMPREHENSION

Dig Deeper

How to Analyze the Text

Use these pages to learn about Comparing and Contrasting, Fact and Opinion, and Author's Word Choice. Then read "Owen and Mzee" again to apply what you learned.

Compare and Contrast

The authors of "Owen and Mzee" thought carefully about how to organize information about two very different animals. Throughout the selection, the authors **compare** and **contrast** the hippo and the tortoise, telling how the two animals are alike and how they are different. The photographs in the selection also show similarities and differences between the two animals.

Look back at page 721. How did Owen and Mzee react differently in their first meeting?

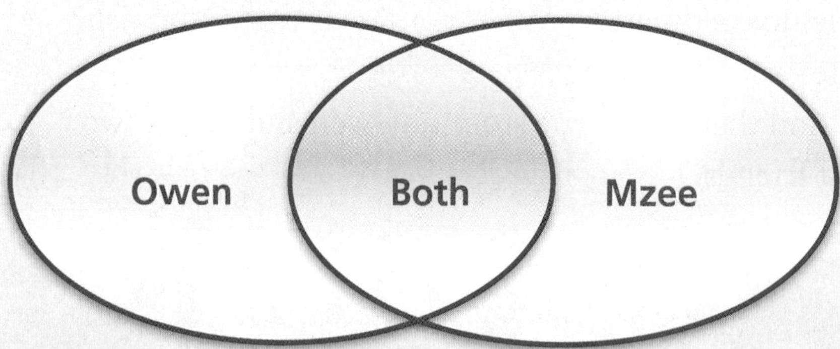

ELACC4RI5 describe the overall structure of a text or part of a text; **ELACC4RI8** explain how an author uses reasons and evidence to support points; **ELACC4L3a** choose words and phrases for effect

Fact and Opinion

Authors of nonfiction include **facts** in their writing. Facts are true statements that can be proved. Authors of nonfiction may also include **opinions,** or statements that express thoughts, feelings, or beliefs. Phrases such as *I think* and words such as *good, bad, beautiful*, and *scary* often signal an opinion. Authors include evidence and details to support both facts and opinions.

Fact: Haller Park is in Kenya.
Opinion: Haller Park is beautiful.

Author's Word Choice

The authors chose their words and phrases carefully to shape your opinion about Owen and Mzee's friendship. They used specific adjectives and verbs to convey feelings. Read this sentence: *The zoo visitors watched the mother nurture her young.* The word *nurture* conveys that the mother took care of her young lovingly. This **word choice** communicates a feeling of love and caring.

Your Turn

RETURN TO THE ESSENTIAL QUESTION

Review the selection with a partner to prepare to discuss this question: *How can animal behavior be like human behavior?* As you discuss, take turns reviewing and explaining the key ideas in your discussion.

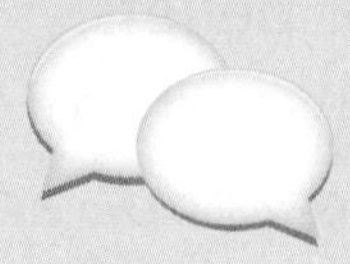

Classroom Conversation

Continue your discussion of "Owen and Mzee" by explaining your answers to these questions:

1. Why do you think Owen and Mzee are drawn to each other?
2. How do Owen and Mzee build "a sense of trust"?
3. Do you agree that our "most important friends are sometimes those we least expected"? Tell why or why not.

IF ANIMALS COULD TALK

Describe Your Life Imagine that Owen and Mzee can talk. Work with a partner. One person should pretend to be Owen. The other person should pretend to be Mzee. Take turns describing your first meeting with the other creature. Tell how your life has changed since that first meeting. Use text evidence in your description.

WRITE ABOUT READING

Response Owen and Mzee live in a wildlife park in Kenya. Using facts and details from the selection, write a paragraph explaining whether you would like to visit the two animals. Include some questions that you might ask Stephen about the animals. Be sure to write a concluding sentence that summarizes your thoughts.

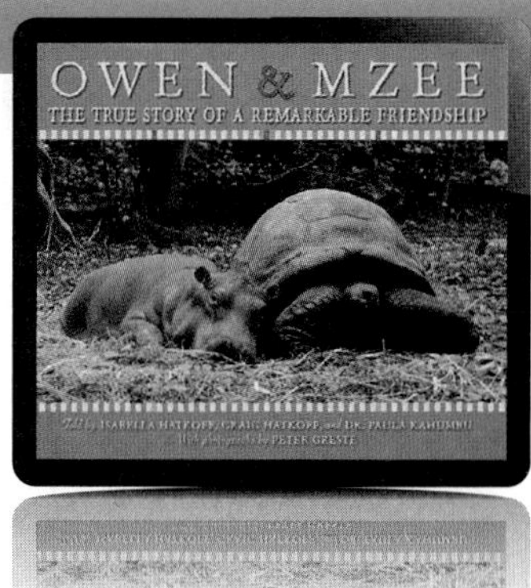

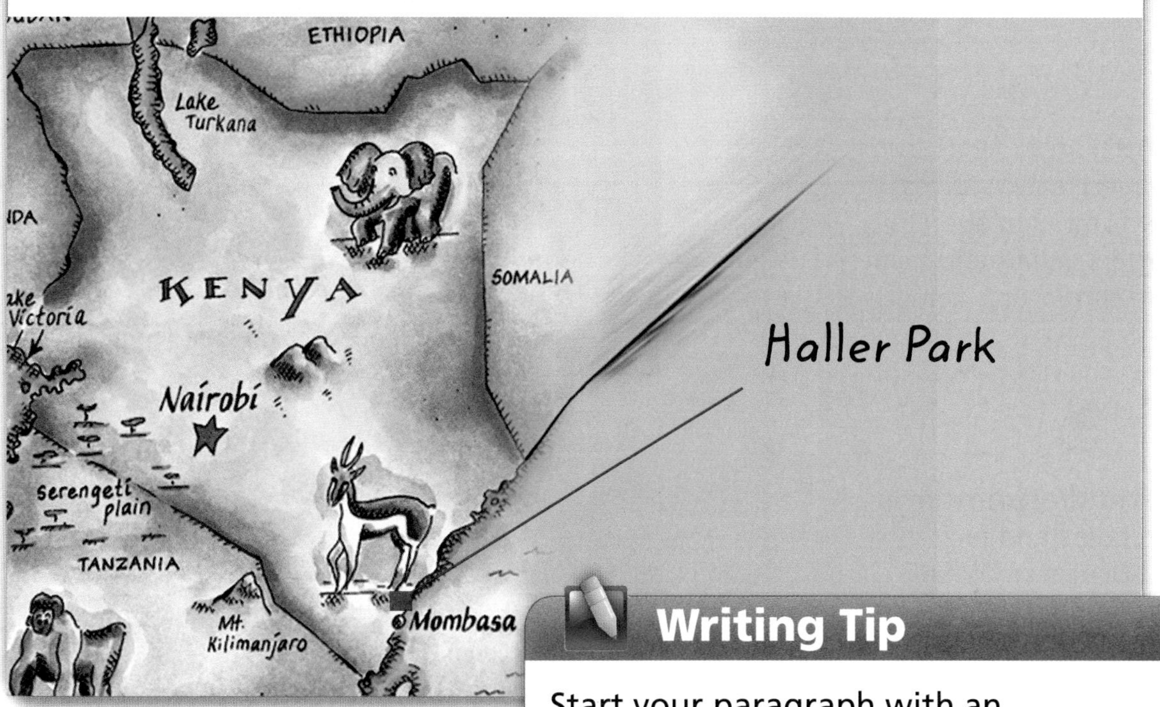

Writing Tip

Start your paragraph with an introductory sentence that clearly introduces your topic. Make sure that you use correct punctuation.

COMMON CORE **ELACC4RI1** refer to details and examples when explaining what the text says explicitly and when drawing inferences; **ELACC4W1a** introduce a topic, state an opinion, and create an organizational structure; **ELACC4W1b** provide reasons supported by facts and details; **ELACC4W1d** provide a concluding statement or section; **ELACC4W9b** apply grade 4 Reading standards to informational texts; **ELACC4SL1d** review key ideas expressed and explain own ideas and understanding

Lesson 24

INFORMATIONAL TEXT

GENRE

Informational text, such as this science article, gives factual information about a topic, organized around main ideas and supporting details.

TEXT FOCUS

Maps and diagrams help readers understand facts in informational text. What information does the diagram on page 734 add to the text of this selection?

ELACC4RI7 interpret information presented visually, orally, or quantitatively; **ELACC4RI10** read and comprehend informational texts

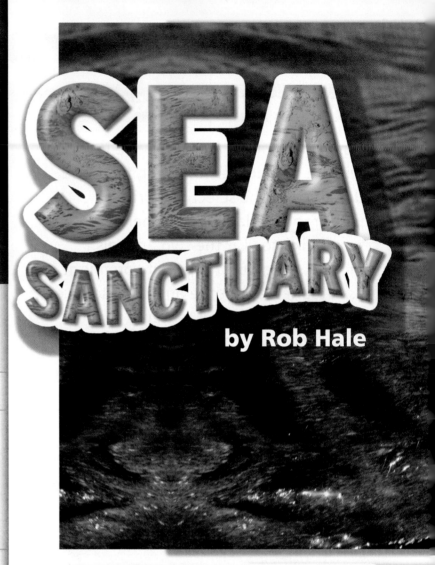

SEA SANCTUARY

by Rob Hale

Monterey Bay National Marine Sanctuary

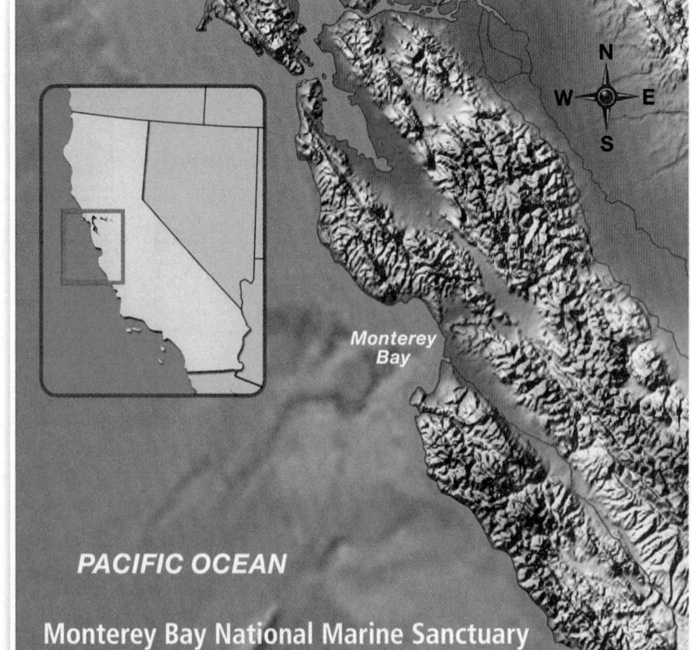

Monterey Bay National Marine Sanctuary covers more than 5,300 square miles.

A sea otter finds plenty of shellfish to eat in Monterey Bay. These animals suffered a drop in numbers because of being hunted for their fur in the early 1900s. Now, they are slowly starting to return to the area.

We often think of a wildlife sanctuary as a jewel of land that has been set aside to keep safe. But there are ocean sanctuaries, too.

The United States government has preserved thirteen important areas as marine, or sea, sanctuaries. The largest of them is California's Monterey Bay National Marine Sanctuary.

This sanctuary is an ecosystem. It is an environment whose nonliving parts, such as water and earth, work with its living parts. Each part is like a companion to another part. "Upwelling" is one example of this. Wind causes cold water to rise to the surface of the ocean. This cold water causes new plants to grow. Then, animals come to eat these plants. This food source is the chief reason why so many species are drawn to Monterey Bay. No enclosure, or closed space, keeps them there. The food does!

Seafood Chain

Each plant and animal in a sanctary is part of a food chain. A necessary bond connects each hunter to its prey. The need for food is why a hungry orca might charge at a sea lion. It is the same reason a sea lion might leave a rockfish exhausted after a chase. One animal depends on another for life.

Flower Garden Banks

Coral reefs and ocean waters are inseparable. Coral reefs can be found 110 miles off the Texas and Louisiana coasts. They are protected by the Flower Garden Banks, a 36,000-acre marine sanctuary.

The coral reefs lie on top of two salt domes, old underwater mountains. Today Flower Garden Banks Sanctuary is home to twenty-three types of coral. Anyone with affection for marine creatures will find many animals there. One might see turtles, manta rays, or the odd intruder, such as the huge whale shark.

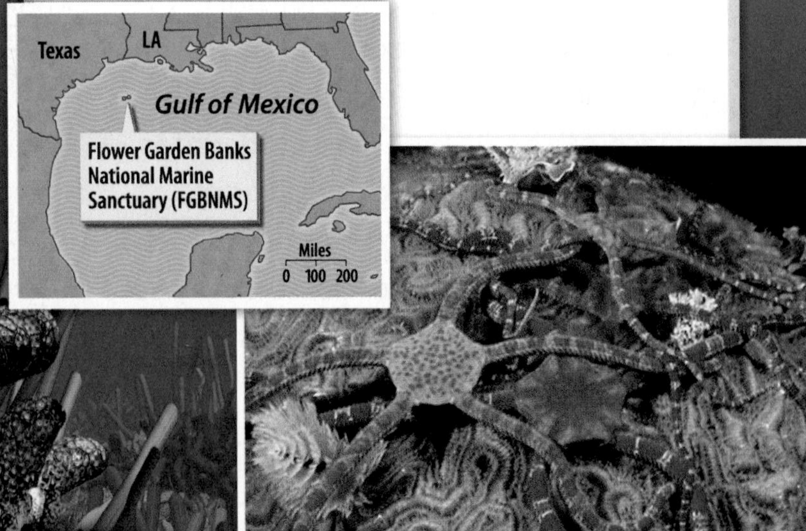

Predators and Prey

A healthy environment keeps each member of the food chain well fed. Orcas eat sea lions. Sea lions eat rockfish. Rockfish eat krill. Krill eat tiny plankton.

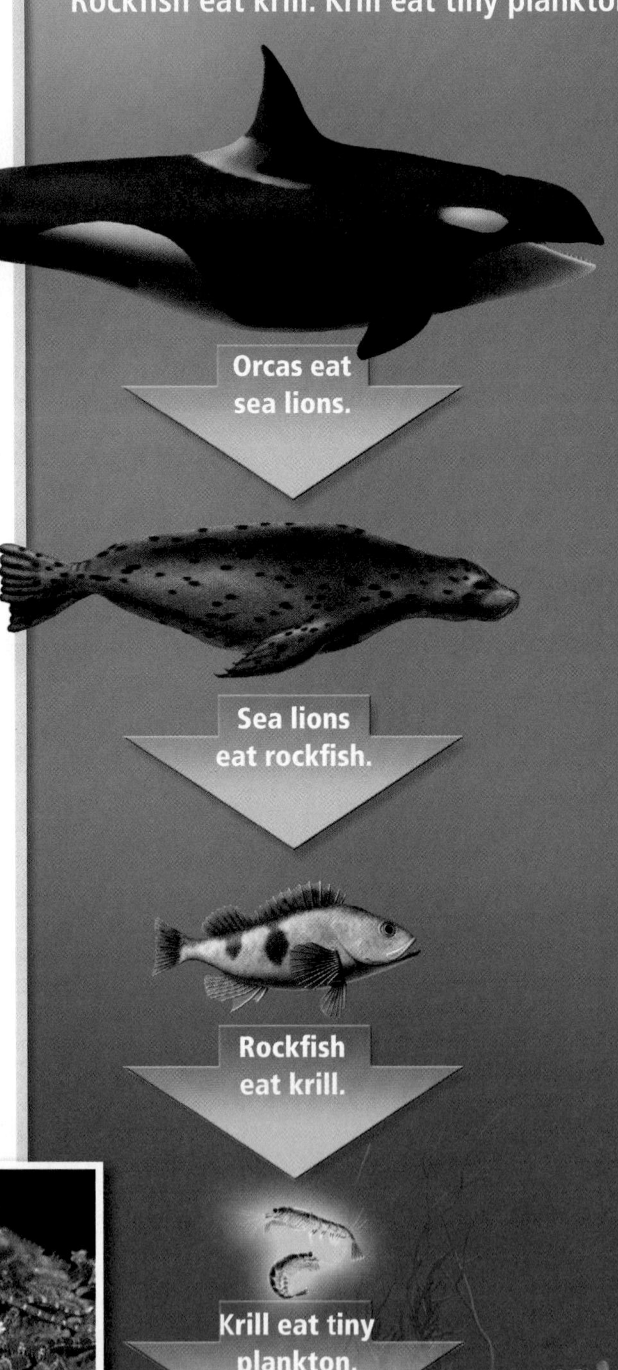

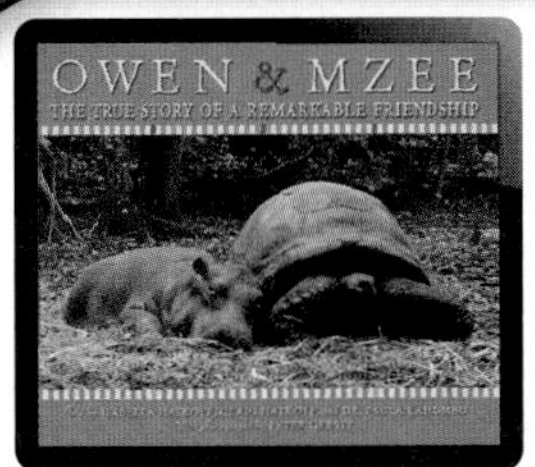

Compare Texts

TEXT TO TEXT

Compare Nonfiction Both "Owen and Mzee" and "Sea Sanctuary" are nonfiction. With a partner, make a Venn diagram to compare and contrast the two selections. Include information about how the texts are organized, the types of graphics and photographs used, and the authors' purposes.

TEXT TO SELF

Write About an Animal Think about a time when you saw an animal in the wild, in a zoo, or in an aquarium. Write a description of the animal and its habitat. Tell how it interacted with nearby animals. Share your writing with a small group.

TEXT TO WORLD

Connect to Science Think about another part of the world where a wildlife sanctuary might help protect a threatened species or habitat. With a partner, use the Internet or other media to find out more information about that animal or habitat. Present your findings to the class.

ELACC4RI5 describe the overall structure of a text or part of a text; **ELACC4RI7** interpret information presented visually, orally, or quantitatively; **ELACC4W7** conduct short research projects that build knowledge through investigation; **ELACC4SL4** report on a topic or text, tell a story, or recount an experience/speak clearly at an understandable pace

ELACC4L2b use commas and quotation marks to mark direct speech and quotations from a text; **ELACC4L2c** use a comma before a coordinating conjunction in a compound sentence

Grammar

How Are Commas Used? A **comma** is needed after an introductory word in a sentence. One or two commas are needed to set off the name of a person being addressed. A comma separates the day and the year in a date as well as the city and the state in a place name. Commas are used to separate items in a series, a list of nouns or actions.

to set off an introductory word; to set off a name

No, Wardell, that is not a warthog.

in a place name

It is the baby hippo that was rescued near Malindi, Kenya, on December 27, 2004.

in a date

to separate items in a series

Villagers, fishermen, and visitors performed the rescue.

A comma is used with a conjunction to form a compound sentence. A comma is also used to introduce quotations.

to join parts of a compound sentence

The tortoise was not very friendly, but he loved being tickled.

in a direct quotation

"I would love to see a baby hippo," remarked Ann.

Work with a partner. Read each sentence and tell how each comma is used.

1. Leah said, "Our zoo has adult hippos, but none of them have babies."
2. "Hey, let's look on the Internet," suggested Ivan.
3. Leah, Ann, and Juan ran to the computer.
4. They found a baby hippo in a zoo in Seattle, Washington.

Sentences with missing commas can be difficult for readers to understand. Check your writing carefully to make sure you have used commas where they are needed.

Sentences with Missing Commas	Sentences with Correct Comma Usage
Sheila Billy and Ava flew into Mombasa Kenya on May 22 2014.	Sheila, Billy, and Ava flew into Mombasa, Kenya, on May 22, 2014.
"Look here Billy" said Sheila.	"Look here, Billy," said Sheila.
Billy exclaimed "The tortoise is eating, so the little hippo is eating, too!"	Billy exclaimed, "The tortoise is eating, so the little hippo is eating, too!"

Connect Grammar to Writing

As you edit your research report next week, make sure that you have used commas correctly. They should be used with introductory words, names, dates, places, direct quotations, compound sentences, and items in a series.

ELACC4W2a introduce a topic and group related information/include formatting, illustrations, and multimedia; **ELACC4W2b** develop the topic with facts, definitions, details, quotations, or other information and examples; **ELACC4W5** ddevelop and strengthen writing by planning, revising, and editing; **ELACC4W7** conduct short research projects that build knowledge through investigation

Informative Writing

Reading-Writing Workshop: Prewrite

my WriteSmart

Go Digital

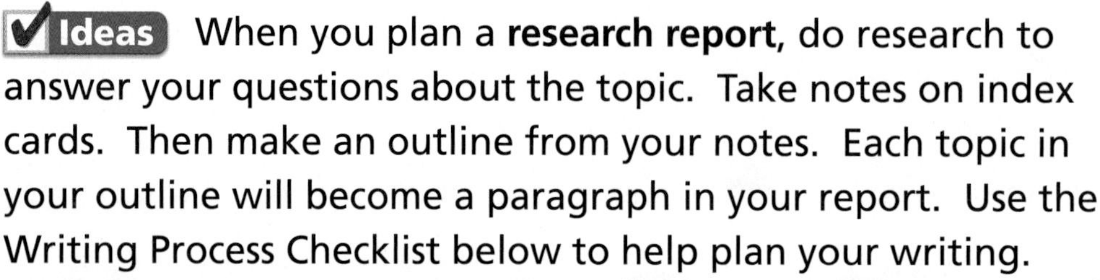

Ideas When you plan a **research report**, do research to answer your questions about the topic. Take notes on index cards. Then make an outline from your notes. Each topic in your outline will become a paragraph in your report. Use the Writing Process Checklist below to help plan your writing.

Maya took notes to answer her questions about hippos. Then she organized all of her notes into an outline.

Writing Process Checklist

▶ Prewrite

- ✔ Did I choose a topic that will interest my audience and me?
- ✔ Did I ask interesting questions about my topic?
- ✔ Did I use dependable sources to find facts?
- ✔ Did I take notes on enough facts?
- ✔ Did I organize my outline with main topics and subtopics?

Draft

Revise

Edit

Publish and Share

Exploring a Topic

What is a hippo's habitat?
-in Africa by rivers and lakes "spend much of the day in the water because the intense heat can rapidly dehydrate them" Langston, Kate. "Hippo Facts." Nature for Kids May 2003: paragraph 1. www.onfourfeet.org/mammals/hippo Nov. 7, 2010.

What do hippos eat?
- mainly plants
- eat at night on grasslands
- about eighty pounds of food a day
Deets, Wayne. The Hippopotamus. New York: Kite Tail Books, 2009. p. 14.

Outline

I. What are hippos?

   A. Huge animals related to pigs

   B. Their name means "river horse"

II. Hippos' water habitat

   A. Live by rivers and lakes in Africa

   B. Spend day in water because "intense heat can rapidly dehydrate them"

   C. In water can watch for danger—eyes near top of head

   D. Walk on river or lake bottom—can hold breath about five minutes

III. What hippos eat

   A. Eat on land at night

   B. Mostly plants

   C. Grab food with lips—sharp teeth only for fighting

   D. Eat about eighty pounds a day—small amount for size

Reading as a Writer

In what way do Maya's facts support her topics? In your outline, where can you add interesting and specific facts, information, and examples?

In my outline, I grouped my facts by topic. I listed them in an order that makes sense. I will use the topic labels as headings in my report.

Lesson

25

ISAAC ASIMOV THE COMPLETE STORIES

Toys! Amazing Stories Behind Some Great Inventions

TARGET VOCABULARY

progress
calculated
dispute
centuries
superior
insert
waste
inspector
mechanical
average

Vocabulary Reader

Context Cards

ELACC4L6 acquire/use vocabulary, including academic and domain-specific

Vocabulary in Context

1 progress

Today's many ways of learning may show society's progress, or improvement.

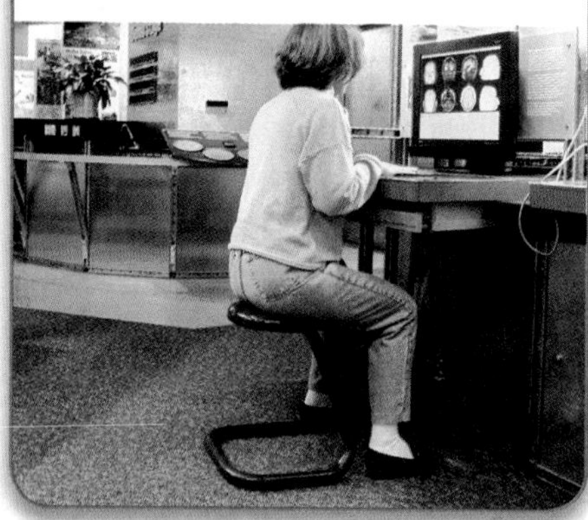

2 calculated

Using machines, many people have calculated answers to math problems.

3 dispute

People dispute the value of TV. Some argue that shows can be educational.

4 centuries

For centuries, or hundreds of years, we've learned a lot from books.

- Study each Context Card.
- Break the longer words into syllables. Use a dictionary to confirm.

5 **superior**

Some people find the Internet superior to, or better than, other ways of learning.

6 **insert**

If you insert a book on disc into a portable CD player, you can learn on the go.

7 **waste**

It's such a waste to throw away old computers. They could be recycled.

8 **inspector**

This inspector checks a disc to make sure there's nothing wrong with it.

9 **mechanical**

Typewriters are mechanical devices for writing that are hardly used anymore.

10 **average**

The average, or typical, reader might prefer printed books to electronic books.

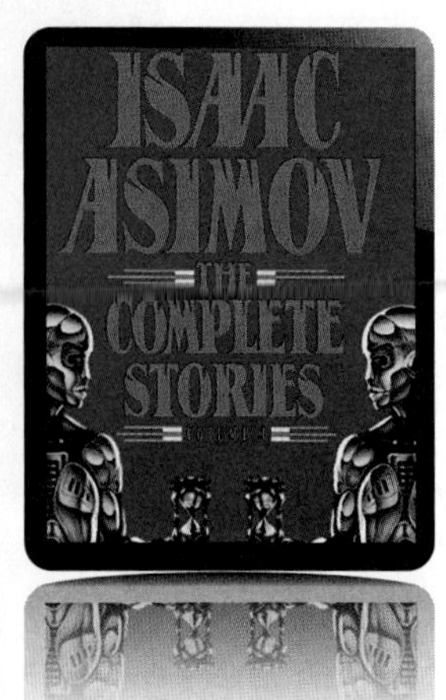

Read and Comprehend

TARGET SKILL

Author's Purpose As you read "The Fun They Had," think about the author's reasons for writing the story. Does he want to entertain, inform, or persuade you? Look for text evidence about the plot and characters as clues to the **author's purpose.** Use a graphic organizer like this one to identify details that will help you figure out the author's purpose.

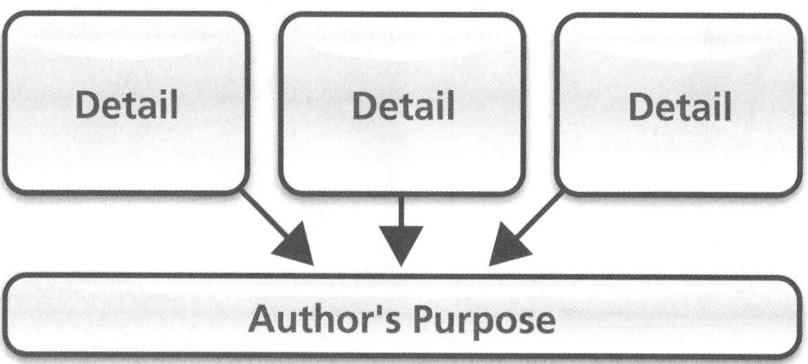

TARGET STRATEGY

Question Ask **questions** before you read, as you read, and after you read. Asking yourself questions can help you better understand the story and figure out the author's purpose. Look for text evidence to help you answer.

COMMON CORE **ELACC4RL1** refer to details and examples when explaining what the text says explicitly and when drawing inferences

PREVIEW THE TOPIC

Inventions

An invention is something that someone thought up and built to solve a problem or to do a job in a better way. Often inventions are devices or gadgets, like the lightbulb or the radio. While new inventions might make our lives easier, they can also complicate our lives in ways the inventors never expected.

"The Fun They Had" features a mechanical teacher, an invention the author has imagined for classrooms of the future. You'll find out whether kids of the future like this invention.

Lesson 25

ANCHOR TEXT

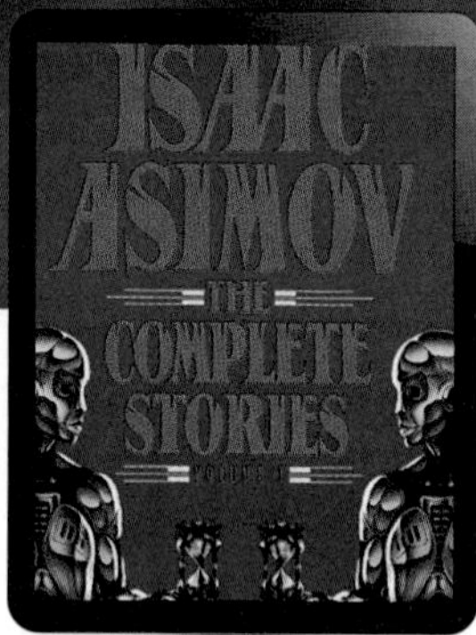

TARGET SKILL

Author's Purpose Use text details to figure out the author's reasons for writing.

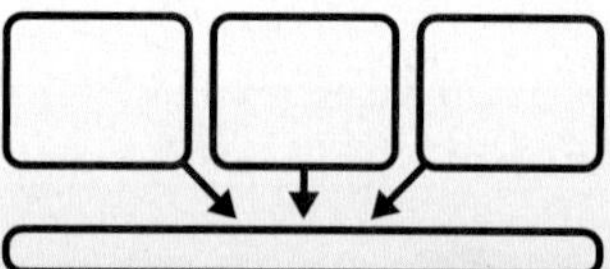

GENRE

Science fiction is a story set in the future and is based on scientific ideas. As you read, look for:

- characters who may or may not act like real people
- technology of the future
- events that cannot happen in real life today

COMMON CORE **ELACC4RL1** refer to details and examples when explaining what the text says explicitly and when drawing inferences; **ELACC4RL3** describe a character, setting, or event, drawing on details; **ELACC4RL10** read and comprehend literature

MEET THE AUTHOR

Isaac Asimov

Isaac Asimov is one of the world's best-known science-fiction writers. His work helped people take science fiction more seriously. Isaac saw his first science-fiction magazine in his father's candy store. After writing his first three hundred books, he said, "Writing is more fun than ever. The longer I write, the easier it gets."

MEET THE ILLUSTRATOR

Alan Flinn

Alan Flinn has been an illustrator for more than twenty years. With author Jim Sukach, he created a book of detective stories called *Elliott's Talking Dog and Other Quicksolve Mysteries.* He has also illustrated *Constellations*, a glow-in-the-dark astronomy book.

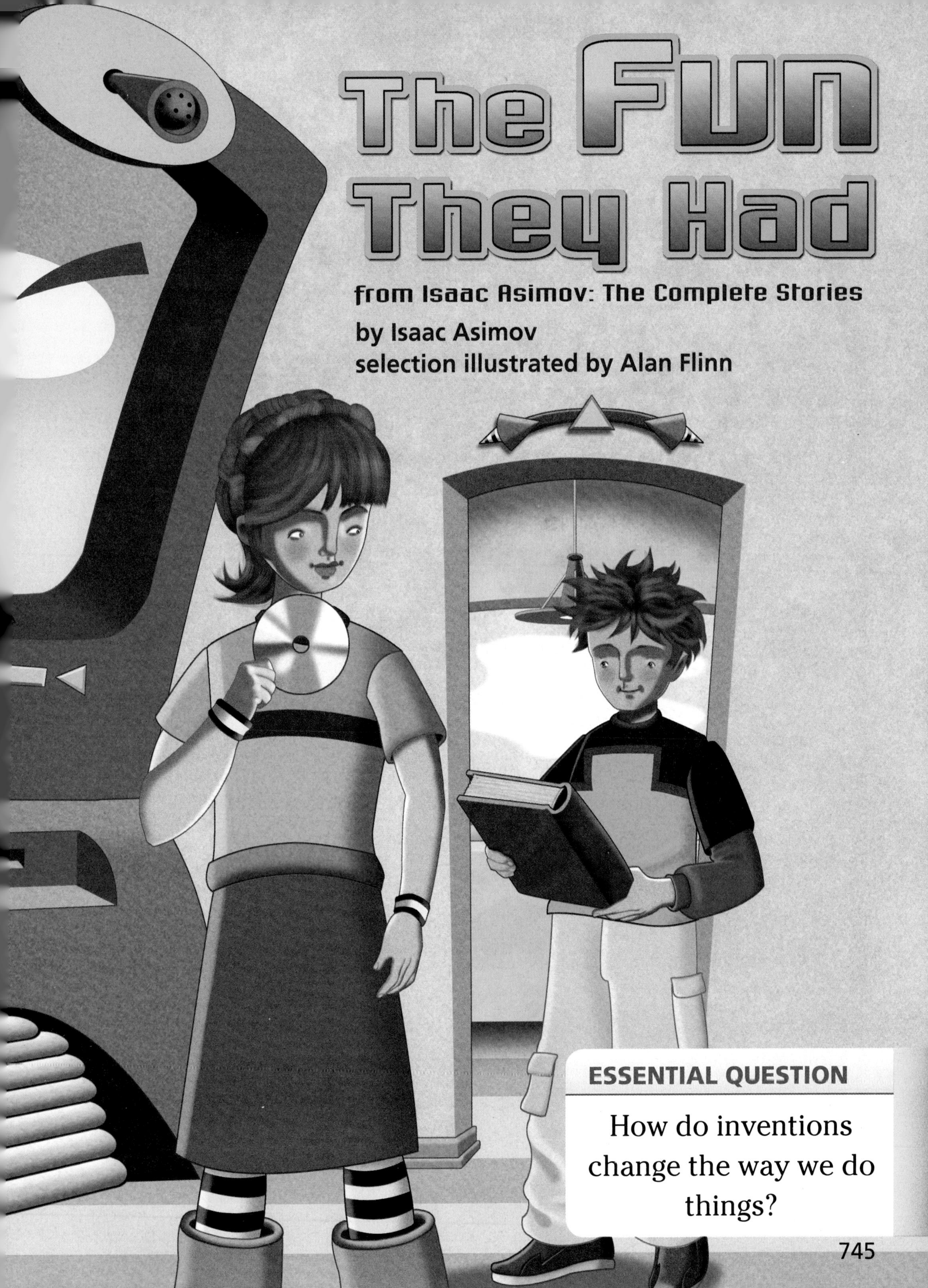

The FUN They Had

from Isaac Asimov: The Complete Stories

by Isaac Asimov

selection illustrated by Alan Flinn

ESSENTIAL QUESTION

How do inventions change the way we do things?

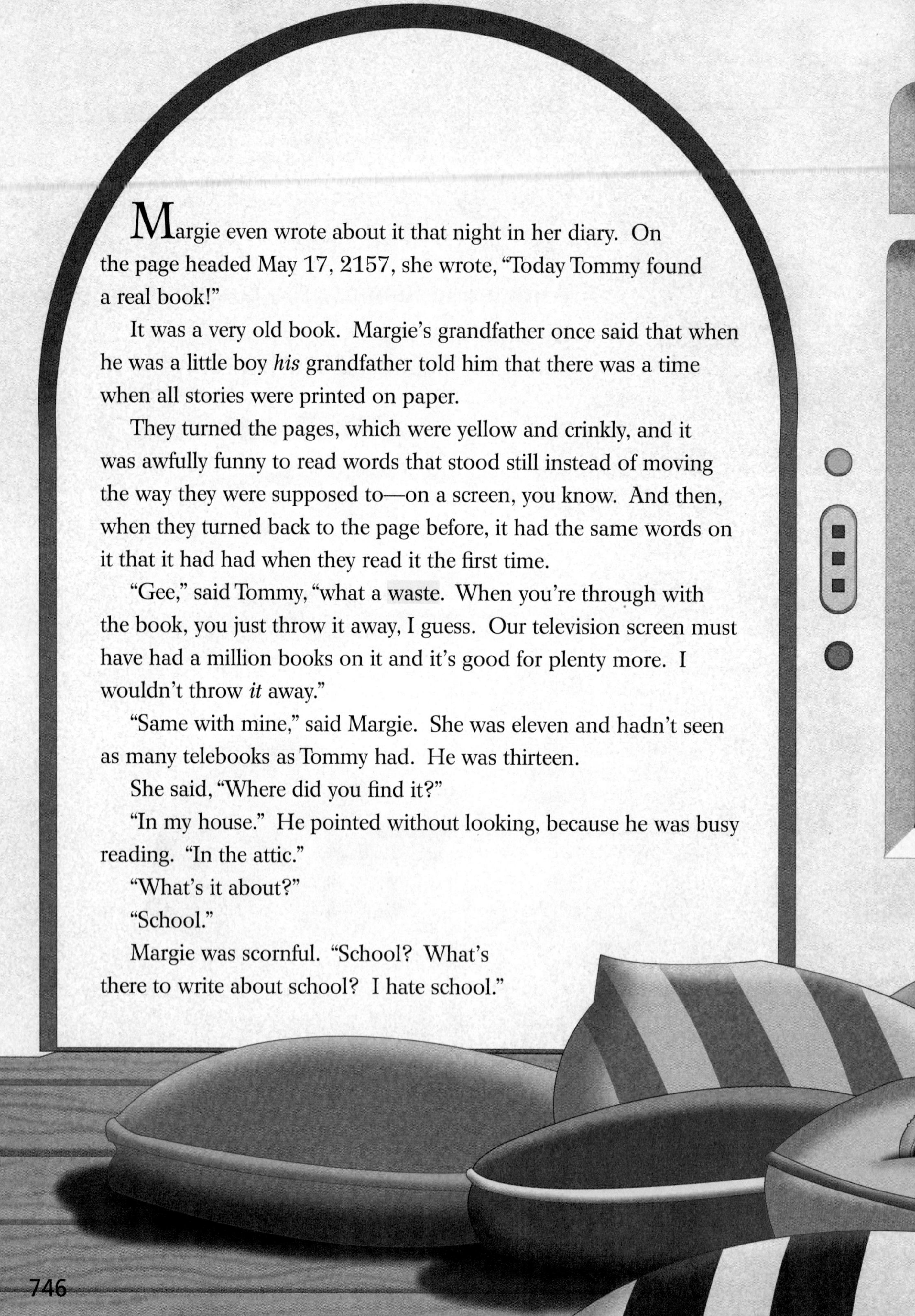

Margie even wrote about it that night in her diary. On the page headed May 17, 2157, she wrote, "Today Tommy found a real book!"

It was a very old book. Margie's grandfather once said that when he was a little boy *his* grandfather told him that there was a time when all stories were printed on paper.

They turned the pages, which were yellow and crinkly, and it was awfully funny to read words that stood still instead of moving the way they were supposed to—on a screen, you know. And then, when they turned back to the page before, it had the same words on it that it had had when they read it the first time.

"Gee," said Tommy, "what a waste. When you're through with the book, you just throw it away, I guess. Our television screen must have had a million books on it and it's good for plenty more. I wouldn't throw *it* away."

"Same with mine," said Margie. She was eleven and hadn't seen as many telebooks as Tommy had. He was thirteen.

She said, "Where did you find it?"

"In my house." He pointed without looking, because he was busy reading. "In the attic."

"What's it about?"

"School."

Margie was scornful. "School? What's there to write about school? I hate school."

ANALYZE THE TEXT

Genre: Science Fiction Many science-fiction stories take place in the future. How does a futuristic setting affect what could happen in the story?

Margie always hated school, but now she hated it more than ever. The mechanical teacher had been giving her test after test in geography and she had been doing worse and worse until her mother had shaken her head sorrowfully and sent for the County Inspector.

He was a round little man with a red face and a whole box of tools with dials and wires. He smiled at Margie and gave her an apple, then took the teacher apart. Margie had hoped he wouldn't know how to put it together again, but he knew how all right, and, after an hour or so, there it was again, large and square and ugly, with a big screen on which all the lessons were shown and the questions were asked. That wasn't so bad. The part Margie hated most was the slot where she had to put homework and test papers. She always had to write them out in a punch code they made her learn when she was six years old, and the mechanical teacher calculated the mark in no time.

The Inspector had smiled after he was finished and patted Margie's head. He said to her mother, "It's not the little girl's fault, Mrs. Jones. I think the geography sector was geared a little too quick. Those things happen sometimes. I've slowed it up to an average ten-year level. Actually, the overall pattern of her progress is quite satisfactory." And he patted Margie's head again.

Margie was disappointed. She had been hoping they would take the teacher away altogether. They had once taken Tommy's teacher away for nearly a month because the history sector had blanked out completely.

ANALYZE THE TEXT

Formal and Informal Language
Does the Inspector use formal or informal language? How does the way he speaks compare to Margie and Tommy's dialogue on page 746?

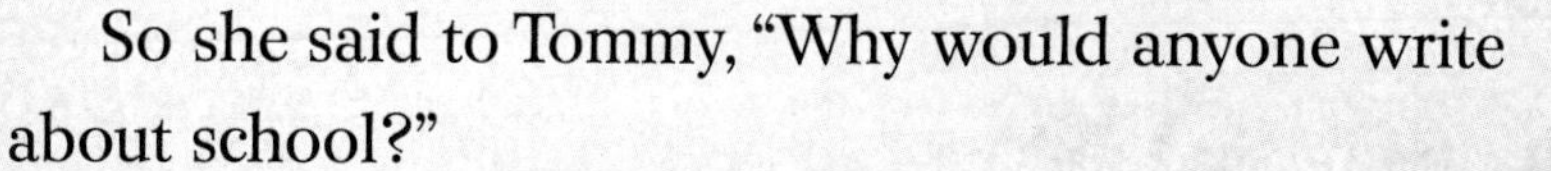

So she said to Tommy, "Why would anyone write about school?"

Tommy looked at her with very superior eyes. "Because it's not our kind of school, stupid. This is the old kind of school that they had hundreds and hundreds of years ago." He added loftily, pronouncing the word carefully, "*Centuries* ago."

Margie was hurt. "Well, I don't know what kind of school they had all that time ago." She read the book over his shoulder for a while, then said, "Anyway, they had a teacher."

"Sure they had a teacher, but it wasn't a *regular* teacher. It was a man."

"A man? How could a man be a teacher?"

"Well, he just told the boys and girls things and gave them homework and asked them questions."

"A man isn't smart enough."

"Sure he is. My father knows as much as my teacher."

"He can't. A man can't know as much as a teacher."

"He knows almost as much, I betcha."

Margie wasn't prepared to dispute that. She said, "I wouldn't want a strange man in my house to teach me."

Tommy screamed with laughter. "You don't know much, Margie. The teachers didn't live in the house. They had a special building and all the kids went there."

"And all the kids learned the same thing?"

"Sure, if they were the same age."

"But my mother says a teacher has to be adjusted to fit the mind of each boy and girl it teaches and that each kid has to be taught differently."

"Just the same they didn't do it that way then. If you don't like it, you don't have to read the book."

"I didn't say I didn't like it," Margie said quickly. She wanted to read about those funny schools.

They weren't even half-finished when Margie's mother called, "Margie! School!"

Margie looked up. "Not yet, Mamma."

"Now!" said Mrs. Jones. "And it's probably time for Tommy, too."

Margie said to Tommy, "Can I read the book some more with you after school?"

"Maybe," he said nonchalantly (nahn shuh LAHNT lee). He walked away whistling, the dusty old book tucked beneath his arm.

Margie went into the schoolroom. It was right next to her bedroom, and the mechanical teacher was on and waiting for her. It was always on at the same time every day except Saturday and Sunday, because her mother said little girls learned better if they learned at regular hours.

The screen was lit up, and it said: "Today's arithmetic lesson is on the addition of proper fractions. Please insert yesterday's homework in the proper slot."

Margie did so with a sigh. She was thinking about the old schools they had when her grandfather's grandfather was a little boy. All the kids from the whole neighborhood came, laughing and shouting in the schoolyard, sitting together in the schoolroom, going home together at the end of the day. They learned the same things, so they could help one another on the homework and talk about it.

And the teachers were people. . . .

The mechanical teacher was flashing on the screen: "When we add the fractions ½ and ¼—"

Margie was thinking about how the kids must have loved it in the old days. She was thinking about the fun they had.

ANALYZE THE TEXT

Author's Purpose Why do you think the author wrote this story? What story details show his purpose? Keep in mind that the story was first published in 1951.

Please
Insert
Yesterday's
Homework
In The
Proper
Slot

COMPREHENSION

Dig Deeper

How to Analyze the Text

Use these pages to learn about Author's Purpose, Science Fiction, and Formal and Informal Language. Then read "The Fun They Had" again to apply what you learned.

Author's Purpose

In "The Fun They Had," the author imagines a time in the future when school is very different from the way it is today. His story can entertain, inform, or persuade you all at the same time. What do you think is his most important purpose?

For clues, look at the **details** about the plot and characters. Look back at the beginning of the story. What does Margie say about school? Use a graphic organizer like this one to help you figure out the **author's purpose** for writing.

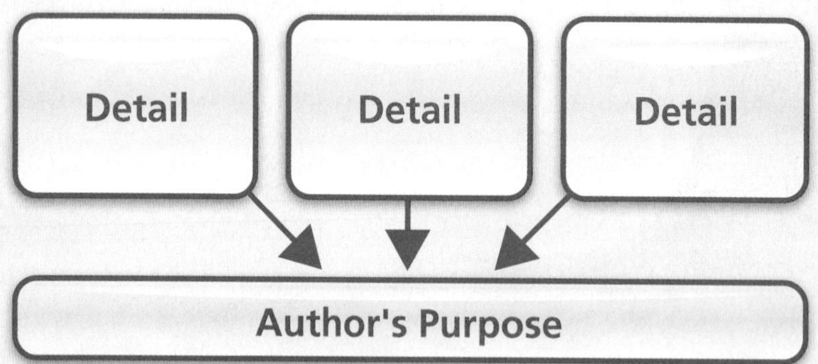

ELACC4RL1 refer to details and examples when explaining what the text says explicitly and when drawing inferences; **ELACC4RL3** describe a character, setting, or event, drawing on details; **ELACC4RL7** make connections between the text and a visual or oral presentation of it; **ELACC4L3c** differentiate contexts that call for formal English and informal discourse

Genre: Science Fiction

"The Fun They Had" is **science fiction.** It is set in the future and features technology that the author could only imagine in 1951. The story describes a mechanical teacher and telebooks. What other futuristic details did the author include to make this science-fiction story fun for readers of the 1950s? How did the illustrator show the details?

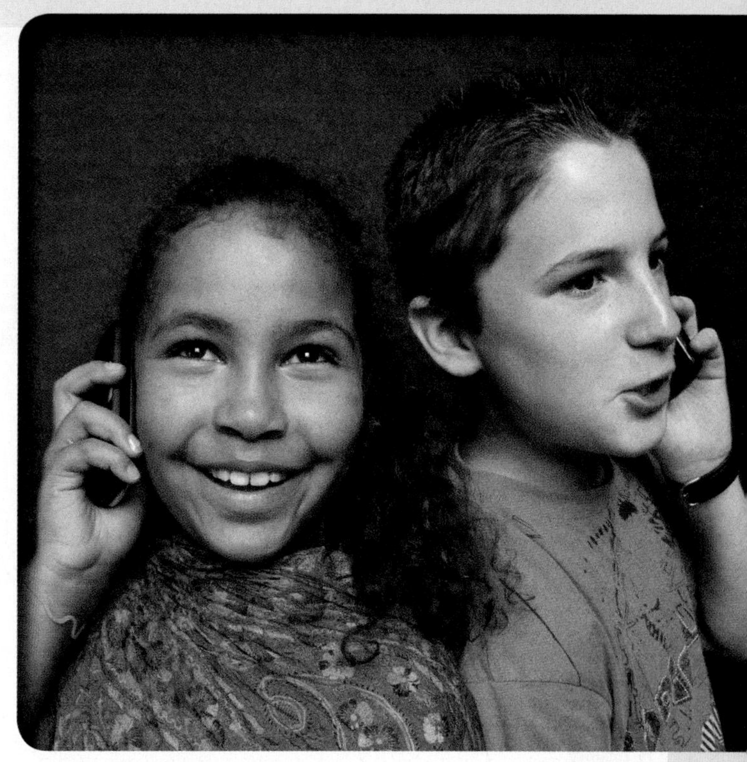

Formal and Informal Language

The author has some characters use **formal language,** which is used when giving a presentation. An example is when the Inspector says, "Actually, the overall pattern of her progress is quite satisfactory." He has other characters use **informal language,** which is used when talking with friends. An example is when Tommy says, "He knows almost as much, I betcha."

Your Turn

RETURN TO THE ESSENTIAL QUESTION

Turn and Talk Review the selection with a partner to prepare to discuss this question: *How do inventions change the way we do things?* Take turns reviewing key ideas in your discussion. Be sure to clearly explain your own ideas using text evidence.

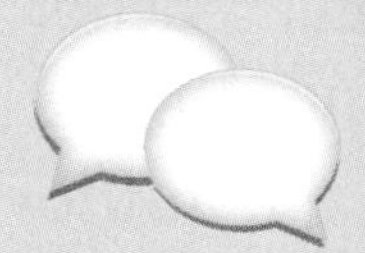

Classroom Conversation

Continue your discussion of "The Fun They Had" by explaining your answers to these questions:

1. How is the technology of today similar to what the author imagined in 1951?
2. What made Margie change her opinion about schools?
3. What are the advantages of having a mechanical teacher? What are the disadvantages?

A PICTURE TELLS A STORY

Connect Illustrations and Text With a partner, look carefully at the illustrations in "The Fun They Had" and review the text. Think about how the illustrations match the descriptions in the story. Then choose one illustration. List the details in the story that the artist likely used to create this artwork. Share your list with another pair of students.

WRITE ABOUT READING

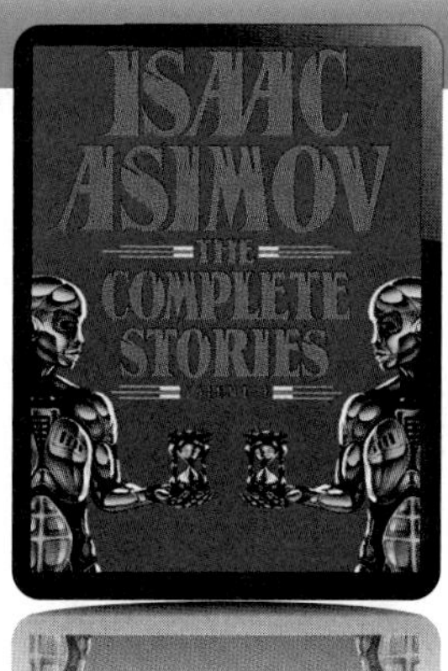

Response How is the future school that the author imagined similar to schools today? How is it different? Write a paragraph comparing and contrasting the two schools. Use facts and examples from your own school experiences, as well as text evidence and quotations from the story, to develop and support your ideas.

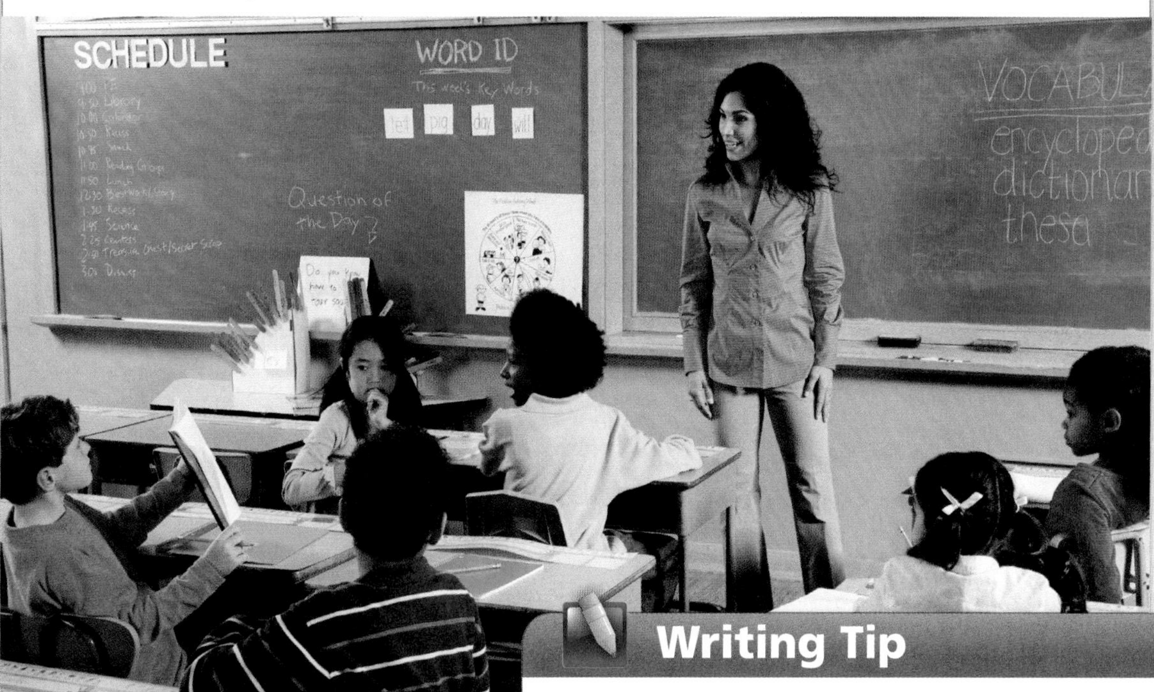

Writing Tip

Organize your paragraph by first explaining how the two schools are the same. Then explain how they are different. Remember to use quotation marks and commas for quotations from the story.

COMMON CORE **ELACC4RL1** refer to details and examples when explaining what the text says explicitly and when drawing inferences; **ELACC4RL7** make connections between the text and a visual or oral presentation of it; **ELACC4W9a** apply grade 4 Reading standards to literature; **ELACC4SL1d** review key ideas expressed and explain own ideas and understanding; **ELACC4L2b** use commas and quotation marks to mark direct speech and quotations from a text

Lesson 25

INFORMATIONAL TEXT

GENRE

Informational text, such as this article, gives facts and details about a topic. Informational text often includes visuals, such as photographs and diagrams.

TEXT FOCUS

Diagrams show the parts of something or how something works. Diagrams usually include labels that name each of the parts. What does the diagram on page 759 show?

ELACC4RI7 interpret information presented visually, orally, or quantitatively; **ELACC4RI10** read and comprehend informational texts

Toys!

Amazing Stories Behind Some Great Inventions

by Don Wulffson

Windup Toys and Automatons

What makes a windup toy work? Turning a key tightens a spring inside the toy. As the spring unwinds, it turns gears, which move the toy's parts.

Today's windup toys are for children, and most of them are relatively simple. Originally, windup toys were for adults—usually royalty—and were often extremely complicated and expensive. Rather than windup toys, they were called automatons and usually featured people, animals, or vehicles of some kind. With the finest craftsmanship, automatons moved by means of elaborate internal clockwork devices; their exterior was formed and decorated by hand, in many cases with the utmost skill and attention to detail.

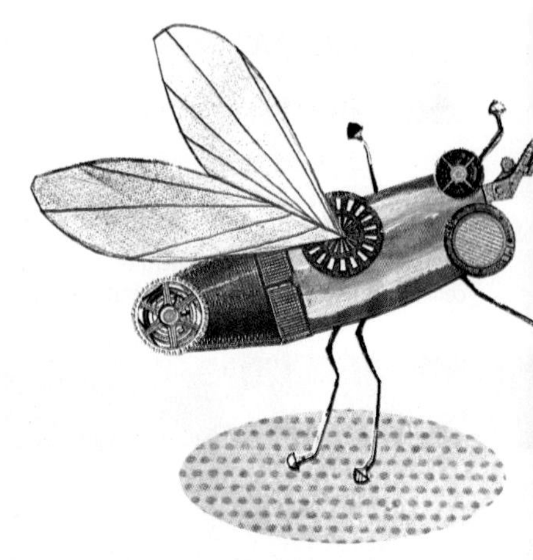

Go Digital

Turning the key on the windup toy tightens the spring. As the spring unwinds, it turns the gears inside the toy, causing the toy to move.

mainspring

end affixed to toy

ratchet wheel

driving gear

end affixed to key

key

axle

gear

In the late 1400s, a German inventor by the name of Karel Grod was often invited to royal banquets. Sitting at the table, Grod would open his hands and release a metal fly that buzzed across the room, circled the long dining table, and then returned to rest on its maker's hand. A few years later, Grod created a life-size mechanical eagle that could fly around town and then return to its original spot.

In 1509, the famous artist and inventor Leonardo da Vinci constructed a mechanical lion to welcome Louis XII to Italy. When the French king was seated on his throne, Leonardo placed the animal on the floor at the opposite end of a great hall. As spectators stared in amazement, the clockwork lion moved slowly toward the king. It stopped in front of him, and, as if in tribute to the king, tore open its chest with its claws. A decorative fleur-de-lis, the symbol of French royalty, tumbled out and fell at the king's feet.

An even more incredible story is told about René Descartes, a renowned French philosopher and scientist of the 1600s. Descartes believed that all living creatures, including people, are basically just highly developed machines. To demonstrate this he constructed a life-size mechanical girl. Shortly after completing the automaton, whom he called Franchina, he took her on a sea voyage. By accident, the captain of the ship set her in motion. Terrified by her sudden movement, the captain ran. The robotic Franchina kept coming toward him. In a panic, the captain grabbed the automaton and threw it overboard.

Perhaps the most fantastic mechanical figures of all time were created by Jean-Pierre Droz, a Swiss watchmaker, and by his son Henri-Louis. One of those made by Jean-Pierre, called the Writer, was a full-size likeness of a young boy seated at a desk. When put into motion, the clockwork child dipped his pen in a bottle of ink, shook off the surplus with a flick of the wrist, then proceeded to write clear and correct sentences. As each line was completed, the hand holding the pen moved to the beginning of the next line.

Superior to the Writer was the Designer, an automaton created by Jean-Pierre's son Henri-Louis. Like an artist studying his model, the automaton paused from time to time as he sketched, examined his work, corrected errors, and even blew the eraser dust from the paper. On one occasion, the Designer was seated before King Louis XVI of France; after working for some time, the automaton put down his pencil and gestured with his hand to his work: a portrait of the French king. Later, when Henri-Louis gave a demonstration in England, his automaton drew portraits of the English monarch and other royalty.

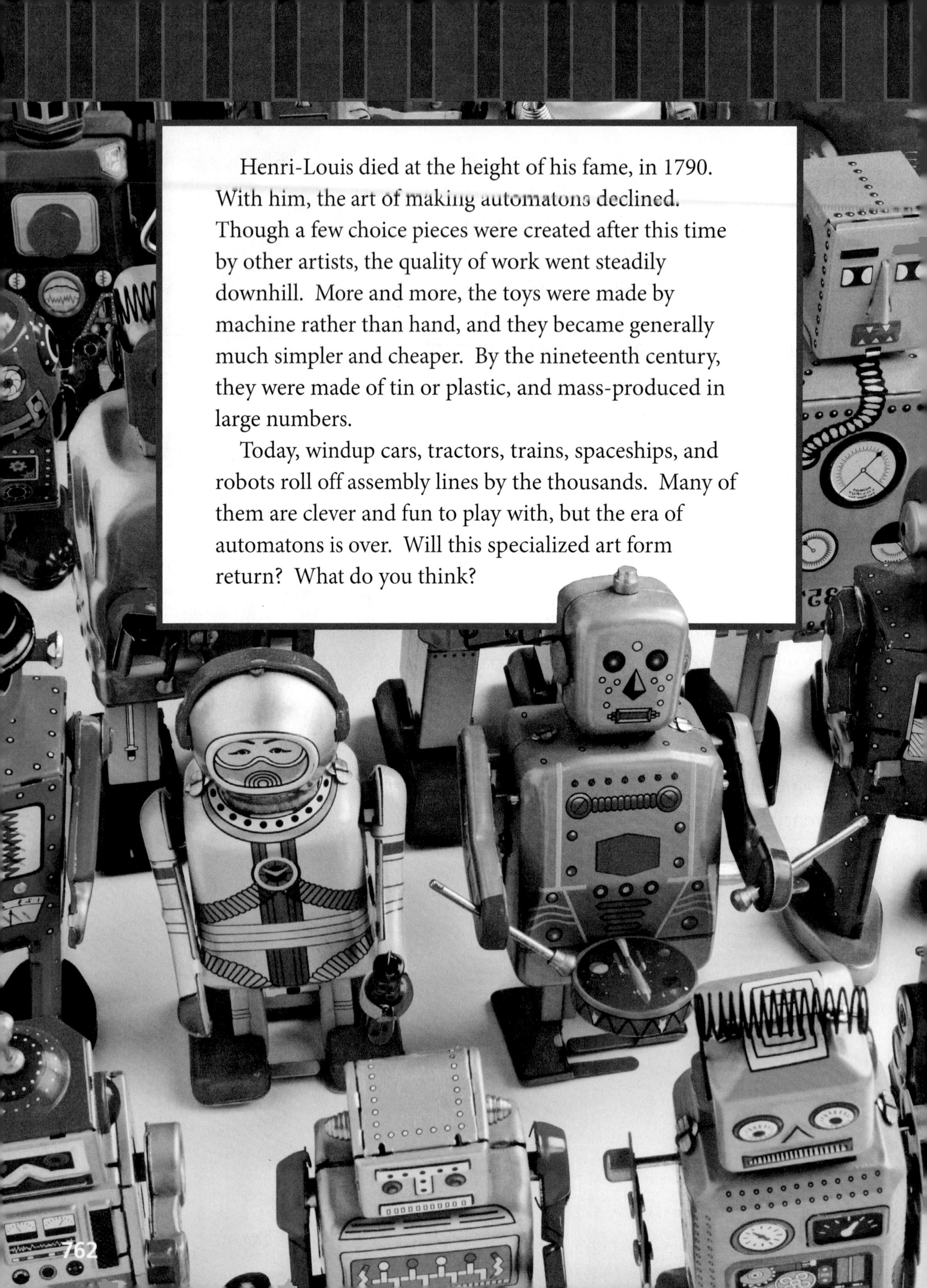

Henri-Louis died at the height of his fame, in 1790. With him, the art of making automatons declined. Though a few choice pieces were created after this time by other artists, the quality of work went steadily downhill. More and more, the toys were made by machine rather than hand, and they became generally much simpler and cheaper. By the nineteenth century, they were made of tin or plastic, and mass-produced in large numbers.

Today, windup cars, tractors, trains, spaceships, and robots roll off assembly lines by the thousands. Many of them are clever and fun to play with, but the era of automatons is over. Will this specialized art form return? What do you think?

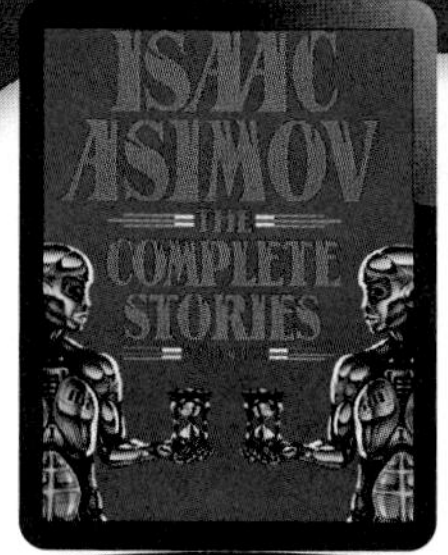

Compare Texts

TEXT TO SELF

Compare Texts About Technology Both "The Fun They Had" and "Toys!" discuss technology. Work with a partner to discuss this question: *What would Margie think about the automatons that were made hundreds of years ago?* Include text evidence from each selection to explain and support your answer.

TEXT TO TEXT

Write About Technology In "The Fun They Had," Margie learns from a mechanical teacher five days a week. Think about a technology product you use often. What if that product had never been invented? Write a paragraph telling how your life would be different if this product did not exist.

TEXT TO WORLD

Make a Chart Compare and contrast "The Fun They Had" to other stories you have read, such as "The World According to Humphrey" (Lesson 21). Think about how the events, characters, setting, theme, point of view, and illustrations are alike and different. With a partner, create a chart that shows the similarities and differences between the stories.

Point of view	Similarities	Differences
Genre		
Setting		

ELACC4RL1 refer to details and examples when explaining what the text says explicitly and when drawing inferences; **ELACC4RL6** compare and contrast the point of view from which stories are narrated; **ELACC4RL9** compare and contrast the treatment of similar themes and topics; **ELACC4RI1** refer to details and examples when explaining what the text says explicitly and when drawing inferences

COMMON CORE **ELACC4L1f** produce complete sentences, recognizing and correcting fragments and run-ons; **ELACC4L2a** use correct capitalization; **ELACC4L2b** use commas and quotation marks to mark direct speech and quotations from a text; **ELACC4L2c** use a comma before a coordinating conjunction in a compound sentence

Grammar

What Are the Mechanics of Writing? Mechanics refers to the correct use of **capitalization** and **punctuation.** Capitalization should be used for proper nouns, such as titles and names of historical events. Documents, languages, names, states, and nationalities are also proper nouns that should be capitalized. Correct punctuation must always be used at the end of a sentence. Apostrophes are needed in contractions and possessive nouns. A comma is needed in a compound sentence.

The [Amazon River Basin: name] is home to the largest rain forest on [Earth: planet].

Why [haven't: contraction] you read the book [The Giant Kapok Tree: book title][?: end punctuation]

[Ty: name] and [Nan: name] read it[,: comma] but I have not read any of the [author's: possessive noun] books.

Try This! **Write the sentences below on another sheet of paper. Capitalize the proper nouns, and add end punctuation, commas, and apostrophes where they are needed.**

1. The book called the amazon is Mikes favorite
2. Isnt that a book about earths rain forests
3. Its about the rain forest but it is also about the animals and the people who live in the amazon.
4. I would love for mrs. ortiz to read that book
5. You cant find it anywhere except the smithville library.

Readers will have an easier time reading and understanding your writing if you use correct capitalization and punctuation. Errors in capitalization and punctuation may confuse readers, and they might not understand what you mean.

Incorrect Capitalization and Punctuation	Correct Capitalization and Punctuation
My aunts newest book is called the strangest river. Its a story about an unusual mammal called the platypus How would you react to an animal that looks like a cross between a beaver and a duck	My aunt's newest book is called The Strangest River. It's a story about an unusual mammal called the platypus. How would you react to an animal that looks like a cross between a beaver and a duck?

Connect Grammar to Writing

As you proofread your research report, correct any errors in capitalization or punctuation.

ELACC4W2a introduce a topic and group related information/include formatting, illustrations, and multimedia; **ELACC4W2b** develop the topic with facts, definitions, details, quotations, or other information and examples; **ELACC4W2c** link ideas within categories of information using words and phrases; **ELACC4W2d** use precise language and domain-specific vocabulary; **ELACC4W2e** provide a concluding statement or section

Informative Writing

Reading-Writing Workshop: Revise

Word Choice In a **research report,** good writers provide facts they have found in reliable sources. Writers develop their topics with clear statements of facts, details, definitions, and quotations. They use headings to identify each main topic and precise language to describe the topic. Writers also use specific words and phrases to connect their ideas.

When Maya revised her report, she used precise language and added definitions of scientific terms. She also added headings.

Writing Process Checklist

Prewrite

Draft

▶ **Revise**

- ✔ **Did I introduce the topic and group related information?**
- ✔ **Did I include facts, definitions, and quotations?**
- ✔ **Did I use a heading for each main topic?**
- ✔ **Does my closing sum up my main ideas?**
- ✔ **Did I use mechanics correctly?**

Edit

Publish

Share

Revised Draft

What Is a Hippopotamus?

Hippopotamuses are huge African ~~animals~~ mammals that may be related to pigs and whales. Their name, however, means "river horse" in Greek.

Water Habitats of Hippos

Hippos live near rivers and lakes in Africa. Because their bodies dehydrate, or dry out, in the sun, hippos spend lots of time in water. They can sense a predator—an animal that would attack them—while underwater. That's because hippos' eyes, nostrils, and ears are on the tops of their heads.

Final Copy

The Amazing Hippopotamus

by Maya Landon

What Is a Hippopotamus?

Hippopotamuses are huge African mammals that may be related to pigs and whales. Their name, however, means "river horse" in Greek.

Water Habitats of Hippos

Hippos live near rivers and lakes in Africa. Because their bodies dehydrate, or dry out, in the sun, hippos spend lots of time in water. They can sense a predator—an animal that would attack them—while underwater. That's because hippos' eyes, nostrils, and ears are on the tops of their heads. Hippos can also walk underwater and can stay there for five minutes. Ceril Mayo said in All About Hippos, "These barrel-shaped beasts have been known to hold their breath for 30 minutes."

Hippos certainly have amazing talents in water. No wonder they seem to be related to whales!

Reading as a Writer

How did Maya treat the sentence she copied from one of her sources? How else could Maya have included this information?

In my final paper, I used precise words and added definitions for topic-specific words. I used capitalization and punctuation correctly for the quotation and title.

Read the passages "Is Cyclocross For You?" and "My First Cyclocross Race." As you read, stop and answer each question using text evidence.

Is Cyclocross For You?

by Rick Spears, Staff Writer

Cyclocross is cross-country bicycle racing. Cyclocross racers spend only part of a race on their bikes because only part of the course is smooth. Other parts of the course present challenges such as sandpits, mud puddles, and piles of wood. When racers reach these obstacles, they have two choices. They can ride over the obstacles, or they can pick up their bikes and run.

You must be a strong athlete with good skills to compete in this sport. Here are some basics you will want to learn and practice before you enter a cyclocross race.

 Which sentence best states the main idea of this passage, and what details has the author given to support the main idea?

Dismounting

To be a top racer, you must be able to dismount from your bike without slowing down. Begin by swinging your right leg over the bike seat. At the same time, move the bike away from your body, making room for your right foot to hit the ground next to your left foot. As your right foot nears the ground, take your left foot off the pedal, put both feet on the ground, and start running!

Carrying Your Bike

As soon as you are running, you have to decide how to carry your bike. You can shoulder it or lift it.

Sometimes you will need to run fast and jump over a series of obstacles. In these cases, you will probably want to shoulder your bike. As your feet hit the ground during a dismount, reach down

COMMON CORE **ELACC4RI1** refer to details and examples when explaining what the text says explicitly and when drawing inferences; **ELACC4RI2** determine the main idea and explain how it is supported by details/summarize; **ELACC4RI6** compare and contrast a firsthand and secondhand account of the same event or topic; **ELACC4RI7** interpret information presented visually, orally, or quantitatively

and grab the bottom of your bike's down tube. Lift up gently and toss the bicycle frame onto your right shoulder. Hold on to the handlebar to keep the bike from bouncing while you run.

At times you may prefer to lift your bike to get through obstacles. Lifting is similar to shouldering, except that you grab the bike's top tube instead of its down tube. Then you lift the bike high enough to get over the obstacles. After clearing the obstacles, set the bike on the ground.

You can probably guess that the top tube is the top bar of the bicycle frame. It extends from just below the handlebar to just below the seat of the bike. The down tube is the slanted bar. It extends from just below the front end of the top tube down towards the pedals.

Remounting

Having successfully dismounted and carried your bike across an obstacle, you will need to remount. As soon as your bike is on the ground, push off with your left leg. Then swing your right leg over the bike seat and slide into riding position. Remounting can be the hardest skill of cyclocross.

Now imagine that you are approaching a single, low obstacle. To clear it without taking time to dismount, do a bunny hop. This means raising your whole body so the bike hops like a rabbit right over the obstacle.

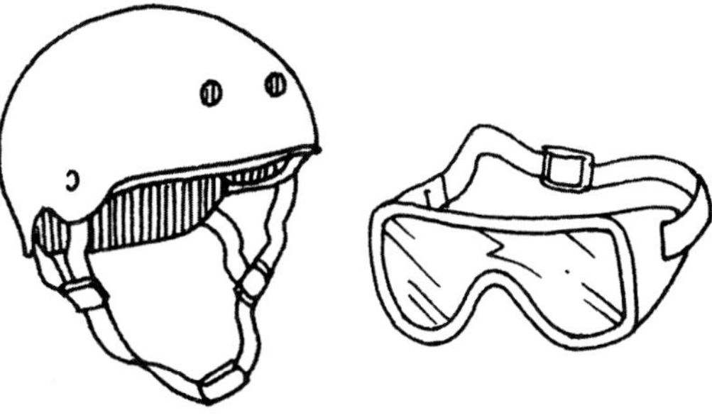

Cyclocross is a great way to stay active and have fun. However, it can be dangerous. Make sure that you are well prepared and have the safety gear you need. Then you will be ready and set. You'll just need to go!

 How does the information in the illustration add to your understanding of the passage?

My First Cyclocross Race

by Alex Woodward

After months of intense training, I was finally ready for my first cyclocross race. The day of the race was chilly, with rain on and off. I knew the course was probably going to be muddy, but I had done some training in muddy conditions. I felt that I was fully prepared.

The first part of the racecourse is smooth and level, and I got off to a good start. I was near the front of the pack, with only five riders ahead of me, but I knew positions could change quickly, especially when you start hitting the rough spots.

The first obstacle we came to was a pile of logs. The lead rider had already remounted by the time I dismounted, but the others ahead of me were still carrying their bikes. I quickly shouldered my bike and tried to run up and over the log pile. The logs were slippery from the rain, which slowed me down. I saw that the other riders seemed to be having some difficulty, too. One slipped, and I was able to get ahead. Now there were only four riders ahead of me.

 How did weather conditions affect the first part of the race? Use details from the passage to support your response.

Soon I found myself running through a muddy bog with my bike on my shoulder. I was glad I had practiced in mud because I was able to keep my footing and make pretty good time. I passed one of the riders who'd been in front of me, so now there were only three.

Around a wide turn on a fairly level stretch, I caught and passed another rider. I didn't think I could catch the leader, but I had hopes of coming in second. Hard as I tried, though, I could not catch up. I came in third, which I thought was not bad for my very first race. I can't wait to race again! Till then, I'll be out there practicing.

 How is the focus of the two articles and the information provided in them alike, and how are they different?

Glossary

This glossary contains meanings and pronunciations for some of the words in this book. The Full Pronunciation Key shows how to pronounce each consonant and vowel in a special spelling. At the bottom of the glossary pages is a shortened form of the full key.

Full Pronunciation Key

Consonant Sounds

b	**b**i**b**, ca**bb**age	kw	**ch**oir, **qu**ick	t	**t**igh**t**, stopp**ed**
ch	**ch**ur**ch**, sti**tch**	l	**l**id, need**le**, ta**ll**	th	ba**th**, **th**in
d	**d**ee**d**, mail**ed**, pu**dd**le	m	a**m**, **m**an, du**mb**	*th*	ba**th**e, **th**is
f	**f**ast, **f**i**f**e, o**ff**, **ph**rase, rou**gh**	n	**n**o, sudd**en**	v	ca**v**e, **v**al**v**e, **v**ine
g	**g**a**g**, **g**et, fin**g**er	ng	thi**ng**, i**n**k	w	**w**ith, **w**olf
h	**h**at, **wh**o	p	**p**o**p**, ha**pp**y	y	**y**es, **y**olk, on**i**on
hw	**wh**ich, **wh**ere	r	**r**oa**r**, **rh**yme	z	ro**s**e, si**z**e, **x**ylophone, **z**ebra
j	**j**u**dg**e, **g**em	s	mi**ss**, **s**au**c**e, **sc**ene, **s**ee	zh	gara**g**e, plea**s**ure, vi**s**ion
k	**c**at, **k**i**ck**, s**ch**ool	sh	di**sh**, **sh**ip, **s**ugar, ti**ss**ue		

Vowel Sounds

ă	p**a**t, l**au**gh	ŏ	h**o**rrible, p**o**t	ŭ	c**u**t, fl**oo**d, r**ou**gh, s**o**me
ā	**a**pe, **ai**d, p**ay**	ō	g**o**, r**ow**, t**oe**, th**ough**	û	c**i**rcle, f**u**r, h**ea**rd, t**e**rm, t**u**rn, **u**rge, w**o**rd
â	**ai**r, c**a**re, w**ea**r	ô	**a**ll, c**augh**t, f**o**r, p**aw**	yo͝o	c**u**re
ä	f**a**ther, ko**a**la, y**a**rd	oi	b**oy**, n**oi**se, **oi**l	yo͞o	ab**u**se, **u**se
ĕ	p**e**t, pl**ea**sure, **a**ny	ou	c**ow**, **ou**t	ə	**a**go, sil**e**nt, penc**i**l, lem**o**n, circ**u**s
ē	b**e**, b**ee**, **ea**sy, pi**a**no	o͝o	f**u**ll, b**oo**k, w**o**lf		
ĭ	**i**f, p**i**t, b**u**sy	o͞o	b**oo**t, r**u**de, fr**ui**t, fl**ew**		
ī	r**i**de, b**y**, p**ie**, h**igh**				
î	d**ea**r, d**ee**r, f**ie**rce, m**e**re				

Stress Marks

Primary Stress ′: bi•ol•o•gy [bī **ŏl′** ə jē]
Secondary Stress ′: bi•o•log•i•cal [bī′ ə **lŏj′** ĭ kəl]

amendment
The base word of *amendment* is the verb *amend*. It comes from the Latin word *emendare*, which means "to correct." The word *mend*, which means "to fix or repair," comes from the same Latin word root. When you *make amends*, you try to correct or mend a wrong you did to someone.

ac•cess (ăk′sĕs′) *n.* Permission or ability to enter or use: *We have* ***access*** *to the playground.*

ac•com•pa•ny (ə **kŭm′** pə nē) *v.* To go along with: *I was told to* ***accompany*** *them to the concert.*

ac•quire (ə **kwīr′**) *v.* To get; gain: *Mona worked hard to* ***acquire*** *her horseriding skills.*

ad•vanced (əd **vănst′**) *adj.* Highly developed or complex; beyond in progress: *The* ***advanced*** *high school student was able to take college courses.*

ad•ver•tise (**ăd′** vər tīz′) *v.* To announce to the public: *Posters sometimes* ***advertise*** *movies.*

af•fect (ə **fĕkt′**) *v.* To cause a change in something or someone: *Problems in the rain forest* ***affect*** *the animals living in it.*

af•fec•tion (ə **fĕk′** shən) *n.* A feeling of fondness or love for a person, an animal, or a thing: *My* ***affection*** *for my dog grew after he brought me the morning paper.*

a•larm (ə **lärm′**) *v.* To fill with sudden fear; frighten: *The family was alarmed when they smelled smoke coming from the kitchen.*

a•lert (ə **lûrt′**) *adj.* Watching out for danger; attentive: *A good driver must always be* ***alert.***

a•mend•ment (ə **mĕnd′** mənt) *n.* A change made to improve, correct, or add something: *An* ***amendment*** *to the United States Constitution limits the President to two full terms in office.*

an•cient (**ān′** shənt) *adj.* Having existed for a long time; very old: *The explorers discovered an* ***ancient*** *temple.*

an•gle (**ăng′** gəl) *n.* A way of looking at something: *There are many different* ***angles*** *from which we could film this movie.*

a•pol•o•gize (ə **pŏl′** ə jīz′) *v.* To make an apology; say one is sorry: *Did you* ***apologize*** *to your mother for burning the pancakes?*

ap•pre•ci•ate (ə **prē′** shē āt′) *v.* To be thankful for: *Will the child* ***appreciate*** *my help?*

ap•prove (ə **pro͞ov′**) *v.* To consent to officially: *The Senate is expected to* ***approve*** *the treaty.*

as•sist (ə **sĭst′**) *v.* To give help; aid: *Did you* ***assist*** *him in moving the box?*

as•so•ci•a•tion (ə sō′ sē **ā′** shən) *n.* A group of people organized for a common purpose: *The students formed an* ***association*** *to help stop global warming.*

av•er•age (**ăv′** ər ĭj) *adj.* Typical or ordinary: *The* ***average*** *kid loves to play.*

av•id (**ăv′** ĭd) *adj.* Very eager: *Terry is an* ***avid*** *mountain climber.*

ă **rat** / ā **pay** / â **care** / ä **father** / ĕ **pet** / ē **be** / ĭ **pit** / ī **pie** / î **fierce** / ŏ **pot** / ō **go** / ô **paw, for** / oi **oil** / o͝o **book**

awe (ô) *n.* A feeling of wonder, fear, and respect: *The astronauts gazed in **awe** back at Earth.*

B

ban (băn) *v.* To forbid by making illegal: *Fishing can be **banned** in certain areas to protect fish.*

beam (bēm) *v.* To smile broadly: *The artist **beamed** when he finished his painting.*

be•tray (bĭ **trā´**) *v.* To be unfaithful to: *When he heard the lie, Tom knew his friend had **betrayed** him.*

blar•ing (**blâr´** ĭng) *adj.* Loud, harsh: *The concert began with a fanfare of **blaring** trumpets.*

boast (bōst) *v.* To praise oneself, one's belongings, or one's actions: *She **boasted** about her good grades.*

bond (bŏnd) *n.* A force that unites; a tie: *I feel a close **bond** with my sister.*

bor•der (**bôr´** dər) *n.* The line where an area, such as a country, ends and another area begins: *The Americans had to cross the Mexican **border** on their way to South America.*

bor•row (**bŏr´** ō) *v.* To get from someone else with the understanding that what is gotten will be returned or replaced: *I want to **borrow** that toy.*

bril•liant (**brĭl´** yənt) *adj.* Very vivid in color: *The sky was a **brilliant** blue.*

bur•gla•ry (**bûr´** glə rē) *n.* The crime of breaking into a building with the intention of stealing: *The unlocked door led to many **burglaries**.*

C

cal•cu•late (**kăl´** kyə lāt´) *v.* To find by using addition, subtraction, multiplication, or division: *I **calculated** the amount of fabric I would need to make the bedspread.*

can•di•date (**kăn´** dĭ dāt´) *n.* A person who seeks or is put forward by others for an office or honor: *The **candidates** walked in the morning parade, shaking people's hands and asking for their votes.*

cap•i•tol (**kăp´** ĭ tl) *n.* The building in which a state legislature meets: *The governor went to the **capitol** to sign a bill that the legislature created.*

capitol

cap•ture (**kăp´** chər) *v.* **1.** To seize and hold, as by force or skill: *The play **captured** my imagination.* **2.** To get hold of, as by force or craft: *The enemy **captured** the general.*

cease (sēs) *v.* To come or bring to an end; stop: *The baby **ceased** crying when she saw the toy.*

o͞o b**oo**t / ou **ou**t / ŭ c**u**t / û f**ur** / hw **wh**ich / th **th**in / *th* **th**is / zh vi**s**ion / ə **a**go, sil**e**nt, penc**i**l, lem**o**n, circ**u**s

concude

One meaning of *conclude* is "to bring to an end; close; finish." *Conclude* comes from the Latin: the prefix *com-* plus *claudere*, "to close." When you decide something or form an opinion, you *conclude* or reach a *conclusion*, bringing your thoughts to a close. The word *include* comes from the same Latin root. When you include people, you "enclose" them.

cen•tu•ry (sĕn´ chə rē) *n.* A period of 100 years: *The United States Constitution was written more than two* ***centuries*** *ago.*

cer•e•mo•ny (sĕr´ ə mō´ nē) *n.* A formal act or series of acts performed in honor of an event or special occasion: *Our school had a graduation* ***ceremony*** *today.*

cham•ber (chām´ bər) *n.* An enclosed space in a machine or in an animal's living space; compartment: *The yellow jackets' nest was in a* ***chamber*** *in the soil next to the house.*

charge (chärj) *v.* To rush or rush at with force; attack: *The soldiers* ***charged*** *the fort.*

chief (chēf) *adj.* Most important: *The* ***chief*** *problem is to decide what to do first.*

churn•ing (chûrn´ ĭng) *adj.* Moving forcefully: *The* ***churning*** *winds picked up dirt.*

civ•i•lized (sĭv´ ə līzd´) *adj.* Having an advanced culture and society: *The* ***civilized*** *city had strict rules.*

clum•sy (klŭm´ zē) *adj.* Done or made without skill: *The* ***clumsy*** *shelter fell apart.*

co•erce (kō´ ûrs´) *v.* To make someone do something, sometimes by force and against his or her will: *It is not nice to* ***coerce*** *someone to do something he or she doesn't want to do.*

com•bi•na•tion (kŏm´ bə **nā´** shən) *n.* The condition of being combined; union: *Salt and pepper make a good* ***combination****.*

com•fort (kŭm´ fərt) *v.* To soothe when sad or frightened: *She tried to* ***comfort*** *the lost child.*

com•pan•ion (kəm **păn´** yən) *n.* A friend or associate: *My dog Sam was my favorite* ***companion****.*

con•cerned (kən **sûrnd´**) *adj.* Worried or anxious: *The* ***concerned*** *citizens went to the town meeting.*

con•clude (kən **klo͞od´**) *v.* To think about something and then reach a decision or form an opinion: *I have* ***concluded*** *that the best way to make a friend is to be one.*

con•dense (kən **dĕns´**) *v.* To change from a gas to a liquid form: *Water in the atmosphere will* ***condense*** *to form clouds.*

con•di•tion (kən **dĭsh´** ən) *n.* General health and fitness: *Athletes train before a competition so they are in good* ***condition****.*

con•fer (kən **fûr´**) *v.* To meet in order to discuss something together: *The doctor is* ***conferring*** *with another doctor.*

ă **r**at / ā **p**ay / â **c**are / ä **f**ather / ĕ **p**et / ē **b**e / ĭ **p**it / ī **p**ie / î **fi**erce / ŏ **p**ot / ō **g**o / ô **p**aw, **f**or / oi **oi**l / o͝o **b**oo**k**

con•fess (kən **fĕs´**) *v.* **1.** To admit that one has done something bad, wrong, or illegal: *This woman **confesses** to eating the apple.* **2.** To own or admit as true: *This girl **confesses**, or admits, that daily care of a dog is hard work.*

con•fi•dence (**kŏn´** fĭ dəns) *n.* Trust or faith in someone else or in something: *The coach had a brief moment of **confidence** in his team before they started losing again.*

con•flict (**kŏn´** flĭkt´) *n.* A clash or struggle, as of ideas, feelings, or interests: *The differences between the rich and the poor cause many **conflicts** about taxes.*

con•sist (kən **sĭst´**) *v.* To be made up: *The biology class today **consisted** of a pop quiz and a lecture on always doing your homework.*

con•struct (kən **strŭkt´**) *v.* To make by fitting parts together; build: *We **constructed** a bookcase.*

con•ti•nent (**kŏn´** tə nənt) *n.* One of the main land masses of the earth: *North America is one **continent**.*

con•vey (kən **vā´**) *v.* To communicate: *The writer wants to **convey** his feelings about his trip to Brazil.*

corps (kôr) *n.* A group of people acting or working together: *We belong to a drum and bugle **corps**.*

crit•ic (**krĭt´** ĭk) *n.* A person whose work is judging the value of books, plays, or other artistic efforts: *There were many **critics** at the premiere of the movie.*

crush (krŭsh) *v.* To press, squeeze, or bear down on with enough force to break or injure: *The tree fell, **crushing** the car.*

cus•tom (**kŭs´** təm) *n.* Something that the members of a group usually do: *Shaking hands when meeting someone is one of many **customs** our society has.*

continent

D

dar•ing (**dâr´** ĭng) *adj.* Boldly courageous; fearless: *The bicyclist made a **daring** ride down the mountain.*

de•bris (də **brē´**) *n.* The scattered remains of something broken or destroyed: *The man used a bulldozer to clear away the **debris** after the storm.*

de•but (dā´ **byōō´**) *n.* A first public appearance, as of a performer: *The juggler had his **debut** on television that night.*

de•clare (dĭ **klâr´**) *v.* To say with emphasis or certainty: *He **declared** that it was bedtime.*

debris

ōō b**oo**t / ou **ou**t / ŭ c**u**t / û f**u**r / hw **wh**ich / th **th**in / *th* **th**is / zh vi**s**ion / ə **a**go, sil**e**nt, penc**i**l, lem**o**n, circ**u**s

ded•i•cate (**dĕd′** ĭ kāt′) *v.* To set apart for a special purpose; devote: *The scientists will **dedicate** themselves to research after graduating from college.*

de•fend (dĭ **fĕnd′**) *v.* **1.** To protect from attack, harm, danger, or challenge: *They **defended** themselves from the wolves with spears.* **2.** *To support or maintain, as by argument; justify: The child **defended** taking the cookie, saying he was hungry.*

dense (dĕns) *adj.* Having the parts packed together closely: *I could not move in the **dense** crowd.*

de•ny (dĭ **nī′**) *v.* To refuse to give; withhold: *He **denied** the rabbit the carrot.*

de•serve (dĭ **zûrv′**) *v.* To be worthy of or have a right to; merit: *You **deserve** the reward.*

de•vise (dĭ **vīz′**) *v.* To think of; plan or invent: *The kids **devised** a plan to hold a bake sale.*

de•vour (dĭ **vour′**) *v.* To eat up in a greedy way: *My dogs always **devour** their meals.*

di•rect•ly (dĭ **rĕkt′** lē) *adv.* In a direct line or way; straight: *My teacher is **directly** responsible for my interest in science.*

dis•cour•aged (dĭ **skûr′** ĭjd) *adj.* Less hopeful or enthusiastic: *After getting a nail in the foot, the **discouraged** child stopped running barefoot.*

dis-

The prefix *dis-* has several senses, but its basic meaning is "not, not any." Thus *discomfort* means "a lack of comfort." *Dis-* comes ultimately from the Latin adverb *dis*, meaning "apart, asunder." *Dis-* is an important prefix that occurs very often in English in words such as *discredit, disrepair, disrespect,* and *disobey.*

dis•o•bey (dĭs′ ə **bā′**) *v.* To refuse or fail to obey: *Why did you **disobey** a direct order to eat your spinach?*

dis•or•der•ly (dĭs **ôr′** dər lē) *adj.* Not behaving according to rules or customs; unruly: *The classroom became **disorderly** after the substitute teacher did not tell the students the rules.*

dis•play (dĭ **splā′**) *n.* A public showing; exhibition: *A **display** of moon rocks is in the museum.*

dis•pute (dĭ **spyo͞ot′**) *v.* To argue about; debate: *In the debate, did the students **dispute** the question of a dress code?*

dream (drēm) *n.* Something hoped for; aspiration: *I have a **dream** of world peace.*

drought (drout) *n.* A period of little or no rain: *The farmers' crops could not grow because of the **drought**.*

du•ty (**do͞o′** tē) *n.* The obligation to do what is right: *The president had a **duty** to serve his country.*

E

ef•fort (**ĕf′** ərt) *n.* The use of physical or mental energy to do something: *Doing it this way will save time and **effort**.*

en•clo•sure (ĕn **klō′** zhər) *n.* An enclosed area: *I kept my pets in an **enclosure** made of wood.*

ă **rat** / ā **pay** / â **care** / ä **father** / ĕ **pet** / ē **be** / ĭ **pit** / ī **pie** / î **fierce** / ŏ **pot** / ō **go** / ô **paw, for** / oi **oil** / o͝o **book**

en•coun•ter (ĕn **koun**′ tər) *n.* **1.** An often unexpected meeting with a person or thing: *I had many* ***encounters*** *with animals as a kid.* **2.** A hostile confrontation: *The two armies had several* ***encounters*** *on the battlefield.*

en•ter•tain•ing (ĕn′ tər **tān**′ ĭng) *adj.* Holding the attention in an agreeable way: *The movie was* ***entertaining****.*

es•cort (ĕs′ **kôrt**′) *v.* To go with as an escort: *Police* ***escorted*** *the senator during the parade.*

e•vap•o•rate (ĭ **văp**′ ə rāt′) *v.* To change into a vapor or gas: *The water will* ***evaporate*** *quickly under the hot sun.*

ex•am•ple (ĭg **zăm**′ pəl) *n.* Someone or something that should be copied; model: *Their courage was an* ***example*** *to all of us.*

ex•cess (**ĕk**′ sĕs′) *adj.* More than is needed or usual: *I brushed the* ***excess*** *salt off my pretzel.*

ex•change (ĭks **chānj**′) *n.* A giving of one thing for another: *I did not feel that the several* ***exchanges*** *I had with that man were fair.*

ex•haust•ed (ĭg **zôst**′ əd) *adj.* Worn out completely; tired: *I was* ***exhausted*** *from the long swim.*

ex•pe•ri•ence (ĭk **spîr**′ ē əns) *v.* To have something happen to oneself: *Some states* ***experience*** *more earthquakes than others.*

ex•traor•di•nar•y (ĭk **strôr**′ dn ĕr′ ē) *adj.* Very unusual; remarkable: *Landing on the moon was an* ***extraordinary*** *event.*

ex•treme (ĭk **strēm**′) *n.* Either of two ends of a scale or range: *In this region we experience* ***extremes*** *in hot and cold weather.*

F

fade (fād) *v.* To become faint or dim: *The music started to* ***fade****.*

faint (fānt) *v.* To lose consciousness for a short time: *She* ***fainted*** *after he took off his mask.*

fault (fôlt) *n.* Responsibility for a mistake or an offense: *Failing the test was my own* ***fault*** *because I did not study.*

fav•or (**fā**′ vər) *n.* A kind or helpful act: *She granted him a* ***favor****.*

feast (fēst) *n.* A fancy meal; banquet: *We prepared a* ***feast*** *for the wedding.*

feat (fēt) *n.* An act or accomplishment that shows skill, strength, or bravery: *The gymnasts performed remarkable* ***feats****.*

feast

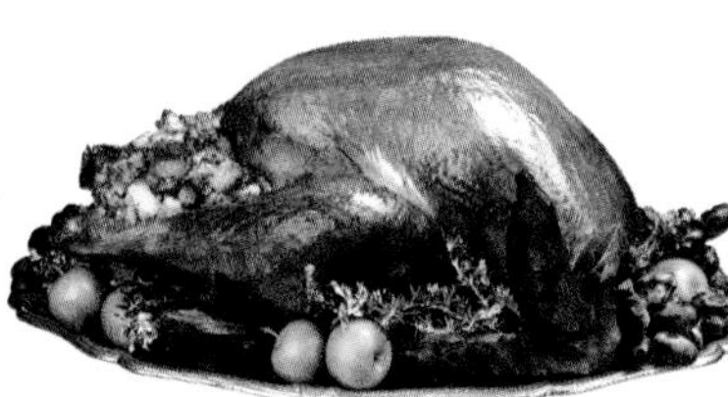

o͞o b**oo**t / ou **ou**t / ŭ c**u**t / û f**u**r / hw **wh**ich / th **th**in / *th* **th**is / zh vi**s**ion / ə **a**go, sil**e**nt, penc**i**l, lem**o**n, circ**u**s

graduate

graduate
Graduate comes from the Latin word root *gradus*, meaning "step." The word *grade*, meaning "a slope that changes a little at a time," also comes from the same word root. *Gradual*, which means "occurring in small steps over time," is another related word.

foam•ing (fō´ mĭng) *adj.* Full of bubbles that form in a liquid such as soap; frothing: ***Foaming** bubbles from the puppy shampoo spilled outside the tub.*

fo•cus (fō´ kəs) *v.* To concentrate or center; fix: *I could not **focus** on the test.*

fos•ter (fô´ stər) *adj.* Receiving, sharing, or giving care like that of a parent, although not related by blood or adoption: *There are three **foster** puppies in our home.*

frac•tured (frăk´ chərd) *adj.* Broken: *The **fractured** television had to be thrown away.*

G

gen•er•ate (jĕn´ ə rāt´) *v.* To bring about or produce: *Water and steam **generated** electricity.*

gen•u•ine (jĕn´ yo͞o ĭn) *adj.* Sincere; honest: *They showed **genuine** interest in my work.*

glare (glâr) *v.* To stare at in an angry way: *She **glared** at her brother.*

glo•ri•ous (glôr´ ē əs) *adj.* Having great beauty; magnificent: *We saw a **glorious** sunset.*

grace•ful (grās´ fəl) *adj.* Showing grace, as in movement: *The deer is a **graceful** animal.*

grad•u•ate (grăj´ o͞o āt´) *v.* To finish a course of study and receive a diploma: *My cousin will **graduate** from high school next Saturday.*

H

hab•i•tat (hăb´ ĭ tăt´) *n.* The place where a plant or an animal naturally lives: *When ecosystems change, animals often have to leave their **habitats**.*

haul (hôl) *v.* To move from one place to another, as with a truck: *I was **hauling** the bed from my house to hers when I heard the news.*

ho•ri•zon (hə rī´ zən) *n.* The line along which the earth and the sky appear to meet: *The sun dropped beneath the **horizon,** and the day grew into the night.*

hor•ri•fy (hôr´ rə fī´) *v.* To surprise unpleasantly: *The farmer was **horrified** to find his cows in the neighbor's field.*

hud•dle (hŭd´ l) *v.* To crowd close or put close together: *We **huddled** around the campfire to keep warm.*

I

im•pass•a•ble (ĭm păs´ ə bəl) *adj.* Impossible to travel on or over: *The heavy rain made the road **impassable**.*

ă **rat** / ā **pay** / â **care** / ä **father** / ĕ **pet** / ē **be** / ĭ **pit** / ī **pie** / î **fierce** / ŏ **pot** / ō **go** / ô **paw, for** / oi **oil** / o͝o **book**

in•de•pen•dent (ĭn´ dĭ **pĕn´** dənt) *adj.* Not dependent: *My brother is not **independent** of Mom and Dad. He receives a monthly check to help pay his rent.*

in•de•scrib•a•ble (ĭn dĭ **skrīb´** ə bəl) *adj.* Something that is too extraordinary to talk about in words: *The light in the sky was **indescribable**.*

in•formed (ĭn **fôrmd´**) *adj.* Having or prepared with information or knowledge: *The **informed** driver knew the correct directions to the city.*

in•jus•tice (ĭn **jŭs´** tĭs) *n.* Unfair treatment of a person or thing: *They protested the **injustice** of not having a snow day.*

in•no•cent (**ĭn´** ə sənt) *adj.* Not guilty of a crime or fault: *The jury found them **innocent**.*

in•sep•a•ra•ble (ĭn **sĕp´** ər ə bəl) *adj.* Impossible to separate or part: *The two best friends were **inseparable**.*

in•sert (ĭn´ **sûrt´**) *v.* To put, set, or fit into: ***Insert** the key in the lock.*

in•sist (ĭn **sĭst´**) *v.* To demand: *I **insisted** on going to the beach.*

in•spec•tor (ĭn **spĕk´** tôr) *n.* A person who makes inspections: *The **inspector** found mold in the walls.*

in•tel•li•gent (ĭn **tĕl´** ə jənt) *adj.* Having or showing the ability to learn, think, understand, and know: *The **intelligent** man read the whole book in five minutes.*

in•tend (ĭn **tĕnd´**) *v.* To have in mind as an aim or goal; plan: *He **intends** to bake his friend a cake for her birthday.*

in•ter•pret•er (ĭn **tûr´** prĭ tər) *n.* A person who translates orally from one language to another: *An **interpreter** was needed to find out what the foreign president was saying.*

in•tro•duce (ĭn´ trə **dōōs´**) *v.* To bring or put in something new or different: *Will you **introduce** the cat to the dog?*

in•trud•er (ĭn´ **trōōd´** ər) *n.* A person who comes in without being invited or wanted: *I called the police after the **intruder** refused to leave my house.*

i•so•late (**ī´** sə lāt´) *v.* To set or keep apart from others: *The sick dog was **isolated** from the others.*

J

jolt (jōlt) *n.* A feeling or something that causes a feeling of sudden shock or surprise: *The audience felt a **jolt** every time the car turned a corner in the movie.*

moisture

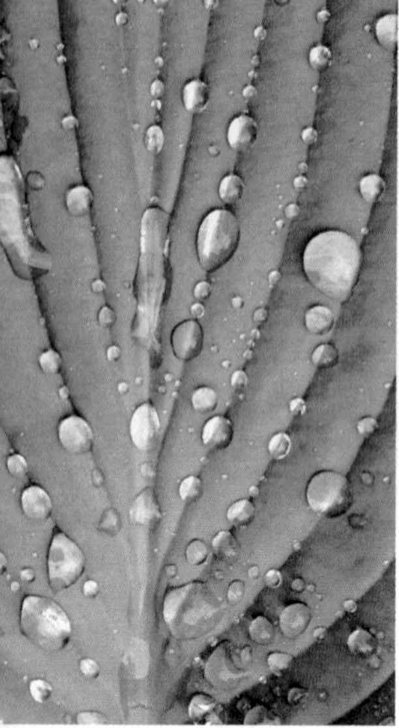

L

land•mark (lănd´ märk´) *n.* A familiar or easily seen object or building that marks or identifies a place: *The Golden Gate Bridge is a* ***landmark*** *of San Francisco.*

leg•is•la•ture (lĕj´ ĭs lā´ chər) *n.* A body of people with the power to make and change laws: *The* ***legislature*** *made a law that forced people to throw away their trash.*

lo•cal (lō´ kəl) *adj.* Of a certain limited area or place: *The town has its own* ***local*** *government.*

lu•mi•nous (lo͞o´mə nəs) *adj.* Giving off light; shining: *The crystal was* ***luminous****.*

M

me•chan•i•cal (mə kăn´ ĭ kəl) *adj.* Of or relating to machines or tools: *It takes* ***mechanical*** *skill to repair a clock.*

mem•o•ra•ble (mĕm´ ər ə bəl) *adj.* Worthy of being remembered: *Our class trip to the circus was a* ***memorable*** *event.*

men•tion (mĕn´ shən) *v.* To speak of or write about briefly: *I* ***mentioned*** *my idea during class.*

mis•judge (mĭs jŭj´) *v.* To judge wrongly: *I* ***misjudged*** *the distance to the boat and fell into the ocean.*

mod•el (mŏd´ l) *adj.* Serving as a model: *Since we have to move, we looked at a number of* ***model*** *homes.*

mois•ture (mois´ chər) *n.* Liquid, as water, that is present in the air or in the ground or that forms tiny drops on a surface: *I wiped away the* ***moisture*** *on the window so I could see outside.*

mood (mo͞od) *n.* A person's state of mind: *Playing with my friends puts me in a happy* ***mood****.*

mourn•ful (môrn´ fəl) *adj.* Feeling, showing, or causing grief; sad: *The* ***mournful*** *owner buried his dog in the back of the yard.*

N

noc•tur•nal (nŏk tûr´ nəl) *adj.* Active at night: *Owls are* ***nocturnal*** *birds.*

nour•ish•ing (nûr´ ĭsh ĭng) *adj.* Helping to promote life, growth, or strength: *The vitamins were parts of a* ***nourishing*** *diet.*

nu•mer•ous (no͞o´ mər əs) *adj.* Including or made up of a large number: *They have* ***numerous*** *problems.*

ă rat / ā pay / â care / ä father / ĕ pet / ē be / ĭ pit / ī pie / î fierce / ŏ pot / ō go / ô paw, for / oi oil / o͝o book

O

ob•sta•cle (**ŏb**´ stə kəl) *n.* Something that blocks or stands in the way: *Fallen rocks and other **obstacles** made it impossible to use the road.*

ob•tain (əb **tān**´) *v.* To gain or get by planning or effort: *We **obtain** good grades when we work hard for them.*

op•por•tu•ni•ty (ŏp´ ər **too**´ nĭ tē) *or* (ŏp´ ər **tyoo**´ nĭ tē) *n.* A good chance, as to advance oneself: *That summer job offers many **opportunities**.*

or•gan•ism (**ôr**´ gə nĭz´ əm) *n.* An individual form of life, such as a plant or an animal: *On the field trip, we looked at sea **organisms** under the microscope.*

out•cast (**out**´ kăst´) *n.* A person blocked from participation in a group or society: *Stormy felt like an **outcast** because he had outgrown Cape Cod.*

o•ver•come (ō´ vər **kŭm**´) *v.* To get the better of; conquer: *I had to **overcome** my fear of heights to climb the mountain.*

P

pa•tient•ly (**pā**´ shənt lē) *adv.* Putting up with trouble, hardship, annoyance, or delay without complaining: *He waited **patiently** for his food to arrive.*

pe•cu•liar (pĭ **kyool**´ yər) *adj.* Not usual; strange or odd: *I smell a **peculiar** odor.*

per•form (pər **fôrm**´) *v.* To carry out; do: *She **performs** very well onstage after a lot of practice.*

per•mis•sion (pər **mĭsh**´ ən) *n.* Consent granted by someone in authority: *Our parents gave us **permission** to go to the movies.*

pol•i•tics (**pŏl**´ ĭ tĭks´) *n.* The science, art, or work of government: *My father felt **politics** got in the way of people doing their regular jobs.*

poll (pōl) *n.* Often **polls.** The place where votes are cast: *I went to the **polls** to vote for the President of the United States.*

pos•i•tive (**pŏz**´ ĭ tĭv) *adj.* Having no doubts; sure: *I'm **positive** that we've met before.*

pos•ses•sion (pə **zĕsh**´ ən) *n.* Something that is owned; a belonging: *They fled the burning building, leaving their **possessions** behind.*

pre•dict (prĭ **dĭkt**´) *v.* To tell about in advance: *Weather reports **predict** the weather.*

pre•fer (prĭ **fûr**´) *v.* To like better: *I **preferred** dancing to jogging.*

pre•serve (prĭ **zûrv**´) *v.* To protect, as from injury or destruction: *It is the police's job to **preserve** the peace.*

---

oo b**oo**t / ou **ou**t / ŭ c**u**t / û f**u**r / hw **wh**ich / th **th**in / *th* **th**is / zh vi**si**on / ə **a**go, sil**e**nt, penc**i**l, lem**o**n, circ**u**s

pri•or (**prī**ʹ ər) *adj.* Coming before in time or order; earlier: *Tell me about your **prior** grades.*

prog•ress (**prŏg**ʹ rĕsʹ) *n.* Steady improvement: *After I passed the test, I realized I was making very good **progress**.*

pro•mote (prə **mōt**ʹ) *v.* To try to sell or make popular, as by advertising; publicize: *Television ads **promote** many products.*

prompt•ly (**prŏmpt**ʹ lē) *adv.* Done or given without delay: *I **promptly** sent my message.*

proof (pro͞of) *n.* Evidence of truth or accuracy: *We have no **proof** that the money was stolen.*

prop•er•ly (**prŏp**ʹ ər lē) *adv.* In a proper manner: *Jim did not hold his fork **properly**.*

pro•pose (prə **pōz**ʹ) *v.* To put forward for consideration; suggest: *I **proposed** a trip to Florida. We went to Ohio instead.*

pub•lic•i•ty (pŭ **blĭs**ʹ ĭ tē) *n.* Information that is given out to let the public know about something or to get its approval: *There was no **publicity** for the new movie, so few people watched it.*

R

rack•et (**răk**ʹ ĭt) *n.* A loud, unpleasant noise: *The several parrots outside my window made a **racket** this morning.*

ra•di•a•tion (rāʹ dē **ā**ʹ shən) *n.* Energy that travels through space as rays or waves: *Sunscreen helps protect people from the sun's **radiation**.*

rage (rāj) *v.* To move with great violence: *Large storms can quickly **rage** through a city.*

rap•id•ly (**răp**ʹ ĭd lē) *adv.* Done in quick or speedy fashion: *She **rapidly** ate her dinner.*

re•act (rē **ăkt**ʹ) *v.* To act in response to something: *The audience **reacted** to the performance with applause.*

re•call (rĭ **kôl**ʹ) *v.* To bring back to mind; remember: *I can't **recall** their phone number.*

reference

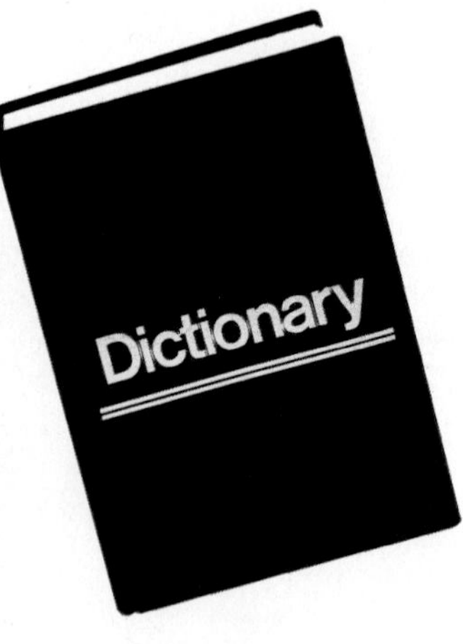

ref•er•ence (**rĕf**ʹ ər əns) *adj.* A type of resource, such as an encyclopedia or dictionary, that gives special information arranged according to a plan or system: *This book has a **reference** glossary.*

reg•is•ter (**rĕj**ʹ ĭ stər) *v.* To show some kind of information, as on a scale or other device: *The scale **registered** the weight of the apples.*

ă rat / ā pay / â care / ä father / ĕ pet / ē be / ĭ pit / ī pie / î fierce / ŏ pot / ō go / ô paw, for / oi oil / o͝o book

re•gret•ful•ly (rĭ **grĕt**´ fə lē) *adv.* Full of regret: *Looking down **regretfully**, she cancelled the party.*

re•in•force (rē´ ĭn **fôrs**´) *v.* To make stronger with more material, help, or support: *The construction crew will **reinforce** this building with a single beam.*

re•ly (rĭ **lī**´) *v.* To be dependent for support, help, or supply: *I **relied** on my brother to give me money for dinner.*

re•mote (rĭ **mōt**´) *adj.* Far away; not near: *The ship sailed near a **remote** island.*

rep•u•ta•tion (rĕp´ yə **tā**´ shən) *n.* The general worth or quality of someone or something as judged by others or by the general public: *The senator has a very good **reputation**.*

re•source (**rē**´ sôrs´) *or* (rĭ **sôrs**´) *n.* Something that is a source of wealth to a country: *Our forests and trees are great natural **resources**.*

re•source•ful (rē´ **sôrs**´ fəl) *adj.* Having access to support or help: *The hiker was very **resourceful**.*

re•ward (rĭ **wôrd**´) *v.* To give a reward for or to: *The son **rewarded** his mother with breakfast in bed.*

ro•tate (**rō**´ tāt´) *v.* To turn on an axis; revolve: *The Earth is constantly **rotating**.*

route (ro͞ot) *n.* A road or lane of travel between two places: *The hikers climbed the mountain, using a well-known **route**.*

rub•ble (**rŭb**´ əl) *n.* Broken or crumbled material, such as brick, that is left when a building falls down: *The building exploded and left **rubble** everywhere.*

ru•in (**ro͞o**´ ĭn) *v.* To damage beyond repair; wreck: *She **ruined** the clay castle by stepping on it.*

S

sat•is•fy (**săt**´ ĭs fī´) *v.* To fulfill or gratify: *The steak **satisfied** my hunger.*

scarce (skârs) *adj.* Not enough to meet a demand: *Food is **scarce** in many countries.*

sched•ule (**skĕj**´ o͞ol) *n.* A program of events, appointments, or classes: *We have a full **schedule** of activities after school.*

scheme (skēm) *n.* A plan or plot for doing something: *He created a **scheme** to break out of prison.*

sea•far•ing (**sē**´ fâr´ ĭng) *adj.* Earning one's living at sea: *The **seafaring** life of a fisherman is dangerous.*

seg•re•ga•tion (sĕg´ rĭ **gā**´ shən) *n.* The act of segregating or the condition of being segregated: *Laws on* ***segregation*** *once kept African Americans and white Americans separate.*

shal•low (**shăl**´ ō) *adj.* Measuring little from bottom to top or from back to front; not deep: *The fish swam in the* ***shallow*** *end of the river.*

short•age (**shôr**´ tĭj) *n.* An amount of something that is not enough: *We donate items to a food pantry when there is a food* ***shortage****.*

storage

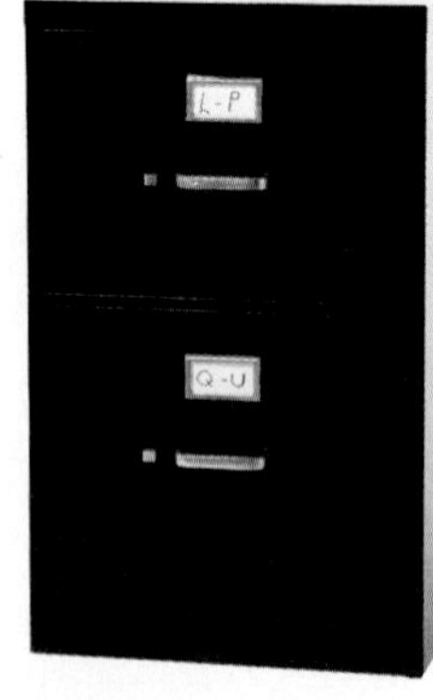

sit•u•a•tion (sĭch´ o͞o **ā**´ shən) *n.* A set of circumstances: *The child knew he was in a bad* ***situation*** *when his mother caught him with his hand in the cookie jar.*

slab (slăb) *n.* A broad, flat, thick piece, as of bread, stone, or meat: *My mother threw a* ***slab*** *of steak on the grill to cook.*

slim•y (**slī**´ mē) *adj.* Like slime in appearance or texture: *The* ***slimy*** *mud made him slip.*

smear (smîr) *v.* To become spread or blurred: *The ink* ***smeared*** *easily.*

so•cial (**sō**´ shəl) *adj.* Living together in communities or groups: *Bees and ants are* ***social*** *insects.*

source (sôrs) *n.* The point where something comes from: *The* ***source*** *of the stream is melting water from the mountain.*

spe•cies (**spē**´ shēz´) *n.* A group of animals or plants that are similar and are able to mate and have offspring: *Scientists discover new* ***species*** *of sea life in the deepest ocean.*

spec•u•late (**spĕk**´ yə lāt´) *v.* To think deeply; ponder; reflect: *I* ***speculated*** *on whether to have fries or mashed potatoes.*

stan•dard (**stăn**´ dərd) *n.* Something that is accepted as a basis for measuring or as a rule or model: *Americans have different* ***standards*** *of living than the Japanese.*

stor•age (**stôr**´ ĭj) *n.* A space or place for storing things: *I kept my belongings in* ***storage*** *when I went away.*

strand (strănd) *v.* To leave in a difficult or helpless position: *They were* ***stranded*** *on the mountain when their car broke down.*

streak (strēk) *v.* To mark or become marked with streaks: *The light seemed to* ***streak*** *across the sky.*

ă **r**at / ā **p**ay / â **c**are / ä **f**a**th**er / ĕ **p**et / ē **b**e / ĭ **p**it / ī **p**ie / î **fier**ce / ŏ **p**o**t** / ō **g**o / ô **p**aw, **f**or / oi **oi**l / o͝o **b**oo**k**

stub•born (**stŭb**ʹ ərn) *adj.* **1.** Continuing to exist; lasting: *I have the* ***stubborn*** *idea that I want to be a teacher when I grow up.* **2.** Unyielding; difficult to deal with: *A* ***stubborn*** *stain ruined the tablecloth.*

stu•di•o (**sto͞o**ʹ dē ōʹ) *n.* The place where an artist works: *The artist was working on his painting in his* ***studio.***

suf•fer (**sŭf**ʹ ər) *v.* To feel or endure pain or distress: *The drought victims* ***suffered*** *from malnutrition.*

sug•gest (səg **jĕst**ʹ) *v.* To offer for consideration or action: *I* ***suggest*** *going to a movie tonight.*

su•pe•ri•or (so͞o **pîr**ʹ ē ər) *adj.* Considering oneself better than others; conceited: *Don't take a* ***superior*** *attitude toward the younger students.*

sup•plies (sə **plīz**ʹ) *n.* Necessary materials used or given out when needed: *After a month of bad weather, the explorers'* ***supplies*** *ran out.*

sus•pect (**səs**ʹ pĕktʹ) *n.* A person suspected, as of a crime: *When I was a child, I was always the* ***suspect*** *when anything broke.*

swell (swĕl) *v.* **1.** To increase in size or volume as a result of internal pressure; expand: *The injured ankle* ***swelled.*** **2.** To increase in force, size, number, or degree: *The army* ***swelled*** *from 100 soldiers to 150 soldiers.*

sym•bol (**sĭm**ʹ bəl) *n.* **1.** Something that stands for or represents something else: *The dove is a* ***symbol*** *of peace.* **2.** A printed or written sign used to represent an operation, action, quantity, and the like: *A red traffic light is a* ***symbol*** *to stop.*

T

tal•ent (**tăl**ʹ ənt) *n.* A natural ability to do something well: *If you stop taking music lessons, you'll waste your* ***talent.***

tar•get (**tär**ʹ gĭt) *adj.* Established goal: *The* ***target*** *date for finishing our report was May 6.*

ten•e•ment (**tĕn**ʹ ə mənt) *n.* An old apartment house that is badly maintained: *My grandfather grew up in a* ***tenement*** *that had holes in the roof.*

ter•ri•to•ry (**tĕr**ʹ ĭ tôrʹ ē) *n.* An area of land; region: *I have never been to any* ***territory*** *south of the equator.*

thrill•ing (**thrĭl**ʹ ĭng) *adj.* Exciting: *The movie was* ***thrilling.***

tid•al (**tīd**ʹ l) *adj.* Relating to or affected by tides: *An earthquake can cause a* ***tidal*** *wave.*

tim•ber (**tĭm**ʹ bər) *n.* A long, heavy piece of wood for building; beam: *The carpenter laid down several* ***timbers*** *that he was going to use to build the house.*

---

o͞o b**oo**t / ou **ou**t / ŭ c**u**t / û f**ur** / hw **wh**ich / th **th**in / *th* **th**is / zh vi**s**ion / ə **a**go, sil**e**nt, penc**i**l, lem**o**n, circ**u**s

trans-
The prefix *trans-* comes from the Latin preposition *trans*, meaning "across, beyond, through." Many common English words begin with *trans-* and have base words from Latin: *transfer*, *transfuse*, *translate*, *transmit*, *transpire*, and *transport*. Another large group of words has *trans-* in combination with English adjectives, as in *transatlantic*, *transcontinental*, and *transoceanic*, meaning "across" or "through" a particular geographic element.

tour (to͝or) *v.* To go on a tour: *We **toured** through Spain.*

tow•er (**tou´** ər) *v.* To rise very high: *The basketball hoop **towered** over the child.*

trace (trās) *n.* A very small amount: *After Julian ate the candy bar, there were **traces** of chocolate on his fingers.*

trans•fer (trăns **fûr´**) *v.* To cause to move from one place to another: *Who **transfers** the money from the house to the bank?*

trans•port (trăns **pôrt´**) *v.* To carry from one place to another: *Can you **transport** this box to China?*

trem•ble (**trĕm´** bəl) *v.* To shake: *He **trembles** in the winter when he doesn't wear a hat.*

tri•umph (**trī´** əmf) *n.* The fact of being victorious: *Becoming a star is a **triumph** most performance artists long for.*

U

un•for•tu•nate (ŭn **fôr´** chə nĭt) *adj.* Not having good fortune; unlucky: *She felt **unfortunate** when she dropped her sandwich.*

V

va•ri•e•ty (və **rī´** ĭ tē) *n.* A number of different things within the same group or category: *The market sells a **variety** of bread.*

vast (văst) *adj.* Very great in area; huge: *The Amazon River flows through a **vast** rain forest.*

vi•o•lence (**vī´** ə ləns) *n.* The use of physical force to cause damage or injury: *The **violence** of war caused many to die.*

vir•tu•al (**vûr´** cho͞o əl) *adj.* A resource available on the Internet or on software: *He looked up the word in a **virtual** dictionary.*

vi•sion (**vĭzh´** ən) *n.* A mental picture produced by the imagination: *I had a **vision** of a pink elephant bouncing on a trampoline.*

W

waste (wāst) *n.* The act of wasting or the condition of being wasted: *If you aren't going to read the newspaper, you should recycle it. It would be such a **waste** if you do not.*

wea•ri•ness (**wîr´** ē nĕs) *n.* Temporary loss of strength and energy resulting from hard physical or mental work: *Chasing the dog for hours caused great **weariness.***

whirling (**wûrl´** ĭng´) *adj.* To spin quickly: *The **whirling** winds messed up her hair.*

wor•thy (**wûr´** thē) *adj.* Having merit or value: *We contribute to **worthy** causes.*

ă **rat** / ā **pay** / â **care** / ä **father** / ĕ **pet** / ē **be** / ĭ **pit** / ī **pie** / î **fierce** / ŏ **pot** / ō **go** / ô **paw**, **for** / oi **oil** / o͝o **book**

wreck•age (rĕk′ ĭj) *n.* The remains of something that has been wrecked: *The **wreckage** of the car was hauled away.*

wreckage

Y

yank (yăngk) *v.* To pull with a sudden, sharp movement: *We **yanked** the heavy door open.*

yearn•ing (yûr′ nĭng) *n.* A deep longing or strong desire: *Grandfather felt a **yearning** to visit his childhood home in the mountains.*

o͞o b**oo**t / ou **ou**t / ŭ c**u**t / û f**u**r / hw **wh**ich / th **th**in / *th* **th**is / zh vi**si**on / ə **a**go, sil**e**nt, penc**i**l, lem**o**n, circ**u**s

Acknowledgments

Main Literature Selections

"Ancestors of Tomorrow/Futuros ancestros" from *Iguanas in the Snow and Other Winter Poems/Iguanas en la nieve y otras poemas de invierno* by Francisco X. Alarcón. Copyright © 2001 by Francisco X. Alarcón. Reprinted by permission of the publisher, Children's Book Press, San Francisco, CA, www.childrensbookpress.org.

Antarctic Journal: Four Months at the Bottom of the World written and illustrated by Jennifer Owings Dewey. Copyright © 2001 by Jennifer Owings Dewey. Reprinted by permission of Houghton Mifflin Harcourt Publishing Company and Kirchoff/Wohlberg, Inc.

Because of Winn-Dixie by Kate DiCamillo. Copyright © 2000 by Kate DiCamillo. Reprinted by permission of the publisher Candlewick Press Inc., and Listening Library, a division of Random House, Inc.

Coming Distractions: Questioning Movies by Frank E. Baker. Copyright © 2007 by Capstone Press. All rights reserved. Reprinted by permission of Capstone Press.

Dear Mr. Winston by Ken Roberts. Copyright © 2001 by Ken Roberts. Reprinted by permission of Groundwood Books Limited, Toronto.

"Dreams" from *The Collected Poems of Langston Hughes* by Langston Hughes, edited by Arnold Rampersad with David Roessel, Associate Editor, copyright © 1994 by The Estate of Langston Hughes. Reprinted by permission of Alfred A. Knopf, a division of Random House, Inc., and Harold Ober Associates, Inc.

"The Dream Keeper" from *The Collected Poems of Langston Hughes* by Langston Hughes, edited by Arnold Rampersad with David Roessel, Associate Editor, copyright © 1994 by The Estate of Langston Hughes. Reprinted by permission of Alfred A. Knopf, a division of Random House, Inc., and Harold Ober Associates, Inc.

The Earth Dragon Awakes: The San Francisco Earthquake of 1906 by Laurence Yep. Copyright © 2006 by Laurence Yep. All rights reserved. Reprinted by permission of HarperCollins Publishers and Curtis Brown, Ltd.

Ecology for Kids by Federico Arana. Originally published as *Ecologia para los ninos*. Text copyright © 1994 by Federico Arana. Text © 1994 by Editorial Joaquin Mortiz, S.A. DE C.V. Reprinted by permission of Editorial Planeta Mexicana, S.A. DE C.V.

The Ever-Living Tree: The Life and Times of a Coast Redwood by Linda Vieira, illustrations by Christopher Canyon. Copyright © 1994 by Linda Vieira. Illustrations copyright © 1994 by Christopher Canyon. All rights reserved. Reprinted by permission of Walker & Company.

"First Recorded 6,000-Year-Old Tree in America" from *A Burst of Firsts* by J. Patrick Lewis. Published by Dial Books for Young Readers. Copyright © 2001 by J. Patrick Lewis. Reprinted by permission of Curtis Brown, Ltd.

"Fog" from *The Complete Poems of Carl Sandburg* by Carl Sandburg. Copyright © 1970 by Lilian Steichen Sandburg, Trustee. Reprinted by permission of Houghton Mifflin Harcourt Publishing Company and La Poesia Del Senor Hidalgo.

The Fun They Had by Isaac Asimov. Copyright © 1957 by Isaac Asimov from Isaac Asimov: The Complete Stories of Vol. 1 by Isaac Asimov. Reprinted by permission of Doubleday, a division of Random House, Inc.

"Giant Sequoias/Secoyas gigantes" from *Iguanas in the Snow and Other Winter Poems/Iguanas en la nieve y otras poemas de invierno* by Francisco X. Alarcón. Copyright © 2001 by Francisco X. Alarcón. Reprinted by permission of Children's Book Press, San Francisco, CA, www.childrensbookpress.org.

Harvesting Hope: The Story of Cesar Chavez by Kathleen Krull, illustrated by Yuyi Morales. Text copyright © 2003 by Kathleen Krull. Illustrations copyright © 2003 by Yuyi Morales. Reprinted by permission of Houghton Mifflin Harcourt Publishing Company and Writer's House, LLC, acting as agent for the author.

Excerpt from *Hurricanes: Earth's Mightiest Storms* by Patricia Lauber. Text copyright © 1996 by Patricia Lauber. Reprinted by permission of Scholastic Inc. SCHOLASTIC'S Material shall not be published, retransmitted, broadcast, downloaded, modified or adapted (rewritten), manipulated, reproduced or otherwise distributed and/or exploited in any way without the prior written authorization of Scholastic Inc.

I Could Do That! Esther Morris Gets Women the Vote by Linda Arms White, illustrated by Nancy Carpenter. Text copyright © 2005 by Linda Arms White. Illustrations copyright © 2005 by Nancy Carpenter. Reprinted by permission of Farrar, Straus & Giroux LLC.

Excerpt from *"Invasion from Mars" from The Panic Broadcast: Portrait of an Event* by Howard Koch. Text copyright © 1940 by Hadley Contril. Text copyright renewed © 1967 by Howard Koch. Reprinted by permission of International Creative Management, Inc.

José! Born to Dance by Susanna Reich, illustrated by Raúl Colón. Text copyright © 2005 by Susanna Reich. Illustrations copyright © 2005 by Raúl Colón. All rights reserved. Reprinted by permission of Simon & Schuster Books for Young Readers, an Imprint of Simon & Schuster Inc., and Adams Literary.

Excerpt from *The Kid's Guide to Money: Earning It, Saving It, Spending It, Growing It, Sharing It* by Steve Otfinoski. Copyright © 1996 by Scholastic Inc. SCHOLASTIC'S Material shall not be published, retransmitted, broadcast, downloaded, modified or adapted (rewritten), manipulated, reproduced or otherwise distributed and/or exploited in any way without the prior written authorization of Scholastic Inc.

The Life and Times of the Ant written and illustrated by Charles Micucci. Copyright © 2003 by Charles Micucci. All rights reserved. Reprinted by permission of Houghton Mifflin Harcourt Publishing Company.

Excerpt from "Lines Written for Gene Kelly to Dance To" from *Wind Song* by Carl Sandburg. Copyright © 1960 Carl Sandburg and renewed 1998 by Margaret Sandburg, Janet Sandburg, and Helga Sandburg Crile. Reprinted by permission of Houghton Mifflin Harcourt Publishing Company.

Me and Uncle Romie: A Story Inspired by the Life and Art of Romare Bearden by Claire Hartfield, illustrated by Jerome Lagarrigue. Text copyright © 2002 by Claire Hartfield. Illustrations copyright © 2002 by Jerome Lagarrigue. Reprinted by permission of Dial Books for Young Readers, a Division of Penguin Young Readers Group, A Member of Penguin Group (USA) Inc., 345 Hudson Street, New York, NY 10014. All rights reserved.

Excerpt from *My Librarian is a Camel* by Margriet Ruurs. Copyright © 2005 by Boyds Mill Press. Reprinted by permission of Boyds Mills Press

My Brother Martin: A Sister Remembers Growing Up with the Rev. Dr. Martin Luther King Jr. by Christine King Farris, illustrated by Chris Soentpiet. Text copyright © 2003 by Christine King Farris. Illustrations copyright © 2003 by Chris Soentpiet. Reprinted by the permission of The Permissions Company and Simon & Schuster Books for Young Readers, an imprint of Simon & Schuster Children's Publishing Division.

Owen and Mzee by Isabella Hatkoff, Craig Hatkoff, and Dr. Paula Kahumbu, photographs by Peter Greste. Copyright © 2006 by Turtle Pond Publications, LLC and Lafarge Eco Systems, Ltd. Photographs copyright © 2006, 2005 by Peter Greste. All rights reserved. Reprinted by permission of Scholastic Press, an imprint of Scholastic Inc., and Turtle Pond Publications, LLC.

Riding Freedom by Pam Muñoz Ryan. Text copyright © 1998 by Pam Muñoz Ryan. Reprinted by permission of Scholastic Press, a division of Scholastic Inc.

The Right Dog for the Job: Ira's Path from Service Dog to Guide Dog by Dorothy Hinshaw Patent, photographs by William Muñoz. Copyright © 2004 by Dorothy Hinshaw Patent. Photographs copyright © 2004 by William Muñoz. All rights reserved. Reprinted by permission of Walker & Company.

Sacagawea by Lise Erdrich, illustrated by Julie Buffalohead. Text copyright © 2003 by Lise Erdrich. Illustrations copyright © 2003 by Julie Buffalohead All rights reserved. Reprinted by permission of Carolrhoda Books, a division of Lerner Publishing Group, Inc.

"The Song of the Night" by Leslie D. Perkins from *Song and Dance*, published by Simon & Schuster.

"Stormalong" from *American Tall Tales*, by Mary Pope Osbourne. Text copyright © 1991 by Mary Pope Osbourne. Reprinted by permission of Alfred A. Knopf, a division of Random House, Inc.

Adapted from "Three/Quarters Time" from *Those Who Rode the Night Winds* by Nikki Giovanni. Copyright © 1983 by Nikki Giovanni. Reprinted by permission of HarperCollins Publishers.

"To You" from *The Collected Poems of Langston Hughes* by Langston Hughes, edited by Arnold Rampersad with David Roessel, Associated Editor, copyright © 1994 by The Estate of Langston Hughes. Reprinted by permission of Alfred A. Knopf, a division of Random House, Inc., and Harold Ober Associates, Inc.

"Weather" from *Always Wondering* by Aileen Fisher. Copyright © 1991 by Aileen Fisher. Reprinted by permission of the Boulder Public Library Foundation, Inc., c/o Marian Reiner, Literary Agent.

"Weatherbee's Diner" from *Flamingos on the Roof* by Calef Brown. Copyright © 2006 by Calef Brown. Reprinted by permission of Houghton Mifflin Harcourt Publishing Company and Dunham Literary as agent of the author.

Excerpt from "Windup Toys and Automatons" from *Toys! Amazing Stories Behind Some Great Inventions* by Don Wulffson. Text copyright © 2000 by Don Wulffson. Reprinted by permission of Henry Holt & Company.

The World According to Humphrey by Betty G. Birney. Copyright © 2004 by Betty G. Birney. Reprinted by permission of G. P. Putnam's Sons, A Division of Penguin Young Readers Group, A Member of Penguin Group (USA) Inc., and Faber & Faber, Ltd.

Credits

Photo Credits

Placement Key: (r) right, (l) left, (c) center, (t) top, (b) bottom, (bg) background

4 (cl) ©Yellow Dog Productions/Getty Images; **4** (bl) ©CORBIS; **4** (bl) ©Bettmann/Corbis; **6** (bl) Artville/ Getty Images; **7** (cl) ©Alan and Sandy Carey/Photo Researchers, Inc.; **7** (bl) ©Robbie Jack/Corbis; **7** (bl) ©Science Source/Photo Researchers, Inc.; **8** (bl) Carolyn Mary Bauman/epa/Corbis; **8** ©U.S. Air Force; **8** (tc) © Brand X Pictures/Getty Images; **9** (bl) Ryan McVay/Getty Images; **9** (b) ©Digital Vision/Getty Images; **10** (cl) Getty Images; **10** (cl) ©SHOUT/Alamy Images; **11** (cl) ©Ariel Skelley/Getty Images; **11** (cl) ©Jeff Greenberg/Image Works, Inc.; **11** (cl) ©Oote Boe Photography/Alamy Images; **11** (bl) Buddy Mays/Corbis; **12** (tl) ©James Randklev/Getty Images; **13** (cr) ©David Courtenay/Oxford Scientific/Getty Images; Blind [**15**] ©Charles Bowman/Age Fotostock America, Inc.; **16** (tr) ©Yellow Dog Productions/ Getty Images; **16** (cl) ©Juan Silva/Getty Images; **16** (cr) ©Alamy Images; **16** (bl) ©Image Source/Getty Images; **16** (br) ©Jupiterimages/Creatas/Getty Images; **17** (tl) ©Blend Images/Alamy Images; **17** (tc) ©Myrleen Ferguson Cat/PhotoEdit; **17** (cr) ©Brian Pieters/Masterfile; **17** (bl) ©Hill Street Studios/Age Fotostock America, Inc.; **17** (bc) ©Terry Vine/Getty Images; **17** (br) ©Getty Images; **19** ©Tony Anderson/Digital Vision/Getty Images; **21** Twentieth Century Fox Film Corporation; **22** (b) Twentieth Century Fox Film Corporation; **23** (t) ©Twentieth Century Fox Film Corporation/Candlewick Press; **25** Twentieth Century Fox Film Corporation; **27** (t) ©Twentieth Century Fox Film Corporation/Candlewick Press; **29** ©Twentieth Century Fox Film Corporation/ Candlewick Press; **30** Twentieth Century Fox Film Corporation; **33** ©Photodisc/Getty Images; **33** ©relaximages/Alamy Images; **34** ©Photodisc/Getty Images; **35** ©Comstock Images/Getty Images; **36** (tr) ©Yellow Dog Productions/Getty Images; **36** (b) ©Purestock/Getty Images; **37** (t) ©Yellow Dog Productions/Getty Images; **39** (tl) ©Yellow Dog Productions/Getty Images; **39** (br) ©Stockdisc Premium/ Getty Images; **39** (br) ©Frank Siteman/PhotoEdit; **43** (br) ©Masterfile; **44** (tl) ©CORBIS; **44** (cl) ©Steve Schapiro/ Corbis; **44** (tr) ©Sebastien Desarmaux/Godong/Corbis; **44** (bl) ©Danny Lyon/Magnum Photos; **44** ©Alamy Images; **44** (tl) ©Bettmann/Corbis; **45** (cl) ©Patrick Durand/Corbis Sygma; **45** (c) ©Kevin Dodge/Corbis; **45** (cr) ©Robert Mass/Corbis; **45** (bl) ©Steve Schapiro/ Corbis; **45** (bc) ©Andrea Thrussell/Alamy Images; **45** (br) ©Dennis MacDonald_correct/PhotoEdit; **46** (bg) ©National Archives at College Park Still Pictures Division; **63** ©Brand X Pictures/Getty Images; **63** ©National Archives at College Park Still Pictures Division; **66** (b) ©CORBIS; **66** (b) ©Bettmann/Corbis; **66** (tl) ©Bettmann/ Corbis; **66** (tr) ©CORBIS; **68** ©Blend Images/Alamy Images, **69** (c) ©Flip Schulke/CORBIS; **69** (tl) ©CORBIS; **69** (tr) ©Bettmann/Corbis; **73** (br) ©Masterfile; **74** Image Ideas/Jupiterimages/Getty Images; **74** ©Rana Faure/Getty Images; **74** Stockbyte/Getty Images; **75** ©Corbis; **75** Photodisc/Getty Images; **75** Photodisc/Getty Images; **75** Comstock/Getty Images; **75** ©EIGHTFISH/Getty Images; **77** Comstock/Getty Images; **93** ©Photodisc/Getty Images; **93** Photodisc/Getty Images; **95** ©Eco Images/ Universal Images Group/Getty Images; **101** Photodisc/ Getty Images; **101** ©Steve Skjold/Alamy Images; **105** (br)

©Masterfile; **106** (cl) ©Yael Kadish/Age Fotostock America, Inc.; **106** (cr) ©Superstock; **106** (bl) ©Michael Newman/PhotoEdit; **106** (br) ©Simon Marcus/Corbis; **107** (cl) ©JG Photography/Alamy Images; **107** (tc) ©Corbis; **107** (cr) ©Will & Deni McIntyre/Corbis; **107** (bc) ©Michael Newman/PhotoEdit; **107** (bc) Corbis; **107** (br) ©MIXA/Getty Images; **123** (tr) ©Brand X Pictures/Getty Images; **124** (b) Digital Vision/Getty Images; **125** ©Andrej CRCEK/Alamy Images; **128** ©PhotoSpin, Inc/Alamy Images; **129** ©Leland Bobbe/Getty Images; **133** (br) ©Rubberball/Superstock; **134** (bc) Corbis; **134** (br) ©Galina Barskaya/Alamy Images; **134** (tr) ©Warren Bolster/Photographer's Choice/Getty Images; **134** (cl) Corel Stock Photo Library - royalty free; **135** (tl) ©Paul Baldesre/Alamy; **135** (tc) ©Kaz Mori/Riser/Getty Images; **135** (tr) ©Masterfile; **135** (bl) ©Jose Luis Pelaez, Inc./Blend Images/Corbis; **135** (bc) ©Associated Press; **135** (br) ©RubberBall/SuperStock; **137** Stockbyte/Getty Images; **155** ©Tetra Images/Houghton Mifflin Harcourt; **155** ©mambo/Alamy Images; **156** (br) Comstock/Getty Images; **161** (t) Corel Stock Photo Library - royalty free; **165** (br) ©Rubberball/Superstock; Blind [**169**] ©PhotoEdit; **170** ©Chabruken/Getty Images; **170** ©Getty Images; **170** ©Corbis; **170** ©Corbis; **171** ©Joseph Sohm-Visions of America/Digital Vision/Getty Images; **171** ©Jose Luis Pelaez Inc/Getty Images; **171** Photodisc/Getty Images; **171** ©Corbis; **171** ©Corbis; **171** Bill Fritsch/Brand X Pictures/Age Fotostock; **173** ©Gamma-Keystone/Getty Images; **187** ©CBS Photo Archive/Getty Images; **187** PhotoDisc/Getty Images; **188** ©Image Source/Getty Images; **188** Jupiterimages/Getty Images; **191** (tl) ©Getty Images; **191** (tr) ©Mark Scheuern/Alamy Images; **192** (tl) ©Getty Images; **192** (tr) ©Time & Life Pictures/Getty Images; **193** (tr) PhotoDisc/Getty Images; **197** (br) ©Masterfile; **198** (tl) Artville / Getty Images; **198** (cl) ©Michael Ochs Archives/Corbis; **198** (cr) ©John Springer Collection/Corbis; **198** (bl) ©Joe Sohm/Visions of America; **198** (br) ©Hulton Archive/Getty Images; **199** (cl) ©Peter Beavis/Getty Images; **199** (c) ©Rob Wilkinson/Alamy Images; **199** (cr) ©Eric O'Connell/Getty Images; **199** (bl) ©Moodboard/Corbis; **199** (bc) ©Photodisc/Alamy Images; **199** (br) ©Purestock/Age Fotostock America, Inc.; **200** (tl) Artville / Getty Images; **201** ©Getty Images; **202** (b) Artville / Getty Images; **202** (tl) Artville / Getty Images; **205** (b) ©Rick Doyle/Corbis; **209** (c) ©New Line Cinema/Zuma Press; **212** (bg) ©Paul Hawthorne/Getty Images; **214** (tl) Artville / Getty Images; **215** Artville / Getty Images; **215** © Alamy; **216** © Corbis; **216** Comstock/Getty Images; **217** © Getty Images; **217** (tl) Artville/ Getty Images; **218** (c) ©Ryan McVay/Photodisc/Getty Images; **219** (t) ©Getty Images; **220** (inset) ©AFP/Getty Images; **221** (tl) Artville / Getty Images; **225** (br) ©Image Source/Superstock; **226** (bl) ©China Span/Keren Su/Alamy Images; **226** (cl) ©Rafael Marcia/Age Fotostock America, Inc.; **226** (cr) ©Daj/Getty Images; **226** (bl) ©Masterfile; **227** (cl) ©neal and molly jansen/Alamy Images; **227** (c) ©Shalom Ormsby/Getty Images; **227** (cr) ©The Photolibrary Wales/Alamy Images; **227** (bl) ©Farinaz Taghavi/Corbis; **227** (bc) ©PhotoDisc/Age Fotostock America, Inc.; **227** (br) ©Michael Mahovlich/Masterfile; **228** (bg) ©Kim Steele/Photodisc/Getty Images; **229** ©AFP/Getty Images; **245** ©Getty Images; **247** L26: © Assorted Imagery By Phil/Alamy; **247** ©Stockbyte/Getty Images; **247** ©Photodisc/Getty Images; **251** (br) ©F. Ruesch/AP Images; **255** (br) ©Sean Justice/Getty Images; **256** (cl) ©myrleen F Cate/PhotoEdit; **256** (cr) ©David Young-Wolff/PhotoEdit; **256** (bl) ©Bill Aron/PhotoEdit; **256** (br) ©Reg Charity/Corbis; **256** (tc) ©Alan and Sandy Carey/Photo Researchers, Inc.; **257** (cl) ©BIG CHEESE PHOTO LLC SPECIAL/Age Fotostock America, Inc.; **257** (c) Layne Kennedy/Corbis; **257** (cr) ©Tony Freeman/PhotoEdit; **257** (bl) ©Jupiterimages/Alamy Images; **257** (bc) ©George Disario/Corbis; **257** (br) ©Bryan Allen/Corbis; **273** ©Jupiterimages/Getty Images; **274** (tr) Ingram; **276** (tr) ©Alan and Sandy Carey/Photo Researchers, Inc.; **276** (bg) ©Atlantide Phototravel/Corbis; **277** (br) ©Alan and Sandy Carey/Photo Researchers, Inc.; **277** (tr) ©Suzanne L. Collins/Photo Researchers, Inc.; **278** (tr) ©Blickwinkel/Alamy Images; **278** (bg) ©Atlantide Phototravel/Corbis; **279** (br) ©Alan and Sandy Carey/Photo Researchers, Inc.; **283** (br) ©Steven Puetzer/Getty Images; **284** (tr) ©Patrick Ward/Alamy Images; **284** (tl) ©Robbie Jack/Corbis; **284** (cl) ©UpperCut Images/Alamy Images; **284** (bl) ©John Norman/Alamy Images; **284** (br) ©Lebrecht Music and Arts Photo Library/Alamy Images; **285** (cl) ©Robbie Jack/Corbis; **285** (c) ©Visions of America, LLC/Jospeh Sohm/Corbis; **285** (cr) ©Alamy Images; **285** (bl) ©Yukmin/Age Fotostock America, Inc.; **285** (bc) ©image100/Alamy Images; **285** (br) ©Ecoscene/Anthony Cooper/Corbis; **287** ©Jeremy Hoare/Alamy Images; **301** Comstock / Getty Images; **301** ©Juice Images/Alamy Images; **302** (tr) Rubberball / Getty Images; **303** ©Getty Images; **304** ©Robbie Jack/Corbis; **304** (tr) ©Robbie Jack/Corbis; **305** ©Time & Life Pictures/Getty Images; **306** ©Corbis Premium RF/Alamy Images; **307** ©Time & Life Pictures/Getty Images; **307** (tr) ©Robbie Jack/Corbis; **311** (br) ©Steven Puetzer/Getty Images; Blind [**315**] ©William Ervin/Science Photo Library; **316** ©Burke/Triolo Productions/Getty Images; **316** ©Brand X Pictures/Alamy; **316** ©Ron Crabtree/Photographer's Choice RF/Getty Images; **316** ©Brand X Pictures/Alamy; **316** ©U.S. Air Force; **316** (tl) © Brand X Pictures/Getty Images; **317** © matthiasengelien.com/Alamy; **317** Getty Images; **317** Adam Crowley/PhotoDisc/Getty Images; **317** © Corbis; **317** PhotoDisc/Getty Images; **317** © Stocktrek Images, Inc. / Alamy; **318** (tl) © Brand X Pictures/Getty Images; **319** Digital Vision/Getty Images; **320** ©Stocktrek Images, Inc./Getty Images; **320** (tl) © Brand X Pictures/Getty Images; **322** © Brand X Pictures/Getty Images; **324** (b) ©Purestock/Getty Images; **325** ©Stocktrek Images, Inc./Getty Images; **326** (tl) © Getty Images Royalty Free; **326** ©Alamy Images; **326** Comstock/Getty Images; **326** ©Ryan McGinnis/Flickr/Getty Images; **326** ©Jan Kupracz/Alamy Images; **328** ©Erik Simonsen/Getty Images; **329** ©Kim Steele/Getty Images; **329** ©Getty Images; **330** (tl) © Brand X Pictures/Getty Images; **331** ©Purestock/Getty Images; **331** ©Purestock/Getty Images; **331** © Getty Images Royalty Free; **332** ©The Washington Post/Getty Images; **332** ©Tobias Helbig/Getty Images; **333** ©Corbis; **333** (tl) © Brand X Pictures/Getty Images; **334** ©U.S. Air Force; **335** Gulf-NOAA/Corbis; **335** (b) ©NOAA / Central Library; **336** ©AFP/Getty Images; **338** ©Getty Images; **338** ©NBAE/Getty Images; **339** Vincent Besnault/PhotoDisc/Getty Images; **339** ©George Doyle/Stockbyte/Getty Images; **339** ©U.S. Air Force; **339** (tl) © Brand X Pictures/Getty Images; **343** (br) ©Amos Morgan/Getty Images; **344** (tl) Carolyn Mary Bauman/epa/Corbis; **344** (cl) ©Jim Cornfield/Corbis; **344** (cr) ©Robert Yager/Getty Images; **344** (bl) ©Lloyd Cluff/Corbis; **344** (br) ©Superstock; **345** (cl) ©PhotoDisc/Alamy Images; **345** (c) ©Corbis; **345** (cr) ©Mark Richards/PhotoEdit; **345** (bl)

©Lloyd Cluff/Corbis; **345** (bc) ©Chuck Franklin/Alamy Images; **345** (br) ©Bettmann/Corbis; **347** W9 2000 INC/ Photodisc Green/Getty Images; **347** ©Photo by H.W. Chadwick/National Archives/Time Life Pictures/Getty Images; **361** ©ROB & SAS/Corbis; **361** ©Digital Vision/ Getty Images; **362** ©Photodisc/Getty Images; **362** M. Freeman/PhotoLink/Photodisc/Getty Images; **363** ©Dorling Kindersley/Getty Images; **364** (bg) Carolyn Mary Bauman/epa/Corbis; **364** (tl) Carolyn Mary Bauman/ epa/Corbis; **366** (inset) Timothy Bethke/Alamy; **367** (tr) Carolyn Mary Bauman/epa/Corbis; **367** (cr) ©Bettmann/ Corbis; **367** (br) Zephyr/Photo Researchers, Inc.; **371** (br) ©Masterfile; **372** (tr) ©Alan and Sandy Carey/Getty Images; **372** (bc) ©Tim Davis/Corbis; **372** Digital Vision/ Getty Images; **372** (br) ©Steve Allen Travel Photography/ Alamy Images; **373** (tl) ©Comstock Images/Jupiterimages/ Getty Images; **373** (bc) ©Comstock Images/Getty Images; **373** (c) ©image100/Corbis; **373** (cr) ©Terrance Klassen/ Alamy Images; **373** (bl) ©Emilio Ereza/Alamy Images; **373** (br) ©Eastcott Momatiuk/Corbis; **375** Eastcott Momatiuk/ Photodisc /Getty Images; **378** (c) ©Jennifer Owings Dewey/Kirchoff Wohlberg, Inc.; **379** (t) ©Jennifer Owings Dewey/Kirchoff Wohlberg, Inc.; **381** (bl) ©Jennifer Owings Dewey/Kirchoff Wohlberg, Inc.; **389** ©Gerald Kooyman/Corbis; **389** Joel Simon/Digital Vision/Getty Images; **389** Comstock/Getty Images; **390** © Adam DeMelo / Alamy; **390** ©Stockbyte/Getty Images; 390 ©HMH; **390** (tl) © JUPITERIMAGES/Brand X/ Alamy; **391** Getty Images; **392** (bg) ©Corbis; **393** (bl) Arco Images GmbH / Alamy; **394** (bg) Mark Karrass/Corbis; **395** (bg) ©Corbis; **396** (tr) Robb Kendrick/Getty Images; **397** (bg) Geoff Renner/Getty Images; **398** (br) Getty Images; **398** (t) Paul Nicklen/National Geographic Society; **399** (bg) Corbis; **400** (bc) AFP/Getty Images; **401** ©Ariel Skelley/Getty Images; **401** ©Radius Images/Corbis; **403** ©Cutcaster; **403** Artville/Getty Images; **405** ©relaximages/Alamy Images; **405** (br) ©Digital Vision/Alamy Images; **406** (br) Digital Vision / Getty Images; **406** (cl) ©Terje Rakke/Getty Images; **406** (cr) ©Redmond Durrell/Alamy Images; **406** (bl) ©Michael Busselle/Corbis; **407** (cl) ©Tony Herbert/Alamy Images; **407** (c) ©Nick Servian/Alamy Images; **407** (bl) ©Jim Corwin/Jupiterimages/Getty Images; **407** (bl) ©Gerald Hinde/Animals Animals/Earth Scenes; **407** (bc) ©Pat Bennett/Alamy Images; **407** (br) ©Paul Conklin/ PhotoEdit; **408** © Radius Images/Corbis; **409** ©H. Lansdown/Alamy Images; **423** ©Digital Vision/Getty Images; **427** (cl) ©Houghton Mifflin Harcourt; **431** ©Digital Vision/Getty Images; **431** (b) ©Digital Vision/Getty Images; **435** (br) ©PhotoDisc/Superstock; **436** (cl) ©Danita Delimont/Gallo Images/Getty Images; **436** (tr) ©Lori Adamski Peek/Stone/Getty Images; **436** (bl) ©Allan Montaine/Phononica/Getty Images; **436** (tl) Ryan McVay/Getty Images; **437** (bl) ©Corbis; **437** (tl) ©Kirk Edwards/The Image Bank/Getty Images; **437** (tc) ©Steve Bowman/Corbis; **437** (tr) ©Corel Stock/Photo Library; **437** (br) ©Image Plan/Corbis; **438** ©Frank Krahmer/ Getty Images; **438** (tl) Ryan McVay/Getty Images; **439** (br) © Diane Macdonald/Stockbyte/Getty Images; **440** (bg) Ryan McVay/Getty Images; **440** (tl) Ryan McVay/Getty Images; **442** (bg) Jorg Greuel/Getty Images; **444** (bg) Paul Sounders/Corbis; **445** (bg) Wayne Lawler/Corbis; **446** (bg) Gary Bell/zefa/corbis; **448** (bg) Bettmann/Corbis; **450** (bg) ©ingmar wesemann/Photodisc/Getty Images; **452** (tl) Ryan McVay/Getty Images; **453** Photodisc/Getty Images; **453** ©ingmar wesemann/Photodisc/Getty Images; **454** ©Photodisc/Alamy Images; **454** Brand X Pictures/ Getty Images; **455** ©Robert Glusic/Photodisc/Getty Images; **455** (tr) Ryan McVay/Getty Images; **459** (tl) Ryan McVay/Getty Images; **463** ©PhotoDisc/Superstock; **467** ©Sean Rowland/Covered Images/ASP via Getty Images; **468** (tc) Getty Images; **468** (cl) ©Bettmann/ Corbis; **468** (cr) Dave G. Houser/Corbis; **468** (bl) ©Corbis; **468** (br) ©North Wind Picture Archives/Alamy Images; **469** (cl) ©Robert Estall/Corbis; **469** (c) ©Digital Vision/Getty Images; **469** (cr) ©J. C. Leacock/Alamy Images; **469** (bl) ©North Wind Picture Archives/Alamy Images; **469** (bc) ©DK Limited/Alamy Images; **469** (br) ©North Wind Picture Archives/Alamy Images; **471** Dynamic Graphics / Getty Images; **487** ©F. Jay Haynes/Corbis; **488** (tl) Getty Images; **488** (c) Getty Images; **489** Getty Images; **489** © Bettmann/CORBIS; **490** © CORBIS; **491** (c) Courtesy Boomtown-Gladys City Boomtown Museum; **491** (tc) Getty Images; **493** (tr) ©Ariel Skelley/Getty Images; **495** (br) ©BananaStock/Age Fotostock America, Inc.; **496** (cl) ©Margaret Miller/Photo Researchers, Inc.; **496** (cr) ©Charles Gupton/Corbis; **496** (br) ©Tim Davis/Corbis; **496** (tc) ©SHOUT/Alamy Images; **497** (cl) Revenge: Ashley Cooper/Corbis; **497** (c) ©Daniel Dempster Photography/Alamy Images; **497** © Blend Images / Alamy; **497** (bc) ©tbkmedia.de/Alamy Images; **497** (br) ©Fred Lord/Alamy Images; **497** ©Juniors Bildarchiv/Alamy Images; **499** Don Farrall/Getty Images; **500** (t) ©William Munoz Photography; **502** (t) ©William Munoz Photography; **503** (b) ©William Munoz Photography; **504** (b) ©William Munoz Photography; **505** (t) ©William Munoz Photography; **506** (b) ©William Munoz Photography; **507** (t) ©William Munoz Photography; **508** (r) ©William Munoz Photography; **509** (r) ©William Munoz Photography; **510** (b) ©William Munoz Photography; 513 ©Huntstock/Alamy Images; **516** ©SHOUT/Alamy Images; **516** (tl) ©SHOUT/Alamy Images; **517** (tr) ©Jean Louis Aubert/Getty Images; **518** (bg) ©Jean B Vernier/Corbis Sygma; **519** ©Don Mason/Blend Images/Getty Images; **519** (tc) ©SHOUT/ Alamy Images; **523** (br) ©Masterfile; **524** Photodisc/Getty Images; **524** (bg) ©Oote Boe Photography/Alamy Images; **525** Alamy; **525** © Steve Skjold / Alamy; **525** ©Mark Karass/Corbis; **525** ©Marilyn Conway/Getty Images; **527** ©Getty Images; **527** Bruno Cossa/Grand Tour/Corbis; **556** (tr) © Dynamic Graphics Group / Creatas / Alamy; **556** (cl) ©Bettmann/Corbis; **556** (bl) Bruce Burkhardt/ Corbis; **556** (br) ©Arthur Rothstein/Corbis; **556** (tc) ©Ariel Skelley/Getty Images; **556** (tc) ©Oote Boe Photography/Alamy Images; **556** (tc) ©Oote Boe Photography/Alamy Images; **557** (tr) ©momentimages/ Tetra Images/Alamy Images; **557** (cl) ©Hulton-Deutsch Collection/Corbis; **557** (c) ©Horacio Villalobos/Corbis; **557** (bl) ©Richard Hutchings/PhotoEdit; **557** (bc) ©Gary Crabbe/Alamy Images; **557** (br) ©Masterfile; **559** ©Corbis; **573** ©Luedke & Sparrow/Getty Images; **573** ©Brand X Pictures/Jupiterimages/Getty Images; **574** Corbis Premium RF/Alamy; **575** ©Getty Images; **576** (tl) ©Ariel Skelley/ Getty Images; **576** (c) ©Iconotec; **576** (bc) ©C Squared Studios/Getty Images//PhotoDisc; **576** (tc) ©C Squared Studios/Getty Images//PhotoDisc; **576** (bg) ©Oote Boe Photography/Alamy Images; **576** (tl) ©Oote Boe Photography/Alamy Images; **577** (br) ©Ariel Skelley/Getty Images; **578** (bg) Yoshio Sawargai/Getty; **578** (tc) ©C Squared Studios/Getty Images//PhotoDisc; **579** (tcl) ©Ariel Skelley/Getty Images; **579** ©Image Source/Getty Images; **579** ©Corbis; **579** (tc) ©Oote Boe Photography/

Alamy Images; **584** (tl) Buddy Mays/Corbis; **584** (cl) © Paul A. Souders/CORBIS; **584** (cr) ©Great Falls Tribune/Robin Loznak/AP Images; **584** (bl) ©Stocktrek/Photodisc/Getty Images; **584** (br) ©Dennis MacDonald/Alamy Images; **585** (tl) ©HMH; **585** (bl) ©Photo Researchers/Martin Shields/Getty Images; **585** (cr) ©Jeremy Woodhouse/Age Fotostock America, Inc.; **585** (bc) ©Getty Images; **585** (br) ©Peter Barritt/Alamy Images; **587** Corbis; **605** ©Getty Images; **606** ©momentimages/Getty Images; **608** (bg) Buddy Mays/Corbis; **608** (tl) Buddy Mays/Corbis; **609** (br) ©Alamy Images; **610** (bg) ©Digital Vision/Getty Images; **611** ©Brand X Pictures/Getty Images; **611** (tr) Buddy Mays/Corbis; **611** (cr) Connie Ricca/Corbis; **615** (br) ©Rubberball/Superstock; Blind [**619**] ©Mitchell Funk/Getty Images; **620** (cl) ©Aura/Getty Images; **620** (cr) ©Dennis Hallinan/Getty Images; **620** ©Getty Images; **620** (bl) ©Stanley Fellerman/Corbis; **621** (cl) ©Don Mason/Corbis; **621** (c) ©Robert Pickett/Corbis; **621** (cr) ©Gary Gerovac/Masterfile; **621** (bl) ©Juniors Bildarchiv/Alamy Images; **621** (bc) ©Steve Lyne/Getty Images; **621** (br) ©Martin Harvey/Getty Images; **623** ©Beau Lark/Corbis; **639** ©Corbis; **639** Getty Images/Photodisc; **640** ©Photodisc/Getty Images; 641 ©Radius Images/Corbis; **645** ©Yasuhide Fumoto/Digital Vision/Getty Images; **645** ©Tony Cordoza/Alamy Images; **645** GK Hart/Vikki Hart/Photodisc/Getty Images; **649** (br) ©Image Source/Superstock; **650** (cl) ©Digital Vision/Getty Images; **650** (cr) © Michael Newman / PhotoEdit Inc.; **650** (br) ©image100/Corbis; **650** (bl) ©Najlah Feanny/Corbis; **651** (cl) Mike Blake/Corbis; **651** (c) ©Susan Steinkamp/Corbis; **651** (cr) Bettmann/Corbis; **651** (bc) ©WireImage/Masterfile; **651** (br) ©Beathan/Corbis; **653** ©Houghton Mifflin Harcourt; **667** Corbis; **670** ©Photodisc/Getty Images; **670** (border) ©Photodisc/Getty Images; **671** ©Library of Congress Prints & Photographs Division; **672** ©Dennis MacDonald/Alamy Images; **673** Vstock LLC/Getty Images; **675** (br) ©imagebroker.net/Superstock; **675** ©JUPITER IMAGES/Getty Images; **679** (br) ©Rubberball/Superstock; **680** (tc) ©l clarke/Spirit/Corbis; **680** (cr) © Brent Waltermire / Alamy; **680** (bl) ©Craig Tuttle/Corbis; **680** (br) ©Alamy Images; **680** (tl) ©James Randklev/Getty Images; **681** (cl) ©Papilio/Alamy Images; **681** (c) ©Corbis; **681** (cr) ©Cartesia/PhotoDisc; **681** (bl) ©Progressive Image/Corbis; **681** (bc) ©Jack Fields/Corbis; **681** (br) ©Leland Bobbe/Getty Images; **683** ©HMH; **683** ©Digital Vision/Getty Images; **701** Getty Images/Photodisc; **701** ©Michael Todd/Alamy Images; **702** Alan Levenson/Corbis; **702** Comstock/Getty Images; **703** Corbis; **704** (tl) ©James Randklev/Getty Images; **704** (b) ©Image Farm Inc./Alamy Images; **705** (bg) ©James Randklev/Getty Images; **705** (l) ©Image Farm Inc./Alamy Images; **705** (t) ©PhotoDisc; **705** (br) ©Andre Jenny/Alamy Images; **706** (l) ©Image Farm Inc./Alamy Images; **706** (bg) ©Corbis; **706** (cr) ©PhotoDisc; **707** (b) ©Michael Nichols/Getty Images; **707** © Adam DeMelo/Alamy; **707** (tr) ©James Randklev/Getty Images; **707** (cr) ©Galen Rowell/Corbis; **711** (br) ©Rubberball/Superstock; **712** (bc) ©Fuse/Getty Images; **712** (tl) ©David Courtenay/Oxford Scientific/Getty Images; **712** (cl) ©Corbis; **712** (cr) ©Alamy Images; **712** (br) ©Jose Luis Pelaez Inc/Getty Images; **713** (cl) ©Kelly Redinger/Age Fotostock America, Inc.; **713** (c) ©Thiery Prat/Corbis; **713** (cr) ©Tim Platt/Getty Images; **713** ©Shaen Adey/ABPL/Animals Animals/Earth Scenes; **713** (bc) ©GoGo Images Corporation/Age Fotostock America, Inc.; **713** (br) ©Jupiterimages/Getty Images; **715** ©IMAGEMORE Co., Ltd./Getty Images; **729** ©Andrew Rutherford/Getty Images; **730** ©Photodisc/Getty Images; **732** ©David Courtenay/Oxford Scientific/Getty Images; **732** (tl) ©David Courtenay/Oxford Scientific/Getty Images; **734** G.P. Schmah/FGBNMS; **735** (tr) ©David Courtenay/Oxford Scientific/Getty Images; **735** Corbis; **735** Corel Stock Photo Library - royalty free; **739** (br) ©PhotoDisc/Superstock; **740** (br) ©Photodisc/Getty Images; **740** (cl) ©Richard Cummins/Corbis; **740** (cr) ©Bonnie Kamin/PhotoEdit; **740** (bl) ©Moodboard/Corbis; **741** (cl) ©Brand X Pictures/Getty Images; **741** (c) ©Elvele Images Ltd/Alamy Images; **741** (cr) ©Don Mason/Corbis; **741** (bl) ©Jeremy Trew/Trewimage/Alamy Images; **741** (bc) ©Liba Taylor/Corbis; **741** (br) ©George Doyle/Getty Images; **743** ©Ryan McVay/Photodisc/Getty Images; **743** Comstock / Getty Images; **743** ©SuperStock RF/SuperStock; **743** ©Paul Fleet/Alamy Images; **755** ©jac Depczyk/Getty Images; **756** ©PhotoDisc/Getty Images; **756** ©Sharon Lapkin/Getty Images; **757** ©BIG CHEESE PHOTO LLC SPECIAL/Alamy Images; **761** ©Ryan McVay/Getty Images; **762** ©Garry Gay/Getty Images; **767** ©Houghton Mifflin Harcourt; **767** (br) ©PhotoDisc/Superstock; G3 (cr) ©Digital Stock; G5 (tr) ©Cartesia/PhotoDisc; G5 (br) ©Digital Stock; G7 (br) ©Artville; G8 (tl) ©Ryan McVay/Getty Images; G10 (cl) Getty Images/Photodisc; G12 (cl) ©Artville; G14 (cl) ©PhotoDisc; G17 (r) ©Corbis

Illustration

96–100 Rèmy Simard; **320–322** Stuart @ KJA; **759–761** Vigg

All other photos: Houghton Mifflin Harcourt Photo Libraries and Photographers.